D1264780

LONDON THEATRES
AND
MUSIC HALLS
1850-1950

by Diana Howard

The Library Association
1970

© Diana Howard, 1970

Published by The Library Association,
7, Ridgmount Street, London, W.C.1.

SBN: 85365 471 9

PRINTED BY Unwin Brothers Limited
THE GRESHAM PRESS OLD WOKING SURREY ENGLAND

Produced by 'Uneoprint'
A member of the Staples Printing Group   (UCO4478)

Contents

Acknowledgments

I am indebted to many people for their help and guidance in the preparation of this work, which was originally prepared as a Library Association Fellowship thesis.

First I must thank Miss Ann Kahn for her advice and help, both during the compilation of the thesis and since its completion; and Mr. J. Middlebrook, formerly of the Greater London Council's Architect's Department for introducing me to the resources of that department, and for giving me the names of individuals and organisations who could help me.

I am very grateful to the staffs of the London and Middlesex Record Offices for giving me much of their time.

I wish to thank Mr. H. R. Beard, Dr. J. F. Arnott and Mr. Ellis Ashton for permitting me to see material in their possession; also the Secretary of the Garrick Club and the Assistant Secretary of the Lord Chamberlain's Office for permission to use material not generally available to the public.

Finally I thank Susan Braybrook and Donald Miller for their skill with typewriter and camera respectively.

February 1969   D. H.

Introduction

SURVEY OF RESOURCES AND SUBJECTS FOR FURTHER RESEARCH.

Research into London's theatres and music halls is handicapped by the absence of a comprehensive collection of material. Theatrical records and publications are scattered through a number of museums, (the British Museum, Victoria and Albert Museum, London Museum, and the British Theatre Museum), through the local collections of public libraries, through the archives of local and central government departments, and through various private collections and societies. The majority of these have very limited financial resources, and they are all primarily interested in the same types of material—notably playbills and prints.

This fragmentation also occurs within the collections themselves; the British Museum, by classifying by type rather than subject, has scattered its theatre material into three departments—the Department of Printed Books, the Department of Manuscripts, and the Department of Prints and Drawings. The Victoria and Albert Museum has material in both the library and the Gabrielle Enthoven Collection. The Westminster City Library has a collection of monographs and bibliographies in the Central Reference Library, St. Martin's Street, as part of the Metropolitan Special Collection, and a collection of prints, programmes and playbills, and cuttings at the Buckingham Palace Road Branch Library in the local collection.

This fragmentation of resources reflects the importance placed on 'theatre' as a subject worthy of separate treatment. Other considerations are allowed to override the subject aspect. Conversely it is the subject matter that attracts people sufficiently for them to 'play' with it, causing for example, playbills of historic interest to be used for interior decoration, and thus destroying them.

The Department of Printed Books of the British Museum is the correct place for the printed books, pamphlets and periodicals; however it also has a collection of theatre scrapbooks and playbills. The Department of Prints and Drawings also has scrapbooks and playbills, besides its excellent collection of theatrical prints. The Department of Manuscripts houses similar material as well as original items such as account books, leases and agreements. This arrangement was probably arrived at by chance donation, and has no functional value.

The Enthoven Collection has become, through the cooperation of theatre managers, virtually a 'copyright' collection of contemporary programmes and other records relating to current productions. This material is being added to the outstanding collection gathered together by Mrs. Gabrielle Enthoven and

given to the Victoria and Albert Museum in 1924. This collection could form the basis of a national theatre archive, which could either be a department of the Victoria and Albert Museum, or affiliated to the National Theatre. This would give a definite 'home' to the subject and enable items such as the scrapbooks and playbills in the British Museum, the programmes, playbills and scrapbooks and prints in the London Museum, and the archive material in the British Theatre Museum to be gathered together in one research centre.

Some attempt is being made by the Enthoven Collection to obtain copies of material in other collections. An example of this is the collection of copies of plans obtained from the London County Council. It should be made financially possible for them to obtain copies of all relevant documents in such collections as the Public Record Office and the State Paper Room of the British Museum. This requires imagination on the part of the grant-giving organisations, and more active support from the various societies concerned with the subject.

At present the societies are continuing the general scattering of resources. The British Drama League, the Society for Theatre Research, and the British Music Hall Society need to pool their resources, and to work together with the Enthoven Collection in acquiring new material. Drama, theatre and variety should be three departments of a single comprehensive collection, not competing against one another.

The Society for Theatre Research has a library that is housed partly in the library of the University of London, and partly on the society's premises. The British Music Hall Society's archives are not easily accessible; accommodation difficulties and lack of help have stopped the adequate cataloguing and indexing of the material in its possession.

It should be the role of these societies, together with the Council for Theatre Preservation, to encourage the preservation of theatrical records of all kinds. At present the Council for Theatre Preservation is occupied with the photographing of theatres in conjunction with the National Buildings Record, and with the physical preservation of the buildings; it has not extended its interest to the archives of the theatres.

One target for the campaign to encourage the preservation of material should be the public libraries. Local historians and archivists in charge of local history collections have recorded and gathered together material on the local theatres of the pre-Nineteenth Century era with great enthusiasm. Little attempt has been made to collect items referring to the music halls, the palaces of variety, and the suburban theatres that flourished during the century following 1850. One librarian may be quoted as saying that her borough was not a theatrical area—even though during the course of the last century at least six music halls and a theatre flourished there. This is the more deplorable when it is remembered that many libraries were active for at least three quarters of the period, and probably actually destroyed a fair number of handbills relating to contemporary performances. It should certainly have been possible for all the buildings to be recorded photographically, yet the libraries that have photographs of their local music halls are in the minority.

There is plenty of scope for the societies if they chose to encourage actively public librarians to value this material. Although this is to some extent advocating the building up of more small collections of theatre material, the public libraries could act in association with the National Theatre Archive, supplying it with copies of items missing from its own collections, and with calendars of their stock.

The creation of such an archive might attract donations from private collectors, or might enable it to bid for such private collections as the Mander and Mitchenson Collection and the Harry Beard Collection should they ever be in danger of being broken up.

It is extraordinary that the much more recent art of the cinema should be served by the British Film Institute and the National Film Archive, while the theatre has nothing comparable. It would also give the United Kingdom a collection to compare with those of the Universities of Harvard and Ohio, and the New York Public Library.

So far the reforms I have been discussing are not within the control of individual researchers, although more vocal expression of their needs might help to accomplish these reforms. There is, however, a considerable amount of basic work for them to do.

The files of *The Era* and *The Stage* need to have published indexes. This would be a monumental task that could only be tackled by a group of people under a strong editor. It would also need financial backing if it were to be published as it would not be commercially self-supporting. This is something that should be sponsored by the Society for Theatre Research as a matter of urgency.

A comprehensive index to the periodicals listed in Part Two would give detailed coverage of all theatrical and music hall events for the period 1850 to 1950. It could not be undertaken by an individual, but could serve as a project for a society.

Secondly, the files of local newspapers need to be searched for references, particularly to music halls. (A select list of the London papers is appended.)

The third indexing task that needs to be undertaken is the indexing of the volumes of Papers of the London County Council's Theatres and Music Halls Committee and its successors. These volumes, which are mines of information, are arranged chronologically and are thus tedious to use when tracing the history of particular buildings.

Finally, theatre historians are needed who will search the records and archives of organisations dealing with associated subjects, such as insurance, brewing, the cinema, and finance.

Insurance records: Insurance companies do not make a practice of preserving their loss records, but the archivist of the Insurance Institute of London's Historic Records Committee has suggested that the larger companies may have some records of interest.

Brewing and cinema records: The brewers are probably more interested in the history of the public houses belonging to their companies than the owners of cinemas are in the previous history of their buildings. One major brewery, at least, has an archivist. The records kept by these firms may contain information on the previous and later history of music halls and theatres that developed out of the public houses, and have since been converted into cinemas and bingo halls.

Financial records: The theatrical companies were usually private companies, and records relating to their financial structure are difficult to obtain. The records at Companies House, City Road (the Register of Companies) require searching and might provide an interesting basis for a history of the theatre business. The financial press covered theatrical mergers. The *London Gazette* lists bankrupts, but could not be used until the names of managers and lessees have been listed in a convenient form.

Legal proceedings: The records of the Home Office contain references to legal proceedings taken against theatres. These are also covered by the records of the Lord Chamberlain and the London County Council, and by *The Era* and *The Stage*.

Fire records: The daily fire reports of the London Fire Brigade which begin in 1866, and are part of the archives of the Greater London Council, contain references to the many fires that took place in the theatres and music halls during the nineteenth century. The *Post Magazine* and *The Times* listed fire losses, and reported on the bigger and more interesting ones.

This is an attempt to indicate possible lines for future research; there are of course many others.

Scope and Arrangement of Contents

i. Scope: (Definition of terms):-

'Theatre': The *Shorter Oxford Dictionary* defines a 'theatre' as 'an edifice especially adapted to dramatic representations, a playhouse'. *Webster's Third New International Dictionary* gives a more detailed definition, 'a building for dramatic performances in modern times usually including a stage with side wings and flies, with dressing rooms for actors and an auditorium often with balconies and boxes'. The *Dictionary of English Law* by Jowitt defines it as 'Any house or place of public resort for the public performance of stage plays', stage plays being 'Tragedy, comedy, farce, opera, burletta, interlude, melodrama, pantomime or other entertainment of the stage or any part thereof unless performed in a booth of a fair'.

'Music Hall': The *Shorter Oxford Dictionary* says a music hall is 'a hall used for musical performances spec. (since about 1885) a hall licensed for singing, dancing and other entertainments exclusive of dramatic performance.' Webster defines it simply as a 'vaudeville theatre', that is, a variety theatre.

These definitions indicate that there is nothing structurally different about theatres and music halls; the difference lies in the sort of entertainment that is being provided. The licensing regulations do not help in the defining of these terms. There were four types of 'permit'—patents, -stage play, music, and music and dancing licences. Originally a hall could be licensed for one type of entertainment only, at one time; later stage play and music and dancing licences were issued concurrently; thus one has to know the type of entertainment being given at a specific performance in order to say 'tonight this hall is being used as a theatre (or music hall).'

'Pleasure gardens' were usually gardens attached to public houses, where food, drink and entertainment were provided. The greatest of these was Vauxhall Gardens, but many smaller gardens flourished during the Eighteenth Century and continued on into the second half of the Nineteenth. The larger gardens frequently had music halls built within their boundaries. The smaller ones had open air stages.

Although it is not possible to separate theatres from music halls, and music halls from pleasure gardens, it seemed that a complete list of all premises licensed for stage plays or variety would provide the basis for this compilation. Closer study of this list showed that the licensing was too general for the purposes of this work. Parish and church halls, town halls, concert halls, museum and exhibition halls, assembly halls, and halls belonging to places of education such as schools, colleges and institutes all received the same types of licences as the theatres and music halls. These were all places of entertainment according to the definitions quoted. In order to

be able to exclude them, it was necessary to find a definition that clearly omitted all types of halls not generally recognised as theatres and music halls, such as those listed above.

A theatre or music hall for the purposes of this work is *a hall that was used by its owner or lessee primarily for the purpose of providing dramatic or variety entertainment by paid performers, to a paying audience, with a view to making a financial profit.* (Theatres that today receive a state grant must be recognised as being in the above category, even if the financial profit is unlikely). This definition includes the music halls of public houses by not requiring elaborate structural and furnishing arrangements, but excludes all halls used primarily for charity and non-profitmaking performances, and those hired by amateur organisations. It also permits the inclusion of halls that slipped through the licensing net and gave dramatic and variety performances illegally.

The general listing of the music halls in public houses may mean the inclusion of some halls that do not in fact meet the requirements of this definition; however a sufficient amount of information is known about the halls that later developed into the music halls, and a sufficient number of handbills, cuttings and reports exist on many of the remainder to make their general inclusion justified.

'London': The County of London was adopted for the geographical limits of this work, as it was the area of London most easily identified from maps and directories. The main difficulty presented by this decision is the fact that in 1850 the 'county' had not been created, and by 1966 it had ceased to exist, except as the Inner London Education Authority area. Until the formation of the County of London, the area in question was divided between the County of Middlesex on the north bank, and the Counties of Surrey and Kent on the south bank of the Thames.

'1850-1950': This period has been chosen as it was the century of the greatest activity in theatre building and management. Virtually the whole history of the music hall is contained in it. In 1850 the music halls were still in the embryo forms of pleasure gardens, tea gardens and music rooms; by 1950 the majority of the variety theatres that had developed during the century had either vanished altogether or had been turned into cinemas. A handful of the theatres that existed before 1850 have survived to the present day; the vast majority were built and demolished or converted for other purposes within this period.

1860 was the peak when the freedom of the theatres, and the popularity of the new variety entertainment were both fully felt. The 1878 Act caused the rapid decline after 1880.

Another reason for selecting this period was its almost total neglect by theatre historians.

'Directory': The directory information is in two sections. The main section is Part I, the A-Z Directory of Theatres and Music Halls. I have attempted to include every theatre and music hall that existed in London during this period, but I cannot claim that it is complete as new music halls are being discovered all the time. The names have been collected from a variety of sources, the main ones being the licensing records, reports, contemporary accounts and newscuttings.

As it was necessary to search the records year by year, I have included the names of the licensees of each building. This was, perhaps, not essential for the purposes of this work, but the interests of theatre research demanded that the opportunity should not be wasted, when the information was readily available.

At the end of many entries the paragraph **Location of other Material** indicates where non-bibliographical material on the building may be seen.

Part III forms the second part of the 'Directory', giving details of the locations mentioned in Part I.

'Bibliography': The bibliographical information is given in two sections. In the entries of the A-Z Directory the bibliographical material is listed under the heading **Literature**.

The second section, Part II Bibliography of General Works, gives the full details of official records, and lists general books and articles. The references have been collected from library catalogues, book trade bibliographies, and from the actual collections listed in Part III. Periodical references were taken from published indexes to periodicals such as the *Subject Index to Periodicals,* from unpublished indexes such as that maintained by the library of the Royal Institute of British Architects, and from collections of cuttings. *The Builder* and *Building News* were systematically searched, and relevant items indexed.

The subject matter of the material listed is confined, in the main, to two topics—the architecture of the buildings, and their management. A great deal has been published on the stage history of this period. Every "name" in the theatre has published his reminiscences or had his career recorded by others. Such works are not included in this compilation, unless they record the theatres rather than performances.

This work is not intended to be a history of the theatre during this period. Its aim is to provide the raw material for future research.

ii. Arrangement

PART I. A-Z DIRECTORY...

Basic plan of entries-

Serial No. NAME

Address (changes of address)

Dates

Former/other names, date where known.

Building details

 Developer

 Architect; Builder/Contractor; Decorator

 Cost

 Capacity

 Auditorium

 Stage

Management

 Lord Chamberlain, 1843-

 Middlesex, Kent or Surrey justices, 1850-

 London County Council, 1889-

Literature

 Official Records

 Contemporary accounts

 Historical accounts

Location of other material

 Plans; illustrations; cuttings; playbills;

 programmes; scrapbooks &c.

The material has been arranged to give a systematic view of the history of the building. The most fully documented theatres and music halls will have entries under each of the above headings; others will have entries under only one or two.

Serial No. Name index refers to the serial number.

Name: under which the entry is given is the last known name, or the name used in 1950. This has been done even when the earlier name is better known. There are two major exceptions to this: the "Old Vic" is used in preference to the Royal Victoria Hall, and Astley's Theatre in preference to the later names of that building.

The descriptive term, 'theatre', 'palace of varieties' etc. is also the last one to be used. The public houses were usually referred to without a descriptive term, for example 'The Red Lion'. The term 'Public House' has been added to the name consistently, even when occasionally the house has been called 'Tavern'. When the actual music hall was known by a different name to the public house to which it was attached, the name of the hall has been used.

All names appear in the name index.

Address: given is that which was used for the longest length of time during the life of the hall. During the Nineteenth and early Twentieth Centuries much 'tidying up' of street names and numbers was done by the Metropolitan Board of Works and the London County Council. The alternative address is given in brackets. The names of the streets given are those current when the hall was in use and do not necessarily include the present name of the street.

Dates: given are either those of the opening and closing of the building, or those of the licensing. The opening and closing dates are given, in the main, for purpose-built theatres and music halls.

It must be stated that licensing dates may be misleading owing to the fact that managers continued to have their halls licensed through habit, until they were warned by the licensing authority. Places licensed for one year only may reflect the intension to provide entertainment rather than the actual provision.

Former/other names: It has been my intention to list all the names by which the hall was known during its existence.

Building details: Information has been gathered from official reports and architectural journals.

Dates: when only one building is involved, the dates, which are given at the beginning of the entry, are not repeated. When more than one building is involved, the dates are given for the subsequent rebuildings.

Developer: the name of the company or individual responsible for commissioning the work and meeting the costs of erection.

Architect, Builder/Contractor, Decorator: the companies or individuals commissioned to plan and build the structure.

Cost: this figure has been taken from reports of accepted tenders, and from the reports of Select Committees.

Capacity: The maximum number of people permitted to view the entertainment, including seating and standing room. The capacity of places of entertainment was continually reduced after 1878; whenever possible the date is given with the capacity.

Auditorium: the tiers, 'boxes' and area seating accommodation. Explanation of abbreviations is given at the beginning of the work.

Stage: Width of the proscenium, and distance from the proscenium to the back wall. Figures obtained from architectural journals and *Who's who in the theatre.*

MANAGEMENT: The names listed here have been collected from the records of the licensing authorities. The person to whom the licence was granted had to be the "actual and responsible manager" of the building. During the Nineteenth Century the licensee was usually either the owner or the lessee. Later, as companies replaced individuals as theatre owners, the licensee was usually either the managing director of the company, or his nominee. From circa 1920 the London County Council granted music and dancing licences to companies, and stage play licences to individuals thus licensing the one building under two names concurrently.

Lord Chamberlain: The names have been collected from the records of the Lord Chamberlain kept in the Public Record Office and the Lord Chamberlain's Office. The names are listed in chronological order, date first. The dash indicates that the person following that date was the licensee until the next date given.

For example:- 29.11.1870- John Smith
13. 6.1879- James Brown
29.11.1879- John Green (to 8.9.1880)
29.11.1881- Mary Jones.

Middlesex, Surrey, and West Kent justices: The names have been collected from records of the Michaelmas Quarter Sessions, now in the hands of the appropriate record office. The licences ran from Michaelmas to Michaelmas.

The terms *No notice, no petition,* and *no application* refer to the procedures for applying for a licence. A new applicant had to post a *notice of intent* on the premises, at the local police station, and with the justices. If this was not done, the licence would not be granted. The applicant could accompany his formal application with a *petition* supporting the application; other managers and interested parties could at this time submit a petition against the granting of the licence.

London County Council: From November 1889 the L.C.C. assumed responsibility for the licensing of those places of entertainment that came within its area, that had previously been licensed by the justices. Applications were made in November; those granted ran from January to December.

Building requirements rather than justices and police reports caused the refusal of many licences, continuing a trend already started under the justices, after the 1878 Act.

LITERATURE:

Official records: The entries for the official records have been abbreviated in order to save space with the continual repetition of the same details. The abbreviations are explained at the beginning of the work; but the *reader should refer to PART II Section ii* for the expanded citation of these records. These two sections must be used in conjunction with one another.

Contemporary accounts: Newspaper and periodical accounts of current events, auction notices, and publicity handouts are listed in chronological order. References to page numbers are given wherever possible; they are sometimes missing from those entries compiled from cuttings.

Historical accounts: Accounts of events that have taken place at least twelve months prior to the writing of the account. This separation of historical and contemporary accounts has been done because of the fact that many theatrical 'histories' are inaccurate. Events and people can easily become misplaced in the writer's memory particularly towards the end of a long career. In the 'popular' works there has been a tendency for stories to be collected from other printed histories, rather than from source material; for example Stuart and Park's *The Variety Stage* has provided information for many later works on the history of the music hall. This is a dangerous practice for, although the original text may be correct, faulty transcription, or the lifting of a sentence from its context, can lead to the establishment and perpetuation of errors of fact. It would be wrong to give the impression that it is a general rule, but it does occur frequently enough to make this type of history suspect, and to limit its value to the historian.

Monographs on individual theatres and music halls are listed in this section only. General works that are given analytical entries under the individual buildings are also listed in Part II Section v, where full details of their publication are given.

LOCATION OF MATERIAL: The limited time available for the compilation of this work has necessitated the indication of sources of non-bibliographical material, rather than the itemizing of them.

Plans: The major collection of theatre plans is in the Greater London Council's Architects Department; the Public Record Office has a small collection. The Enthoven Collection has copies of plans of fifty five theatres from the G.L.C. collection.

The G.L.C. Architects Department has re-surveyed the theatres approximately every ten years; thus the series of plans for one theatre shows how the building was altered during its 'career'. The non-current plans are now housed in the Record Office.

Illustrations; Prints; Drawings and Photographs: This material is badly scattered. There is no comprehensive collection, although the National Buildings Record is aiming to have a comprehensive collection of photographs for the Twentieth Century.

Programmes and playbills: There are many locations of this material. I have listed some. Collections that I was unable to index include The British Music Hall Society archives, the British Drama League Collection, and the major American university collections, at Harvard and Ohio. I was unable to get access to the Mander and Mitchenson Collection. All these sources should be searched by any one compiling a history of an individual building.

PART II. Bibliography of general works:

Section i. Brief list of *theatre bibliographies*. As will be seen there are very few, and with the exception of the Boston Catalogue and the Lowe, they are of limited use.

Section ii. *The calendar of official records,* which must be used to clarify the abbreviated entries in Section I, is the major source for any researcher into the original records. It is on these records that future study should be directed.

Sections iii & iv. *Selected lists of newspapers and periodicals.* These lists have be included as an indication of the range of material available to researchers.

Section v. *Other publications* include monographs on the history of the theatre in general, and those on specific years and decades. It does not include monographs or articles on individual theatres (for this see Section I), nor does it include theatre biography. The exceptions to this are biographies directly referring to theatre promotion and management.

PART III Location of material: directory of collections.
Directory of sources listed in Section I.

Name index to buildings: Indexes to serial numbers, all names listed in Section I.

Abbreviations

A.	Amphitheatre	m.d.l.	music and dancing licence
Ar.	Area	Mich.	Michaelmas
Aug.	August	Mss.	Manuscript
B.	Balcony	Mx.	Middlesex
B.M.	British Museum	n.d.	no date
B.S.	Balcony stalls	Nov.	November
Bx.	Boxes	Oct.	October
C.	Circle	p.	page
D.C.	Dress circle	P.	Pit
Dec.	December	Part.	Parterre
Faut.	Fauteuils	pp.	pages
Feb.	February	P.R.O.	Public Record Office
G.	Gallery	ports.	portraits
G.C.	Grand circle	Prom.	Promenade
G.L.C. Arch. Dpt.	Greater London Council *Architects Department*	P.S.	Pit stalls
		Q.S.	Quarter Sessions
Illus.	Illustrations	Rpt.	Report
Jan.	January	S.	Stalls
L.C.	Lord Chamberlain's records in the Public Record Office	S.B.	Side balconies
		Sel. Com.	Parliamentary Select Committee
L.C.C. Th. & M-H. Com. App.	London County Council. *Theatres and Music Halls Committee.* Applications and other records, of this and subsequent committees	Sept.	September
		s.p.	stage play licence
		Sy.	Surrey
L.C.O.	Lord Chamberlain's Office, St. James's Palace, theatre files	U.C.	Upper Circle
		U.G.	Upper Gallery
M.B.W.	Metropolitan Board of Works	W.Kt.	West Kent

PART I

A – Z DIRECTORY OF THEATRES, MUSIC HALLS AND PLEASURE GARDENS, WITH BIBLIOGRAPHIES

1

ABBEY PUBLIC HOUSE

Between 6 & 10 Violet Hill, St. John's Wood.

Licensed: 1857-1867

Management

Middlesex justices:

Mich.	1857-	Henry Wilkin
"	1864-	William Bent
"	1865-	James Hodges
"	1867	*No notice, no petition*

Literature

Official records:

Mx. Mich. Q.S. 1857-1867.

2

ADAM AND EVE PUBLIC HOUSE

Adam and Eve Terrace, St. Giles-in-the-Fields, Holborn.

Licensed: 1854-1863.

Management

Middlesex justices:

Mich.	1854-	Thomas Lee
"	1855-	Henry Schabel
"	1857-	Robert Edward Gaye
"	1859	*No petition*
"	1860-	William Francis
"	1861-	Benjamin Strutton
"	1862-	Robert Roscoe
"	1863	*No petition*

Literature

Official records:

Mx. Mich. Q.S. 1854-1863.

3

ADAM AND EVE PUBLIC HOUSE

29, St. John St. Road, Clerkenwell.

Licensed: 1854-1875

Management

Middlesex justices:

Mich.	1854-	Joseph Ferrar
"	1855-	Frederick Parr
"	1856-	Abraham Trew
"	1860-	Richard Dunn
"	1874-	Kate Wallcraft
"	1875	*No petition*

Literature

Official records:

Mx. Mich. Q.S. 1855-1875.

4

ADAM'S ARMS PUBLIC HOUSE

11, Hampstead Street, St. Pancras.

Licensed: 1852-1862.

Management

Middlesex justices:

Mich.	1852-	James Phillips
"	1861-	Robert Price
"	1862	*No petition*

Literature

Official records:

Mx. Mich. Q.S. 1852-1862.

5

ADELAIDE GALLERY, THEATRE OF VARIETIES

Adelaide Street West, Strand.

Licensed: 1850-1862.

Former names

Adelaide Gallery, Exhibition Rooms 1850
Royal Adelaide Theatre 1853
Adelaide Gallery and Marionette Theatre 1855-1859

Management

Middlesex justices:

Mich.	1850-	Thomas Bartlett Simpson
"	1852-	Charles Cooper
"	1857-	William Palmer
"	1861-	John Burns Bryson
"	1862	Agostino Gatti and Giacomo Monico *refused licence.*

Literature

Official records:

Mx. Mich. Q.S. 1850-1862.

Contemporary accounts:

1909 BUILDER, 1909 Oct. 30. p. 457.—Note of history and report on formation of new restaurant.

Location of other material

Playbills and programmes:

Enthoven Collection; London Museum.

6

ADELPHI THEATRE

409-412 (formerly 411-2), Strand.

Opened: 27 November 1806

Former names

Sans Pareil 1806-1819
Adelphi Theatre 1819-1829
Theatre Royal, Adelphi 1829-1858
Theatre Royal, New Adelphi 1858-1867
Royal Adelphi Theatre 1867
Century Theatre 1901-1902
Adelphi Theatre 1902-1930
Royal Adelphi Theatre 1930-1940

Building details

1st building:

Architect: Samuel Beazley

Builder: Mr. Jay of London Wall

2nd building:

Opened: 27.12.1858

Architect: T.H. Wyatt

Builder: J. Willson

Decorators: Frederick Sang and J.H. Parsons

Capacity: 1500

Auditorium: P. 500; S. 69; C. 100; U.C. 182; G. 360; Bx. 96.

Renovations, 1879.

Architect: Green Chadwick

Decorators: Mr. Crossley, and J.M. Allen

Reconstruction, 1887, incorporating 409-410 Strand.

Architect: Spencer Chadwick

Capacity: 2135

3rd building:

Opened: 11.9.1901

Architect: Ernest Runtz

Contractor: Frank Kirk

Capacity: 1297; (1916) c. 1500.

Auditorium: (1916) S. 206; B.S. 126; B.S. Bx. AA-HH; U.C. 256; Bx. A-H.

Stage: 64' wide by 87' deep.

4th building:

Opened: 3.12.1930

Architect: Ernest Schaufelberg

Contractors: Pitcher Construction Company

Capacity: 1400

Auditorium: S. 547; D.C. 420; U.C. 385; Bx. A-D.

Stage: 36' wide, by 27'9" high, by 49' deep.

Management

Lord Chamberlain:

29. 9.1843-		Thomas Gladstone
"	1844-	Benjamin Webster
"	1874-	Frederick Balsir Chatterton
"	1878-	Agostino and Stefano Gatti
"	1885-	Stefano Gatti
1. 9.1900-		George Edwardes
28. 9.1901-		Tom Buffen Davis
20. 4.1908-		George Edwardes
15.10.1915-		Joseph Archibald Edward Malone
1.12.1916-		Alfred Butt (to 30.11.1919)
24. 9.1920-		George Grossmith and Edward Laurillard
1.10.1921-		Thomas Francis Dawe and William Cooper
1.12.1923-		Charlton Mann and William Cooper
"	1924-	Horace Fry and William Cooper
"	1926-	William Clifford Gaunt
"	1931-	George Brinton McLellan
"	1932-	James Ernest Sharpe
"	1933-	Thomas Henry Bostock (to 30.11.1940) (Not licensed)
"	1942-	Thomas Henry Bostock
"	1943-	Jack Hylton (Through 1950)

London County Council:

1940-   Musical Plays Limited (through 1950)

Literature

Official records:

G.L.C. Arch. Dpt. Th. case 416; L.C.C. Th. & M-H. Com. App. Nov. 1939-; L.C.C. Th. & M-H. Com. Papers 1888-; LC1/507-752; LC7/13-17, 20-48; L.C.O. 345 and 374; M.B.W. Rpt. 1882, pp. 5-18; Sel. Com. 1866, 1877 and 1892.

Contemporary accounts:

1858 BUILDER, 1858 Sept. 4, pp. 599-600. —Description.
BUILDER, 1858 Dec. 11, pp. 833-4. —Detailed description, plan.
BUILDING NEWS, 1858 Dec. 24, pp. 1278-9. —Description.
ILLUSTRATED LONDON NEWS, 1858 Dec. 18. Supplement pp. 579-80. —Detailed description; illus of auditorium; plan.
ILLUSTRATED NEWS OF THE WORLD, 1858 Dec. 25. —Description and drawing of auditorium.
BUILDER, 1858 Dec. 25, p. 871. —Detailed description of decor.

1865 ADELPHI THEATRE. Return of takings for 1865. (*In* Westminster. Local Collection.)

1879 BUILDING NEWS, 1879 Feb. 28, p. 241. —Renovations.

1883 BUILDER, 1883 Feb. 17, p. 227. —Report of M.B.W.'s summons of Gattis' for not carrying out required alterations.

1886 BUILDER, 1886 Nov. 27, p. 763—Report that Gattis' to purchase the Hampshire Hog, 410 Strand, and Nell Gwynne Tavern for extension.

1887 SATURDAY REVIEW, 1887 July 2. State of the London theatres, No. 3. —Detailed description.

1893 BUILDER, 1893 Feb. 4, p. 94—Report on need for alterations.

1901 SKETCH, 1901 March 6, p. 270 'New Century Theatre (late Adelphi)'—Description and illus.
BUILDER, 1901 March 16, p. 256—Brief report

of remodelling and summary of history.
BUILDING NEWS, 1901 Sept. 6, p. 310 'Century
Theatre'—description.
BUILDER, 1901 Sept. 7, p. 217.—Detailed report.
SKETCH, 1901 Sept. 11, p. 311 —Report on stage.
Illus.
1930 ARCHITECTS' JOURNAL, 1930 Dec. 3, p. 824,
828~30.—'Trigonometry in the theatre'.—Building
details.
ARCHITECT, 1930 Dec. 5, pp. 761-763 —Details
of building.
BUILDER, 1930 Dec. 5, pp. 960-962 —Building
details. Illus.
BUILDER, 1930 Dec. 5, p. 970 —'Revolving stage
at the Adelphi'. —Description and illus.
ARCHITECT, 1930 Dec. 11, pp. 825-829 —Further details.
ARCHITECT AND BUILDING NEWS, 1930 Dec.
19.—Building details.
1931 ARCHITECTURE ILLUSTRATED, 1931 Feb.
—Building details.
1950 THEATRE ownership. p. 73 and p. 106

Historical accounts:

1877 BLANCHARD, E. L.
History of the Adelphi Theatre. 10 p.
in ERA ALMANACK, 1877
'The playgoer's portfolio'.
1904 BAKER, H. Barton.
The history of the London stage and its players.
pp. 413-438.
1925 CHANCELLOR, E. B.
The pleasure haunts of London. pp. 123-125.
c. 1930 MAYES, Ronald
Romance of London theatres, Nos. 12, 63 and
152.
1930 NOTES & QUERIES, 1930 June 14, pp. 419-422
'The story of the Adelphi Theatre'.

1946 SCOTT, Harold.
The early doors. pp. 93—
1952 PULLING, Christopher
They were singing. p. 177-8 —On pantomime and
variety.
1959 ENCICLOPEDIA dello spettacolo. Vol. 6, Col.
1615.
1963 MANDER, R. and MITCHENSON, J.
The theatres of London. 2nd edition. pp. 14-20.

Location of other material

Plans:

Enthoven Collection 3 sheets (1931)
G.L.C. *Architects Department.*
Public Record Office, LC7/49 6 sheets.

Illustrations:

Enthoven Collection.
Westminster Local Collection.

Programmes and playbills:

British Museum; Enthoven Collection; Garrick Club;
Guildhall Library; London Museum; Westminster
Local Collection.

7

ADMIRAL KEPPEL PUBLIC HOUSE

Marlborough Road (*later* 77 Fulham Road), Chelsea.

In use between 1790-1856.

Management

Middlesex justices:

Mich. 1852-	Benjamin Watts
" 1859	*No petition.*

Adelphi Theatre 1858 (6)

(Victoria & Albert Museum, Crown copyright)

Literature

Official records:

Mx. Mich. Q.S. 1852-1859.

Historical accounts:

1860 CROKER, Thomas Crofton
A walk from London to Fulham... (Revised edition). William Tegg, 1860. pp. 75-76. illus.
—Notes old building pulled down 1856 and new one erected by Benjamin Watts.

1907 WROTH, Warwick
Cremorne and later London gardens. p. 93.

8

ALBERT PALACE

Prince of Wales Road, Battersea Park.

Opened: 1884. *Closed:* 1888.

Building details

Developer: Baron Grant —from the shell of the Dublin Exhibition, 1872.

Architect: Messrs. F. & H. Francis.

Capacity: (of gardens) 3900.

Area: (of palace and gardens) 10 acres

Entertainments were given in a number of places within the palace, e.g. Connaught Hall; The Nave; Outdoor Theatre.
The grounds were auctioned in 1893.

Management

Surrey justices:

Mich. 1884-	Henry Risborough Sharman
" 1886-	William Holland
" 1887-	Charles Henry Weatherly

London County Council:

| 1890- | Frederick William Hindmarsh; but licence retained as building no longer in use. Licence refused Nov. 1892 |

Literature

Official records:

G.L.C. Arch. Dpt. Th. case 032; L.C.C. Th. & M-H. App. Nov. 1889-92; Sel. Com. 1892; Sy. Mich. Q.S. 1884-1888.

Contemporary accounts:

1884 BUILDER, 1884 Oct. 25, p. 551. —Brief report of permission to build large concert room at west end of Albert Exhibition Building.

1885 GRAPHIC, 1885 June 13. —Description, illus.

1888 TIMES, 1888 Feb. 4, Aug. 2, Oct. 9, Oct. 10. —Letters on closure.

1893 BUILDER, 1893 Aug. 19, p. 134. —Account of proposed sale and note of history, with description of organ.
SOUTH WESTERN STAR, 1893 Aug. 26, —Account of auction.

Historical accounts:

1952 PULLING, Christopher.
They were singing... p. 179.

Location of other material

Plans: Battersea Local Collection, G.L.C. *Architects Department.*

Illustrations: Battersea Local Collection

Cuttings, playbills &c: Enthoven Collection, Guildhall Library.

9

ALBERT PUBLIC HOUSE

17, Grays Inn Lane, Holborn.

Licensed: 1854-1861.

Management

Middlesex justices:

| Mich. 1854- | Patrick Carroll |
| " 1861 | *No petition.* |

Literature

Official records:

Mx. Mich. Q.S. 1854-1861.

10

ALBERT SALOON

Shepherdess Walk (*later* 106 Shepherdess Walk) Hoxton.

Licensed: 1843-1851

Building details

Site: Shaftesbury Street—Wenlock Street—Cropley Street—Shepherdess Walk.

The saloon had two stages built at right angles—proscenium of one opening into the garden, and that of the other into the saloon for wet weather. Report in *Shoreditch Observer* 22. 1. 1898, in which it is referred to as the Albert Theatre, states that it was never successful and years later the Saloon was turned into the headquarters of the Tower Hamlets Volunteers.

Management

Lord Chamberlain:

29. 9. 1843-	Henry Brading
" 1850-	William Borrow
" 1852	*Not licensed as out of repair.*
" 1853	*Reported closed.*

Literature

Official records:

LC7/13; Sel. Com. 1866.

Historical accounts:

1907 WROTH, Warwick.
Cremorne and later London gardens. pp. 68-69.

1910 EVENING NEWS, 1910 July 22.
'Talks about old London: reminiscences of the oldest clown— Alfred Giovanelli'.

1925 CHANCELLOR, E. B.
The pleasure haunts of London. p. 411.
SHERSON, Erroll.
London's lost theatres... pp. 326-327.

Location of other material

Illustrations: Enthoven Collection: sketch of stage, 1845.

Programmes and playbills: British Museum, pre-1850. Guildhall Library pre 1850.

11

ALBION HALL

Albion Square, Dalston.

Licensed: 1850-1894.

Former name

Kingsland, Dalston and De Beauvoir Town Literary and Scientific Institution 1850-1868.

Building details

Area: 1440 sq.'

Capacity: 400.

Management

Middlesex justices:

Mich. 1850-	James Kent Vote
" 1853-	James Alexander Hughes.
" 1854-	William Shaw
" 1857-	William Horry
" 1867-	William Smith Horry
" 1869-	James Cox
" 1870-	Henry Budd
" 1871-	Walter Lloyd Horry
" 1874-	William Smith Horry
" 1887-	Richard William Jarrett
" 1888	Henry Charles Rawll

London County Council:

1890-	Henry Charles Rawll
1892-	Arthur Cheese
Nov. 1894	*No application.*

Literature

Official records:

L.C.C. Th. & M.H. Com. App. Nov. 1889-1893.
Mx. Mich. Q.S. 1850-1888.

12

ALBION PUBLIC HOUSE

Albion Road, (*formerly* Webb Lane) Hammersmith.

Licensed: 1848-1855.

Management

Middlesex justices:

Mich. 1849-	James Henry Wills
" 1851-	William Brown
" 1853-	James Cowderoy
" 1855	*No petition.*

Literature

Official records:

Mx. Mich. Q.S. 1848-1855.

13

ALBION PUBLIC HOUSE

Albion Road, Stoke Newington.

Licensed: 1861-1864.

Management

Middlesex justices:

Mich. 1861-	William Jonathan Smith
" 1863-	Thomas Chapman
" 1864	*No petition.*

Literature

Official records:

Mx. Mich. Q.S. 1861-1864.

14

ALBION PUBLIC HOUSE

36, Lauriston Road (*formerly* Grove Street), Hackney.

Licensed: 1856-1892.

Building details

Concert hall situated on the first floor, giving a total area of 488 sq'. Hall closed as a result of the 1878 Act.

Albert Palace 1885 (8)

(Wandsworth Public Libraries)

Management

Middlesex justices:

Mich.	1856-	William Dupree
"	1863-	Thomas Robinson Schrier
"	1864-	William Bristow
"	1865-	John Henry Bristo (as on application).
"	1873-	Isabella Watkinson
"	1874-	John Doughty
"	1876-	William Thomas Roberts
"	1877-	William Shearman
"	1879-	Henry Thomas Vickress
"	1881-	George Frederick Upward
"	1882-	Joseph Edwin Lane
"	1884-	Samuel Sherwell Pound
"	1886-	Caroline Pound

London County Council:

1890- Clara Sawyer Clarke (licence retained)
Nov. 1891 *Not licensed.*

Literature

Official records:

L.C.C. Th. & M-H. Com. App. Nov. 1889-90.
Mx. Mich. Q.S. 1856-1888.

Location of other material

Plans: G.L.C. Architects Department

15

ALBION PUBLIC HOUSE

210-211, Shadwell High Street, Shadwell.

Licensed: 1854-1876

Management

Middlesex justices:

Mich.	1854-	William Worthan
"	1857-	George Grumbridge and James Ward
"	1859-	William Creighton
"	1867-	James Clewley and Robert Samuel Keymer
"	1868-	James Clewley
"	1873-	John Stott
"	1875-	Henry Muddle
"	1876	*Licence refused.*

Literature

Official records:

Mx. Mich. Q.S. 1854-1876.

16

ALBION PUBLIC HOUSE

York Road, St. Pancras.

Licensed: 1862-1867

Management

Middlesex justices:

Mich.	1862-	James Henry Clowting
"	1867	*No petition.*

Literature

Official records:

Mx. Mich. Q.S. 1862-1867.

17

ALDWYCH THEATRE

Aldwych, Strand.

Opened: 23rd December 1905

Building details

Developer: Seymour Hicks

Architect: W. C. R. Sprague

Builder: Walter Wallis of Balham

Capacity: (1950) 1100

Auditorium: (1950) S. 378; D.C. 299; U.C. 109; G. 350;
Bx. A-H.

Stage: 31'10" wide, 30' high, 37' deep.

Management

Lord Chamberlain:

23.12.1905- Charles Frohman (Theatre closed
from end of 1908)
1.10 1909- Philip Yorke
1.11.1909- Sidney Marler (died Jan. 1910)
Theatre in the hands of the liquidators of the Law
Guarantee, Trust and Accident Society.
3.2.1910- Frederick Melville
8.5.1911- Herbert Sleath (to 12.6.1911)
Letter dated 2.11.1911 - liquidators of Law Guarantee, Trust and Accident Society sold out to Joseph
Beecham.
1.12.1911- Albert Archdeacon
4.7.1912- Alfred McLeod Loader
27.2,1915- Donald Baylis (to 1.12.1918)
Letter 27.7.1917 - Donald Baylis approached Sir
Thomas Beecham (owner) to permit the Australian
Y.M.C.A. the use of the theatre as a recreation hall.
13.8.1917 permission granted.
Letter 30.9.1919 - A. E. Abrahams (owner) gave 7
yr. lease to C. B. Cochran to start as soon as the
theatre restored.
31.10.1919- C. B. Cochran
30.10.1922- Tom Walls and Leslie Henson
1.12.1927- Tom Walls
1.12.1933- David Albert Abrahams
(1940-41 Not licensed)
1.12.1941- David Albert Abrahams (through 1950)

Literature

Official Records:

G.L.C. Arch. Dpt. Th. case 417; L.C.C. 374 and 428.

Contemporary accounts:

1905 BUILDING NEWS, 1905 Dec. 29, p. 918—Brief
description.
ERA, 1905 Dec. 30, p. —Building description.
TIMES, 1905 Dec. 30. —Report of opening.
1950 THEATRE ownership. p. 54, 58, 87.

Historical accounts:

c. 1930 MAYES, Ronald.
Romance of London theatres. No. 4

1959 ENCICLOPEDIA dello spettacolo. Vol. 6 Col. 1615.
1963 MANDER, Raymond *and* MITCHENSON, Joe
The theatres of London. 2nd edition. pp. 21-25.
1965/6 BRITISH THEATRE MUSEUM. 'Sixty years at the Aldwych' [Catalogue] of 6th exhibition.

Location of other material

Plans: G.L.C. *Architects Department*

Programmes and playbills:

British Museum Library; Enthoven Collection; Garrick Club; London Museum; Westminster Local Collection.

18

ALEXANDRA HALL

Charlton.

Licensed: 1866-1884

Former name

Alexandra Assembly Rooms.

Management

West Kent justices:

Mich. 1866-	Edgar Drewett
" 1869-	Thomas Simpson
" 1872-	Edgar Drewett
" 1873-	Edwin Shalless
" 1876-	Alfred William Johnson Budds
" 1884	*Not licensed.*

Literature

Official records:

W. Kt. Mich. Q.S. 1866-1883.

19

ALEXANDRA THEATRE and HIGHBURY BARN

19, Highbury Park, Islington.

Opened as a place of entertainment: 1740. *Closed:* 1871

Former names

Willoughby's Tea Rooms
Royal Alexandra Theatre.

Building details

1865 rebuilding:

'The Royal Alexandra... erected on a portion of my extensive property adjoining the Highbury Barn gardens. (The old barn of the Manor of Highbury was opened as a pleasure resort in 1740). The theatre only having stalls... a commodious balcony similar to the dress circle in other theatres, and a most comfortable pit'. *(from publicity handout)*

Cost: £20,000

Capacity: 1900

Management

Middlesex justices:

Mich. 1852-	Archibald Hinton
" 1865-	Edward Giovannelli
" 1871	*Licence refused to* E. T. Smith.

Lord Chamberlain:

| 16.5.1865- | Edward Giovannelli |
| 5.4.1871- | E. T. Smith (to 29.9.1871). |

Literature

Official records:

LC7/15, 22-23; Mx. Mich. Q.S. 1852-1871; Sel. Com. 1866 and 1877.

Contemporary accounts:

1857 RITCHIE, J. Ewing. The night side of London. pp. 152-7.
1865 GIOVANNELLI, Edward. Publicity circular. (Copy in Islington Local Collection.)
CITY PRESS, 1865 May 20.—Description.
ERA, 1865 May 21.—Description.
TIMES, 1865 May 22.—Description.
DAILY TELEGRAPH, 1865 May 22. —Description.
MORNING POST, 1865 May 23. —Description.
MORNING ADVERTISER, 1865 May 23. —Description.

Historical accounts:

1871 ERA Almanack, 1871 pp. 3-4.
1883 WILLIAMS, Michael
Some London theatres past and present. pp. 33-46.
1908 DAILY TELEGRAPH, 1908 Jan. 25.
'The old gardens: outdoor amusements in London'.
—Brief history of Highbury Barn.
1925 CHANCELLOR, E. B.
The pleasure haunts of London. pp. 380-82.
SHERSON, Erroll.
London's lost theatres... pp. 289-291.
c. 1930 MAYES, Ronald
Romance of London theatres, No. 71.
1952 PULLING, Christopher
They were singing... p. 11, 170.
1955 ISLINGTON. Public Libraries.
Islington and the theatre (exhibition). p. 8.

Location of other material

Plans: G.L.C. *Architects Department*

Programmes and Playbills:

Islington Local Collection (1 playbill); Enthoven Collection.

20

ALEXANDRA THEATRE

Between 67-69, Stoke Newington Road, Stoke Newington.

Opened: 27 December 1897. *Closed:* October 1950.

Former names

New Alexandra Theatre 1897-
Palace Theatre of Varieties 1906-9

Building details

Owner: F. W. Purcell

Architect: Frank Matcham

Capacity: (1897) c. 3000

Auditorium: (1897) S. 200; P. 600; D.C. 200; U.C. 400;
G. 600; Bx. 25.
After the 1939-45 war, although the building retained
the name of Alexandra Theatre, it was used for a
variety of different purposes. including boxing tourna-
ments.

Management

Lord Chamberlain:

27.12.1897-   Frederick William Purcell
Letter 7.6.1905- from F.W. Purcell stating that
theatre had been purchased by H.G.D. Bennett.
31.10.1905-   Henry George Dudley Bennett
                (to 31.10.1907)
 4.12.1906   Letter stating theatre now licensed
                by L.C.C.
 1. 3.1909-   Oswald Stoll for Moss Empires Ltd.
 1.11.1911-   George Ernest Williams
14. 2.1916-   Frank Allen
Letter 17.5.1917- theatre taken over by Hackney and
Shepherds Bush Empire Palaces Ltd.
23. 5.1917-   Oswald Stoll (to 30.11.1919)
 1.12.1921-   Arthur William Pearce (to 28.9.1931)

From this time the Lord Chamberlain's licence was
subsidiary to that of the L.C.C.

 1.12.1931-   George Edward Woodman
  "   1932-   Arthur William Pearce
  "   1934-   George Barclay
  "   1939-   Stanley Thomas Wootton
  "   1946-   Abraham Adolph Dubens
  "   1948-   Nathan Gersh Beitler
  "   1949-   Abraham Adolph Dubens

London County Council:

1932-   Standard Cinema Properties Ltd.
1933-   Alexandra Theatre (Stoke Newington) Ltd.
1935-   Alexandra Theatre (Lessees) Ltd.
1940-   Alexandra Theatre (Stoke Newington) Ltd.
1947-   Boojan Properties and Productions Ltd.

The theatre was closed during the war years.

Literature

Official records:

G.L.C. Arch. Dpt. Mss. Index;
G.L.C. Arch. Dpt. Th. case 457.
L.C.C. Th. & M-H. Com. App. Nov. 1931+
L.C.C. Th. & M-H. Com. Papers. 1896+
LC7/44-48; L.C.O. 346 and 374.

Contemporary accounts:

1896 BUILDER, 1896 Oct. 24, p. 339.—Brief report of
     proposed new theatre.
1897 BUILDING NEWS, 1897 Dec. 31, p. 960.—Brief
     description.
1898 BUILDER, 1898 Jan. 1, p. 24.—Brief description
     of theatre nearing completion.

Historical accounts:

c. 1930 MAYES, Ronald.
        Romance of London theatres, No. 193.

1960 HEASMAN, R. W.
     Alexandra Theatre, Stoke Newington. 11p.
     Typescript.—Gives brief history and list of
     plays—compiled from local papers.
     (*In* Stoke Newington Local Collection).

Location of other material

Plans: G.L.C. *Architects Department;*
Enthoven Collection, 1929 (2 sheets)

Programmes and playbills:

Enthoven Collection; Guildhall Library; London
Museum; Westminster Local Collection.

21

ALHAMBRA

Church Street, Woolwich.

Licensed: 1869-1872.

Management

West Kent justices:

Mich. 1869-   William Heathman
  "   1872   *No application.*

Literature

Official records:

W. Kt. Mich. Q.S. 1869-1871.

22

ALHAMBRA PALACE

27, Leicester Square, and 23-25, Charing Cross Road,
Westminster.

Opened: 18th March 1854. *Closed:* 1st September 1936.

Former names:

Panoptican of Science and Art 1854-58
Great United States Circus 1858
Alhambra Palace 1858-
Royal Alhambra Palace 1863-
Royal Alhambra Theatre
Theatre Royal, Alhambra
Alhambra Theatre of Varieties
Alhambra Theatre
New Alhambra Theatre

Building details

1st building:

Building erected as Panoptican of Science and Art.

Architect: Messrs. Finden and Lewis.

Cost: £100,000

Exhibition capacity: 5000

In 1858 E. T. Smith took it over for 'entertainments'.

Capacity: 2208.

In 1860 major alterations were made, and a stage
built in order that it could be used as a music hall.

Contractor: William Beverley.

Cost: £120,000

(Above) Alhambra Palace (22)

(Greater London Council Photograph Library)

(Left) Royal Panoptican of Science and Art 1851 (22)

(The Builder)

Alexandra Theatre, Stoke Newington, c. 1950 (20)

(Greater London Council Photograph Library)

Capacity: 3,500

Auditorium: Prom. 140; P. 128; P.S. 140; Faut. 251; Bx. 274; S.B. 175; B.S. 261; G. 632; U.G. 205.

In 1864 further alterations carried out for Frederick Strange.

Architect: J.H.Rowley.

Builder: W.Bass.

—a fourth gallery erected.

Destroyed by fire 7th December 1882.

2nd building:

Opened: 3rd December 1883

Architect: Messrs. John Perry and Frederick Reed.

Contractor: W.Bass.

1888 Redecoration:

Architect: E.Clark.

Contractor: Campbell Smith & Co.

1892 Reconstruction:

Circle extended by reduction of boxes.
New electrical plant installed.

Architect: Messrs. Clark and Pollard.

Capacity: (1912) 2336 with 838 standing.

Auditorium: (Seating) Part. 588; G.C. 166; B. 226; A. 160; G. 298.

1897 A new 'grand entrance' made.

Architect: W.M.Brutton.

—Demolished November 1936.

Site now occupied by Odeon Cinema.

Management

Middlesex justices:

Mich.	1858-	Edward Tyrrell Smith
"	1861-	William Wilde, Jnr.
"	1865-	Frederick Strange
"	1870	*Licence refused.*

Lord Chamberlain:

24. 4.1871-	Frederick Strange
16. 3.1872-	John Baum
3. 4.1875-	Joseph Arnold Cave
4. 2.1876-	Frederick Christopher Leader
3. 7.1877-	Thomas Kittle
12.11.1877-	Charles Morton
5. 6.1880-	James Killingsworth
6. 4.1881-	Howard Paul
29. 9.1881-	Sydney Alport
8. 2.1882-	James Howell (to 28. 9. 1884)

Licences granted to run concurrently with L.C.C. music and dancing licences...

October 1912-	Henry William Woodford
1. 3.1913-	Dudley John Gayford (to 1936)

London County Council:

1890-	Edwin Winder
1892-	James Howell
1893-	Albert Augustus Gilmer
1895-	Henry William Woodford
1915-	Dudley John Gayford
1926-	Alhambra Company Ltd. (to 1936)

10

Literature

Official records:

G.L.C. Arch. Dpt. Mss. Index;
G.L.C. Arch. Dpt. Th. case 7;
L.C.C. Th. & M-H. Com. App. Nov. 1889-1935;
L.C.C. Th. & M-H. Com. Papers 1882-1936;
LC7/14-17, 25-31, 89; L.C.O. 143 and 374;
M.B.W. Rpt. 1882; Mx. Mich. Q.S. 1858-72 and 1884-88;
Sel. Com. 1866 and 1892.

Contemporary accounts:

1851 BUILDER, 1851 Dec. 20, pp. 802-3.—Description, plan. illus.
1852 ILLUSTRATED LONDON NEWS, 1852 Jan. 31. —Description.
1853 BUILDER, 1853 May 7 and 14, pp. 290-1 and 308-9 —Paper read by architect T. Hayter Lewis to R.I.B.A. on 18th April 1853. Description.
1854 BUILDER, 1854 March 11, p. 137.—Description of decoration on opening of building.
ILLUSTRATED LONDON NEWS, 1854 March 18 —Description.
ROYAL PANOPTICAN OF SCIENCE AND ART. The illustrated handbook... by W. White. (B.M. 7956 b. 36)
1858 ILLUSTRATED LONDON NEWS, 1858 April 3. —Description.
ILLUSTRATED LONDON NEWS, 1858 June 12. —Note on the conversion of the building into the 'Great United States Circus'.
1860 ERA, 1860 Dec. 2.—Description
ERA, 1860 Dec. 9.—Detailed description giving names of designers, artists, &c.
ERA, 1860 Dec. 16.—Description of opening
1864 ERA, 1864 Dec. 25.—Description of alterations and entertainment.
1869 ROYAL ALHAMBRA PALACE, Illustrated handbook... by W. White. Nicholls Bros. 1869. (B.M. 10350 bb 35 (5)).
1871 DAILY TELEGRAPH, 1871 April 27.—Report on reopening and conversion from a music hall into a theatre, after refusal of a music and dancing licence.
ERA, 1871 April 30.—Description of reopening.
1880 BUILDER, 1880 Nov. 27, p. 657.—Report of auction of freehold land including that on which the theatre stood.
1881 BUILDING NEWS, 1881 Dec. 2, p. 745.—Brief description of repairs and alterations.
BUILDER, 1881 Dec. 3 and 10, pp. 707, and 739-40.—Report of redecoration and some structural alterations including widening of proscenium and illumination of dome by electric light.
DAILY NEWS, 1881 Dec. 5.—Description of new decorations.
1882 BUILDER, 1882 June 3, p. 670.—Description and illus of shoring.
BUILDER, 1882 Dec. 9, pp. 761-2.—Description of fire.
ERA, 1882 Dec. 9.—Report of fire.
ILLUSTRATED LONDON NEWS, 1882 Dec. 16. —Illus. of destruction of theatre by fire.
1883 BUILDER, 1883 Feb. 24, p. 235.—Brief report of proposed building.
BUILDER, 1883 April 21, p. 553.—List of tenders.
BUILDER, 1883 June 16, pp. 810, 814 and 816. —Description of proposed new theatre. Illus. of foyer of second tier and auditorium.
BUILDING NEWS, 1883 Aug. 31, p. 343.—Detailed description.

ERA, 1883 Sept. 8, 'The new Alhambra'—progress report.
BUILDER, 1883 Oct. 20, p. 541.—Brief report on gas lighting.
BUILDER, 1883 Oct. 27, p. 574.—Report that auditorium to be lit by Strode and Company's patent ventilating sun-burner.
BUILDER, 1883 Nov. 10, pp. 636-7.—Description.
The ERA, 1883 Nov. 10.—Detailed description.
ALHAMBRA THEATRE ROYAL (Publicity leaflet). Reopened December 3rd, 1883. 16p. illus. (Copy in Enthoven Collection).
1884 BUILDER, 1884 April 12, p. 531 —Report of alterations.
DAILY NEWS, 1884 April 14.—Brief description of decorations.
1887 SATURDAY REVIEW, 1887 June 11. The state of the London theatres... No. 1.—Detailed description.
1888 BUILDING NEWS, 1888 April 6, p. 493.—Description of new decorations.
BUILDER, 1888 April 7, p. 249.—Description of decorations.
1892 BUILDER, 1892 Sept. 24, p. 251.—Report of partial rebuilding.
ALHAMBRA THEATRE. The Alhambra alterations and decorations. London, 1892. (B.M. 1882 c. 2 (124)).
1896 BUILDING NEWS, 1896 Oct. 30, p. 631.—Note of building of extension to back of theatre. Illus. of Charing Cross Road elevation.
SACHS, Edwin O. and WOODROW, E. A. E. Modern opera houses and theatres. Vol. 1, pp. 42-3.—Description, dimensions, plates and plans.
1897 SKETCH, 1897 March 3.—Article by John Hollingshead on 'The Alhambra extension'.
1898 SACHS, Edwin O. and WOODROW, E. A. E. Modern opera houses and theatres. Vol. 3. plates, plans.
1907 BUILDING NEWS, 1907 May 17, pp. 683-4. —Description of partial reconstruction and redecoration.
1937 ILLUSTRATED LONDON NEWS, 1937 Jan. 9. —Drawing by Bryan de Grineau of demolition.

Historical accounts:

c. 1863 ROYAL ALHAMBRA PALACE
Programme of entertainments. J. Ring, c. 1863. 8p.—Includes an account of the building.
1904 BARKER, H. Barton.
History of the London stage and its players. pp. 343-4.—Its history as a theatre.
1915 DANCING TIMES, 1915 Feb.-June. Articles by Mark E. Perugini: 'The story of the Alhambra, 1854-1912'. illus.
c. 1930 MAYES, Ronald
Romance of London theatres No. 2.
1935 HADDON, Archibald
The story of the music-hall... Numerous references.
1938 DISHER, M. Willson
Winkles and champagne...—Numerous references.
1946 SCOTT, Harold
Early doors. pp. 153+
1952 PULLING, Christopher
They were singing...—Numerous references.
1959 ENCICLOPEDIA dello spettacolo, Vol. VI Col. 1615-6.
GUEST, Ivor Forbes

The Alhambra ballet. Brooklyn Dance Perspectives Inc., 1959. 72p. illus. (Dance perspectives 4).
1966 GREATER LONDON COUNCIL
Survey of London, Vol. 34, 1966. pp. 495-9. plans, plates.
1968 MANDER, Raymond and MITCHENSON, Joe
The lost theatres of London. pp. 15-50. 7 illus.

Location of other material

Plans:

Enthoven Collection, 1930s (3 sheets).
G.L.C. *Architects Department.*
Middlesex Record Office. Dep. Plan 643 (1862).
Public Record Office, LC7/50.

Programmes and playbills:

British Museum Library; Enthoven Collection; Guildhall Library; London Museum; Westminster Local Collection.

23

ALMA MUSIC HALL

at Alma Public House, 29 Alma Street, Islington.

Licensed: 1856-c. 1922.

Building details

Concert room on the first floor attached to public house known as the 'The Alma Music Hall'.

Capacity: 300 (later reduced to 100).

Management

Middlesex justices:

Mich. 1856-	Solomon Deacon
" 1860-	John Peter Craven
" 1867-	George Skinner
" 1868	*Licence refused owing to Sunday trading.*
" 1870-	George Skinner
" 1873-	Edmund Harsthorn
" 1874-	James Savill
" 1875-	Alfred John Saltmer
" 1879-	Elizabeth Wadkin
" 1882-	Edward Cole

London County Council:

1890-	Edward Cole
1891-	Charles Elledge
1895-	Walter Elledge
1897-	John Webb
1900-	Isabella Webb

Nov. 1903 *Not listed as a theatre or music-hall.*

Literature

Official records:

G.L.C. Arch. Dpt. Mss. Index; G.L.C. Arch. Dpt. Th. case 10; L.C.C. Th. & M-H. Com. App. Nov. 1889-1902. Mx. Mich. Q.S. 1856-68; 1871-88. Sel. Com. 1892.

Location of other material

Plans: G.L.C. *Architects Department.*

24

ALWYNE CASTLE PUBLIC HOUSE

St. Paul's Road, Islington.

Licensed: 1855-c. 1861.

Management

Middlesex justices:

Mich. 1855-   George Frederick Kerchner
" 1862   *Manager reported having left property.*

Literature

Official records:

Mx. Mich. Q.S. 1855-62.

25

AMBASSADORS' THEATRE

Tower Street, and West Street, Holborn.

Opened: 5th June 1913.

Building details

Developer: Ambassadors' Theatre Ltd. (originally called Casino Theatre Ltd.) Directors: J. F. H. and A. C. Jay, and Prince Littler.

Architect: W. G. R. Sprague.

Builder: Kingerlec and Sons of Oxford.

Capacity: (1950) 490.

Auditorium: S. 210; B. S. 122; U. C. 54; Bx. A-C.

Stage: 24'6" wide, 17'10" high, 20'6" deep.

Management

Lord Chamberlain:

5. 6.1913-   John Herbert Jay
1.12.1933-   Frank Rolison Littler
1.12.1937-   John Herbert Jay
(1940-1941 not licensed).
1.12.1941-   John Herbert Jay (through 1950).

Literature

Official records:

G.L.C. Arch. Dpt. Th. case 2009; L.C.O. 374 and 533.

Contemporary accounts:

1912 BUILDER, 1912 Nov. 1, p. 505. —Brief report that theatre to be built.
1913 ERA, 1913 June 7. —Building description.
1950 THEATRE ownership. . . pp. 64 and 95.

Historical accounts:

c. 1930 MAYES, Ronald. Romance of London theatres, No. 20.
1959 ENCICLOPEDIA dello spettacolo, Vol. 6, Col. 1616.
1963 MANDER, Raymond, *and* MITCHENSON, Joe. The theatres of London. 2nd ed. pp. 26-29.

Location of other material

Plans: G.L.C. *Architects Department.*

Programmes and playbills:

British Museum Library; Enthoven Collection; Garrick Club; Guildhall Library; London Museum; Westminster Local Collection.

26

AMERSHAM HALL

411, New Cross Road, Deptford.

Licensed: 1885-after 1903

Former names

Conservative Club Hall 1885-1888

Building details

Described by L.C.C. as a small music hall with stage, on the ground floor of the building.

Capacity: 250.

Management

West Kent justices:

Mich. 1885-   Robert Wallbutton
" 1888-   Ernest Collard
" 1889   *Licence refused*

London County Council:

1890-   Stephen Winn
1896-   William Albert Schultz
Nov. 1903 *not listed as theatre or music-hall.*

Literature

Official records:

G.L.C. Arch. Dpt. Mss. Index;
L.C.C. Th. & M-H. Com. App. Nov. 1889-1902;
Sel. Com. 1892; W. Kt. Mich. Q.S. 1885-1889.

27

AMHERST ARMS PUBLIC HOUSE

Shacklewell, Hackney.

Licensed: 1854-1862.

Management

Middlesex justices:

Mich. 1854-   John Blake
" 1862   *No petition.*

Literature

Official records:

Mx. Mich. Q.S. 1854-62.

28

ANCHOR AND HOPE PUBLIC HOUSE

50, Edward Street, Stepney.

Licensed: 1855-1863.

Management

Middlesex justices:

Mich.	1855-	James Prevost
"	1860-	James Wrangham
"	1861-	James Pottinger
"	1863	*No petition.*

Literature

Official records:

Mx. Mich. Q.S. 1855-63.

29

ANCHOR HILL AND COFFEE PALACE

130-132, King Street, Hammersmith.

Licensed: 1880-1882.

Management

Middlesex justices:

Mich.	1880-	Charles Ashby
"	1882	*Licence not renewed.*

Literature

Official records:

Mx. Mich. Q.S. 1880-82.

30

ANGEL PUBLIC HOUSE

4, Back Road, St. George in the East, Stepney

Licensed: 1855-1856.

Management

Middlesex justices:

Mich.	1855-	Jane Willer
"	1856	*No petition.*

Literature

Official records:

Mx. Mich. Q.S. 1855-56.

31

ANGEL AND CROWN PUBLIC HOUSE

Tabernacle Square, Shoreditch.

Licensed: 1862-1875.

Management

Middlesex justices:

Mich.	1862-	Charles William Neale
"	1864-	George Smith Medus
"	1867-	Francis Frebout
"	1871-	Walter Boston
"	1875	*No petition.*

Literature

Official records:

Mx. Mich. Q.S. 1862-74.

32

APOLLO MUSIC HALL

at Red Cross Public House, 25, Hare Street, Bethnal Green.

Licensed: 1854-1871.

Building details

Cost: £ 3 000

Capacity: 600

Correspondence with the L.C.C. 1890-1891, refers to a proposal by the proprietor Mr. Hay to clear away partitions and floors at the back of the building to restore them to their former position as the 'Apollo Music Hall'. Nothing materialized.

Management

Middlesex justices:

Mich.	1854-	William Davis
"	1861	*Licence refused to* William Walker
"	1861-	Mr. Sleigh
"	1862-	Michael Abrahams
"	1867-	Mary Ann Agar
"	1869-	Israel Martin
"	1871	*No petition.*

Literature

Official records:

G.L.C. Arch. Dpt. Th. case 040/127;
Mx. Mich. Q.S. 1854-71;
Sel. Com. 1866 and 1877.

33

APOLLO THEATRE

Shaftesbury Avenue, Westminster.

Opened: 21st February 1901.

Proposed name:

(not adopted) Mascot Theatre.

Building details

Developer: Henry Lowenfeld

Architect: Lewin Sharp

Builder: Walter Wallis

Capacity: (1950) 893

Auditorium: S. 162; D.C. 250; U.C. 138; P. (not numbered): Bx. A-J.

Stage: 30′ wide, 24′ high, 24′ deep.

Management

Lord Chamberlain:

29. 9.1901-	Henry Lowenfeld
1. 11.1904-	Tom Buffen Davis
30. 9.1920-	George Grossmith and Edward Laurillard
1. 10.1921-	Thomas Francis Dawe and William Cooper
1. 12.1923-	Charlton Mann and William Cooper
1. 12.1924-	Horace Fry and William Cooper
" 1926-	William Clifford Gaunt
" 1930-	George Brinton McLellan

" 1932-   James Ernest Sharpe
" 1933-   Thomas Henry Bostock
(1940-1941 not licensed)
" 1941-   Thomas Henry Bostock
" 1943-   Prince Littler, (through 1950).

Literature

Official records:

G.L.C. Arch. Dpt. Th. case 418;
L.C.C. Th.& M-H. Com. Papers 1889+;
LC7/48; L.C.O. 104 and 374.

Contemporary accounts:

1900   BUILDER, 1900 Aug. 25, p. 180. —Note of proposed theatre.
1901   BUILDING NEWS, 1901 Feb. 22, pp. 260-1. —Brief description.
       BUILDER, 1901 Feb. 23, p. 194. —Note of erection.
1950   THEATRE ownership... pp. 58 and 88.

Historical accounts:

1904   BAKER, H. Barton
       The history of the London stage and its players. pp. 533-4.
c. 1930 MAYES, Ronald
       Romance of London theatres, No. 30.
1952   PULLING, Christopher
       They were singing... A number of brief references.
1959   ENCICLOPEDIA dello spettacolo, Vol. 6 Col. 1616.
1963   LONDON. County Council.
       Survey of London: St. James's. Vol. 31-32.1963 pp. 52, 71, 76-7. Plates 34a, 34, plan.
       MANDER, Raymond, *and* MITCHENSON, Joe.
       The theatres of London, 2nd. ed. pp. 30-34.

Location of other material

Plans: G.L.C. Architects Department;
Enthoven Collection, 1943? (2 sheets)

Programmes and playbills:

British Museum Library; Enthoven Collection;
Garrick Club; Guildhall Library; London Museum;
Westminster Local Collection.

34

APPROACH PUBLIC HOUSE

47, Approach Road, Bethnal Green.

Licensed: 1861-1889.

Building details

Area: 40' × 20'.

Capacity: 100.

The hall was closed as a result of the 1878 Act.

Management

Middlesex justices:

Mich. 1861-   Abraham Keymer
"   1863-   George Glave
"   1864-   Charles Entwhistle
"   1868-   Thomas Lloyd.

London County Council:

Nov. 1889 *Licence refused.*

Literature

Official records:

G.L.C. Arch. Dpt. Th. case 040/4.
Mx. Mich. Q.S. 1861-1888.

35

ARTS THEATRE CLUB

6-7, Great Newport Street, St. Martin's Lane,
Westminster.

Opened: 20th April 1927.

Building details

Developers: Walter Payne, Bronson Albery and W.E. Gillespie.

Architect: P. Morley Horder.

Capacity: (1950) 324

Auditorium: (1950) S. 218; C. 106; Bx. A-B.

Stage: 20'6" wide, 13' high, 18' deep.

Management

As a theatre club this building came outside the licensing regulations.

Literature

Official records:

G.L.C. Arch. Dpt. Th. case 3313.

Contemporary accounts:

1927   NEW STATESMAN, 1927 May 28, pp. 214-5. 'Experimental theatre (Arts Theatre Club)' by W. J. Turner.
       NEW STATESMAN, 1927 June 4, pp. 246-7. —Correspondence.

Historical accounts:

c. 1930 MAYES, Ronald
       Romance of London theatres, No. 203.
1963   MANDER, Raymond, *and* MITCHENSON, Joe
       The theatres of London, 2nd ed. pp. 258-259.
1966   GREATER LONDON COUNCIL
       Survey of London, Vol. 34, 1966. p. 346.

Location of other material

Plans: G.L.C. Architects Department

Programmes and playbills:

Enthoven Collection; Garrick Club;
Westminster Local Collection.

36

ASHBY CASTLE PUBLIC HOUSE

10, Upper Ashby Street, Northampton Square,
Finsbury.

Licensed: 1856-1858.

Management

Middlesex justices:

Mich. 1856- Walter Cannon
"   1858 *No petition.*

Literature

Official records:

Mx. Mich. Q.S. 1856-58.

37

ASSEMBLY HOUSE PUBLIC HOUSE

298, Kentish Town Road, St. Pancras.

Licensed: 1848-1890, (with interruptions).

Management

Middlesex justices:

Mich. 1848-	James Wise
" 1850-	Mary Wise
" 1852-	Charles Crane (to Mich. 1853)
" 1857-	Joseph Creech (to Mich. 1858)
" 1860-	Henry Bryon
" 1862-	Benjamin Catchpole
" 1863-	Mary Ann Catchpole (licence rarely used.)
" 1878-	William Harwood
" 1884-	John Ernest Gerlach
" 1886-	George Alexander Bacon

London County Council:

1890 George Alexander Bacon
Nov. 1890 *Licence refused.*

Literature

Official records:

L.C.C. Th. & M-H. Com. App. Nov. 1889-1890.
Mx. Mich. Q.S. 1848-52, 1857. 1860-88.

38

ASTLEY'S THEATRE

6 and 7, Westminster Bridge Road, Lambeth.

Opened: 1770 *Closed:* 1893.

Former names

Royal Saloon 1791-
Royal Grove 1794-
Astley's Amphitheatre of Arts 1795-
Royal Amphitheatre 1804-
Davis's Royal Amphitheatre 1823?-
Royal Amphitheatre (Astley's) 1825-
Batty's Amphitheatre 1842-
Theatre Royal, Westminster c. 1862-
New Westminster Theatre Royal c. 1862-
Astley's Theatre 1863-
Theatre Royal, Astley's c. 1867-
Sanger's Grand National Amphitheatre 1883-

Building details

1st building:

1775 Amphitheatre partially covered and seated.
1782 Ring covered.

2nd building:

Opened: 1784.

Philip Astley constructed first completely covered amphitheatre with stage.

Destroyed by fire: 1794.

3rd building:

Opened: Easter Monday 1795. *Closed, destroyed by fire:* 1803.

4th building:

Opened: 1804. *Destroyed by fire:* 1830.

5th building:

Opened: 1831? *Destroyed by fire:* 1841.

6th building:

Opened: 1842.

Reconstructed 1862:

Architect: R. W. Griffiths.

Builder: Messrs. Patrick & Son.

Capacity: 3780.

Reconstructed 1872:

Architect: J. T. Robinson.

Builder: Mr. Snowden.

Capacity: (1882) 2407.

Auditorium: S. 360; P. 769; D.C. 176; A. 176; G. 677; Bx. 249.

Closed as unsafe: 1893

Demolished: 1893.

Management

Lord Chamberlain:

29. 9. 1843-	William Batty
28. 3. 1853-	William Cooke
29. 9. 1860-	William Batty
1. 12. 1862-	Dion Boucicault
29. 9. 1863-	William Batty
23. 11. 1863-	Edward Tyrell Smith
27. 10. 1866-	William Hamilton Codrington Nation (to 26. 10. 1868)
23. 3. 1869-	Charles Gaddener (*or* Gardener) (to 28. 9. 1869)
30. 10. 1869-	James Harwood (to 28. 9. 1870)
26. 12. 1870-	John Baum (to 18. 3. 1871)
29. 9. 1871-	John Sanger, and George Sanger
29. 9. 1874-	John Sanger
29. 9. 1885-	George Sanger (to 28. 9. 1892).

Literature

Official records:

G.L.C. Arch. Dpt. Th. case 07;
LC1/526, 546, 547; LC7/12-17, 20-39, 89;
M.B.W. Rpt. 1882, pp. 13-23;
Sel. Com. 1866, 1877 and 1892.

Contemporary accounts:

1850-51 TALLIS'S DRAMATIC MAGAZINE, 1850-1, pp. 57 and 89.

1862 BUILDING NEWS, 1862 Dec. 26, p. 492+
—Description.
BUILDER, 1862 Dec. 27, p. 927. —Report of
rebuilding.
1872 BUILDER, 1872 Oct. 26, p. 841. —Proposed
reconstruction.
1893 BUILDER, 1893 Feb. 4, p. 94. —Report that
theatre was in an unsafe condition.
DAILY TELEGRAPH, 1893 March 7.
'Astley's Amphitheatre' —report of demolition
and brief history.
BUILDER, 1893 March 25, pp. 229-30. —Report
of demolition and brief history.

Historical accounts:

1879 DRAMATIC NOTES, 1879, pp. 72-3. —Historical
account.
1893 GRAPHIC, 1893 March 18, pp. 275-6. Illus.
—History of theatre in process of being
demolished.
1904 The MICROCOSM of London... Vol. 1 p. 19+
—Description.
BAKER, H. Barton
History of the London stage and its players...
pp. 384-9.
1913 SANGER, George
Seventy years a showman.
Dent, 1913. 215p.
1925 CHANCELLOR, E. B.
The pleasure haunts of London. pp. 420-22.
SHERSON, Erroll
London's lost theatres... pp. 52-76.
c. 1930 MAYES, Ronald
Romance of London theatres, No. 33.
1950 CONNOISSEUR, 1950 Dec. pp. 186-9. —'Hash-
ley's (Astley's) Amphitheatre', by A. V.
Sutherland-Graeme.
1951 LONDON. County Council.
Survey of London. Vol. 23, 1951. pp. 70-72.
1952 PULLING, Christopher
They were singing... Historical references.
1959 ENCICLOPEDIA dello spettacolo. Vol. 6 Col.
1616.

Location of other material

Plans: G.L.C. *Architects Department.*
Public Record Office. LC7/51. 4 sheets dated
1. 10. 1872. —Plans of proposed alterations for the
Sangers.

Illustrations: Enthoven Collection; Lambeth. Local
Collection; London Museum.

Programmes and playbills:

British Museum Library; Enthoven Collection;
Garrick Club; Guildhall Library; Lambeth Local
Collection; London Museum.

Illustrations, playbills & cuttings:

London Museum Library *in* The Pleasure gardens of
South London. Vol. II. pp. 83-93.

39

ATHENAEUM

Camden Road, Islington.

Opened: 1871 *to after* 1903

Building details

Architect: F. R. Meeson.

Contractors: Messrs. Gough and Lawton.
'Community centre' including meeting halls, libraries
and a large hall for theatrical and musical performances.

Management

Middlesex justices:

Mich. 1871-   John Heaton
  "   1875-   Allan Booth (to Mich. 1889)

London County Council:

1894-   Allan Booth
1895-   William Edward Beale
Nov. 1903 *Not listed as a theatre or music-hall.*

Literature

Official records:

G.L.C. Arch. Dpt. Th. case 14;
L.C.C. Th. & M-H. Com. App. Nov. 1893-1902;
L.C.C. Th. & M-H. Com. Papers, 1888+;
Mx. Mich. Q.S. 1871-1888.

Contemporary accounts:

1871 BUILDER, 1871 March 25, p. 231. —Brief
description.
BUILDER, 1871 July 8, p. 524 —Report on the
opening of the first part.
1873 BUILDING NEWS, 1873 Jan. 17, p. 88
—Description.

Location of other material

Plans: G.L.C. *Architects Department.*

40

ATHENAEUM

Highbury New Park.

Licensed: 1882-1889

Former names

Highbury Athenaeum.

Building details

Concert hall on the ground floor, with minor hall on
first floor.

Capacity: 1060

Auditorium: S. 800; G. 60; Platform 200.

Management

Middlesex justices:

Mich. 1882-   Charles Horsley (to Mich. 1889)

London County Council:

Nov. 1889 *No licence issued.*

Literature

Official records:

G.L.C. Arch. Dpt. Mss. Index;
G.L.C. Arch. Dpt. Th. case 149;
L.C.C. Th. & M-H. Com. Papers 1889+;
Mx. Mich. Q.S. 1882-1888.

Location of other material

Plans: G.L.C. *Architects Department.*

41

ATHENAEUM

Tottenham Court Road.

Mentioned by Alladyce Nicoll *in* 'Late Nineteenth Century Drama'. —Plays produced there in 1887-9. British Museum Library has one programme for 26th January 1893, (No. 342).

42

BAGNIGGE WELLS PUBLIC HOUSE

1, Bagnigge Wells Road, (*later* Kings Cross Rd.) Kings Cross.

Licensed: 1848-1871

Management

Middlesex justices:

Mich.	1848-	William Negus
"	1852-	William Baldock Page
"	1854-	George Jackson
"	1858-	Martin Saint Ledger
"	1861-	George Wyatt
"	1863-	George David Hall
"	1868-	Henry Howard
"	1869-	George David Hall
"	1870-	Nathaniel Webb Willmore
"	1871	*Licence refused on police report.*

Literature

Official records:

Mx. Mich. Q.S. 1848-1871

Location of other material

Handbills: Guildhall Library, pre. 1850

43

BAKER'S ROOMS

107, Upper Street, Islington.

Licensed: 1852-1860

Management

Middlesex justices:

Mich.	1852-	Daniel Sebbon Baker, Jnr.
"	1860	*No application*

Literature

Official records:

Mx. Mich. Q.S. 1852-1859

44

BALD FACED STAG PUBLIC HOUSE

64, Clifton Street, Shoreditch.

Licensed: 1860-1890

Management

Middlesex justices:

Mich.	1860-	James Lewis Minton
"	1871-	John Billing
"	1872-	Alfred Brickell
"	1880-	Henry Adolphus Crowhurst Gray
"	1883-	Ann Pettit
"	1885-	John Vian

London County Council:

Mich. 1890-	John Vian
Nov. 1890	*Refused, owing to 1878 Act*

Literature

Official records:

G.L.C. Arch. Dpt. Th. case 040/5;
L.C.C. Th. & M-H. Com. App. Nov. 1889-1890;
Mx. Mich. Q.S. 1860-1888 (gives address as Worship St.).

Location of other material

Plans:

G.L.C. *Architects Department.* No. 040/5

45

BALHAM EMPIRE

75, High Road, Balham.

Licensed: 1890-1909

Former name

Balham Music Hall (to Nov. 1902)

Building details

In March 1890 a certificate was issued and licence granted to the former swimming bath that had been converted into a hall for concerts &c.

1897-8 Altered for stage plays.
1900   Further alterations.

Architect: W. Hancock

Capacity: 766

Auditorium: Ar. 500; B. 250; Bx. 16.

1904 Stage play licence refused.
1909 Converted into cinema 'Theatre de Luxe'.

Management

London County Council:

1901-	John Dickeson
1904-	Alfred William Deer
1906	John Dickeson
1907	Peter Gotto
1908-	Eugene Winter
1909	Frederick Richard Griffiths
Nov. 1909	*Licensed as a cinema*

Literature

Official records:

G.L.C. Arch. Dpt. Mss index;
G.L.C. Arch. Dpt. Th. case 2367;
L.C.C. Th. & M-H. Com. App. Nov. 1900-1909;
L.C.C. Th. & M-H. Com. Papers 1888+.

1900 BUILDER:1900, August 11. p. 137. Brief note of conversion of music hall at Balham on site of old swimming pool. Architect. W. Hancock.

Location of other material

Plans: G.L.C. Architects Department.

Programmes and playbills: Enthoven Collection

46

BALHAM HIPPODROME

105, Balham Hill, High Road, Balham.

Licensed: 1899-1939

Former names

Royal Duchess Theatre 1899-1903
Duchess Palace   1903-1906
Duchess Theatre   1906-1909

Building details

Developer: London Theatres of Varieties and Barrasford Ltd.,

Architect: W. G. R. Sprague.

Cost: £35,000.

Capacity: 1,268, (1899) 2,500

Auditorium: S. 106; P. 450; D.C. 86; B. 160; G. 410; Bx. 56.

Management

London County Council:

1900-	William George Robert Sprague
1903	Henry Thomas Brickwell
1904	W. G. R. Sprague
1905-	Walter Gibbons
1913-	Charles Gulliver
1921-	Isabel Katherine Sprague
1923-	Stuart Laurance
1925-32	London and Counties Theatres Ltd. (m.d.) Stuart Laurance (sp)
1935-37	William Greenville Arrowsmith (m.d. & sp)
1938	John Robert Avery (m.d.); Richard John Trebilco (sp)
1939	Robert Lear Productions Ltd. (m.d.); Jack Frederick Colley (sp)

Literature

Official records:

G.L.C. Arch. Dpt. Mss index;
G.L.C. Arch. Dpt. Th. case 19;
L.C.C. Th. & M-H. Com. App. Nov. 1899-1938;
L.C.C. Th. & M-H. Com. Papers 1898+.

Contemporary accounts:

1899 BUILDER. 1899, Sept. 2. p. 224 Brief note on near completion.
BUILDING NEWS. 1899, Sept. 22. p. 368. Brief description.
c. 1930 MAYES, Ronald Romance of London theatres No. 169.

Location of other material

Plans: G.L.C. *Architects Department.*

Programmes: British Museum. Library.

Playbills, newscuttings &c. Enthoven Collection.

47

BANK OF FRIENDSHIP PUBLIC HOUSE

22, Harford Street (*Prior to 1882* 1, Bancroft Place) Mile End.

Licensed: 1862-1889

Building details

Auditorium: 1,880 sq'

Management

Middlesex justices:

Mich.	1862-	Thomas Hemingway
"	1869-	Mary Jane Hemingway
"	1881-	Fanny Chown and Kate Hemingway
"	1882-	Albert Toombs
"	1886-	Emma Toombs

Not licensed by the L.C.C.

Literature

Official records:

Mx. Mich. W.S. 1862-1888.

48

BARING MUSIC HALL

at Baring Arms Public House, 55, Baring Street, New North Road, Shoreditch.

Licensed: 1854-1887

Building details

A small music hall on the first floor of the public house.

Capacity: 160

Auditorium: 42' long, by 13'6" - 16' wide.

Management

Middlesex justices:

Mich.	1854-	Solomon Deacon
"	1856-	Edmund Deacon
"	1858-	Charles Cornelius Maynard
"	1860-	Charles Neville
"	1863-	Richard Neville
"	1864-	Thomas Baker
"	1867-	Rebecca Rivett
"	1871-	Joseph Rixsen
"	1874-	George Fisher
"	1875-	George Chapman
"	1879-	William Hyde
"	1885-	Edward Ambrose Jefferies
"	1886-	Charles Capon
"	1887	*Application withdrawn, owing to 1878 Act.*

Literature

Official records:

G.L.C. Arch. Dpt. Th. case 040/6; Mx. Mich. Q.S. 1854-1887.

Location of other material

Plans: G.L.C. *Architects Department.*

49

BARLEY MOW PUBLIC HOUSE

Before 2, New Gravel Lane, Shadwell.

Licensed: 1851-1853

Management

Middlesex justices:

Mich. 1851-	Thomas Lloyd
" 1852-	George Wortham
" 1853	*No application*

Literature

Official records:

Mx. Mich. Q.S. 1851-1852.

50

BARNSBURY HALL

Barnsbury Street, Islington.

Licensed: 1864-1871, and 1872-1885

Building details

Capacity: 400

Auditorium: Area, 1, 150 sq'

Management

Middlesex justices:

Mich. 1864-	William Henry Conquest
" 1871	*Licence refused*
" 1872-	William Henry Conquest
" 1880-	William Conquest
" 1885	*Application withdrawn, owing to 1878 Act.*

Literature

Official records:

G.L.C. Arch. Dpt. Th. case 040/7; Mx. Mich. Q.S. 1864-1885; Sel. Com. 1892.

Location of other material

Programmes: Enthoven Collection.

51

BATTERSEA PALACE

32, York Road, Battersea.

Licensed: 1886-1924

Former names:

Royal Standard Music Hall 1886 (Used before opening)
Washington Music Hall 1886-1900
Standard (Washington) Music Hall (at various times)
Battersea Palace of Varieties 1900
Washington Music Hall 1901
New Battersea Empire 1902
Battersea Empire 1903-1908
Palace Theatre of Varieties 1910
Battersea Palace 1917

Building details

1876   Surrey justices granted music licence to Royal Standard Public House on condition it was not used as a music hall.
1886   (M.B.W. Minutes 1. 8. 1886 para 63) application for permission to build hall at rear of public house.

Capacity: 600 (seated)

Auditorium: Ar. 383; B. 277.

Management

Middlesex justices:

Mich. 1886-   George Washington Moore

London County Council:

1890-	George Washington Moore
1898-	Robert Rhodes
1899-	William Clark Kirk
1901	Leopold Leach
1902	George Washington Moore
1903-	James McGuinness
1907	George Washington Moore
1908	Joseph Nolan
1909-	Frank Macnaghten
1912-1924	Frederic Baugh
Nov. 1924	*Not licensed as theatre or music hall.*

Washington Music Hall   (51)

(Gerald Forsythe)

Literature

Official records:

G.L.C. Arch. Dpt. Mss index;
G.L.C. Arch Dpt. Th. case 21;
L.C.C. Th & M-H. Com. App. Nov. 1889-1923;
L.C.C. Th. & M-H. Com. Papers 1886+; Sel. Com. 1892;
Sy. Mich. Q.S. 1876, 1886-1888.

Contemporary accounts:

1886   BUILDER. 1886, May 15th. p. 731. Tenders.
1887   SATURDAY REVIEW. 1887, Sept. 3rd. The State
       of London music halls. No. 4.
1889   SOUTH LONDON PRESS. 1889, Jan. 19th. p. 5.
       Report that as George Washington, proprietor too
       busy, theatre will be managed by his son George
       Moore.
       GREEN, Richard Judd, *and* DAMER, John.
       Clapham Junction and its people: a peep show.
       (1889) p. 53-7. —Description of Washington.
n.d.   YOUNG, Douglas and G. *Auctioneer.*
       [Auction details: ground plan and description]
       (Copy in Battersea Public Library).

Location of other material

Plans: G.L.C. *Architect's Department.*

Illustrations and cuttings: Battersea Local Collection

52

BATTY'S HIPPODROME

Opposite Broad Walk, Kensington.

In existence between: 1851 and 1853

Other name

Royal Hippodrome

Building details

Architect: Mr. Taylor

Contractors: Messrs. James Haward and William
                      Thomas Nixon.
Used for Circus performances.

Literature

Contemporary accounts:

1850   JOHN BULL. 1850, p. 582. —Description.
1851   BUILDER. 1851, May 10th. p. 298-9. Description
       and plans.
       ILLUSTRATED LONDON NEWS. 1851, May 10th.
       Illus. of chariot race.
       LADY'S NEWSPAPER. 1851, May 31st. p. 1. Re-
       port on entertainment, illus. of events.
       THEATRICAL JOURNAL. 1851, May. Descrip-
       tion.

Historical accounts:

1907   WROTH, Warwick.
       Cremorne and later London Gardens. p. 30-33.
1925   CHANCELLOR, E. B.
       The pleasure haunts of London. p. 422.
1952   PULLING, Christopher.
       They were singing. p. 180. (Note of existence)

Location of other material

Newscuttings: Kensington Public Library.

Programme: British Museum Library.

Folder of cuttings, playbills &c. Enthoven Collection.

53

BAXENDALE ARMS PUBLIC HOUSE

164, Columbia Road, Bethnal Green.

Licensed: 1891-1893

Building details

A small music hall on the ground floor attached to the
public house.

Capacity: 150 (varies)

Management

London County Council:

1891-   Charles Wood
Nov. 1894 Room to be used only for private parties.

Literature

Official records:

G.L.C. Arch. Dpt. Mss index; L.C.C. Th. & M-H. Com.
App. Nov. 1890-1894; Sel. Com. 1892..

54

BAXTER ARMS PUBLIC HOUSE

30, Baxter Road, Essex Road, Islington.

Licensed: 1868-1889

Building details

Concert hall on 1st floor of public house.

Auditorium: 670 sq'

Management

Middlesex justices:

Mich. 1868-	Charles Walker	
" 1871-	George Parsons	
" 1872-	Charles Edward Richardson	
" 1874-	Louisa Putland	
" 1875-	Frederick Vaughan	
" 1876-	Henry Salmon	
" 1877-	Harriet Le Maitre	
" 1878-	John Edward Tunstall	
" 1880-	Richard Humphreys	
" 1883-	Charles Harris	
" 1885-	George Mansfield	

Not licensed by the L.C.C. owing to 1878 Act.

Literature

Official records:

G.L.C. Arch. Dpt. Th. case 040/8.
Mx. Mich, Q.S. 1868-1888.

Location of other material

Plans: G.L.C. *Architect's Department.*

55

BAYSWATER PUBLIC HOUSE

Paddington.

Licensed: 1848-1860

Also known as

Royal Albert Saloon
Wale's Bayswater Tavern.

Management

Middlesex justices:

Mich. 1848-	William Wale	
" 1856-	Frances Sarah Wale	
" 1858-	John David Wale	
" 1860	*No application.*	

Literature

Official records:

Mx. Mich. Q.S. 1848-1859.

Location of other material

Newscutting (advertisement): Enthoven Collection.

56

BECKFORD'S HEAD PUBLIC HOUSE

122, (formerly 38) Old Street. (-pre Nov. '64)
Shoreditch.

Licensed: 1852-1883

Management

Middlesex justices:

Mich. 1852-	Thomas Lee
" 1854-	Valentine Roberts
" 1855-	Joseph Mead
" 1856-	Francis Hungate
" 1857-	James Hicks
" 1858-	John Herbert
" 1862-	George Young
" 1863-	John Thomas Dowles
" 1864-	George Gurney
" 1865-	John Henry Giles
" 1875-	William Warner
" 1876-	Edwin Horsfall
" 1877-	Charles Humphreys
" 1878-	George Sanger
" 1883	Thomas Smith *absconded.*

Literature

Official records:

Mx. Mich. Q.S. 1852-1883.

57

BEDFORD HEAD PUBLIC HOUSE

5, Upper King Street, Holborn.

Licensed: 1854-1861

Management

Middlesex justices:

Mich. 1854-	John Brown
" 1855-	James Hepple
" 1856-	Charles Philippe Feuillan
" 1858-	Matthew Henry Fulford
" 1859-	George John Tilling
" 1861-	Auguste Jean Baptiste Amand
" 1862	*No application.*

Literature

Official records:

Mx. Mich. Q.S. 1854-1861.

58

BEDFORD THEATRE

93-95, Camden High Street,

(*formerly,* Grove St., to 1888, *then* 80-2, Arlington St.)
Camden Town.

Opened c. 1824-   *Closed after* 1950. *Demolished* 1969.

Former names

Bedford Arms Tavern and Tea Garden c. 1824-1861
Bedford Music Hall 1861-1896
New Bedford Palace of Varieties,
officially, New Bedford Theatre 1896-
Bedford Palace of Varieties -1924
Bedford Music Hall 1924-1941

Building details

1861 Theatre built

Developer: R. C. Thornton

Cost: £5,000

1896-8 Reconstructed.

Architect: Bertie Crewe

Contractor: W. Johnson & Co.

Capacity: 1,168

Auditorium: P. & S. 488; C. 238; G. 426; Bx. 16.

Management

Middlesex justices:

Licensed prior to 1840

Mich. 1848-	Henry Willard
" 1852-	Daniel Lovett
" 1856-	James Bliss
" 1858	*Not licensed*
" 1861-	Robert Clint Thornton
" 1867-	Edward Weston
" 1868-	George Forbes, E. A. Chaston and H. Kelly, *trade assignees of E. Weston, bankrupt.*
" 1870-	Alfred Trotman
" 1877-	George Fredericks
" 1885-	Henry Hart

London County Council:

1890-	Henry Hart
1896-	Thomas Flower Maltby
1899-	Benjamin Pearce Lucas
1920-	Harry Goodson

1921-	Charles Gulliver
1925-	Bedford Music Hall Ltd.
1933-	Associated British Cinemas Ltd.
1940-	Bedford Theatre (Camden Town) Ltd.
1941-	Brisford Entertainments Ltd.
1942-	F. J. B. Theatres (London) Ltd.
1950	Bedford Theatre (London) Ltd.

Lord Chamberlain:

18.12.1911-	Benjamin Pearce Lucas
14.12.1919-	Harry Goodson
1.12.1919-	Charles Downing Allen
1.12.1920-	Charles Gulliver
1.12.1928-	Harry Goodson
1.12.1932-	Ralph Bromheed
1.12.1934-	Arthur Stanley Moss
1.12.1939-	Harry Goodson
1.12.1940-	Walter Matthew Morris
1.12.1941-	Frederick John Butterworth
1.12.1946-	Albert James Matthews
1.12.1949-	Patricia Dorothy Nye

Literature

Official records:

G.L.C. Arch. Dpt. Th. Case 223; L C.C. Th. & M-H. Com. App. Nov. 1889+; L.C.C. Th. & M-H. Com. Papers 1889+; Mx. Mich. Q.S. 1848-1857, 1861-1888; L.C.O. 374 and 500.

Contemporary accounts:

1899 BUILDING NEWS. 1899, Feb. 10th. p. 196—
Description

Historical accounts:

1907 WROTH, Warwick
Cremorne and the later London Gardens. p. 95.
c. 1930 MAYES, Ronald.
Romance of London theatres, No. 143.
1935 HADDON, Archibald.
The story of the music hall from Cave of
Harmony to Cabaret. p. 27, 40.
1961 REYNOLDS, E.
Recreations and leisure in St. Pancras ... p. 21-
27.
1964 FLETCHER, Geoffrey S.
London overlooked. Illus. of exterior (frontis)
and prompt side box.

Location of other material

Illustrations:

Camden P. L. (Swiss Cottage).
incl. originals of G. S. Fletcher illus. *see above.*

Plans: G.L.C. Architects Department;
Enthoven Collection (2 sheets)

Programmes and playbills: Enthoven Collection

59

BEE HIVE PUBLIC HOUSE

20, Christian Street, (*pre 1863:* King Street) Stepney.

Licensed: 1854-1868

Management

Middlesex justices:

| Mich. 1854- | George William Matthews |
| " 1855- | John James Pearce |

" 1861-	Frederick Hofsommer
" 1865-	Charles Tingey and Thomas Hume Tingey
" 1867-	Richard Cook
" 1868-	*Licence refused to Balthaser Hewser.*

Literature

Official records:

Mx. Mich. Q.S. 1854-1868.

60

BEE HIVE PUBLIC HOUSE

27, Crombie's Row, Commercial Road, Stepney.

Licensed: 1855-1857

Management

Middlesex justices:

Mich. 1855-	William Thursfield Taylor
" 1856-	John Wardhaugh
" 1857	*No application.*

Literature

Official records:

Mx. Mich. Q.S. 1855-1856.

61

BEE HIVE PUBLIC HOUSE

18, Wellington Street, Deptford.

Licensed: 1852-1859

Management

West Kent justices:

Mich. 1852-	John Hight
" 1853-	Thomas Greenwood
" 1854-	Edward Clinton
" 1855-	William Gordon Crow
" 1858-	Jane Willer
" 1859	*No application.*

Literature

Official records:

W. Kt. Mich. Q.S. 1852-1858.

62

BELGRAVE PUBLIC HOUSE

(1, Upper) Ebury Street, Westminster.

Licensed: 1849-1863

Management

Middlesex justices:

Mich. 1849-	John Griffin
" 1852-	John Edmonds
" 1855-	Anthony Anderson
" 1863	*No applications.*

Literature

Official records:

Mx. Mich. Q.S. 1849-1862.

63

BELL PUBLIC HOUSE

38, Kilburn High Road, Kilburn.

Licensed: Pre 1850-1889

Former names

Bell Tavern, Kilburn Wells—to 1851
Bell Public House and London and Birmingham
Railway Tavern
Bell Tavern, Manchester Terrace, Kilburn—to 1873

Building details

The concert hall was situated on the 1st floor of the
public house: area 453 sq'.

Management

Middlesex justices:

Mich. 1850-	John Cruwys
" 1851-	Eliza Cruwys
" 1852-	John Shepherd
" 1858-	Elizabeth Shepherd
" 1860-	Charles Hawkins
" 1866-	Mary Ann Davison
" 1870-	Luke Muncey
" 1876-	Henry James
" 1877-	Richard Jandrell
" 1878-	Francis William A. Cossey
" 1884-	William Harwood
" 1886-	Hatsell Garrard

Not licensed by the L.C.C. owing to 1878 Act.

Literature

Official records:

G.L.C. Arch. Dpt. Th. case 040/97.

Mx. Mich, Q.S. 1848-1888.

64

BELL PUBLIC HOUSE

Middlesex Street, Stepney.

Licensed: 1855-1863

Management

Middlesex justices:

| Mich. 1855- | John Bremer |
| " 1863 | *No application for renewal.* |

Literature

Official records:

Mx. Mich. Q.S. 1855-1862.

65

BELL PUBLIC HOUSE

116, St. George Street, Tower, Stepney.

Licensed: 1851-1884

Building details

Area: 690 sq'.

Management

Middlesex justices:

Mich. 1851-	John Whiteley
" 1862-	William Duncan Neeson
" 1867-	Thomas Castle, Junior
" 1869-	Edward Holt
" 1870-	Henry Whithey Knight
" 1872-	William Ward
" 1876-	Charles Lamb
" 1879-	Arthur Nicholas Bartlett
" 1882-	Henry Bushell
" 1883-	Joseph Wood
" 1884	*Application withdrawn.*

Literature

Official records:

Mx. Mich, Q.S. 1851-1884.

66

BELL AND ANCHOR PUBLIC HOUSE

Hammersmith Turnpike.

Licensed: From before 1850-1852

Management

Middlesex justices:

To Oct. 1852 John Curtis

Literature

Official records:

Mx. Mich, Q.S. pre 1850-1852.

67

BELMONT PUBLIC HOUSE

Belmont Wharf, York Road, Kings Cross.

Licensed: 1862-1863

Management

Middlesex justices:

| Mich. 1862- | Charles Rich |
| " 1863 | *No application.* |

Literature

Official records:

Mx. Mich, Q.S. 1862.

68

BELVIDERE PUBLIC HOUSE

1, Penton Street, Finsbury.

Licensed: 1861-1880

Management

Middlesex justices:

Mich. 1861-	Alfred Buckingham
" 1867-	Thomas Goswell
" 1875-	William Goosey
" 1880	*Application refused.*

Literature

Official records:

Mx. Mich, Q.S. 1861-1880.

69

BENYON ARMS PUBLIC HOUSE

Hereford Terrace, De Beauvoir Road, Hackney.

Licensed: 1860-1861

Management

Middlesex justices:

Mich. 1860-	William Miller
" 1861-	*No application.*

Literature

Official records:

Mx. Mich. Q.S. 1860.

70

BIJOU THEATRE

at His Majesty's Theatre, Haymarket.

In use: c. 1860-1868

This theatre was formerly the concert room in the theatre. It was used mainly by amateur companies.

Management

Lord Chamberlain:

18. 9.1860 (one day) and 9.11.1860-31.12.1860
          Limited licence to Edward Tyrrell Smith
18. 7.1861 Henry Montague for the play
27. 7.1861 'The Christie Minstrel's Entertainment'.
21.11.1861 Charles Matthews
 2. 2.1867 James Henry Mapleson (to September
          1868)

Literature

Official records:

LC 7/13 and 15.

Historical accounts:

1925 SHERSON, Erroll.
    London's lost theatres. p. 324-325.

71

BIRD CAGE PUBLIC HOUSE

Virginia Row (*pre 1854* Barnet Street)
Bethnal Green.

Licensed: 1850-1878

Management

Middlesex justices:

Mich. 1850-	Alexander Mills
" 1851-	Richard Algar
" 1852-	Richard Algar and Robert Bowell
" 1853-	Edward Barker Johnson
" 1854-	John Leighton

" 1858-	Caroline Leighton
" 1862-	Samuel Wray
" 1863-	Henry Havelock Billingshurst
" 1864-	Peter Harrison Richardson
" 1865-	William Aitken
" 1872-	Barbara Aitken
" 1876-	Eliza Sophia Billinghurst
" 1878	*No application.*

Literature

Official records:

Mx. Mich. Q.S. 1851-1878.

72

BISHOP BONNER PUBLIC HOUSE

21, Bonner Lane, Old Ford Road, Bethnal Green.

Licensed: 1865-1898

Building details

Capacity: 100

Management

Middlesex justices:

Mich. 1865-	William Lloyd
" 1867-	Jessey Lloyd
" 1870-	James Pasmore
" 1874-	Jonathan Foster
" 1875-	William Lorrieux Harrison
" 1876-	Thomas Nicholls
" 1877-	John Hay
" 1879-	Ellen Kate Lawrence
" 1880-	John Souter
" 1882-	Geoffrey Watkins
" 1883-	John Glancy
" 1884-	Isaac Hayward
" 1885-	Eliza Hayward
" 1886-	William Mark Gange

London County Council:

Mich. 1890-	William Mark Gange
" 1893-	John William Seeley
" 1896-	Colin John Lunn
" 1897-	Urbane Blanchett
" 1898	Daniel Dupuy

Literature

Official records:

L.C.C. Th. & M-H. Com. App. Nov. 1889-1897.
Mx. Mich. Q.S. 1865-1888.
Sel. Com. 1892.

73

BISHOPSGATE HALL

202, Shoreditch High Street, Shoreditch.

Licensed: 1881-1890

Management

Middlesex justices:

Mich. 1881-	John and Richard Douglass

London County Council:

1890 Andrew Melville
Nov. 1890 *Licence refused.*

Literature

Official records:

L.C.C. Th. & M-H. Com. App. Nov. 1889-1890.
Mx. Mich. Q.S. 1881-1888.

74

BLACK BULL PUBLIC HOUSE

Freeschool Street, Southwark.

Licensed: 1861-1867

Management

Surrey justices:

Mich. 1861-	Alfred Oliver	
" 1864-	Maria Charlotte Hales	
" 1867-	Benjamin Toombs	
" 1868	*No application.*	

Literature

Official records:

Sy. Mich. Q.S. 1861-1867.

75

BLACK BULL PUBLIC HOUSE

Lewisham High Road, Lewisham.

Licensed: 1859-1860

Management

West Kent justices:

Mich. 1859-	John Hall Saunders	
" 1860	*No application.*	

Literature

Official records:

W. Kt. Mich. Q.S. 1859.

76

BLACK DOG PUBLIC HOUSE

101, Bethnal Green Road, *(formerly,*45, Church Street
to 1870) Bethnal Green.

Licensed: 1856-1890

Building details

Concert room on the first floor of the public house.

Management

Middlesex justices:

Mich. 1856-	Henry Hall	
" 1864-	Mary Hall (Administratix)	
" 1865-	Thomas Pond	
" 1873-	Ann Pond	

" 1875-	William John Burran	
" 1877-	Samuel Pritchett	
" 1878-	Arthur Henry Lyon	
" 1882-	Alfred William Howell	
" 1883-	Edwin Davis Estall	
" 1885-	Thomas Barrow	
" 1888-	Emma Gordon	

London County Council:

1890-	Frederick Samuel Wallis	
Nov. 1890	*Not licensed as result of 1878 Act.*	

Literature

Official records:

G.L.C. Arch. Dpt. Th. Case 040/10;
L.C.C. Th. & M-H. Com. App. Nov. 1889;
Mx. Mich. Q.S. 1856-1888.

77

BLACK DOG PUBLIC HOUSE

Denmark Street, St. George E., Stepney.

Licensed: 1859-1862

Management

Middlesex justices:

Mich. 1859-	John Rohrs	
" 1861-	Wilhelm Rohrs	
" 1862	*Licence refused to Charles Alber.*	

Literature

Official records:

Mx. Mich. Q.S. 1859-1862.

78

BLACK DOG PUBLIC HOUSE

112, Vauxhall Walk, Lambeth.

Licensed: prior to 1850-1889

Management

Surrey justices:

Mich. 1849-	Thomas Collis	
" 1854-	James Went	
" 1857-	Charles Smith	
" 1862-	William Blackney	
" 1864-	Louisa Price	
" 1865-	Edmund Meacock	
" 1867-	Henry Bennett	
" 1874-	John Wilson	
" 1876-	George Skegg	
" 1878-	Robert Thomas Fitch	
" 1879-	Robert James Fitch (sic)	
" 1880-	Robert Thomas Fitch	
" 1885-	George Tildesley	
" 1886-	Henry Broadbridge	

Not licensed by L.C.C. as result of 1878 Act.

Literature

Official records:

G.L.C. Arch. Dpt. Th. case 040/11;
Sy. Mich. Q.S. pre 1850-1888.

Location of other material

Plans: G.L.C. *Architect's Department*

79

BLACK EAGLE PUBLIC HOUSE

140, Brick Lane, Spitalfields E., Whitechapel.

Licensed: 1869-1889

Building details

Concert room on the first floor, 39' 8" × 19' 1" × 12'. Area 736 sq'

Management

Middlesex justices:

Mich. 1869-		John Newman
"	1875-	Peter Yorde Reeland
"	1877-	James Bradgate
"	1882-	Richard Fresta Brettingham
"	1888-	Elisa Cesarine Brettingham

Not licensed by the L.C.C. Result of 1878 Act.

Literature

Official records:

G.L.C. Arch. Dpt. Th. case 040/12;
Mx. Mich. Q.S. 1869-1888.

80

BLACK HORSE PUBLIC HOUSE

215, Kingsland Road, (*formerly* 1, York Place) Shoreditch.

Licensed: 1862-1890

Building details

Room on first floor used as a music hall. Irregular shape with a small platform. Area 544 sq'

Management

Middlesex justices:

Mich. 1862-		James Gill
"	1864-	James Moore
"	1866-	Edwin Lewellin
"	1867-	Thomas George Watkinson
"	1870-	Isabelle Watkinson
"	1872-	Ann Henrietta Winn
"	1873-	Edward Stokes
"	1874-	James Licence
"	1876-	Arthur Humphryes
"	1878-	George Moore

London County Council:

	1890-	Albert William Norris— *Licence retained*
Nov.	1890-	*As result of 1878 Act licence not renewed.*

Literature

Official records:

G.L.C. Arch. Dpt. Th. case 040/14;
L.C.C. Th. & M-H. Com. Nov. 1889;
Mx. Mich. Q.S. 1862-1888.

Location of other material

Plans: G.L.C. *Architect's Department.*

81

BLACK HORSE PUBLIC HOUSE

4, Well Street, Wellclose Square, St. George E., Tower, Stepney.

Licensed: 1890

Building details

Concert room on the first floor; 30' × 16' × 10'. *Area:* 411 sq'

Management

London County Council:

	1890-	Ambrose Henry Bellinger
Nov.	1891-	*As result of 1878 Act, not relicensed.*

Literature

Official records:

G.L.C. Arch. Dpt. Th. case 040/13;
L.C.C. Th. & M-H. Com. App. Nov. 1889-1890.

Location of other material

Plans: G.L.C. *Architect's Department.*

82

BLACK HORSE AND WINDMILL PUBLIC HOUSE

Fieldgate Street, Whitechapel.

Licensed: 1854-1863

Management

Middlesex justices:

Mich. 1854-		William Drake
"	1859-	John Henry Schulte
"	1862-	Frederich Itter
"	1863	*Licence refused.*

Literature

Official records:

Mx. Mich. Q.S. 1854-1863.

83

BLACK SWAN PUBLIC HOUSE

School House Lane, Stepney.

Licensed: 1854-1861

Management

Middlesex justices:

Mich. 1854-		John Stephens
"	1861	*Not relicensed.*

Literature

Official records:

Mx. Mich. Q.S. 1854-1860.

84

BLOCKMAKER'S ARMS PUBLIC HOUSE

1, Ashley Crescent, (*later* 133, Shepherdess Walk)
Shoreditch.

Licensed: 1852-1890

Management

Middlesex justices:

Mich.	1852-	William Thomas Hamilton
"	1855-	Job Copeman
"	1862-	Edmund Francis Chown
"	1874-	George Wood
"	1878-	Alfred Fairs
"	1882-	George Wood
"	1885-	William Dempster
"	1886-	Sydney Byatt

London County Council:

	1890-	Sydney Byatt
Nov.	1890	*Not licensed.*

Literature

Official records:

L.C.C. Th. & M-H. Com. App. Nov. 1889;
Mx. Mich. Q.S. 1852-1888.

85

BLUE ANCHOR PUBLIC HOUSE

21, Dock Street, Wapping.

Licensed: 1854-1883

Management

Middlesex justices:

Mich.	1854-	Joseph Sanders
"	1857-	Edward Jones
"	1867-	Edward Harris
"	1878-	Henry John William Bose
"	1883	*Licence refused as it had been seldom used.*

Literature

Official records:

Mx. Mich. Q.S. 1854-1883.

86

BLUE ANCHOR PUBLIC HOUSE

67, Whitechapel Road, Stepney.

Licensed: 1854-1882

Management

Middlesex justices:

Mich.	1854-	George Church
"	1857-	Constantine John Collins
"	1858-	Joseph Chapman
"	1859-	George Church
"	1873-	Harriett A. Medlock
"	1874-	William Scott
"	1875-	William Josiah Knight
"	1879-	John Eberhardt Schnabel
"	1881-	John Henry Aitken
"	1882	*Not relicensed.*

Literature

Official records:

Mx. Mich. Q.S. 1854-1881.

87

BLUE ANCHOR PUBLIC HOUSE

92, York Street, Westminster.

Licensed: 1852-1855

Management

Middlesex justices:

Mich.	1852-	George Slater
"	1853-	Thomas Russell Curling
"	1854-	John Wildey
"	1855	*Not relicensed.*

Literature

Official records:

Mx. Mich. Q.S. 1852-1854.

88

BLUE COAT BOY PUBLIC HOUSE

32, Dorset Street, Christchurch, Spitalfields.

Licensed: 1860-1862

Management

Middlesex justices:

Mich.	1860-	Thomas Bailey
"	1862	*Application withdrawn.*

Literature

Official records:

Mx. Mich. Q.S. 1860-1862.

89

BOLTONS THEATRE CLUB

65, Drayton Gardens and 26, Thistle Grove. Kensington.

Theatre club opened on 15th January 1947 in the disused Bolton's cinema. Now the Paris-Pullman Cinema.

Management

As a theatre club not subject to licensing laws.

Literature

Official records:

L.C.C. Arch. Dpt. Th. case 619.

Historical accounts:

1947 The STORY of the Boltons Theatre first season.
Marsland Publications, 1947. 63p. illus.
1950 FERGUSON, Rachel.
Royal Borough. J. Cape. 1950. p. 270-272.

Location of other material

Plans: G.L.C. Architects Department.

Illustrations:

Kensington News, 1948. Drawing of Drayton Gardens showing exterior. (Royal Borough No. 2).
Copy in Kensington Local Collection

Programmes:

Enthoven Collection.
Garrick Club. 1947-1951.

90

BOROUGH MUSIC HALL

172, Union Street, Borough.

Opened: pre 1850- c. 1889

Former names

Salmon Concert Room/Salmon Public House
Alexandra Music Hall
Raglan Music Hall

Building details

The Hall, built prior to 1866.
It was burnt down on 28th September, 1871.

Cost: £6,000

Rebuilt by Henry Hart of the Raglan Music Hall, Theobalds Road, with George Wane as manager, 26.12.1872.

Capacity: 1,000

Burnt down again on 13.11.1883

Rebuilt 1887

Capacity: 906

Management

Surrey justices:

Mich. 1849-		Augusta Maria Crispin and Maria Harris
"	1853-	Maria Harris
"	1859-	Robert Gear
"	1870-	George Walker
"	1877-	William Brown
"	1879-	Samuel Hart
"	1880-	Catherine Grouse

Literature

Official records:

G.L.C. Arch. Dpt. Th. case 06;
Sel. Com. 1892; Sy. Mich. Q.S. pre 1850-1888

Contemporary accounts:

PEEPING Tom: a journal of town life. No. 3.
London Concert Rooms: Boro' Music Hall. Union Street. 2p. illus.

Historical accounts:

1895 STUART, C.D. *and* PARK, A.J.
The variety stage. Mentions opening by Henry Hart in 1872 with George Wane as manager.
1935 HADDON, Archibald.
The story of the music hall. Illus. opp. p. 42. interior 1860's.
1954 WILSON, A.E.
East end entertainment. p. 229-230.

Location of other material

Cuttings, playbills &c. Enthoven Collection.

91

BOUDOIR THEATRE (Little French Theatre)

Pembroke Gardens. Kensington.

L.C.C. Theatre and Music Hall Committee minutes 28.6.1911 p. 598 reports that stage plays were performed here without a licence.
Later it became the Pembroke Hall.

Literature

Official records:

G.L.C. Arch. Dpt. Th. case 1521.

Historical accounts:

1950 FERGUSON, Rachel.
Royal Borough.
J. Cape. p. 265-266.

Location of other material

Programmes: London Museum.

92

BOW PALACE

156-8, Bow Road, Bow (*formerly* High Street, Bow and *prior to 1882* Stratford, Bow)

Licensed: 1855-1923

Former names

Three Cups Public House and Music Hall 1855-1889
Bow Music Hall (Three Cups) 1889-1892
Marlow's Music Hall (name used on programmes) c. 1889-1892
Eastern Empire 1892-1903
Palace Theatre, Bow 1903-1917
Tivoli Theatre, Bow 1917-1918

Building details

Hall situated at the rear of the Three Cups Tavern.

Capacity: 300

2nd building: 1892

Capacity: 2,078

Auditorium: (seating) Ar. 484; B. 260; G. 300.

In 1923 building used as cinema.

Management

Middlesex justices:

Mich. 1855-		William Ufindell
"	1856-	James Holmes
"	1858-	Frederick Ward
"	1863-	Mary Ann Ward
"	1865	*No application*
"	1866-	Henry Hodge
"	1867-	John James Kinggett
"	1868-	William Cole
"	1869-	Henry Preece
"	1871-	Lewis Henry Claridge
"	1872-	Frederick Vanderkiste

"	1874-	Elizabeth Vanderkiste
"	1876-	Sarah Prideaux
"	1877-	Charles Calhery
Nov.	1878-	Matthew Richard Barrett
"	1879-	Alfred Probyn
"	1881-	James John Bolton
"	1884-	Frederick Lovegrove
"	1885-	Arthur William Palmer and John Hawkins
"	1887-	John Hawkins

London County Council:

	1890-	William Marlow
	1895-	Alexander Jackson Leese
	1899-	Frank William Macnaghten
	1912-	Frederic Baugh
Nov.	1912	*Not licensed by L.C.C.*
	1918-	Edward Walter Rice
	1919-	Artie James Oswick
	1921-	Robert Isaac Barnett, and Hyman Coher
	1922-	Robert Isaac Barnett
Nov.	1923	*Licensed as a cinema.*

Lord Chamberlain:

8. 5.1911-	Frederic Baugh
28. 5.1917-	Edward Walter Rice
14.10.1918-	Artie James Oswick
? 1920-	Robert Isaac Barnett, and Hyman Coher
30.11.1920-	Robert Isaac Barnett (to 30.11.1923).

Literature

Official records:

G.L.C. Arch. Dpt. Mss. index;
G.L.C. Arch. Dpt. Th. case 244;
L.C.C. Th. & M-H. Com. App. Nov. 1889-1911,
1917-1923; L.C.C. Th. & M-H. Com. Papers, 1888+;
L.C.O. 473;
Mx. Mich. Q.S. 1855-1864, 1865-1888.

Contemporary accounts:

1923 EAST LONDON OBSERVER, 1923 Nov. 17.
Report on opening as a cinema.

Location of other material

Plans: G.L.C. *Architects Department*

Newscuttings and programmes &c. Poplar Local Collection.

Playbills: Guildhall Library (1 item for Marlow's).

93

BOWER THEATRE

Stangate Street, Lambeth.

Licensed: 1837-1877.

Former names

Bower Music Hall
Bower Saloon
at Dukes's Public House 1837-1864
Bower Operetta House
Bower Theatre 1864-1875
Stangate Music Hall/Theatre 1875-1877
Names occasionally prefixed by 'Royal'.

Building details

Builder: Philip Phillips

Rebuilt: 1875.

Finally after 6. 9. 1877 converted into a warehouse for Price's Patent Candles.

Management

Lord Chamberlain:

29. 9.1843-	George Alfred Hodson
Oct. 1845-	James Biddles
Oct. 1854-	Thomas Henry
21.12.1855-	Victor Isaac Hazelton
28. 9.1876-	Robert Maw (to 6.9.1877)

Literature

Official records:

LC7/3-16; 20-23; 89.
Sel. Com. 1877.

Historical accounts:

1877	ILLUSTRATED SPORTING AND DRAMATIC NEWS, 1877, Oct. 20th.—Brief history and illus.
1895	STUART, C. D. *and* PARK, A. J. Variety stage. p. 38-39.
1925	SHERSON, Erroll London's lost theatres. p. 314-317.
c.1930	MAYES, Ronald The romance of London theatres: No. 83 and 172.
1946	SCOTT, Harold Early doors. p. 57 et seq.

Location of other material

Programmes and playbills:

Lambeth Local Collection; British Museum Library; Enthoven Collection; Guildhall Library.

Bower Theatre, Lambeth 1877 (93)

(British Museum)

Scrapbook:

London Museum Library: The PLEASURE gardens of South London, Vol. II. pp. 226-7

94

BRECKNOCK ARMS PUBLIC HOUSE

Maiden Lane.

Licensed: pre 1850-1856

Management

Middlesex justices:

Mich. 1848-	Thomas Bruce and John William Gibson
" 1851-	Henry James Vincent
" 1852-	John Morgan
" 1854-	Frederick Butcher
" 1857	*No application*

Literature

Official records:

Mx. Mich. Q.S. 1848-1856.

95

BRICKLAYERS ARMS PUBLIC HOUSE

77, Adam Street, Rotherhithe.

Licensed: 1862-1868

Management

Surrey justices:

Mich. 1862-	John Cadd
" 1868-	Samuel Cadd
" 1869	*No application*

Literature:

Official records:

Sy. Mich. Q.S. 1862-1868.

96

BRIDGE HOUSE PUBLIC HOUSE

55, Whitmore Road, Shoreditch.

Licensed: 1865-1890

The L.C.C. records state that it was first licensed by the Middlesex justices at Clerkenwell Assizes in 1849 to John Matthew Westcott.

Management

Middlesex justices: (from printed lists)

Mich. 1865-	George Henry Squires
" 1867-	James Strawson
" 1874-	Alfred Johnson
" 1877-	William Oyler
" 1888-	George Stevens

London County Council:

1890-	George Stevens
Nov. 1890-	*Not relicensed as a result of 1878 Act.*

Literature

Official records:

G.L.C. Arch. Dpt. Th. Case 040/17;
Mx. Mich. Q.S. 1865-1888.

97

BRITANNIA MUSIC HALL

58, Blackfriars Road, Southwark.

Place of Entertainment: 18th century to 1886

Former names

Bijou Music Hall
Rotunda Assembly Room
Rotunda Music Hall.

Later name

The Ring.

Building details

Capacity: 150

Management

Surrey justices:

Mich. 1876-	William Tompson Wyatt
" 1879-	John Hoodless, Jnr.
" 1880-	Harry Wallace
" 1885-	John Kembrey
" 1886	*Not relicensed.* Closed because of cock-fighting.

Literature

Official records:

G.L.C. Arch. Dpt. Th. case 013; LC7/14;
Sel. Com. 1892; Sy. Mich. Q.S. 1876-1885

Historical accounts:

c. 1930	MAYES, Ronald The romance of London theatres, No. 73.
1946	SCOTT, Harold The early doors. p. 54 et seq.
1952	PULLING, Christopher They were singing. p. 136, 176.

Location of other material

Playbills: Enthoven Collection (1 bill)

98

BRITANNIA MUSIC HALL AND PUBLIC HOUSE

139, Tooley Street, Southwark.

Licensed: 1855-1882

Former name

Colonel Wardle Public House *prior to 1864*

Building details

The concert room was situated on the first floor.

Area: 540 sq'

Management

Surrey justices:

Mich.	1855-	Peter Haslip
"	1864-	George Thomas Liscoe
"	1868-	Charles Hearn
"	1870-	Edward Daniel
"	1872-	John Marriott
"	1873-	William Hart
"	1876-	Robert King
"	1878-	Robert Wheeler
"	1881-	Charles Hughes
"	1882-	William Webber Greenslade. *On condition it is not turned into a music hall*

Literature

Official records:

G.L.C. Arch. Dpt. Th. case 040/18;
Sy. Mich. Q.S. 1855-1882.

Location of other material

Plans: *G.L.C. Architects Department.*

99

BRITANNIA PUBLIC HOUSE

1, Britannia Row, Islington.

Licensed: 1852-1863

Management

Middlesex justices:

Mich.	1852-	Robert Bragg
"	1863	*No application*

Literature

Official records:

Mx. Mich. Q.S. 1852-1862.

100

BRITANNIA PUBLIC HOUSE

157, City Road.

Licensed: 1866-1886

Building details

Concert room with area of c. 800 sq'

Management

Middlesex justices:

Mich.	1866-	Thomas Keen
"	1872-	John Wollond
"	1874-	George Jones
"	1875-	William Drummond Spragg
"	1877-	John Temple
"	1878-	William Stephens
"	1879-	John Jacob Jex
"	1882-	Charles Gilbert
"	1884-	Charles Hillary Laurence
"	1886	*Application withdrawn*

Literature

Official records:

Mx. Mich. Q.S. 1866-1885.

101

BRITANNIA PUBLIC HOUSE

759, Commercial Road, (*formerly* 1, St. Ann's Place)
Stepney.

Licensed: 1851-1884

Former name

Britannia Commercial Hotel *prior to 1863*

Building details

Area of concert hall 660 sq'

Management

Middlesex justices:

Mich.	1851-	George Thomee
"	1858-	Joseph Bagent
"	1861-	John Sutton
"	1863-	William Wheeler's *application not granted*
"	1864-	William Wheeler
"	1865-	George Absell
"	1869-	Sarah Harwood
"	1872-	George Clark
"	1874-	William Brown
"	1878-	Richard Brown
"	1884	*Application withdrawn.*

Literature

Official records:

Mx. Mich, Q.S. 1851-1884.

102

BRITANNIA PUBLIC HOUSE

279, Mare Street, (*formerly* Church St.)
Hackney.

Licensed: 1855-1890

Building details

Area: 600 sq'

Management

Middlesex justices:

Mich.	1855-	Bartholomew Francis Fowler
"	1864-	Charles Law
"	1865-	Thomas Cracknell
"	1867-	William Pitt Steggall
"	1875-	William Keith
"	1876-	Thomas Lawrence Finch
"	1879-	George John Kelly
"	1880-	Thomas White
"	1885-	Thomas Heath and William Ball
"	1886-	William Ball and Ellen Heath
"	1887-	William Ball, Emma Ball and Ellen Heath

London County Council:

	1890	Henry Hopkins
Nov.	1890	*Not licensed*

Literature

Official records:

L.C.C. Th. & M-H. Com. App. Nov. 1889.
Mx. Mich. Q.S. 1855-1888.

103

BRITANNIA PUBLIC HOUSE

Prospect Place, St. George in the East, Wapping.

Licensed: 1854-1872

Management

Middlesex justices:

Mich. 1854-	James Pitcher	
" 1863-	Charles Joseph Morbey	
" 1864-	Thomas Parsons	
" 1867-	John David Gibb	
" 1872	Richard Carnell *refused licence for harbouring questionable characters.*	

Literature

Official records:

Mx. Mich, Q.S. 1854-1872.

104

BRITANNIA SALOON

Ratcliff Highway.

In use 1850

Licensed: 1856-1860

Former name

Royal French Circus and Britannia Saloon.

Management

Middlesex justices:

Mich. 1856-	George Bonner and William Lovell
" 1860	*No application*

Literature

Official records:

Mx. Mich. Q.S. 1856-1859.

Contemporary accounts:

1850 ERA. 1850 Jan 13. p. 5. 'Unlicensed theatricals' M. Benoit Tournaire v R. S. Tharne of The Pavilion, Whitechapel.

105

BRITANNIA THEATRE

188, High Street, Hoxton.

1841-1923 became a cinema. Destroyed 1940.

Former name

Britannia Saloon (prior to 1858)

Building details

The original saloon was built at the back of the tavern, and opened Easter Monday, 1841.
The theatre was built in 1858.

Developer: Samuel Lane

Architects: Finch Hill, and Paraire

Builders: Messrs. Hollards and Hannen

Decorators: Messrs. White and Parlby and W. Homann

Capacity: 3, 923 (in 1866)—later limited to 2, 972

Auditorium: S. 330; P. 730; D.C. 460; G. 1, 380; Bx. 72 (A-F)

Cost: £12, 744

Stage: 76' wide, 60' deep. Proscenium opening 34' × 37' high.

Management

Lord Chamberlain:

29. 9.1843-	Samuel Lane
29.12.1871-	Mrs. Sara Haycraft Lane
16. 8.1899-	Alfred Lane Crauford
29. 9.1899-	William Samuel and Alfred Lane Crauford
1.11.1904-	Samuel Bury (*Owner* Thomas Barrasford)
31.10.1905-	Frederick Baugh
31.10.1908-	Thomas Barrasford, Jnr.
27.12.1909-	Elles Brammall (but surrendered 15.10.1910)
3.10.1910-	George Oliver Conquest
10. 4.1911-	Alfred Lane Crauford
8. 5.1911-	Thomas Morton Powell
20.10.1913-	John Challis Vine (used almost exclusively as a cinema) to 30.11.1914)
22.12.1917-	Barry Thomas Underwood (specifically for pantomime which did not run) to 2.2.1918

London County Council:

	1913-	Thomas Morton Powell
	1915-	Harry Thomas Underwood
Nov.	1923	*Listed as a cinema*

Literature

Official records:

G.L.C. Arch. Dpt. 419;
L.C.C. Th. & M-H. Com. App. Nov. 1912, 1914-1923;
L.C.C. Th. & M-H. Com. Papers 1888
LC7/13-17, 7/20-48, 7/89; L.C.O. 168;
M.B.W. Rpt. 1882. p. 35-45.

Contemporary accounts:

1858 BUILDING NEWS, 1858 July 2, p. 685.—Tenders.
BUILDING NEWS, 1858 Aug. 6, p. 785.—Description.
BUILDER, 1858, Sept. 25th. p. 644-645 Description of plans in 'New theatres: Hoxton and Whitechapel'.
BUILDING NEWS, 1858 Oct. 15, p. 1026.—Report of strike.
BUILDING NEWS, 1858 Nov. 12, p. 1123—Description.
BUILDER, 1858 Nov. 13, p. 762-63.—Detailed description. Illus. of auditorium.
BUILDER, 1858 Nov. 20, p. 772.—Decorations.
ILLUSTRATED TIMES, 1858, Dec. 11th The theatrical lounger: The new Britannica (Description of new building).
ILLUSTRATED NEWS OF THE WORLD, 1858 Dec. 25th. Illustrations and description.

1859 BUILDING NEWS, 1859 April 15, p. 352—Roof details.

1883 BUILDER, 1883 Aug. 4, p. 168.—Brief report that work required by M.B.W. completed.

1887 SATURDAY REVIEW, 1887 July 30. 'The state of the London theatres...No. 7'.

1896 SKETCH, 1896 June 24. 'Saturday night at the Britannica'.

1899 ERA, 1899 Aug. 19. 'Death of Mrs. Sara Lane: Obituary'.
STAGE, 1899 Aug. 24.—Report of Mrs. Lane's funeral.

1904 SHOREDITCH OBSERVER, 1904, July 30th. 'The Hoxton Playhouse'. (Report of auction—highest bid £6,800 bought in at £8,000).

1913 STAR. 1913, Oct. 16th. 'Old Brit' glories to be revived. Reopening as musichall next Monday. (Report on reopening after extensive redecoration).

Historical accounts:

1879 DRAMATIC NOTES. 1879, p. 74-5.

1895 STUART, C.D. *and* PARK, A.J.
The Variety Stage. p. 37-38.

1904 BAKER, H. Barton
History of the London stage and its players p. 379-80.

1909 EVENING NEWS. 1909, Sept. 15th & 16th.
Talks about old London: history of Britannia Theatre.
314th and 315th talks by T.E.T. of Margaret Street, Clerkenwell.

1924 REFEREE. 1924, Jan. 27th and Feb. 3rd.
True stories of the stage and its players, 1864-1924, by Carados (H. Chance Newton) Tales of the 'Old Brit'.

1925 CHANCELLOR, E. Beresford
The pleasure haunts of London. p. 135.

c. 1930 MAYES, Ronald.
The romance of London theatres, No. 19.

1933 CRAUFORD, Alfred L.
Sam and Sallie: a romance of the stage. Cranley and Day, 1933. 352p.
HACKNEY GAZETTE, 1933, March 1st.
'Shoreditch and the drama'. 1 column history.

1934 TIMES, 1934, March 21st.
The Britannia Music Hall: film based on its history. (Proposed by Gaumont British)—Includes history.

1935 TIT-BITS. 1935, Feb. 23rd.
Shakespeare went to this cinema. Hoxton's part in the fight for stage liberty, by Leslie Wood. (Report of film project to star Jessie Matthews, and brief history of theatre).

1940 STAR. 1940, Dec. 17th.
From gallery to stalls. 11. Pantomime memories by A. E. Wilson.

194- WILSON, A.E.
Pantomime pageant. p. 110 et seq.

1945 EVENING NEWS. 1945, June 13th.
Hitler passed this way No. 57 (Note, with before and after illus. of bombing).

1946 SCOTT, Harold.
Early doors. p. 70 et seq.

1952 WILSON, A.E.
East end entertainment. Chapters XIV and XV.

1953 TIMES, 1953, Dec. 16th.
'The Queen of Hoxton' Sara Lane of the Old Britannia. (Britannia festivals—particularly that of 1898).

1959 ENCICLOPEDIA dello spettacolo.
Vol. VI Col. 1616/7.

Location of other material

Plans:

Public Record Office: LC7/53. Plan for proposed alteration to staircase.
Edward Clark. Architect.
Plans of part of dress circle and ground level.
G.L.C. *Architects Department.*
Enthoven Collection, 1927 (4 Sheets)—A cinema.

Programmes and play bills:

British Museum; Enthoven Collection; Guildhall Library.

Newscuttings and playbills:

Shoreditch Local Collection.

106

BRITISH QUEEN PUBLIC HOUSE

Ferdinand Street, St. Pancras.

Licensed: 1860-1862

Management

Middlesex justices:

Mich. 1860-	John Overend
Mich. 1862	*No application*

Literature

Official records:

Mx. Mich. Q.S. 1860-1861

107

BRITISH QUEEN PUBLIC HOUSE

Langley Place, Commercial Road, E., Stepney.

Licensed: 1851-1862

Britannia Theatre c. 1855 (105)

(Hackney Public Libraries)

Management

Middlesex justices:

Mich. 1851- John Phillips
" 1862   *Licence refused* as Phillips had been selling spirits.

Literature

Official records:

Mx. Mich. Q.S. 1851-1862.

108

BRIXTON THEATRE

Coldharbour Lane, Brixton, Lambeth.

Opened: 21st September, 1896. *Demolished* by a high explosive bomb 8th November, 1940.

Renamed (during final months of its existence) Melville Theatre

Building details

Architect: Frank Matcham

Contractor: Mr. Wheeler

Capacity: 1,504

Auditorium: (seating) S. 233; P. 261; D.C. 220; G. 412; Bx. 12.

Management

Lord Chamberlain:

29.9.1896-   Charles Rider-Noble
4.8.1899-   Edward George Saunders
25.7.1901-   Edmund Lockwood and Frederick Mouillot to 28.9.1902
Nov. 1905-Oct. 1906   Ernest Stevens
4th March, 1907   William George Grimes
31st Oct. 1907-Nov. 1934   Frederick Melville
December 1936-Nov. 1938   Frederick Melville
December 1938-8th Nov. 1940
   Bert Ernest Hammond

Literature

Official records:

G.L.C. Arch. Dpt. Th. case 420; LC7/43-48; L.C.O. 287 & 374.

Contemporary accounts:

1894 BUILDER. 1894, April 28th. p. 333. Report of proposed new theatre.
1896 BUILDER. 1896, Oct. 10th. p. 295. Brief note of opening.

Location of other material

Plans: G.L.C. *Architect's Department.*

Programmes:

British Museum. Nov. 1900, 1926-1938.
Enthoven Collection.

109

BROADWAY THEATRE

Broadway, New Cross.

Opened: 27th December 1867 *Used as a cinema after* c. 1911.

Building details

Architect: W. C. R. Sprague

Contractor: Walter Wallis of Balham.

Cost: £35,000

Capacity: 1,372

Accommodation: P. 556; S. 74; D.C. 96; B. 156; G. 450; Ex. 40.

Stage: 80' × 40' deep.

Management

London County Council:

1900-   William Edward Allen
1903-   Edmund Lockwood
1905-   Frederick Mouillot
1907-   Louis Calvert
1909-   Oswold Stoll
1912-   Sir Horace Edward Moss
1914-   Frank Allen
1917-   Charles Warren Lovesy
1918-   William Edward Allen
1920-   Charles Warren Lovesy
1921-   Samuel Carson Allen
1923-   Albert Clavering
Nov. 1923   *Listed as a cinema.*

Literature

Official records:

G.L.C. Arch. Dpt. Th. case 41; L.C.C. Th. & M-H Com. App. Nov. 1899-1923; L.C.C. Th. & M-H. Com. Paper 1897+.

Contemporary accounts:

1896 BUILDER. 1896, Dec. 19th. p. 525. Brief note of new theatre to be built.
1897 BUILDER. 1897, April 17th. p. 360. Description of proposed theatre
   BUILDING NEWS: 1897, Dec. 24. p. 903 —Description.
   BUILDER. 1897, Dec. 25th. p. 538. —Report of new theatre to be opened following Monday.
1922 BUILDER. 1922, Dec. 1st. p. 839. 'Formerly a theatre for stage plays - more lately a cinema'. Description, illus. and plans of ventilating plant.

Historical accounts:

c. 1930   MAYES, Ronald
   The romance of London theatres. No. 182.

Location of other material

Plans: G.L.C. *Architect's Department.*

Illustrations, cuttings &c.:

Deptford Local Collection.

Programmes:

Enthoven Collection.
Guildhall Library (one item for 1913)

110

BROMLEY ARMS PUBLIC HOUSE

Fairfield Road, Bow.

Licensed: 1868-1883

Building details

Concert room and area of 450 sq′

Management

Middlesex justices:

Mich.	1868-	Jacob Merchant
″	1871-	George Mitton
″	1874-	Edgar Spencer Easlea
″	1875-	James Mills
″	1883	*No application.*

Literature

Official records:

Mx. Mich. Q.S. 1868-1882.

111

BROOKDALE HALL

Brookdale Road, Catford.

Licensed: 1886-7

Building details

Music room on first floor. 38′ × 22′8″.

Area: 860 sq

Capacity: 180 (later given as 92)

Closed as result of 1878 Act.

Management

West Kent justices:

Mich.	1886-	John Harrison
″	1887	*Not licensed.*

Literature

Official records:

G.L.C. Arch. Dpt. Th. case 040/19;
Sel. Com. 1892; W. Kt. Mich. Q.S. 1886.

Location of other material

Plans: G.L C .Architect's Department.

112

BROWN BEAR PUBLIC HOUSE

44, Albert Gate, Knightsbridge.

Licensed: 1851-1886

Management

Middlesex justices:

Mich.	1851-	Joseph Piercy
″	1868-	Christopher Elgie
″	1876-	Annie Cook
″	1877-	James Gosden
″	1879-	Mary Ann Gosden
″	1880-	Joshua Beardwell
″	1886	*Application withdrawn.*

Literature

Official records:

Mx. Mich. Q.S. 1851-1886.

113

BROWN BEAR PUBLIC HOUSE

65, Broad Street, Holborn.

Licensed: 1854-1855

Management

Middlesex justices:

Mich.	1854-	George Barnard Eagle
″	1855	*No application.*

Literature

Official records:

Mx. Mich. Q.S. 1854.

114

BROWN BEAR PUBLIC HOUSE

77, Leman Street, Whitechapel.

Licensed: pre 1850-1866

Management

Middlesex justices:

Mich.	1848-	William Brand
″	1859-	Henry Dittmar
″	1865-	Margaret Caroline Dittmar
″	1866	*Neclaus Sturcke refused licence.*

Literature

Official records:

Mx. Mich. Q.S. 1848-1866.

115

BROWNLOW ARMS PUBLIC HOUSE

13, Brownlow Street, Drury Lane, Holborn.

Licensed: 1852-3 and 1858-9

Management

Middlesex justices:

Mich.	1852-	John Cole
″	1853	*No application*
″	1858-	Herbert Elliott
″	1859	*Reported Closed.*

Literature

Official records:

Mx. Mich. Q.S. 1852 and 1858-9.

116

BUCKINGHAM THEATRE

153, Buckingham Palace Road, Westminster.

Opening date unknown. *Closed:* 1885

Building details

The theatre was on the upper floor, measuring 107′ × 21′.

Area: 2,240 sq′

There were no fixed seats but room for 300 persons. It consisted of two rooms - 1st room was 52′ × 16′ 9″ and lighted from 6 skylights. 2nd room 55′ × 25′ including stage and 2 dressing rooms. On 20th Feb, 1885 pronounced totally unfit for use as a theatre and was closed under the 1878 Act.

Owner: W. Northington of 136, Buckingham Palace Road.

Literature

Official records:

G.L.C. Arch. Dpt. Th. case 040/20.

Contemporary accounts:

1885 BUILDER. 1885, March 7th. p. 362.
Metropolitan Board of Works reported on the unsafe state of the building.

Location of other material

Plans: G.L.C. *Architects Department*

117

BUILDERS ARMS PUBLIC HOUSE

Russell Street, Chelsea.

Licensed: 1855-1862

Management

Middlesex justices:

Nov. 1855-	George Dobson	
" 1856-	James Tufnell	
" 1859-	George Alison	
" 1861-	Elizabeth Sarah Hallat	
" 1862	*No application*	

Literature

Official records:

Mx. Mich. Q.S. 1855-1861

118

BUILDERS ARMS PUBLIC HOUSE

50, Stebondale Street, *(from 1885* No. 99) Poplar.

Licensed: 1865-1891

Building details

A concert room was on the ground floor adjoining the Public House. 34′ × 11′ 6″.
Finally closed as a result of the 1878 Act.

Management

Middlesex justices:

Mich. 1865-	Henry Thomas Curline	
" 1887-	Alexander Andrew Wallace	

London County Council:

Mich. 1890-	Alexander Andrew Wallace	
" 1891-	Jane Campbell May	
Nov. 1891	*Not licensed.*	

Literature

Official records:

G.L.C. Arch. Dpt. Th. case 040/21.
Mx. Mich. Q.S. 1865-1888.

119

BULL PUBLIC HOUSE

Kingsland High Street, Hackney.

Licensed: 1859-1874

Management

Middlesex justices:

Mich. 1859-	Joseph Francis Pool	
" 1861-	James Hickley	
" 1862-	George Perkins	
" 1867-	William Sanger	
" 1870-	Samuel Hall	
" 1874	*Licence not renewed.*	

Literature

Official records:

Mx. Mich. Q.S. 1859-1873.

120

BULL AND BUSH PUBLIC HOUSE

North End, Hampstead.

Licensed: 1867-1889

Management
Middlesex justices:

Mich. 1867-	Henry Humphreys	

London County Council:

Nov. 1889 *Application for licence withdrawn.*

Literature

Official records:

L.C.C. Th. & M-H. Com. App. Nov. 1889.
Mx. Mich. Q.S. 1867-1888.

121

BURDETT HALL

15, Burdett Road, Limehouse.

Licensed: 1866-1876

Management

Middlesex justices:

Mich. 1866-	Peter Campbell	
" 1876	*Licence refused.*	

Literature

Official records:

Mx. Mich. Q.S. 1866-1876.

122

BUTCHER'S ARMS PUBLIC HOUSE

York Road, Islington.

Licensed: 1855-1862

Management

Middlesex justices:

Mich. 1866-	William Dudley
" 1862	*No application.*

Literature

Official records:

Mx. Mich. Q.S. 1855-1861.

123

CAMBERWELL EMPIRE

The Triangle, Denmark Hill, Camberwell.

Opened: 1894

Ceased to be used for live entertainment: 1924
Demolished: 1937

Former names

Metropole Theatre 1894-1906
Theatre Metropole and Opera House
Camberwell Empire 1906-1918
Camberwell Theatre and Picture Palace 1918
then Camberwell Empire and Picture Palace

Building details:

Developer: John Brennan Mulholland

Architect: Bertie Crewe and W. G. R. Sprague

Capacity: (1894) 2,050: (1903) 1,596

Auditorium: (1894) S. 100; P. 800; D.C. 350; G. 800.
(1903) S. 85; P. 400; D.C. 104; B. 103; G. 352.
N.B. Boxes included with figure for level.

The Odeon Cinema now stands back from the site of
the Empire.

Management

London County Council:

1905-	John de Freece
1907	Donald Munro
1908-	Percy Ford
1911-	Cissie Lawson
1914	Oscar Berry
1915-	John Ennis Lawson
1918	Charles Gulliver
1920-	Henry Seddon
1924	Arthur Israel Cohen

Lord Chamberlain:

1. 6.1912-	Cissie Lawson
1.12.1913-	Oscar Berry
1.12.1914-	John Ennis Lawson
1.12.1916-	Charles Gulliver
19. 6.1918-	Henry Seddon (sub-let by C. Gulliver)
1.12.1923-	Arthur Israel Cohen (to 30.11.1926)

Literature

Official records:

L.C.C Arch. Dpt. Mss. index; L.C.C. Arch. Dpt. Th.
case 55; L.C.C. Th. & M-H. Com. App. Nov. 1904-1923.
L.C.C. Th. & M-H. Com. Paper 1893+.
LC7/42-48; L.C.O. 374 & 516.

Contemporary accounts:

1893 BUILDER. 1893, Nov. 18th. p. 337. Report that
L.C.C. had accepted drawings.
1937 SOUTH LONDON PRESS. 1937, Aug. 10th. Illus.
of exterior and note of demolition for road
widening.

Historical accounts:

c. 1930   MAYES, Ronald
The romance of London theatres. No. 175.

Location of other material

Plans: G.L.C. *Architects Department*

Illustrations: Camberwell Public Library.

Newscuttings: Camberwell Public Library.

Programmes: Guildhall Library (3 items)

124

CAMBERWELL PALACE

23-31, Denmark Hill, Camberwell.

Opened: 1899

Former name

Oriental Palace of Varieties. 1896-1899

Oriental Palace 1896 (124)

(Southwark Public Libraries)

Building details

Architect: E. A. E. Woodrow

Builder: C. Gray Hill

Capacity: 2,117

Auditorium: (seated) S. 665; B. 400; G. 456; Bx. 32.

Management

London County Council.

1897-	George Venner
1910-	Thomas Masters
1913-	Charles Gulliver
1925-	New Camberwell Palace Ltd.
1928-	Greater London Theatres and Cinemas Ltd.
1929-	Summers Brown
1932	Loughborough Playhouse Ltd.
1933-	Associated British Cinemas Ltd.
1940-	Loughborough Playhouses Ltd.
1943-	Suburban Century Cinemas Ltd.
1946-	Regis Entertainments Ltd.

Lord Chamberlain:

4.12.1911-	Thomas Masters
2. 7.1912-	Charles Gulliver
1.12.1928-	Summers Brown
1.12.1931-	George Barclay
1.12.1932-	Ralph Bromhead
1.12.1934-	Arthur Moss
1.12.1939-	Ernest Geering
1.12.1943-	Archie Shenburn (after Roy George Futroye)

Literature

Official records:

G.L.C. Arch. Dpt. Th. case 56; L.C.C. Th. & M-H. Com. App. Nov. 1896+:
L.C.C. Th. & M-H. Com. Papers 1896+;
L.C.O. 374 & 498.

Contemporary accounts:

1899 BUILDER. 1899, July 22nd. p. 86. Brief note of erection.
BUILDER. 1899, Dec. 2nd. p. 516. Report of opening. Description.
BUILDING NEWS. 1899, Dec. 8th. p. 762. Brief description.
1950 THEATRE ownership... p. 126 & p. 131.

Location of other material

Plans: G.L.C. *Architect's Department.*

Programmes, playbills & cuttings:

Enthoven Collection; Lambeth Local Collection

125

CAMBRIDGE THEATRE

Earlham Street, Seven Dials, Holborn.

Opened: 4th Sept. 1930

Building details

Architect: Wimperis, Simpson & Guthrie

Builder: Gee, Walker & Slater

Interior decorator: S. Chermayeff

Capacity: 1255

Auditorium: (seating) S. 486; D.C. 301; U.C. 422.

Stage: 33' wide; 26' high; 32' deep.

Management

Lord Chamberlain:

1.12.1930-	Bertie A. Meyer
1.12.1931-	George Brinton McLellan
1.12.1932-	James Ernest Sharpe
1.12.1933-	Thomas Henry Bostock

(Letter dated 13.10.1941 stated theatre used for film trade shows and concerts)

1.12.1942-	Thomas Henry Bostock
1.12.1943-	Prince Littler
1.12.1947-	Joy Pomeroy
1.12.1949-	Clifford Middleton. *Receiver*
1.12.1950-	Tom Arnold and Emile Littler

London County Council:

4.11.1938-	Cambridge Theatre Co.
1948-	Cambridge Theatre Properties Ltd.

Literature

Official records:

G.L.C. Arch. Dpt. Th. case 4155; L.C.O. 204 & 374.

Contemporary accounts:

1930 CAMBRIDGE THEATRE. Souvenir of Cambridge Theatre, Seven Dials. Open. 3rd September, 1930. Photos. and description.
STAGE. 1930, Sept. 4th. Building description.
BUILDER. 1930, Sept. 5th. p. 382-5. Illus. building details.
ARCHITECTS' JOURNAL. 1930, Oct. 8th. p. 824, 828-30. Building details.
ARCHITECTURAL REVIEW. 1930, Oct. p. 159-164.
ARCHITECT. 1930, Oct. 10th. p. 491-2. Building details.
ARCHITECT AND BUILDING NEWS. 1930, Oct. 10th. p. 491-496. Photo. plans. Building details.
TIMES. 1930, Nov. 29th. Building details.
c. 1930 MAYES, Ronald
The romance of London theatres. No. 145.
1931 ARCHITECTURE ILLUSTRATED. 1931, April. Building details.
MODERNE BAUFORMEN. 1931, May. p. 217-24. Das neue Cambridge-theater in London.
1950 THEATRE ownership... p. 62.

Historical accounts:

1959 ENCICLOPEDIA dello spettacolo. Vol. 6 col. 1, 617
1963 MANDER, Raymond *and* MITCHENSON, Joe
The theatres of London. 2nd ed. p. 35-37.

Location of other material

Plans:

Enthoven Collection, 1928. (2 sheets)
G.L.C. *Architects Department.*

Programmes:

Enthoven Collection; Garrick Club. 1930-1952;
Holborn Local Collection; Westminster Local Collection.

CAMDEN ARMS PUBLIC HOUSE

1, Randolph Street (*formerly* Great Randolph Street)
Camden Town.

Licensed: pre 1850 to 1891

Building details

Concert room on first floor. 31′ 9″ × 17′ 4″.
Area: 540 sq
By 1891 used as a billiard room.

Management

Middlesex justices:

Mich. 1850-	Harry Bonham Hall
″ 1851-	Maria Briant Hall
″ 1852-	Joseph Lanham
″ 1865	Robert Forbes
″ 1866-	James Carter
″ 1868	James Argent
″ 1869-	Charles Godfrey Kurtz
″ 1876-	John Wheeler
″ 1882-	Thomas Joseph Shelton

London County Council:

1890-1   Thomas Joseph Shelton
Nov. 1891 *No application*

Literature

Official records:

G.L.C. Arch. Dpt. Th. case 040/22;
L.C.C. Th. & M-H. Com. App. Nov. 1889-90;
Mx. Mich. Q.S. 1848-1888.

Location of other material

Plans: G.L.C. *Architects Department.*

127

CAMDEN THEATRE

Camden High Street, and Crowndale Road, Camden
Town.

Opened: 1901 By 1924 in use as a cinema.
Later B.B.C. studio.

Former names

Royal Camden Theatre	(Never licensed as this)
Camden Theatre	1901-1914
Camden Hippodrome	1914-1940

Building details

Architect: W. G. R. Sprague

Cost: £50,000

Capacity: 2,434

Auditorium: (Seating) P. and S. Bx. 725; D.C. and Bx.
156; B. and Bx. 240; G. 520.

Stage: 75′ wide, 60′ high, 40′ deep.

Management

Lord Chamberlain:

Letter 16.12.1903	Frank Curzon has licence transferred from E.G. Saunders.

1. 8.1904-	
16. 9.1908	Robert Arthur

(29. 5.1908 Law case Rex. v. Arthur, Gibbons, Deer
& Terrell for giving variety performances - convicted)

14.12.1908-	
31.10.1909	Albert Maxsted
31.10.1912	Joseph Clavering
1.12.1928	William Henry Bickerton
1.12.1930	Ernest W. P. Peall
1.12.1940-	
30.11.1945	Edmund Crisp

London County Council:

1910	Sidney Marler
1911	Charles Gulliver
1912	William Ernest Mansell
1913-	Henry Thomas Underwood
1915-	Albert Simmons
1917-	Joseph Charles Clavering (to 1924)

Literature

Official records:

G.L.C. Arch. Dpt. Mss index;
G.L.C. Arch. Dpt. Th. case 58;
L.C.C. Th. & M-H. Com. App. Nov. 1909-1924;
L.C.C. Th. & M-H. Com. Papers 1899+;
LC7/47-48; LCO 211 and 374.

Contemporary accounts:

1900 SKETCH. 1900, Oct. 17th. "More new theatres.'
illus. of exterior of 'Royal Camden Theatre.'
BUILDING NEWS. 1900, Dec. 28th. p. 933.-Brief
description.
1901 BUILDER. 1901, Jan. 5th. p. 23. Report of new
building.

Camden Theatre 1900 (127)

(Victoria & Albert Museum, Crown copyright)

Historical accounts:

c.1930   MAYES, Ronald
           The romance of London theatres. No. 121.

Location of other material

Plans: G.L.C. *Architects Department.*

Programmes:

Garrick Club (one only); British Museum Library.
No. 474; Enthoven Collection; London Museum;
St. Pancras Local Collection.

128 CAMEL PUBLIC HOUSE

16, Phillipp Street, Kingsland Road, Shoreditch.

Licensed: 1866-1891

Management

Middlesex justices:

Mich. 1866-	Henry Carwood
" 1868	William Joseph Gibbons
" 1869	Giles Lewis
" 1870	Charles Gilbert
" 1871	James Stracey
" 1872-	William Burrell
" 1874	William Phillippe
" 1875	Thomas Walker
" 1876	Ann Stern
" 1877	Alfred George Johnson
" 1878	Thomas Treeby
" 1879	Gore William Frood
" 1880	Alfred Aberg
" 1881	James Lilley
" 1882	John Selby Nesbitt James
" 1883	Walter William Cowlrick
" 1884	William Lee
" 1885	Charles Grieveson
" 1886	Samuel Smith
" 1887	Henry John Newman
" 1888	Alfred Till Whalley

London County Council:

1890	David Arthur Barnes
1891	Alfred Hutchin
Nov. 1891	*Not licensed.*

Literature

Official records:

L.C.C. Th. & M-H. Com. App. Nov. 1889-1890.
Mx. Mich. Q.S. 1866-1888.

129

CANTERBURY MUSIC HALL

143, Westminster Bridge Road, (*formerly* Upper
Marsh) Lambeth.

Opened: 1851

After 1927 not licensed as a theatre or music hall,
although having L.C. licence.

Destroyed: 1942

Former names

Canterbury Arms Public House (pre 1850-1851.
Licensed by this name to 1861)
Canterbury Hall 1851-1887
Canterbury Music Hall 1887-1904
(Royal) Canterbury Theatre of Varieties }
    "   Palace of Varieties   } 1904-1912
Canterbury Music Hall 1912-1914
Canterbury Theatre of Varieties 1914-1922
Canterbury Music Hall 1923+

Building details

1848 Charles Morton took over Canterbury Arms.
1851 Canterbury Hall opened.
1854 Reconstruction.

Cost: £25,000

Capacity: 1,500

1876 Reconstruction

Architect: Albert Bridgman

Builder: W.H. Bracher & Son, Great Ormond St.

Interior decoration: E.W. Bradwell
Sliding roof designed and patented by F. Villiers and
executed by Mr. Somerville of Upper Thames Street.

Management

Surrey justices:

Mich. 1851-	Charles Morton
" 1868-	William Holland
" 1871-	Frederic Villiers
" 1880-	Edward Garcia
" 1881-	Gerald George Whitehead
" 1882-	William John Alt
" 1883-	George Adney Payne

London County Council:

1890-	George Adney Payne
1909-	Henry Wells
1914-	Julius Fuld
1919-	Henry Brickwell
1923-	Hyman Hyams
1926-7	Mrs. Jessie Hyams

Lord Chamberlain:

10. 1.1912-	Henry Wells
1.12.1913-	Henry Brickwell
19.12.1921-	H. Hyams
1.12.1925-	Mrs. J. Hyams
1.12.1928-	Alfred E. Corrick
1.12.1929-	Ernest W.P. Peall
1.12.1940-30.11.1942	Sid Hyams

Literature

Official records:

G.L.C. Arch. Dpt. Th. case 60;
L.C.C. Th. & M-H. Com. App. Nov. 1889-26;
L.C.C. Th. & M-H. Com. Papers 1888+.
L.C.O. 374 and 508.
Sy. Mich. Q.S. 1851-1888.

Contemporary accounts:

1856 ILLUSTRATED LONDON NEWS. 1856, Dec. 6th.
          —Description of the 'new Hall'. Illus. of interior.
1857 RITCHIE, J. Ewing. The night side of London.
          p. 58-65.

1858 BUILDER. 1858, Nov. 6th. p. 746. —Fine arts and singing rooms 'Canterbury Hall Gallery' —description.

1876 THE CANTERBURY Theatre of Varieties and its associates, with some account of Lambeth and its vicinity. London. 1876. 28p. ports, plates, map.

1887 SATURDAY REVIEW. 1887, Aug. 20th. The state of London ... music halls ... No. 2.

1890 BUILDER, 1890 Aug. 9, p. 114. —Report of re-arrangement and redecoration of interior.

1909 CANTERBURY THEATRE OF VARIETIES. Souvenir, 1200-1907. 55th anniversary commemoration of the Canterbury ... December 5th 1907. Annals old and new. 16p. (B.M. 011795. h. 56).

Historical accounts:

c. 1930 MAYES, Ronald
The romance of the London theatres, No. 105.

1935 HADDON, Archibald
The story of the music hall ... pp. 25-8, other refs.

1946 SCOTT, Harold
Early doors ... pp. 50+, 133+ and other refs.

1952 PULLING, Christopher
They were singing ... p. 175, 181, 183.

1959 ENCICLOPEDIA dello spettacolo. Vol. 6, Col. 1617.

Location of other material

Plans: G.L.C. *Architects Department.* Enthoven Collection.

Programmes and playbills:

British Museum Library. 1879-83
Enthoven Collection.
Guildhall Library.
Lambeth Local Collection

130

CANTERBURY PUBLIC HOUSE

Woolwich.

Licensed: 1854-1869.

Management

West Kent justices:

Mich.	1854	William Hare
"	1857-60	Charles Job
"	(1861-5	no records)
"	1866-8	George Moreland

Literature

Official records:

W. Kt. Mich. Q.S. 1854-1868.

131

CAPE OF GOOD HOPE PUBLIC HOUSE

787, Commercial Road, E. (*formerly* St. Anne's Place, Commercial Rd.) Stepney.

Licensed: 1862-1890

Building details

Concert room on the first floor, by Oct. 1890 used as a masonic lodge.
The concert room was closed as a result of the 1878 act.

Management

Middlesex justices:

Mich.	1862	Andrew Benjamin Penny
"	1863-	William Davies
"	1886	Frederick Henry Salmon
"	1887+	Charles Busbridge

London County Council:

1890 Henry Busbridge (Retained)

Literature

Official records:

G.L.C. Arch. Dpt. Th. case 040/23;
L.C.C. Th. & M-H. Com. App. Nov. 1889;
Mx. Mich. Q.S. 1862-1888.

132

CARDINAL WOLSEY PUBLIC HOUSE

King Henry Street, Islington.

Licensed: 1859-1862, 1864-1869

Management

Middlesex justices:

Mich.	1859-	Raymond Wheeler
"	1861-	Frederick Wortham
"	1862-	William Hart
"	1863	*No application*
"	1864	George Everett
"	1865	William Hunter
"	1866-8	Octavius Neely
"	1869	*Refused.*

Literature

Official records:

Mx. Mich. Q.S. 1859-1869.

133

CARLTON PUBLIC HOUSE

Carlton Road, St. Pancras.

Licensed: 1855-1857

Management

Middlesex justices:

Mich. 1855 and 1856 Robert Clint Thornton

Literature

Official records:

Mx. Mich. Q.S. 1855-1856.

134

CARLTON THEATRE

62-65, Haymarket, Westminster.

Opened: 27th April, 1927. *It became a cinema:* 1929

Building details

Developer: Carlton Theatre Co.

Architect: F. T. Verity and S. Beverley.

Contractor: Arthur Vigor Ltd.

Management

Lord Chamberlain:

1. 12. 1927-30. 11. 1929 John Cecil Graham

Literature

Official records:

G.L.C. Arch. Dpt. Th. case 3286.
L.C.O. 374 and 556.

Contemporary accounts:

1927 ARCHITECT. 1927, April 29th. p. 732-6, 742.
illus. —Building details.
ARCHITECTS JOURNAL. 1927, May 11th.
p. 647-52. illus. —Article by S. C. Ramsay.
BUILDER. 1927, April 29th. p. 677, 679, 682,
684. illus. of interiors and front elevation.
—Description.
CARLTON THEATRE. Opening souvenir, 1927.
illus. (sketches), ports and description. 40p.
(Copy in Enthoven Collection)

Historical accounts:

1965 MANDER, Raymond *and* MITCHENSON, Joe.
The Theatres of London, 2nd ed. p. 266.
1960 LONDON. County Council.
Survey of London. Vol. XXIX.
L.C.C. 1960. p. 213-214.

Location of other material

Plans: G.L C. *Architects Department.*

Programmes: Garrick Club (1 only);
Enthoven Collection.

135

CASINO THEATRE

22, Old Compton Street, Cambridge Circus,
Westminster.

Opened: 3rd April, 1930.

Former names

Prince Edward Theatre 1930-36
London Casino   1936-46 and after 1950

Building details

Developer: Hay Hill Syndicate

Architect: Edward Albert Stone

Contractor: Griggs and Son

Interior decorators: Marc-Henri and Laverdet

Capacity: 1, 800

Stage: 44′ wide, 24′ high, 35′ deep.

Building has been used for various purposes: a
theatre, trade cinema, a cabaret-restaurant, a club and
now for cinerama.

Management

Lord Chamberlain:

3. 4. 1930-	Henry Thomas Richardson
1. 12. 1934-	*Not licensed*
1. 12. 1935-	E. A. Stone
1. 12. 1936-	Thomas William Bowyer
1. 12. 1937-	William Duncan Stewart
1. 12. 1939-	Alfred Esdaile
[1. 12. 1942-	John Edward Harding: Queensbury All Services Club]
1. 12. 1946-	Emile Littler
1. 12. 1947-	Tom Arnold and Emile Littler

London County Council:

1931-	Hay Hill Syndicate Ltd.
1946-1950	Arnlit Ltd.

Literature

Official records:

G.L.C. Arch. Dpt. Th. case 4160.
L.C.O. 225 and 374.

Contemporary accounts:

1930 PRINCE EDWARD THEATRE. Programme
of 'Rio Rita' for 3rd April, 1930. —Description.
ARCHITECT AND BUILDING NEWS. 1930,
April. —Description.
ARCHITECTURE ILLUSTRATED. 1930, July.
—Description.
1936 ARCHITECTURE ILLUSTRATED. 1936, May.
—Description.

Historical accounts:

1931 CHANCELLOR, E. B.
The romance of Soho. p. 239-40.
c. 1930 MAYES, Ronald
The romance of London theatres, No. 137.
The Prince Edward.
1952 PULLING, Christopher
They were singing. . . p. 226.
1963 MANDER, Raymond *and* MITCHENSON, Joe.
The theatres of London. 2nd ed. p. 38-40.
1966 GREATER LONDON COUNCIL
Survey of London. Vol. 33. 1966.   pp. 199-200.

Location of other material

Plans: G. L. C. *Architects Department.*

Programmes:

Enthoven Collection; Westminster Local Collection

136

CASTLE MUSIC HALL

Castle Public House, 188, Camberwell Road,
Camberwell.

Licensed: 1875-1889

Other names

Castle Public House
Godfrey's Music Hall

Management

Surrey justices:

Mich. 1875–		Charles Mackay
"	1882	George Henry Wolfe
"	1883	Charles Norden
"	1884	Alfred James Deer
"	1885	Charles Godfrey
"	1886–	Thomas William Wragg
"	1888	John Syer

On 19th October, 1888, the Metropolitan Board of Works approved the drawings for a new music hall. The music hall was not completed in accordance with the plans, and in 1889 the L.C.C. licence granted to Augustus Frederick Leech was retained; it was not relicensed.

Literature

Official records:

G.L.C. Arch. Dpt. Th. case 676; Sel. Com. 1892; Sy. Mich. Q.S. 1875–1888.

137

CASTLE PUBLIC HOUSE

1, Belinda Street, Islington.

Licensed: 1861–1864

Management

Middlesex justices:

Mich. 1861		William Turner
"	1862–	Frederic Robert Salter
"	1864	Joseph P. Vezey *refused.*

Literature

Official records:

Mx. Mich. Q.S. 1861–1864.

138

CASTLE PUBLIC HOUSE

37, City Road, Shoreditch.

Licensed: 1862–1864

Management

Middlesex justices:

Mich. 1862	Joseph Ferrar
"	1863 John Robert Gwynn

Literature

Official records:

Mx. Mich. Q.S. 1862–1863.

139

CASTLE PUBLIC HOUSE

Goodman's Stile, Whitechapel.

Licensed: 1851–1863

Management

Middlesex justices:

Mich. 1851–		Friederich Junge
"	1855–	Gerhard Kaemens
"	1863	*Refused.*

Literature

Official records:

Mx. Mich. Q.S. 1851–1863.

140

CASTLE PUBLIC HOUSE

Kentish Town Road, St. Pancras.

Licensed: 1850–1873

Management

Middlesex justices.

Mich. 1849–		John Ecles Lawford
"	1851–	Simon Willsment
"	1853–	James Jones
"	1869–	William Jones
"	1873	*No application.*

Literature

Official records:

Mx. Mich. Q.S. pre 1850–1872.

Location of other material

Handbills: Guildhall Library (1 item for 1833)

141

CAT AND SHOULDER OF MUTTON PUBLIC HOUSE

1, Duncan Place, London Fields, Hackney.

Licensed: 1850–1883

Management

Middlesex justices:

From prior to 1850– Richard Sobee
Mich. 1858–		Edward Smith
"	1865–	George Adams
"	1867–	Alfred Stace
"	1873–	John Elves
"	1875–	Edward Mills
"	1880–	Richard Robert Sharp Scott
"	1883	*Refused, as licence seldom used.*

Literature

Official records:

Mx. Mich. Q.S. pre 1850–1883.

142

CATHERINE WHEEL PUBLIC HOUSE

46, Great Windmill Street, Piccadilly.

Licensed: prior to 1850–1857

Management

Middlesex justices:

Pre	1850-	John Dodson
Mich.	1851-	George Whyte
"	1852-	James Holt
"	1854-	Edward Smith
"	1855-	Henry Osborn
Mich.	1857	Abraham Shelley

Literature

Official records.

Mx. Mich. Q.S. pre 1850-1857.

143

CHANTICLEER THEATRE

34, Clareville Street, Kensington.

Licensed: 1937-1940

Other names

formerly Webber-Douglas Theatre,
later   Webber-Douglas School

Premises rented by the Chanticleer Theatre Club,
director Greta Douglas...a non-profit making members club...presenting plays of quality...from the
Webber-Douglas School of Singing and Dramatic Art.

Management

London County Council:

1937-1940 Walter Henry George Johnstone-Douglas

Literature

Official records:

G.L.C. Arch. Dept. Th. case 3336;
L.C.C. Th & M-H. Com. App. Nov. 1936-39.

Historical accounts:

1944	THEATRE ARTS. 1944, June. p 29.
	—London's little theatres: the work of the Gate-
	way and the Chanticleer.
	NEW STATESMAN. 1944, July 15th. p 40
	—The Chanticleer.
1950	FERGUSON, Rachel
	Royal borough. J. Cape, 1950. p. 266.

Location of other material

Plans: G.L.C *Architects Department.*

Programmes: Enthoven Collection.

144

CHELSEA PALACE

232-242, King's Road, Chelsea.

Opened: 13th April, 1903. *Closed:* 1957 except for one
season.

Former name

Chelsea Palace of Varieties

Building details

Developer: Chelsea Palace Syndicate

Architect: Messrs. Wylson and Lang

Contractor: C. T. Kearley

Capacity: 2,524

Auditorium: (seating) P. 784; S. 168; C. & Bx. 431; G. 513.

Management

London County Council:

1903-	Henri Gros
1910-	Ilford Ibbetson
1925-	Variety Theatres Consolidated *and* Ilford Ibbetson (sp)
1931-	Variety Theatres Consolidated *and* Adney W. Gibbons (sp)
1942-	Variety Theatres Consolidated and Otto Knifton (sp)

Literature

Official records:

G.L.C. Arch. Dpt. Mss index; G.L.C. Arch. Dpt. Th.
case 70;
L.C.C. Th. & M-H. Com. App. Nov. 1902+;
L.C.C. Th. & M-H. Com. Papers 1902+.

Contemporary accounts:

1902	BUILDING NEWS. 1902, Oct. 24th. p 571 illus. of exterior.—Description. BUILDER. 1902, Oct. 25th. p. 376.—Brief description.
1950	THEATRE ownership. p 126.

Location of other material:

Plans: G.L.C. *Architects Department.*

Programmes:

British Museum Library. (March 1940. No. 474)
Chelsea Public Library: Programmes and Playbills
relating to recruitment meetings & war charities.
—Chelsea Miscellany. Vol. 14.

Programmes, Newscuttings &c: Enthoven Collection

145

CHEQUERS PUBLIC HOUSE

13, Provinence Row, Finsbury.

Licensed: 1806-1877

Management

Middlesex justices:

Mich.	1860-	Sarah Pugh
"	1868-	George Frederick Calver (i.e. Kalber)
"	1875-	George Barnett Boulter
"	1876-	Alfred Leggett
"	1877-	*Refused.*

Literature

Official records:

Mx. Mich. Q.S. 1860-77.

146

CHERRY TREE PUBLIC HOUSE

Bowling Green Lane, Finsbury.

Licensed: 1854-1875

Management

Middlesex justices:

Mich.	1854-	John Shergold
"	1865-	Samuel Shergold
"	1870-	John Shergold
"	1875-	*Not licensed.*

Literature

Official records:

Mx. Mich. Q.S. 1854-1874.

147

CHERRY TREE PUBLIC HOUSE

64, Kingsland Road, Shoreditch.

Licensed: 1866-1891

Other name

The Old Cherry Tree Public House

Building details

A concert room on the first floor over the kitchen and part of the yard. 27'8" × 23'6".

Area: 612'— later reduced below 500'

Average audience 70.

The hall was closed as a result of the 1878 Act.

Management

Middlesex justices:

Mich.	1866-	Thomas Birds
"	1871-	Thomas Franklin
"	1872-	William Ringer
"	1874-	Thomas Stock
"	1876-	Samuel Mead

London County Council:

1890-91 George Witherall
Nov. 1891 *Not relicensed.*

Literature

Official records:

G.L.C. Arch. Dpt. Th. case 040/98;
L.C.C. Th & M-H. Com. App. Nov. 1889-90;
Mx. Mich. Q.S. 1866-1888

148

CHERRY TREE PUBLIC HOUSE

St. Leonard's Road, Bromley.

Licensed: 1854-1862

Management

Middlesex justices:

Mich.	1854-	Thomas Price
"	1857-	George Hamilton
"	1861-	Eliza Smith
"	1862-	*No application.*

Literature

Official records:

Mx. Mich Q.S. 1854-1861.

149

CHESHIRE CHEESE PUBLIC HOUSE

Grosvenor Row, Pimlico.

Licensed: 1861-1873

Management

Middlesex justices:

Mich.	1861-	Alfred Watson
"	1864-	James Watson
"	1873-	*No application.*

Literature

Official records:

Mx. Mich. Q.S. 1861-1872.

150

CHILDE HAROLD PUBLIC HOUSE

Railway Street, Bromley.

Licensed: 1861-1874

Management

Middlesex justices:

Mich.	1861-	Thomas Edward Bowkett
"	1863	George Bowkett
"	1864-	Thomas Edward Bowkett
"	1867-	Charles Hood
"	1869	Robert Green Grimes
"	1870-	Thomas Edward Bowkett
"	1874-	*No application.*

Literature

Official records:

Mx. Mich. Q.S. 1861-1873.

151

CHILDREN'S THEATRE

81, Endell Street, Holborn.

Licensed: 1927-1931

Management

Lord Chamberlain:

1.12.1927-30.11.1931 Joan Lowson (Known as Joan Luxton)

London County Council:

Licensed from 1928 to 1931 Joan Lowson.

Literature

Contemporary accounts:

1930 NATION. 1930, Sept. 6th p. 704.
Reopening of the Children's Theatre.

Location of other material

Programmes: Enthoven Collection

152

CITY MUSIC HALL

Dr. Johnson Hotel, Supper and City Concert Rooms,
Bolt Court, Fleet Street.

Opened: c. 1835   *Closed:* 1863

Former name

Dr. Johnson's Concert Room

Later name

In 1895 part of the premises of the Albert Club.

Proprietor
Name on handbills at Guildhall is J. Wilton.

Literature

Contemporary accounts:

1857   RITCHIE, J. Ewing
The night side of London, 1857. p 113-119.

Historical accounts:

1895   STUART, C. D. *and* PARK, A. J.
The variety stage p. 31-33.

Location of other material

Handbills: Guildhall Library (2 items)

153

CITY ARMS PUBLIC HOUSE

273, City Road, (*formerly* Bridge Place, City Road)
Shoreditch.

Licensed: 1854-1865

Management

Middlesex justices:

| Mich. | 1854- | Erasmus Lawrence |
| " | 1865 | *No application.* |

Literature

Official records:

Mx. Mich. Q.S. 1854-1864.

154

CITY OF GLOUCESTER PUBLIC HOUSE

1, St. Leonard's Street, (*formerly* St. Leonard's Terrace) Chelsea.

Licensed: 1854-1891

Management

Middlesex justices:

Mich.	1854-	William Skelton
"	1857-	John Samuel Hittinger
"	1861	*License refused*
"	1862-	Issac Munro
"	1864	Charles Gratton Bill
"	1865-	William Hendebourck
"	1872	Hannah Hendebourck
"	1873-	Edward Austin
"	1879	Hannah Austin
"	1880	Alfred Samuel Block
"	1881-	John Block
"	1884	Cubitt Cooke
"	1885-	Alfred Hubbard

London County Council:

| | 1890- | Frederick Gurney |
| Nov. 1891 | | *Opposed and refused.* |

Literature

Official records:

L.C.C. Th. & M-H. Com. App. Nov. 1889-1891;
Mx. Mich Q.S. 1854-1888.

155

CITY OF LONDON PUBLIC HOUSE

Albert Terrace, York Road, Kings Cross.

Licensed: 1855-7 and 1869-1872

Management

Middlesex justices

Mich.	1855-6	Frederick Bishop
"	1869	Benjamin Robesson
"	1870	William Henry Caldecourt
"	1871-2	James Blyth

Literature

Official records:

Mx. Mich. Q.S. 1869-1872.

156

CITY OF LONDON THEATRE

35 and 36, Norton Folgate, Bishopsgate.

Opened: 1835.   *Closed:* 1871 (Destroyed by fire)

Former name

City Theatre

Later name

Great Central Hall (1874+)

Building details

Architect: Samuel Beazley

Capacity: (1865) 2,500

Rebuilt as Great Central Hall

Management

Lord Chamberlain:

1st licence:29th Sept. 1843 Charles James James
(cancelled 22.4.1844)

22. 4.1844-	Frederick Fox Cooper	
1. 7.1844-	Christopher Cockerton	
29. 9.1848-	John Johnson and Richard Nelson Lee	
29. 9.1863-	Richard Nelson Lee	
28.11.1868-	Richard Homer Gibbs	
15. 6.1869-	William Henry Squier (to 28.9.1870)	

Middlesex justices:

Mich.	1874-	George Ling and George Palmer
"	1887	*Not relicensed.*

Literature

Official records:

G.L.C. Arch. Dpt. Th. case 025;
L.C. 7/13-15, 20-23;
Mx. Mich. Q.S. 1874-1887.
Sel. Com. 1866, 1872, 1892.

Contemporary accounts:

1850/1	TALLIS's DRAMATIC MAGAZINE. 1850/51. p. 29 & 90.
1871	ILLUSTRATED LONDON NEWS. 1871, Oct. 28th. p. 416. —Illus. of the destruction of the theatre.

Historical accounts:

1883	WILLIAMS, Michael Some London theatres. p. 42-79.
1904	BAKER, H. Barton History of the London stage and its players. p. 407-8.
1925	SHERSON, Erroll London's lost theatres...p. 37-8.
c.1930	MAYES, Ronald The romance of London's theatres, No. 167
1952	WILSON, A. E. East end entertainment. Chapters XII and XIII.

Location of other material

Programmes and Playbills:

British Museum Library. 1831-56; Enthoven collection; Guildhall Library; London Museum.

157

CITY OF NORWICH PUBLIC HOUSE

Wentworth street, Christchurch, Whitechapel.

Licensed: 1855-1868

Management

Middlesex justices:

Mich.	1855-	Frederick Gehringer
"	1868	*Refused owing to 2 a.m. closing*

Literature

Official records:

Mx. Mich Q.S. 1855-1868.

158

CITY OF ROME PUBLIC HOUSE

Roman Road, Islington.

Licensed: 1860-1862

Management

Middlesex justices:

Mich.	1860-	Martha Clarke
"	1862	*Refused*

Literature

Official records:

Mx. Mich. Q.S. 1860-1862.

159

CITY OF YORK PUBLIC HOUSE

9, River Terrace, York Road, Islington.

Licensed: 1854-1891

Building details

Room on the first floor used as a club and concert room. 29'6" × 17'5".

Area: 513 sq.'

Management

Middlesex justices:

Mich.	1854	Margaret Burnman
"	1855-	John Burnman
"	1861-	Frank Squire
"	1866-	John Squire
"	1871-	Frank Squire
"	1882-	Frank Patrick

London County Council:

	1890-1	Edward Gentry
Nov.	1891	*Not licensed.*

Literature

Official records:

G.L.C. Arch. Dpt. Th. case 040/24;
L.C.C. Th. & M-H Com. App. Nov. 1889-90;
Mx. Mich. Q.S. 1854-1888.

160

CLAY HALL PUBLIC HOUSE

Old Ford Road, Bow.

Licensed: 1859-1883

Management

Middlesex justices:

Mich.	1859	George Rumsey
"	1860-	Robert Twocock
"	1875-	Sarah Jane Twocock
"	1877-	Robert William Neall
"	1883-	*No application.*

Literature

Official records:

Mx. Mich Q.S. 1859-1882.

161

COACH AND HORSES PUBLIC HOUSE

380, Mile End Road, (*formerly* Roadside, Mile End Old Town) Stepney.

Licensed: 1859-1889

Management

Middlesex justices:

Mich.	1859-	Charles Stanton
"	1868-	Robert Stanton
"	1875	Frederick Garner
"	1876	James Venters
"	1877	Rudolph Henry Pickel
"	1878-	James George Speaight
"	1883-	Jane Amelia Speaight

London County Council:

Nov.	1889	*Licence refused.*

Literature

Official records:

L.C.C. Th. & M-H. Com. App. Nov. 1889;
Mx. Mich. Q.S. 1859-1888.

162

COACH AND HORSES PUBLIC HOUSE

1-3, Mitchell Street (*later* 182 Great Mitchell Street) St. Luke's, Finsbury.

Licensed: 1856-1888

Building details

1st floor contains in front a Concert Room of irregular form, 26'7" × 23'7"
Closed as a result of 1878 Act.

Management

Middlesex justices:

Mich.	1856	Major Aldridge
"	1861-	Richard League
"	1863-	Henry Denford
"	1865-	James Lumsden
"	1867-	Thomas Conway
"	1869-	James Bale
"	1873-	Thomas Greaves
"	1876-	John Jones

London County Council:

	1890	John Jones
Nov.	1890	*Not relicensed.*

Literature

Official records:

G.L.C. Arch. Dpt. Th. case 040/27;
L.C.C. Th. & M-H. Com. App. Nov. 1889;
Mx. Mich. Q.S. 1856-1888.

163

COACH AND HORSES PUBLIC HOUSE

29, Ray Street, Clerkenwell.

Licensed: 1854-1861

Licensed by the Middlesex justices from 1854 to 1861 to Charles Rennoldson. Not relicensed in 1861 after Rennoldson's death.

Management

Middlesex justices:

Mich.	1854-	Charles Rennoldson
"	1861	*Not relicensed. Licensee dead*

Literature

Official records:

Mx. Mich. Q.S. 1854-1861.

164

COAL HOLE PUBLIC HOUSE

Fountain Court, Strand.

Opened during 1820's. Closed and demolished during Strand widening.

Management

Middlesex justices:

Only licence recorded after 1850:-
Mich. 1861 to Charles Samworth.
" 1862 *Refused.*

Literature

Official records:

Mx. Mich. Q.S. 1861-2.

Historical accounts:

n.d.	RENTON, Nicholas. Autobiography of a fast man. (Manager of the Coal Hole).
1895	STUART, C.D., *and* PARK, A.J. The variety stage...p. 21-24.
1935	HADDON, Archibald. The story of the music hall...p. 12.
1938	DISHER, M.W. Winkles and champagne...p. 5, 6, 8.
1952	PULLING, Christopher They were singing...p. 172.

see also TERRY'S THEATRE

165

COBHAM'S HEAD PUBLIC HOUSE

1, Cobham Row, Clerkenwell.

Licensed: 1854-1862

Management

Middlesex justices:

Mich.	1854-	Joseph Brown
"	1857-	Edward Francklin Pickering
"	1859-	Charles Somers
"	1862	*No application.*

Literature

Official records:

Mx. Mich. Q.S. 1854-1861.

166

COCK PUBLIC HOUSE

77, Longacre, Westminster.

Licensed: 1879-1881

Management

Middlesex justices:

Mich. 1879-   George Curtis
  " 1881   *Not relicensed.*

Literature

Official records:

Mx. Mich. Q.S. 1879-1881.

167

COCK AND HOOP PUBLIC HOUSE

West End, Hampstead.

Licensed: 1855-1890

Management

Middlesex justices:

Mich.	1855-	Handell Hawgood
"	1858-	Israel Hurst
"	1866-	John Hall
"	1886	Charlotte Susannah Hall
"	1887	Richard Titcombe
"	1888	George Robinson

London County Council:

| | 1890 | George Robinson |
| Nov. | 1890 | *Licence refused.* |

Literature

Official records:

L.C.C. Th. & M-H. Com. App. Nov. 1889-90;
Mx. Mich. Q.S. 1855-1888.

168

COLLIN'S MUSIC HALL

10-11, Islington Green, Islington.

Opened: 1862   *Closed:* 1958

Former names

Lansdowne Arms Public House 1851-2, 55-9
Lansdowne Music Hall 1862
Collin's Music Hall 1863+
Collin's Theatre of Varieties 1897
Islington Hippodrome. By 1908 and during 1914-18 war.

Collin's Music Hall (168)

(Islington Public Libraries)

Collin's Music Hall (168)

(Greater London Council Photograph Library)

Building details

The Islington Borough Guide states that the first actual music hall there was founded by Mr. Montgomery, the proprietor of the public house, in 1862. It was never licensed to him.

Cost: £4,000

Capacity: 600

1897 Rebuilt.

Architect: Messrs. Drew Bear, Perks & Co.

Contractor: C. Dearing & Co.

Capacity: (1897) 1,800 *later* 1,444

Auditorium: (seating) S. & Bx. 489; B. & Bx. 239; G. 290.

Management

Middlesex justices: licensed throughout as Lansdowne Arms.

Mich. 1851	William Belton, Jnr.
" 1852	Henry Anthony Westcott
" 1855	William Belton, Jnr.
" 1856-	John Scargill
" 1859	*Not licensed-reported closed.*
" 1863-	Samuel Vagg (i.e. Sam Collins)
" 1865-	Anne Vagg
" 1868-	Henry Watts
" 1881-	Herbert Sprake

London County Council:

1890-	Herbert Sprake
1898-	Thomas Richards
1904-	Charles Dearing
1910-	Herbert Sprake
1912-	Samuel Patrick Derbyshire
1913-	John Percy Mitchelhill
1920-	Charles Gulliver
1925-	Productions (Richmond) Ltd.
1928	Semyl Bernstein (i.e. Samuel Berney)
1929-	Collins Music Hall and Samuel Berney
1932	Frederick Hy. Smith and Samuel Harte
1933	Frederick Green, Cumberland Clark and Jack Doig
1934	*Not licensed.*
1935-	New Entertainments Ltd.
1937-	Loughborough Playhouse Ltd.
1940	Mrs. Jessie Lake
1941-	Lew Lake

Lord Chamberlain:

26.1.12-25. 3.19	John P. Mitchellhill
25.3.19-30.11.27	Charles Gulliver for Productions (Richmond) Ltd.
Dec. 27-Nov. 31	Samuel Berney
1931/2	Frederick Hy Smith
1932/3	Jack Alex. Doig
1933/4	John Southern
1934/6	Worland Sidney Wheeler
1936/7	Edward Rind
1937/8	David Albert Abrahams
1938/9	Edward Walter Rice
1939/40-	Lewis Hy. Arthur Lake

Literature

Official records:

G.L.C. Arch. Dpt. Mss index;
G.L.C. Arch. Dpt. Th. case 80;

L.C.C. Th. & M-H. Com. App. Nov. 1889-1950;
L.C.C. Th. & M-H. Com. Papers 1889+;
L.C.O. 374 and 478; Mx. Mich. Q.S. 1851-1888;
Sel. Com. 1866, 1877, 1892.

Contemporary accounts:

1887 SATURDAY REVIEW. 1887, Sept. 3rd. The state of the London... music hall, No. 4.
1897 STANDARD. 1897, Dec. 24th.—Description of building alterations.
BUILDING NEWS, 1897. Dec. 31st. p. 960—Brief description of rebuilding
1898 BUILDER. 1898, Jan, 15th. p. 66.-Brief report of rebuilding.
1945 ILLUSTRATED. 1945, Dec. 15th. 3p. illus. Article reports auction to take place shortly.
1946 ISLINGTON GAZETTE, 1946, Feb. 1st.—Report of auction which took place 23.1.1946.
1950 THEATRE ownership. p. 127 & 311.
1958 TIMES. 1958, Sept. 15th.—Report on fire that marked final end.

Historical accounts:

c.1930 MAYES, Ronald
The romance of London theatres. No, 89.
Collins Music Hall.
1934 COLLIN'S Music Hall.
12p. illus (sights and sounds of London series).
Exteriors, 1834 and 1934, and interiors of auditorium and bar.
1935 HADDON, Archibald
The story of the music hall...
(Various references).
1938 DISHER, M. W.
Winkles and champagne... Various references.
1946 SCOTT, Harold.
Early doors. pp. 125+.
1950 POPE, W. Macqueen
The melodies linger on... Various references.
1955 ISLINGTON. Public Libraries.
Islington and the theatre (exhibition catalogue). pp. 10-11.
1958 WHAT'S ON IN LONDON, 1858 Jan. 10.
—One page general article.

Location of other material

Plans: G.L.C. *Architects Department;*
Enthoven Collection. (4 sheets)

Programmes:
British Museum Library.
Enthoven Collection.
Guildhall Library.
Islington Local Collection.

Newscuttings and illustrations:
Enthoven Collection. Islington Local Collection

169

COLOSSEUM

Regent's Park.

Erected: 1824-6. *Removed:* 1875.

Building details

Architect: Decimus Burton.
-Designed to hold a panoramic view of London.

Management

Middlesex justices:

Mich. 1850-	David Montague
" 1859-	George Henry Bachhoffner
" 1863-	John Burns Bryson
" 1864	*Not licensed.*

Literature

Official records:

Mx. Mich. Q.S. 1850-1864.

Historical accounts:

1925 SHERSON, Erroll
London's lost theatres...p. 323.
c. 1930 MAYES, Ronald
The romance of London theatres, No. 96.
The Colosseum.
1938 LONDON. County Council.
Survey of London. Vol. 19, 1938. p. 123. plate.
1961 REYNOLDS, E.
Recreation and leisure in St. Pancras...
Chapter II.

Location of other material

Playbills: Guildhall Library. (15 items pre-1850)

170

COMEDY THEATRE

Panton Street, Westminster.

Opened: 15th October, 1881.

Proposed names

Lyric Theatre April 1881
Alexandra Theatre June 1881

Former name

Royal Comedy Theatre

Building details

Architect: Thomas Verity

Capacity: (1880) 1,055

Auditorium: (seating) (1882) S. 265; P. 185; Bx. A-N, 56; U.C. 120; A & G 240.

1911 Alterations.

Architect: Frank E. Whiting and Walter S. Peto

Contractors: Messrs. Battley, Sons and Holness

Capacity: (1881) approx. 1300 (1950-) 708

Auditorium: (1881) p. 400; S. 140; D.C. 120; U. Bx. 126; A. 100; G. 300.
(1950) S. 258; D.C. 99; U.C. 109; Bx. A-N.

Stage: 24' 6" wide, 26' high, 24' 6" deep.

Management

Lord Chamberlain:

15.10.1881-	Alexander Henderson
During 1884	Violet Melnotte (let to Charles Hawtrey from 1892)
6. 1.1888	Charles Henry Hawtrey
1.12.1893-	Joseph William Comyns Carr
1.12.1896-	Charles Henry Hawtrey
1.12.1898-	William Greet
1.12.1905-	Arthur Chudleigh
1.12.1921-	Paul Murray
13. 5.1922-	John Eugene Vedrenne
1.12.1924-	Archibald Nettlefold
1.12.1944-	George Duke Midgley
1.12.1948	Harold Hyam Wingate

(During these years the theatre was frequently sublet to other managers, including-

1902-	Frank Curzon
1906-11	Charles Frohman
1916	C. B. Cochran
1916	Andre Charlot, and again in 1930's)

Literature

Official records:

G.L.C. Arch. Dpt. Th. case 421; L.C.C. Th. & M-H. Com. Papers. 1888-; LC1/507-752; LC7/17, 28-48; L.C.O. 76 & 347; M.B.W. Rpt. 1882 p. 53-60.

Contemporary accounts:

1881 BUILDER. 1881, April 2nd. p. 422.—Report of proposal of J. H. Addison to build 'Lyric Theatre'.
BUILDER. 1881, June 18th. p. 764 and 773, illus. —Description of new theatre in course of construction 'Alexandra'.
BUILDING NEWS. 1881, Sept. 9th. p. 341, col. c. —Note of erection.
BUILDING NEWS, 1881 Oct. 14, p. 493.—Description.
TIMES. 1881, Oct. 17th.—Royal Comedy, brief description.
BUILDER. 1881, Oct. 29th. p. 559.—Letter of complaint about new theatre.
DAILY TELEGRAPH. 1881, Oct. 14th.—Building description.
ERA. 1881, Oct. 15th.—Building description
1882 BUILDER. 1882, April 15th. p. 468.—Letter reporting separation of pit and gallery entrances.
1887 SATURDAY REVIEW. 1887, June 11th. The state of the London theatres...No. 1.

Comedy Theatre 1881 (170)

(The Builder)

1911 BUILDER. 1911, Oct. 27th. p.487.—Report of
alterations and decorations including reconstruction of entrance.
1950 THEATRE ownership. p.73 and 107.

Historical accounts:

1904 BAKER, H. Barton
History of the London stage and its players.
p.314-6.
c.1930 MAYES, Ronald
The romance of London theatres. No.44.
The Comedy.
1955 THEATRE Notebook, 1955, Oct.-Dec. p.17-20.
1959 ENCICLOPEDIA dello Spettacolo. Vol.6, col.
1617.
1963 MANDER, Raymond *and* MITCHENSON, Joe
The theatres of London. 2nd ed. p.47-51.

Location of other material

Plans:

G.L.C. *Architects Department;*
Enthoven Collection (2 sheets)
Public Record Office. LC7/54. 11 sheets. 13.4.1881.

Programmes:

British Museum. (Programmes) 21 parts.
1889-1925. 11797 f.4.; Enthoven Collection;
Garrick Club. 1881-1949; Guildhall Library (80 items);
London Museum; Westminster Local Collection.

171

COMET PUBLIC HOUSE

7, Christian Street, St. George in the East, Wapping.

Licensed: 1854-1872.

Management

Middlesex justices:

Mich. 1854-	Peter Carms	
" 1862-	Johann Mehrtens	
" 1863-	Sarah Ann Mehrtens	
" 1866-	Peter Heitmann	
" 1872	*Licence refused for permitting riotous conduct.*	

Literature

Official records:

Mx. Mich. Q.S. 1854-1872.

172

COMMERCIAL PUBLIC HOUSE

Battersea Park Road, Battersea.

Licensed: 1881-1888

Management

Surrey justices:

Mich. 1881-	Stephen Henry Duffield
" 1888	*Not licensed.*

Literature

Official records:

Sy. Mich. Q.S. 1881-1887.

173

COMMERCIAL PUBLIC HOUSE

Kings Road, Chelsea.

Licensed: 1850-1889

Management

Middlesex justices:

Mich. 1848-	Richard Smith
" 1855-	George Valentine Davis
" 1858	William Smith and Henry Hoather
" 1859-	Thomas Neal
" 1861-	Henry French Lonsdale
" 1864-	John Morrison
" 1871-	William Newton
" 1875-	William Thomas Phillips
" 1877-	John Carter

Not licensed by the L.C.C.

Literature

Official records:

Mx. Mich. Q.S. pre 1850-1888

174

COMPASSES PUBLIC HOUSE

94, Fulham High Street, Fulham.

Licensed: 1867-1873

Management

Mich. 1867-1873 William Hanley

Literature

Official records:

Mx. Mich. Q.S. 1867-1872.

175

COOPER'S ARMS PUBLIC HOUSE
52, Huntingdon Street, Hoxton.

Licensed: 1865-1868

Management

Middlesex justices:

Mich. 1865-1868 William Davis

Literature

Official records:

Mx. Mich. Q.S. 1865-1867.

176

COOPER'S ARMS PUBLIC HOUSE

28, Hampden Street, St. Pancras.

Licensed: 1861-1862

Management

Middlesex justices:

Mich. 1861   Richard Henry Price
"   1862   *No answer to relicensing notice.*

Literature

Official records:

Mx. Q.S. 1862. (refers to 1861 licensing).

177

COPENHAGEN HOUSE PUBLIC HOUSE

Maiden Lane, Islington.

Licensed: 1854-1858

Management

Middlesex justices:

Mich. 1853-   John Garratt
"   1855-   Alfred Beckett
"   1858   *Not licensed.*

Literature

Official records:

Mx. Mich. Q.S. 1854-1857.

178

CORONET THEATRE

103-111, High Street, Notting Hill.

Opened: 28th November, 1898. By 1923 in use as a cinema.

Building details

Architect: W.G.R. Sprague (*Building News* gives Frank Matcham as architect)

Cost: £25,000

Capacity: 1,143

Auditorium: S. 93; P. 350; D.C. 120; B. 125; G. 415; Bx. 40.
Stage: 65' wide by 40' deep.

'The Architect' reported it in use as a cinema in 1916.

Management

London County Council:

20.12.1898-1904	Edward George Saunders
1905-11	Robert Arthur
1912	William Ernest Mansell
1913	William Herbert Chantrey, then Horace William Rowland to 1915
1916-17	William Herbert Chantrey
1918-20	Thomas Frank Gillett
1921-23	Claude Hardwick Knight Bovill
Nov. 1923	*Licensed as a cinema.*

Literature

Official records:

G.L.C. Arch. Dpt. Mss index;
G.L.C. Arch. Dpt. Th. case No. 82;
L.C.C. Th. & M-H. Com. App. Nov. 1898-1923;
L.C.C. Th. & M-H. Com. Papers. 1898+.

Contemporary accounts:

1897   BUILDING NEWS. 1897, Nov. 26th. p. 759—Brief description.
1898   BUILDER. 1898, Jan. 15th. p. 61-2.—Description and plan. Illus. of exterior.
       BUILDING NEWS. 1898, Dec. 2nd. p. 784.—Brief description.
       BUILDER. 1898, Dec. 3rd. p. 511.—Report of opening.
1899   ARCHITECT. 1899, Oct. 27th.—plate of exterior elevation (photo)

Historical accounts:

c. 1930 MAYES, Ronald
        The romance of London theatres, No. 132.

Location of other material

Plans: G.L.C. *Architects Department.*

Programmes:

Enthoven Collection; Garrick Club. 1899-1909; British Museum. Library. 1900-1913. Nos. 342, 336, 436, 346, 474; London Museum; Westminster Local Collection.

Newscuttings &c. Paddington Local Collection.

179

CORUNNA MUSIC HALL

General Moore Public House, 59, Stewarts Road. Battersea.

Licensed: 1869-1889

Building details

Hall 29' 6" × 19' 6", superficial area 530'. (8th March, 1889)

Coronet Theatre 1898 (178)

(The Builder)

Size of hall later reduced to 19' 6" × 19' 6", i.e. 380' 3" area.

Management

Surrey justices:

Mich. 1869-	George Mills
" 1871-	Septimus Smith
" 1874-	John Edmunds
" 1878-	Charles Frederick Fenton
1881-	Elisha Harrison

Letter from J. A. Ruddick to L.C.C. (28. 9. 1889) states he has omitted by an oversight to renew licence.

Literature

Official records:

G.L.C. Arch. Dpt. Th. case. No. 040/30; Sy. Mich. Q.S. 1869-1889.

Location of other material

Plans: G. L. C. *Architects Department.*

180

COSMOTHECA MUSIC HALL

27, Bell Street, Edgware Road, St. Marylebone.

Licensed: 1857-1869

Management

Middlesex justices:

| Mich. 1857- | Joseph Cave (to 1869). |
| By Mich. 1876 | Joseph Cave was still trying to renew his licence. |

Literature

Official records:

Mx. Mich. Q.S. 1857-1859.

Historical accounts:

Brief mention only in C. Pulling's 'They were singing'.

181

COURT THEATRE

Lower George Street, Chelsea.

Opened: 16th April, 1870. *Closed:* 22nd July, 1887, and demolished.

Former names

New Chelsea Theatre
Belgravia Theatre
Royal Court Theatre

Building details

Theatre opened in a converted chapel—The Ranelagh Chapel.

1871 Interior altered:

Architect: Walter Emden

1882 Alterations:

Architect: Alexander Peebles

Capacity: (1882) 728

Auditorium: (1882) P. 148; S. & Bx. 173; D.C. & B. 165; A. & Bx. 70; G. 172.

Stage: 44' × 26'

The theatre was rebuilt on another site. *See* Royal Court Theatre.

Management

This theatre was not licensed by the Lord Chamberlain or Mx. Q.S. although the 1877 Select Committee states it was licensed by the magistrates.

Information from programmes:-

1870-	Arthur Morgan and B. Oliver
1871-	Marie Litton
1875-	John Hare
1879-	Wilson Barrett
1881-	Marie Litton
1881-	John Clayton and Arthur Cecil.

Literature

Official records:

M.B.W. Rpt. 1882. p. 71-85.

Contemporary accounts:

1870 ERA. 1870, April 17th.—Description.
1871 DAILY TELEGRAPH. 1871, Jan. 27th.
—Report of opening.
1871 SUNDAY TIMES. 1871, Jan.—Report.
ILLUSTRATED LONDON NEWS. 1871, Feb. 4th.
—Description of alterations.
1872 BUILDER. 1872, Jan. 6th. p. 14.—Reply to letter about wooden stairs leading from street to pit.
1882 BUILDER. 1882, Oct. 21st. p. 542.—Note of considerable structural alterations and new porch.
1887 SATURDAY REVIEW. 1887, July 2nd. The state of the London theatres. No. 3.
DAILY TELEGRAPH. 1887, July 23rd.—Report of last performance before demolition.
BUILDER. 1887, Aug. 13th. p. 256.—Report of demolition.

Historical accounts:

1879 DRAMATIC NOTES. 1879. p. 58-62.
1904 BAKER, H. Barton
History of the London stage and its players.
p. 501-5.
c. 1930 MAYES, Ronald
The romance of London theatres,
No. 146: The old Court Theatre, 1870-1887.
No. 228: Chelsea Theatre

Location of other material

General collection (excluding plans): Chelsea Local collection.

Programmes:

Enthoven Collection; Guildhall Library; London Museum; Westminster Local Collection.

182

COVENT GARDEN, THE ROYAL OPERA HOUSE

Bow Street, Westminster.

Opened: 7th December, 1732.

Other names

Theatre Royal in Covent Garden	1732
Theatre Royal, Covent Garden	1769
Royal Italian Opera, Covent Garden	1847
Royal English Opera, Covent Garden	
Royal Opera, Covent Garden	1897
Royal Opera House	1939

Building Details

1st theatre:

Opened: as Theatre Royal in Covent Garden, 7th Dec. 1732 under John Rich.

Capacity: 1,879

Burnt down: 20th August, 1808.

2nd theatre:

Opened: 18th Spetember, 1809, under John Philip Kemble. 6th April, 1847, reopened having been converted into an opera house.

Capacity: 3,000

Destroyed by fire: 5th March, 1856.

3rd theatre: (i.e. present theatre)

Opened: 15th May, 1858, under Frederick Gye. (Closed 1939-1945 when in use as a dance hall)

Architect: Edward M. Barry

Contractor: Messrs. Lucas Bros.

1900-2 Alterations:

Architect: E.O. Sachs
Contractor: Messrs. Colls & Sons.
Capacity: (1882) 2,299; (1912) 2,316; (1950) 1,952.

Auditorium:

(1882) P. tier 118; P. 462; S. 136; C. tier 314; U. tier 185; A. 387; G. 697.
(1912) S. 558; 1st C. 148; 2nd C. 148; 3rd. C. 206; 4th C. 400; G. 137.

Stage: (1950) 44' 3" wide, 37' high, 74' deep.

Management

A patent theatre, and therefore not licensed.

Literature

Official records:

G.L.C. Arch. Dpt. Mss. index. L.C.C. Th. & M-H. Com. Papers, 1888-; LC7/13, 20-31, 33-48.
M.B.W. Rpt. 1882, p. 18-27.
Sel. Com. 1892. paras. 1821-7, 2214-8, 2513-22.

Contemporary accounts:

c. 1828-56 SHEPHERD, Thomas *and* ELMES, James Metropolitan improvements. p. 196-201. plates.
1832-56 GENTLEMAN'S MAGAZINE. Topographical history. Vol. 1. p. 138-145. 100th anniversary. 1832. Part II. p. 586-590.
1847 ILLUSTRATED LONDON NEWS. 1847, May 6th. p. 268. illus. Ceiling of the Royal Italian Opera.
1850 ERA. 1850, Feb. 10th. p. 12. Theatrical bankruptcy.
ERA. 1850, March 3rd. p. 12-13. Theatrical speculation: The Royal Italian Opera Lefevre v. Chappell.

(1856) F.P.A. JOURNAL. 1954, April. No. 25. Historic fires: Royal Italian Opera House, Covent Garden, 1856. p. 218-222. illus.
1856 BUILDER. 1856, March 8th. p. 132-3.—Destruction of Covent Garden theatre.
BUILDER. 1856, March 15th. p. 137-139. —Inquiry into the destruction of Covent Garden Theatre.
ILLUSTRATED LONDON NEWS. 1856, March 15th. p. 276-77, illus. of fire.
ILLUSTRATED TIMES. 1856, March 15th. —Royal visits to the ruins. illus.
PICTORIAL TIMES. 1856, March 15th, p. 168-169.—Reports and illus.
BUILDER. 1856, March 22nd. p. 165-166. —Inquiry into the destruction ... (completed).
ILLUSTRATED LONDON NEWS. 1856, March 22nd. p. 299-300.—Illus. Poem 'The fire spirit' —Report of meeting of renters.
ILLUSTRATED LONDON NEWS. 1856, March 29th. p. 307.—Description of theatre.
1857 BUILDER. 1857, March 7th. p. 138.—Site of new theatre.
BUILDING NEWS. 1857, Aug. 14th. p. 857. —Description of proposed building.
BUILDING NEWS. 1857, Oct. 23rd. p. 1118. —Notes on rebuilding.
BUILDER. 1857, Oct. 24th. p. 610-611.—Description of proposed building. Illus. of facade.
1858 BUILDER. 1858, April 3rd. p. 236.—Report on progress.
BUILDER. 1858, April 24th. p. 273-4.—Leading article describing new theatre in detail.
BUILDING NEWS. 1858, May 14th. p. 510-511. —Detailed description.
BUILDER. 1858, May 15th. p. 325-6.—Description of stage.
BUILDING NEWS. 1858, May 21st. p. 537 —Correction.
BUILDER. 1858, May 22nd. p. 345-7, p. 355. —Illus. of auditorium. Leading article on the occasion of the opening of the theatre: including estimate of accommodation.
1859 BUILDER. 1859, March 19th. p. 200.—Question of exits from places of entertainment.
BUILDER. 1859, April 2nd. p. 235-7.—Report on improvements. Plan on level of Grand Tier. Illus. of auditorium.
1859 BUILDER. 1859, April 16th. p. 268-69.—Further description of structure. Longitudinal section.
BUILDING NEWS. 1859, May 13th. p. 446.—Right of light dispute.
1860 BUILDER. 1860, Feb. 11th. p. 85-7, and Feb. 18th. p. 102-3.—Paper by the architect E. M. Barry on the construction and rebuilding of the Italian Opera House, read to the R.I.B.A.
1862 GYE, Frederick. Narrative addressed to the Duke of Bedford, of the negotiations between Frederick Gye and the Duke's agent (Charles Parker) relative to the rebuilding of the present Covent Garden theatre and the Floral Hall. London, 1862.
1864 ROYAL Italian opera, Covent Garden. Season, 1864 (Prospectus). London, Miles & Co., 1864. 20p.
1882 BUILDER. 1882, Nov. 11th. p. 632-3.—Report of the Metropolitan Board of Works on the state of the theatre.
1887 SATURDAY REVIEW. 1887, July 9th. The state of the London theatres. No. 4.
1890 BUILDER. 1890, Aug. 9th. p. 107. Report of auction of ground lease and theatrical properties.

1892 BUILDER. 1892, May 28th. p. 413. Brief report on poor use of electric light in theatre.

1898 SACHS, E. O. and WOODROW, E. A. E. Modern opera houses and theatres. Vol. III. illus.
SACHS, E. O. Stage construction. illus.

1901 BUILDER. 1901, June 1st. p. 538-9.—Plan of stage as remodelled. Plan of stalls corridor level. Section through stage portion.
SKETCH. 1901, April 3rd. and April 24th. —Reconstruction of the opera stage. illus. ports.

1902 BUILDER. 1902, May 24th. p. 521.—Detailed report of structural alterations carried out 1900-2. including almost total turn over to electricity.

1904 The MICROCOSM of London. Vol. I. p. 212+. —Description and regulation.
The MICROCOSM of London. Vol. 3. p. 259-264. —Covent Garden new theatre.
BUILDING NEWS. 1904, Aug. 5th. p. 205.—Brief report that plans drawn up for theatre in the Strand to replace C.G.—Denial in B N. 1904, Aug. 12th. p. 240.
BUILDER. 1904, Aug. 13th. p. 185.—Brief report of project for erection of opera house in Aldwych on land between St. Mary le Strand and St. Clement Danes, as Duke of Bedford proposes to demolish Covent Garden for improvement of market.

1946 NEWSWEEK. 1946, March 4th. p. 78. 'Covent Garden Theatre re-opened after wartime use as a dance-hall'.

1950 THEATRE ownership. p. 73.

Historical accounts:

1879 DRAMATIC NOTES. 1879, p. 1-2

1897 WYNDHAM, Henry Saxe
The annals of Covent Garden, 1732-1897. Chatto & Windus, 1906. 2v.

1904 BAKER, H. Barton
History of the London stage and its players... pp. 113-46, 208-10, 546.

1906 BUILDER, 1906 July 14, pp. 38-9. —General history.

1908 TREVOR, Harry
Royal Opera, Covent Garden: jubilee souvenir. Dover St. Studios, 1908. 52p. illus.

1925 CHANCELLOR, E. B.
The pleasure haunts of London... pp. 88-96, 428-30.

1930 CHANCELLOR, E. B.
The annals of Covent Garden and its neighbourhood. Hutchinson, 1930. pp. 265 et seq.

c.1930 MAYES, Ronald
The romance of London theatres, Nos. 15 and 111.

1933 NOTES AND QUERIES, 1933 Jan. pp. 61-2. Footlights: introduction at Drury Lane and Covent Garden.

1934 PLAY PICTORIAL, 1934, Vol. 64, No. 382, p. 55. The annals of the Royal Opera House, Covent Garden.

c.1940 WILSON, A. E.
Pantomime pageant... pp. 20+, 40+, 50+ and other references.

1946 SCOTT, Harold
Early doors. —Various references.

1948 COUNTRY LIFE, 1948 June 25, pp. 1278-81. Covent Garden Opera House, by Christopher Hussey.
SHAWE-TAYLOR, Desmond
Covent Garden. Parish, 1948. 71p.

1958 ROSENTHAL, Harold D.
The Covent Garden centenary (a brief history) 3p.—A talk given to the Society for Theatrical Research, Tuesday, 21st Jan. 1958.

1958 ROSENTHAL, Harold D.
The Royal Opera House, Covent Garden, 1858-, 1958. London, 1958. Unpaged. illus.
ROSENTHAL, Harold D.
Two centuries of opera at Covent Garden. Putnam, 1958. 849p. illus., facsims.

1959 ENCICLOPEDIA dello spettacolo.
Vol. 6, Col. 1618-9.

1963 MANDER, Raymond, *and* MITCHENSON, Joe
The theatres of London, 2nd ed. pp. 52-58.

Location of other material

General collection:

Royal Opera House, Covent Garden. (By letter or appointment only.)

Plans: G.L.C. *Architects Department;* Enthoven Collection (7 sheets).

Programmes and playbills:

British Museum Library;
Enthoven Collection;
Garrick Club; Guildhall Library;
London Museum;
Westminster Local Collection.

Prints:

Enthoven Collection; Guildhall Library; Garrick Club; London Museum; Westminster Local Collection.

183

CRANBOURN PUBLIC HOUSE

3, Great Newport Street (formerly Cranbourn St.) Westminster.

Licensed: 1852-1860.

Management

Middlesex justices:

Mich. 1852-	George Palk Ager	
" 1854-	Richard Willoughby	
" 1858-	Deborah Willoughby	
" 1860	*No application.*	

Literature

Official records:

Mx. Mich, Q.S. 1852-1860.

184

CRAVEN HEAD PUBLIC HOUSE

98-9, Drury Lane, Parish of St. Clement Danes.

Licensed: 1854-1862

Management

Middlesex Justices:

Mich. 1854-	Robert Hales	
" 1856-	Edward Parfitt	
" 1862	*No application.*	

Literature

Official records:

Mx. Mich, Q.S. 1854-1861.

185

CREMORNE GARDENS

Chelsea.

Opened: 1831   *Closed:* 1877 after protests by the
Chelsea Vestry.

Building details

12 acres west of Battersea Bridge between King's
Road and the river. Originally known as the Chelsea
Farm, it was the residence of Lord Cremorne. In
1831 it was opened by 'Baron de Beaufair' as Cremorne Stadium for sports. In the 1840's it was under
the management of Renton Nicholson. It became a
pleasure gardens and included circus, theatres and
side shows.
Among the theatres listed a bijou theatre, the Marionette Theatre, and the 'Theatre Royal'.
Lots Road Power Station now stands on the centre of
the site.

Management

Middlesex justices:

Mich.	1850-	Charles Cooper
"	1852-	Thomas Bartlett Simpson
"	1861-	Edward Tyrrell Smith
"	1870	John Baum
"	1871	*Licence refused*
"	1874-	John Baum
"	1877	*Opposed and refused.*

Literature

Official records:

LC7/22; Mx. Mich. Q.S. 1850-1877.

Contemporary accounts:

1850 ERA. 1850, Feb. 17th. p. 10.—Bankruptcies of
       Cremorne & Vauxhall Gardens.
1857 RITCHIE, J. Ewing. The night side of London.
1861 The PLAYERS. 1861, May 11th. Cremorne
       theatres.—Report of application by Mr. Simpson
       for a stage play licence for the Marionette
       Theatre and the Ballet Theatre.
1864 LONDON JOURNAL. 1864, p. 21+.—Illus. of
       interior of new theatre and ball room.
1878 FURBER, PRICE & FURBER. Catalogues of the
       sales, April 8th-25th, 1878. (A copy in 'Papers
       upon the history of Cremorne Gardens', p. 111-
       114) in Chelsea Public Library.
       BUILDER. 1878, April 20th. p. 414.—Report of
       sale.

Historical accounts:

1871 ERA Almanac. p. 5.
1907 WROTH, Warwick
       Cremorne and the later London gardens. p. 1-24.
1908 DAILY TELEGRAPH. 1908, Jan. 25th.
       The Old Gardens: outdoor amusements in
       London.—Brief history.
1925 CHANCELLOR, E. B.
       The pleasure haunts of London. p. 396-406.

c. 1930 MAYES, Ronald
         The romance of London theatres, No. 166.
1946 SCOTT, Harold
       Early doors. p. 64+.
1952 PULLING, Christopher
       They were singing. p. 45, 171-3.

Location of other material

General collection: Chelsea Public Library.
Papers upon the history of Cremorne Gardens,
Chelsea, 1840-1878. 2v.—Scrapbooks containing news-
cuttings, programmes, posters. &c.

Illustrations: Chelsea Public Library.
A collection of prints and printed matter concerning
Cremorne Gardens, including 2v. history.

Programmes and Playbills: British Museum.
A collection of programmes, newspaper cuttings,
tickets &c. 1845-1885 (BM 1880 c 9) also 1846-1971
No. 363.
Guildhall Library; London Museum.

186

CRITERION THEATRE

221, Piccadilly Circus (formerly Regent Circus)
Westminster.

Opened: 21st March, 1874.

Building details

Theatre built in basements of Criterion Restaurant
which stands on the site of the White Bear, a posting
inn dating from the late Seventeenth Century.

1st building:

Developers: Felix, Spiers and Christopher Pond

Architects: Thomas Verity

Contractors: George Smith & Co.

Capacity: 675

Auditorium: (1882) S. 110; P. 205; B. 120; G. 160; Bx. 80.
Closed by M.B.W. owing to improbability of an
audience escaping in the case of fire.

2nd building:

Architect: Thomas Verity

Contractor: William Webster

Capacity: (1950) 560

Stage: 25' 4" wide, 16' 3" high, 19' 6" deep.

Management

Lord Chamberlain:

21st March, 1874	Felix William Spiers and Christo-
	pher Pond
28. 9.1879	Felix William Spiers
28. 9.1889	Joshua Ellis, Secretary to Spiers &
	Pond Ltd.
28. 9.1896	Henry Godbold (to 28.9.1902)
During 1903 licensed to Spiers and Pond.	
1.11.1904	Ernest Frederick Bugler
31.10.1909	Charles Wyndham (to 31.10.1910)
15.11.1909	Ernest Frederick Bugler
1. 9.1917	Charles Edward Cottier
1.12.1923	Mary Wyndham

1.12.1931   Howard James Wyndham
             (to 30.11.1941)
A memorandum notes that Criterion in hands of the
B.B.C. for the duration of the war plus six months.
1.12.1945   Howard James Wyndham and Bronson
             James Albery
1.12.1947-1950 Bronson James Albery

Middlesex justices:

1874-1880   Felix William Spiers and Christopher
             Pond
1881-1889   Felix William Spiers

London County Council:

1890-1896   Joshua Ellis
1897-1901   Henry Godbold

Literature

Official records:

G.L.C. Arch. Dpt. Th. case No. 422;
L.C.C. Th. & M-H. Com. App. Nov. 1889-1900;
L.C.C. Th. & M-H. Com. Papers 1872+;
LC7/16-17, LC7/24-48, LC7/89; L.C.O. 89 and 374.
M.B.W. Rpt. 1882. p. 83-93; Mx. Mich. Q.S. 1874-1888.
Sel. Com. 1892.

Contemporary accounts:

1879   DRAMATIC NOTES. 1879. p. 41-43.—Report
        of opening.
        R.I.B.A. Transactions, 1879, Jan. 1st. IV The
        modern restaurant, by Thomas Verity. Plans.
        BUILDER. 1879, Jan. 18th and Jan. 25th. p. 72
        and 75-6; p. 109. 'Criterion Restaurant and
        Theatre' from a paper by Thomas Verity ...
        read at the R.I.B.A.
1882   BUILDER. 1882, Nov. 11th. p. 632-3. —The safety
        of London theatres: report of M.B.W. that
        theatre totally unsafe.
1884   DAILY TELEGRAPH. 1884, April 6th. 'Criterion
        Theatre'—Report of rebuilding.
        DRAMATIC NOTES. 1884, April 16th. —Building
        description.
        DAILY NEWS. 1884, April 17th. 'Report of
        opening of rebuilt theatre.'
        BUILDER. 1884, April 19th. p. 558.—Description
        of extensive reconstruction.
        ERA. 1884, April 19th. —Building description.
1887   SATURDAY REVIEW. 1887, July 2nd.—State of
        the London theatres—No. 3.
1889   SACHS, E.O. *and* WOODROW, E.A.E. Modern
        opera houses and theatres... Vol. III p. 39, 61-2.
        —Plans of area, tiers and auditorium, view of
        auditorium.
1903   PEMBERTON, Thomas Edgar
        The Criterion Theatre. Eyre and Spottiswoode,
        1903. 76p. illus., ports., facsims.

Historical accounts:

1904   BAKER, H. Barton
        History of the London stage and its players,
        p. 506-9.
1930?   MAYES, Ronald
        Romance of London theatres, No. 16. Criterion.
1939   THEATRE WORLD. 1939, Nov. p. 186-7.
        'The story of the Criterion Theatre', by E.
        Johns.
1959   ENCICLOPEDIA dello spettacolo. Vol. 6.
        Col. 1619.

1960   LONDON. County Council.
        Survey of London, Vol. 29, 1960. p. 254-6
1963   MANDER, Raymond *and* MITCHENSON, Joe
        The theatres of London, 2nd. ed. p. 59-63.

Location of other material

Plans: G.L.C. *Architects Department;*
Enthoven Collection (3 sheets);
Public Record Office. LC7/55 (Five sheets.)

Programmes:

British Museum. Library. 1888-1936 (11797. f. 7)
1877-1915 (listed in Register)
Garrick Club 1875-1953;
Enthoven Collection; Guildhall Library;
London Museum; Westminster Local Collection.

187

CROOKED BILLET PUBLIC HOUSE

32, St. George Street, St. George in the East, Stepney.

Licensed: 1854-1886.

Management

Middlesex justices:

Mich. 1853-   Thomas Stone
  "   1854-   John Lewis
  "   1873-   Henry James Lewis
  "   1879-   Matilda Mead Walter
  "   1885   *Application by Henry Bullwinkel
               withdrawn.*

Literature

Official records:

Mx. Mich. Q.S. 1854-1885.

188

CROSBY HALL

More's Garden, Chelsea Embankment.

Location of the 'Theatre in Eyre' a theatre club.
Westminster local collection has programme.

189

CROSS KEYS COFFEE TAVERN

42, Hampstead Road, St. Pancras.

Licensed: 1881-1883

Management

Middlesex justices:

Mich. 1881-   William Morgan
  "   1882-   Charles Leonard
  "   1883   *Not renewed.*

Literature:

Official records:

Mx. Mich. Q.S. 1881-1882.

190

CROSS KEYS MUSIC HALL

Cross Keys Public House, 80, Theobalds Road, (No. 58 before 1884, then 68 until 1885). Holborn.

Licensed: 1867-1889

Building details

A small music hall on the first floor of the public house. Opened twice a week for musical performances.

Area: 30' × 29' × 9' 9"

Capacity: 80-100

In 1887 reported that it had ceased to be used for entertainment and was being converted into a dining room, following the 1878 Act.

Management

Middlesex justices:

Mich. 1867-	James George Burden
" 1870-	William Cable
" 1873-	George Cole
" 1874-	Richard Isaac Beard
" 1883-	Charles Henry Belsey

Literature

Official records:

G.L.C. Arch. Dpt. Th. case 040/31;
Mx. Mich. Q.S. 1867-1888.
Sel. Com. 1892.

Location of other material

Plans: G.L.C. *Architects Department.*

191

CROWN MUSIC HALL

Crown Public House, 44, Clerkenwell Green, Clerkenwell.

Licensed: 1852-1888

Other name

Apollo Concert Room (Crown Public House) (Jan. 1841)

Building details

Area: approx. 500'

Capacity: 100

Management

Middlesex justices:

Mich. 1852-	Joseph Wade
" 1856-	John Smith
" 1865-	Sarah Smith
" 1868-	James Smith
" 1869-	Jarvis Maples
" 1875-	John Billing
" 1878-	Thomas Lansdowne
" 1880-	Archibald William Caddell
" 1887	*Maria Bryer refused licence.*

Literature

Official records:

Mx. Mich. Q.S. 1852-1888.
Sel. Com. 1892.

Location of other material

Playbills:

Finsbury Public Library.
Playbill for Jan. 1841. S. Bird proprietor.

192

CROWN PUBLIC HOUSE

Broad Street, Golden Square, Westminster.

Licensed: 1855-1863.

Management

Middlesex justices:

Mich. 1855-	James Frederick Hallatt
" 1856-	John Smith
" 1859-	John King
" 1861-	Frederick Gedge
" 1863	*No application.*

Literature

Official records:

Mx. Mich. Q.S. 1855-1862.

193

CROWN PUBLIC HOUSE

223, Landsmere Terrace, Old Ford Road, Bethnal Green.

Licensed: 1862-1891

Management

Middlesex justices:

Mich. 1862-	John Robert Bowen
" 1865-	John Steptow
" 1874-	Emanuel Gregory
" 1875-	William Beale

London County Council:

1890-91	William Beale, *but licence retained.*
Nov. 1891	*Licence refused.*

Literature

Official records:

L.C.C. Th. & M-H. Com. App. Nov. 1889-1891.
Mx. Mich. Q.S. 1862-1888.

194

CROWN PUBLIC HOUSE

Lavender Hill, Battersea.

Licensed: 1870-1875.

Management

Surrey justices:

Mich. 1870-1875 Samuel Bowker

Literature

Official records:

Sy. Mich. Q.S. 1870-1874.

195

CROWN PUBLIC HOUSE

74, Mile End Road, Stepney.

Licensed: 1865-1869.

Management

Middlesex justices:

Mich.	1865-	John Richard Winson
"	1866-	John Everard
"	1867-	Cord Campe
"	1868-	Abraham Reynolds
"	1869	*Licence refused.*

Literature

Official records:

Mx. Mich. Q.S. 1865-1869.

196

CROWN PUBLIC HOUSE

8, New Winchester Street, Clerkenwell.

Licensed: 1854-1863.

Management

Middlesex justices:

Mich.	1854-	Vincent Simpson
"	1859-	John Dalton
"	1860-	Robert Wilby
"	1862-	Charles Hughes
"	1863	*No application.*

Literature

Official records:

Mx. Mich. Q.S. 1854-1863.

197

CROWN PUBLIC HOUSE

356, Oxford Street, Westminster.

Licensed: 1855-1862

Management

Middlesex justices:

Mich.	1855-	William McDonald
"	1860-	John Ignatius Pick
"	1862	*No application.*

Literature

Official records:

Mx. Mich. Q.S. 1855-1861.

198

CROWN PUBLIC HOUSE

Rupert Street, Whitechapel.

Licensed: 1855-1863.

Management

Middlesex justices:

Mich.	1855-	Louis William Strauss
"	1859-	Henry Betjemann
"	1861-	Sarah Betjemann
"	1863	*Licence refused.*

Literature

Official records:

Mx. Mich. Q.S. 1855-1863.

199

CROWN PUBLIC HOUSE

60, Shadwell High Street, Shadwell.

Licensed: 1858-1884

Management

Middlesex justices:

Mich.	1858-	John Wells
"	1859-	Edward Stanner Stevens
"	1866-	Ann Murray Stevens
"	1874-	Alfred Stevens
"	1879-	George Andrew Crook
"	1884	*Licence refused.*

Literature

Official records:

Mx. Mich. Q.S. 1858-1884.

200

CROWN PUBLIC HOUSE

York Road, St. Pancras.

Licensed: 1855-1858.

Management

Middlesex justices:

Mich. 1855-1858 George Fish

Literature

Official records:

Mx. Mich. Q.S. 1855-1858.

201

CROWN AND ANCHOR PUBLIC HOUSE

Charles Street (later Parker's Row) Neckinger St. Dockhead, Bermondsey.

Licensed: 1862-3 and 1870-1

Management

Surrey justices:

Mich.	1862-	George Price (to Mich. 1863)
"	1870-	John M. Bottomley (to Mich. 1871)

Literature

Official records:

Sy. Mich. Q.S. 1862 and 1870.

202

CROWN AND ANCHOR PUBLIC HOUSE

Cheshire Street, Bethnal Green.

Licensed: 1856-1863

Management

Middlesex justices:

Mich.	1856-	Eleanor Cooke
"	1857-	John Marvel Smith
"	1863	*No application.*

Literature

Official records:

Mx. Mich. Q.S. 1856-1863.

203

CROWN AND ANCHOR PUBLIC HOUSE

Upper Albany Street *(later* Albany Street) St. Pancras.

Licensed: 1854-1878

Managment

Middlesex justices:

Mich.	1854-	Robert Warrington Colling
"	1857-	Thomas Lloyd Jones
"	1860-	Daniel Williams
"	1870-	Charles Chrisfield
"	1874-	William Henry Piggott
"	1876-	Frederick William Clark
"	1877-	Frederick Bishop
"	1878	*No application.*

Literature

Official records:

Mx. Mich. Q.S. 1854-1877.

204

CROWN AND ANCHOR PUBLIC HOUSE

37, Woolwich High Street, Woolwich.

Licensed: 1875-1889

Building details

A concert room with a platform in one angle, on the 1st floor fronting the High Street.
35'6" × 18'5" × 12'
Area: 588' exclusive of platform.

The hall was closed as a result of the 1878 Act.

Management

West Kent justices:

Mich.	1875-	Louisa and McJon Carter
"	1876	John Aillud

Literature

Official records:

G.L.C Arch. Dpt. Th case 040/33;
W. Kt. Mich. Q.S. 1875-1888.

205

CRYSTAL PALACE THEATRE

Sydenham.

Licensed: 1890-1900

Building details

Capacity: (1892) 1, 739

Management

London County Council:

1890-1897	Henshaw Russell
1898-1900	Henry Gillman

Literature

Official records:

L.C.C. Th. & M-H. Com. App. Nov. 1889-1899.
L.C.C. Th. & M-H. Com. Papers 1889-1900.
Sel. Com. 1866, 1877, and 1892.

Contemporary accounts:

1883 BUILDER. 1883, Aug. 18th. p. 211—Report of proposal.

Location of other material

Programmes:

British Museum Library. 1858-1895 (Listed in B.M. . Register); Enthoven Collection; Westminster Local Collection.

206

CUMBERLAND HEAD AND GREEN GATE PUBLIC HOUSE

220, City Road, (formerly Bath Street and City Rd.) St. Luke's, Finsbury.

Licensed: 1851-1891

Management

Middlesex justices:

Mich.	1851-	Henry Miller
"	1860-	William John Ward
"	1869-	George Read Peerless
"	1873-	William Hurran
"	1885-	George Tomalin

London County Council:

1890-1891 Frederick Searle
-Retained in 1891 and not renewed.

Literature

Official records:

L.C.C. Th. & M-H. Com. App. Nov. 1889-1890.
Mx. Mich. Q.S. 1851-1888.

207

CYDER CELLARS

20, Maiden Lane, Covent Garden.

Opened: during the 18th C.—William Rhodes, brother of proprietor of Coal Hole ran it in 1820's.

Licensed: 1854-1862

Management

Middlesex justices:

Mich. 1854-	Charles Brumfit	
" 1858-	John Hart	
" 1862	*Licence refused.*	

Literature

Official records:

Mx. Mich. Q.S. 1854-1862.

Historical accounts:

1895 STUART, C. D. *and* PARK, A. J.
    The variety stage. p. 25-28.
1935 HADDON, Archibald
    The story of the music hall. p. 12-13.
1938 DISHER, M. W.
    Winkles and champagne... p. 6 & 14. fig. 13.
1946 SCOTT, Harold
    Early doors. p. 42+, 116+ and other refs.
1952 PULLING, Christopher
    They were singing... p. 172-3.

208

DALSTON THEATRE

12, Dalston Lane, (formerly Rosebery Place) Hackney.

Opened: 1886   By 1923 in use as a cinema.

Former names

Dalston Circus   1886
North London Colosseum Theatre   1887+
also North London Colosseum and Amphitheatre
North London Colosseum and National Hippodrome
London Colosseum and National Amphitheatre (In
'East end entertainment')
Dalston Colosseum   1894
Dalston Theatre of Varieties   1897-on provisional
                                    licences
Dalston Theatre   25-7-1898+

Later names

Dalston (picture) Theatre; Gaumont Theatre.

Building details

1st building:

-Premises used as a circus.

Capacity: (1890) 1,030

1890 Lord Chamberlain's licence withdrawn on re-
commendation of the L.C.C.

Reconstruction, 1897:

Opened: 25th September, 1898.

Architect: Messrs. Wylson and Long.

Contractor: Kirk & Kirk

Capacity: 3,516

Auditorium: S. & Bx. C-J 416; P. 666; D.C. & Bx. A-B
416; G. 500.

Management

Lord Chamberlain:

30. 10. 1886-	Alfred Barrett Brandreth
10. 9. 1888-	Charles Ambrose Wilkes
10. 1. 1890-	Harry Herbert Hamilton (to 28. 9. 1890)
25. 7. 1898-	Milton Bode and Edward Compton
8. 1. 1914-	James Langdon Lee (to 8. 10. 1919)

-Postcard from Lee stated his lease has expired on
24. 6. 1919.
Lord Chamberlain granted no further licences.

London County Council:

Nov. 1894 and 1895 prov. licences granted to Frank
Kirk.
Nov. 1896 and 1897 prov. licences granted to Charles
Edgar Liles.
1917-1918 James Langdon Lee
1922-1923 Harry Thomas Underwood (Probably a
                 cinema)
Nov. 1923   listed as a cinema.

Literature

Official records:

G.L.C. Arch. Dpt. Mss index;
G.L.C. Arch. Dpt. Th. case 423;
L.C.C. Th. & M-H. Com. App. Nov. 1894-7, 1917-18,
1922-23;
L.C.C. Th. & M-H. Com. Papers 1885+;
LC7/17, 34, 45-8.

Contemporary accounts:

1897 BUILDER. 1897, June 5th. p. 516. -Note of new
    theatre.

Historical accounts:

c. 1930   MAYES, Ronald
       The romance of London theatres, No. 160.
1954   WILSON, A. E.
       East end entertainment... p. 230.

Location of other material

Plans: G.L.C. Architects Department.

Programmes:

Enthoven Collection; Guildhall Library (4 items);
Westminster Local Collection

209

DALY'S THEATRE

2 & 8, Cranbourne Street, Leicester Square,
Westminster.

Opened: 27th June 1893.   *Closed:* 25th September,
1937.

Building details

Architect: Spencer Chadwick

Contractor: Frank Kirk

Cost: £60,000

Auditorium: S. 244; B.S. 140; U.C. 170; Bx. A-K.
1937 rebuilt by E. A. Stone and T. R. Somerford,
Architects, as Warner Theatre.

Management

Lord Chamberlain:

28. 9.1893-	Augustin Daly
28. 9.1899-	George Edwardes
12.10.1915-	Dorothy Julia Gwynne Sherbrooke (George Edwardes' daughter)
7. 5.1920-	Robert Evett
1.12.1921-	Harold Morton
1.12.1926-	Cecil Paget (to 30.11.1937)

London County Council:

1933-1937   British Amalgamated Theatres Ltd.

Literature

Official records:

G.L.C. Arch. Dpt. Th. case 424;
L.C.C. Th. & M-H. Com. App. Nov. 1932-1936;
L.C.C. Th. & M-H. Com. Papers 1893+;
LC1/601-752, LC7/40-48; L.C.C. 282 and 374.

Contemporary accounts:

1890 BUILDER. 1890, Nov. 1st. p. 340.—Report of new theatre to be built for George Edwardes.
1891 DAILY GRAPHIC. 1891, Oct. 31st. -'The Daly Theatre': report of foundation stone ceremony.
DAILY TELEGRAPH. 1891, Oct. 31st. -'A new London theatre': report of foundation stone laying.
BUILDING NEWS. 1891, Nov. 13th. p. 682. -Brief description and front elevation.
BUILDER. 1891, Nov. 14th. p. 368-9. -Description, exterior elevation section and plan of new theatre.
1893 DALY'S THEATRE (Publicity pamphlet) c. June 27th, 1893. -Note of new productions. G. E. SKETCH. 1893, June 14th, p. 381. 'A chat with London's latest theatre architect'. illus of exterior.
DAILY GRAPHIC, 1893 June 28. -Description.
ERA, 1893 July 1.—Report of opening.
BUILDER. 1893, July 8th. p. 29. -Brief report of decorations.
SKETCH. 1893, Sept. 20th. -Note of opening. illus. of interior of auditorium.
1896 SACHS, E. O. *and* WOODROW, E. A. E. Modern opera houses and theatres. Vol. 1. p. 38-9. -Illus. include elevation, plans of each level, sections, general view and view of proscenium.
Text includes description and dimensions.
1898 As above. Vol. III. p. 17, 62, 71, 73 and 87. -Illus. include diagram of box-front line, lounge, elevation of proscenium frame, skeleton plans and section of auditorium.
Text includes cost and dimensions.
1937 BUILDER, 1937, July 30th. -Report of rebuilding.

Historical accounts:

1899 DALY'S THEATRE
Souvenirs of plays produced at Daly's Theatre. London, 1899.
1930? MAYES, Ronald
Romance of London theatres, No. 49.
1944 WINSLOW, D. Forbes
Daly's: the biography of a theatre. W. H. Allen, (1944). 220p. illus. ports.
1959 ENCICLOPEDIA dello spettacolo. Vol. 6. Col. 1619.

1966 GREATER LONDON COUNCIL Survey of London, Vol. 34, 1966. pp. 355-357. plans, plates.
1968 MANDER, Raymond *and* MITCHESON, Joe. The lost theatres of London. p. 51-57. 2 illus.

Location of other materials

Plans: G.L.C. *Architects Department;* Enthoven Collection (3 sheets);

Programmes: Enthoven Collection; Guildhall Library; London Museum; Westminster Local Collection.

210

DAUNTLESS HALL

38, Lisson Grove, St. Marylebone.

Licensed: 1880-1893

Building details

Area: 870'

Capacity: 300

Daly's Theatre (209)

(Greater London Council Photograph Library)

Management

Middlesex justices:

Mich. 1880-   Charles Harris

London County Council:

1890-93   Charles Harris
Nov. 1893   *Licence refused.*

Literature

Official records:

L.C.C. Th. & M-H. Com. App. Nov. 1889-93.
Mx. Mich. Q.S. 1880-1888; Sel. Com. 1892.

211

DEACON'S MUSIC HALL

Sir Hugh Myddelton Public House, Myddelton Place, Finsbury.

Opened: 14 December, 1861.   Demolished for construction of Rosebery Ave.

Building details

Cost: £5,000

Capacity: 800

1884 - Enlarged

Capacity: 1,032

Management

Middlesex justices:

Mich. 1861-   James Deacon
  " 1885-   Henry Edward Davis

London County Council:

1890-91   Henry Edward Davis
Nov. 1891   *Not renewed.*

Literature

Official records:

Fire Brigade Report. 1877.
G.L.C. Arch. Dpt. Th. case 029;
L.C.C. Th. & M-H. Com. App. Nov. 1889-90;
Mx. Mich. Q.S. 1861-88; Sel. Com. 1866, 1877, 1892.

Contemporary accounts:

1887   SATURDAY REVIEW, 1887, Aug. 27th. The state
        of the London... music halls... No. 3.

Historical accounts:

1907   WROTH, Warwick
        Cremorne and later London gardens. p. 52-3.
1930?   MAYES, Ronald
        The romance of London theatres, No. 216.
1933   ERA. 1933, July 5th.
        -Obituary of H. E. Davis (Manager of Deacon's
        at its close in 1891)
1935   HADDON, Archibald
        The story of the music hall... p. 27 and 41
1938   DISHER, M. W.
        Winkles and champagne. p. 3. -Mentioned as
        Sir Hugh Myddleton (sic) Tavern.

Location of other material

Plans: G.L.C. *Architects Department:*

Illustrations: Enthoven Collection. postcard c.1890. exterior.

Playbills and cuttings:

Finsbury Local Collection.
Guildhall Library (1 programme for 1875)

212

DENISON ARMS PUBLIC HOUSE

1, Northampton Street, Kings Cross.

Licensed: 1854-1861

Management

Middlesex justices:

Mich. 1854-   William Freeman
  " 1859-   John Chapman
  " 1861   *No application.*

Literature

Official records:

Mx. Mich. Q.S. 1854-1860.

213

DEPTFORD THEATRE

Church Street, Deptford.

In use: 1840   *Closed:* 1857

Former name

Royal Deptford Theatre

Building detail

Building a school, warehouse and chapel before being converted into a theatre.

Capacity: 900

By 1895 site known as Theatre Wharf.

Management

Jan. 1842   Mr. Laws
  " 1853   J. C. Neville

Literature

Historical accounts:

1895   STURDEE, Thankful
        Old Deptford: Reminiscences.
        London, 1895. p. 23.
        Plate of watercolour with text.
1935   KENTISH MERCURY. 1935, Nov. 15th.

Location of other material

Playbills: Deptford Local Collection (1842 and 1853).

214

DEVONSHIRE ARMS PUBLIC HOUSE

Bristowe Street, Shoreditch.

Licensed: 1862-1890

Management

Middlesex justices:

Mich. 1862-	Thomas How Bromley	
" 1864-	Henry Owles	
" 1870-	William Henry Bedding	
" 1874-	Charles John Jarvis	
" 1875-	George Skinner	
" 1878-	John Billing	
" 1881-	George Foord	
" 1884-	George Samuel	
" 1886-	William John Spring	

London County Council:

1890	William Edward Hodges

Literature

Official records:

L.C.C. Th. & M-H. Com. App. Nov. 1889;
Mx. Mich. Q.S. 1862-1888.

215

DEVONSHIRE CASTLE PUBLIC HOUSE

Grove Road, Upper Holloway.

Licensed: 1859-1861

Management

Middlesex justices:

Mich. 1859	George William Seager
" 1860	Mary Elizabeth Wood
" 1861	*No application.*

Literature

Official records:

Mx. Mich. Q.S. 1859-1861.

216

DICK WHITTINGTON COFFEE TAVERN

9, Highgate Hill, Islington.

Licensed: 1882-1899

Building details

Capacity: 110

Management

Middlesex justices:

Mich. 1882-	Charles Leonard

London County Council:

1890-1899	Charles Leonard
Nov. 1899	*No application.*

Literature

Official records:

L.C.C. Th. & M-H. Com. App. Nov. 1889-1898;
Mx. Mich. Q.S. 1882-1888;
Sel. Com. 1892.

217

DOLPHIN PUBLIC HOUSE

Mare Street, Hackney.

Licensed: pre 1850-1852

Management

Middlesex justices:

Mich. 1850-1852	John James Homer

Literature

Official records:

Mx. Mich. Q.S. pre 1850-1852.

218

DOLPHIN PUBLIC HOUSE

134, Old Street, Shoreditch.

Licensed: 1852-1856

Management

Middlesex justices:

Mich. 1852-1856	William Smith

Literature

Official records:

Mx. Mich. Q.S. 1852-1856.

219

DOMINION THEATRE

Tottenham Court Road, Holborn.

Opened: 3rd October, 1929. From 1932 used mainly as a cinema.

Building details

Built on the site of Meux's Horseshoe Brewery.

Deptford Theatre (213)

(Lewisham Public Libraries)

Built under direction of R.H. Gillespie.

Architects: William and T. R. Milburn

Builders: Messrs. Bovis.

Capacity: (at opening) 2,800

Management

Lord Chamberlain:

1.12.1929-	Richard Henry Gillespie
	—*as a theatre*
1.12.1932	William Herbert Chantrey
	—*as music hall & cinema*
1.12.1933-	Ernest William Pashley Peall
1.12.1940-	Edmund Albert Crisp
1.12.1948-	Richard Herbert Dewes

London County Council:

| 1929-1933 | Dominion Theatre Ltd. |
| 1934-1939 | Dominion Theatre (1933) Ltd. |

Literature

Official records

G.L.C. Arch. Dpt. Th. case 4061. L.C.O. 112 and 374.

Contemporary accounts:

1928 ARCHITECT. 1928, Dec. 15th. p. 724-7. illus.
—'Simplification of theatre construction'.
1929 ARCHITECTS JOURNAL. 1929, Oct. 2nd. p. 484-90.—Building details.
STAGE. 1929, Oct. 3rd.—Building description.
ARCHITECT. 1929, Oct. 4th. p. 407-13.—Building details.
ARCHITECT AND BUILDING NEWS. 1929, Oct. 4th.—Building news.
BUILDER. 1929, Oct. 4th. p. 546, 548, 555-560.
—Detailed description, photographs, plans and sections.

Historical accounts:

c. 1930 MAYES, Ronald
The romance of London theatres, No. 134.
1963 MANDER, Raymond *and* MITCHENSON, Joe
The theatres of London. 2nd ed. p. 267-8.

Location of other material

Plans: G.L.C. Architects Department.

Programmes:

Enthoven Collection; Westminster Local Collection.

220

DRURY LANE, THEATRE ROYAL

Catherine Street, *(formerly* Brydges Street)
Westminster.

Opened: 7th May, 1663.

Building details

1st theatre opened on 7th May, 1663 as Theatre Royal
on Bridges St.

2nd theatre opened on 26th March, 1674: Theatre
Royal in Drury Lane.
From 1783 it became known as Theatre Royal, Drury
Lane.

3rd theatre opened 12th March, 1794. Burnt down 24th
February, 1809.

4th and present theatre opened 10th October, 1812.

Redeveloped by The Committee of Management.

Architect: Benjamin Wyatt.

Cost: £151,672

Capacity: 3,060.

1817: Gas lighting installed.
1820: Portico added.
1822: Interior reconstructed:

Architect: Samuel Beazley.

Cost: £22,000.

1831: Colonnade added (Columns from Regent Street
Quadrant).

1841: Interior reconstructed:

Architect: Samuel Beazley

1870: Alterations:

Architect: Messrs. Nelson & Harvey.

Builder: Messrs. Bracher & Sons.

Decoration: Messrs. Green & King.

Capacity: c.3,000.

Auditorium;(1882) P. 732; Bx. A-X; S. 126; D.C. 220;
1st. C. 175; B. 460; L.G. 684; U.G. 164.

1922: Interior reconstruction:

Architect: F. Emblin-Walker, assisted by F. Edward
Jones.

Cost: £150,000.

Capacity: 2,247.

Auditorium: S. c.490; P. 296; c. 147; U.C. 448; Bx. A-P,
AA-HH; plus G.

Stage: 42' wide × 80' deep.

Management

A patent theatre, and therefore not licensed.

Literature

Official records:

G.L.C. Arch. Dpt. Th. case 456;
L.C.C. Th. & M-H. Com. Papers 1887+;
LC7/13, 20-32, 34-48;
L.C.O. 202;
M.B.W. Rpt. 1882. pp. 28-47;
Sel. Com. 1892.

Contemporary accounts:

1813 WYATT, B.D.
Observations on the design for the Theatre
Royal, Drury Lane, as executed in 1812.
London, 1813. plates, plans, diagrs.
1828 SHEPHERD, Thomas, *and* ELMES, James. Metropolitan improvements... pp. 201-206. plate.
1847 BUILDER, 1847 Oct. 2, p. 465 & 471. plate of interior.—Detailed description.
1850 BUILDER, 1850 Nov. 9, p. 538.—Decoration at
theatre for ball and the coming season.
TALLIS'S DRAMATIC MAGAZINE, 1850-51, p. 83,
115, 149, 184, 216, 249.

1858 BUILDING NEWS. 1858, Dec. 17th. p. 1257, col. B.—Note on roof construction.

1859 BUILDING NEWS. 1859, Jan. 28th, p. 84.—Report on repairs required.
BUILDER. 1859, Feb. 5th. p. 87-8.—Inspection of theatres: Drury Lane. Report and comments.

1868 BUILDING NEWS. 1868, April 3rd. p. 226.—Report of alterations to auditorium.

1870 BUILDER. 1870, Feb. 12th. p. 131. Report of theatre architect M. Nelson to proprietors & c. Dispute over state of repairs.
BUILDING NEWS. 1870, April 22nd. p. 304. —Description of alterations.

1871 BUILDER. 1871, April 22nd. p. 304.—Brief description of reconstruction of interior.

1874 BUILDING NEWS. 1874, March 20th. p. 327. —Brief description of conversion into opera house.

1875 BUILDING NEWS. 1875, Aug. 27th. p. 223.—Repairs and alterations.

1876 BUILDING NEWS. 1876, Sept. 29th. p. 327.—Note of repairs and renovations.
BUILDER. 1876, Dec. 30th. p. 1, 269. 'Drury Lane management: lack of order at paybox balcony.'

1878 BUILDER. 1878, June 15th. p. 624. The letting of Drury Lane Theatre: report on call for tenders and requirements laid down.

1879 BUILDER. 1879, Dec. 13th. p. 1, 369. Note reporting C. J. Phipps appointed architect to company in place of Marsh Nelson, resigned.

1880 BUILDER. 1880, Aug. 7th. p. 186. Report of auction of four renters' shares.

1882 BUILDER. 1882, Oct. 14th. p. 506. Result of arbitration on M.B.W. requirements.

1887 SATURDAY REVIEW. 1887, June 11th. 'The state of the London theatres... No. 1.

1889 BUILDER. 1889, Sept. 21st. p. 208. Description of redecoration. Illus. of theatre.

1891 BUILDING NEWS. July 21st. p. 93.—Theatre to be demolished.

1893 BUILDER. 1893, July 29th. p. 82. Brief summary of history; end of ground lease. Duke of Bedford unwilling to renew. *Erratum* 1893, Aug. 12th. p. 127.

1896 BUILDER. 1896, Sept. 12th. p. 216. Brief report of completion of extensive alterations.

1897 BUILDER. 1897, Sept. 18th. p. 226. Report of redecoration. Architect Philip E. Pilditch, contractor Messrs. Campbell Smith & Co.

1898 BUILDING NEWS. 1898, Sept. 30th p. 483.—Description of installation of electric power to assist in scene changes.
BUILDER. 1898, Dec. 17th. p. 566. Report on installation of electric power for driving moving stage machinery, by Thames Ironworks Co.
SACHS, E. *and* WOODROW, E. A. E.
Modern opera houses and theatres. Vol. III p. 115. Stage: view of hydraulic bridges in sloping position. III S. p. iv.

1899 BUILDING NEWS. 1899, May 12th. p. 658.—Note of extension to theatre at rear.

1901 BUILDING NEWS. 1901, June 28th. p. 861.—Brief description of alterations.
BUILDER. 1901, Aug. 31st. p. 199. Report of structural alterations—including reconstruction of stalls, grand and 1st circles.

1904 The MICROCOSM of London. Vol. 1. p. 288 +. —Description.
BUILDER. 1904, March 26th. p. 337-338. Detailed report of L.C.C. requirements for structural alterations.

BUILDER. 1904, July 23rd., Aug. 27th., Sept. 3rd., p. 102, 235, 257.—Brief note of arbitrations; note that theatre to be closed until December for carrying out of alterations required by L.C.C. in accordance with arbitration award. A.G.M. comments on L.C.C. requirements.
BUILDING NEWS. 1904, Aug. 5th. p. 204.—Note of disagreement over L.C.C. requirements.
BUILDING NEWS. 1904, Dec. 2nd. p. 812.—Description of alterations being made under L.C.C. order.

1908 BUILDER. 1908, May 23rd. p. 610. Brief note that reconstruction of parts damaged by the recent fire commenced under Mr. Pilditch. Hoped to be completed by Autumn.
BUILDER. 1908, July 4th. p. 9. Detailed description of extensive alterations to the stage including addition of 30' to size.

1908 BUILDING NEWS, 1908, Sept. 18th. p. 391.—Summary of history and description of reconstruction of stage destroyed by fire on 25. 3. 1908
BUILDER. 1908, Sept. 19th. p. 308-9. Description of rebuilding of stage destroyed by fire on March 25th. Contractor: Messrs. Dove Brothers Ltd.,

1910 GRAPHIC. 1910, Jan. 1st. p. 13. 'Drury Lane theatre: behind the scenes'.

1911 BUILDER. 1911, Aug. 25th. p. 225. Report of structural alterations in progress, also redecoration.
BUILDING NEWS. 1911, Aug. 25th. p. 276.—Report of structural alterations.

1912 ILLUSTRATED LONDON NEWS. 1912, Oct. 19th. p. 568. 'Drury Lane centenary.'

1915 BUILDER. 1915, Nov. 12th. p. 354A. Description and photograph of orginal staircase.

1922 DRURY LANE THEATRE
The new Theatre Royal, Drury Lane: then and now. Theatre Royal, Drury Lane Ltd. 1922. 19p. illus.—Includes description of rebuilding and brief history.
BUILDER. 1922, April 14th. p. 558d. The reconstruction of Drury Lane Theatre: detailed report. Photos. of auditorium, staircase and rotunda.

1931 R.I.B.A. Journal. 1931, Jan 24th. p. 176-8. First sprinkler system at Drury Lane theatre, A.V. Sutherland-Green.

1939 ILLUSTRATED LONDON NEWS. 1939, Dec. 2nd. p. 830-1. 'Drury Lane theatre in a new role: headquarters of the entertainment front.'

1944 THEATRE ARTS. 1944, May. p. 285-7. 'Old Theatre Royal Drury Lane as ENSA headquarters in wartime'.

1946 EVENING STANDARD. 1946, Aug. 28th. 'Most famous theatre is reborn as ENSA leave Drury Lane.'

1950 THEATRE ownership. p. 58 and 89.

Historical accounts:

1879 DRAMATIC NOTES. 1879. p. 2-5.

1881 DORAN, John
Drury Lane
1881. 2v.
STIRLING, Edward
Old Drury Lane: fifty years recollections of author, actor and manager.
Chatto, 1881, 2v.

1903 GORDEN, Charles.
Old time Aldwych. p. 259 and 360-62.

1904 BAKER, H. Barton
History of the London stage and its players.
p. 45-106.
1906 BUILDER. 1906, July 14th. p. 39-40.
History of theatre
1907 The PICTURE history of Drury Lane and
souvenir programme... March 5th, 1907. 20p.
1918 PARKER, Louis N.
The pageant of Drury Lane Theatre, 1663-1918...
(The story of Drury Lane by Austin Brereton)
24p. 1918.
1921 GRAPHIC. 1921, July 23rd. p. 103.
'Sixth Drury Lane Theatre'.
1922 The NEW Theatre Royal Drury Lane: then and
now. London, 1922. (11795 p. 4)
1925 CHANCELLOR, E. B.
The pleasure haunts of London... p. 81-88.
c. 1830 McKECKNIE, Samuel
Popular entertainments.—Number of refs.
MAYES, Ronald
The romance of London theatres. No. 17, 110,
Drury Lane.
1930 CHANCELLOR, E. B.
The annals of Covent Garden and its neighbourhood. Hutchinson, 1930. p. 258 et seq.
1933 NOTES AND QUERIES. 1933, Jan. p. 61-2.
P. J. Crean: Footlights (introduction at Drury
Lane and Convent Garden)
1938 DISHER, M. W.
Winkles and champagne... —large number of
refs.
1945 COUNTRY LIFE. 1945, June 18th and Aug. 3rd.
p. 1002 and 209. Dates, plans, of successive
buildings &c.
194-? WILSON, A. E.
Pantomime pageant... p. 13+; 51+; 80+; 100.
and 27 other refs.
1946 POPE, W. J. Macqueen
Theatre Royal, Drury Lane. W. H. Allen, 1946.
BUILDER, 1946, Aug. 9th.—Theatre Royal, Drury
Lane.
JOURNAL OF THE LONDON SOCIETY. 1946,
Nov. p. 43-8.—The history of Drury Lane Theatre.
1951 FEASLEY, L.
On the boards of old Drury. Harrap, 1951.
1958 OPERA, 1958 Feb., pp. 94-6.
Opera at Drury Lane from 1887.
1959 ENCICLOPEDIA dello spettacolo. Vol. 6, Col.
1619-20.
1963 MANDER, Raymond, and MITCHENSON, Joe.
The theatres of London. 2nd ed. pp. 64-71.
THEATRE WORLD, 1963 Jan.
Drury Lane— 1812-1963, by Neville M. Bligh.
3p. illus.
THEATRE WORLD, 1963 May.
Tercentenary of Drury Lane, by Neville M.
Bligh. 4p. illus.—History to 1812.

Location of other materials

Plans: G.L.C. *Architects Department;* Enthoven Collection (7 sheets); Public Record Office LC1/508.

Programmes and playbills:

British Museum Library; Enthoven Collection; Garrick
Club; Guildhall Library; Westminster Local Collect-
tion; London Museum.

Prints: British Museum; Enthoven Collection; London
Museum; Westminster Local Collection.

68

221

DUCHESS THEATRE

Catherine Street, Aldwych.

Opened: 25th November 1929.

Owners: West End and Country Theatres Ltd.; Duchess
Theatre Ltd. (1930)

Promoter: Arthur Gibbon.

Architect: Ewen S. Barr.

Builder: F. G. Minter Ltd.

Interior decorator: Marc Henri and Laverdet

Later redone by: Mary Wyndham-Lewis

Capacity: 491

Management

Lord Chamberlain:

1. 12. 1929   Martin Henry
1. 12. 1930-   John Henry Mitchelhill
1. 12. 1938-   Michael Hillman
Letter 23. 10. 1941 Theatre not relicensed owing to
complications in estate of late Michael Hillman and to
fact that theatre damaged by enemy action.
1. 12. 1942-   James Sharp
1. 12. 1946-   Marianne Davis

Literature

Offical records:

G.L.C. Arch. Dpt. Th. case 4156.
L.C.O. 147 and 374.

Contemporary accounts:

1929 BUILDER. 1929, Nov. 29th. p. 913-5, 923, 949.
Photos., plans, section.
ARCHITECT. 1929, Nov. 29th. p. 659-60.—Building details.
ARCHITECT AND BUILDING NEWS. 1929, Nov.
—Building details.
1931 ARCHITECTURE ILLUSTRATED. 1931, June.
—Building details.
1937 HILLIER, PARKER, MAY AND ROWDEN. Auctioneers. The Duchess Theatre... for sale by
auction... on Wednesday, December 8th, 1937.
12p. illus.
(Copy in Enthoven Collection)
1950 THEATRE ownership.—Various references.

Historical accounts:

c. 1930 MAYES, Ronald
The romance of London theatres, No. 205.
1959 ENCICLOPEDIA dello Spettacolo.
Vol. 6. Col. 1620.
1963 MANDER, Raymond and MITCHENSON, Joe.
The Theatres of London, 2nd ed. p. 72-75.

Location of other materials:

Plans: G.L.C. *Architects Department.*

Programmes:

Enthoven Collection; Westminster Local Collection;
London Museum.

222

DUCHESS OF CLARENCE PUBLIC HOUSE

Vauxhall Bridge Road, Westminster.

Licensed: pre 1850-1857

Management

Middlesex justices:

Mich.	1848-	Walter Swift Walford
"	1850-	Thomas How Bromley
"	1857	*Not licensed.*

Literature

Official records:

Mx. Mich. Q.S. pre 1850-1856

223

DUCHESS OF KENT PUBLIC HOUSE

Bridge Street, *(later* 179, Morning Lane) Homerton, Hackney.

Licensed: 1868-1890

Building details

The hall on the first floor was irregular in shape with an area of 470 sq.
The platform was placed in an angle.
It was closed as a result of the 1878 Act.

Management

Middlesex justices:

Mich.	1868-	George William Watkinson
"	1875-	James Tanner
"	1887-	Frederick Valentine Foster

London County Council:

	1890-	Frederick Valentine Foster
Nov. 1890		*Not licensed:*

Literature

Official records:

G.L.C. Arch. Dpt. Th. case. 040/35;
L.C.C. Th. & M-H. Com. App. Nov. 1889-90;
Mx. Mich. Q.S. 1868-1888.

224

DUCHESS OF YORK PUBLIC HOUSE

90, Kingsland Road, Shoreditch.

Licensed: 1862-1883

Management

Middlesex justices:

Mich.	1862-	William Payne
"	1873-	Edward Binge
"	1882-	David Meiklejohn Partridge
"	1883	*No application.*

Literature

Official records:

Mx. Mich. Q.S. 1862-1883.

225

DUKE OF BRIDGEWATER PUBLIC HOUSE

Macclesfield Street, *(later* Graham Street) St. Luke's, Finsbury.

Licensed: 1859-1885

Management

Middlesex justices:

Mich.	1859-	Maurice Harden Dale
"	1862-	Friedrich Luhke
"	1863	*No application.*
"	1885	Hastings John Reeve

Literature

Official records:

Mx. Mich. Q.S. 1859-62 and 1885.

226

DUKE OF CLARENCE PUBLIC HOUSE

1, Eyre Street Hill, Holborn.

Licensed 1854-1857

Management

Middlesex justices:

Mich.	1854-	James Francis Hookham.
	1857	*No application*

Literature

Official records

Mx. Mich. Q.S. 1854-1857

227

DUKE OF CLARENCE PUBLIC HOUSE

154, Manor Place, Walworth.

Building details

The concert hall was on the first floor. It was irregular in shape, 25' × 38', area of 950'.
Accommodation for 240 people.
Closed as a result of the 1878 Act.

Literature

Official records:

G.L.C. Arch. Dpt. Th. case 040/36.

228

DUKE OF CLARENCE PUBLIC HOUSE

106, Scawfell Street, *(formerly* Cumberland Street) Shoreditch.

Licensed: 1858-1890

Building details

Concert room was situated on the first floor, 27'8" × 27'8" × 10'
Excluding projections and stage, hall of an area of 687'.
Closed as a result of the 1878 Act.

Management

Middlesex justices:

Mich.	1858	Charles Entwistle
"	1859-	John William Allan
"	1863	Frances Belchamber
"	1864-	Edward Clayton
"	1866-	William Young Angus
"	1871-	Julius Simon
"	1876-	George Wocha
"	1882-	James Griffiths
"	1887-	Henry John Cook

London County Council:

1890	Henry John C(r)ook
Nov. 1890	*Not relicensed.*

Literature

Official records:

G.L.C. Arch. Dpt. Th. case 040/37.
L.C.C. Th. & M-H. Com. App. Nov. 1889.

Location of other material

Plans: G.L.C. *Architects Department.*

229

DUKE OF CONNAUGHTS COFFEE TAVERN

33, New Road, Woolwich.

Licensed: 1881-1902

Later name

Royal Assembly Rooms (1891-)

Building details

The concert room was on the 2nd floor over the coffee house. Large alterations were required by the L.C.C. in 1892 and 1900.

Management

West Kent justices:

Mich. 1881-	Frederick Johnson	

London County Council:

1890-	Frederick Johnson
1902-	William Entwisle
Nov. 1902	*Not relicensed.*

Literature

Official records:

G.L.C. Arch. Dpt. Mss. index.
L.C.C. Th. & M-H. Com. App. Nov. 1889-1902.
Sel. Com. 1892.
W. Kt. Mich. Q.S. 1881-1888.

Location of other material

Handbills: Guildhall Library (1 item for 1883)

230

DUKE OF CORNWALL PUBLIC HOUSE

St. Nicholas, Deptford.

Licensed: before 1847- 1854

Management

West Kent justices:

Mich.	1847-	James Dunster
"	1851-	Thomas Parkins
"	1852-	Charles Carter Lewis
"	1854	Henry Gore.

Literature

Official records:

W. Kt. Mich. Q.S. 1847, 1851-1854.

231

DUKE OF HAMILTON PUBLIC HOUSE

New End, Hampstead.

Licensed: 1860-1890

Management

Middlesex justices:

Mich.	1860-	William Goulding
"	1878-	Mary Ann Sophia Goulding
"	1881-	John William Banger
"	1882-	Frederick William Smith

London County Council:

1890-	Frederick William Smith
Nov. 1890	*Licence refused*

Literature

Official records:

L.C.C. Th. & M-H. Com. App. Nov. 1889-1890.
Mx. Mich. Q.S. 1860-1888.

232

DUKE OF KENT PUBLIC HOUSE

Old Kent Road, Lambeth.

Licensed: 1862-1864

Management

Surrey justices:

Mich.	1862	Edwin Hayward
"	1863	Charlotte Ireland
"	1864	*above name crossed out in pencil.*

Literature

Official records:

Sy. Mich. Q.S. 1862-1864.

233

DUKE OF RICHMOND PUBLIC HOUSE

176, Queen's Road, Dalston.

Licensed: 1865-1890

Management

Middlesex justices:

Mich.	1865	Thomas Anthony Langden
"	1866-	John Elves

"	1872-	Ebenezer Ferry
"	1875	William Rider
"	1876-	George John Kelly
"	1878	John Cherry
"	1879-	Sophia Shears
"	1881-	Henry Kining
"	1884	John Ash
"	1885	Samuel Thomas Alexander Sheen
"	1886-	William Frederick Garrett
"	1888	Robert Kemp

London County Council:

1890	Robert Kemp
Nov. 1890	*Not relicensed.*

Literature

Official records:

L.C.C. Th. & M-H. Com. App. Nov. 1889.
Mx. Mich. Q.S. 1865-1888.

234

DUKE OF WELLINGTON PUBLIC HOUSE

52, Cyprus Street, (*formerly* Wellington Street) Old
Ford Road, Bethnal Green.

Licensed: 1854-1891

Building details

The music room was situated on the first floor. Its
dimensions were 29' 8" × 14' 9" (area 425'). It was
closed as a result of the 1878 Act.

Management

Middlesex justices:

Mich.	1854	William Joseph Parker
"	1855-	Samuel Turner
"	1864	Alfred Copping
"	1865	Henry John Hayward
"	1866-	Mary Hayward
"	1868-	Charles Blackburn Baker
"	1873-	Richard Rier
"	1880	Henry Bridges
"	1881-	William Henry Worton

London County Council:

1890 & 1891	William Henry Worton
Nov. 1891	*Licence not renewed*

Literature

Official records:

G.L.C. Arch. Dpt. Th. case 040/40.
L.C.C Th. & M-H. Com. App. Nov. 1889-1890.
Mx. Mich. Q.S. 1854-1888.

Location of other material:

Plans: G.L.C. Architects Department

235

DUKE OF WELLINGTON PUBLIC HOUSE

92, Drury Lane, Westminster.

Licensed: 1856-1875

Management

Middlesex justices

Mich.	1856-	Richard Thomas Reeves
"	1872	James Bishop
"	1873-	Alfred Charles Mountford
"	1875	*No Application*

Literature

Official records:

Mx. Mich. Q.S. 1856-1874.

236

DUKE OF WELLINGTON PUBLIC HOUSE

Shepherd Street, Christchurch.

Licensed: 1860-1868

Management

Middlesex justices:

Mich.	1860-	Samual Watkins
"	1864-	Charles Borthwick Ward
"	1867-	William King
"	1868	*Thomas Holman refused licence.*

Literature

Official records:

Mx. Mich. Q.S. 1860-1868.

237

DUKE OF WELLINGTON PUBLIC HOUSE

Wellington Road, Holloway.

Licensed: 1855-1862

Management

Middlesex justices:

Mich.	1855-	Charles Warr
"	1862	*No application*

Literature

Official records:

Mx. Mich. Q.S. 1855-1861

238

DUKE OF WIRTEMBURG PUBLIC HOUSE

Hatfield Street, Christchurch.

Licensed: Before 1850-1869

Management

Surrey justices:

Mich.	1849-	Thomas Marshall
"	1851	Henry Smith
"	1851-	Benjamin Habberton Ellis
"	1864-	Thomas Batten White
"	1869	*Not renewed*

Literature

Official records:

Sy. Mich. Q.S. pre 1850-1868.

239

DUKE OF YORK PUBLIC HOUSE

8, Charlotte Place, St. Pancras.

Licensed: 1854-1860

Management

Middlesex justices:

Mich. 1854-   Charles Thomas Wood
"   1858-   Thomas Fowler
"   1859   Edward Taylor
"   1860   *Licence refused to* John Adams.

Literature

Official records:

Mx. Mich. Q S. 1854-1860.

240

DUKE OF YORK PUBLIC HOUSE

14, Gloucester Street, Clerkenwell.

Licensed: 1854-1864

Management

Middlesex justices:

Mich. 1854-   Reuben Edward Nye
"   1858   Mary Nye
"   1859   *No application*
"   1860-   William Field Mourgue
"   1864   *No application*

Literature

Official records:

Mx. Mich. Q.S. 1854-58, 1860-1863.

241

DUKE OF YORK PUBLIC HOUSE

28 & 29, Stockbridge Terrace, Pimlico.

Licensed: 1851-1889

Management

Middlesex justices:

Mich. 1851-   Thomas Wil(l)cox
"   1863-   Peter Osgood
"   1866-   Edwin John Dyne
'"   1869-   Frederick Mattews
"   1871-   Edwin John Dyne
'"   1877   Joseph John Leftwich
"   1878   Lewis Ascott
"   1883-   Sidney Stops

Not licensed by the L.C.C.

Literature:

Official records:

Mx. Mich. Q.S. 1851-1888.

242

DUKE OF YORK PUBLIC HOUSE

7, York Road, Kings Cross.

Licensed: 1854-1860

Management

Middlesex justices:

Mich. 1854-   George Grendon
"   1860   Petition in the name of James E. Miles *refused.*

Literature

Official records:

Mx. Mich. Q.S. 1854-1860.

243

DUKE OF YORK'S THEATRE

St. Martin's Lane, Westminster.

Opened: 10th September, 1892.

Former names

Trafalgar Square Theatre 1892-1894
Trafalgar Theatre 1894-Sept. 1895

Building details

Developers: Frank Wyatt and Violet Melnotte

Architect: Walter Emden

Builder: Frank Kirk

Capacity: (1950) 900

Auditorium: S. 256; D.C. 116; U.C. 132; Bx. A-O.

Stage: 26' 4" wide, 24' high, 35' 6" deep.

Redecorated 1950

Decorator: Cecil Beaton

Management

Lord Chamberlain:

29. 2. 1892-   Michael Lirenston
Jan. 1893-   Violet Melnotte
Oct. 1894-   Frank and Violet Wyatt (i.e. Melnotte)
Oct. 1895-   Charles Cartwright and Henry Dana
Oct. 1896-   Michael Levenston
Oct. 1897-   Application by Michael Levenston on behalf of St. Martin's Syndicate Ltd., not granted as he was bankrupt.
Oct. 1897   Frank Wheeler
Oct. 1998-   Charles Frohman
8. 5. 1915-   Boileau Wooldridge Lestocq (i.e. William Lestocq)
3. 7. 1916-   Violet Melnotte-Wyatt
17. 7. 1920-   Philip Michael Faraday
30. 11. 1922-   Violet Melnotte Wyatt
1. 12. 1928-   William Mathias Hutter
1. 12. 1933-   Violet Melnotte Wyatt
1. 12. 1935-   Archibald Patrick Moore
1. 12. 1939-   Joseph Wyatt
1. 12. 1945   G. A. Glover
1. 12. 1946-   Marianne Davis (to after 1950)

Literature

Official records:

G.L.C. Arch. Dpt. Th. case 425;
L.C.C. Th. & M-H. Com. Papers 1890-;
L.C. 1/582, L.C. 7/39-48. L.C.O. 350 and 374.

Contemporary accounts:

1891 BUILDING NEWS. 1891, June 12th. p. 802-3.
—Description, elevation, section and plan.
BUILDING NEWS. 1891, Nov. 27th. p. 773-4.
'The new Trafalgar Theatre': description. 2
plates of plans, sections and elevations.

1892 TRAFALGAR SQUARE THEATRE. The Trafalgar Square Theatre. Allen, 1892. 7p. plan.
DAILY GRAPHIC. 1892, Sept. 1st & 2nd. The Trafalgar Square Theatre.—Report and description.
ERA. 1892, Sept. 3rd.—Building description

1896-8 SACHS, Edwin *and* WOODROW, E. A. E.
Modern opera houses and theatres. Vols. I and III.—Plans, sections, descriptions and dimensions.

1910 HOWE, P. P. The repertory theatre, 1910.—The Frohman season.

1950 ARCHITECTS JOURNAL. 1950, Nov. 30th. and Dec. 7th. p. 442 and 471. Interior and foyer and lighting.

Historical accounts:

c. 1930 MAYES, Ronald
The romance of London theatres, No. 8.

1950 THEATRE ownership. p. 70.

1959 ENCICLOPEDIA dello Spettacolo
Vol. 6. Col. 1621.

1963 MANDER, Raymond *and* MITCHENSON, Joe
The theatres of London. 2nd ed. p. 76-80.

Location of other material

Plans: G.L.C. *Architects Department;* Enthoven Collection 1949 (4 sheets)

Programmes: Enthoven collection; Guildhall Library; London Museum, Westminster Local Collection.

244

DUKE'S THEATRE

42, High Holborn, Holborn.

Opened: 6th October 1866 *Burnt down:* 4th June, 1880

Former names

Holborn Theatre
Theatre Royal, Holborn 1869
Royal Holborn Theatre 1870
Mirror Theatre 1875-1880

Building details

Developer: Sefton Parry

Architect: Finch, Hill & Paraire

Builder: Mr. Simpson

Decorators: Kittle & Balliscombe & Mr. Houmann

Management

Lord Chamberlain:

29. 9.1866-	Sefton Parry
1. 4.1868-	Fanny Josephs
24. 4.1869-	Barry Sullivan
21. 3.1870-	Sefton Parry
25. 9.1871-	Richard Mansell (to 17.10.1871) —Closed by Sefton Parry, as the lessee could not carry on.
26. 3.1872-	Joseph Fell.
3. 3.1873-	William Hamilton Codrington Nation. (to 3.6.1873)
1.10.1873-	Ernest Valuay and Alexis Petron (to 31.3.1874)
4. 4.1874-	Walter Joyce and William Ridewood Field
6. 7.1874-	Morris James Guiver
16. 4.1875-	Horace Wigan
8. 1.1876-	Francis Cowley Burnaud
12. 4.1876-	Thomas Mowbray (to 28.9.1876)
29. 9.1876-	Lewis Brockman
31. 3.1877-	Thomas Mowbray
Nov. 1878-	Charles Wilmot (to 4.6.1880-)

Literature

Official records:

LC7/15-17, LC7/22-26, LC7/89.
Sel. Comm. 1877 and 1892.

Contemporary accounts:

1865 BUILDER, 1865 July 29, p. 540.— Proposed 'Holborn Theatre Royal' approached through 43 High Holborn and 1 & 2 Brownlow Mews.

1866 BUILDING NEWS, 1866 Sept. 14, p. 608.
—Description.
ILLUSTRATED LONDON NEWS, 1866 Oct. 3.
illus of interior.
BUILDER. 1866 Oct. 6, p. 745.—Description.
ERA. 1866 Oct. 7.—Detailed description giving dimension.
BUILDING NEWS, 1866 Oct. 12, p. 674.
—Description.
BUILDER, 1866 Nov. 3, pp. 819-20.—Letter about pit and gallery entrances.

1879 DRAMATIC NOTES, 1879 pp. 64-5.

1880 DAILY NEWS, 1880 July 5th.—Burning of the Duke's Theatre (on 4th July): report.
DAILY TELEGRAPH, 1880 July 5th. Report of fire.
BUILDER, 1880 July 10, p. 63.—Report of fire.
ERA, 1880, July 11.—Fire report.

Historical accounts:

1904 BAKER, H. Barton
The history of the London stage and its players.
pp. 326-7. (indexed as Holborn Theatre).

1925 SHERSON, Erroll
London's lost theatres, ... pp. 189-198. (N.B. Sherson confused the two Holborn Theatres).

c. 1930 MAYES, Ronald
The romance of London theatres, No. 127.

1956 PRYCE, F. R.
Holborn Theatre Royal, *in* Holborn in Brief. (Copy in Holborn Local Collection).

1957 THEATRE WORLD, 1957 June.
Lost London theatres, by N.M. Bligh. No. 8. The story of the Holborn Theatre. 2p. illus.

1968 MANDER, Raymond *and* MITCHENSON, Joe
The lost theatres of London. pp. 186-204. 2 illus.

Location of other material

Plans: Public Record Office. LC7/87. 3 sheets.

Programmes and playbills: British Museum Library; Enthoven Collection; Guildhall Library; Holborn Local Collection; London Museum; Westminster Local Collection.

245

DUKE'S HEAD PUBLIC HOUSE

155, Flood Street, (*formerly* 1, Queen Street) Cheyne Walk.

Licensed: 1856-1888

Management

Middlesex justices:

| Mich. 1856- | William John Gross |
| " 1888 | *No application.* |

Literature

Official records:

Mx. Mich. Q.S. 1856-1888.

246

DUKE'S HEAD PUBLIC HOUSE

Roadside, Whitechapel.

Licensed: 1852-1859

Management

Middlesex justices:

| Mich. 1852- | William Gardner |
| " 1859 | *No application* |

Literature

Official records:

Mx. Mich. Q.S. 1852-1859

247

DURANT ARMS PUBLIC HOUSE

35, Durant Street, Bethnal Green.

Building details

Music room on the first floor over the bar, 36′ 2″ × 13′ 9″ with a platform.
Area 467′ 2″, i.e. not sufficiently large to bring it within the scope of the 1878 Act, but closed down because of it.

Literature

Official records:

G.L.C. Arch. Dpt. Th. case 040/41.

248

EAGLE TAVERN MUSIC HALL

Shepherdess Walk, City Road.

Licensed: 1884-1887, but in use by 1857.

Former name

Royal Eagle Music Hall.

Building details

The hall was on the first floor of the public house, on the east side of Shepherdess Walk.
The hall measured 60′ × 32′ × 19′. At the north-east angle was a saloon 24′ × 14′ 16″ communicating with the hall, which was divided by dwarf partition into three parts.
Total capacity: 300.
By 13.5.1887 the hall was closed. The billiard room on the ground floor was converted into a concert room, but the area was not sufficient to bring it within the scope of the 1878 Act.

Management

Middlesex justices:

Mich. 1884-	Thomas Broom
" 1885-	C. Arthur McCluer
" 1887	George Chutter *refused licence.*

Literature

Official records:

G.L.C. Arch. Dpt. Th. case 040/41;
Mx. Mich. Q.S. 1884-7; Sel. Com. 1892.

Contemporary accounts:

1857 RITCHIE, J. Ewing. The night side of London. pp. 211-220.
1884 ENTRACTE, 1884 Dec. 13. 'Royal Eagle'. Report on proposed re-opening.

Historical accounts:

1898 SHOREDITCH OBSERVER, 1898 Jan. 22. Chapters of Old Shoreditch, No. VII. Description of development by T. Rouse.
1907 WROTH, Warwick
Cremorne and later London gardens. pp. 57-67. illus.
1935 HADDON, Archibald
The story of the music hall. pp. 15, 17 and 39.
1938 DISHER, M. W.
Winkles and champagne. pp. 9, 38; fig. 12.
see also GRECIAN THEATRE

249

EAGLE AND CHILD COFFEE TAVERN

45, Old Compton Street, Soho.

Licensed: 1881-1889

Management

Middlesex justices:

Mich. 1881-	Edward Plummer
" 1882-	John Field
" 1883-	William Henry Brewster (to 1889)

Not licensed by the London County Council.

Literature

Official records:

Mx. Mich. Q.S. 1881-1888.

250

EARL GREY PUBLIC HOUSE
44, Mile End Road, Stepney.

Licensed: 1854-1890.

Management

Middlesex justices:

Mich.	1854-	Mary Ann Roper
"	1855-	Sutton le Neve
"	1857-	William Brown
"	1873-	Thomas Jennings

London County Council:

1890	Thomas Jennings
Nov. 1890	*Application withdrawn.*

Literature

Official records:

L.C.C. Th. & M-H. Com. App. Nov. 1889-90.
Mx. Mich. Q.S. 1854-1888.

251

EARL OF ABERDEEN PUBLIC HOUSE
Bridport Place, Hoxton, Shoreditch.

Licensed: 1854-1857, and 1861-1863.

Management

Middlesex justices:

Mich.	1854-	Peter Smith
"	1855-	William James Lewis
"	1857	*No application*
"	1861-	Frank Baker
"	1863	*No application.*

Literature

Official records:

Mx. Mich. Q.S. 1854-57, and 1861-1863.

252

EARL OF ABERDEEN PUBLIC HOUSE
Grove Road, Bethnal Green.

Licensed: 1860-1869.

Management

Middlesex justices:

Mich.	1860-	William Henry Whiter
"	1861-	George Stewart Sim
"	1869	*No application.*

Literature

Official records:

Mx. Mich. Q.S. 1860-68.

253

EARL OF CHATHAM PUBLIC HOUSE
Hughes Fields, Deptford

Licensed: to 1851.

Management

West Kent justices:

Mich.	1846-51.	Alexander Spence.
"	1851	*No application.*

Literature

Official records:

W. Kt. Mich. Q.S. 1846-1850.

254

EARL OF ELLESMERE PUBLIC HOUSE
19, Chisenhale Road, Bethnal Green.

Licensed: 1866-1890.

Building details

Concert hall situated on the first floor of the public house, 34′ 10″ × 15′ 11″.
Its raised platform was used once a week for concerts.

Capacity: 100.

Management

Middlesex justices:

Mich.	1866-	John Hall
"	1877-	Thomas Richard Honey
"	1879-	James Johnson
"	1885-	Alfred John Bullock
"	1887-	Richard Collis.

London County Council:

1890 Richard Collis —on 5th May 1890 he was charged under the 1878 Act with not meeting the L.C.C.'s requirements. The hall was closed.

Literature

Official records:

G.L.C. Arch. Dpt. Th. case 040/43;
L.C.C. Th & M-H. Com. App. Nov. 1889;
Mx. Mich. Q.S. 1866-1888.

Contemporary accounts:

1890 STANDARD, 1890 May 5.—Report on the case.

255

EAST LONDON THEATRE
236-7, Whitechapel Road, Stepney.

Opened: 1834 *Closed as a place of live entertainment:* 1897.

Former names

Earl of Effingham Saloon	1834-
New Garrick Theatre	Use forbidden 29.9.1850
Effingham Saloon	
Effingham Theatre	29.9.1861-
New East London Theatre	1867-
East London Theatre	
Jewish Theatre	

Later names

Wonderland
Drill Hall.

Building details

Capacity: 2150

2nd building:

Opened: 1867.

Burnt down: 16.3.1879.

3rd building:

Rebuilt as The Wonderland—a theatre of Yiddish plays.
1897 Report that building to be used as museum and
exhibition hall. It became a boxing hall, and later a
drill hall.

Management

Lord Chamberlain:

29.9.1843-	Thomas Sims
	(Performances stopped between 23.1. 1846 and 19.2.1846 as building reported unsafe.)
	(29.9.1850 Letter from Lord Chamberlain telling Sims not to use the name 'New Garrick Theatre' on playbills.)
4.6.1852-	James George Armstrong
29.9.1852-	West Digges
2.3.1853-	James George Armstrong
28.4.1856-	Morris Abrahams (to 28.9.1880).

London County Council:

1896 Drill Hall (Wonderland) licensed to William
Muskerry Tilson.

Literature

Official records:

G.L.C. Arch. Dpt. Th. case 574;
L.C.C. Th. & M-H. Com. App. Nov. 1895-6.
LC7/13-16, 20-26, and 89.

Contemporary accounts:

1867 BUILDING NEWS, 1867 Oct. 18, p.726.—Report
of rebuilding.
1879 BUILDER, 1879 March 22, p.328.—Report of its
destruction by fire on previous Sunday.

Historical accounts:

1893 EDWARDS, Francis. *bookseller*.
Playbills: a collection and some comments.
pp.31-34.
1904 BAKER, H. Barton.
History of the London stage and its players, p.
409. (Indexed under Effingham Saloon).
1925 SHERSON, Erroll.
London's lost theatres... pp.47-48.
c.1930 MAYES, Ronald.
The romance of London theatres, No. 225.
1951 ROSE, Millicent
The east end of London. Cresset Press, 1951.
p.224.—Brief entry.
1954 WILSON, A. E.
East end entertainment.—Various references.

Location of other material

Plans: G.L.C. *Architects Department.*

Newscuttings, programmes and playbills:
Stepney. Local Collection.

Programmes: Enthoven Collection.

256

EASTERN COLISSEUM

Globe Road, Mile End.

Licensed: 1858-59.

Management

Middlesex justices:

Mich.1858-		Henry Savage
"	1859	*No application.*

Literature

Official records:

Mx. Mich. Q.S. 1858-1859.

257

EASTERN TEMPERANCE HALL

246, Whitechapel Road, Stepney.

Licensed: 1854-1873.

Former name:

Eastern Temple (to 1863)

Management

Middlesex justices:

Mich.1854-		Frederick Brickel Sheppard
"	1858-	Charles William Henry Taylor
"	1861-	William Winningale
"	1870-	Francis Palmer
"	1873	*No application*

Literature

Official records:

Mx. Mich. Q.S. 1854-1872.

258

EASTNOR CASTLE PUBLIC HOUSE

42, Union Street, St. Pancras.

Licensed: 1854-1856, and 1861-1867.

Management

Middlesex justices:

Mich.1854-		Charles Paternoster
"	1856	*No application*
"	1861-	Arthur John North
"	1862-	Esau Stevens
"	1865-	Joseph Gladman
"	1867	*No application.*

Literature

Official records:

Mx. Mich. Q.S. 1854-56, and 1861-67.

259

EDINBORO' CASTLE PUBLIC HOUSE

Mornington Road, Regent's Park.

Licensed: 1857-1858.

Management

Middlesex justices:

Mich. 1857-   Frederick Weidenback Whichelo
               (to Mich. 1858).

Literature

Official records:

Mx. Mich. Q.S. 1857-1858.

260

EDINBORO' CASTLE PUBLIC HOUSE

St. John's Terrace, Rhode's Well, Mile End.

Licensed: pre 1850-1873.

Management

Middlesex justices:

Mich.	1848-	James Mullet
"	1863-	Peter Lole and Jeremiah Holloway
"	1864-	Jeremiah Holloway
"	1865-	Henry Evans
"	1867-	Robert Atkins
"	1869-	William Dundock
"	1873	*No application*

Literature

Official records:

Mx. Mich. Q.S. pre 1850-1872.

261

EDINBOROUGH CASTLE PUBLIC HOUSE

Woolwich.

Licensed: pre 1850-1852.

Management

West Kent justices:

Mich.	1850-	Thomas Reynolds
"	1852	*No application.*

Literature

Official records:

W. Kt. Mich. Q.S. 1850-1851.

262

EIGHT BELLS PUBLIC HOUSE

18, Ironmonger Row, Finsbury.

Licensed: 1852-1860, and 1861-1863.

Management

Middlesex justices:

Mich.	1852-	Charles Clarke
"	1853-	William Blake Stannard
"	1855-	George Wentworth
"	1857-	Robert Dansie
"	1858-	Gabriel Treadwell
"	1860	*No licence granted.*
"	1861-	John Frederick Edwards
"	1862-	Henry Aley
"	1863	*No petition.*

Literature

Official records:

Mx. Mich. Q.S. 1852-1862.

263

ELEPHANT AND CASTLE PUBLIC HOUSE

1, Kings Road, Pancras Road, St. Pancras.

Licensed: 1854-1891.

Building details

Concert room on the first floor of the public house, 23' × 20'. Closed as a result of the 1878 Act.

Management

Middlesex justices:

Mich.	1854-	Samuel Hierons
"	1855-	Mary Ann Hierons
"	1865-	Charles Peckham
"	1868-	Richard Holmes Hammond
"	1881-	George H. P. Measor
"	1882-	Alfred Shaw
"	1887-	Charles Christopher Robertson
"	1888-	Eliza Hinton

London County Council:

1890 Eliza Hinton (Licence retained).
1891 George William Barnes
Nov. 1891 *Licence not renewed.*

Literature

Official records:

G.L.C. Arch. Dpt. Th. case 040/44;
L.C.C. Th. & M-H. Com. App. Nov. 1889-1891;
Mx. Mich. Q.S. 1854-1888.

264

ELEPHANT AND CASTLE THEATRE

24-28, New Kent Road, Southwark.

Opened: 1872 *In use as a cinema by* 1928.

Other names

Theatre Royal, Elephant and Castle.

Building details

1st building:

Architect: Messrs. Dean & Son, and Matthews.

Contractors: Giles Bennett, of Vauxhall.
Building was erected as a public hall, but was never completed. It was converted into a theatre. This building was burnt down on 26th March, 1878.

2nd building:

Opened: June 1879.

Architect: Frank Matcham.

Contractor: Messrs. Brass of Chelsea.

Decorator: Messrs Pashley, Newton and Young.

Capacity: (1882) 2203.

Auditorium: (1882) S. 96; P. 637; Bx. 610; G. 900, Bx. A-J 40.

Reconstructed: 1882

Reconstructed: 1902.

Management

Lord Chamberlain:

26. 12. 1872-	Edward Tyrrell Smith
29. 9. 1873-	Thomas Preston Mead
4. 3. 1874-	Frank Wallis
29. 9. 1874-	Richard Freeborne
17. 4. 1875-	John Aubrey (to 28. 9. 1878)

After rebuilding:

30. 5. 1879-	John Aubrey
29. 9. 1880-	George Parkes and William Tanner
29. 9. 1881-	George Parkes
27. 10. 1883-	Joseph Arnold Cave
14. 10. 1887-	Walter Burton Preen
8. 4. 1888-	Henry Vassall d'Esterre
29. 9. 1897-	Henry William d'Esterre (son of above)
29. 9. 1898-	Henry Vassall d'Esterre
19. 10. 1904-	Ernest Edward Norris, manager in the absence of the lessee d'Esterre.
31. 10. 1906-	Henry Vassall d'Esterre
31. 10. 1907-	Henry William d'Esterre

Theatre sold to Charles Barnard.

23. 3. 1908-	Charles Daniel Barnard
31. 10. 1926-	Sidney Barnard
31. 10. 1928	*Not licensed as theatre or music-hall.*

Literature

Official records:

G.L.C. Arch. Dpt. Th. case 426;
L.C.C. Th. & M-H. Com. Papers, 1888-1928.
LC1/525-767; LC7/15-17, 24-31, 33-48, and 89;
M.B.W. Rpt. 1882, pp. 93-103.

Contemporary accounts:

1872   BUILDER, 1872 Aug. 10, p. 621. —Brief description.
1878   TOUCHSTONE, 1878 March 30. "Destruction of the Elephant and Castle Theatre" —report.
       BUILDING NEWS, 1878 June 7, p. 589. —Note that theatre to be rebuilt.
       BUILDER, 1878 Aug. 3, p. 812. —Description of plans to rebuild theatre.
1879   DRAMATIC NOTES, 1879, p. 71
       BUILDING NEWS, 1879 June 6, p. 647. —Description.
       BUILDER, 1879 June 7, p. 636. —Description of new theatre on opening.

1883   BUILDER, 1883 March 24, p. 394. —Report of M.B.W.'s required alterations.
1887   SATURDAY REVIEW, 1887 July 30. The state of London theatres. . . No. 7.
(1908?) HILLIER, PARKER, MAY & ROWDEN. *Estate Agents & Valuers.* Schedule of fixtures and fittings appurtances at the Theatre Royal, Elephant and Castle, to be included in the purchase. n.d. (Copy in Enthoven Collection).

Historical accounts:

1904   BAKER, H. Barton
       History of the London stage and its players, p. 400.
c.1930 MAYES, Ronald
       The romance of London theatres, No. 21.
1967   EAST, John M.
       'Neath the mask. . . pp. 212-226.

Location of other material

Plans: G.L.C. Architects Department

Public Record Office. LC7/56 5 sheets dated 7.11.1872
                              5 sheets dated 17. 5.1878

Programmes and playbills:

Enthoven Collection; British Museum Library. 1 programme (11795 p. 29); Guildhall Library; Westminster Local collection.

265

EMBASSY THEATRE

Eton Avenue, Hampstead.

Opened: 11th September 1928. *Finally closed:* 1955.

Later

Central School of Speech and Drama.

Building details

Formerly the Hampstead Conservatoire of Music, the building was adapted by Andrew Mather. It was run by the Embassy Theatre Ltd., a company promoted by John Herbert Jay. In 1930 Alec Rea took over, and the Embassy Playgoers' Association was formed. April 1932 Ronald Adams purchased the shares and took control. In 1933 the Embassy School of Acting was opened. The theatre was damaged during the war, by bombing. In 1945 it was restored and reopened by Anthony Hawtrey. 1957 lease sold to the Central School of Speech and Drama.

Capacity: 678

Auditorium: S. 362; P. 98, C. 240.

Management

London County Council:

1928-	Embassy Theatre Ltd. (m.d.l)
1940-	Embassy (Swiss Cottage) Ltd. (m.d.l) (not licensed 1941-1945).
1928-	John Herbert Jay (s.p.)
1935-	Harry Walter Lawrence (s.p.)
1936-	Ronald Adams (s.p.)
1940	Jack de Leon (s.p.) (Not licensed 1941-1945)
1946-	Anthony Hawtrey (through 1950) (s.p.)

Literature

Official records:

G.L.C. Arch. Dpt. Th. case 143;
L.C.C. Th. & M-H. Com. App. Nov. 1928-.

Contemporary accounts:

n.d. EMBASSY THEATRE LIMITED List of original
      shareholders. (Typescript in Hampstead Local
      Collection. H. 792)
1931 BOOKMAN, 1931 Jan. p. 274 The Embassy, Swiss
      Cottage.
1938 THEATRE WORLD, 1938 Jan. The Embassy,
      by George Fearon, in an interview with Ronald
      Adam.

Historical accounts:

c. 1930 MAYES, Ronald
         The romance of London theatres, No. 201.
1950 THEATRE ownership. p. 127 and 142.
1959 ENCICLOPEDIA dello spettacolo. Vol. 6 Col. 1621.

Location of other material

Plans: G.L.C. *Architects Department*

Programmes and playbills:

British Museum Library. 'Embassy successes,
1946-8'. (11783 ff. 71);
Enthoven Collection; Westminster Local Collection.

266

EMPIRE THEATRE

5-6, Leicester Square, Westminster.

Opened as a place of entertainment: 1849

Former names

Saville House	1849-
Linwood Gallery	1856-
El Dorado	1862-
Criterion Music Hall	1863
Imperial Music Hall	1864-5
Royal Denmark Theatre	1869
Alcazar	1880
Royal London Panorama	1880
Pandora Theatre	1882
Empire Theatre	1884-

Building details

Saville House:

Destroyed by fire, 11. 3. 1865.

Royal Denmark Theatre:

Architect: Edward C. Robins.

Pandora Theatre/Empire Theatre:

Opened: 17. 4. 1884.

Architect: Thomas Verity succeeded by J. & A. E. Bull.

Contractor: Messrs. Merritt and Ashby succeeded by
            Messrs. Bywater Bros.

Cost: £25,000.

Capacity: 3000, (1912) 1726.

Auditorium: S. & P. 586; Bx. C. and Bx. 176; G.C. 150;
G. 162.
1893 a new foyer erected.

Architect: Frank Verity.

Empire Cinema:

Rebuilt 1928. Opened: 8 Nov. 1928

Architect: Frank Matcham and Thomas W. Lamb.

Contractor: Anglo-Scottish Construction Company Ltd.

Capacity: 3500.

Auditorium: S. 2000; D.C. 1500.

Stage: 54′ wide by 35′ deep.

This building was used for live as well as film per-
formances.
Closed May 1961.
Rebuilt 1963 as dance hall and cinema.

Management

Lord Chamberlain:

28. 11. 1843 Licence requested by S. A. Emery for
              Saville House. Licence refused.

Middlesex justices:

Mich. 1850-	Richard Pridmore, for Saville House.
″ 1855	*No petition.*
″ 1856-	Frederick Frampton, for Saville House.
″ 1857-	George Reeve, for the Linwood Gallery. (He had been refused a licence the previous year.)
″ 1858	*No petition.*
″ 1863-	James Ellis, for Criterion.
″ 1864-	Stephen Pott, for Imperial Music Hall.
″ 1865	*Licence refused.*

Lord Chamberlain:

15. 4. 1884-	George Hunt
29. 9. 1885-	Daniel Nicols (to 28. 9. 1887).

Elephant & Castle Theatre (264)

(Greater London Council Photograph Library)

Middlesex justices:

Mich. 1887-   George Edwardes.

London County Council:

1890-	George Edwardes
1908-	Harry James Hitchins
1912-	Walter Dickson
1916-	Alfred Butt
1925-	Empire Palace Ltd.
1927-	William Herbert Chantrey
Nov. 1927	*Not licensed as theatre being reconstructed.*
1929-	New Empire Ltd.
1930	*Licensed as a cinema.*

Lord Chamberlain:

1.12.1923-	Alfred Butt (to 30.11.1924).
" 1929-	William Tustin
" 1932-	William Webb
" 1935-	George Webb
" 1937-	Matthew Raymond
" 1946-	Cecil Maitland (through 1950).

Literature

Official records:

G.L.C. Arch. Dpt. Th. case 102;
L.C.C. Th.& M-H. Com. App. Nov. 1889-;
LC7/13, 17, 31-33;
Mx. Mich, Q.S. 1850-4; 1856-7; 1863-5; 1887-8;
Sel. Com. 1892.

Contemporary accounts:

1865 ILLUSTRATED LONDON NEWS, 1865 March 11, illus. —Destruction of Saville House.

1869 BUILDING NEWS, 1869 Dec. 24, plate after p.477. —Front elevation of the Royal Denmark Theatre and Winter Garden.

1870 BUILDING NEWS, 1870 March 18, p. 210. —Announcement that "prospectus issued by Denmark Theatre and Winter Garden Company which is formed to erect theatre... on site of Saville House.

1880 DAILY NEWS, 1880 Jan. 19. 'The Theatres' column—report on proposed plans for site of Saville House, and review of defunct plans.
BUILDER, 1880 July 10, p. 60.—Speculative theatre building. Re: The Alcazar Company. Petition for winding up company by E. L. Paraire, architect.
BUILDER, 1880 July 17, p. 96. —Actual building under construction is Royal London Panorama.

1881 BUILDER, 1881 Aug. 20, and Aug. 27, pp. 250 and 282. —Report of arbitration on architect's charges.

1882 BUILDER, 1882 March 25, p. 372. —Royal London Panorama to be converted into theatre.

1883 BUILDER, 1883 Jan. 6, p. 30. —Messrs. Vaughan & Brown of Kirby Street responsible for gas engineering.
BUILDING NEWS, 1883 March 2, p. 248. —Description.
BUILDER, 1883 March 3, p. 274. —Report of visit of members of the Architectural Association. Description of building in course of erection. Due to open at Easter.
BUILDER, 1883 June 23, p. 867. 'The theatre building mania in London'. —Report of failure of Pandora Theatre Co. Contractors Messrs. Merritt & Ashby bankrupt.

1884 BUILDING NEWS, 1884 Feb. 29, pp. 313-4. —Detailed description. Third attempt to complete.
BUILDER, 1884 April 12, p. 530. —Report that opening to take place Monday next: originally built as Pandora.
DAILY NEWS, 1884 April 16. 'The Empire Theatre'. —Description of building to be opened on 17th.
ERA. 1884 April 19.—Report of opening and description.
MORNING POST, 1884 April 18. Description and report of opening.
ILLUSTRATED LONDON NEWS, 1884 April 26. Illus. of foyer, auditorium, staircase, promenade and exterior.

1887 BUILDER, 1887 Dec. 17, p. 865. —Description. Architect: Messrs. Romaine-Walker & Tanner.
DAILY TELEGRAPH, 1887 Dec. 23. 'Empire Theatre of Varieties' opens as variety theatre.
ERA, 1887 Dec. 24. —Report.

1894 DAILY GRAPHIC, 1894 May 15, p. 70. 'The other side of the pictures' (Tableaux vivants).

1894 BUILDER, 1894 Nov. 3, p. 307. —Report on closure, L.C.C.'s requirements impracticable.
DAILY GRAPHIC, 1894 Nov. 5, p. 69. —Reopening: disgraceful rowdyism.

1897 SACHS, E. O. and WOODROW, E. A. E. Modern opera houses and theatres... Vol. 2, pp. 39-40. Illus. —Description and dimensions.

1898 SACHS, E. O. Stage constructions. —Plan and details of rostrums from 'Faust' ballet.

1905 BUILDER, 1905 April 1, p. 350. —Report of proposal to close in order to carry out L.C.C. requirements. Includes brief history of site.

1927 TIMES, 1927 Jan. 21. 'End of the Empire'.
GRAPHIC, 1927 Jan. 29, p. 168. 'The passing of the Empire Theatre'.
ILLUSTRATED LONDON NEWS, 1927 Feb. 5. —Report on the closing of the Empire, by J. T. Grein.

1928 BUILDER, 1928 Nov. 16, p. 790, pp. 800-06. 'The new Empire Cinema'. —Description.
ARCHITECT, 1928 Dec. 7, pp. 724-7. illus. 'Simplification of theatre construction'.

1961 TIMES, 1961 May 27. 'Last days of the Empire: Dan Leno to Ben Hur'.

Historical accounts:

1884 EMPIRE THEATRE.
Programme. April 17th 1884.
—Contains history of site and description of building. (Copies in Enthoven Collection and British Museum Library).

1888 BUILDER, 1888 Jan, 14, pp. 267.
History of the site.

1895 RIMBAULT, E. F.
Soho and its associations... edited by George Clinch. Dulau & co., 1895. p. 186.

1904 BAKER, H. Barton
History of the London stage and its players. pp. 344-5. —Its history of the building as a theatre.

1905 EMPIRE THEATRE
'The Empire: past and present, 1884-1905'. 20p. (Copy in the Enthoven Collection).

1931 CHANCELLOR, E. B.
The romance of Soho. pp. 240-1.

c. 1930 MAYES, Ronald.
The romance of the London theatres, Nos. 116 and 148.

1935 HADDON, Archibald
The story of the music hall... pp. 19, 85, 125-9,
150.
1946 SCOTT, Harold.
Early doors. pp. 154 et seq.
SHORT, Ernest.
Fifty years of vaudeville. Numerous references.
1952 PULLING, Christopher
They were singing... —Various references.
1959 ENCICLOPEDIA dello spettacolo. Vol. 6
Col 1621-2.
1962 GUEST, Ivor Forbes
The Empire Ballet.
Society for Theatrical Research, 1962. 111p.
plates (annual publication No. 9).
1966 GREATER LONDON COUNCIL
Survey of London, Vol. 34,
1966, pp. 464-70. Plans, plates.
1968 MANDER, Raymond and MITCHENSON, Joe.
The lost theatres of London. pp. 58-79. 3 illus.

Location of other material

Plans: G.L.C. *Architects Department.*

Programmes and playbills:

British Museum Library; Enthoven Collection;
Guildhall Library, London Museum; Westminster
Local Collection.

267

EMPRESS THEATRE OF VARIETIES

Carlton Grove (Brighton Terrace), Brixton.

Opened: Boxing Day 1898

Other name

Empress Music-Hall

Later name

Granada Cinema.

Building details

Architects: Messrs. Wylson and Long

Capacity: 1260

Auditorium: A. 580; B. 240; G. 440.

Stage: 60′ wide × 40′ deep.

Management

Lord Chamberlain:

19. 12. 1898-	William Henry Burney
29. 9. 1899-	William John Grimes (to 28. 9. 1900)
10. 1. 1912-	Ilford Ibbetson (music hall licence)
1. 12. 1932-	Walter Payne
1. 12. 1949-	Reginald Charles Bromhead.

London County Council:

1898-	William Henry Burney (Provisional licence)
1900-	Edwin Vine Page
1905-	Nelson Francis
1912-	Ilford Ibbetson
1925-	Syndicate Varieties Ltd.
1932-	Empress Theatre of Varieties Ltd. (to Dec. 1942)
1946-	Empress Theatre of Varieties Ltd. (through 1950).

Literature

Official records:

G.L.C. Arch. Dpt. Th. case 103;
L.C.C. Th. & M-H. Com. App. Nov. 1897-;
LC1/692 and 712;
LC7/46; L.C.O. 374 and 506.

Contemporary accounts:

1897 BUILDER, 1897 May 8, p. 426. —New theatre to
be called 'The Empress'.
1898 BUILDING NEWS, 1898 Dec. 23, p. 823 —Brief
description.

Location of other material

Plans: G.L.C. *Architects Department.*

Folder of cuttings, playbills etc. Enthoven Collection

268

EMPRESS OF RUSSIA PUBLIC HOUSE

132, St. John Street Road (*formerly* 1, Owen's Row).
Clerkenwell.

Licensed: 1885-1889

Building details

Music hall on the first floor, originally formed from
three small rooms.
Closed as a result of the 1878 Act.

Management

Middlesex justices:

Mich. 1885-   Frederick Frampton Beard.

Not licensed by the London County Council.

Literature

Official records:

G.L.C. Arch. Dpt. Th. case 040/45;
L.C.C. Th. & M-H. Com. App. Nov. 1889;
Mx. Mich. Q.S. 1855-88.

Location of other material

Plans: G.L.C. *Architects Department*

269

ENNISMORE ARMS PUBLIC HOUSE

Ennismore Gardens, Westminster.

Licensed: pre 1850-1853.

Management

Middlesex justices:

Mich. 1850-	James Broggreff
" 1851-	Edward Clarke
" 1853	*No petition*

Literature

Official records:

Mx. Mich. Q.S. pre 1850-1853.

270

ENTERPRISE COFFEE TAVERN

37, Peckham High Street, Peckham.

Licensed: c. 1880-85.

Building details

Concert hall on the ground floor behind the coffee shop.

Capacity: 150

The small stage at the north end was fitted with wood and canvas proscenium; the space at the rear was used as dressing rooms.
Closed as a result of the 1878 Act.

Literature

Official records:

G.L.C. Arch. Dpt. Th. case 040/46.

Location of other material

Plans: G.L.C. *Architects Department.*

271

ENTERPRISE PUBLIC HOUSE

Blenheim Road, Islington.

Licensed: 1866-1869.

Management

Middlesex justices:

Mich. 1866-   Thomas Ackland
 "   1869   *No petition.*

Literature

Official records:

Mx. Mich. Q.S. 1866-1869.

272

ETON PUBLIC HOUSE

Adelaide Road, Hampstead.

Licensed: 1856-1866.

Management

Middlesex justices:

Mich. 1856-   John Cuming
 "   1866   *No petition.*

Literature

Official records:

Mx. Mich, Q.S. 1856-1865.

273

EVAN'S MUSIC-AND-SUPPER ROOMS

43, King Street, Covent Garden.

Licensed: 1854-1882 (In use as a place of entertainment prior to 1854).

Later names

Grand Hotel   1854-
Falstaff Club   1880-

Building details

Originally the residence of Sir Kenelm Digby during the reign of Charles II.
1773 it was converted into a family hotel by David Lowe.
Later W.C. Evans converted the basement dining saloon into a song-and-supper room.
1844 John Green (Paddy Green) reconstructed the supper room, converting it into a cafe and vestibule to a new hall.

Architect: Finch Hill.

Cost: £20,000

Capacity: 1000

Management

Middlesex justices:

Mich. 1854-   John Green
 "   1871-   James Barnes
 "   1872-   Barnes Amor
 "   1879   *Licence refused.*
 "   1880-   Barnes Amor
 "   1881-   Harrington Edgar O'Reilly
 "   1882   *Not renewed.*

Literature

Official records:

G.L.C. Arch. Dpt. Th. case 3349.
Mx. Mich. Q.S. 1854-1882;
Sel. Com. 1866 and 1877.

Contemporary accounts:

1855   BUILDER, 1855 Dec. 22, pp. 622-3. —Description of the new singing room of Evans' Hotel. Engraving of interior.
1866? TOWNSEND, G.H. Evans's Music and Supper rooms, Covent Garden. Odds and ends about Covent Garden... London, 1866?
1881   BUILDER; 1881 June 11 and 18, p. 744 and 781. —Report of possible sale and conversion into a club.

Historical accounts:

1895   STUART, C.D., *and* PARK, A.J.
       The Variety stage. pp. 14-21.
1933   DAILY MAIL, 1933 Dec.
       Illus of old time music hall in Covent Garden. (Copy in Enthoven Collection.)
1935   HADDON, Archibald
       The story of the music hall. —Various references.
1938   DISHER, M.W.
       Winkles and champagne. pp. 13, 15 and 17.
1946   SCOTT, Harold
       The early doors. pp. 21+, 43+, and 117+
1952   PULLING, Christopher
       They were singing... p. 111, 168, and 173-5.

Location of other materials

Plans: G.L.C. *Architects Department.*

Playbills: Guildhall Library (10 items. 1856-69)

EVERYMAN THEATRE

Holy Bush Vale, Hampstead.

Opened: 15th September 1920   *Closed as a theatre:*
Nov. 1933

Later name

Everyman Cinema Theatre.

Building details

Originally the Hampstead Drill Hall..
Converted at cost of £10,000.
1929 theatre closed for a short time owing to financial
difficulties.
Everyman Theatre Guild formed with Sir Gerald du
Maurier as president.
August 1931 the Everyman Theatre Club was formed.
Theatre finally closed in November and reopened as
a cinema on 26th December 1933.

Management

London County Council: (s.p.)

1921-	Norman MacDermott (1921 licensed as Hampstead Drill Hall).
1927-	George Garstin Carr
1928-	Milton Rosmer
1930-	Malcolm Morley
1932-	Consuelo Mary de Reyes
1933-	Charles Frederick Wales
1934-	Consuelo Mary de Reyes
Nov. 1943	*Not licensed as theatre.*

London County Council: (m.d.l.)

1928-	Everyman Productions Ltd.
1932-	Consuelo Mary de Reyes
1933-	Theatrical Service Ltd.
1934-	Consuelo Mary de Reyes
1935-	Repertory Entertainments Ltd.
Nov. 1943	*Not licensed.*

Literature

Official records:

G.L.C. Arch. Dpt. Th. case 144;
L.C.C. Th. & M-H. Com. App. Nov. 1920-1942.

Contemporary accounts:

1920	HAMPSTEAD AND HIGHGATE EXPRESS, 1920 Aug. 7 and Sept. 11.—Reports on opening. ARCHITECTS JOURNAL, 1920 Dec. 22, p. 675. 2 figs. FRIENDS of the Everyman Theatre. n.d. 9p. —Gives aims of enterprise and lists productions. (Copy in Hampstead Local Collection.)
1928	EVERYMAN theatre in danger. 1928. 4p. —Appeal for support. (Copy in Hampstead Local Collection.)

Location of other material

Plans: G.L.C. *Architects Department.*

Programmes: Enthoven Collection; Westminster
Local Collection

EXMOUTH ARMS PUBLIC HOUSE

1, Exmouth Street, Hampstead Road.

Licensed: 1858-1869

Management

Middlesex justices:

Mich.	1858-	William Woodin
"	1859-	William Glasgow
"	1862-	Thomas Austin
"	1864-	John Elliott
"	1866-	John Ruddock
"	1868-	Alfred Baker Vicary
"	1869	*Refused on police report.*

Literature

Official records:

Mx. Mich. Q.S. 1858-1869.

FALCON PUBLIC HOUSE

Victoria Park Square, Cambridge Road,
Bethnal Green.

Licensed: 1861-1887.

Management:

Middlesex justices:

Mich.	1861-	James Macaire
"	1878-	George Butler
"	1885-	Frederick Powell
"	1887	*Licence refused:*

Literature:

Official records:

Mx. Mich. Q.S. 1861-1887.

FATHER RED CAP PUBLIC HOUSE AND MUSIC HALL

Cambridge High Street, Camberwell.

Licensed: 1857-1889.

Management

Surrey justices:

Mich.	1857-	Walter Hooker
"	1859-	Eliza Williams
"	1862-	Thomas Kitchin
"	1865-	James Job
"	1880-	John Gannaway
"	1884-	George Henry Wrigglesworth
"	1886-	Henry King. (through 1889)

Application to L.C.C. withdrawn by Henry King, Nov.
1889.

Literature

Official records:

L.C.C. Th. & M-H. Com. App. Nov. 1889;
Sel. Com. 1892; Sy. Mich. Q.S. 1857-1888.

Location of other material

Playbills:

Camberwell Local Collection contains transcript of a playbill (in private hands).
'A grand extra night of music and drama on Monday, 2nd December 1867, at the 'Father Red Cap' Music Hall, Camberwell Green'.
c.f. CAMBERWELL CALLING, 1965 Jan. p. 2. 'Night out'.

278

FINSBURY PARK EMPIRE

St. Thomas's Road and Prah Road, Finsbury Park.

Opened: 5th September 1910   *Closed:* 7th May 1960.

Building details

Built for Moss Empires' Ltd.

Cost: £45,000.

Capacity: approx. 2000.

Auditorium: P. 513; S. 407; G.C. & Bx. 391; B. 375; G. 452.

Management

London County Council:

1909–	Oswald Stoll
1912–	Sir Horace Edward Moss
1914–	Frank Allen
1921–	Richard Henry Gillespie
1925–	Moss Empires' Ltd. (through 1950)

Lord Chamberlain:

This licence was subsidiary to the L.C.C. licence.

1.11.1911–	Sir Horace Edward Moss
1.12.1913–	Frank Allen
1.12.1920–	Richard Henry Gillespie
1.12.1947–	V. C. Parnell.

Literature

Official records:

G.L.C. Arch. Dpt. Mss. Index;
G.L.C. Arch. Dpt. Th. case 108;
L.C.C. Th. & M-H. Com. App. Nov. 1908–;
L.C.C. Th. & M-H. Com. Papers 1905–;
L.C.O. 374 and 497.

Contemporary accounts:

1910   BUILDER, 1910 Sept. 24, p. 351. 'New variety theatres...'
1950   THEATRE ownership. p. 127

Location of other material

Plans: G.L.C. *Architects Department*

Programmes: Enthoven Collection; Westminster Local Collection.

Programmes & Cuttings

Islington Local Collection; Enthoven Collection.

279

FIRST SURREY LIGHT HORSE MUSIC HALL

166, Drummond Road, Bermondsey.

Licensed: 1867-1890.

Building details

Hall situated on the first floor of the public house.

Area 47' × 27'.

It had a raised stage, and contained dressing and refreshment rooms.

Capacity: 250.

Closed as a result of the 1878 Act.

It had generally been used twice a week.

Management

Surrey justices:

Mich.	1867–	Joseph Aley
"	1870–	William Henry Green
"	1880–	William Spain
"	1881–	William Henry Green
"	1882–	Thomas McCluer Butt
"	1887–	Joseph Samuel Bullimore
"	1888–	Henry George Wier.

London County Council:

1890	Isaac Levy
Nov. 1890	*Licence not renewed.*

Literature

Official records:

G.L.C. Arch. Dpt. Th. case 040/156
L.C.C. Th. & M-H. Com. App. Nov. 1889;
Sel. Com. 1892; Sy. Mich. Q.S. 1867-1888.

Location of other material

Plans: G.L.C. *Architects Department.*

280

FLORA GARDENS

Wyndham Road, Lambeth.

Licensed: 1853-1862.

Management

Surrey justices:

Mich.	1853–	Richard Lewis
"	1855–	David Humphreys
"	1857–	Frederick Hell(e)well
"	1862	*No petition.*

Literature

Official records:

Sy. Mich. Q.S. 1853-1861.

Historical accounts:

WROTH, Warwick
Cremorne and later London gardens. 1907. pp. 79-80.
—Gives it as being in existence 1849-1857, 1851-4 under James Ellis.

Location of other material

Playbills:

Camberwell Local Collection.
London Museum (in The Pleasure Gardens of South
London. Vol. II. pp. 230-1.)
Guildhall Library.

281

FORESTERS HALL

65, Carlisle Street, Edgware Road.

Licensed: 1867-1871.

Management

Middlesex justices:

Mich.	1867-	Harry Enderson
"	1869-	Charles Sinclair
"	1871	*Refused to* Edwin Croueste.

Literature

Official records:

Mx. Mich. Q.S. 1867-1871.

282

FORESTERS HALL

15, Clerkenwell Road (*formerly* Wilderness Row),
St. Luke's, Finsbury.

Licensed: 1872-1886.

Building details

Area: 2900 sq'.

Capacity: 1600.

Closed as a result of the 1878 Act.

Management

Middlesex justices:

Mich.	1872-	Charles Cannon, W. C. Price, H. T. Swatton, and F. K. Cotton.
"	1876-	*As above* excluding F. K. Cotton.
"	1877-	*As above* with T. J. Dawson.
"	1878-	Ebenezer Arnold, W. C. Price, H. T. Swatton and T. J. Dawson.
"	1886	*Application withdrawn.*

Literature

Official records:

G.L.C. Arch. Dpt. Th. case 040/50;
Mx. Mich. Q.S. 1872-1886; Sel. Com. 1892.

Location of other material

Plans: G.L.C. Architects Department.

283

FORESTERS HALL

Raglan Street, Forest Hill.

Licensed: 1869-1887.

Building details

The hall was on the first floor of a detached building.

Area: 1675 sq'.

Capacity: 300.

The ground floor of the building was used as kitchens,
dressing rooms &c.

Management

West Kent justices:

Mich.	1869-	John S. Hood, W. Roe and John Foreman.
"	1872-	John Foreman and John Perkins.
"	1873-	John S. Hood, John Foreman and John Perkins.
"	1877-	John Foreman and John Perkins.
"	1879-	John Foreman, John Perkins and John S. Sharp.
"	1881-	John S. Sharp. John Foreman and William Dunford.
"	1888	*Not relicensed.*

Literature

Official records:

G.L.C. Arch. Dpt. Th. case 040/51;
W. Kt. Mich. Q.S. 1869-1887.

284

FORESTERS MUSIC HALL

93-95, Cambridge Road (*formerly* Dog Row.)
Bethnal Green.

Licensed: c. 1825   *Closed as a theatre:* 1917.

Former names

Artichoke Public House to 1889
Foresters Music Hall 1889-1901, 1904-16
Royal Foresters Music Hall 1901-04
New Lyric Music Hall 1916-7
New Lyric Theatre   "

The building ultimately became a cinema on the
Odeon circuit.
The cinema was closed in 1962 and the building is
now derelict (1964).

Management

Middlesex justices:

	c. 1850	Mr. Buckhurst.
Mich.	1854-	Thomas Jones.
"	1858-	George John Rogers.
"	1866-	Abraham Charles Moss.
"	1870-	William Stafford Street and Thomas Kite.
"	1871-	Robert Fort.
"	1879-	Charles Merion.
"	1880-	Edward G. Chapman, Jnr.
"	1881-	James Seaward.
"	1884-	Sarah Graydon.
"	1888-	William Lusby.

London County Council:

1890-	William Lusby
1898-	Gilbert Hustings Macdermott.
1902-	William Henry Pannell.
1904-	Frank Macnaghten
1912	*Licensed as a cinema.*

21. 11. 1911-   Frederick Baugh.
26.   2. 1916-   Harry Steinwoolf   (to 30. 11. 1917).

Literature

Official records:

G.L.C. Arch. Dpt. Mss. Index;
G.L.C. Arch. Dpt. Th. case 113;
L.C.C. Th. & M-H. Com. App. Nov. 1889-1911;
L.C.O. 374 and 466; Mx. Mich. Q.S. 1854-1888;
Sel. Com. 1892.

Historical accounts:

1901   ERA. 1901 May 11. Obituary of G. H. Mac-
dermott. illus.
c. 1930   MAYES, Ronald.
The romance of London theatres, No. 186.
1949   RULE, Leonard G. 'Foresters' lives again...'
in The CIRCLE, New series No. 1, Nov. 1949.
1954   WILSON, A. E.   East end entertainment. pp.
215-7.

Location of other material

Plans: G.L.C. *Architects Department;*
Enthoven Collection.

Cuttings & Illustrations: Bethnal Green Local
Collection.

Programmes: Enthoven Collection.

285

FORTUNE THEATRE

Russell Street, Covent Garden.

Opened: 8th November 1924.

Building details

Built for: Laurence Cowen.

Builder: Boris, Ltd.

Architect: Ernest Schaufelberg.

Capacity: (1950) 473.

Auditorium: S. 195; B. 107; U.C. 122; Bx. 20.

Stage: 25′ wide × 26′ deep.

Management

Lord Chamberlain:

1. 12. 1924-   Laurence Cowen
1. 12. 1927-   Tom Walls
1. 12. 1930-   Wilfred Henry Grainger (receiver for
mortgage).
1. 12. 1932-   Laurence Cowen
1. 12. 1933   David Albert Abrahams (through
1950).

Literature

Official records:

G.L.C. Arch. Dpt. Mss. Index; G.L.C. Arch. Dpt. Th.
case 2963;
L.C.O. 282 and 374.

Contemporary accounts:

1922   BUILDER, 1922 Oct. 27, p. 620 and 638.
—Description and drawings of proposed new
theatre.
1924   BUILDER, 1924 Jan. 11, p. 64.
—Illus. of progress.
BUILDER, 1924 May 2, p. 714 and 718-20.
—Detailed description, photographs and plans.
The ERA, 1924 Oct. 30.
FORTUNE THEATRE
Programme for 8th Nov. 1924.
—Contains history of original Fortune in Golden
Lane, and description of the new theatre.
1925   [ZANGWILL, I.]
A brochure issued by the Fortune Theatre, con-
taining a letter by I. Zangwill on his manage-
ment of the theatre.
1931   [AUCTION CATALOGUE]
For sale by auction 16th Jan. 1931. 8p. illus.
1931   THEATRE WORLD, Feb. 1931.
—Announcement of amateur shows.
1932   THEATRE WORLD, Aug. 1932.
—Announcement of amateur shows.
1950   THEATRE ownership... p. 64.

Historical accounts:

c. 1930   MAYES, Ronald
The romance of London theatres, No. 130.
1963   MANDER, Raymond, *and* MITCHENSON, Joe
The theatres of London, 2nd edition. pp. 81-84.

Location of other material

Plans: G.L.C. *Architects Department.*

Programmes:

Enthoven Collection; London Museum; Westminster
Local Collection.

286

FORUM THEATRE

1-4, Greenwood Place, and 9-17 Highgate Road,
Kentish Town.

Licensed: 1935-1939.

Management

Lord Chamberlain:

1. 12. 1935-   Arthur Stanley Moss (to 1. 12. 1939)
—As a music hall.
1. 12. 1939   *Application withdrawn.*

Literature

Official records:

G.L.C. Arch. Dpt. Th. case 1415;
L.C.O. 374 and 469.

Location of other material

Plans: G.L.C. *Architects Department.*

287

FOUNTAIN PUBLIC HOUSE

Deptford Broadway.

Licensed: 1874-1888.

Other name

Old Fountain Public House and Music Hall.

Management

West Kent justices:

Mich.	1874-	James McPherson.
"	1888	*Not relicensed owing to the 1878 Act.*

Literature

Official records:

G.L.C. Arch. Dpt. Th. case 040/101;
W. Kt. Mich. Q.S. 1874-1888.

288

FOUNTAIN PUBLIC HOUSE

Sandy Hill, Woolwich.

Licensed: Pre 1850-1860

Management

West Kent justices:

Mich.	1850-	Alfred William Young.
"	1852-	Hammond Upton.
"	1860	*Not relicensed.*

Literature

Official records:

W. Kt. Mich. Q.S. 1850-60.

289

FOX AND BULL PUBLIC HOUSE

Knightsbridge.

Licensed: pre 1850-1857.

Other name

Royal Harmonic Hall.

Management

Middlesex justices:

Mich.	1848-	George Benns
"	1854-	George Blizard
"	1857	*Not relicensed.*

Literature

Official records:

Mx. Mich. Q.S. pre 1850-1856.

Location of other material

Playbills:

Guildhall Library have scrapbook containing playbill dated 22nd March 1841 for:- 'Royal Harmonic Hall, Fox and Bull Tavern.'

290

FOX AND COCK PUBLIC HOUSE

Grays Inn Lane, Holborn.

Licensed: 1854-1858.

Management

Middlesex justices:

Mich.	1854-	Barry O. Meara Mullins
"	1855-	John Joseph Geary
"	1856-	Hugh Wickstead
"	1857-	Michael Duffy
"	1858-	*Not licensed.*

Literature

Official records.

Mx. Mich. Q.S. 1854-1858.

291

FOX AND FRENCH HORN PUBLIC HOUSE

Clerkenwell Green, Finsbury.

Licensed: 1860-1866.

Management

Middlesex justices:

Mich.	1860-	Leopold Gilling
"	1862-	Elizabeth Gilling
"	1866	*No application.*

Literature

Official records:

Mx. Mich. Q.S. 1860-1865

292

FREEMASON'S PUBLIC HOUSE

Great Queen Street, Holborn.

Licensed: 1878-1898.

Management

Middlesex justices:

Mich.	1878-	Edwin Dawkins
"	1886-	Alfred Madell

London County Council:

	1890-	Joshua Ellis
	1897-	Henry Godbold
Nov.	1898	*Not relicensed.*

Literature

Official records:

L.C.C. Th. & M-H. Com. App. Nov. 1889-97;
Mx. Mich. Q.S. 1878-88.

293

FREEMASON'S ARMS PUBLIC HOUSE

Salmon's Lane, Limehouse.

Licensed: 1856-1891.

Management

Middlesex justices:

Mich.	1856-	Charles Thomas Pike (through 1888)

London County Council:

1890-	Charles Thomas Pike
Nov. 1891	*No application.*

Literature

Official records:

L.C.C. Th. & M-H. Com. App. Nov. 1889-1890;
Mx. Mich. Q.S. 1856-1888.

294

FREEMASON'S ARMS PUBLIC HOUSE

19, Suffolk Street, Kings Cross.

Licensed: 1855-1868.

Management

Middlesex justices:

Mich.	1855-	Richard Ryall
"	1858-	Charles Thomas Sutton
"	1860-	Cornelius David Watkins
"	1861-	George Tilley
"	1868	*No petition.*

Literature

Official records:

Mx. Mich. Q.S. 1855-1868.

295

GAIETY THEATRE

354, Strand, Westminster.

Opened: 1862 *Closed:* 4th July 1903.

Former name

Strand Musick Hall (1864-68).

Building details

1st building:

Architect: E. Bassett Keeling.

Contractors: Messrs Trollope and Sons.

Decorations: George Foxley

2nd building:

Opened: 21.12.1868.

Architect: C.J. Phipps.

Cost: £15,000

Capacity: 1126.

Auditorium: S. 160; P. 200; B. 126; Bx. 240; G. 400.

Management

Middlesex justices:

Mich.	1864-	Robert Syers
"	1866-	*Licence refused.*
"	1885-	Felix William Spiers

Lord Chamberlain:

19.12.1868-	John Hollingshead
1.12.1886-	George Edwardes (to July 1903).

Literature

Official records:

G.L.C. Arch. Dpt. Th. case 04;
L.C.C. Th. & M-H. Com. Papers 1888-1903;
LC7/15-17, 24-48, and 89;
M.B.W. Rpt. 1882, pp. 47-62.
Mx. Mich. Q.S. 1864-6, 1885-8;
Sel. Com. 1892, App. 392-95 and para. 24 & 25.

Contemporary accounts:

1862	BUILDER, 1862 Oct. 25, p. 768.—Report on proposed erection.
1864	ERA, 1864 Oct. 16.—Report of opening and detailed description.
1868	TIMES, 1868 Dec. 11.—'New Gaiety Theatre' description.
	ERA, 1868 Dec. 13.—Detailed description.
	BUILDING NEWS, 1868 Dec. 25, p. 879—Detailed description.
	BUILDER, 1868 Dec. 26. pp. 941-2—Detailed decription.
	ERA, 1868 Dec. 27.—Report of opening.
1869	BUILDING NEWS, 1869 Jan. 1.—Plate after p. 32 —plan & illus. of auditorium.
	ILLUSTRATED LONDON NEWS, 1869 Jan. 2, p. 20.—Illus. of auditorium and description of theatre.
	BUILDING NEWS, 1869 March 19, p. 251. Plates of lunettes by N.S. Marks.
1879	DRAMATIC NOTES, 1879. pp. 22-28.
1882	SHAW, E.M. Report of Gaiety Theatre, 1882.
1886	DAILY TELEGRAPH, 1886 Sept. 27.—Report of redecoration.
1887	SATURDAY REVIEW, 1887 June 18. State of the London theatres...No. 2.
1889	BUILDING NEWS, 1889 Sept. 20, pp. 380-1. —Description of 'Indian' style redecoration.
	BUILDER, 1889 Sept. 21, p. 214.—Description of redecoration.
1896	SKETCH, 1896 April 22, pp. 571-2. 'Behind the scenes. No. IV. The Gaiety Theatre'.
1903	BUILDER, 1903 Sept. 12., pp. 266-77.—Report on old Gaiety (in process of demolition) and its site.
	DAILY GRAPHIC, 1903 July 6, p. 4 'Last night at the Gaiety': report.

Historical accounts:

1871	The STRAND musick hall: historic of ye bylding... (anon.) The Strand Musick Hall, 1871, 16p.
1898	HOLLINGSHEAD, John. Gaiety chronicles... Archibald Constable, 1898. 493p. illus., ports., facsims.
1903	GORDON, Charles Old time Aldwych...p. 12, 207, 209-213.
	HOLLINGSHEAD, John. 'Good Old Gaiety' an historiette and remembrance. Gaiety Theatre Co., 1903. 78p. ports.
1904	BAKER, H. Barton. History of the London stage and its players. pp. 338-42, and p. 542.
c.1930	MAYES, Ronald The romance of London theatres, No. 67 and 190.
1935	HADDON, Archibald. The story of the music hall, p. 41.

For items on the history of both Gaiety Theatres see list at end of entry 296

Location of other material

Plans:

G.L.C. *Architects Department;* Enthoven Collection, 1903 (3 sheets).

Public Record Office. LC7/57.—Section, elevations and plans.

Programmes & playbills:

Enthoven Collection; Guildhall Library; London Museum.

296

GAIETY THEATRE

Aldwych.

Opened: 26th October 1903 *Closed after* 1950.

Building details

The second Gaiety was built on corporate property to reinstate the old theatre which was demolished for the formation of the Aldwych. The L.C.C. contributed £50,000 to the cost of rebuilding.

Architect: Ernest Runtz, and George McLean Ford.

Contractor: Henry Lovatt.

Capacity: 1267.

Auditorium: S. & Bx. 241; P. 270; D.C. & Bx. 196; U.C. & Bx. 260; G. 300.

Proscenium 30' × 32'

Management:

Lord Chamberlain:

1.11.1904-	George Edwardes
11.12.1916-	Alfred Butt
23.10.1920-	George Grossmith and Edward Laurillard
1.10.1921-	Thomas Francis Dawe and William Cooper
1.12.1922-	Robert Evett and William Cooper
1.12.1924-	Horace Fry and William Cooper
1.12.1926-	William Clifford Gaunt
1.12.1931-	George Brinton McLellan
1.12.1932-	James Ernest Sharpe
1.12.1933-	Thomas Henry Bostock (not licensed after 1939).

Literature

Official records:

G.L.C. Arch. Dpt. Th. case 427;
L.C.C. Th. & M-H. Com. Papers 1900-;
L.C.O. 240 and 374.

Contemporary accounts:

1899 BUILDER, 1899 Oct. 28, p. 400. 'London theatres old and new'.—Report on plans of Mr. Runtz.
1901 BUILDING NEWS, 1901 Aug. 23, p. 243.—Note and plate of exterior of proposed theatre.
1902 SKETCH, 1902 May 14.—Illus. of exterior, description of proposed interior.
      BUILDING NEWS, 1902 Sept. 26, p. 430.—Note, plans & plate of Strand elevation.
1903 SKETCH, 1903 Sept. 30.—Illus. of interior.
      TATLER, 1903 Oct. 14.—Description.
ERA, 1903 Oct. 17.—Detailed description.
BUILDING NEWS, 1903 Oct. 23, pp. 542-3. 'New Gaiety'—article on rebuilding, including detailed description.
BUILDER, 1903 Oct. 24, p. 413.—Description.
BUILDERS JOURNAL & ARCHITECTS RECORD, 1903 Nov. 4, pp. 182-6.
1904 ARCHITECTS REVIEW, 1904 March, pp. 89-93
      BUILDER, 1904 May 7, pp. 499-500.—Report of arbitrator's sitting, Gaiety v. L.C.C. Claim by theatre for £25,000.
1905 BUILDER, 1905 Dec. 30, pp. 699-700.—Detailed description of Gaiety Theatre, Hotel and Restaurant.
      BUILDING NEWS, 1905 Feb. 24, p. 298.—Report of payment of £17,217 to Gaiety Company for additional expenditure incurred by ornate character of building required.

Historical accounts:

1913 NAYLOR, S.
      Gaiety and George Grossmith.
      Stanley Paul, 1913.
c. 1930 MAYES, Ronald.
      The romance of London theatres, No. 99.
1948 POPE, W. Macqueen
      Gaiety, glamour and girls: a glimpse of the Old Gaiety Theatre. *in* The QUEEN, 1948 Nov. 24.
1950 BUILDER, 1950 June 21, p. 86. illus.
      'Gaiety Theatre to make way 1or an office block'.—history.

Gaiety Theatre, Aldwych (296)

(Greater London Council Photograph Library)

Location of other material:

Plans: G.L.C. *Architects Department.*

Programmes and playbills:

Enthoven Collection; London Museum; Westminster
Local Collection.

Works covering the history of both theatres:

1923 JUPP, James.
      The Gaiety stage door: thirty years'
      reminiscences of the theatre.
      Cape, 1923. 352p.
1925 CHANCELLOR, E. B.
      The pleasure haunts of London... pp. 138-9.
1949 POPE, W. Macqueen.
      Gaiety: theatre of enchantment.
      W. H. Allen, 1949. 498p. plates.
1952 PULLING, Christopher
      They were singing... pp. 182, 193-6, 210, 213,
      220, 231.
1959 ENCICLOPEDIA dello spettacolo, Vol. 6, Col.
      1622-3.
1968 MANDER, Raymond *and* MITCHENSON, Joe.
      The lost theatres of London. pp. 80-119. 6 illus.

297

GALLERY OF ILLUSTRATION

14, Regent Street, Westminster.

Licensed: 1856-1873.

Building details

Cost: £5000

Capacity: 500

Management

Lord Chamberlain:

26. 1. 1856-   Thomas Grieve and William Telbin.
Oct. 1860-   Special limited licences for Mr.
               German Reed's Entertainment—
               Thomas German Reed.
Not licensed after 1875.

Middlesex justices:

Mich. 1855-   Thomas Grieve
  "   1856-   Thomas German Reed
  "   1871-   *No petition.*

Literature

Official records:

LC7/13, 15 and 23.
Mx. Mich. Q.S. 1856-71.

Historical accounts:

1952 PULLING, Christopher
      They were singing... pp. 137-9.

Location of other material

Programmes: Enthoven Collection.

298

GARRICK PUBLIC HOUSE

70, Leman Street, Whitechapel.

Licensed: 1856-1896.

Other name

Garrick Hall of Varieties.

Management

Middlesex justices:

Mich. 1856-   William Davis
  "   1859-   John Morris
  "   1864-   Benjamin Phillips
  "   1867-   Frederick Hofsommer
  "   1877-   Eli Perry
  "   1878-   Solomon Temple
  "   1882-   William Martin Assiter
  "   1886-   Alfred Herring

London County Council:

      1890   Charlotte Reeves
      1891-   Arthur Leopold Simons
      1893   Alfred Church
      1894-   Charlotte Reeves
      1896   David Packman
Nov. 1896   *Licence refused.*

Literature

Official records:

G.L.C. Arch. Dpt. th. case 026;
L.C.C. Th. & M-H. Com. App. Nov. 1889-96;
Mx. Mich. Q.S. 1856-1888.

Location of other material

Plans: G.L.C. *Architects Department.*

299

GARRICK THEATRE

Charing Cross Road, Westminster.

Opened: 24th April 1889.

Building details

Built for: W. S. Gilbert

Architect: Walter Emden, with C. J. Phipps.

Contractor: Messrs. Peto.

Capacity: 773.

Auditorium: S. 419; D.C. 132; U.C. 114; Bx. A-L.

Management

Lord Chamberlain:

10. 4. 1889-   John Hare
 1. 12. 1896-   William Greet
 1. 12. 1897-   Harry Thomas Brickwell
 1. 12. 1900-   Arthur Bouchier
 4. 5. 1910-   Gilbert Portious
12. 5. 1910-   Herbert Sleath
13. 6. 1910-   Herbert Sleath and Arthur Bouchier
 1. 12. 1913-   Arthur Bouchier
 1. 12. 1914-   Herbert Sleath and Arthur Bouchier
15. 10. 1915-   Thomas Dott
 8. 10. 1917-   Gilbert Heron Miller
 1. 4. 1918-   Charles Blake Cochran
 1. 12. 1924-   David Albert Abrahams (except
                1940-1)
 1. 12. 1946-   Gilbert Brown (through 1950).

London County Council:

1935-1940   Abram Emanuel Abrahams.

Literature

Official records:

G.L.C. Arch. Dpt. Mss Index; G.L.C. Arch. Dpt. Th.
case 428;
L.C.C. Th. & M-H. Com. App. Nov. 1934-39.
L.C.C. Th. & M-H. Com. Papers 1888-;
LC1/525-752; LC7/36-48;
L.C.O. 352 and 374;
Sel. Com. 1892.

Contemporary account:

1888 BUILDER, 1888 May 26, p. 384.—Report on
      proposed new theatre.
      BUILDER, 1888 June 30, pp. 468-9.—Description,
      plan and section, illus. of exterior elevation.
1889 ERA, 1889 April 17.—Description.
      DAILY TELEGRAPH, 1889 April 24.—Descrip-
      tion.
1889 STAGE, 1889 April 24.-Description.
      BUILDING NEWS, 1889 April 26, p. 605—Note of
      opening.
      BUILDING NEWS, 1889 May 3, p. 638—Correction
      BUILDING NEWS, 1889 May 10, p. 673—Correc-
      tion.
      BUILDER, 1889 May 4, p. 330.—Detailed des-
      cription.
1897 SACHS, E.O., *and* WOODROW, E.A.E.
      Modern opera houses and theatres. Vol. 2, p. 38.—
      Description, dimensions, plans, elevations and
      sections.
1950 THEATRE ownership... pp. 73-4, and 107-8.

Historical accounts:

1904 BAKER, H. Barton.
      History of the London stage and its players.
      pp. 526-8.
c. 1930 MAYES, Ronald.
      The romance of London theatres, No. 24.
1963 MANDER, Raymond *and* MITCHENSON, Joe.
      The theatres of London. 2nd ed. pp. 85-89.

Location of other material

Plans:

G.L.C. *Architects Department.*
Public Record Office. LC7/49. 10 sheets.

Programmes:

British Museum Library; Enthoven Collection;
Guildhall Library; London Museum; Westminster
Local Collection.

300

GARRICK THEATRE

70, Leman Street, Whitechapel.

Opened: January 1831 *Closed:* c. 1881

Other names

Albert and Garrick Royal Amphitheatre 1854
New Albert Theatre 1873
New Prince's Theatre 1878
Prince's Theatre 1878
Garrick Theatre 1831-, 1879-

Building details

1st building:

Developer: Benjamin Conquest.

Burnt down: Nov. 1846.

2nd building:

Opened: 1854

Reconstructed: 1873.

Reconstructed: 1879.

Capacity: 462.

Auditorium: S. 54, P. 230; B. 70; G. 108.

Management

Lord Chamberlain:

29. 9.1843-   Benjamin Oliver Conquest (to
               4. 11. 1946).
19. 12.1854-   Lawrence Levy
29. 10.1864-   John Seymour
26. 12.1864-   Charles Edwards (to 28. 9. 1865).
(Not licensed 28. 9. 1865-26. 12. 1867)
26. 12.1867-   Lawrence Levy
13. 3.1868-   Charles Spencer Crowder (to
               21. 5. 1869).
 2. 4.1870-   Linda Bertram (to 2. 5. 1870)
18. 8.1870-   James Richards
 2. 8.1873-   Thomas Burdett Howe (to
               29. 12. 1873)
27. 2.1875-   John Walter Scott (to 28. 8. 1875)
24. 12.1875-   Thomas Eplett and George Gill
               (to 28. 9. 1876)
20. 4.1878-   Arthur Henderson
30. 5.1879-   May Bulwer
29. 11.1880-   Charles Wentworth (to Nov. 1881).

Literature

Official records:

G.L.C. Arch. Dpt. Th. case 026;
LC7/13-16, 20-23, 26-29.
M.B.W. Rpt. 1882, pp. 103-111.
Sel. Com. 1866, 1877, and 1892.

Contemporary accounts:

1846 ILLUSTRATED LONDON NEWS, 1846 Nov. 7.
      —Garrick burnt down.
1873 BUILDER, 1873 Sept. 13, pp. 720-21. 'The last
      of the 'Gaffs''.

Historical accounts:

1893 EDWARDS, Francis. *Bookseller*
      Playbills: a collection and some comments.
      pp. 25-30.
1904 BAKER, H. Barton.
      History of the London stage and its players.
      p. 406.
1925 CHANCELLOR, E. B.
      The pleasure haunts of London... pp. 132-3.
      SHERSON, Erroll.
      London's lost theatres... pp. 38-9.
c. 1930 MAYES, Ronald
      The romance of London theatres, No. 162.
1953 FLEETWOOD, Frances.
      Conquest: the story of a theatre family. pp.
      32-54.

1954 WILSON, A. E.
    East end entertainment.
    -Chapter IX. Ups and downs at the Garrick.
1959 ENCICLOPEDIA dello spettacolo. Vol. 6, Col.
    1623.
    -Leman Street and Charing Cross Road.

Location of other material

Plans:

G.L.C. *Architects Department*
Public Record Office. LC7/58. Ground plans and
sections.

Programmes and playbills:

British Museum Library, Playbills 399;
Enthoven Collection; Guildhall Library;
Stepney Local Collection.

301

GATE THEATRE

18, Chepstow Villas, Kensington.

In use: c. 1944-

Other names

Gateway Theatre
Threshold Theatre
Chepstow (Theatre) Club.
Actors Theatre
Estonian Theatre

Management

A theatre club, not licensed by the authorities.

Literature

Official records:

G.L.C. Arch. Dpt. Th. case 745.

Historical accounts:

1944 THEATRE ARTS, 1944 June, p. 29.
    'London's little theatres: the work of the Gate-
    way and the Chanticleer.'
1950 FERGUSON, Rachel.
    Royal borough. J. Cape, 1950. pp. 267-268.

Location of other material

British Museum Library. (Prospectus for 1932-3
season).

302

GATE THEATRE

18, Villiers Street, Charing Cross.

Opened: 30th October 1925 *Closed:* c. 1942.

Management

A theatre club, not licensed by the authorities.
Managers: 1925- Peter Godfrey; 1933- Norman
Marshall.

Location of other material

Programmes:

Enthoven Collection; London Museum; Westminster
Local Collection.

In Spring 1966, reported that theatre was to reopen
as Villiers Theatre.

303

GATTI'S PALACE OF VARIETIES

214-6, Westminster Bridge Road, Lambeth.

Opened: 1865
Closed as a theatre; 1924.
Demolished: 1950.

Also known as

Gatti's-in-the-Road
Gatti's-over-the-Water
Gatti's Music Hall.

Building details

Rebuilt: 1883.

Architect: Mr. Bolton of Lincolns Inn Fields.

Contractor: G. Gaisford.

Capacity: 1183.

Auditorium: A. 454; B. 236.

Blitzed in 2nd World War, later demolished for road
widening.

Management

Surrey justices:

Mich.	1865-	Carlo Gatti
"	1878-	Maria Gatti and Rosa Corazza.
"	1879-	Giacomo and Luigi Corazza.

London County Council:

	1890-	Giacomo and Luigi Corazza
	1911-	William Hutton
	1912	John Hinton Bailey
	1913-	Hector Munro
Nov.	1925	*Not listed as theatre or cinema.*

Literature

Official records:

G.L.C. Arch. Dpt. Mss. Index;
G.L.C. Arch. Dpt. Th. case 122;
L.C.C. Th. & M-H. Com. App. Nov. 1889-1924;
Sel. Com. 1877 and 1892; Sy. Mich. Q.S. 1865-88.

Contemporary accounts:

1883 BUILDER, 1883 March 24, pp. 394-5.—Descrip-
    tion of rebuilt theatre.
1887 SATURDAY REVIEW, 1887 August. The state of
    the London. . .music halls, No. 2.

Historical accounts:

c. 1930 MAYES, Ronald
    The romance of London theatres, No. 206.
1935 HADDON, Archibald
    The story of the music hall. pp. 15, 37, 41.
1938 DISHER, M.W.
    Winkles and champagne. pp. 28, 90, 103, 114.

Location of other material

Plans:

G.L.C. *Architects Department.*
Enthoven Collection. 1914 (1 sheet)-cinema.

Folder of newscuttings, playbills &c. Enthoven Collection.

304

GEORGE PUBLIC HOUSE

Fosters' Building, St. Luke's, Finsbury.

Licensed: 1864-1869.

Management

Middlesex justices:

Mich. 1864-	Joseph Springett
" 1867-	Thomas Jones
" 1869	*Licence refused.*

Literature

Official records:

Mx. Mich. Q.S. 1864-1869.

305

GEORGE PUBLIC HOUSE

91 (formerly 108), Old Street. Shoreditch.

Licensed: 1852-1879.

Management

Middlesex justices:

Mich. 1852-	Joseph Mincer Pugh
" 1855-	William Bowden
" 1861-	John Baker
" 1862-	Alfred John Bowden
" 1873-	Thomas Layborn
" 1879	*No licence granted.*

Literature

Official records:

Mx. Mich. Q.S. 1852-1879.

306

GEORGE AND DRAGON PUBLIC HOUSE

15, Hoxton Market, Shoreditch.

Licensed: 1861-1868.

Former name

George Public House.

Management

Middlesex justices:

Mich. 1861-	Thomas Smith
" 1865-	James Fletcher
" 1868	*Licence refused owing to sale of exciseable liquors.*

Literature

Official records:

Mx. Mich Q.S. 1861-1868.

307

GEORGE AND VULTURE PUBLIC HOUSE

Haberdasher Street, Pitfield Street, Hoxton.

Licensed: 1863-1867.

Management

Middlesex justices:

Mich. 1863-	James Blyth
" 1866-	Ingle Few
" 1867	*No petition.*

Literature

Official records:

Mx. Mich. Q.S. 1863-1867

Gatti's Palace of Varieties, Lambeth (303)

(Greater London Council Photograph Library)

308

GEORGE THE FOURTH PUBLIC HOUSE

Edward Street, Regent's Park.

Licensed: 1854-1860.

Management

Middlesex justices:

Mich. 1854-		Horatio Mearing
"	1858-	Thomas Alfred Young
"	1860	*No petition.*

Literature

Official records:

Mx. Mich. Q. S. 1854-1860.

309

GEORGE THE FOURTH PUBLIC HOUSE

Royal Mint Street, Whitechapel.

Licensed: 1856-1858.

Management

Middlesex justices:

Mich. 1856-		Martin St. Ledger
"	1858-	*No petition.*

Literature

Official records:

Mx. Mich. Q. S. 1856-1858.

310

GIPSY QUEEN PUBLIC HOUSE

166, Malden Road, Kentish Town.

Licensed: 1861-1892

Management

Middlesex justices:

Mich. 1861-		George Hill
"	1862-	Mary Frances Hill
"	1863-	Henry Hill
"	1866-	Benjamin Young
"	1868-	John Young
"	1869-	John Pick
"	1870-	Walter William Cann
"	1874-	William Wilce Key
"	1875-	Susannah Page
"	1876-	James Albert Woollhead
"	1878-	Charles Clarke
"	1884-	Walter Pellant
"	1888-	Arthur Sherras

London County Council:

	1890-	Thomas Henry Payne (licence retained).
Nov.	1891-	*No application.*

Literature

Official records:

L.C.C. Th & M-H Com. App. Nov. 1889-90;
Mx. Mich. Q. S. 1861-1888.

311

GLASS HOUSE PUBLIC HOUSE

344, Edgware Road, St. Marylebone.

Licensed: 1879-1881.

Management

Middlesex justices:

Mich. 1879-		George Curtis.
"	1881-	*No petition.*

Literature

Official records:

Mx. Mich Q. S. 1879-1881.

312

GLOBE PUBLIC HOUSE

Lower road, (*Formerly* Evelyn Street) Deptford.

Licensed: 1859-1882.

Management

West Kent Justices:

Mich. 1859-		Vincent Lambert Pascoe
(1861-1865 Records missing)		
Mich. 1866-		Philip James Shelley
"	1876-	John Palmer Morton
"	1877-	John Welshman
"	1882	*No application.*

Literature

Official records:

W. Kt. Mich. Q. S. 1859-60, 1866-81.

313

GLOBE PUBLIC HOUSE

Charles Street, Hatton Garden, Holborn.

Licensed: 1854-1862.

Management.

Middlesex justices:

Mich. 1854-		John Draper
"	1857-	Joseph Skidmore Draper
"	1859-	George Hockley
"	1860-	James Fraser
"	1862	*No petition.*

Literature

Official records:

Mx. Mich. Q. S. 1854-1861.

314

GLOBE PUBLIC HOUSE

Elizabeth Street, St. George in the East.

Licensed: 1855-1868.

Management.

Middlesex justices:

Mich. 1855-   Thomas Midgley
  "   1857-   Margaret Midgley
  "   1868   *Licence refused because of Sunday trading.*

Literature

Official records:

Mx. Mich. Q. S. 1855-1868.

315

GLOBE THEATRE

Francis Street, Newington.

Active 1850's

Former name: Newington hall.

Southwark Local Collection includes transcripts of playbills announcing performances of Othello and other plays.
1855 Transcript of playbill dated 15. 11. 1855 first names hall 'Globe'.
1856 Names of F. Preece and Alfred Nicholls are given as managers on transcript dated 6. 10. 1856.

316

GLOBE THEATRE

Newcastle Street, Strand.

Opened: 28th November 1868.   *Closed:* March 1902.

Other name

Royal Globe Theatre.

Building details

Built on the site of Lyon's Inn, the theatre was constructed on part of the foundation, which had been laid for the Strand Hotel.

Built for: Sefton Parry.

Builder: Samuel Simpson.

Capacity: Approx. 1000.

Auditorium: S. 172; P. 277, D. C. 102; U. C. 72; A. 55; G. 204; Bx. 44.

Management

Lord Chamberlain:

28. 11. 1868-	Sefton Parry
27. 12. 1869-	Fanny Josephs
29. 9. 1870-	Bessie Alleyne
21. 4. 1871-	Richard Mansell
7. 10. 1871-	Henry James Montague
26. 9. 1874-	Francis Charles Fairlie
1. 1. 1875-	Alexander Henderson
16. 4. 1876-	Francis Charles Fairlie
29. 10. 1880-	George Philips
17. 1. 1881-	William Augustus Burt
21. 10. 1881-	Francis Maitland
29. 9. 1884-	Charles Henry Hawtrey

4. 12. 1887-	Wilson Barrett
1. 10. 1888-	John Lart
21. 12. 1888-	Richard Mansfield
22. 10. 1889-	Robert Rodford
29. 9. 1890-	George Paget
9. 1. 1891-	Norman Forbes Robertson
28. 9. 1891-	Edward Michael
28. 9. 1893-	William Sidney Penley
28. 9. 1898-	Romer Williams
28. 9. 1900-	William Greet (to 1902)

Literature

Official records:

G.L.C. Arch. Dpt. Th case 012;
L.C.C. Th. & M-H. Com. Papers 1888-1909;
LC 1/508-752; LC7/15-17, 24-48, and 89;
M.B.W. Rpt. 1882, pp 111-125;
Sel. Com. 1877 and 1892.

Contemporary accounts:

1868	ERA, 1868 Nov. 29—Detailed description of opening.
	BUILDER, 1868 Dec. 5, p 885—Description.
1869	ILLUSTRATED LONDON NEWS, 1869 Jan. 16. Illus of Interior.—Description.
1870	ERA. 1870 Oct. 9—Description of re-decoration
1879	DRAMATIC NOTES, 1879 pp. 47-8
1887	SATURDAY REVIEW, 1887 June 18. The state of London theatres, No. 2.

Historical accounts:

1903	GORDON, C.
	Old time Aldwych. . . pp 242-4.
1904	BAKER, H. Barton
	History of the London stage and its players. pp. 330-4.
1925	CHANCELLOR, E. B.
	The pleasure haunts of London. p. 140.
	SHERSON, Erroll
	London's lost theatres. . . pp. 237-253.
c. 1930	MAYES, Ronald.
	The romance of London theatres, No. 84.
1958	THEATRE WORLD, 1958 Oct.
	Lost London theatres, by N. M. Bligh. No. 12. The story of the Globe, East Strand. 3p. illus.
1968	MANDER, Raymond *and* MITCHENSON, Joe. The lost theatres of London. pp. 130-143. 2 illus.

Location of other material

Plans: G.L.C *Architects Department.*

Programmes and playbills:

Enthoven Collection; London Museum; Westminster Local collection.

317

GLOBE THEATRE

Shaftesbury Avenue, Westminster.

Opened: 27th December 1906

Former name

Hicks Theatre (to July 1909)

Building details

Built for: Charles Frohman and Seymour Hicks, in association with Jacobus-Marler Estates Ltd.

Architect: W. G. R. Sprague.

Builder: Walter Wallis of Balham.

Capacity: 970.

Auditorium: S. 261; P. 114; D.C. 189; U.C. 150; G. 150; Bx. 16.

Stage: 30' wide, 21' 1" high, 38' deep.

Management

Lord Chamberlain:

24.12.1906-	Charles Frohman (to 25.12.1913-end of lease).
1. 1.1914-	Alfred Beyfus.
9. 3.1914-	Alfred Butt
1.12.1930-	Maurice Browne
1.12.1933-	Harold Gosling (through 1950).

Literature

Official records:

G.L.C. Arch. Dpt. Mss. Index;
G.L.C. Arch. Dpt. Th. case 430;
L.C.C. Th. & M-H. Com. Papers 1904-;
L.C.O. 374 and 446.

Contemporary accounts:

1904 BUILDER, 1904 Aug. 27, p. 221—Brief report of new theatre for Mr. and Mrs. Hicks.
1906 BUILDER, 1906 Dec. 29, P. 750—Brief report of erection, with description.

Historical accounts

c.1930	MAYES, Ronald	
	The romance of London theatres, No. 36.	
1959	ENCICLOPEDIA dello spettacolo, Vol. 6. Col. 1623-5.	
	—Covers all Globe Theatres.	
1963	LONDON. County Council.	
	Survey of London. St. James. Vols. 31 and 32. pp. 71, 78-81. Plates 36a, 37a, Plan of dress circle (1924).	
1963	MANDER, Raymond *and* MITCHENSON, Joe	
	The theatres of London. 2nd edition. pp. 90-94.	

Location of other material

Plans: G.L.C. *Architects Department;* Enthoven Collection 1906 (4 sheets).

Programmes and Playbills:

Enthoven Collection; Guildhall Library; Westminster Local Collection.

318

GLOBE AND FRIENDS PUBLIC HOUSE

13, Morgan Street, St. George-in-the-East.

Licensed: 1855-1868.

Management

Middlesex justices:

Mich. 1855-	James Spikes
" 1868	*Licence refused to* Edward Hibbered.

Literature

Official records:

Mx. Mich. Q. S. 1855-1868.

319

GLOUCESTER PUBLIC HOUSE

King Street, (*later* King William Street), Greenwich.

Licensed: 1869-1902.

Building details

Capacity: 250.

Management

West Kent Justices:

Mich. 1869-	William Fisher
" 1873-	Kate Helena Fisher
" 1878-	Frederick Malyon

London County Council:

1890-	Frederick Malyon
1891-	William Hillyard
1894-	Frederick Maylon
Nov. 1902-	*Not licensed.*

Literature

Official records:

L.C.C. Th & M-H. Com. App. Nov. 1889-1901;
Sel. Com. 1892;
W. Kt. Mich. Q. S. 1869-1888.

320

No entry.

321

GOLDEN EAGLE PUBLIC HOUSE

234, Shadwell High Street, Shadwell.

Licensed: 1854-1885.

Management

Middlesex justices:

Mich. 1854-	William Abraham Scott
" 1856-	James Lugg
" 1860-	George Potterell
" 1861-	William Pinsent Hummerton
" 1862-	Robert Ross
" 1863-	Charles Edward Williams.
" 1865-	George Hayman
" 1867-	John Booty
" 1873-	Walter Sargent
" 1877-	Thomas Gibbs
" 1878-	William James Playle
" 1881-	Thomas Ould
" 1885	*Licence refused.*

Literature

Official records:

Mx. Mich. Q. S. 1854-1885.

322

GOLDEN LION PUBLIC HOUSE

Britannia Street, St. Pancras.

Licensed: 1854-1864.

Management

Middlesex justices:

Mich.	1854-	John Greenwood
"	1861-	George Lewin
"	1864	*No petition.*

Literature

Official records

Mx. Mich. Q. S. 1854-1864.

323

GOLDEN LION PUBLIC HOUSE AND PALACE OF VARIETIES

14, Sydenham Road, Lower Sydenham.

Licensed: 1855-1897.

Management

West Kent Justices:

Mich.	1855-	James Trehearne
"	1859-	Susannah Trehearne

(Records missing 1860-1865)

Mich.	1866-	William Smith
"	1868-	Alfred Field
"	1874-	James Lovell Batley
"	1875-	John Joseph Dawson
"	1876-	Benjamin Picking
"	1877-	Thomas Grinham
"	1880-	William Luke Mason
"	1883-	Frank Thomas Mason
"	1884	William Cobb

London County Council:

1890-	William Cobb
1891-	Alfred Kindred
1893-	James Blenkin
1895-	Thomas Masters
1896-	Arthur Baxter Howard
1897-	Sophia Dutchess
Nov. 1897	*Not relicensed.*

Literature

Official records:

L.C.C. Th.& M-H. Com. App. Nov. 1889-1896.
W. Kt. Mich. Q. S. 1855-60, 1866-88.

324

GOLDEN LION PUBLIC HOUSE

4, Warwick Place, Bedford Row, Holborn.

Licensed: 1852-1853.

Management

Middlesex justices:

Mich.	1852-	William Crouch
"	1853-	*No petition.*

Literature

Official records:

Mx. Mich. Q. S. 1852-1853

325

GOLDSMITH'S ARMS PUBLIC HOUSE

47, Little Sutton Street, Clerkenwell.

Licensed: 1860-1881.

Management

Middlesex justices:

Mich.	1860-	George Clarke
"	1865-	George Frederick Priest
"	1866-	Robert Morgan Holt Griffith
"	1868-	George Clarke
"	1872-	Henry Salmon
"	1873-	Charles Pay
"	1874-	William Davis
"	1875-	Randall Joseph Niner
"	1877-	Alexander Sharpe Naylor
"	1878-	Henry Hawley
"	1879-	Henry Walker
"	1881	*Petition arrived too late to be granted.*

Literature

Official records:

Mx. Mich. Q.S. 1860-1881.

326

GOOD DUKE HUMPHREY COFFEE TAVERN

15, Park Row, Greenwich.

Licensed: 1855-1901.

Building details

Capacity: 700

Management

West Kent justices:

Mich.	1855-	Frederick Eliot Duckham (through 1889)

London County Council:

1890-	*Not licensed.*
1891-	Edward W. Ratcliffe
1892-	Eugene Samuel Glover
1893-	Major General James de Havilland
Nov. 1901	*Not licensed.*

Literature

Official records:

L.C.C. Th.& M-H. Com. 1890-1900;
Sel. Com. 1892; Wt. Kt. Mich. Q.S. 1885-1888.

GOSPELL OAK PUBLIC HOUSE

Circus Road, St. Pancras.

Licensed: 1856–1865.

Management

Middlesex justices:

Mich.	1856–	Thomas Marsden
"	1857–	Henry Marsden
"	1859–	Thomas Marsden
"	1864–	Thomas Clegg
"	1865	*No petition.*

Literature

Official records:

Mx. Mich. Q.S. 1856–1865.

328

GRAFTON THEATRE

133, Tottenham Court Road, St. Marylebone.

Licensed: 1930–1940.

Management

London County Council:

1930–	Judith Wogan
1932–	Grafton Theatre Ltd.
1937–	Associated London Properties Ltd.
1938–	Inaugurated Plays Ltd.
Nov. 1940	*Not licensed.*

Lord Chamberlain:

1.12.1930–	Judith Wogan
1.12.1937–	Lionel Trevor Westlake (to 30.11.1938)
1.12.1939–	David Farrar (to 30.11.1940).

Literature

Official records:

G.L.C. Arch. Dept. Th. case 721;
L.C.C. Th. & M-H. Com. App. Nov. 1929–1939;
L.C.O. 181 and 374.

Contemporary accounts:

1932 THEATRE WORLD, 1932 May.—Announcement that auditorium was to be made available to London societies.

Historical accounts:

1952 PULLING, Christopher
They were singing...p. 161.

Location of other material

Plans: G.L.C. *Architects Department*

Programmes: Enthoven Collection.

329

GRAND THEATRE

Putney Bridge Approach, Fulham High Street, Fulham.

Opened: 23rd August 1897   *From* c. 1912 frequently used as a cinema.

Other names:

Fulham Theatre
Shilling Theatre

Building details

Architect: W. G. R Sprague

Capacity: (1897) 2239. (1914) 1411.

Auditorium: S. 175; P. 329; D.C. 95; B. 135; G. 367; Bx. 31.

Management

London County Council:

1897–	Alexander Francis Henderson
1906–	Robert Arthur (Fulham Theatre)
1912–	Sidney Cooper
Nov. 1914	Avigdor Lewis Birnstingl (retained).
1917–	William Patrick Mackintosh (to Dec. 1923)
1925	Partnership Players Ltd. (m.d.l.) Anthony Ellis (s.p.l.)
Nov. 1925	*Not licensed.*
1930–1931	London Cinema Ltd. (m.d.l.) William McNeill (s.p.l.)
1934–1935	Shilling Theatre Ltd. (m.d.l.) John Stevenson (s.p.l.)
1948–1950	Ernestine Mary Ann Shirley.

Literature

Official records:

G.L.C. Arch. Dpt. Mss. Index;
L.C.C. Th. & M-H. Com. App. Nov. 1897–

Contemporary accounts:

1893 BUILDER, 1893 July 29, p. 85.—Note that plans had been accepted.
1897 BUILDING NEWS, 1897 Aug. 20, p. 256.—Description.
BUILDER, 1897 Sept. 4, p. 190.—Note of opening.

Historical accounts:

c. 1930 MAYES, Ronald
The romance of London theatres, No. 128.

Location of other material

Plans: G.L.C. *Architects Department;*
Enthoven Collection, 1896 (3 sheets).

Programmes:

Enthoven Collection; Fulham Local Collection;
Guildhall Library; Westminster Local Collection.

330

GRAND THEATRE

21, St. John's Hill, Clapham Junction.

Opened: 1900

Other names

New Grand Theatre of Varieties 1900–1912
Grand Theatre of Varieties 1912–1927

Building details

Architect: E. A. Woodrow.

Builder: Gray Hill of Coventry.

Capacity: (1900) 3000.

Auditorium: P.; S.; C.; G.

Stage: 68' wide, 28' deep.

Management

London County Council: (m.d.l.)

1905-	Frederick Williams
1910-	Charles Gulliver
1911-	Frederick Williams
1912-	John Williams
1925-	London Theatres of Varieties Ltd.
1928-	Greater London Theatres and Cinemas Ltd.
1929-	Summers Brown
1932-	Grand Theatre (Clapham) Ltd.
1938-	London and District Cinemas Ltd.
1940-	Loughborough Playhouse Ltd.
1942-	George Barclay
1945-	Mrs. Katherine Mary Shea.
1946-	Nat Tennens
1949-	Sunniside Trust Co. Ltd.

London County Council: (s.p.l.)

1915-	Charles Gulliver
1928-	Summers Brown
1932-	Albert Matthews
1934-	Maurice Cheeper
1935-	Frederick Charles Lander
1939-	Leslie Ogilvie
1940-	Samuel William Dixon
1945-	Harry James Shea (i.e. Shea-Barclay).
1949-	William John Chegwidden
1950	Mark Sheckman.

Literature

Official records:

L.C.C. Th. & M-H. Com. App. Nov. 1904-.

Contemporary accounts:

1900 BUILDING NEWS, 1900 March 23, p. 400.—
Brief description of building being erected, to
replace the Grand Hall, on the adjoining site.
BUILDER, 1900 June 2, p. 548.—Foundation
stone laying, 16. 5. 1900.
BUILDER, 1900 Dec. 1, p. 495-6.—Brief description.

Historical accounts:

c. 1930 MAYES, Ronald
The romance of London theatres, No. 189.

Location of other material

Plans: G.L.C. *Architects Department.*

Programmes:

Enthoven Collection; Westminster Local Collection.

331

GRAND THEATRE

Streatham High Road, and Gleneagle Road, Streatham.

Licensed: 1890-1903.

Former Name:

Streatham Town Hall (n.b. Name misleading, not
municipal building.)

Management

London County Council:

1891-	Frederick Martin
1892-	Edward Smee
1897-	Henry George Astbury
Nov. 1903	*Not listed as theatre or music hall..*

Literature

Official records:

L.C.C. Th. & M-H, Com. App. Nov. 1891-.

332

GRANGE PUBLIC HOUSE

Mayfield Road, Dalston.

Licensed: 1869-1883.

Grand Theatre, Fulham (329)

(Greater London Council Photograph Library)

Management

Middlesex justices:

Mich.	1869-	Joseph Nation
"	1872-	Marion Nation
"	1873-	George Osmond
"	1874-	Walter John Barnes
"	1883	*Licence refused as it was seldom used.*

Literature

Official records:

Mx. Mich. Q.S. 1869-1883.

333

GRANVILLE THEATRE OF VARIETIES

Fulham Broadway, Walham Green.

Opened: 19th September 1898 *Closed:* 1956.

Building details

Architect: Frank Matcham.

Builder: Gray Hill of Coventry.

Capacity: 1122

Auditorium: Ar. 289; B, 210, G. 280.

Management

London County Council: (m.d.l.)

1898-	Herbert Campbell
1905-	Robert Astley
1914-	John Williams
1925-	Granville Theatre of Varieties (Walham Green) Ltd.
1939-	Amusement Developments Ltd. (Not licensed Nov. 1939 and Nov. 1940).
1942-	G.T.V. Entertainments Ltd. (through 1950)

London County Council: (s.p.l.)

1925-	John Williams
1939-	Charles Thomas Hawtree
1942-	Archie Allerton Shenburn. (through 1950)

Literature

Official records:

G.L.C. Arch. Dpt. Mss. Index;
G.L.C. Arch. Dpt. Th. case 125;
L.C.C. Th. & M-H. Com. App. Nov. 1897-.

Contemporary accounts:

1898 BUILDING NEWS, 1898 Sept. 9, pp. 375-6.—Description.
BUILDER, 1898 Sept. 10, p. 236.—Report of laying of commemoration stone.—Description.
1950 THEATRE ownership. p. 127.
1956 TATLER, 1955 Sept. 21.—Illus. of theatre in use as television studio. Closed 1956.

Historical accounts:

c. 1930 MAYES, Ronald.
The romance of London theatres, No. 178.

Location of other material

Plans: G.L.C. *Architects Department.*

Prospectus: Original prospectus, 1897 *in* Fulham Local Collection.

Programmes: Enthoven Collection.

334

GRASSHOPPER PUBLIC HOUSE

Bakers Row, (*formerly;* 15 Charles Street), Mile End.

Licensed: 1856-1883.

Management

Middlesex justices:

Mich.	1856-	James Towsey
"	1861-	James Johnson
"	1867-	Sarah Susannah Johnson
"	1874-	Charles Hinds
"	1879-	Benjamin Pearce Lucas
"	1883	*Licence refused as seldom used.*

Literature

Official records:

Mx. Mich. Q.S. 1856-1883.

335

GREAT EASTERN PUBLIC HOUSE

Ashwell Road, Bethnal Green.

Licensed: 1866-1890.

Management

Middlesex justices:

Mich.	1866-	Robert Martin Copeman
"	1875-	Henry Shephard
"	1876-	Henry Crease
"	1878-	Edward Brown
"	1887-	John Krappen.

London County Council:

	1890	John Krappen
Nov.	1890	*Not relicensed.*

Literature

Official records:

L.C.C. Th. & M-H. Com. App. Nov. 1889-90.
Mx. Mich. Q.S. 1866-1888.

336

GRECIAN THEATRE

City Road, Shoreditch.

Opened: c. 1825 *Closed:* 1882.

Former names

Shepherd and Shepherdess Gardens replaced 1825
Grecian Saloon 1832-1846
also Coronation Pleasure Ground 1838-1846.

Building details

Rebuilt 1858:

Developer: George Conquest.

Rebuilt 1876-7:

Opened: 29.10.1877

Architect: J.T.Robinson.

Builder: John Garrud of Spitalfields.

Capacity: c.1850.

Auditorium: S. 300; P. 420; Bx. C. 340; G. 660; Bx. 72.

Stage: 71' wide, and 30' deep.

Management

Lord Chamberlain:

29.9.1843-	Thomas Rouse
25.3.1851-	Benjamin Oliver Conquest
15.3.1879-	Thomas George Clark (to 29.10. 1882).

Middlesex justices:

Mich.	1848-	Thomas Rouse
"	1851-	Benjamin Oliver Conquest
"	1879-	Thomas George Clark
"	1882-	William Booth (of the Salvation Army).
"	1883	*No petition.*

Literature

LC7/13-17, 20-29, and 89.
M.B.W.Rpt. 1882, pp. 125-136;
Mx.Mich.Q.S. pre 1850-1882;
Sel.Com. 1877 and 1892.

Contemporary accounts:

1850-1   TALLIS'S DRAMATIC MAGAZINE, Nov. 1850-June 1851, p. 90.
1857   RITCHIE, J.E. The night side of London.—Chapter.
1872   DAILY TELEGRAPH, 1872 Sept. 28.—Report on George Conquest's management.
OBSERVER, 1872 Sept. 29. 'The stage in the suburbs: No. 3'.—History and description.
1877   BUILDER, 1877 Nov. 3, pp. 1105 and 1107.—Description, plan, illus. of auditorium.
TOUCHSTONE, 1877 Nov. 3. 'The New Grecian'.—Report of opening on previous Monday.
1879   REFEREE, 1879 March 23. 'Dramatic & musical gossip'.—Report on change of management.
1881   DAILY TELEGRAPH, 1881 Dec. 28. 'Panic at the new Grecian Theatre'.
1882   WEEKLY DISPATCH, 1882 Dec. 10. Queen's Bench Division: a theatrical case. Sennett v. Clark. (Report).
BUILDER, 1882 May 27, p. 656.—Report that theatre is up for sale.
1883   DAILY TELEGRAPH, 1883 July 4.—Report of action against General Booth in the Queen's Bench Division.
1898   BUILDER, 1898 May 21, p. 487.—Report of Charity Commission's scheme for the 'Bishopsgate Foundation'. Includes brief history of the site.
1899   BUILDER, 1899 Oct. 28, p. 400. 'London theatres old and new': report of demolition.

1901   DAILY TELEGRAPH, 1901 May 15.—Obituary of George Conquest.
STAGE, 1901 May 16.—Obituary.
ERA, 1901 May 18.—Obituary.

Historical accounts:

1895   HOLLINGSHEAD, John.
My lifetime...
STUART, C.D., *and* PARK, A.J.
The variety stage. pp. 35-37.
1904   BAKER, H. Barton
History of the London stage and its players. pp. 376-8.
1907   WROTH, Warwick
Cremorne and later London gardens. pp. 57-67.
1908   DAILY TELEGRAPH, 1908 Jan. 25.
'Old gardens: outdoor amusements in London'.
1910   EVENING NEWS, 1910 July 22.
Talks about old London: reminiscences of the oldest clown—Alfred Giovannelli.
1925   CHANCELLOR, E.B.
The pleasure haunts of London. pp. 406-410.
SHERSON, Erroll
London's lost theatres. pp. 9-23.
1926   JOHN O'LONDON'S WEEKLY, 1926 April 17.
'Letters to Gog and Magog—'Pop goes the weasel'.—Article on the song and the theatre.
c. 1930   MAYES, Ronald.
The romance of London theatres, No. 27 and 209.
1938   DISHER, M.W.
Winkles and champagne. p. 9, 13, 36 and 46.
1946   SCOTT, Harold
The early doors. pp. 166+
1951   HACKNEY GAZETTE, 1951 Jan. 26.
'Echoes of the past No. 53: End of the Grecian'.
1952   PULLING, Christopher
They were singing...p. 171, 176, 195 and 201.
1953   FLEETWOOD Frances
Conquest: the story of a theatre family. pp. 59-131, pp. 245-260.
1961   THEATRE WORLD, 1961 Jan. *and* Feb.
Lost London theatres, by N.M.Bligh. No. 15: The story of the Eagle or Grecian, 1832-1882. 8p. ports.

Location of other material

Plans: Public Record Office. LC7/87.

Grecian Theatre (336)

(Islington Public Libraries)

Enthoven Collection; Finsbury Local Collection; Guildhall Library (items include bound collection of playbills 1832-1882).

337

GREEN DRAGON PUBLIC HOUSE

Poplar High Street, Poplar.

Licensed: 1859-1868.

Management

Middlesex justices:

Mich.	1859-	Thomas Graves
"	1860-	George Frederick Wickers
"	1868	Henry John Marsh *refused licence.*

Literature

Official records:

Mx. Mich. Q.S. 1859-1868,

338

GREEN DRAGON PUBLIC HOUSE

Spring Garden Place (*formerly* Beast Lane), Ratcliff.

Licensed: 1850-1889.

Management

Middlesex justices:

Mich.	1850-	Thomas Walter
"	1852	*No application.*
"	1853-	Lewis Sulsh
"	1854-	Thomas Walter
"	1855	*No application..*
"	1856-	Thomas Walter
"	1879-	Alfred Walter
"	1887-	Septimus Phillips.

Literature

Official records:

Mx. Mich. Q.S. 1850-1888.
Sel. Com. 1892.

339

GREEN GATE MUSIC HALL

City Road.

Playbill: in Enthoven Collection. Proprietor W. Hurran. No date.

340

GREEN GATE PUBLIC HOUSE

Pentonville Road.

Mentioned by Warwick Wroth in *Cremorne and later London gardens.* He mentions that it had concert room and stage, and was in use in the 1850s.

341

GREEN LANE MUSIC HALL

Green Lane, Battersea.

In use c. 1880.

Other name

St. Mary's Temperance Hall & Green Lane Schools.

Building details

Hall stands 56' back from Green Lane, and was approached through the passage between buildings on street front.

Capacity: 430.

Auditorium: Ar. 300; G. 130.

Music hall concerts held every Monday and Saturday under the proprietorship of J. W. Butterfield. At other times it was used as a dancing academy. It was closed as a result of the 1878 Act.

Literature

Official records:

G. L. C. Arch. Dpt. Th. case 040/138.

Location of other material

Plans: G.L.C. *Architects Department.*

342

GREEN MAN HOTEL

Blackheath, Lewisham.

Licensed: 1850-1902.

Management

West Kent justices:

Mich.	1850-	Ann Whitmarsh. (1861-1865 records missing).
Mich.	1869-	Samuel John Jerrard
"	1871-	Henry James Pettit
"	1875-	Sarah Dimbleby
"	1877-	Thomas Hagger
"	1878-	Eliza Susan Orchard

London County Council:

	1890-	Eliza Susan Orchard
	1895-	James Parsons
Nov.	1903	*Not listed as a theatre or music hall.*

Literature

Official records:

L.C.C. Th. & M-H. Com. App. Nov. 1889-1902.
W. Kt. Mich. Q.S. 1850-60, 1869-88.

343

GREEN MAN PUBLIC HOUSE

12, Jame Street, St. George-in-the-East.

Licensed: 1855-1858.

Management

Middlesex justices:

Mich. 1855–	John James Chown.	
" 1858	*No application.*	

Literature

Official records:

Mx. Mich. Q.A. 1855-1858.

344

GREEN MAN PUBLIC HOUSE

Plumstead Village.

Licensed: 1866-1899.

Building details

Capacity: 180.

Management

West Kent justices:

(Records missing 1861-1865)

Mich. 1866–	William Williamson.	
" 1874–	George Pike Weaver.	

London County Council:

	1890–	George Pike Weaver.
	1895–	Richard Edward Dipple.
Nov.	1899	*Not licensed.*

Literature

Official records:

L.C.C. Th. & M-H. Com. App. Nov. 1889-98;
Sel. Com. 1892; W. Kt. Mich. Q.S. 1866-88.

345

GREEN MAN PUBLIC HOUSE

71, Shacklewell Lane, Hackney.

Licensed: 1859-69, 1870-1890.

Management

Middlesex justices:

Mich. 1859–	James Linton	
" 1869	*No application.*	
" 1870–	Henry Guilliam Worlock	
" 1872–	Edward Clement Hobday	
" 1873–	John Hughes	
" 1874–	Henry Hodges	
" 1876–	Thomas Christian Cubbon	

London County Council:

	1890–	Thomas Charlton
Nov.	1890	*Licence refused as no repairs done.*

Literature

Official records:

L.C.C. Th. & M-H. Com. App. Nov. 1889-90;
Mx. Mich. Q.S. 1859-1888.

346

GREENWICH HIPPODROME

Stockwell Street, and Nevada Street (*formerly* Silver Street), Greenwich.

Licensed: 1855-1924.

Former names

Rose and Crown Public House	1855–
Rose and Crown (Crowder's Music Hall)	1889–
known as Crowder's Music Hall	1871–
Rose and Crown Palace of Varieties	By Nov. 1900
Greenwich Palace of Varieties	1901–
Palace of Varieties, Greenwich	
Parthenon Palace of Varieties	1906–11

Building details

Rebuilt 1871:

Opened: 28th October 1871.

Developer: C. S. Crowder.

Rebuilt 1895:

Architect: Mr. Hancock

Capacity: 750

Auditorium: Ar. 350; B. 200; G. 200.

Management

West Kent justices:

Mich. 1855–	John Green	
(1861-1865 records missing).		
Mich. 1866–	John Samuel Emerton	
" 1868–	Ann Emerton	
" 1871–	Charles Spencer Crowder	
" 1878–	Alfred Ambrose Hurley.	

London County Council:

	1890–	Alfred Ambrose Hurley
	1901–	Geoffrey Charles Best
	1903–	David Barnard
	1912–	Edward Walter Rice
	1913–	Harry Thomas Underwood
	1915–	John Edward Charles Stubbs.
Nov.	1924	*Not licensed as a theatre or music hall.*

Literature

Official records:

G.L.C. Arch. Dpt. Mss. Index;
G.L.C. Architects Department case 245;
L.C.C. Th. & M-H. Com. App. Nov. 1889-1923;
Sel. Com. 1892; W. Kt. Mich. Q.S. 1855-1888.

Location of other material

Plans: G.L.C. *Architects Department.*

Playbills and newscuttings:

Greenwich Local Collection;
Guildhall Library (1 bill for Crowder's 1883)

Note: Building demolished 1965, and currently (Feb. 1966) being replaced by new 'Greenwich Theatre'.

347

GREENWICH THEATRE

75, London Road, Greenwich.

Opened: 1864   *From:* 1910 used as a cinema.

Former names

Morton's Theatre 1889-96, 1900-01
Morton's Model Theatre 1897-99
Carlton Theatre 1902-08
Prince of Wales' Theatre.
Theatre Royal, Greenwich. Occasionally.
At other times known as Greenwich Theatre.

Building details

Capacity: 721.

Auditorium: P. 240; Bx. C. 153; G. 328.

Management

The records of stage play licences granted by the West Kent justices do not appear to have survived.

London County Council:

1890-	William Morton
1901-	Arthur Carlton
1911-	George Herbert Gray
Nov. 1911	*Not licensed as a theatre or music hall.*

Literature

Official records:

G.L.C. Arch. Dpt. Th. case 129;
L.C.C. Th. & M-H. Com. App. Nov. 1889-1911;
M.B.W. Dpt. 1882, pp. 137-147;
Sel. Com. 1892.

Historical accounts:

1904	BAKER, H. Barton. History of the London stage and its players. p. 400.

Location of other material

Plans: G.L.C. *Architects Department.*

Playbills and cuttings: Greenwich Local Collection.

Programmes: Enthoven Collection.

348

GREYHOUND PUBLIC HOUSE

72, Ball's Pond Road, Islington.

Licensed: 1869-1871.

Management

Middlesex justices:

Mich.	1869-	Thomas Masters
"	1870-	Edwin Rice
"	1871	*No application.*

Literature

Official records:

Mx. Mich. Q.S. 1869-71.

349

GREYHOUND PUBLIC HOUSE

Battersea.

Licensed: 1868-1871.

104

Management

Surrey justices:

Mich.	1868-	Richard Cassius Gurney
"	1869-	William Pratt Barrett
"	1871	*No petition.*

Literature

Official records:

Sy. Mich. Q.S. 1868-70.

350

GREYHOUND PUBLIC HOUSE

Greenwich

Licensed: 1854-55.

Management

West Kent justices:

Mich.	1854-	Benjamin Suffrein
"	1855	*No application.*

Literature

Official records:

W. Kt. Mich. Q.S. 1854.

351

GREYHOUND PUBLIC HOUSE

Gretton Place, near Victoria Park, Bethnal Green.

Licensed: 1856-1866.

Management

Middlesex justices:

Mich.	1856-	Henry Flint
"	1866	*No application.*

Literature

Official records:

Mx. Mich. Q.S. 1856-1865.

352

GRIFFIN PUBLIC HOUSE

Leonard Street, Shoreditch.

Licensed: 1854-1891.

Management

Middlesex justices:

Mich.	1854-	Joseph Goodliffe
"	1855-	George Heaverman
"	1862-	James Johnson Smith
"	1866-	Samuel Robert Pether
"	1867-	Thomas Swindell
"	1872-	Emily Newton
"	1873-	John Housley
"	1874-	John Webb
"	1876-	Harriet Sarah Naylor
"	1877-	Frederick Henry Salmon
"	1878-	George Miles O'Reilly

Literature

Official records:

L.C.C. Th. & M-H. Com. App. Nov. 1889-90;
Mx. Mich. Q.S. 1854-1888.

353

GRIFFIN PUBLIC HOUSE AND MUSIC HALL

99, Shoreditch High Street (*formerly* Holywell Street)
Shoreditch.

Licensed: 1856-1889.

Management

Middlesex justices:

Mich.	1856-	William Smith
"	1866-	John Hamlin
"	1876-	James Blumson
"	1877-	George Neary
"	1882-	Mary Catherine Walsh
"	1884-	John Henry Williams
"	1885-	Alfred Neary.

Literature

Official records:

Mx. Mich. Q.S. 1856-1888; Sel. Com. 1892.

354

GROSVENOR ARMS PUBLIC HOUSE

Grosvenor Street, Mile End.

Licensed: 1854-1863.

Management

Middlesex justices:

Mich.	1854-	Richard Bishop
"	1855-	Alfred Walters
"	1856-	George Bint
"	1862-	Mary Gobert
"	1863	*No petition.*

Literature

Official records:

Mx. Mich. Q.S. 1854-1863.

355

GROSVENOR HALL

200, Buckingham Palace Road, Westminster.

Licensed: 1876-1903.

Building details

Capacity: 500.

Management

Middlesex justices:

| Mich. 1876- | Herbert Bulkley Praed and Henry Arthur Hunt. |

London County Council:

| 1890- | Herbert Bulkley Praed and Henry Arthur Hunt. |
| Nov. 1903 | *Not licensed as a theatre or music hall.* |

Literature

Official records:

L.C.C. Th. & M-H. Com. App. Nov. 1889-1903;
Mx. Mich. Q.S. 1876-1888; Sel. Com. 1892.

356

GUN PUBLIC HOUSE AND MUSIC HALL

117, Shoreditch High Street, (*formerly* Holywell Street), Shoreditch.

Licensed: 1854-1889.

Building details

The concert room was on the first floor over the public bar, 36′ × 26′ 6″.

Management

Middlesex justices:

Mich.	1854-	William Lock
"	1861-	Charlotte Moor Lock
"	1866-	Henry Lock
"	1870-	Moss Henry Nathan
"	1875-	William Blumson
"	1877-	John Coe
"	1878-	William Fowler
"	1881-	Joseph Gobby.

Not licensed by the London County Council.

Literature

Official records:

G.L.C. Arch. Dpt. Th. case 040/56;
Mx. Mich. Q.S. 1854-1888.

357

GUN PUBLIC HOUSE

97, New Road, Woolwich.

Licensed: 1868-1891.

Building details

The concert room was on the first floor, and had an area of 555 sq′. In 1889 it was used every night by about 60 visitors. Later that year it was reduced below 500 sq′. On 27th February 1891 it was reported that the hall was no longer in use owing to the 1878 Act.

Management

West Kent justices:

Mich.	1868-	Charles Gordon
"	1872-	Arabella Gordon
"	1873-	William Vail

	1874-	James Richard Dovey
	1879-	Thomas Barriskill
	1883-	William Armstrong
	1886-	Eliza Armstrong

London County Council:

| 1890 | Eliza Armstrong (licence retained). |
| Nov. 1891 | *No application.* |

Literature

Official records:

G.L.C. Arch. Dpt. Th. case 040/57;
L.C.C. Th. & M-H. Com. App. Nov. 1889-1890;
W. Kt. Mich. Q.S. 1868-1888.

Location of other material

Plans: G.L.C. *Architects Department.*

358

GUY OF WARWICK PUBLIC HOUSE

9, Gray's Inn Lane, Holborn.

Licensed: 1856-57, and 1861-1865.

Management

Middlesex justices:

Mich. 1856-	George Manning
" 1857-	Liberty Pitt
" 1858	*No petition.*
" 1861-	Henry Hunt
" 1863-	Francis Kirby Evans
" 1864-	George Formon Gratton
" 1865	*Licence refused.*

Literature

Official records:

Mx. Mich. Q.S. 1856-7, 1861-65.

359

HACKNEY EMPIRE

381-391, Mare Street, Hackney.

Opened: 1901

Building details

Architect: Frank Matcham

Builders: F. and H. F. Higgs

Decorators: Messrs. De Jong & Co.

Capacity: 3,000

Auditorium: S. 418; P. 455; B. 312; C. 327; C. 596; Bx. 24.

Management

London County Council:

1901-	Oswald Stoll
1925-	Hackney and Shepherd's Bush Empire Ltd.
1942-	Hackney and Shepherd's Bush Empire Palaces Ltd.

Lord Chamberlain:

| 27.11.1911- | Oswald Stoll |
| 1.12.1942- | Prince Littler |

Literature

Official Records:

G.L.C. Arch. Dpt. Mss Index;
G.L.C. Arch. Dpt. Th. case 133;
L.C.C. Th. & M-H. Com. App. Nov. 1900+;
L.C.C. Th. & M-H. Com. Papers. 1897+;
L.C.C. 374 and 491.

Contemporary accounts:

| 1901 | BUILDER, 1901, Dec. 7th, p. 517.—Brief report of erection. BUILDING NEWS, 1901, Dec. 13th, p. 795. —Description. |

Location of other material

Plans: G.L.C. *Architects Department.*
Cuttings: Hackney Local Collection (few only)

Cuttings, playbills &c.

Enthoven Collection; Guildhall Library (1 item)

360

HACKNEY THEATRE

Glenarm Road, Hackney.

Licensed: 1875 and 1884

Former name

Clapton Park Theatre (1872-76)

Building details

Architect: J. T. Robinson

Capacity: approx. 600

Auditorium: S. 90; P. 110; B. 160; C. 210; Bx. 15.

Management

Lord Chamberlain:

20.1.1875+   Thomas Turner

ceased to be licensed 30.6.1884.

Literature

Official records:

G.L.C. Arch. Dpt. Th. case 033; LC7/16-17;
LC7/24-29; M.B.W. Rpt. 1882, p. 45-53;
Sel. Com. 1877 and 1892.

Location of other material

Plans: G.L.C. *Architects Department*

Public Record Office, LC7/61. Plans of various levels, and transverse section.

361

HALF MOON AND PUNCHBOWL PUBLIC HOUSE

Buckle Street, Whitechapel.

Licensed: 1854-1863

Management

Middlesex justices:

Mich. 1854	Lewis Kurler
" 1855-	Caspar Mihr
" 1863	*Licence refused.*

Literature

Official records:

Mx. Mich. Q.S. 1854-1863.

362

HALIFAX ARMS PUBLIC HOUSE

Halifax Street, Mile End New Town.

Licensed: 1859-1862

Management

Middlesex justices:

| Mich. 1859- | William Fryer |
| " 1862 | *No petition.* |

Literature

Official records:

Mx. Mich. Q.S. 1859-1862.

363

HAMMERSMITH PALACE OF VARIETIES

82, King Street, Hammersmith.

Licensed: 1880-1944

Former Names

Town Hall, Hammersmith -1883
Town Hall and Temple of Varieties 1883-5
Temple of Varieties 1885-1898

Building details

1898: reconstructed.

Architect: W. M. Brutton

Builder: Messrs. Godson and Sons

Capacity: 2,815

Auditorium: S. 315; P. 538; B. & Bx. 474; G. 518

1910: alterations carried out under Frank Matcham & Co.

Reopened 24.1.1910.

Management

Middlesex justices:

Mich. 1880	Donald Sinclair Watson
" 1881-	Penniston Dunn
" 1884-	Acton Phillips, Snr.

London County Council:

1890-	Acton Phillips, Snr.
1893-	Acton Francis Phillips
1899-	John Charles Coe

1910-	Thomas Henry Masters
1913-	Charles Gulliver
1925-	Hammersmith Palace Ltd. (m.d.l.) Charles Gulliver (s.p.l.)
1927	Hammersmith Palace of Varieties Ltd. Charles Gulliver (s.p.l.)
1928	Greater London Theatres and Cinemas Ltd. Summers Brown (s.p.l.)
1929-	Summers Brown
1931-	Metropolitan & Provisional Cinematograph Theatres Ltd. (m.d.l.) Victor Sheridan (s.p.l.)
1934-	Electric Palaces Ltd. William Robinson (s.p.l.)
1936-	Metropolitan and Provisions Cinematograph Theatres Ltd. and Victor Sheridan and (37) Theodore Kanssen and (38) Arthur James Hillier
1942-	Audio Film Corporation Ltd. and Richard Edward Marcoso
1943-	Suburban Century Cinemas Ltd. and Archie Allerton Shenburn
Nov. 1945	*Not licensed as theatre or music hall.*

Literature

Official records:

G.L.C. Arch. Dpt. Mss. Index;
G.L.C. Arch. Dpt. Th. case 137;
L.C.C. Th. & M-H. Com. App. Nov. 1889-1945;
Mx. Mich. Q.S. 1880-1888; Sel. Com. 1892.

Hackney Empire (359)

(Greater London Council Photograph Library)

1887 SATURDAY REVIEW. 1887, Sept. 3rd. The state
of the London. . . music halls, No. 4.
1898 BUILDER. 1898, Nov. 26th. p. 490-1.—Description.

Location of other material

Plans: G.L.C. *Architects Department.*

Programmes, playbills and Cuttings:
Enthoven Collection;
Guildhall Library (1 item);
Hammersmith Local Collection.

364

HAND AND FLOWER PUBLIC HOUSE

King's Road, Fulham.

Licensed: 1852-1884

Management

Middlesex justices:

Mich.	1852-	Henry Barr
"	1867-	Mary Ann Barr
"	1869-	Francis Bateman
"	1871-	Francis Gorringe
"	1883	Joshua William Hollot
"	1884	*Application withdrawn.*

Literature

Official records:

Mx. Mich. Q.S. 1852-1884.

365

HARE MUSIC HALL AND PUBLIC HOUSE

505, Cambridge Road, (*formerly* Cambridge Heath
Bethnal Green.

Licensed: 1858-1889

Building details

Music hall, which was situated on the first floor of
the public house, was L shaped and had an area of
627 sq′. Accommodating 120 people, it was used as a
music hall twice a week; on other nights it was used
as a billiard room.

In 1886 plans were drawn up for a new concert room
on the west side of the public house, but this did not
materialize. Concert room finally closed as a result
of the 1878 Act.

Management

Middlesex justices:

Mich.	1858-	Henry Silly
"	1863-	Abraham Keymer
"	1873-	Sarah Jull
"	1876	John North
"	1877-	Sidney Edwards

London County Council:

| Nov. 1889 | Application not granted as repairs required were stated to be too costly to complete. |

Literature

Official records:

G.L.C. Arch. Dpt. Th. case 040/59;
L.C.C. Th. & M-H. Com. App. Nov. 1889;
Mx. Mich. Q.S. 1858-88;
Sel. Com. 1892.

Location of other material

Plans: G.L.C. *Architects Department.*

366

HARE AND HOUNDS PUBLIC HOUSE

Chalk Farm Lane, St. Pancras.

Licensed: pre 1850-1862

Management

Middlesex justices:

Mich.	1850-	Edward Cole Price
"	1852-	Elijah Evans Land
"	1856	Henry Coomber Bridger
"	1857-	Isaac Gadsby
"	1862	*Not relicensed.*

Literature

Official records:

Mx. Mich. Q.S. 1850-1862.

367

HARE AND HOUNDS PUBLIC HOUSE

Stoke Newington Road, Stoke Newington.

Licensed: 1851-1861

Management

Middlesex justices:

Mich.	1851-	Edward Mannakee
"	1856	James Wrangham
"	1857-	Charles Ethelstan Allen
"	1861	*No application.*

Literature

Official records:

Mx. Mich. Q.S. 1851-1861.

368

HARE AND HOUNDS PUBLIC HOUSE

Upper Street, Islington.

Licensed: 1856-1857

Management

Middlesex justices:

| Mich. | 1858- | Thomas Smith |
| " | 1857 | *No petition.* |

Literature

Official records:

Mx. Mich. Q.S. 1856-1857.

HAVELOCK ARMS PUBLIC HOUSE

24, Grays Inn Road, St. Andrew's, Holborn.

Licensed: 1859-1871

Management

Middlesex justices:

Mich. 1859-	Isaac Bliss
" 1867-	George Carey
" 1869-	Johnathan M.A. Pollard
" 1871	*No application.*

Literature

Official records:

Mx. Mich. Q.S. 1859-1871.

370

HAVERING ATTE BOWER PUBLIC HOUSE

Ann Street, Stepney.

Licensed: 1854-1863

Management

Middlesex justices:

Mich. 1854-	James Davis
" 1858	James Allen
" 1859	David Charles Waters
" 1860	(?) Charles Waters
" 1861	*Licence not granted* to George Bailey
" 1862	Richard Fisher Barton
" 1863	*No application.*

Literature

Official records·

Mx. Mich. Q S. 1854-1862.

371

HAYMARKET, THEATRE ROYAL

7-8, Haymarket, Westminster.

Opened: 29th December, 1720.

Former names

The Little Theatre in the Hay-Market	1720-
Theatre Royal in the Haymarket	1766-
Haymarket Theatre	1853-
Theatre Royal Haymarket	1855-

Building details

1st theatre:

Opened: under John Potter

2nd theatre:

Opened: 4th July, 1821, under David Morris.

Site: Immediately to south of the first theatre.

Reconstructed 1879:

Opened: 31st January, 1880.

Architect: C. J. Phipps

Contractors: Laing & Sons

Decorators: Messrs. Geo. Jackson & Sons & Edward Bell

Capacity: 1, 159 seated

Auditorium: S. 249; B. 172; 1st C. 187; 2nd C. 174; G. 244; Bx. 132.

Reconstructed 1904:

Opened: 2nd January, 1905

Capacity: 978

Auditorium: S. 311; D.C. 211; U.C. 192; G. 126; Bx. 110

Stage: 27' wide × 38' deep.

Management

Lord Chamberlain:

29. 9.1843-	Benjamin Webster (*as* Little Theatre in the Haymarket)
28. 3.1853-	John Baldwin Buckstone (Sept. 1853 Haymarket Theatre)
18. 5.1878-	John Sleeper Clarke (to 30.9.1879)
31. 1.1880-	Squire Bancroft Bancroft
29. 9.1888-	Herbert Beerbohm Tree
16.10.1888-	Squire Bancroft Bancroft
28. 9.1889-	Herbert Beerbohm Tree
28. 9.1896-	Frederick Harrison
1.12.1927-	Horace Watson
1.12.1935-	Stuart Watson (through 1950)

Literature

Official records:

G.L.C. Arch. Dpt. Mss Index;
G.L.C. Arch. Dpt. Th. case 429,:
L.C.C. Th. & M-H. Com. Papers 1888+;
LC1/508-752; LC7/13-17, 20-48, 89;
L.C.O. 278 and 374;
M.B.W. Rpt. 1882 p. 147-161;
Sel. Com. 1866, 1877 and 1892.

Contemporary accounts:

1850 BUILDER. 1850, Oct. 19th. p. 500.—Description of redecoration including construction of new royal box.
1851 TALLIS'S DRAMATIC MAGAZINE. Nov. 1850-June 1851. p. 26, 51, 84, 116, 150, 184, 217, 249.
1853 BUILDER. Oct. 22nd. p. 653.—'Improvements in the Haymarket Theatre'. Architect: G. Somers Clarke.
1858 BUILDER. 1858, July 17th. p. 487.—The entrance to the Haymarket: letter on dangerous condition of pit entrance.
1872 BUILDER. 1872, Nov. 9th. p. 883.—Brief description of redecoration of interior.
1879 GRAPHIC. 1879, Oct. 25th.—Report of closure and rebuilding. Note of history.
DRAMATIC NOTES. 1879, p. 8-12.
BUILDER. 1879, Dec. 27th. p. 1, 438.
—Description of complete internal reconstruction.
1880 BUILDER. 1880, Jan. 3rd. p. 23.—Further details of new Haymarket Theatre.
DAILY NEWS. 1880, Feb. 2nd.—Haymarket: description of extensive alterations.
BUILDING NEWS. 1880, Feb. 6th. p. 159.—Description of internal reconstruction.
SUNDAY TIMES. 1880, Feb. 8th. 'The reopening of the Haymarket' (description).

1885 SUNDAY TIMES. 1885, Sept. 27th. Haymarket Theatre—Report of theatre's reopening under Edward Russell and Bashford following retirement of Bancrofts.

1897 SACHS, E. *and* WOODROW, E. Modern opera houses and theatres. Vol. III p. 30 and p. 62. Plans.

1903 BUILDER. 1903, Sept. 5th. p. 245. Note of L.C.C. requirements of alterations and note on history.

1904 BUILDER. 1904, June 4th. p. 601. Note of C. Stanley Peach having prepared plans for alterations, plus note on history.

1950 THEATRE ownership. p. 74, p. 108.

Historical accounts:

1822 GENTLEMAN'S MAGAZINE. 1822. p. 201-204, and 406-408.
(Vol. I p. 123-135)

1873 BLANCHARD, E. L.
History of the Haymarket.
in Era Almanac, 1873 p. 1-16.

1903 MAUDE, Cyril
The Haymarket Theatre.
Richards, 1903. 239p. 18 plates.

1904 BAKER, H. Barton
History of the London stage and its players.
p. 211-244.

1913 ? THE PALL MALL restaurant in the Haymarket: its historical site, early associations and present popularity, 1713-1913.
—Ch. II The story of the Little Theatre on the site of the Pall Mall Restaurant, 1720-1820.

1925 CHANCELLOR, E. B.
The pleasure haunts of London... p. 96-105.

c. 1930 MAYES, Ronald
The romance of London theatres. No. 65 and 80.

1932 LEVERTON, W. H.
Through the box-office window: Memories of fifty years at the Haymarket, (by) the box office manager. 1932.

1940 LONDON. County Council.
Survey of London. Volume 20.
L.C.C. 1940. p. 98-100. 6 plates.

1948 POPE, W. J. Macqueen
Haymarket: theatre of perfection. 1948.

1959 ENCICLOPEDIA dello spettacolo.
Vol. 6. Col. 1, 626.

1963 MANDER, R. *and* MITCHENSON, J.
The theatres of London. 2nd ed. p. 95-102.

Location of other material

Plans:

G.L.C. *Architects Department;*
Enthoven Collection, 1924 (3 sheets);
Public Record Office. LC7/62. 28.10.1879. Eight plans and sections.

Programmes and playbills:

British Museum Library; Enthoven Collection; Garrick Club 1790+ —Strongest for 18th century; Guildhall Library (750 items); London Museum; Westminster Local Collection.

Prints:

British Museum; Enthoven Collection; London Museum; Westminster Local Collection.

372

HELVETIA MUSIC HALL

King's Arms Public House, 6 & 7 (*later* 23-25) Old Compton Street, Westminster.

Licensed: 1858-1891, but ceased to be a music hall Nov. 1886.

Building details

The music hall was situated on the first floor.

Area: 39' × 16' 9''.

Capacity: 100
From November 1886 the hall was used as a billiard room. It was closed through the 1878 Act.

Management

Middlesex justices:

Mich. 1858-	Joseph Medworth
" 1863-	John Ford Hallet
" 1869-	*Not licensed.*
" 1872-	John Wheeler
" 1877-	John Dawson
" 1880-	Charles Leder
" 1884-	James Wanner
" 1885-	H. J. Hirst
" 1887-	Herman Rossberg

London County Council:

1890	Herman Rossberg
Nov. 1891	*No application.*

Literature

Official records:

G.L.C. Arch. Dpt. Th. case 040/60;
L.C.C. Th. & M-H. Com. App. Nov. 1889-1890;
Mx. Mich. Q.S. 1858-68, 72-88; Sel. Com. 1892.

373

HENRY THE EIGHTH PUBLIC HOUSE

King Henry Street, Islington.

Licensed: 1853-1856

Management

Middlesex justices:

Mich. 1853-	John Taylor
" 1856	*No petition.*
" 1857	*Licence refused* to Robert Townsend

Literature

Official records:

Mx. Mich. Q.S. 1853-1857.

374

HIGHBURY PARK PUBLIC HOUSE

Highbury New Park, Islington.

Licensed: 1854-1872

Management

Middlesex justices:

Mich. 1854-	Job Palmer
" 1862-	Samuel Martin
" 1872	*Not licensed.*

Literature

Official records:

Mx. Mich. Q.S. 1854-1872.

HIS MAJESTY'S THEATRE

Haymarket.

Opened: 9th April, 1705.

Former names

Queen's Theatre 1705-1714
King's Theatre 1714-1837
Her Majesty's Theatre 1837-1901
His Majesty's Theatre 1901-1952

Also known as

Italian Opera House

Later name

Her Majesty's Theatre, on accession of Elizabeth II.

Building details

1st building:

Opened under: William Congreve

2nd building:

Opened: 26.3.1791, by William Taylor.

Reconstructed 1818.

1866: Alteration of proscenium.—Stage boxes removed and proscenium frame brought forward 10'.

Stage: 87' wide × 34' deep.

3rd building:

Built: 1868-69.

Opened as theatre: 28.4.1877.

Developer: Colonel Mapleson.

Architect: Charles Lee, Sons and Pain.

Contractor: George Trollope & Sons.

Stage: 95' wide × 55' deep.

4th building:

Opened: 28.4.1897.

Developer: Herbert Beerbohm Tree.

Capacity: approx. 1,319.

Auditorium: S.486; D.C.281; U.C.382; G.170.

Stage: 34' wide × 45' 6" deep.

Management

Lord Chamberlain:

29. 9.1843-	Benjamin Lumley (until 28.9.1858) except for 1852/3 season when theatre closed
15. 3.1860-	Edward Tyrrell Smith
29. 9.1861-	James Henry Mapleson
19.11.1866-	Edmund Falconer
2. 2.1867-	James Henry Mapleson
29. 9.1882-	Frederick Rye (provisional)
24. 3.1883-	F. Christopher Leader
14. 4.1884-	John Richard Hunter Taylor
29. 9.1884-	Samuel Hayes
26.12.1884-	Frederic La Fargue
19. 5.1885-	Ercole Boracchi and Enrico Corti
29. 9.1885-	Charles Henry Hawtrey (to 30.11.1885)

27. 2.1886-	Edward Carillon
24. 4.1886-	Michaelm Peopold Mager
4. 6.1887-	James Henry Mapleson
12.11.1887-	John Glendower Owen
30. 7.1889-	Henry John Leslie (to 28.9.1890)
28. 9.1897-	Herbert Beerbohm Tree
27. 7.1917-	Joseph David Langton (on death of Tree)
9.11.1918-	William Webb and Alan Parsons
1.12.1923-	George Grossmith and J.A.E. Malone
1.12.1926-	William Clifford Gaunt
1.12.1931-	George Brinton McLellen
1.12.1932-	James Ernest Sharpe
1.12.1933-	Thomas Henry Bostock
1.12.1943-	Prince Littler (through 1950)

Literature

Official records:

G.L.C. Arch. Dpt. Mss Index;
G.L.C. Arch. Dpt. Th. case 431;
L.C.C. Th. & M-H. Com. Papers 1895-; L.C. 1/525-752;
L.C. 7/13-17, 20-48; L.C.O. 334 and 374;
Lord Chamberlain's Office. Warrant folio. No. 30.
1773+ (In Public Record Office).
M.B.W. Rpt. 1882. p. 169-181;
Sel. Com. 1866, 1877 and 1892.

Her Majesty's Theatre 1869 (375)

(The Builder)

Contemporary accounts:

1850 BUILDER. 1850, Oct. 5th. p. 476.—Paragraph describing alterations made necessary by season of Promenade Concerts.

1851 TALLIS'S DRAMATIC MAGAZINE. Nov. 1850-June 1851. p. 183.

1853 SCOTT, James, *auctioneer*
Her Majesty's Theatre: a catalogue... 17. 3. 1853. 170 p. (in Westminster Local Collection).

1856 HER MAJESTY'S THEATRE
A list of subscribers for the season, 1856. (B.M. 840. a. 38).

1860 BUILDER. 1860, April 21st. p. 255.—Note on improvements.

1863 BUILDINGS NEWS. 1863, March 20th, p. 224.—Redecoration by Messrs. Green and King.

1865 BUILDER. 1865, Jan. 28th. p. 69. —The ceiling of Her Majesty's.

1866 BUILDING NEWS. 1866, Nov. 9th. p. 747.—Note of alteration to proscenium.

1867 POST. 1867, Dec. 7th 9th, and 11th. Destruction of Her Majesty's Theatre by fire—report.
STANDARD. 1867, Dec. 7th. Total destruction of Her Majesty's Theatre by fire—report.
STAR. 1867, Dec. 7th, 8th, 9th and 10th. Destruction of Her Majesty's Theatre by fire—report.
TELEGRAPH. 1867, Dec. 7th, 9th and 10th.—Great fire: total destruction of Her Majesty's.
TIMES. 1867, Dec. 7th, 9th and 10th. Burning of Her Majesty's Theatre.
BUILDER. 1867, Dec. 14th. p. 903. Report of destruction of theatre by fire on 6. 12. 1867.
ILLUSTRATED LONDON NEWS. 1867, Dec. 14th.—Notice of fire and appeal for artists and theatre. Illus.
BUILDER. 1867, Dec. 28th, p. 945.—Letter commenting on the high standard of acoustics of the destroyed theatre.

1868 BUILDER. 1868, May 16th. p. 362.—List of tenders.
BUILDER. 1868, May 23rd. p. 379.—Report of foundation stone laying.
BUILDER. 1868, Nov. 28th. p. 872-3.—Report on rebuilding.
BUILDER. 1868, Dec. 12th. p. 911-12.—Plans of old and new theatres: a comparison.

1869 BUILDING NEWS. 1869, April 2nd. p. 299-300.—Detailed description and plan.
BUILDER. 1869, June 26th. p. 509.—Description and illus. of interior.
BUILDER. 1869, July 3rd. p. 526.—Longitudinal section.

1874 BUILDING NEWS. 1874, April 17th. p. 436.—Brief report that theatre to be auctioned.
BUILDING NEWS. 1874, May 22nd. p. 574.—Brief report of sale.
BUILDER. 1874, May 23rd. p. 447.—Report of sale.

1875 BUILDER. 1875, Nov. 27th. p. 1, 072.—Brief report on proposal to convert it into a West End Stock Exchange.

1881 STANDARD. 1881, Jan 21st.—Fire at Her Majesty's Theatre.

1884 BUILDER. 1884, Nov. 29th. p. 743. —Report of summons by M.B.W. for failing to remedy defects.

1889 DAILY TELEGRAPH. 1889, Aug. 19th.—Report and description of redecoration for promenade concerts.
BUILDER. 1889, Nov. 16th. 'Note pages'.—Brief description.

1890 DAILY CHRONICLE. 1890, Jan. 30th.—Closing of Her Majesty's Theatre (due to bankruptcy)—report.

1892 BUILDER. 1892, May 21st. p. 394.—Brief report of proposed demolition to make way for new hotel.

1892 BUILDER. 1892, July 30th. p. 82. Proposal to build 'Palais des Beaux-Arts'.

1895 BUILDER. 1895, May 25th. p. 390. Report that question asked in Commons about site. Protest that it should have been demolished before plans for new buildings drawn up.

1896 BUILDER. 1896, Feb. 8th. p. 123.—Report of commencement of building.
SKETCH. 1896, July 15th. 'Mr. Tree's new theatre'.
BUILDING NEWS. 1896, July 31st. p. 147.—Description and plate of front elevation.
BUILDER. 1896, Aug. 1st. p. 103.—Description of plans. Report of laying of foundation stone.

1897 HER MAJESTY'S THEATRE.—Description. 1897. 3p. illus.
SACHS, E. *and* WOODROW, E. A. E.
Modern opera houses and theatres ... Vol. II. p. 35/6, 68, 73/4, 88.—Descriptive text, plans elevations. ditto ... Vol. III Costs and dimensions. illus. pp. 17 (&c).
BUILDER. 1897, March 13th. p. 251.—Report of Architectural Association visit—Description.
BUILDING NEWS. 1897, April 30th. p. 629.—Brief description.
BUILDER. 1897, May 8th. p. 421. -Detailed description.
BUILDING NEWS. 1897, May 14th. p. 703.—Description and plate of facade.

1898 SACHS, E.
Stage construction... —General view of stage.

1899 HER MAJESTY'S THEATRE
'Souvenirs' of plays produced at Her Majesty's Theatre, by H. Beerbohm Tree. London, 1899.

1905 BUILDING NEWS. 1905, Sept. 29th. p. 431.—Report of crack above proscenium which caused theatre to be temporarily closed.

1950 THEATRE ownership ... p. 58 & 89.

Historical accounts:

1864 LUMLEY, Benjamin
Reminiscences of the opera. Hurst, 1864. 448p. port.—Author was, for 20 years, director of the theatre.

1865 BUILDER. 1865, Feb. 11th. p. 103.—Brief note of history.

1867 ERA. 1867, Dec. 15th.

1868 ERA ALMANACK. 1868, p. 34-37.
SHEPHERD, T. *and* ELMES, J.
Metropolitan improvements. p. 274. plate.

1904 The MICROCOSM of London. Vol. 2, p. 213+.
BAKER, H. Barton
History of the London Stage and its players. p. 163-210, 535-9, 546.
Also indexed under Haymarket Opera House.

1925 CHANCELLOR, E. B.
The Pleasure haunts of London, p. 425-8.

c. 1930 MAYES, Ronald
The romance of London's theatres, Nos. 47, 55 and 118.

1946 SHORT, Ernest
Fifty years of vaudeville.—Various references.

1949 COUNTRY LIFE. 1949, Feb. 4th.
'Opera in the Haymarket' by Rachel Caro.—History of site, building plans and subsequent changes.

DRAMA. 1949, May. p. 16-19.
The story of His Majesty's by W. MacQueen Pope.
1957 ARUNDELL, Dennis
The critic at the Opera. 1957.
1960 LONDON. County Council.
Survey of London. Vol. 29, Chapter VIII.
p. 223-250, plates.—History of theatre and architectural plans.
1963 LONDON. County Council.
Survey of London. Vol. 31. p. 76, 276, 278 and 303.
MANDER, Raymond *and* MITCHENSON, Joe.
The theatres of London. 2nd ed. p. 103-109.

Location of other material

Plans:

G.L.C. *Architects Department.*
Enthoven Collection, 1963 (3 sheets).
Public Record Office. LC7/63. 28.5.1860. 12 sheets of plans, sections.

Programmes and playbills:

British Museum Library; Enthoven Collection; Garrick Club; Guildhall Library; London Museum; Westminster Local Collection.

Cuttings, Souvenirs and programmes: London Museum.

376

HOLBORN EMPIRE.

242-5, High Holborn, Holborn.

Opened: November, 1857. *Closed by bombing* 1941. *Demolished* 1961.

Former names

Seven Tankards and Punch Bowl Public House
National Hall, Holborn/National Schoolrooms
Weston's Music Hall
Royal Music Hall 30. 11. 1868
Royal Holborn Empire
Royal Holborn Theatre of Varieties 1892-1906.

Building details

1857:

Developer: Charles Weston

Architects: Messrs. Finch and Paraire

Contractor: Messrs. Patrick & Sons

Decorations: Messrs. Homann and Beensen

1887:

Architects: Messrs. Lander and Bedells.

Auditorium: Area and Balcony

1892: Alterations and redecoration.

1897: New frontage.

1906:

Architect: Frank Matcham

Cost: £30,000

Capacity: 2,000

Auditorium: Area, Circle and Gallery

Weston's National Music Hall 1858 (376)

(Victoria & Albert Museum, Crown copyright)

Management

Middlesex justices:

Mich. 1857-	Edward Weston	
"	1866-	John Samuel Sweasey and William Holland
"	1968-	John Samuel Sweasey
"	1881-	William Thomas Purkiss
"	1886-	William Thomas Purkiss and Samuel Adams

London County Council:

1890-	Spencer William Thomas Tyler
1892-	John Hollingshead
1893-	John Brill
1903-	Harry Lundy
1905-	Walter Gibbons
1913-	Charles Gulliver
1925-	Holborn Empire Ltd.
1929-	General Theatre Corporation Ltd.
1947-	Moss' Empires Ltd.

Lord Chamberlain:

30.11.1911-	Walter Gibbons
2. 7.1912-	Charles Gulliver
1.12.1928-	Hubert Peter Morrison
1.12.1930-	Ernest William Pashley Peall
1.12.1940-	Horace Stanley White
1.12.1943	*Not relicensed.*

Literature

Official records:

G.L.C. Arch. Dpt. Mss Index;
G.L.C. Arch. Dpt. Th. case 152;
L.C.C. Th. & M-H. Com. App. Nov. 1889-;
L.C.C. Th. & M-H. Com. Papers 1882-;
L.C.C. 374 and 496; Mx. Mich. Q.S. 1857-1888;
Sel. Com. 1866, 1877 and 1892.

Contemporary accounts:

1857 BUILDING NEWS. 1857, Aug. 14th. p. 857.—Note of rebuilding.
BUILDING NEWS. 1857, Nov. 13th. p. 1, 203. —Detailed description.
ERA. 1857 Nov. 17.—Detailed description of opening.

1858 BUILDING NEWS. 1858, Feb. 26th. p. 214. Illus. of interior.

1859 BUILDER. 1859, March 19th. p. 200.—Note on exits.

1887 DAILY TELEGRAPH. 1887, Sept. 10th. The Royal Music Hall—description of new hall.
ERA. 1887, Sept. 17.—Report of opening.

1888 BUILDER. 1888, April 28th, p. 310.—Report of fire precautions.

1892 ERA. 1892 Sept. 17—Report of alterations and redecorations.

1896 ERA. 1896 March 7—Report of sale.

1905 BUILDER, 1905 Aug. 9, p. 213—Note on reconstruction.

1906 ERA. 1906 Jan. 27.—Detailed description of rebuilding.

1906 BUILDER. 1906, Feb. 3rd. p. 124.—Brief description

1940 DAILY MAIL. 1940, Oct. 16th. Photo. of bombed and gutted theatre.

Historical accounts:

c. 1930 MAYES, Ronald
The romance of London's theatres No. 107.

1935 HADDON, Archibald
The story of the music hall ... p. 27-29, 40, 75-7, 194.

1938 DISHER, M.W.
Winkles and champagne ... p. 22, 90.

1959 ENCICLOPEDIA dello spettacola. Vol. 6. col. 1, 626-7.

1968 MANDER, Raymond *and* MITCHENSON, Joe.
The lost theatres of London, pp. 168-185.

Location of other material

Plans:

G.L.C. Architects Department;
Enthoven Collection (2 sheets)
Holborn Local Collection (Royal Music Hall);
Middlesex Record Office. Ground plan by Edward Clark, 1881 (M & D 13/6)

Programmes, playbills and cuttings:

British Museum Library; Enthoven Collection;
Guildhall Library; Holborn Local Collection;
Westminster Local Collection

377

HOLBORN THEATRE

85, High Holborn, Holborn.

Opened: 25 May 1867. *Closed:* as a theatre: c 1887

Former names

New Royal Amphitheatre 1867
Royal Amphitheatre and Circus 1867
Grand Cirque & Amphitheatre 1873
National Amphitheatre 1873
National Theatre 1873
Holborn Amphitheatre 1874
Hamilton's Royal Amphitheatre 1878
Royal Connaught Theatre 1879
Alcazar Theatre 1882
International Theatre 1883
Holborn Theatre 1884

Later

West Central Hall 1887
Holborn Stadium
Stadium Club

Building details

Architect: Thomas Smith.

Builder: Thomas Ennor.

Reconstruction: 1876

Reconstruction: 1879

Redecorated: 1881

Management

Lord Chamberlain:

14. 5.1867-	William Charman and Thomas McCollum	
19. 9.1870-	William Charman	
8.11.1872-	Charles Weldon	
29. 9.1873-	Frederick Strange	
26.12.1873-	William Charman	
29. 9.1874-	George Frederick MacDouogh	

19.12.1874-	John Hollingshead (to 18.6.1875)
6. 8.1875-	James Newsome
13.12.1875-	Francisco Rizareli and Dominogo Rizareli
11. 6.1877-	Alfred Duboys de Lavigerie
29. 9.1877-	James Taylor (to 30.3.1878)
16.11.1878-	Harry Herbert Hamilton
25.10.1879-	James Wyllie Currans
9.12.1879-	John Vale (Official receiver) (to 28.9.1880)
8. 1.1881-	Charles Morton (to 5.3.1881)
3.12.1883-	Marguerite Dinorben
12. 4.1884-	George Rignold
29. 9.1884-	William Rignold
12. 9.1885-	William Thomas Purkiss

London County Council:

1890 William Thomas Purkiss (West Central Hall)

Literature

Official records:

G.L.C. Arch. Dpt. Th. case 2, 944;
L.C.C. Th. & M-H. Com. App. Nov. 1889;
L.C.C. Th. & M-H. Com. Papers, 1883-; (*Under* Alcazar Theatre)
LC7/15-17, 23-17, 31-33; M.B.W. Rpt. 1882. p. 61-71;
Sel. Com. 1877 and 1892.

Contemporary accounts:

1867 ERA. 1867, May 5th.—Description.
BUILDER. 1867, May 25th. p. 367.—Brief description of new theatre built on site of Horse Bazaar.
ERA. 1867. May 26th.—Further description including accommodation details.
ILLUSTRATED LONDON NEWS. 1867, June 22nd. p. 610 and 630.—Interior of auditorium and description.
ILLUSTRATED LONDON NEWS. 1867, Nov. 22nd. —Description of new building.
1873 ERA. 1873, Oct. 12.—Report of reopening.
1876 BUILDER. 1876, Feb. 19th. p. 172.—Conversion to adapt it for skating and promenade concerts.
1878 ERA. 1878, Nov. 17.—Report of opening under Harry Hamilton.
1879 BUILDER. 1879, Nov. 1st. p. 1, 212-3.—Description of complete internal reconstruction to make theatre seating 3, 000.
DAILY TELEGRAPH. 1879, Nov. 3rd.—Description of conversion, by J.W. Currans.
DRAMATIC NOTES. 1879. p. 77.
1881 DAILY TELEGRAPH. 1881, Jan. 10th.—Report of redecorations; Charles Norton as new manager.
1882 BUILDER. 1882, Oct. 21st. p. 542.—Note of Sale.
1883 DAILY NEWS. 1883, Dec. 24th.—Report of reopening as International Theatre.
DAILY TELEGRAPH. 1883, Dec. 24th.—Report of reopening.
ERA. 1883, Dec. 29th.—Reopening as the International.
1884 DAILY NEWS. 1884, Aug. 25th.—Disgraceful riot (owing to no performance and failure to return money).
ERA 1884, Aug. 30.—Description of riot.
1887 BUILDER. 1887, July 16th. p. 120.—Report of conversion into public hall.
1889 BUILDER. 1889, April 6th. p. 270. Report of reopening, and brief note of history.

Historical accounts:

1904 BAKER, H. Barton
History of the London stage and its players. p. 327. —'Holborn Amphitheatre'.
1925 SHERSON, Erroll
London's lost theatres ... p. 188-189. 'Royal Amphitheatre'.
c. 1930 MAYES, Ronald
Romance of London theatres, No. 92.
1946 SCOTT, Harold
The early doors ... p. 104+.
1957 THEATRE WORLD. 1957, Sept.
Lost London theatres, by N.M. Bligh. No. 9. The story of the Royal Amphitheatre, Holborn. 3p. illus.
PRYCE, F.R. in 'Holborn in Brief'.
1968 MANDER, Raymond *and* MITCHESON, Joe
The lost theatres of London. pp. 144-167.

Location of other material

Plans:

G.L.C. *Architects Department.*
Public Record Office. LC7/65. 4 sheets.

Programme and playbills:

Enthoven Collection; Garrick Club; Guildhall Library; Holborn Local Collection; Westminster Local Collection.

Prints: Holborn Local Collection (3 only)

378

HOLE IN THE WALL PUBLIC HOUSE

Kirby Street, Liberty of Saffron Hill, Holborn.

Licensed: 1860-1863

Management

Middlesex justices:

Mich. 1860		William Hearn
"	1861-	Richard Woodlow Parsonson
"	1863	*No application*
"	1864	*Licence refused* to John Thomas Bayford.

Literature

Official records:

Mx. Mich. Q.S. 1860-1864.

379

HOLLAND ARMS PUBLIC HOUSE

Brixton Hill.

Licensed: 1873-1874

Management

Surrey justices:

Mich. 1873-		Edward Dawson
"	1874	*No petition.*

Literature

Official records:

Sy. Mich. Q.S. 1873.

380

HOLLOWAY EMPIRE

564, Holloway Road, Islington.

Opened: 4th December, 1899. By 1924 used as a cinema.

Former name

Empire Theatre of Varieties.

Building details

Architect: W. G. R. Sprague

Builder: Mr. Longden of Sheffield

Capacity: 1, 210

Auditorium: S. 260; Faut. 49; P. 175; C. 260; G. 450; Bx. 16.

Stage: 65' wide × 35' deep.

Theatre finally sold for demolition 31. 3. 1953.

Management

London County Council:

1899-	Oswald Stoll
Nov. 1910	*Not licensed.*
1916-	Harry Thomas Underwood
Nov. 1923	*Listed as a cinema.*
1947	Joseph Bloom, Leslie Bloom and Thomas Jenkins trading as Bloom Bros.
1949	Holloway Empire Ltd.

Lord Chamberlain:

7. 8.1899-	Oswald Stoll (to 28. 9.1899)
1.12.1947-	Jay Pomeroy
1.12.1949	*In hands of Official Receiver.*

Literature

Official records:

G.L.C. Arch. Dpt. Mss. Index;
G.L.C. Arch. Dpt. Th. case 157;
L.C.C. Th. & M-H. Com. App. Nov. 1898+;
L.C. 1/712, LC7/46; L.C.O. 47 and 374.

Contemporary accounts:

1899 BUILDING NEWS. 1899, Dec. 8th. p. 762.—Brief description.
BUILDER. 1899, Dec. 16th. p. 565.—Report of opening and brief description.
1903 HOLLOWAY EMPIRE
(Programme) Grand matinee. Thursday, Oct. 22nd. 1903.—includes two page description of theatre. (Copy in Enthoven Collection)

Location of other material

Plans: G.L.C. *Architects Department.*

Programmes: Enthoven Collection.
Islington Local Collection.

381

HOOP AND GRAPES PUBLIC HOUSE

68, Cable Street, Stepney.

Licensed: 1890-1892

Building details

Concert hall, with platform, was situated on the ground floor at the rear of the public house; it had an area of 477 sq'. After it was closed owing to the 1878 Act, it was converted into a Bagatelle Room.

Management

London County Council:

1890-	Jane Raycroft
Nov. 1892	*No application.*

Literature

Official records:

G.L.C. Arch. Dpt. Th. case 040/62;
L.C.C. Th. & M-H. Com. 1889-1891.

Location of other material

Plans: G.L.C. *Architects Department.*

382

HOOP AND GRAPES PUBLIC HOUSE

112, St. George Street, St. George in the East.

Licensed: 1852-1884

Management

Middlesex justices:

Mich.	1852	Joseph Thomas Winter
"	1853	*Not licensed*
"	1854-	John Ward
"	1863-	James Shepherd
"	1865-	Henry King
"	1868-	Thomas Thompson
"	1876-	Thomas Clegg
"	1880-	Henry Johns
"	1884	*Licence refused.*

Literature

Official records:

Mx. Mich. Q.S. 1852-1884.

383

HOP POLE PUBLIC HOUSE

60, Bath Street, City Road, St. Lukes, Finsbury.

Licensed: 1854-1874

Former name

The Barley Mow and Hop Pole Public House

Management

Middlesex justices:

Mich.	1854	Henry Collard
"	1855-	Alfred Oliver
"	1860-	John Giles (as the Hop Pole)
"	1862	*Refused*
"	1863-	John Giles
"	1865-	George Walter Davis
"	1869	George Frederick Pursell
"	1870-	William Gibbs
"	1874	*Licence refused* to George Belby.

Literature

Official records:-

Mx. Mich. Q.S. 1854-1874.

384

HOPE MUSIC HALL

Hope Public House, 63 (*later* 23) Banner Street, Finsbury.

Licensed: 1860-1898

Building details

Capacity: 150

Management

Middlesex justices:

Mich. 1860	John Harrison
" 1861-	Henry Webb
" 1865-	Henry Morgan
" 1869-	William Hartrill Brady
" 1873	John James Gibson
" 1874	Ellen Durahm
" 1875-	Robert Dean
" 1880-	Jame Cousins
" 1883	Henry Luker
" 1884	Ernest Nicholson
" 1885-	Henry Gobby
" 1888	John James Cousins

London County Council:

1890	Charles Alfred Creasey
1891	Thomas Bonner
1892	Ernest Franklin
1893	Joseph Richard Archbell
1894-	Charles Henry Farmer
1898-	John Martin
Nov. 1898	*Not licensed*

Literature

Official records:

G.L.C. Arch. Dpt. Th. case 047;
L.C.C. Th. & M-H. Com. App. Nov. 1889-1898;
Mx. Mich. Q.S. 1860-1888; Sel. Com. 1892.

385

HOPE PUBLIC HOUSE

16, Blackmore Street, Clare Market.

Licensed: 1854, and 1856-60

Management

Middlesex justices:

Mich. 1854-	William Driver
" 1855	*No petition*
" 1856-	John Pearson
" 1857-	Frederick Charles Ponu
" 1858-	Thomas James Marrable
" 1859-	George Hardy
" 1860	*William Cole refused licence.*

Literature

Official records:

Mx. Mich. Q.S. 1854-1860.

386

HOPE PUBLIC HOUSE

47, Stanhope Street, Hampstead Road, St. Pancras.

Licensed: 1864-1889

Management

Middlesex justices:

Mich. 1864-	Horatio Chipp
" 1874	Veere Woodman
" 1875-	Sarah Maria Woodman
" 1879-	Moses Mercer Ward (through 1888)

Literature

Official records:

Mx. Mich. Q.S. 1864-1888.

Holloway Empire c. 1899 (380)

(Ellis Ashton Collection, British Music Hall Society)

387

HOPE AND ANCHOR PUBLIC HOUSE

14, Hereford Street, Lisson Grove.

Licensed: 1854-1857

Management

Middlesex justices:

Mich. 1854-   Joseph Whiteman
"   1857   *No petition.*

Literature

Official records:

Mx. Mich. Q.S. 1854-1857.

388

HORN PUBLIC HOUSE AND ASSEMBLY ROOMS

Kennington (Park) Road, Lambeth.

Licensed: 1857-1898

Management

Surrey justices:

Mich. 1857-   John Martin
"   1859-   James Martin
"   1861-   William Davis
"   1866-   Alexander Whittet
"   1873-   Joseph Eaton
"   1877-   John William Frederick Cox
"   1880-   John Thomas Smith
"   1882-   William Thomas Buxton

London County Council:

1890-   William Thomas Buxton
1894-   Edmund Ferguson
Nov.   1898   *Licence refused for private gain or trade.*

Literature

Official records:

L.C.C. Th. & M-H. Com. App. Nov. 1889-1898;
Sy. Mich. Q.S. 1857-1888.

Location of other material

Playbills, illustrations & cuttings:

London Museum Library *in* The Pleasure Gardens of South London. Vol. II pp. 97-120.

389

HORNS PUBLIC HOUSE

Whitechapel High Street, Whitechapel.

Licensed: 1855-1857

Management

Middlesex justices:

Mich. 1855-   Michael Myers
"   1857   *No petition.*

Literature

Official records:

Mx. Mich. Q.S. 1855-1857.

390

HORNS AND CHEQUERS PUBLIC HOUSE

Thames Place, Limehouse Hole, Poplar.

Licensed: 1869-1891

Building details

Concert hall on the first floor, area 627' 7" plus stage. Used one day a week for concerts. Hall closed by the Act of 1878.

Management

Middlesex justices:

Mich. 1869   William Bundock
"   1870-   James Ashpool
"   1872-   Thomas Bairstow
"   1877-   Daniel Birkbeck
"   1885-   John James Silvester

London County Council:

1890-   John James Silvester
Nov.   1891   *Not licensed.*

Literature

Official records:

G.L.C. Arch. Dpt. Th. case 040/64;
L.C.C. Th. & M-H. Com. App. Nov. 1889-91.

391

HORSE AND GROOM PUBLIC HOUSE

Mare Street, Hackney.

Licensed: 1866-1868

Management

Middlesex justices:

Mich. 1866-   John Boyd
"   1868   *Licence refused.*

Literature

Official records:

Mx. Mich. Q.S. 1866-1868.

392

HORSE SHOE MUSIC HALL

Horse Shoe Public House, 26, Clerkenwell Close, Finsbury.

Licensed: 1856-1886

Building details

Small music hall, 37' × 26', on the first floor of the public house.

Capacity: 150

Hall closed owing to the 1878 Act.

Management

Middlesex justices:

Mich. 1856-	Benjamin Hayne
" 1862-	George Major
" 1864-	Robert Goodwin
" 1866-	John Callow
" 1869-	Edward Stokes
" 1872-	Frederick Henry Clarke
" 1874	Richard Philipps
" 1875-	Richard Darter
" 1877	George Lovell
" 1878-	James Smith
" 1885	Andrew George Kelso
" 1886	*Application withdrawn.*

Literature

Official records:

G.L.C. Arch. Dpt. Th. case 040/65;
Mx. Mich. Q.S. 1856-1886; Sel. Com. 1892.

Location of other material

Plans: G.L.C. *Architects Department.*

393

HOXTON HALL

64 B, Hoxton High Street, Hoxton.

Licensed: 1864-1871

Also known as
McDonald's Music Hall.

Building details

Hall empty from 1872 to 1877, from this date to 1885
it is listed as a music hall in Shoreditch ratebooks.
From the 1890's until the present day it has been used
by the Quakers as a meeting place. In 1963 a music
hall performance was given there to celebrate its
centenary.

Management

Middlesex justices:

Mich. 1864	James Mortimer
" 1865	Francis Day and Joseph Sawyer
" 1866-	James McDonald Jnr.
" 1871	*Licence refused.*

Literature

Official records:
Mx. Mich. Q.S. 1864-1871.

394

HUNGERFORD PALACE MUSIC HALL
Hungerford Market, Charing Cross.

Licensed: 1858-1862

Also known as

Hungerford Hall
Hungerford Music Hall
Hungerford Market Music Hall
Music Hall, Hungerford Market.

Hoxton Hall (393)

(Greater London Council Photograph Lib›

Management

Middlesex justices:

Mich. 1858-   Carlo Gatti, Giovanni Gatti and
               Guiseppe Monico
"   1862   *Reported demolished.*

Literature

Official records:

Mx. Mich. Q.S. 1858-1861.

Contemporary accounts:

1857   RITCHIE, J. Ewing
        The night side of London. p. 144-151.

Historical accounts:

1946   SCOTT, Harold
        Early doors... p. 143.

395

IMPERIAL THEATRE

Newington Causeway.

Theatre partly constructed, but never used.

Literature

Contemporary accounts:

1872   BUILDER, 1872, April 13th. p. 280. Description of new theatre to be built. Architect Albert Bridgemann, Contractors, W.& B. Lacey.
1874   BUILDER, 1874, March, 21st. p. 247. Report of new theatre to be built by financier. Architect, Elliott and Warren, Contractor Mr. Wheeler.—Detailed description of plans.
1880   BUILDER, 1880, April 3rd. p. 419.—Conversion of intended theatre into factory.

396

IMPERIAL THEATRE

Tothill Street, Westminster.

Opened: 15th April, 1876. *Closed:* November 1907.

Former names

Aquarium Theatre
Royal Aquarium Theatre

Building details

Theatre built at west end of the Royal Aquarium.

Architect: A. Bedborough.

Contractor: Messrs. Lucas

Capacity: 1, 293

Auditorium: S. 244; P. 133; B. 202; U.C. 163; G. 214.

1898: Extensive alterations.

Architect: Walter Emden.

Reconstructed: 1901

Architect: F. T. Verity

Builders: John Allen & Sons Ltd., Kilburn

Capacity: 1, 150

Stage: 62' wide × 40' deep.

Mrs. Langtry sold theatre to Wesleyan Methodists who in turn sold it to the company owning the Royal Albert Music Hall, Canning Town, who re-erected it stone by stone as the Music Hall of Dockland.

Management

Lord Chamberlain:

15. 4. 1876-   Stephen Samuel Coleman
29. 9. 1877-   William Wybrow Robertson
20. 3. 1879-   Marie Litton
30. 8. 1880-   William Edgcumbe Rendle
29. 9. 1881-   Anthony Pemberton Hobson
 2. 3. 1885-   Thomas Mowbray
 8. 3. 1886-   David de Pinna (to 31. 5. 1886)
29. 9. 1891-   James Watson Wilkinson (to 10. 1.1903)

Literature

Official records:

G. L. C. Arch. Dpt. Mss. index;
G.L.C. Arch. Dpt. Th. case 01;
L.C. C. Th. & M-H. Com. Papers 1889-1908;
LC7/16-17, 24-32, 44-48, 89;
M.B.W. Rpt. 1882, p. 181 & 193;
Mx. Mich. Q.S. 1875-1888 ('Royal Aquarium');
Sel. Com. 1877 and 1892.

Contemporary accounts:

1875   BUILDER. 1875, May 1st.—Illus. of theatre.
1876   ERA. 1876, Jan 16th.—Description of Aquarium—theatre secondary.
        BUILDER. 1876, Jan. 22nd.—Illus of theatre.
        ERA. 1876, Jan. 23rd.—Description.
        ERA. 1876, April 16th.—Description of theatre.
1879   DRAMATIC NOTES. 1879, pp. 44-47.
1898   ERA. 1898, April 16th—Report of reopening, alterations made to meet L.C.C. requirements.
1901   BUILDER. 1901, March 16th. p. 271.—Brief note on reopening after Mrs. Langtry's reconstruction of building. Architect: F. T. Verity.
        BUILDER. 1901, April 27th. p. 422-3.—Detailed description of rebuilt theatre.
1908   BUILDER. 1908, Jan. 4th. p. 25.—Report that it is offered for sale on Feb. 5th. Note of history.

Historical accounts:

1904   BAKER, H. Barton
        History of the London stage and its players. p. 532-3.—'Aquarium Theatre'.
1925   SHERSON, Erroll
        London's lost theatres... Chapter XIV. p. 295-305.
c. 1930 MAYES, Ronald
        Romance of London theatres. No. 23.
1946   SCOTT, Harold
        Early doors... p. 163+.
1952   PULLING, Christopher
        They were singing... p. 192-3.
1954   WILSON, A. E.
        East end entertainment... p. 221.
1957   THEATRE WORLD. 1957, March.
        Lost London theatres, by N. M. Bligh. No. 7 The story of the Aquarium or the Imperial Theatre, Westminster. 3p. illus.
1959   ENCICLOPEDIA dello spettacolo. Vol. 6. col. 1615.

1968 MANDER, Raymond *and* MITCHENSON, Joe.
The lost theatres of London. pp. 205-217.

Location of other material

Plans:

G.L.C. *Architects Department;* Public Record Office,
LC7/64. 6 sheets of plans and sections.

Programmes and playbills:

British Museum Library; Enthoven Collection;
Garrick Club; Guildhall Library; London Museum;
Westminster Local Collection.

397

IRONMONGERS ARMS PUBLIC HOUSE

7, Lizard Street, Old Street.

Licensed: 1848-1890

Building details

Concert room on the first floor of the premises,
39′ × 16′; it was closed as a result of the 1878 Act.

Management

Middlesex justices:

Mich.	1848-	John Andrew Jones
"	1851-	Philip Wildee
"	1861-	James Thomas Humphrey
"	1875-	Emma Matilda Humphrey
"	1877-	John Collins
"	1880-	James William Edwards Eve
"	1885-	Elizabeth Emma Clarke
"	1888	Henry Caldecourt

London County Council:

1890 Henry Caldecourt (licence retained).

Literature

Official records:

G.L.C. Arch. Dpt. Th. case 040/66;
L.C.C. Th. & M-H. Com. App. Nov. 1889;
Mx. Mich. Q.S. 1848-1888.

Location of other material

Plans: G.L.C. *Architects Department.*

398

IRONMONGER'S ARMS PUBLIC HOUSE

210, West Ferry Road, Millwall, Poplar.

Licensed: 1861-1891

Building details

Concert room on the first floor over the public house
bar, 39′ 4″ × 16′ 6″, with an area of 458 sq′ without
the stage. Hall had fixed seating round it. Hall eventu-
ally closed as a result of 1878 Act.

Management

Middlesex justices:

Mich.	1861-	Nicholas Knight
"	1864	Richard Burley
"	1865-	Charles Darling
"	1882-	John Douglas Charrington
"	1886-	Justin McSwiney

London County Council:

	1890-	Justin McSwiney
Nov.	1891	*No application*

Literature

Official records:

G.L.C. Arch. Dpt. Th. case 040/67;
L.C.C. Th & M-H. Com. App. Nov. 1889-1890;
Mx. Mich. Q.S. 1861-1888.

399

ISLAND QUEEN PUBLIC HOUSE

34, Hanover Street, Islington.

Licensed: 1857-1889

Management

Middlesex justices:

Mich.	1857-	Henry William Wild
"	1860-	Paul Puzey
"	1863-	William Benwell
"	1865-	Walter William Cannaway
"	1867-	George Cox
"	1870-	William Augustus Smith
"	1872-	Alfred Gurney
"	1875-	Harry Kettle
"	1878	Henry Cross
"	1879-	Edward Charles Mears
"	1885-	Charles Frederick Hyde
"	1888	Alfred William Knotts

Literature

Official records:

Mx. Mich. Q.S. 1857-1888.

400

ISLINGTON EMPIRE

40, Islington High Street, *(formerly* 40, Upper St. *)*
Islington.

Opened: 1860 *Last proper variety show:* February
1932.

Former names

Philharmonic Hall 1860-
Philharmonic Theatre 1874-
Grand Theatre 1888-
Empire, Islington 1908-
Islington Palace 1912-
Islington Empire 1918-

Building details

1st building:

Architects: Finch, Hill & Paraire

Cost: £20,000

Capacity: 1,500

1870: Alterations

Reopened with new stage and promenade.

1874: Redecoration

Opened as Philharmonic Theatre

Capacity: 758 seated

Auditorium: S. 148; P. 337; B. & C. 285; Bx. 48.

2nd building:

Opened: 4.8.1883.

Architect: Frank Matcham

Destroyed: 29.12.1887

3rd building:

Opened: 1.12.1888

Architect: Frank Matcham

Decorations: Messrs. Campbell, Smith & Co.

Capacity: c. 3,000

Destroyed by fire: February 1900

4th building:

Opened: 1901

Architect: Frank Matcham

Contractor: Messrs. Dearing & Sons

Decorator: Messrs. F. de Jong & Co.

Management

Middlesex justices:

Mich. 1860-	Frederick Sanders and Edward Lacey
" 1864-	Frederick Sanders and Samuel Adams
" 1865-	George Turnham and Samuel Adams
" 1867-	Samuel Adams
" 1869-	Francis Robinson
" 1870-	Charles Morton
" 1871	*Licence refused.*

Lord Chamberlain:

21.12.1870-	Charles Morton
29.9.1873-	Charles Head
29.9.1874-	Richard Shepherd
29.9.1875-	J.D. Solomon
29.9.1877-	Frederick Wilson
17.11.1877-	Charles Head (to 28.9.1882)
4.8.1883-	Charles Wilmot
27.11.1896-	William McLean Borrodaile
26.12.1900-	Harry Shrubsole (to 1902)

London County Council:

1908-	Walter Gibbons
1913-	Charles Gulliver
1925-	London Theatres of Varieties Ltd.
1928	Greater London Theatres and Cinemas Ltd.
1929-	Summers Brown
1931-	Metropolitan and Provincial Cinematograph Theatres Ltd.
Nov. 1931	*Not Licensed.*
1933-1942	Associated British Cinemas Ltd.

Lord Chamberlain—subsidiary licence:

4.12.1911-	Walter Gibbons
2.7.1912-	Charles Gulliver
1.12.1927-	Summers Brown
1.12.1930-	Victor Sheridan
1.12.1932-	Ralph Sidney Bromhead
1.12.1934-	Arthur Stanley Moss (to 1939)

Literature

Official records:

G.L.C. Arch. Dpt. Mss. index; G.L.C. Arch. Dpt. Th. case 230;
L.C.C. Th. & M-H. Com. App. Nov. 1907-1941;
L.C.C. Th. & M-H. Com. Papers 1888+;
L.C. 7/15-17, 24-29, 32-48; L.C.O. 374, 494 and 538;
M.B.W. Rpt. 1882, p. 231-241.
Mx. Mich. Q.S. 1860-1871.

Contemporary accounts:

1874 BUILDING NEWS. 1874, Sept. 18th. p. 360.—Note of decoration.
1882 BUILDER. 1882, May 13th. p. 599.—Brief report that Frank Matcham is preparing entire reconstruction.
1883 DAILY TELEGRAPH. 1883, Aug. 6th. 'The Grand Theatre'—Description.
BUILDER. 1883, Sept. 1st, and 8th. p. 305 and 312.—Description of new theatre.
1887 SATURDAY REVIEW. 1887, July 9th. 'The state of the London theatres'...No. 4.
DAILY TELEGRAPH. 1887, Dec. 29th, 30th and 31st 'Destruction of the Grand Theatre at Islington'.
1887 GLOBE, 1887, Dec. 29th (4th edition)—The Grand Theatre, Islington, destroyed by fire: report.
1888 BUILDING NEWS. 1888, Jan. 6th. p. 64.—Letter on burning of theatre.
GRAPHIC. 1888, Jan 7th. 'The burning of the Grand'.
DAILY TELEGRAPH. 1888, Dec. 3rd. 'Grand Theatre': report of rebuilding.
ILLUSTRATED SPORTING AND DRAMATIC NEWS. 1888, Dec. 8th.—Illustration of new interior.
1896 SACHS, E.O. and WOODROW, E.A.E. Modern opera houses and theatres...Vol. 1. p. 41.—Illus. plates, plans and sections.
1900 SKETCH. 1900, March 7th.—Illus. of fire at the Grand Theatre.
BUILDING NEWS, 1900, Dec. 28th. p. 933.—Description.
1901 BUILDER. 1901, Jan. 5th. p. 13.—Report of rebuilding after fire in February 1900.
1906 BUILDER. 1906, April 7th. p. 385.—Report of proposed sale: summary of history.

Historical accounts:

1898 SOLDENE, Emily
My theatrical and musical recollections. Downey, 1898. p. 107-134, her memories of the Philharmonic and Charles Morton.
1904 BAKER, H. Barton
History of the London stage and its players, p. 382.
1925 SHERSON, Erroll
London's lost theatres...p. 262-277
c. 1930 MAYES, Ronald
The romance of London theatres, No. 41.

1938 DISHER, M.W.
Winkles and champagne...p. 15, 94.
1956 POPE, W. J. Macqueen
Nights of gladness...p. 86+.

Location of other material

Plans:
G.L.C. *Architects Department.*
Enthoven Collection (2 sheets)
Public Record Office. LC7/60, Plans of alterations, 1871-1878. Plans for hall, with section, 1870.

Programmes and playbills:

British Museum Library; Enthoven Collection; Guildhall Library. (57 items); Islington Local Collection; Westminster Local Collection.

401

ISLINGTON PALACE

Royal Agricultural Hall, Upper Street, Islington.

Opened: 1869-

Former names

Berner's Hall
New Concert Hall
Mohawkes Hall
Empire Music Hall
Islington Palace

Later

Blue Hall Cinema
Gaumont Cinema

Management

London County Council:

Licensed by the L.C.C. as part of the Royal Agricultural Hall which it adjoined.

Lord Chamberlain:

21.12.1908-31.1.1909 Francis Joseph Petter (returned 13.3.1909).

Literature

Official records:

G.L.C. Arch. Dpt. Th. case 344; L.C.O. 151; Sel. Com. 1892.

Contemporary accounts:

1955 ISLINGTON. Public Libraries. Islington and the theatre (exhibition). p. 8

Location of other material

Plans: G.L.C. *Architects Department.*

Playbills, Programmes & cuttings:
Islington Local Collection; Guildhall Library (14 items for Agricultural Hall 1867-1893).

402

JACK STRAW'S CASTLE PUBLIC HOUSE

Hampstead.

Licensed: 1856-1888

Islington Empire (400)

(Ellis Ashton Collection, British Music Hall Society)

Grand Theatre 1888 (400)

(British Museum)

Management

Middlesex justices:

Mich. 1856-	Robert Ware
" 1875	Henry Charles Fulloon
" 1876-	John Lane
" 1879	Thomas Aynsley Cook
" 1880-	John Lane

Literature

Official records:

Mx. Mich. Q. S. 1856-1888.

403

JERUSALEM PUBLIC HOUSE

1, St. John Square, Finsbury.

Licensed: 1851-1889

Former names

Old Jerusalem Public House.

Management

Middlesex justices:

Mich. 1851-	Benjamin Foster
" 1863-	Samuel Wickens
" 1874-	William Charles Gay

London County Council:

Nov. 1889 Owen Hood's *application refused.*

Literature

Official records:

Mx. Mich. Q. S. 1851-1888.

404

JEW'S HARP PUBLIC HOUSE

Edward Street, Regents Park.

Licensed: 1853-1864

Management

Middlesex justices:

Mich. 1853-	Thomas Burnick
" 1854	Robert Polworth
" 1855-	John Crabbe
" 1861	William Rippin
" 1862	Thomas Windmill
" 1863	Alexander Hargreaves
" 1864	Alfred Wilson *refused licence.*

Literature

Official records:

Mx. Mich. Q. S. 1854-1864.

405

JOHN BULL PUBLIC HOUSE

3, Brewer Street, Clerkenwell.

Licensed: 1859-1882

Management

Middlesex justices:

Mich. 1859-	Joseph Knowles
" 1864-	Abraham Hanwell Tomkins
" 1869	Daniel Milton
" 1870	John Waller
" 1871-	William Reeves
" 1873-	Joseph Bailey
" 1878-	Alfred Hinton
" 1880	William Styles Linforth
" 1881	John Chitterbuck
" 1882	*Licence not renewed.*

Literature

Official records:

Mx. Mich. Q. S. 1859-1882.

406

JOHN OF JERUSALEM PUBLIC HOUSE

164, St. John Street, Finsbury.

Licensed: 1866-1890

Management

Middlesex justices:

Mich. 1866-	Randall Dean
" 1870-	Joshua Watkins
" 1875	Mary Ann Watkins
" 1876-	Thomas Francis Haslip
" 1878-	Edward Thomas Huish
" 1885-	William Bray

London County Council:

1890 William Bray
Nov. 1890 *Not relicensed*

Literature

Official records:

L.C.C. Th. & M-H. Com. App. Nov. 1889;
Mx. Mich. Q. S. 1866-1888.

407

JOLLY ANGLERS PUBLIC HOUSE

42, Bath Street, St. Luke's, Finsbury.

Licensed: 1865-1890

Management

Middlesex justices:

Mich. 1865-	James Bond
" 1875-	Charles Coleman
" 1888	Thomas Henry Rice

London County Council:

1890 William Tofield

Literature

Official records:

L.C.C. Th. & M-H. Com. App. Nov. 1889;
Mx. Mich. Q. S. 1865-1888.

408

JOLLY ANGLERS PUBLIC HOUSE

Lea Bridge, Hackney.

Licensed: 1852-1890

Management

Middlesex justices:

Mich. 1852-	William Wicks
" 1864-	John Charles Kay
" 1866-	Robert Sargent
" 1873-	Masterman Hardy Willson Hill
" 1878-	Elonza Eversden
" 1882-	Joseph Kendall
" 1884-	Frederick Henry Fullcher

London County Council:

1890	Frederick Henry Fullcher
Nov. 1890	*Application withdrawn owing to works required.*

Literature

Official records:

L.C.C. Th. & M-H. Com. App. Nov. 1889-1890;
Mx. Mich. Q. S. 1852-1888.

409

JOLLY SAILOR PUBLIC HOUSE

6, Back Road, Shadwell.

Licensed: 1854-1857

Management

Middlesex justices:

Mich. 1854-	John Shirley
" 1857	*No petition,*

Literature

Official records:

Mx. Mich. Q. S. 1854-1857.

410

JOLLY SAILOR PUBLIC HOUSE

182, St. George Street, Ratcliffe Highway.

Licensed: 1853-1888

Building details

Concert hall 28' 10" × 46', with raised platform 4' high.

Management

Middlesex justices:

Mich. 1853	Henry Brand
" 1854-	Mary Ann Brand
" 1857-	Georgiana Sophia Marshall
" 1865-	Peter Lawson
" 1879-	Augusta Larsen
" 1881-	Georg Ludwig Cumprecht
" 1887	*Licence refused.*

Literature

Official records:

G.L.C. Arch. Dept. Th. case 040/69;
Mx. Mich. Q.S. 1854-1887.

Location of other material

Plans: G.L.C. *Architects Department.*

411

JOLLY TANNERS MUSIC HALL AND PUBLIC HOUSE

36, Alice Street, Bermondsey.

Licensed: 1861-1893

Also known as

Jolly Tanners Public House
Jolly Tanners Assembly Rooms

Management

Surrey justices:

Mich. 1861-	Thomas Lewis Green
" 1868-	William Henry Green and James Joseph Green
" 1870-	John Stacey
" 1878-	James Copelin
" 1880	Thomas Clarke
" 1881	William Thomas Clarke
" 1882-	Henry Robert Cole
" 1885	*Not licensed*
" 1886-	Thomas Newber
" 1888	James Piper

London County Council

1890-	James Piper
Nov. 1891	*Not licensed*
1893	Henry Montgomery Graham *as Jolly Tanners Music Hall*
Nov. 1893	*Not licensed*

Literature

Official records:

L.C.C. Th. & M-H. Com. App. Nov. 1889-1893;
Sy. Mich. Q.S. 1861-1888; Sel. Com. 1892.

412

KENNINGTON THEATRE

Kennington Park Road, Kennington.

Opened: 26th December, 1898.

Former name

Princess of Wales' Theatre

Building details

Architect: W. G. R. Sprague

Builder: Walter Wallis

Decorator: Messrs. De Jong

Capacity: 1, 347

Auditorium: P. 346; S. & Bx. 310; D.C. & Bx. 257; G. & Bx. 434.

Stage: 80' wide × 50' deep.

Management

Lord Chamberlain:

1. 12. 1899-	Robert Arthur
23. 9. 1912-	Milton Bode and Edward Compton
16. 7. 1918-	Virginia Frances Compton Mackenzie
10. 5. 1919-	William Herbert Percy
1. 12. 1921-	John Morgan
1. 12. 1925-	Michael Leonard Abrahams
1. 12. 1928-	William Henry Bickerton
1. 12. 1930-	Ernest William Pashley Peall (Secretary of United Picture Theatres Ltd.)
1. 12. 1934-	John Morgan
1. 12. 1935	*Not relicensed.*

London County Council:

1922-	John Morgan
1925-	Kennington Theatre Ltd.
1926-	Michael Leonard Abrahams
Nov. 1926	*Not licensed as theatre or music-hall.*

Literature

Official records:

G.L.C. Arch. Dpt. Mss. index;
G.L.C. Arch. Dpt. Th. case 432;
L.C.C. Th. & M-H. Com. App. Nov. 1921-25;
L.C.C. Th. & M-H. Com. Papers 1897+;
LC1/712, 731 and 752; LC7/45-48;
L.C.O. 337 and 374.

Contemporary accounts:

1898 BUILDING NEWS. 1898, April 1st. p. 470.
—Description.
BUILDER. 1898, April 2nd. p. 334.—Brief note on proposed new theatre.
BUILDER. 1898, July 30th. p. 108.—Description of plans, note of foundation stone laying by Henry Irving.
SOUTH LONDON PRESS. 1898, Dec. 24th. 'Princess of Wales' Theatre: the new dramatic temple at Kennington'. Illus. of exterior.
BUILDING NEWS. 1898, Dec. 30th. p. 952.
—Brief description.
1899 BUILDER. 1899, Feb. 4th. p. 118.—Description, plan and exterior elevation.
1949 SOUTH LONDON PRESS. 1949, Nov. 11th. 'Theatre site for Sale'.—Report of proposed compulsory purchase order.
EVENING NEWS. 1949, Nov. 29th.—Report that flats to be built on site.

Historical accounts:

c. 1930 MAYES, Ronald The romance of London theatres. No. 95.
1949 SOUTH LONDON PRESS. 1949, Nov. 18th.
—Note of history.

Location of other material

Plans: G.L.C. *Architects Department.*

Photographs: Enthoven Collection

Programmes and playbills:

British Museum Library; Enthoven Collection; Garrick Club; Lambeth Local Collection; Westminster Local Collection.

413

KENTON ARMS PUBLIC HOUSE

Kenton Road, Hackney.

Licensed: 1862-1869

Management

Middlesex justices:

Mich. 1862-		Dowman Carrington
"	1864	Benjamin Beach
"	1865	Thomas Flandell
"	1866-	Charles George Hollot
"	1869	*No application.*

Literature

Official records

Mx. Mich. Q.S. 1862-1869.

414

KILBURN EMPIRE

9-11, The Parade, Kilburn High Road, Kilburn, Hampstead.

Opened: c. 1906.

Former names

New Kilburn Empire
Kilburn Vaudeville Theatre

Building details

Capacity: 1, 913

Auditorium: S. 133; P. 496; C. 454; G. 546.

Management

London County Council:

Nov. 1905	*Prov. Licence* to Walter Stephens (to be erected)
Nov. 1906-8	*Prov. Licence* to Harry Warden and Stanley Chilcott
1909-	Francis Joseph Pepper
1925-	London Theatres of Varieties & F. J. Pepper (spl)
1928	Greater London Theatres and Cinemas Ltd. & Summers Brown (spl)
1929-30	Summers Brown
1931-	Metropolitan & Provincial Cinematograph Theatres Ltd.
	and 1931- Victor Sheridan
	1937 Theodore Kanssen
	1938- Arthur Hillier
1942-	Kilburn Varieties Ltd.
	and 1942 Richard Ed. Marcoso
	1943- Frederick J. Butterworth
1947-	Nat Tennens

Literature

Official records:

G.L.C. Arch. Dpt. Mss. index;
G.L.C. Arch. Dpt. Th. case 231;
L.C.C. Th. & M-H. Com. App. Nov. 1905+;
L.C.C. Th. & M-H. Com. Papers. 1904+.

Location of other material

Plans: G.L.C. *Architects Department.*

Programmes and playbills

British Museum Library; Enthoven Collection; Hampstead Local Collection; London Museum; Westminster Local Collection;

415

KILBURN PALACE

256, Belsize Road, Hampstead.

Opened: 1886. *Reopened* as Cinematograph Theatre 2nd Aug. 1909.

Former name

Kilburn, Theatre Royal.

Building details

Theatre built on the site of the old Kilburn Town Hall which had been licensed before 1878.
1895 Premises reconstructed, and fireproof curtain provided.

Capacity: 514

Auditorium: Area 300; D.C. 214.

Rebuilding, 1899:

Architect: Palgrave & Co.

Management

London County Council:

Building hitherto licensed as Kilburn Town Hall

1896	Julien Davis Solomon
1897-	Henry Harvey Morell
1900-	Julien Davis Solomon
1908-	Richard Chadwick
Nov. 1916	*Licensed as Kilburn Picture Palace to* J. Clavering

Literature

Official records:

G.L.C. Arch. Dpt. Mss. index;
G.L.C. Arch. Dpt. Th. case 356;
L.C.C. Th. & M-H. Com. App. Nov. 1895-1916.

Contemporary accounts:

1899 BUILDING NEWS. 1899, May 26th. p. 711. plate & plan.—Proposed theatre to be built on site of Theatre Royal.

Location of other material

Plans: G.L.C. *Architects Department.*

Kilburn Empire   (414)

(Ellis Ashton Collection, British Music Hall Society)

Kennington Theatre 1899   (412)

(The Builder)

Programmes:
Enthoven Collection;
Guildhall Library (5 items for 1898)

416
KING AND PRINCE OF WALES PUBLIC HOUSE

1, Brick Street, Piccadilly.

Licensed: 1851-1858

Management
Middlesex justices:

| Mich. 1851- | George Loomis |
| " 1858 | *No petition.* |

Literature
Official records:
Mx. Mich. Q.S. 1851-1857.

417
KING AND QUEEN PUBLIC HOUSE

1, Foley Street, St. Marylebone.

Licensed: 1864-1888

Management
Middlesex justices:

Mich. 1864-	William Fisher
" 1866-	John Rogers
" 1882-	Sarah Jane Petherbridge
" 1884-	Sarah Jane Carrington (same as above)
" 1886-	Charles Trery Sinclair
" 1888	*Refused*

Literature
Official records:
Mx. Mich. Q.S. 1864—1888.

418
KING AND QUEEN PUBLIC HOUSE
Harrow Road, Paddington.

Licensed: 1850-1868.

Management
Middlesex justices:

Mich. 1850-	Frederick Smith
" 1855-	William James Smith
" 1868	*Not licensed.*

Literature
Official records:
Mx. Mich. Q.S. 1848-1867.

419
KING OF PRUSSIA PUBLIC HOUSE
Somerset Place, Hoxton New Town.

Licensed: 1851-1856

Management
Middlesex justices:

| Mich. 1851- | John Arnold |
| " 1856 | *No petition.* |

Literature
Official records:
Mx. Mich. Q.S. 1851-1856.

420
KING'S HALL
83/5, Commercial Road, Stepney.

Licensed: 1890-1903.

Also known as
Phoenix Temperance Hall.

Management
Middlesex justices:

| Mich. 1875- | Thomas Reilly |

London County Council:

1890-	Thomas Reilly
Nov. 1897	*Not licensed:*
1899-	Frank Moss
1902-	Moses Cohen
Nov. 1903	*Not licensed as theatre or music hall*

Literature
Official records:
L.C.C. Th. & M-H. Com. App. Nov. 1889-1903;
Mx. Mich. Q.S. 1875-1888.

421
KING'S THEATRE
Hammersmith Road, Hammersmith

Opened: 26th December 1902.   *Demolished:* 1963

Building details
Architect: W. G. R. Sprague.
Capacity: 3,000
Auditorium: S. 156; P. 542; D.C. 302; G. 786.

Management
London County Council:

1903-	John Brennan Mulholland
1926-	Mrs. Aimee Louise Mulholland
1946-	Thomas Joseph Pigott, for J. B. Mulholland's trustees.
1948-	John Victor Mulholland.

Literature
Official records:
G.L.C. Arch. Dpt. Mss. index;
G.L.C. Arch. Dpt. Th. case 1883;
L.C.C. Th. & M-H. Com. Nov. 1902+

Contemporary accounts:

1901 BUILDER, 1901 Sept. 21, p. 257.—Note that Charity Commission concur with plan to build theatre upon land belonging to trustees of charitable endowment.
1903 BUILDER, 1903 Jan. 3, p. 20.—Report of opening.
1904 SKETCH, 1904 Sept. 28. Illus. of interior and exterior.
1950 THEATRE ownership. p. 128.

Historical accounts:

c. 1930 MAYES, Ronald
　　　The romance of London theatres, No. 82.
1965 TABS, 1965 June, pp. 15-21. plan and section. 'How did they do it? of the King's Hammersmith.' by Frederick Bentham.

Location of other material

Plans: G.L.C. *Architects Department;* Enthoven Collection.

Programmes and playbills &c.

British Museum Library; Enthoven Collection; Garrick Club; Hammersmith Local Collection; London Museum; Westminster Local Collection.

422

KING'S ARMS PUBLIC HOUSE

114, Cheyne Walk, (*formerly* Davies Place, and Ryley Street) Chelsea.

Licensed: 1852-1903

Building details

Capacity: 140

Management

Middlesex justices:

Mich.	1852-	John Sparks Alexander
"	1860-	Edward George Chapman
"	1862-	Thomas Crane
Mich.	1869-	James Hayward Hughes
"	1873-	James Copelin
"	1875	James Hayward Hughes
"	1876-	William John Fickling

London County Council:

1890- Nov. 1903	William John Fickling *Not licensed as theatre or music hall*

Literature

Official records:

L.C.C. Th. & M-H. Com. 1889-1903; Mx. Mich. Q.S. 1852-1888; Sel. Com. 1892.

423

KING'S ARMS PUBLIC HOUSE

Church End, Shoreditch.

Licensed: 1860-1862

Management

Middlesex justices:

Mich.	1860-	William Walker
"	1862	*Licence refused.*

Literature

Official records:

Mx. Mich. Q.S. 1860-1862.

424

KING'S ARMS PUBLIC HOUSE

Fieldgate Street, Stepney.

Licensed: 1855-1863

Management

Middlesex justices:

Mich.	1855-	Johan Jockim Gerkes
"	1863	*Licence refused.*

Literature

Official records:

Mx. Mich. Q.S. 1855-1863.

425

KING'S ARMS PUBLIC HOUSE

2, Houghton Street, St. Clement Danes.

Licensed: 1854-1862

Management

Middlesex justices:

Mich.	1854-	William Potter
"	1857-	Henry Shynn
"	1861	George Jessup

King's Theatre (421)

(Hammersmith Public Libraries)

Literature

Official records:

Mx. Mich. Q.S. 1854–1861.

426

KING'S ARMS PUBLIC HOUSE

Greenwich.

Licensed: 1850–1857

Management

West Kent justices:

Mich.	1850–	Thomas William Thame
"	1851–	Christopher Paine (Payne)
"	1854–	Charles Carter Lewis
"	1858	*Not licensed.*

Literature

Official records:

W. Kt. Mich. Q.S. 1848–1857.

427

KING'S ARMS PUBLIC HOUSE

Kennington Lane, Kennington.

Licensed: 1861–1865

Management

Surrey justices:

Mich.	1861–	John Hickman
"	1865	*No petition.*

Literature

Official records:

Sy. Mich. Q.S. 1861–1864.

428

KING'S ARMS PUBLIC HOUSE

2, Kensington High Street, Kensington.

Licensed: 1850–1875 (except 1855–60)

Management

Middlesex justices:

Mich.	1850–	Mary Anderson (to 1855)
"	1860–	Harriette Paton
"	1872–	James Copelin
"	1875	*Not renewed.*

Literature

Official records:

Mx. Mich. Q.S. 1848–1854, 1860–1874.

Location of other material

Kensington Local Collection has two posters announcing entertainments.

429

KING'S ARMS PUBLIC HOUSE

Kingsland Green, Hackney.

Licensed: 1861–1883

Management

Middlesex justices:

Mich.	1861–	James Keymer
"	1869–	John Edward Bonny
"	1879–	Margaret Rich
"	1882	Harper Roads
"	1883	*No application.*

Literature

Official records:

Mx. Mich. Q.S. 1861–1883.

430

KING'S ARMS PUBLIC HOUSE AND PALACE OF VARIETIES

230, Mile End Road, Stepney.

Licensed: 1850–1885

Also known as

King's Arms Hall of Varieties *or* Palace of Varieties Eastern Saloon

Building details

The small music hall on the level of the first floor at the rear of the public house. The entrance to the hall was in Beaumont Street.

Capacity: 200

Stage: 21′ 6″ × 10′

Closed as a result of the 1878 Act.

Management

Middlesex justices:

Mich.	1850–	Moss Phillips
"	1855–	Henry Levy
"	1859–	Louis William Strauss
"	1867	Caroline Strauss
"	1868–	James Edmonds
"	1873	William Alfred Gale
"	1874	Henry Edward Wilson
"	1875	George Cole
"	1876	Maria and Lewis Lazarus
"	1877–	Barnet Cross
"	1880–	Charles Edwards
"	1882–	Thomas Mc'Govarin
"	1885	George Woodman *refused licence.*

Literature

Official records:

G.L.C. Arch. Dpt. Th. case 040/72;
Mx. Mich. Q.S. 1848–1885; Sel. Com. 1892.

Location of other material

Plans: G.L.C. *Architects Department.*

Playbills:

L.C.C. have playbill for 12. 10. 1885.
Guildhall Scrapbook contains playbills for 11. 10. 1841
and 18. 10. 1841.

431

KING'S ARMS PUBLIC HOUSE

39, Mitchell Street, (*formerly* 3, Little Mitchell
Street), St. Luke's.

Licensed: 1862-1890

Building details

Music room on the first floor of public house was
irregular in shape, 35′ 3″ × 25′ 10″ at widest part
and 13′ 3″ at narrowest part.

Closed as a result of the 1878 Act.

Management

Middlesex justices:

Mich. 1862	Henry James Wells	
" 1863	Benjamin Hayden	
" 1864-	William Henry Cooper	
" 1875-	Thomas William Pealling	
" 1877	John Harper	
" 1878	Alfred Coote	
" 1879	James Creagh	
" 1880-	Edward Alexander West	
" 1882	Edward Horace Cox	
" 1883-	Launcelot Frederick Holt	
" 1886-	Richard James Morley	
" 1888	Launcelot Frederick Holt	

London County Council:

1890	Frederick Fielder
Nov. 1890	*Not licensed.*

Literature

Official records:

G.L.C. Arch. Dpt. Th. case 040/75;
L.C.C. Th. & M-H. Com. App. Nov. 1889;
Mx. Mich. Q.S. 1862-1888.

432

KING'S ARMS PUBLIC HOUSE AND COURT HOUSE FOR THE LIBERTY OF THE TOWER

Neptune Street, Tower.

The G.L.C. Architects Department, Theatre file
040/74 states that music hall on the 1st floor was
closed as a result of the 1878 Act.

433

KING'S ARMS PUBLIC HOUSE

Woolwich.

Licensed: 1860-1867

Management

West Kent justices:

Mich. 1860- Alexander Melville Blest
(Records missing for 1861-65)
Mich. 1867 *No petition.*

Literature

Official records:

W. Kt. Mich. Q.S. 1860 and 1866.

434

KING'S CROSS THEATRE

60, Liverpool Street (later Birkenhead St. and 1/3
Euston Rd.) St. Pancras.

Opened: 4th March 1830. Opened to the public May
1832. *Demolished after* 1879.

Other names

Panharmonium, or Royal Panharmonium 1820's
Royal Theatre
Royal Clarence Theatre 1832
New Lyceum Theatre 1838
Regent Theatre 1840
Argyll Theatre after 1840
Cabinet Theatre 1854
Cabinet Assembly Rooms
Century Theatre
Royal King's Cross Theatre.

Building details

Erected: c. 1820 as part of Panharmonium project of
Gesvaldo Lanza

Architect: Stephen Geary

Capacity: 360

Later used for political and religious meetings.

Management

Middlesex justices:

Mich. 1854-	John Brydon (as Cabinet Theatre)	
" 1857	*No petition.*	
" 1859	John Brydon (as Cabinet Assembly Rooms)	
" 1862	*No application.*	

Lord Chamberlain:

29. 9. 1862-	John Brydon
29. 9. 1870-	Edgar Bradley
29. 9. 1871-	John Brydon (returned 27. 4. 1872)
15. 4. 1872-	Frederick Belton
29. 9. 1873-	John Brydon
29. 9. 1874-	George Fleming
29. 9. 1874-	Harry Crouch
29. 9. 1879	*Not licensed.*

Literature

Official records:

G.L.C. Arch. Dpt. Th. case 1442;
LC 7/13-15, 21, 24-26; Mx. Mich. Q.S. 1854-1861.

Contemporary accounts:

1869 ERA ALMANACK, 1869. p. 34.—Description.
1877 BUILDER, 1877, Feb. 24th. p. 174.—Report of
      auction.
      LUMLEY, Messrs. E. & H.
      Particulars and conditions of sale of the King's
      Cross Theatre. The Mart, Tokenhouse Yard,
      February 20th, 1979. 'This well-known and long
      established bijou theatre... with possession...'
1879 BUILDER, 1879, July 12th. p. 785.—Report of
      sale.

Historical accounts:

1890 CLINCH, George.
Marylebone and St. Pancras: their history, cele-
brities, buildings and institutions. Truslove,
1890. pp. 182 et seq.

1903 ST. PANCRAS NOTES AND QUERIES, 1903 p. 106
Letter by Walter Brown originally published in
St. Pancras Guardian, 6.9.1901.

1904 BAKER, H. Barton.
History of the London stage and its players
...p. 381.

1907 WROTH, Warwick.
Cremorne and the later London gardens. p. 54
et seq.—Panharmonium Gardens Theatre.

1925 SHERSON, Erroll.
London's lost theatres... pp. 317-319.

c. 1930 MAYES, Ronald.
The romance of London theatres, Nos. 155 and
226.

1952 LONDON. County Council
Survey of London. Vol. 24.
L.C.C. 1952. p. 110. plates.

1953 THEATRE WORLD, 1953 April.
A lost London theatre. The story of the Royal
Clarence, King's Cross, by N.M. Bligh. 2p. illus.

Location of other material

Programmes and playbills &c.

Enthoven Collection; Guildhall Library; St. Pancras
Local Collection.

435

KING'S HEAD PUBLIC HOUSE

Church Street, Deptford.

Licensed: 1854-1879.

Management

West Kent justices:

Mich.	1854-	Joseph Huggett
"	1878	Richard Thomas Satter
"	1879	*No petition.*

Literature

Official records:

W. Kt. Mich. Q.S. 1854-1878.

436

KING'S HEAD PUBLIC HOUSE

7, Cumberland Street, St. Pancras.

Licensed: 1858-1870.

Management

Middlesex justices:

Mich.	1858-	John Christian Deedy
"	1865	Frederick Pewtress
"	1866-	Frederick Anderson
"	1870	*Licence refused following police complaint.*

Literature

Official records:

Mx. Mich. Q.S. 1858-1870.

132

437

KING'S HEAD PUBLIC HOUSE

18, Duke Street, Lincoln's Inn Fields, Holborn.

Licensed: 1854-71, 1873-78.

Management

Middlesex justices:

Mich.	1854-	Elizabeth Groves
"	1856-	George Edward Noone
"	1858	Timothy Elliott
"	1859-	Henry Amber
"	1861-	Charles Howard
"	1863-	Richard Southworth
"	1867-	William Macaire
"	1871	*No application.*
"	1873-	William Macaire
"	1875-	Robert Burrows
"	1877	David James Rohan
"	1878	*No application.*

Literature

Official records:

Mx. Mich. Q.S. 1854-1877.

438

KING'S HEAD PUBLIC HOUSE

257, Kingsland Road, Shoreditch.

Licensed: 1859-1890

Former name

The Old Kings Head Public House

Building details

Concert room was on the first floor, of irregular
shape with an area of 894 sq'. A small platform and
canvas proscenium was fixed at the north end of the
room.

Capacity: 200

The hall was closed as a result of the 1878 Act.

Management

Middlesex justices:

Mich.	1859-	Mary Randall
"	1861-	Mary Ann, Matilda and Louisa Randall
"	1863-	William Riley
"	1871-	William Winyard
"	1874-	James Moore
"	1876-	Robert Hownam Ludgate
"	1878	Charles Salter Pinn
"	1879	James Lilley
"	1880	Frederick Harcourt Smith
"	1881-	James Griffin

London County Council:

| | 1890- | James Griffin |
| Nov. | 1891 | *Not relicensed.* |

Literature

Official records:

G.L.C. Arch. Dpt. Th. case 040/77;
L.C.C. Th. & M-H. Com. App. Nov. 1889-1890;
Mx. Mich. Q.S. 1859-1888.

KING'S HEAD PUBLIC HOUSE

Knightsbridge.

Licensed: 1851-1858

Management

Middlesex justices:

Mich. 1851-	Charles Hickman
" 1854-	Thomas Kibble
" 1858	*Not relicensed.*

Literature

Official records:

Mx. Mich. Q.S. 1851-1858.

440

KING'S HEAD PUBLIC HOUSE

Lea Bridge, Clapton.

Licensed: 1862-1863

Management

Middlesex justices:

| Mich. 1862- | John Hammond |
| " 1863 | *No petition.* |

Literature

Official records:

Mx. Mich. Q.S. 1862-1863.

441

KING'S HEAD PUBLIC HOUSE

11, Little Woodstock Street, St. Marylebone.

Licensed: 1865-1868

Management

Middlesex justices:

Mich. 1865	Frederick Fox
" 1867	Thomas Garrett
" 1868	*No application.*

Literature

Official records:

Mx. Mich. Q.S. 1867-1868.

442

KING'S HEAD PUBLIC HOUSE

West Norwood High Street, West Norwood.

Licensed: 1857-1891

Management

Surrey justices:

Mich. 1857-	Alfred Charles Dronett
" 1881	Edward Watkins Alderson
" 1882	William Jacob Morris
" 1883	Lousia Ann Morris

" 1884	George Bennett
" 1885-	George Thies
" 1887-	Robert Reed

London County Council:

| 1890- | Robert Reed |
| Nov. 1891 | *No application.* |

Literature

Official records:

L.C.C. Th. & M-H. Com. App. Nov. 1889-1890;
Sy. Mich. Q.S. 1857-1888.

443

KINGSWAY THEATRE

Great Queen Street, Holborn.

Opened: 9th December 1882. *Bombed:* 1941.
Demolished: after 1950

Former names

Novelty Theatre 1882
Folies Dramatique March 1883
Novelty Theatre Dec. 1883
Jodrell Theatre Sept. 1888
Novelty Theatre 1889
New Queen's Theatre 1890
Eden Palace of Varieties 1894
Novelty Theatre 1895
Great Queen Street Theatre 1900
Kingsway Theatre Sept. 1907+

Building details

Architect: Thomas Verity.

Builder: Messrs. Kirk and Randell of Woolwich.

Decorator: E. W. Bradwell.

Reconstruction: 1900.

Reopened: 24.5.1900.

Architect: Murray & Foster, under John Murray.

Contractors: Messrs. Campbell, Smith & Co.

Decoration: Gerald Moira and F. Lynn Jenkins.

Capacity: 650.

Auditorium: S. 293; D.C. 96; G. 135; Bx. 32.

Alterations: 1907.

Architect: F. W. Foster.

Management

Lord Chamberlain:

8.12.1882-	George Somers Bellamy
26. 3.1883-	Francis Charles Fairlie
17.12.1883-	Miss Nelly Harris
1. 9.1885-	Willie Edouin
13. 5.1886-	John Lewis Nathan
10.10.1888-	Karl Samuel
19.11.1889-	John Lewis Nathan
4. 8.1891-	Samuel Tolhurst
2. 1.1891-	Mary Ann Brian
28. 9.1892-	Herbert Such
1. 3.1894-	Charles Morritt
23.12.1895-	John Tomsson and Thomas Gilbert Perry

28. 9.1896-	Victoria St. Lawrence
20.12.1897-	William Sydney Penley
27. 9.1907-	Lena Ashwell
18. 9.1916-	Frank Rolison Littler
1.12.1936-	Mark Wolfe
1.12.1938-	John Herbert Jay
15.10.1941	Memorandum states that theatre not to be relicensed owing to war damage.

London County Council:

1917	Lena Ashwell (new licence for music and dancing)
1938	Burlington Property Co. Ltd.
1939 & 1940	John Herbert Jay

Literature

Official records:

G.L.C. Arch. Dpt. Mss. Index;
G.L.C. Arch. Dpt. Th. case 433;
L.C.C. Th. & M-H. Com. App. Nov. 1916 and 1937-39;
L.C.C. Th. & M-H. Com. Papers 1881+;
LC7/17, 31-48;
L.C.O. Files 60 and 374; Sel. Com. 1892.

Contemporary accounts:

1881 ERA. 1881, June 18.—Note on proposed theatre.
BUILDER. 1881, June 25th. p. 809. Report of proposal to build theatre.
1882 BUILDER. 1882, Feb. 4th. p. 146.—Site of proposed theatre scheduled by Central Metropolitan Railway Company.
1882 ERA. 1882. Aug. 12.—Description.
BUILDER. 1882, Aug. 26th. p. 263.—Report on theatre nearing completion.
BUILDER. 1882, Sept. 2nd. p. 319.—Description.
ILLUSTRATED SPORTING AND DRAMATIC NEWS. 1882, Oct. 7th.—Illus of exterior and description.
NOVELTY THEATRE. Theatre publicity handout, 9.12.1882.—Description.
ERA. 1882, Dec. 16.—Detailed description of opening.
PICTORIAL WORLD. 1882, Dec. 30th.—Illus of interior.
1883 BUILDER. 1883, June 23rd. p. 867.—Notes lack of success; rarely open for long.
1885 BUILDER. 1885, Jan. 10th. p. 89.—Report of sale.
1892 BUILDER. 1892, April 30th. p. 345.—Report of auction to take place 20.5.1892.
1898 BUILDER. 1898, April 23rd. p. 403.—Report of extensive alterations.
1900 ERA. 1900, May 26th.—Description of rebuilding.
BUILDING NEWS. 1900, June 1st. p. 750.—Note of reconstruction.
BUILDER. 1900, June 9th. p. 565.—Report of reopening.
1907 BUILDER. 1907, Aug. 24th. p. 228.—Note of alterations required by Lena Ashwell, also note of history.
n.d. SHAW, George Bernard
To the audience at the Kingsway Theatre—a personal appeal. 4p.

Historical accounts:

1904 BAKER, H. Barton
History of the London stage and its players. p. 518.

c. 1930 MAYES, Ronald
The romance of London theatres, No. 138 and 22.
1955 Newspaper reports on possible reopening by English Stage Co. 21.7.1955
1959 ENCICLOPEDIA dello spettacolo. Vol. 6. col. 1627.
1960 THEATRE WORLD. 1960, June and August.
Lost London theatres, by N. M. Bligh. No. 14.
The story of the Novelty or Kingsway, 1882-1940. 7 p. illus.
1968 MANDER, Raymond *and* MITCHENSON, Joe.
The lost theatres of London. pp. 219-241. 2 illus.

Location of other material

Plans:

G.L.C. *Architects Department;* Enthoven Collection, 1915 (2 sheets); Public Record Office LC7/69, 2 sets, 4.2.1882 and 23.3.1899, Plans, sections and elevations.

Programmes and playbills:

British Museum Library; Enthoven Collection; Garrick Club; Guildhall Library; Holborn Local Collection; London Museum; Westminster Local Collection.

444

KNIGHTSBRIDGE HALL

66 (formerly 22), Knightsbridge High St., Knightsbridge.

Licensed: 1883-1890 and 1893-1897.

Former name

Humphrey's Hall

Also known as

Japanese Village (1887)

Building details

Hall incorporated Sun Music Hall. q.v.

Capacity: 550

Management

Middlesex justices:

Mich. 1883-   James Charlton Humphreys

London County Council:

1890-	James Charlton Humphreys
Nov. 1890	*Licence refused.*
1893-	James Charlton Humphreys
Nov. 1897	Refused as hall used in connection with a bicycle business for previous 12 m.

Literature

Official records:

G.L.C. Arch. Dpt. Th. case 028; L.C.C. Th. & M-H. App. Nov. 1889-1897; Mx. Mich. Q.S. 1883-88; Sel. Com. 1892.

Contemporary accounts:

1887 SATURDAY REVIEW. 1887, Aug. 27th. State of London's... music halls No. III—Para. on Japanese Village at Humphrey's Hall.

445

LAMB PUBLIC HOUSE

Kingsland Road, Hackney.

Licensed: 1852-1859, and 1868-1889.

Management

Middlesex justices:

Mich.	1852	George Kirby
"	1854	John Walter Freeman
"	1859	*Licence refused.*
"	1868-	Joseph Hornes
"	1872	Henry Smith
"	1873	Mary Ann Cripps
"	1874	John Joseph Alford
"	1875-	Richard Beyman Meck
"	1877-	Frederick John Dudley and John James Sherren
"	1881	Alice Mary Sherren
"	1882	Eleanor Sherren
"	1883	George Robert Gwynne
"	1887-	Henry Levy

Literature

Official records:

Mx. Mich. Q.S. 1852-1859, 1868-1888.

446

LAMB PUBLIC HOUSE

Metropolitan Cattle Market, Islington.

Licensed: 1866-1869

Management

Middlesex justices:

Mich.	1866-	Thomas Norris
"	1869	*No petition.*

Literature

Official records:

Mx. Mich. Q.S. 1866-1869.

447

LAMB PUBLIC HOUSE

Wick Road, Hackney Wick.

Licensed: 1862-1863

Management

Middlesex justices:

Mich.	1862-	Abraham Gadd
"	1863	*Licence refused.*

Literature

Official records:

Mx. Mich. Q.S. 1862-1863.

448

LAMB PUBLIC HOUSE

Wilmot Street, and Three Colts Lane, Bethnal Green.

Licensed: 1861-1877

Management

Middlesex justices:

Mich.	1861	Oliver Foster
"	1862	Wallis Ritchie and Frederick Ritchie
"	1863-	John Henry Collins
"	1866	William Parker
"	1867	Eugene Mansfield and Charles E.C. Medwin
"	1869-	Charles E.C. Medwin
"	1876	John Cammack
"	1877	*No application.*

Literature

Official records:

Mx. Mich. Q.S. 1861-1877.

Historical accounts:

1895 STUART, C.D. *and* PARK, A.J.
      The Variety Stage.—Brief mention.
1950 POPE, W. Macqueen
      The Melodies linger on.—Brief mention.

449

LARKHALL PUBLIC HOUSE

Larkhall Lane, Lambeth.

Licensed: 1850-1864

Management

Surrey justices:

Mich.	1850-	Charles Richard Dean
"	1864	*No petition.*

Literature

Official records:

Sy. Mich. Q.S. 1850-1864.

450

LAUREL TREE PUBLIC HOUSE

Brick Lane, Christchurch.

Licensed: 1860-1884

Management

Middlesex justices:

Mich.	1860-	Henry John King and Richard Fox
"	1862-	John Grist
"	1871-	Henry John Mansell
"	1874-	John Ash
"	1884	*Licence refused* to Charles John Ash

Literature

Official records:

Mx. Mich. Q.S. 1860-1884.

451

LEAPING BEAR PUBLIC HOUSE

146 (later 13), Old Street, Shoreditch.

Licensed: 1854-1866

Management

Middlesex justices:

Mich. 1854-   James Short
"   1866   *No petition.*

Literature

Official records:

Mx. Mich. Q.S. 1854-1865.

452

LEBECK'S HEAD PUBLIC HOUSE

Shadwell High Street, Shadwell.

Licensed: 1854-1862.

Management

Middlesex justices:

Mich. 1854-   Albert Lankeman
"   1857-   Emma Mahalah Lankenau (?)
"   1859-   John Stichbury
"   1862   *No application.*

Literature

Official records:

Mx. Mich. Q.S. 1854-1861.

453

LEICESTER SQUARE THEATRE (OF VARIETIES)

39-41, Leicester Square, Westminster.

Opened: 19th December, 1930. Used as a cinema from June 1931.

Proposed names

Buchanan Theatre
Olympic Theatre

Building details

Developers: Walter Gibbons in association with Jack Buchanan

Architect: Andrew Mather

Contractors: Gee Walker and Slater Ltd.

Capacity: 2, 000

1931 R.K.O. bought theatre from bankrupt Walter Gibbons. They installed a revolving stage. The interior redesigned by Edward Carrick.
-Note: In 1892 it had been proposed to build a variety theatre on the same site. Architect: G. H. Greatback.

Management

London County Council:

1931-   Buchanan Estates Ltd.
1932-   Radio-Keith Orpheum
1933-   Leicester Square Estates
1949-   Odeon Associated Theatres

Lord Chamberlain: (subsidiary to L.C.C. licence)

1. 12. 1931-   William Herbert Thornton
1. 12. 1932-   Walter Gibbons

136

1. 12. 1933-   Alexander Stevenson
1. 12. 1937-   John Allison Webb
1. 12. 1939-   Ernest Stanley Luke
1. 12. 1946-   Richard Herbert Dewes

Literature

Official records:

G.L.C. Arch. Dpt. Th. case 4162;
L.C.C. Th. & M-H. Com. App. Nov. 1930-;
L.C.O. 232 and 374.

Contemporary accounts:

1892 BUILDER. 1892, Oct. 8th. p. 287.—Report of new theatre to be built on west side of St. Martins Street, Leicester Sq.
1930 BUILDER. 1930, Dec. 10th. p. 1040, 1042-4. plates.—Description.

Historical accounts:

1963 MANDER, Raymond *and* MITCHENSON, Joe
The theatres of London, 2nd ed. p. 271-2.
1966 GREATER LONDON COUNCIL
Survey of London, Vol. 34, 1966. p. 506. plate.

Location of other material

Plans: G.L.C. Architects Department.

Programmes and playbills:

Enthoven Collection.
Westminster Local Collection.

454

LEWISHAM HIPPODROME

135 and 139, Rushey Green, Catford.

Opened: 13th February, 1911.

Building details

Built for Walter Gibbons and Charles Gulliver.

Architect: Frank Matcham

Capacity: 3, 222

Auditorium: P. 434; S. 574; C. 590; G. 830; Bx. 20.

Management

London County Council:

1909   Arthur Algernon Welesley Grist
1910-   Charles Gulliver
1925-   London Theatres of Varieties, and Charles Gulliver
1928-   Empire Kinema (Lewisham) Ltd., and Sidney Lewis Bernstein
1932-   Lewisham Theatres Ltd., and Sidney Lewis Bernstein
1934   Loughborough Playhouse Ltd. and David Albert Abrahams
1935-   B & J Theatres Ltd. and Cecil Emanuel Blush
1938-   "   John Idris Lewis
1939   "   Ernest A. Vincent.

Not licensed 1941-2
1943   British Union Varieties Ltd. and Ernest A. Vincent.
1944-   "   Cecil Orlando Schofield
1947-   S A Varieties Ltd. and L. Morely-Clarke

Literature

Official records:

G.L.C. Arch. Dpt. Mss. Index;
G.L.C. Th. case 195;
L.C.C. Th. & M-H. Com. App. Nov. 1908+.

Location of other material

Plans: G.L.C. *Architects Department.*

Programmes: Enthoven Collection.

455

LILLIE ARMS PUBLIC HOUSE

North End, Fulham.

Licensed: 1850-1851

Management

Middlesex justices:

Mich. 1850- Henry Balls
" 1851 *No petition.*

Literature

Official records:

Mx. Mich. Q.S. 1850.

456

LION PUBLIC HOUSE

Holloway Road, Islington.

Licensed: 1861-1864

Management

Middlesex justices:

Mich. 1861- George Albert Palmer
" 1864 *No petition.*

Literature

Official records:

Mx. Mich. Q.S. 1861-1864.

457

LION PUBLIC HOUSE

Tapp Street, Bethnal Green.

Licensed: 1854-1866

Management

Middlesex justices:

Mich. 1854	Elizabeth Gilbert
" 1855	Hannah Wheeler Grimes
" 1856-	Elizabeth Gilbert
" 1857-	George Ward Gilbert
" 1860-	Clement Houghton
" 1866	*No application.*

Literature

Official records:

Mx. Mich. Q.S. 1854-1866.

458

LITTLE THEATRE

16, John Street, (*later* John Adam Street) Adelphi.

Opened: 11th October, 1910. *Destroyed:* 16.4.1941.
Demolished: 1949

Building details

Owner: George Drummond

Architect: Messrs. Hayward and Maynard

Contractors: Messrs. Macey and Sons.

The former banking hall of Coutts in John Street was converted into a theatre.

Capacity: 309

Auditorium: S. 199, Bx. 12; B. 98.

1912 A balcony and 4 new boxes were constructed. The original architect was used, the contractors were Bovis Ltd.

Lewisham Hippodrome (454)

(Lewisham Public Libraries)

Little Theatre 1910 (458)

(The Builder)

1917 The theatre was damaged by bombing.
1919 Reconstructed as before.
1920 Reopened.
1941 Again closed through war damage.

Management

Lord Chamberlain:

11. 10. 1910-	Gertrude Kingston (to 30. 11. 1915)
24. 2. 1920-	John Eugene Vedrenne
2. 8. 1920-	Jose Gerlad Levy
1. 12. 1936-	Lionel Louis Falck
1. 12. 1942	*Not relicensed as closed.*

London County Council:

1909	a provisional licence to George Drummond
1913-	Gertrude Kingston
Nov. 1916	*Not relicensed:*

Literature

Official records:

G.L.C. Arch. Dpt. Mss. Index;
G.L.C. Arch. Dept. Th. case 84;
L.C.C. Th. & M-H. Com. App. 1909, 1912-1916;
L.C.O. 372 and 461.

Contemporary accounts:

1910 BUILDER. 1910, April 23rd. p. 471.—Report of conversion of banking hall.
BUILDING NEWS. 1910, June 10th. p. 783. 'A bijou theatre in the Adelphi'.—Description and illus. of construction of boxes.
BUILDER. 1910, Sept. 24th. p. 351.—Report of proposed opening and note on previous use.
LITTLE THEATRE
[Souvenir programme] 11th October 1910.
—Descriptions.
ERA. 1910, Oct. 15.—Description and report of opening.
BUILDER. 1910, Nov. 12th. p. 581-583.—Description, section and plan, and photos. of auditorium.
1914 BUILDER. 1914, March 20th. p. 357 and 359.
—Report of alterations to auditorium, made in 1912. Photos. and plan.
1920 LITTLE THEATRE. (Publicity leaflet), under management of Vedrenne and Vernon. 9 p. illus. seating plan.
The STAGE, 1920 Feb. 26.—Description and report of reopening.
SPECTATOR. 1920, Sept. 25. p. 402-3. 'Little Theatre'.
1949 TIMES. 1949, Aug. 4th. Demolition—'Change in The Adelphi—work on the Little Theatre site.'
SPHERE. 1949, Aug. 20th.—Illus. of bombed theatre.
LISTENER. 1949, Nov. 14th. 'End of the Little Theatre' report of talk by Sybil Thorndike.

Historical accounts:

c. 1930 MAYES, Ronald
The romance of London theatres. No. 64.
1937 LONDON. County Council.
Survey of London. Vol. 28.
L.C.C. 1937. p. 112. plan.
1946 SHORT, Ernest
Fifty years of Vaudeville. various references.
1959 ENCICLOPEDIA dello spettacolo. Vol. 6.
col. 1627.

1962 THEATRE WORLD. 1962, March.
Lost London theatres, by N. M. Bligh.
No. 16. The Little Theatre, 1910-1941. 5p.
(N.B. Two articles in this series numbered 16).
1968 MANDER, Raymond *and* MITCHENSON, Joe
The lost theatres of London. pp. 242-252.
2 illus.

Location of other material

Plans: G.L.C. *Architects Department.*

Programmes and playbills:

British Museum Library;
Enthoven Collection;
Garrick Club; Guildhall Library;
London Museum;
Westminster Local Collection.

459

LITTLE DRIVER PUBLIC HOUSE

Bow Road, Bow.

Licensed: 1850-1873

Management

Middlesex justices:

Mich. 1850	James Green
" 1851-	Eliza Green
" 1862-	Stephen Green
" 1866-	George Pillbeam
" 1871-	Charles Good
" 1873	*No application.*

Literature

Official Records:

Mx. Mich. Q.S. 1850-1872.

460

LOAD OF HAY PUBLIC HOUSE

Haverstock Hill, Hampstead.

Licensed: 1874-1882.

Management

Middlesex justices:

Mich. 1874	Charles Eugene Salmon
" 1875	Horace Besant
" 1876	George Hutchins
" 1877-	Sarah Ann Applegarth
" 1881	Charles Norden
" 1882	*No application.*

Literature

Official records:

Mx. Mich. Q.S. 1874-1882.

461

LONDON COLISEUM

St. Martin's Lane, Westminster.

Opened: 24th December, 1904.

Also known as

Coliseum Theatre

Building details

Built for Oswald Stoll

Architect: Frank Matcham

Capacity: 3, 389

Auditorium: S. & Bx. 517; D. C. & Bx. 518; Grand Tier
& Bx. 556; B. 498.

Stage: 55' wide and 92' deep.

Management

London County Council:

1904-   Oswald Stoll
1924-   Coliseum Syndicate Ltd.

Lord Chamberlain:

23. 12. 1905-   Oswald Stoll (to 31. 10. 1906)
 9. 1. 1912-   Oswald Stoll
 1. 12. 1942-   Prince Littler

Literature

Official records:

G.L.C. Arch. Dpt. Mss. Index; G.L.C. Arch. Dpt. 198;
L.C.C. Th. & M-H. Com. App. Nov. 1903+;
L.C.O. 374 and 427.

Contemporary accounts:

1902 BUILDER. 1902, Oct. 11th. p. 327.—Note of proposed new theatre.
1904 ERA. 1904, Dec. 17th.—Building description.
1950 THEATRE ownership. p. 56 and 86.

Historical accounts:

1930 CROXTON, Arthur
Crowded nights and days.
c. 1930 MAYES, Ronald
The romance of London theatres, No. 56.
1935 HADDON, Archibald
The story of the music hall. p. 111-121 and 125-
129. Many references.
1938 DISHER, MW.
Winkles and champagne.—various references.
1946 SHORT, Ernest
Fifty years of vaudeville.—various references.
1952 PULLING, Christopher
They were singing... p. 12, 187, 199-200.
1954 TIMES. 1954, Nov. 24th.
'Fifty years of the Coliseum'.
SPHERE. 1954, Dec. 25th.
'Half a century of the London Coliseum'. illus.
1957 BARKER, Felix
The house that Stoll built: the story of the Coliseum theatre. Muller. 1957. 256 p. illus.
1959 ENCICLOPEDIA dello spettacolo. Vo. 6. col. 1617.
1963 MANDER, Raymond *and* MITCHENSON, Joe
The theatres of London. 2nd ed. p. 41-46.

Location of other material

Plans: G.L.C. *Architects Department.*

Enthoven Collection, 2 sheets. 1946.

Programmes and playbills:

British Museum Library; Enthoven Collection;
Garrick Club; Guildhall Library;
Westminster Local Collection.

462

LONDON HIPPODROME

Cranbourne Street, Westminster.

Opened: 15th January, 1900.

Also known as

Hippodrome Theatre

Now known as

The Talk of the Town

Building details

Built for Moss Empires Ltd.

Architect: Frank Matcham

Contractors: Messrs. Whitford and Co.

Opened as a circus, with a large water tank.
1909 Circus area seated to form stalls. Reopened
2. 8. 1909.

Capacity: 2020

Auditorium: S. 386; C. 468; G. 474; Bx. 64.

Management

London county Council:

1899-   Horace Edward Moss (Provisional for
first months)
1914-   Frank Allen
1921   Richard Henry Gillespie

Lord Chamberlain:

1. 12. 1913-   Frank Allen
1. 12. 1920-   Richard Henry Gillespie
1. 12. 1947-   Valentine Charles Parnell

Literature

Official records:

G.L.C. Arch. Dpt. Mss. Index;
G.L.C. Arch. Dpt. Th. case 200;
L.C.C. Th. & M-H. Com. App. Nov. 1898-1920;
LC7/46; L.C.O. 374 and 491.

Contemporary accounts:

1904 PEARSON'S magazine. 1904. Running a great
variety show, by Turner Morton. p. 254-263.
illus. of lighting, fires, etc.
1950 THEATRE ownership. p. 59

Historical accounts:

1924 BENNETT, Will. A.
London Hippodrome. 25th birthday souvenir.
London Hippodrome, 1924. 32 p. illus.
c. 1930 MAYES, Ronald
The romance of London theatres, No. 52.
1935 HADDON, Archibald
The story of the music hall. various references.
1937 DISHER, M. W.
Winkles and champagne. various references.
1946 SCOTT, Harold
The early doors... p. 180+.
SHORT, Ernest
Fifty years of vaudeville. various references.
1959 ENCICLOPEDIA dello spettacolo. Vol. 6. col.
1626.

1963 MANDER, Raymond *and* MITCHENSON, Joe
The theatres of London. 2nd ed. p. 269-70.
1966 GREATER LONDON COUNCIL
Survey of London, Vol. 34, 1966. pp. 357-359.
plan, plates.

Location of other material

Plans: G.L.C. *Architects Department.*

Enthoven Collection, 1915 (4 sheets)

Programmes and playbills:

British Museum Library; Enthoven Collection;
Garrick Club; Guildhall Library; London Museum;
Westminster Local Collection.

463

LONDON PALLADIUM

Argyll Street, Westminster.

Opened: 1871

Former names

Corinthian Bazaar 1870
Hengler's Grand Cirque 1871
National Skating Palace 1884
Palladium Theatre 1910

Building details

Site was that of Argyll House, the London home of
the Dukes of Argyll. House sold in 1860, and bonded
wine cellars were sunk.
1870: Corinthian Bazaar erected.
1871: Opened as Hengler's Grand Cirque.

Architect: J. T. Robinson

Capacity: 1,090

Auditorium: S. 110; Partere 225; Amphi. 594; Bx. 79;
Reserved seats 82.

Metropolitan Board of Works condemned building as
it was constructed of wood.

2nd building: 1884

Architect: C. J. Phipps

3rd building:

Opened: 26.12.1910.

Architect: Frank Matcham

Capacity: 3,435

Auditorium: S. 2,393; G.C. 640; U.C. 690.

Stage: 90' wide × 45' deep.

Management

Lord Chamberlain:

31. 8.1871-	Charles Hengler (as Hengler's)
5.11.1887-	Frederick Charles Hengler and Albert Henry Hengler
5.12.1889-	John Michael Hengler
29.10.1890-	Albert Henry Hengler
28. 9.1891-	John Michael Hengler
28. 9.1895-	Donald Gordon Cameron
28. 9.1896-	Charles C. Baker
28. 9.1879-	Herbert Alfred Deed (as National Skating Palace) (to Sept. 1902)

140

20.11.1911-	Thomas Henry Masters
2. 7.1912-	Charles Gulliver
1.12.1928-	Hubert Pater Morrison
1.12.1930-	Ernest William Pashley Peall
1.12.1940-	Horace Stanley White
1.12.1947-	Valentine Charles Parnell

London County Council

1896	Donald Gordon Cameron
1897	Charles Caryll Baker
1898-	Herbert Alfred Deed
1903	Joseph Fishburn
1910-	Thomas Henry Masters
1913-	Charles Gulliver
1925-	Capital Syndicate Ltd.
1929-	General Theatre Corporation Ltd.
1947-	Moss' Empires Ltd

Literature

Official records:

G.L.C. Arch. Dpt. Mss. Index;
G.L.C. Arch. Dept. Th. case 148;
L.C.C. Th. & M-H. Com. App. Nov. 1895+;
L.C.C. Th. & M-H. Com. Papers 1892+;
LC1/507; LC7/15-17, 24-30, 32-48, **89**;
M.B.W. Rpt. 1882, p. 161-169; Sel. Com. 1892.

Contemporary accounts:

1883 BUILDER. 1883, July 21st. p. 95 'Hengler's
Circus in auction market...'
1910 BUILDER. 1910, Sept. 24th. p. 351.—Brief description.
BUILDING NEWS. 1910, Dec. 23rd. p. 896-7.
—Detailed description. Illus. of exterior and
auditorium.
ERA. 1910, Dec. 14th.—Description.
1950 THEATRE ownership. p. 60.

Historical accounts:

c. 1930 MAYES, Ronald
The romance of London theatres, No. 72.
1935 HADDON, Archibald
The story of the music hall.
—Various references.
1937 DISHER, M. W.
Winkles and champagne...—various references.
Illus.
HOUSE OF WHITBREAD, 1937, July.
London's theatres. 2-The Palladium. 4p. illus.
1949 MOSS' EMPIRES LTD.
(London Palladium) Jubilee, 1899-1949. 16p.
illus., ports.
1952 BEVAN, Ian.
Top of the bill.
PULLING, Christopher
They were singing... p. 135 and 200. (Henglers);
226, 231, 232.
1959 ENCICLOPEDIA dello spettacolo. Vol. 6, Col.
1629-30.
1963 LONDON. County Council.
Survey of London, St. James'. Vol. 31-2.—History,
illus., and plans.
MANDER, Raymond *and* MITCHENSON, Joe
The theatres of London, 2nd ed. p. 126-9.

Location of other material

Plans:

G.L.C. *Architects Department.*
Enthoven Collection (1 sheet)

Public Record Office. Dated 17.3.1871, Transverse section and ground plan.

Programmes and playbills:

British Museum Library;
Enthoven Collection; Garrick Club;
Westminster Local Collection.

464

LONDON PAVILION

3 and 4, Tichborne Street, Westminster.

Opened: 23.2.1861   *Demolished:* 26th March 1885.

Building details

A hall had been built on the site of the stable yard of the *Black Horse Inn.* It was used as a waxwork exhibition and later as a skating rink. In 1859 Loibl and Sonhammer opened it as a 'sing-song' saloon. On 23.2.1861, the saloon was reopened as a music hall called the London Pavilion. It cost £12,000 and had a capacity of 2,000 later reduced to 1,750. In 1878 the Metropolitan Board of Works paid £109,347 for the site, for street improvements.

Management

Middlesex justices:

Mich. 1860-		Emil Loibl
"	1866-	Emil Loibl and Charles Sonhammer
"	1874-	Emil Loibl
"	1879-	Robert Edwin Villiers (to 1885)

Literature

Official records:

Mx. Mich. Q.S. 1860-1885; Sel. Com. 1866 and 1877.

Historical accounts:

c.1930   MAYES, Ronald
         The romance of London theatres, No. 151.
         'Old London Pavilion.'

465

LONDON PAVILION

3-5, Piccadilly,

Opened: 30.11.1885   *Converted into a cinema:* 1934.

Also: Pavilion Theatre.

Building details

Architect: J. E. Saunders

Contractors: Peto Bros.

Built after the demolition of the music hall in Tichborne Street. 1886 Reconstructed. Tables removed and tip-up seats installed. The tip-up seats and seat reservations were innovations.

1900 Reconstructed.

Architect: Wylson and Long

1918 Reconstructed.

1934 Converted into a cinema

Architects: C. Nicholas & J. E. Dixon-Spain.

Management

Middlesex justices:

Mich. 1886-   Robert Edwin Villiers.

London County Council:

1890	Edwin Adam Villiers
1891-	Edwin Thomas
1895-	Edward Swanborough
1898-	Frank Glenister
1925-	London Pavilion Ltd.
1946-	United Artists Corporation Ltd.

Lord Chamberlain:

10. 1.1912-	Frank Glenister
1.12.1922-	Walter Payne
1.12.1949-	Reginald Charles Bromhead

Literature

Official records:

G.L.C. Arch. Dpt. Mss. Index;
G.L.C. Arch. Dept. Th. case 202;
L.C.C. Th. & M-H. Com. App. Nov. 1889-;
L.C.O. 374 and 501;
Mx. Mich. Q.S. 1886-1888; Sel. Com. 1892.

Contemporary accounts:

1885   SPORTING AND DRAMATIC NEWS. 1885, Dec. 12th.—Illus. of exterior and auditorium.

London Pavilion, Tichborne
Street, c. 1870   (464)

(Greater London Council Photograph Library)

BUILDER. 1885, Dec. 26th. p. 911.
—Description and plans.

1930 ARCHITECTURE ILLUSTRATED. 1930, Oct.
—Conversion into cinema.

Historical accounts:

c.1930 MAYES, Ronald
        The romance of London theatres, No. 5.
1935 HADDON, Archibald
        The story of the music hall. p. 62-74 and other refs.
1937 DISHER, M. W.
        Winkles and champagne... various refs.
1946 SHORT, Ernest,
        Fifty years of vaudeville.—various references.
1952 PULLING, Christopher.
        They were singing... Various references.
1959 ENCICLOPEDIA dello spettacolo. Vol. 6, Col. 1627.
1963 LONDON. County Council.
        Survey of London. St. James'. Vol. 31-2. History, illus., and plans.
        MANDER, Raymond *and* MITCHENSON, Joe
        The theatres of London, 2nd ed. p. 277-8.

Location of other material

Plans: G.L.C. Architects Department.

Programmes and Playbills:

British Museum Library; Enthoven Collection; Garrick Club; Guildhall Library; Westminster Local Collection.

466

LORD DUNCAN PUBLIC HOUSE

Duncan Place, Hackney.

Licensed: 1859-1883

Management

Middlesex justices:

Mich.	1859-	Charles Stewart
"	1882	Rienzi Hillier
"	1883	*Licence refused as it had not been used.*

Literature

Official records:

Mx. Mich. Q.S. 1859-1883.

467

LORD HIGH ADMIRAL PUBLIC HOUSE

Salisbury Street, Agar Town.

Licensed: 1854-1860

Management

Middlesex justices:

Mich.	1854	William Haynes
"	1855-	John Wyer
"	1860	*Not relicensed.*

Literature

Official records:

Mx. Mich. Q.S. 1854-1860.

468

LORD NELSON PUBLIC HOUSE

5, Clements Inn Passage, Clare Market.

Licensed: 1858-1871

Management

Middlesex justices:

Mich.	1858-	Samuel Gilbert
"	1860-	Alfred Feist
"	1871	*No application.*

Literature

Official records:

Mx. Mich. Q.S 1858-1870.

469

LORD NELSON PUBLIC HOUSE

42, Devas Street, (*formerly* Park Street) Stepney.

Licensed: 1863-1890

Building details

Concert room was situated on the first floor, 25′ × 15′ 6″ × 9′ 8″. It was finally closed as a result of the 1878 Act.

Management

Middlesex justices:

Mich.	1863-	George Boys
"	1888	George Henry Smith

London County Council:

1890	George Henry Smith
Nov. 1890	*Not relicensed.*

Literature

Official records:

G.L.C. Arch. Dpt. Th. case 040/80;
L.C.C. Th. & M-H. Com. App. Nov. 1889-1890;
Mx. Mich. Q.S. 1863-1888.

Location of other material

Plans: G.L.C. Architects Department.

470

LORD NELSON NEW MUSIC HALL

Lord Nelson Public House, Duke's Row, New Road, St. Pancras.

Licensed: 1852-1862   *Demolished:* 1887.

Also known as

Euston Music Hall
New Music Hall
Frampton's Music Hall
Music Hall, Euston Square

Building details

Capacity: 1,000

Management

Middlesex justices:

Mich. 1852-		David Smith
"	1858	Sarah Smith—later transferred to Frederick Frampton
"	1858-	Frederick Frampton
"	1862	*Licence refused to Jhan Kranchy.*

Literature

Official records:

Mx. Mich. Q.S 1852-1862.

Historical accounts:

1895 STUART, C.D. *and* PARK, A.J.
The variety stage.—Brief mention.
1937 DISHER, M.W.
Winkles and champagne...illus. (interior) p.12.
(*From* Paul Pry. Nov. 29, 1856)

Location of other material

Programmes and playbills:

St. Pancras Local collection.

471

LORD NELSON PUBLIC HOUSE

145, Whitechapel Road, (*formerly* Roadside, White-chapel) Stepney.

Licensed: 1852-1882.

Management

Middlesex justices:

Mich. 1852-		Edmund Gilbert
"	1870-	Mary Ann Green Scarlett
"	1876	Robert Barber
"	1877	James Hall
"	1878	Robert Henry Donegar
"	1879-	Stephen Beaumont
"	1882	*Licence refused to William Oakley.*

Literature

Official records:

Mx. Mich. Q.S. 1852-1882.

472

LORD RAGLAN MUSIC HALL AND PUBLIC HOUSE

158, Burrage Road, Plumstead.

Licensed: 1866-1889

Building details

The music Hall was situated on the first floor of the public house. It had an area of 1,257 sq.' including the small stage. It was closed as a result of the 1878 Act.

Management

West Kent justices:

Mich. 1866		Henry Sargent Vant
"	1867-	William James Raymond
"	1874-	Harvey Hammond

"	1876-	William Alfred Tucker
"	1881	James Mandy
"	1882	James Baker
"	1885	Henry Vallom

Not relicensed by the L.C.C. in Nov. 1889

Literature

Official records:

G.L.C. Arch. Dpt. Th. case 040/82; W. Kt. Mich. Q.S. 1866-1888.

Contemporary accounts:

1882 BUILDER. 1882, Feb. 25th. p. 239.—Brief report that M.B.W. was taking proceedings against owners.

473

LORD RAGLAN MUSIC HALL AND PUBLIC HOUSE

26, Theobalds Road, Holborn.

Licensed: 1855-1878

Former name

The Golden Horse Public House

Also known as

Raglan Music Hall.

Management

Middlesex justices:

Mich. 1855		Alfred Maddick
"	1856	Frederick Russell
"	1857-	Henry Hart
"	1877	George Parkes
"	1878	*Reported demolished.*

Literature

Official records:

Mx. Mich. Q.S. 1855-1877; Sel. Com. 1886 & 1877.

Contemporary accounts:

1859 BUILDER. 1859, March 19th. p. 200.—Note on exits.

Historical accounts:

1952 PULLING, Christopher
They were singing...p. 178.

Location of other material

Playbills &c:

Holborn Local Collection (one, undated); Enthoven Collection.

474

LORD RAGLAN PUBLIC HOUSE

St. Anne's Road, Burdett Road, Stepney.

Closed: 1893

Building details

Music hall was situated on the ground floor; 43′6″ × 12′ × 15′9″, seating approximately 100 people. It was closed in 1893 as a result of the 1878 Act, when John Henry Worledge, the proprietor was prosecuted.

Literature

Official records:

G.L.C. Arch. Dept. Th. case 040/81.

475

LORD SOUTHAMPTON PUBLIC HOUSE

2, Southampton Road, St. Pancras.

Licensed: 1868-1890

Management

Middlesex justices:

Mich. 1868-   William James Wetenham

London County Council:

1890   William Thomas Dawson
Nov. 1890   *Licence refused.*

Literature

Official records:

L.C.C. Th. & M-H. Com. App. Nov. 1889-1890.
Mx. Mich. Q.S. 1868-1888.

476

LYCEUM THEATRE

Wellington Street, Strand.

Opened as a place of entertainment: 1765.

Other names

Theatre Royal, Lyceum
Theatre Royal, English Opera House
English Opera House
Royal Lyceum Theatre

Building details

1st building: 1765

Exhibition hall and academy for Society of Artists, called The Lyceum.

Architect: James Payne

2nd building: 1790

Theatre erected on site for music and dancing.

3rd building:

1795 A Dr. Arnold commenced new theatre adjoining Lyceum. Not completed.
1809 S. J. Arnold (son of above) completed theatre for English Opera.

4th building:

1812 rebuilt

Architect: Samuel Beazley

144

Cost: £80,000

Destroyed by fire 16th February, 1830

5th building:

Opened: 12th July, 1834

Architect: Samuel Beazley

Contractors: Messrs. Peto and Grissell

Redecorated a number of times, particularly in 1882, 1885 and 1893.

6th building:

Opened: 31st December, 1904

Architect: Bertie Crewe

Management

Lord Chamberlain:

15.11.1843-	Louis George Tullien
22. 1.1844-	Samuel Anderson Emery
29. 1.1844-	Edward Parratt
8. 4.1844-	Mary Anne Keeley
20. 6.1847-	Charles Gaderer
29. 9.1847-	Charles James Mathews
14. 5.1855-	Frederick William Allcroft
3. 9.1855-	Mr. Anderson (details not completed)
15. 4.1856-	Frederick Gye
29. 9.1856-	Charles Dillon
11. 4.1857-	Frederick Gye
29. 9.1857-	Charles Dillon
17. 7.1858-	George Webster
26. 8.1858-	Edmund Falconer
1.11.1858-	Louis Jullien
20.12.1858-	Edmund Falconer
26.11.1859-	Mme Celeste Elliott
9. 4.1860-	William Brough
9. 5.1860-	Emile Laurent
29. 9.1860-	Celeste Elliott
8. 6.1861-	James Henry Mapleson Jnr.
19. 8.1861-	Edmund Falconer
10. 1.1863-	Charles Albert Fechter
21.12.1867-	Edward Tyrrell Smith
28. 9.1869-	Charles Allerton
21. 1.1870-	William Lauderdale Mansell
17. 9.1870-	Edmund Falconer
2. 1.1871-	Tito Mattei
19. 4.1871-	John Mitchell
31. 8.1871-	Hezekish Linthicum Bateman (died 22.3.1875)
23. 3.1875-	Sidney Frances Bateman
29. 9.1878-	Henry Irving
4. 4.1899-	Joseph Comyns Carr (to 1903)

London County Council:

1905-1906   Thomas Barrasford

Lord Chamberlain:

28. 1.1907-	Henry Richard Smith
26. 5.1910-	Walter Melville
23. 4.1920-	Frederick Melville
30.11.1922-	Walter and Frederick Melville
1.12.1937-	Frederick Melville
1.12.1938-	Bert Ernest Hammond (to Nov. 1939)

London County Council:

1937	Walter and Frederick Melville
1938	Frederick Melville
1939	Bert Ernest Hammond

Literature

Official records:

G.L.C. Arch. Dpt. Mss. Index;
G.L.C. Arch. Dept. Th. case 434;
L.C.C. Th. & M-H. Com. App. Nov. 1904-1905, 1936-
1938; L.C.C. Th. & M-H. Com. Papers 1882-;
LC1/507-752; LC7/13-17; 20-48 and 89;
L.C.O. 374 and 447; Sel. Com. 1866, 1877 and 1892.

Contemporary accounts:

1834 The MIRROR OF LITERATURE, AMUSEMENT
       & INSTRUCTION, 1834, Aug. 2nd. No. 675.—Des-
       cription of the new English Opera House, Strand.
1847 BUILDER. 1847, Oct. 16th. p. 489-90, 494.
       —Detailed description and plan.
       BUILDER. 1847, Oct. 23rd. p. 506-7. plate.
       —Description of decoration.
1856 ILLUSTRATED LONDON NEWS. 1866, April
       19th. p. 408.—Description and illus. of auditorium.
1878 BUILDER. 1878, Sept. 28th. p. 1002.—Report of
       quarrel resulting in Mrs. Bateman going to
       Sadlers Wells and Irving assuming management
       of Lyceum.
1882 BUILDER. 1882, Jan. 14th. p. 56.—Description
       of redecoration.
       BUILDER. 1882, Feb. 18th. p. 208.—Note of
       report of M.B.W. on state of exits.
1885 BUILDING NEWS. 1885, Sept. 11th. p. 427-8.
       —Detailed description of redecoration.
       BUILDER. 1885, Sept. 12th. p. 375.—Report of
       redecoration.
1887 SATURDAY REVIEW. 1887, July 2nd. The state
       of the London theatres... No. 3.
1893 BUILDING NEWS. 1893, Dec. 22nd. p. 845.—Brief
       description of alterations.
1902 BUILDING NEWS. 1902, July 23rd. p. 133.—Re-
       port of proposed demolition.
       BUILDER. 1902, Aug. 9th. p. 122.—Report that
       shareholders to sell rather than carry out
       alterations required by L.C.C. —also note of
       history.
1903 FAREBROTHER, ELLIS & CO. *Surveyors and
       auctioneers.* (Lyceum Theatre) Particulars,
       plans and conditions of sale of the... freehold
       estate... To be sold by auction... on Thursday,
       the 23rd April, 1903.—Copy in Westminster
       Local Collection.
1904 BUILDER. 1904, March 5th. p. 245.—Report that
       Bertie Crewe appointed architect to rebuild
       theatre as music hall. Only portico and back
       wall to remain.
1906 BUILDER. 1906, Dec. 1st. p. 639.—Report of
       court order for sale of property.
1939 ILLUSTRATED LONDON NEWS, 1939, April
       15th.—Illus. of exterior, report of proposed
       demolition. Not carried out because of war.
       NEW STATESMAN. 1939, July 8th. p. 47-8.
       'The end of the Lyceum' by D. MacCarthy.

Historical accounts:

1850 TALLIS'S DRAMATIC MAGAZINE. Nov. 1850-
       June 1851.—Various references.
1875 ERA ALMANACK. 1875. History of the Lyceum
       Theatre. p. 1-7
1879 DRAMATIC NOTES. 1879. p. 13-18
1883 WILLIAMS, Michael.
       Some London theatres... p. 117-215.
1893 FITZGERALD, P. H.
       Henry Irving: a record of twenty years at the
       Lyceum. London, 1893. ports.

1897 CALVERT, W.
       Sir Henry Irving and Miss Ellen Terry. A
       record of over twenty years at the Lyceum
       Theatre. London, 1897. 2pt.
1899 HOLLINGSHEAD, John
       A lyceum historiette. Nassau Press, 1899. 14p.
1902 BUILDING NEWS. 1902, Aug. 22nd. p. 275.
       —Note on history of site.
1903 BRERETON; Austin
       The Lyceum & Henry Irving. 1903.
       GORDON, Charles
       Old Time Aldwych... 1903. p. 187 and 196-202.
1904 BAKER, H. Barton
       History of the London stage and its players.
       p. 274-308.
1925 CHANCELLOR, E. B.
       The pleasure haunts of London... p. 117-121.
1930 CHANCELLOR, E. B.
       The annals of Covent Garden and its neighbour-
       hood. p. 271-3.
c. 1930 MAYES, Ronald
       The romance of London theatres. Nos. 45, 177
       and 100.
1935 HADDON, Archibald
       The story of the music hall. p. 79.
1952 WILSON, Albert Edward.
       The Lyceum... (1771-1945) Yates, 1952? 208p.
       plates.
1959 ENCICLOPEDIA dello spettacolo. Vol. 6, Col.
       1627-8.
1963 MANDER, Raymond *and* MITCHENSON, Joe.
       The theatres of London... 2nd ed. p. 273-6.

Location of other material

Plans:

G.L.C *Architects Department.*
Public Record Office. LC7/66   9 sheets, 13. 4. 1875.
                               4 sheets, 2. 8. 1881.

Programmes and playbills:

British Museum Library; Enthoven Collection;
Garrick Club; Guildhall Library; London Museum;
Westminster Local Collection.

Scrapbooks:

British Museum Print Room includes
IRVING COLLECTION
Portraits, theatre programmes... 6v.

Documents &c.

British Theatre Museum has collection of Irving
relics.

477

LYRIC OPERA HOUSE

Bradmore Grove, Hammersmith.

Opened: 17th November, 1888

Former names

Lyric Hall
Lyric Theatre

Building details

Architect: Isaac Mason

Reconstructed:

Opened: 17.11.1890

Architect: F. & H. Francis & Sons

Reconstructed:

Opened: 20.7.1895

Architect: Frank Marcham

Capacity: 800

Stage: 23' 10" wide × approx 17' deep.

Management

London County Council:

Nov. 1889-90	*Licence refused.*
1892	Charles Cordingley
1893-	Acton Francis Phillips
1905-	Samuel T. T. James
1908	Acton Phillips
1909-	Wentworth Croke
1915	Bertie Frederic Coleman Crump
1916	Edward Walter Rice
1917-	Acton Phillips
1919	Margaret Shelley
1920-	Nigel Ross Playfair
1935	De Frece Vaudeville Entertainments Ltd. and Cecil Wells
1936	Arthur Phillips
1937	Charles Cecil Courtney Lewis
1938-	William Reginald Clemens
1940	Brandon Cremer
1945	Associated Theatre Seasons and John Baxter Somerville.

Literature

Official records:

G.L.C. Arch. Dpt. Th. case 208;
L.C.C. Th. & M-H. Com. App. Nov. 1889-;
Sel. Com. 1892.

Contemporary accounts:

1899	ERA. 1899, Oct. 21st.—Illus. description of improvements.
1950	THEATRE ownership... p. 128.

Historical accounts:

1925	PLAYFAIR, Nigel The story of the Lyric, Hammersmith.
1930	PLAYFAIR, Nigel Hammersmith Hoy.
c. 1930	MAYES, Ronald The romance of London theatres, No. 93.
1959	ENCICLOPEDIA dello spettacolo, vol. 6, col. 1628
1963	MANDER, Raymond *and* MITCHENSON, Joe The theatres of London, 2nd ed. p. 226-231.
1967	EAST, John M. 'Neath the mask... pp. 94-150.

Location of other material

Plans: G.L.C. *Architects Department.*
Enthoven Collection (2 sheets).

Programmes and playbills:

British Museum Library; Enthoven Collection; Garrick Club; Hammersmith Local Collection.

478

LYRIC THEATRE

29, Shaftesbury Avenue, Westminster.

Opened: 17th December, 1888.

Building details

Developer: Henry J. Leslie

Architect: C. J. Phipps

Builder: Messrs. Stephens and Bastow

Capacity: 1,306

Auditorium: S. 178; P. 180; D-C. 167; U-C. 230; G. 375.

Stage: 29' 6" wide × 36' deep.

Management

Lord Chamberlain:

28. 9.1890	Henry John Leslie
29. 9.1890-	Horace Sedger
24. 6.1896-	William Greet
25. 4.1914-	Edward Coryton Engelbach
13. 3.1916-	Frederick William Tibbetts
1.12.1929-	Albert Charles Belsey
1.12.1932-	James Ernest Sharpe
1.12.1933-	Thomas Henry Bostock
1.12.1943-	Prince Littler

Literature

Official records:

G.L.C. Arch. Dpt. Mss. Index;
G.L.C. Arch. Dept. Th. case 435;
L.C.C. Th. & M-H. Com. Papers 1888-;
LC1/525-752; LC7/36-48; L.C.O. 333 and 374;
Sel. Com. 1892.

Contemporary accounts:

1888	BUILDER. 1888, Feb. 4th. p. 89.—Description of proposed theatre. BUILDER 1888, Oct. 13th. p. 273.—Note that Messrs. Campbell, Smith & Co. are to do decorations. LYRIC THEATRE (Publicity leaflet) 9p.—Details of building at opening on 17.12.1888. (Copy in Enthoven Collection) PALL MALL BUDGET. 1888, Dec. 20th. The Lyric Theatre.—Description and illustration of exterior. BUILDER. 1888, Dec. 22nd and 29th. p. 453-4, p. 478.—Detailed description.
1889	ILLUSTRATED SPORTING AND DRAMATIC NEWS. 1889, Jan 12th.—Illus. of interior and exterior. The THEATRE. 1889, Feb.
1892	BUILDER. 1892, May 21st. p. 407.—Report of proposed sale.
1897	SACHS, E.O., and WOODROW, E.A.E. Modern opera houses and theatres.—Illus., diagrs. plans, in all 3 vols.
1898	SACHS, E.O. Stage construction.—Plan and section of bridges.
1933	ARCHITECT AND BUILDING NEWS, 1933, Jan. p. 14. ARCHITECTURAL REVIEW. 1933, Jan. p. 7. —New decorations at the Lyric Theatre.
1950	THEATRE ownership. p. 59 and 90.

Historical accounts:

1904 BAKER, H. Barton
History of the London stage and its players.
p. 523-5.

c. 1930 MAYES, Ronald
The romance of London theatres, No. 7.

1959 ENCICLOPEDIA dello spettacolo. Vol. 6. col.
1628.

1963 LONDON. County Council.
Survey of London. St. James'. Vol. 31-32. p. 38,
48, 50, 52, 71, 74-6. illus., plan.
MANDER, Raymond *and* MITCHENSON, Joe
The theatres of London, 2nd ed. p. 110-115.

Location of other material

Plans: G.L.C. *Architects Department.*

Programmes and playbills:

British Museum Library; Enthoven Collection;
Garrick Club; Guildhall Library; London Museum;
Westminster Local Collection.

479

MACCLESFIELD ARMS PUBLIC HOUSE

Macclesfield Street, City Road.

Licensed: 1851-1878

Management

Middlesex justices:

| Mich. 1851- | Benjamin Dudley |
| " 1854- | George Burdon |

Lyric Opera House   (477)

(Hammersmith Public Libraries)

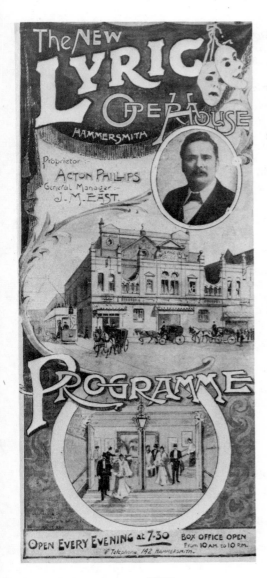

Lyric Opera House   (477)

(Hammersmith Public Libraries)

Lyric Theatre, Shaftesbury Avenue 1889   (478)

(British Museum)

"	1867-	Charles Thomas Cutton
"	1872-	Charles Blount Tabernacle
"	1875-	Arthur Christopher Peake
"	1876-	George Davey
"	1878	*No application.*

Literature

Official records:

Mx. Mich. Q.S. 1851-1877.

480

MAGPIE MUSIC HALL AND PUBLIC HOUSE

Battersea Park Road, (*formerly* Lower Wandsworth Road) Battersea.

Licensed: 1869-1880.

Also known as

Battersea Music Hall and Palace of Varieties

Management

Surrey justices:

Mich.	1869-	Daniel Barrett
"	1874-	John Barrett
"	1879-	Stephen Henry Duffield
"	1881	*No application.*

Literature

Official records:

Sy. Mich. Q.S. 1869-1880.

Historical accounts:

WILSON, A. E.
Pantomime pageant... 'Mentions that Ada Blanche began her career in 1874 at the Magpie, Battersea'.

Contemporary advertisement:

1875. The ENTR'ACTE and limelight... 1875, May 22 No. 308

481

MAGPIE AND STUMP PUBLIC HOUSE

37, Cheyne Walk, Chelsea.

Licensed: 1873-1886

Management

Middlesex justices:

Mich.	1873-	Edward Goodson Alford
"	1878-	Joseph Picton
"	1881	Thomas Henry Lownds
"	1882-	John Price
"	1885	George Bubear
"	1886	*Licence refused to Frank Baker.*

Literature

Official records:

Mx. Mich. Q.S. 1873-1886.

482

MANCHESTER ARMS PUBLIC HOUSE

Manchester Road, Poplar.

Licensed: 1859-1884

Management

Middlesex justices:

Mich.	1859-	Charles Davis
"	1862	William Willis
"	1863	George Boulton Hipgrave
"	1864-	John Backway
"	1866-	William Herbert
"	1868-	George Sadler Jnr.
"	1884	*Licence refused.*

Literature

Official records:

Mx. Mich. Q.S. 1859-1884.

483

MANOR THEATRE

Kenmure Road, Hackney.

Licensed: 1891-1903

Former names

Manor House, Church Street
Assembly Room, Mare Street (later Brett Street)
Manor Assembly Rooms & Club
Tee-To-Tum Club, Manor Rooms

Management

Lord Chamberlain:

| 1. 12. 1896- | Samuel Archibald Went |
| 15. 10. 1903 | E. Gerber *does not renew licence.* |

London County Council:

1891	James Bond
1892	Patrick Robertson Buchanan
1893-	Samuel Archibald Went
1903	*No longer licensed as theatre or music hall.*

Literature

Official records:

L.C.C. Th. & M-H. Com. App. Nov. 1889-1903;
LC1/657-752; LC7/43-48; L.C.O. 231.

484

MANOR HOUSE

Green Lane, Stoke Newington.

Licensed: 1852-1903

Building details

Concert room was on the ground floor attached to the public house.

Capacity: 300

Management

Middlesex justices:

Mich. 1852–   James Toomer
"   1871   John Charles Kay
"   1872–   Samuel Perrin
"   1876–   Stephen Ballinger Metcalf
"   1884–   Samuel Perrin
"   1887–   Morris Benjamin

London County Council:

1890   Morris Perrin
1891–   James Swinford
Nov. 1903   *No longer listed as a theatre or music hall*

Literature

Official records:

G.L.C. Arch. Dpt. Mss. Index.
L.C.C. Th. & M-H. Com. App. Nov. 1889–1903;
Mx. Mich. Q.S. 1852–1888; Sel. Com. 1892.

485

MANOR HOUSE PUBLIC HOUSE

Walworth.

Licensed: 1856–1862

Management

Surrey justices:

Mich. 1856–   William Wale
"   1862   *No petition.*

Literature

Official records:

Sy. Mich. Q.S. 1856–1861.

Historical account:

n.d.   PAUL PRY. No. 19.—Article on Manor House.
Copy in The Pleasure Gardens of South London.
Vol. II. p. 200. in London Museum Library).

486

MANSFIELD PUBLIC HOUSE

Mansfield Road, Kentish Town.

Licensed: 1862–1863

Management

Middlesex justices:

Mich. 1862–   John Frost
"   1863   *Licence refused.*

Literature

Official records:

Mx. Mich. Q.S. 1862–1863.

487

MARKET HOUSE PUBLIC HOUSE

Randall Street, Poplar.

Licensed: 1865–1868.

Management

Middlesex justices:

Mich. 1865   Henry Peter Speedy
"   1866–   Elizabeth Newton
"   1868   *Licence refused owing to sale of malt liquor.*

Literature

Official records:

Mx. Mich. Q.S. 1865–1868.

488

MARLBOROUGH THEATRE

383, Holloway Road, Islington.

Opened: 5th October, 1903. By 1919 in use as a cinema. *Demolished:* 1962.

Building details

Built for: F.W. Purcell

Architect: Frank Matcham

Builders: Messrs. Patman and Fatheringham

Capacity: 2, 612

Auditorium: P. 481; S. 358; D.C. 172; U.S. 331; G. 537: Bx. 64.

Management

Lord Chamberlain:

1. 11. 1904–   Frederick William Purcell
30. 4. 1906–   Ernest Stevens
22. 2. 1916–   John Joseph Hilyer (to 22. 2. 1918)

London County Council:

1914–   Ernest Stevens
1917–   John Joseph Hilyer
1919–   Henry Seddon. *Marlborough Picture Theatre.*

Literature

Official records:

G.L.C. Arch. Dpt. Mss. Index;
G.L.C. Arch. Dpt. Th. case 436;
L.C.C. Th. & M-H. Com. App. Nov. 1913–1919;
L.C.C. Th. & M-H. Com. Papers. 1900–1919.

Contemporary accounts:

1903   BUILDER. 1903, Oct. 10th. p. 369.—Report of erection.
ISLINGTON GAZETTE. 1903, Oct. 3rd.—Report of opening.

Historical accounts:

c. 1930   MAYES, Ronald
The romance of London theatres, No. 95.

Location of other material

Plans: G.L.C. *Architects Department.*

Programmes and playbills:

Enthoven Collection; Guildhall Library; Islington Local Collection.

489

MARQUIS CORNWALLIS PUBLIC HOUSE

Old Ford Road, Bethnal Green.

Licensed: 1857-1865

Management

Middlesex justices:

Mich. 1857-   James Brown
  "   1865   *No petition.*

Literature

Official records:

Mx. Mich. Q.S. 1857-1865.

490

MARSHAL KEATE PUBLIC HOUSE

Preston Road, Poplar.

Licensed: 1862-1877

Management

Middlesex justices:

Mich. 1862-   Joseph Matthew Hocking
  "   1877   *No petition.*

Literature

Official records:

Mx. Mich. Q.S. 1862-1877.

491

MARYLEBONE MUSIC HALL

32-3, Marylebone High Street, St. Marylebone.

Licensed: 1856-1900

At the Rose of Normandy Public House.

Building details

Developer: 'Sam Collins'

Capacity: 800

Cost: £8,000

Management

Middlesex justices:

Mich. 1856-   John Page
  "   1858-   Samuel Vagg (i.e. Sam Collins)
  "   1861-   Robert Frederick Botting

London County Council:

1890-   Robert Frederick Botting
1894-   William Albert Shaw
1896   Henry Hart
1897-   Edward Hart
Nov. 1900   *Not licensed.*

Literature

Official records:

G.L.C. Arch. Dpt. Th. case 3264;
L.C.C. Th. & M-H. Com. App. Nov. 1889-1900;
Mx. Mich. Q.S. 1856-1888; Sel. Com. 1866 and 1892.

Contemporary accounts:

1887   SATURDAY REVIEW. 1887, Sept. 3rd. The state of the London...music halls...No. 4.

Historical accounts:

1952   PULLING, Christopher
    They were singing...p. 169 and 175.
1959   BRITISH BROADCASTING CORPORATION
    Abroad to Marrowbone. 1959. 24p. illus.—
    Includes brief account of the music hall.

Location of other material

Plans: G.L.C. *Architects Department.*

Programmes and playbills: Marylebone Local Collection; Enthoven Collection (1 bill).

492

MERCURY THEATRE

2, Ladbroke Road, Nottinghill Gate.

Opened: 19th October, 1933

Former names

Horbury Hall
Ballet Club (Private theatre)

Building details

Capacity: 130

Stage: 18' wide × 11' 6" deep. No platform.

Management

London County Council:

1934-   Mrs. Cyvia Myrian Dukes
1941-   New Mercury Ltd., and Ashley Dukes

Literature

Official records:

G.L.C. Arch. Dpt. Th. case 824; L.C.C. Th. & M-H. Com. App. Nov. 1933-1950.

Historical accounts:

1950   FERGUSON, Rachel
    Royal Borough. Cape 1950. p. 265.
[1962   CLARKE, Mary
    Dancers of Mercury: the story of the Ballet Rambert. Black. 1962. 240 p.—Little or no mention of the theatre.]

Location of other material

Plans: G.L.C. *Architects Department.*

Programmes and playbills:

Enthoven Collection; Garrick Club; Kensington Local Collection; Westminster Local Collection.

493

METROPOLITAN THEATRE

267, Edgware Road, Paddington.

Opened: 1836 *Closed:* 6th December, 1962.

Former names

White Lion Public House
Turnham's Grand Concert Hall

Building details

The White Lion Inn dated from 1524.
1836 rebuilt as hall or concert room.

1862 Rebuilt:

Reopened 8.12.1862.

Built at cost of £25,000. Capacity 2,000.

1864 Easter Monday. Reopened as Metropolitan Music Hall.

1897 Rebuilt.

Architect: Frank Matcham

Capacity: 1,855.

Auditorium: S.310; P.282; B.402; G.567.

Management

Middlesex justices:

Mich. 1850-	George Anthony Smith and Frederick Smith
" 1854-	William Clark
" 1858-	Charles Davis
" 1862	John Turnham
" 1863-	James Miller
" 1865-	Robert Meacock
" 1867-	Edwin Winder
" 1871-	George Richard Speedy
" 1873-	Walter Gooch
" 1876-	George Speedy
" 1879-	Henry George Lake
" 1888	William James Lake

London County Council:

1890-	William James Lake
1892	Henry George Lake
1893-	Henri Gros
1911-	Ilford Ibbetson
1925-	Metropolitan Theatre of Varieties Ltd.

Lord Chamberlain:

10. 1.1912-	Ilford Ibbetson
1.12.1932-	Walter Payne
1.12.1949-	Reginald Charles Bromhead.

Literature

Official records:

G.L.C. Arch. Dpt. Mss. Index; G.L.C. Arch. Dpt. Th. case 213; L.C.C. Th. & M-H. Com. App. Nov. 1889-; L.C.O. 374 and 507; Mx. Mich. Q.S. 1850-1888; Sel. Com. 1866, 1877, and 1892.

Contemporary accounts:

1877 ERA ALMANACK. 1877
1887 SATURDAY REVIEW. 1887, Aug. 20th. The state of the London...music halls...No. 2.

1897 BUILDING NEWS. 1897, Aug. 20th. p. 256—Brief description of rebuilding.
BUILDER. 1897, Aug. 21st. p. 156. Report of proposed reconstruction.
ERA. 1897, Dec. 25th.
1898 BUILDER. 1898, Jan 1st. p. 24.—Brief description of reconstruction.
SKETCH. 1898, June 1st.—Brief history, and illus. of exterior.
1950 THEATRE, ownership. p. 128.

Historical accounts

c. 1930 MAYES, Ronald
The romance of London theatres, No. 78.
1935 HADDON, Archibald
The story of the music hall...Various references.
1946 SCOTT, Harold
The early doors. p. 211+.
1952 PULLING, Christopher
They were singing. p. 182.
1959 ENCICLOPEDIA dello spettacolo. Vol. 6, Col. 1628.
1963 MANDER, Raymond *and* MITCHENSON, Joe
The theatres of London. 2nd ed. p. 232-4.

Location of other material

Plans: G.L.C. *Architects Department;* Enthoven Collection, 1921 (3 sheets).

Photographs: Paddington Local Collection.

Programmes and Playbills:

British Museum Library;
Enthoven Collection; London Museum;
Paddington Local Collection;
Westminster Local Collection.

494

MILE END EMPIRE

95, Mile End Road, Stepney.

Licensed: By 1848-1933

Former names

Eagle Public House
Lusby's Summer and Winter Garden
Lusby's Music Hall
Paragon Music Hall
Mile End Empire. 1912+.

Building details

1885 Rebuilding.

Architect: Frank Matcham.

Builders & Developer: C. Crowder & G. Payne

Management

Middlesex justices:

Mich. 1848-	John Ealy
" 1851-	William Dix
" 1855-	Henry Gould Hayward
" 1861-	Edward Hayward
" 1870-	Ann Hayward
" 1874-	William Lusby
" 1878-	Charles Spencer Crowder and George Adney Payne

" 1883- Charles Spencer Crowder
" 1887- Alfred Aspinall Thoidon

London County Council:

1890-	Alfred Aspinall Thoidon
1892-	John Arthur Tressidder
1894-	William Potier
1899-	Frederick Miller
1909-	Edward Rawlings
1911	David Jacob Cashstein
1912	Jacob Rosenberg
1913-	Alexander Bernstein
1921-	Henry Goide
Nov. 1923	*Listed as a cinema.*

Lord Chamberlain:

30. 3.1912-	Alexander Bernstein
Dec. 1913	*not in use as a theatre*
1.12.1929	William Henry Bickerton
1.12.1930-	Ernest William Pashley Peall (to 1933).

Literature

Official records:

G.L.C. Arch. Dpt. Mss. Index; G.L.C. Arch. Dpt. Th. case 247; L.C.C. Th. & M-H. Com. App. Nov. 1889-; Mx. Mich. Q.S. 1859-88; Sel. Com. 1892.

Contemporary accounts:

1885 BUILDING NEWS. 1885, May 22nd. p. 808.
—Description of rebuilding.
BUILDER. 1885, May 23rd. p. 748.—Description.
1887 SATURDAY REVIEW. 1887, Aug. 27th. The state of the London...music halls...No. 3.
1896 SACHS, E. O. *and* WOODROW, E. A. E. Modern opera houses and theatres... Vol. III. Plans and section.
1906 PARAGON THEATRE OF VARIETIES. Souvenir ...21st anniversary...F.F.W. Oldfield & Co. 1906. (B.M. 011795.f.9).

Historical accounts:

1954 WILSON, A. E.
East end entertainment. p. 217, 219.

Location of other material

Plans: G.L.C. *Architects Department.*

Playbills: Enthoven Collection (1 bill for Lusby's 1881).

495

MILLER'S GRAND MUSIC HALL

Charles Square, Shoreditch.

Active 1864

Proprietor: H. H. Miller

Shoreditch Public Library has one playbill for 21st June 1864

496

MILWARD'S COFFEE TAVERN AND MUSIC HALL

144, Whitechapel Road, Stepney.

Licensed: 1882-1891

Former name Railway Coffee Tavern

Building details

The hall was situated at the back of the tavern on the ground floor, 36′ × 14′. The small stage was at the northern end of the hall with a wood and canvas proscenium; a small staircase to one side of the stage led to the dressing room above it.

When the licence was refused in 1891 Mr. Milward's solicitor denied that the hall was being used for anything more than odd 'benefits' for members of temperance groups. The hall was closed as a result of the 1878 Act.

Management

Middlesex justices:

Mich. 1882-	George Alfred Milward

London County Council:

1890-	George Alfred Milward
Nov. 1891	*Not licensed.*

Literature

Official records:

G.L.C. Arch. Dpt. Th. case 040/121; L.C.C. Th. & M-H. Com. App. Nov. 1889-90; Mx. Mich. Q.S. 1882-1888.

497

MITFORD CASTLE PUBLIC HOUSE

129, Cadogan Terrace, Bow.

Licensed: 1866-1889.

Building details

The concert room was on the first floor over the public house. Capacity 120.

Management

Middlesex justices:

Mich. 1866-	Harvey Greenfield
" 1876	Elizabeth Phillipas
" 1877-	Moses Piper
" 1879	William Augustus Eykyn
" 1880-	George Hillier

London County Council:

1890	George Hillier
1891-	Frederick Kingwell
1893	Edwin Edbrooke
1894-	Baptiste De Bolla
1896	Francis Collingwood
1897	James Johnson
1898	Frederick Dabs
1899-	Arthur Pollard
Nov. 1903	*Not licensed as theatre or music hall.*

Literature

Official records:

G.L.C. Arch. Dpt. Mss. Index; L.C.C. Th. & M-H. Com. App. Nov. 1889-1903; Mx. Mich. Q.S. 1866-1888; Sel. Com. 1892.

MITRE MUSIC HALL

145, Woolwich High Street, Woolwich.

Licensed: 1855-1901

Also known as

Plume's Music Hall

Building details

Capacity: 150

Management

West Kent justices:

Mich. 1855-   Charles Thomas Green
(records for 1861-1865 missing)
Mich. 1870-   William Henry Plume
  "   1880-   John Plume

London County Council:

1890-   John Plume
1898-   George Robert Park
Nov. 1901   *Licence refused*

Literature

Official records:

G.L.C. Arch. Dpt. Th. case 1992; L.C.C. Th. & M-H.
Com. App. Nov. 1889-1901; Sel. Com. 1892; W. Kt. Mich.
Q.S. 1855-60; 1866-88.

Location of other material

Plans: G.L.C. *Architects Department.*

Playbills: Guildhall Library. (1 item)

499

MONARCH PUBLIC HOUSE

Hampstead Road, St. Pancras.

Licensed: 1854-1863.

Management

Middlesex justices:

Mich. 1854-   Edward Hobday
  "   1856-   Frederick Shelley
  "   1859-   Lutje Otten
  "   1861-   Robert Wiskar
  "   1863   *No application.*

Literature

Official records:

Mx. Mich. Q.S. 1854-1863.

500

MONARCH TEMPERANCE COFFEE HOUSE

166, Bethnal Green Road, Bethnal Green.

Licensed: 1884-1890

Building details

The lower concert hall was at the rear of the premises. A second hall was opened on the first floor. They were closed as a result of the 1878 Act.

Management

Middlesex justices:

Mich. 1884-   Joseph Norris

London County Council:

1890   Joseph Norris
Nov. 1890   *Not licensed.*

Literature

Official records:

G.L.C. Arch. Th. case 040/85; L.C.C. Th. & M-H. Com.
App. Nov. 1889; Mx. Mich. Q.S. 1884-1888.

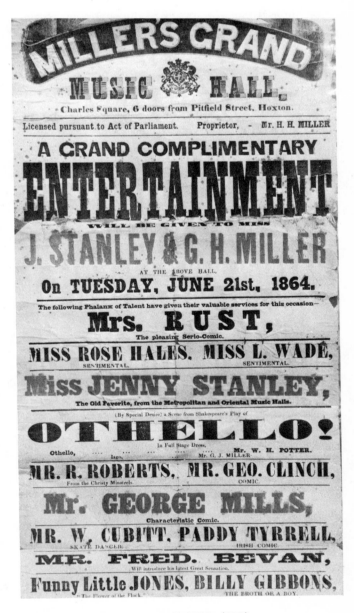

Miller's Grand Music Hall 1864 (495)

(Hackney Public Libraries)

Location of other material

Plans: G.L.C. *Architects Department.*

501

MONTPELIER PALACE

18, Montpelier Street, Newington.

Licensed: 1853-1919.

Former names

Montpelier Tavern
Montpelier Music Hall c. 1890
Empire Music Hall 1902-
Walworth Empire 1906-7
Montpelier Palace/Assembly Rooms 1908-
(names alternate)

Building details:

Music hall was at the back of the public house. In 1891 the greater part of the hall was burnt down, but was reconstructed almost immediately.

Capacity: 662

Auditorium: P. 142; S. 170

Management

Surrey justices:

Mich. 1853	Thomas Hall
" 1854-	John Owen
" 1856-	John Steptoas
" 1859-	William Fountain
" 1864-	Joseph Langham
" 1866	James Edbrooke
" 1867-	John Dobson Allatt
" 1878-	William Tanner
" 1886-	Robert Benjamin Greenwood

London County Council:

1890-	Samuel Hart
1894-	George Edwards
1899-	Ezra Albert Pilgrim
1901-	Francis Albert Pinn
1903-	Benjamin Dent Weston
1907-	Isadore Bloom
1909-	Frederick Stephens
1911-	Walter George Newnam
1913-	Selina Hartry Newnam
1915-	William Thomas Collins
Nov. 1919	*Not licensed.*

Literature

Official records:

G.L.C. Arch. Dpt. Mss. Index; G.L.C. Arch. Dpt. Th. case 217; L.C.C. Th. & M-H. Com. App. Nov. 1889-1918; Sel. Com. 1892; Sy. Mich. Q.S. 1853-1888.

Contemporary accounts:

1891 STANDARD. 1891, Sept. 14th. 'Destruction of a music hall'.—(cutting in Southwark Public library)

Location of other material

Plans: G.L.C. *Architects Department.*

502

MOORE ARMS PUBLIC HOUSE

4, Halsey Terrace, (later 61-3, Cadogan Street) Chelsea.

Licensed: 1860-1891

Management

Middlesex justices:

Mich. 1868-	Abraham Hardy
" 1876-	William Charles Grant
" 1879-	William Brown
" 1882	Eliza Brown
" 1883-	Harry Jordan
" 1888	Robert Hicks

London County Council:

1890-	Robert Hicks (licence retained)
Nov. 1891	*Not relicensed.*

Literature

Official records:

L.C.C. Th. & M-H. Com. 1889-1891; Mx. Mich. Q.S. 1868-1888.

503

MORLEY COFFEE PALACE

133, Mare Street, Hackney.

Licensed: 1884-1890

Building details

The concert room was at the back of the coffee shop.
Area: 38' × 15'.

Platform with two small dressing rooms beneath it. The hall was closed as a result of the 1878 Act.

Management

Middlesex justices:

Mich. 1884-	James Tite

London County Council:

1890	James Tite
Nov. 1890	*No application.*

Literature

Official records:

G.L.C. Arch. Dpt. Th. case 040/87; L.C.C. Th. & M-H. Com. App. Nov. 1889; Mx. Mich. Q.S. 1884-1888.

504

MORPETH CASTLE PUBLIC HOUSE

Old Ford Road, Bethnal Green.

Licensed: 1855-57, 1858-65, 1869-89.

Management

Middlesex justices:

Mich. 1855-	William White (to 1857)	
" 1858-	Arthur Lake	
" 1860-	Thomas George Stanton	
" 1865	*No petition.*	
" 1869	William Tant	
" 1870-	Albert Masterson	
" 1872-	John Frederick Burward	
" 1875	William Buckley	
" 1876-	John Giles	
" 1878-	Henry Josiah Moore	
Nov. 1889	*Licence refused as work not done*	

Literature

Official records:

L.C.C. Th. & M-H. Com. App. Nov. 1889;
Mx. Mich. Q.S. 1855-1888.

505

MORTIMER ARMS PUBLIC HOUSE

Mortimer Road, Hackney.

Licensed: 1866-1867

Management

Middlesex justices:

Mich. 1866-	George Alfred Pape	
" 1867	*No petition.*	

Literature

Official records:

Mx. Mich. Q.S. 1866-1867.

506

MORTON ARMS PUBLIC HOUSE

51, Exmouth Street, Stepney.

Licensed: 1880-1881

Management

Middlesex justices:

Mich. 1880-	George Curtis	
" 1881	*No petition.*	

Literature

Official records:

Mx. Mich. Q.S. 1880-1881.

507

MOTHER SHIPTON PUBLIC HOUSE

Prince of Wales Road, St. Pancras.

Licensed: 1854-1860.

Management

Middlesex justices:

Mich. 1854-	Robert Wilby	
" 1857-	Thomas Marsden	
" 1859	Frederick Cole	
" 1860	*No application.*	

Literature

Official records:

Mx. Mich. Q.S. 1854-1859.

508

MULBERRY TREE MUSIC HALL AND PUBLIC HOUSE

133, Stepney Green, Stepney.

Licensed: 1865-1903

Building details

The concert room was on the first floor of the public house, with a capacity of 180, (later capacity reduced to 110). In 1890 large alterations were carried out.

Management

Middlesex justices:

Mich. 1865-	William Percy Harvey	
" 1875-	Alfred Walter Clark	
" 1882-	Leonard Carden	
" 1886-	Henry Lyons	

London County Council:

1890-	Henry Lyons	
1893	William Simpson	
1894	George Willey	
1895	Herbert Edward Edwards	
1896-	Arthur Nelson Crouch	
1898	Isaac Smith	
1899	John Douglas	
1900-	Emma Douglas	
1902-	James Thomas Huxley	
Nov. 1903	*Not licensed as a theatre or music hall.*	

Literature

Official records:

G.L.C. Arch. Dpt. Mss. Index; L.C.C. Th. & M-H. Com. App. Nov. 1889-1903; Sel. Com. 1892.

509

NAG'S HEAD PUBLIC HOUSE

39, Leather Lane, Holborn.

Licensed: 1854-1856

Management

Middlesex justices:

Mich. 1854-	Robert Chamberlain	
" 1856	*No notice, no petition.*	

Literature

Official records:

Mx. Mich. Q.S. 1854-1856.

510

NAG'S HEAD PUBLIC HOUSE

Oxford Street, St. James, Westminster.

Licensed: 1851-1862

Management

Middlesex justices:

Mich.	1851-	Robert Tritton
"	1859-	Henry Saunders Lamb
"	1862	*Licence refused, as premises licensed to sell spirits by Excise.*

Literature

Official records:

Mx. Mich. Q.S. 1851-1862.

511

NATIONAL OPERA HOUSE

Victoria Embankment.

Under construction: 1875

Also known as

Grand National Opera House

Building details

Building never completed.
It was constructed on the site of Northumberland House. The site was held under an arrangement with the M.B.W. dated 14.1.1875 for eighty years.
The opera house, which was leased to Mr. Mapleson for thirty years, was due to be completed by 1.3.1881.

Architect: Francis Fowler

Contractor: Mr. Webster

Capacity: (proposed) 3,000

Literature

Official records:

M.B.W. Th. & M-H. Com. Papers. 1875-.

Contemporary accounts:

1875 BUILDER. 1875, Feb. 6th. p. 131.—Report on proposed plans.
BUILDER. 1875, May 1st. p. 400.
BUILDER. 1875, June 12th. p. 528.—Brief description, illus.
BUILDER. 1875, July 31st. p. 682.—Dispute over encroachment of embankment.
BUILDER. 1875, Sept. 11th. p. 829.—First brick laid.
BUILDER. 1875, Dec. 18th. p. 1138.—Foundation stone laid.
GRAND NATIONAL OPERA COMPANY LTD. Prospectus. (LC7/68. P.R.O.)

Location of other material

Plans: LC7/68. 10 sheets 1″ to 8′ scale.

512

NAVY ARMS PUBLIC HOUSE

6, Queen Street, Woolwich.

Licensed: 1875-1889

Building details

Concert room was at the rear of the building on the first floor, 26′ 6″ × 17′ 2″ × 10′ 6″. Closed as a result of the 1878 Act.

Management

West Kent justices:

Mich.	1875	Thomas Parsons
"	1876-	William Watson
"	1884-	Henry Wakeling.
"	1888	William Prance

London County Council:

Nov. 1889	Licence granted to William Prance but retained.
Nov. 1890	*Not granted.*

Literature

Official records:

L.C.C. Th. & M-H. Com. Papers. Nov. 1889-1890;
W. Kt. Mich. Q.S. 1875-1888.

513

NELL GWYNNE PUBLIC HOUSE

Bull Inn Court, Strand.

Licensed: 1855-1857

Management

Middlesex justices:

Mich.	1855-	Frederick Frampton
"	1857	*No petition, no application.*

Literature

Official records:

Mx. Mich. Q.S. 1855-1857.

see also Adelphi Theatre.

514

NEW THEATRE

St. Martin's Lane, Westminster.

Opened: 12th March, 1903.

Building details

Architect: W. G. R. Sprague

Contractors: Messrs. Owen Lucas and Pyke

Capacity: c. 938

Auditorium: S. 396; D.C. 185; U.C. 158; G. 180; Bx. 48.

Stage: 31′ 6″ wide × 37′ 6″ deep (to centre)

Manager

Lord Chamberlain:

1903-	Charles Wyndham
1.12.1919-	Mary Wyndham
1.12.1931-	Howard James Wyndham
1.12.1945-	Howard James Wyndham and B. J. Albery
1.12.1947-	Bronson J. Albery.

Literature

Official records:

G.L.C. Arch. Dpt. Mss. Index; G.L.C. Arch. Dpt. Th. case 437; L.C.C. Th. & M-R. Com. Papers. 1900-; L.C.O. 140 and 374.

Contemporary accounts:

1900 BUILDER. 1900, June 16th. p. 594.—Brief report of proposed new theatre. Report architect to be Frank Matcham.
1901 BUILDER. 1901, Aug. 24th. p. 178.—Note that W.G.R. Sprague to draw up plans.
1903 BUILDING NEWS. 1903, March 13th. p. 370.—Brief description.
   BUILDER. 1903, March 21st. p. 315.—Brief description.
   NEW THEATRE. Souvenir programme. 1903.—Gives description.

Historical accounts:

c. 1930 MAYES, Ronald
   The romance of London theatres No. 32.
1959 ENCYCLOPEDIA dello spettacolo. Vol. 6, Col. 1628.
1963 MANDER, Raymond, *and* MITCHENSON, Joe.
   The theatres of London. 2nd ed. p. 116-121.

Location of Other Material

Plans: G.L.C. *Architects Department.*

Programmes:

British Museum Library; Enthoven Collection; Garrick Club; Guildhall Library; London Museum; Westminster Local Collection.

515

NEW CLOWN PUBLIC HOUSE

136, St. John Street Road (formerly 62, then 121) Clerkenwell.

Licensed: 1852-1891

Also known as

The Clown Public House (c. 1863)

Management

Middlesex justices:

Mich.	1852-	William Tyler
"	1859-	Frederick Charles Agg
"	1861-	Philip Jagels
"	1877-	Mary Ann Jagels
"	1888	William Thomas Richardson

London County Council:

| 1890- | William Thomas Richardson |
| Nov. 1891 | *Not licensed.* |

Literature

Official records:

L.C.C. Th. & M-H. Com. App. Nov. 1889-1890.
Mx. Mich. Q.S. 1852-1888.

516

NEW CROSS EMPIRE

New Cross Road and Watson Street, New Cross.

Opened: 1899

Former names

Deptford Empire Theatre of Varieties
New Cross Empire Theatre of Varieties

New Cross Empire 1899 (516)

(Lewisham Public Libraries)

Building details

Architect: Frank Marcham

Capacity: c. 2, 000

Auditorium: S. 290; P. 466; B. 240; U.C. 254; G. 406.

Management

London County Council:

1899-	Oswald Stoll
1912-	Sir Horace Edward Moss
1914-	Frank Allen
1921-	Richard Henry Gillespie
1925-	Moss' Empires Ltd., and Richard Henry Gillespie
1947-	People's Entertainment Society Ltd., and Joseph Henry Walker
1949-	Parl Theatrical Productions Ltd., and Frank Sydney Webb

Literature

Official records:

G.L.C. Arch. Dpt. Mss. Index; G.L.C. Arch. Dpt. Th. case 224; L.C.C. Th. & M-H. Com. App. Nov. 1898-; L.C.C. Th. & M-H. Com. Papers 1896-.

Contemporary accounts:

1899 BUILDER. 1899, Aug. 19th. p. 182.—Report of opening and brief description.
1950 THEATRE ownership. p. 128.

Location of other material

Plans: G.L.C. *Architects Department.*

Illustrations and programmes: Deptford Local Collection.

Programmes &c. Enthoven Collection.

517

NEW CROWN PUBLIC HOUSE

Paul Terrace, Balls Pond.

Licensed: 1852-1855

Management

Middlesex justices:

| Mich. 1852- | Samuel Shannon |
| " 1855- | *No notice, no petition.* |

Literature

Official records:

Mx. Mich. Q.S. 1852-1855.

518

NEW EASTERN ALHAMBRA

7, Winckworth Place, Shoreditch.

Licensed: 1861-1863.

Management

Middlesex justices:

| Mich. 1861- | Samuel Tyzack |
| " 1863- | *Licence refused.* |

Literature

Official records:

Mx. Mich. Q.S. 1861-1863.

519

NEW GLOBE PUBLIC HOUSE

Mile End Road, Stepney.

Licensed: 1850-1866

Management

Middlesex justices:

Mich. 1848-	Thomas Gardner
" 1859-	Benjamin Vernon
" 1861-	Richard Norden
" 1866	*No application.*

Literature

Official records:

Mx. Mich. Q.S. 1848-1866.

520

NEW LINDSEY THEATRE

Kensington.

In use: 1949-1950.

Formerly

Lindsey Hall

Building details

Capacity: 164

Stage: 20' wide × 16' deep

Management

Not licensed as theatre club.

Literature

Historical accounts:

1950 FERGUSON, Rachel Royal borough. p. 269.

Location of other material

Programmes:

Enthoven Collection.
Westminster Local Collection.

521

NEW SOUTHAMPTON ARMS PUBLIC HOUSE

Camden Town High Street, St. Pancras.

Licensed: 1866-1890

Management

Middlesex justices:

Mich. 1866-	Samuel Bloomfield
" 1872-	John Winder
" 1877-	Denis James Donovan
" 1882-	John Tappenden
" 1884-	William Ash

London County Council:

1890	Herbert Hames Cathie
Nov. 1890	*Application withdrawn.*

Literature

Official records:

L.C.C. Th. & M-H. Com. App. Nov. 1889-90;
Mx. Mich. Q.S. 1866-1888.

522

NEW VAUXHALL GARDENS

Camberwell.

Licensed: 1862-1873

Management

Surrey justices:

Mich. 1862-	Henry King
" 1864-	William Walter Wale
" 1867-	Walter Wastell
" 1873	*No application.*

Literature

Official records:

Sy. Mich. Q.S. 1862-1872.

Location of other material

Programmes: Enthoven Collection

523

NEW YIDDISH THEATRE

Adler Street, Commercial Road.

Licensed: 1945-1947

Former name

Folkhouse

Management

Lord Chamberlain:

1.12.1944-   Nathan Gersh Beitler (to 1.12.1947)

Literature

Official records:

L.C.O. 374- and 534.

Location of other material

Programmes: Enthoven Collection

524

NEWINGTON BUTTS MUSIC HALL

107, Newington Butts.

Building details

Concert room attached to a coffee palace, 37' 7"
× 24' 10".

Capacity: 100

Closed as a result of the 1878 Act.

Literature

Official records:

G.L.C. Arch. Dpt. Th. case 040/90;
Sel. Com. 1892.

525

NEWMARKET PUBLIC HOUSE

St. Paul's Road, Camden Town.

Licensed: 1866-1871

Management

Middlesex justices:

Mich. 1866-	Charles Buckhurst
" 1871	*Licence refused.*

Literature

Official records:

Mx. Mich. Q.S. 1866-1871.

526

NORTH POLE MUSIC HALL AND PUBLIC HOUSE

131, Greenwich Road, Greenwich.

Licensed: 1850-1889

Building details

The music hall was situated on the first floor over
the bar. It had accommodation for 150 people, with
fixed seating round the walls, and loose chairs across
the middle. No concerts were reported after c. 1885.
After 1890 report of proposed rebuilding.

Management

West Kent justices:

Mich. 1850	Richard Harrison
" 1851-	William Henry Wright
" 1853-	John Gibb
" 1856-	David Croft
" 1859-	Charles Peckham
(1861-6 records missing)	
" 1866-	William Francis Shand
" 1868-	Henry Gordon
" 1873	Emma Castle
" 1874-	William Sturch
" 1877-	Henry Medcalf
" 1882-	Henry Robert Towers

London County Council:

Nov. 1889 and 1890 *Licence refused.*

Literature

Official records:

G.L.C. Arch. Dpt. Th. case 040/43; L.C.C. Th. & M-H.
Com. App. Nov. 1889-1890; Sel. Com. 1892;
W. Kt. Mich. Q.S. 1850-60, 66-88.

Location of other material

Plans: G.L.C. *Architects Department.*

527

NORTH POLE PUBLIC HOUSE

190, New North Road, (*formerly* 7, Bear's Place)
Islington.

Licensed: 1854-1869

Management

Middlesex justices:

Mich. 1854-	John Thornett	
"	1856	*No notice, no petition.*
"	1857-	James Shepherd
"	1859	*Licence refused.*
"	1862-	John Palmer
"	1865	James Nuttall
"	1866-	John William Oliver
"	1869	*No notice, no petition.*

Literature

Official records:

Mx. Mich. Q.S. 1854-1869.

528

NORTH STAR PUBLIC HOUSE

College Villas Road, Hampstead.

Licensed: 1867-1868

Management

Middlesex justices:

Mich. 1867-	John Dent	
"	1868	*No notice, no petition.*

Literature

Official records:

Mx. Mich. Q.S. 1867-1868.

529

NORTHAMPTON ARMS PUBLIC HOUSE

Northampton Street, Cambridge Road, Bethnal Green.

Licensed: 1860-1889

Building details

The small hall was on the ground floor, attached to
the public house, with accommodation for 100 people.

Management

Middlesex justices:

Mich. 1860-	Richard Thomas Frederick Davey	
"	1862	Elizabeth Davey
"	1863	Frederick Barnett
"	1864	Sarah Jull
"	1865-	Edward Mills
"	1868	James Huxley
"	1869-	James Sullivan
"	1872-	Thomas Scott
"	1875-	Walter Scott
"	1877-	Robert Charles Shaw
"	1888	William Shaw

London County Council:

1890-	William Charles Thomas Hine (Licence granted but retained)
1893-	George Frederick Hine
Nov. 1903	*Not listed as theatre or music hall.*

Literature

Official records:

G.L.C. Arch. Dpt. Mss. Index;
L.C.C. Th. & M-H. Com. App. Nov. 1889-1903;
Mx. Mich. Q.S. 1860-1888; Sel. Com. 1892.

530

NORTHUMBERLAND ARMS PUBLIC HOUSE

King's Cross Road (*formerly* Bagnigge Wells Road)
St. Pancras.

Licensed: pre 1850-1874

Management

Middlesex justices:

Mich. 1848-	William Greenwood	
"	1862-	Edward Newton
"	1864-	Frederick Bailey Strange
"	1869-	William Henry Whiter
"	1874	*Licence refused to George Tompkins*

Literature

Official records:

Mx. Mich. Q.S. 1850-1874.

531

ODELL ARMS PUBLIC HOUSE

Park Walk, Chelsea.

Licensed: 1860-1870

Management

Middlesex justices:

Mich. 1860-	John Edward Allen	
"	1863-	William Henry Haynes
"	1869	Ann Loosemore
"	1870	*No notice, no petition.*

Literature

Official records:

Mx. Mich. Q.S. 1860-1870.

532

OFFORD ARMS PUBLIC HOUSE

388, Caledonian Road, Islington.

Licensed: 1854-1890

Building details

The concert room was on the first floor, and was L shaped, and divided into two rooms by movable partitions. It was closed as a result of the 1878 Act.

Management

Middlesex justices:

Mich. 1854-	James Greenwood	
" 1860-	Mathew Hitchcox	
" 1864	Martin Spence Baylis	
" 1865-	Thomas Gibbs	
" 1874-	Alexander Brown	
" 1876	Mathew Newman	
" 1877-	Charles Mills	
" 1883-	John Gerlach	

London County Council:

1890	Thomas Hurdle
Nov. 1890	*Licence refused.*

Literature

Official records:

G.L.C. Arch. Dpt. Th. case 040/96; L.C.C. Th. & M-H. Com. App. Nov. 1889-1890; Mx. Mich. Q.S. 1854-1888.

533

OLD COMMODORE PUBLIC HOUSE

Old Montague Street, Whitechapel.

Licensed: 1850-1870

Management

Middlesex justices:

Mich. 1850-	John Stainforth	
" 1853-	John Farrington Peters	
" 1863-	William John Peters	
" 1865-	William Savage	
" 1870	*Licence refused* to Isaac Bird.	

Literature

Official records:

Mx. Mich. Q.S. 1850-1870.

534

OLD COMMODORE PUBLIC HOUSE

209, Poplar High Street, Poplar.

Licensed: 1855-1890

Also known as

Commodore Arms Public House

Building details

Concert hall was on the ground floor at the rear of the public house. It measured 38' × 15' exclusive of the platform. The hall was closed as a result of the 1878 Act.

Management

Middlesex justices:

Mich. 1855-	Timothy Blackman	
" 1858	*No notice, no petition.*	
" 1859-	Harriet Hannah Blackman	
" 1863-	William Ford Lukes	
" 1882	Thomas W. Finnes and Richard Broomfield	
" 1883	Charles Webb and Richard Broomfield	
" 1884	John Edwin Spencer	
" 1885-	Richard Broomfield	

London County Council:

1890	Richard Broomfield
Nov. 1890	*Licence refused.*

Literature

Official records:

G.L.C. Arch. Dpt. Th. case 040/99; L.C.C. Th. & M-H. Com. App. Nov. 1889-1890; Mx. Mich. Q.S. 1859-1888.

535

OLD CROWN PUBLIC HOUSE

Upper Holloway.

Licensed: 1854-1856

Management

Middlesex justices:

Mich. 1854-	John Colson	
" 1856	*No notice, no petition.*	

Literature

Official records:

Mx. Mich. Q.S. 1854-1856.

536

OLD CROWN PUBLIC HOUSE

Hornsey Lane and Highgate Hill, Islington.

Licensed: 1899-1903

Building details

Hall licensed subject to the undertaking that no money shall be taken at the doors for the admission of the public to entertainments covered by the council's licence.

Capacity: 108

Management

London County Council:

1899-	Charlotte Griffiths
Nov. 1903	*Not licensed as theatre or music hall.*

Literature

Official records:

G.L.C. Arch. Dpt. Mss. Index;
L.C.C. Th. & M-H. Com. App. Nov. 1899-1903.

537

OLD DUNDEE ARMS PUBLIC HOUSE

51, Wapping Street,

Licensed: 1854-1858

Management

Middlesex justices:

Mich. 1854-   John Samuel James
"   1858   *No notice, no petition.*

Literature

Official records:

Mx. Mich. Q.S. 1854-1858.

538

OLD FOUNTAIN PUBLIC HOUSE

3, Baldwin Street, City Road, St. Luke's, Finsbury.

Licensed: 1860-1891

Building details

The Concert room was on the first floor of the public house, and was L shaped, measuring 21'11" and 29' in length, and 15' wide. It was closed as a result of the 1878 Act.

Management

Middlesex justices:

Mich. 1860-   Alfred Paradise
"   1862-   Vincent Lambert Pascoe
"   1869-   William Thomas Tubbs
"   1871-   Charles Sims
"   1873-   William Phillips
"   1878   William Finch
"   1879-   Richard James Burden

London County Council:

1890-   Richard James Burden
Nov. 1891   *Not licensed*

Literature

Official records:

G.L.C. Arch. Dpt. Th. case 040/100; L.C.C. Th. & M-H. Com. App. Nov. 1889-1890; Mx. Mich. Q.S. 1860-1888.

Location of other material

Plans: G.L.C. Architects Department

539

OLD KING JOHN'S HEAD PUBLIC HOUSE

90, Mansfield Street, Shoreditch.

Licensed: 1856-1890

Management

Middlesex justices:

Mich. 1856-   Joseph James Stratton
"   1860   Charles Forster
"   1861   William Bennett
"   1862   John Grove

"   1863   George Drury
"   1864-   William Burtwell
"   1866-   James Smith
"   1871-   Andrew Rogers
"   1884-   Andrew Rogers' widow (i.e. Mary Rogers)

London County Council:

1890   Mary Rogers
Nov. 1890   *Licence refused.*

Literature

Official records:

L.C.C. Th. & M-H. Com. App. Nov. 1889-1890; Mx. Mich. Q.S. 1856-1888.

540

OLD MARGATE TOWN PUBLIC HOUSE

George Row, Bermondsey.

Licensed: 1872-1873

Management

Surrey justices:

Mich. 1872-   John Moffatt Bottomley
"   1873   *Not licensed.*

Literature

Official records:

Sy. Mich. Q.S. 1872

541

OLD MERMAID PUBLIC HOUSE

364, Mare Street, Hackney.

Licensed: 1869-1890

Management

Middlesex justices:

Mich. 1869   William James Holt
"   1870   Henry Bull
"   1871   William Abraham
"   1872   Alfred Homer
"   1873   Francis Trundle
"   1874   Abraham Bryant
"   1875   William Reid Bulman
"   1876   Walter Vyse
"   1877-   William Henry Brinkworth
"   1879-   Leonard Joseph Abington

London County Council:

1890   Leonard Joseph Abington
Nov. 1890   *Licence refused.*

Literature

Official records:

L.C.C. Th. & M-H. Com. App. Nov. 1889-1890; Mx. Mich. Q.S. 1869-1888.

542

OLD ROSE MUSIC HALL AND PUBLIC HOUSE

42, Tanner Street, Bermondsey.

Building details

Concert room on the 1st floor of the public house, with unfixed seating for 100 people. The hall measured 33'10" × 16'2". It was closed as a result of the 1878 Act.

Management

No licensing records traced.

Literature

Official records:

G.L.C. Arch. Dpt. Th. case 040/104; Sel. Com. 1892.

543

OLD SWAN PUBLIC HOUSE

Queen's Road West, Chelsea.

Licensed: 1859-1873.

Management

Middlesex justices:

Mich. 1859-	Frederick James Fell
" 1862-	James Dike Nicholson
" 1866-	George Vigurs
" 1873	*No notice, no petition.*

Literature

Official records:

Mx. Mich. Q.S. 1859-1872.

544

OLD THREE COLTS PUBLIC HOUSE

Old Ford Road, St. Mary, Stratford, Bow.

Licensed: 1857-1872.

Management

Middlesex justices:

Mich. 1857-	William Thomas Hudson
" 1865-	James Lewis Beech.
" 1866-	Edward Cross
" 1870-	Benjamin Farmer
" 1872	*Licence refused.* Fined forty shillings and costs for illegal Sunday trading.

Literature

Official records:

Mx. Mich. Q.S. 1857-1872.

545

'OLD VIC' (i.e. Royal Victoria Hall)

The Cut, Lambeth.

Opened: 11th May, 1818

Former names

Royal Coburg Theatre 1818
Royal Victoria Theatre 1. 7. 1833

Old Vic 1922 (545)

(Greater London Council Photograph Library)

Victoria Theatre
New Victoria Palace
Royal Victoria Hall and Coffee Tavern 27. 12. 1880

Building details

Architect: Rudolph Cabanel of Aachen

Material for foundations etc. taken from demolished Savoy Palace.

1871: Reconstructed

Architect: J. T. Robinson

Contractor: Thomas Snowdon

1927: Minor repairs

1940: Closed by war damage.

1950: Reconstructed

Architect: Douglas W. Rowntree

Capacity: 1, 454

Stage: 29'6" wide × 30' deep.

Management

Lord Chamberlain:

29. 9.1843-	David Webster Osbaldiston
8. 1.1851-	Miss Eliza Vincent
9. 4.1855-	Joseph Johnson Towers
24.12.1862-	Frederick Fenton and Frederick Frampton
22. 5.1867-	William James Rofs
29. 9.1867-	Joseph Henry Arnold Cave
23.12.1871-	Romaine Delatoire
29. 9.1873-	Charles Thomas Burleigh
29. 9.1874-	William Thomas Frewer
27.12.1875-	William Henry Swanborough
25. 3.1876-	John Aubrey
29. 9.1878-	Joseph (written as John) Henry Arnold Cave and Albert West (to 28. 9. 1880)

Surrey justices:

Mich. 1880-	Emma Cons, Secretary of Coffee Music Halls Co. Ltd.

London County Council:

1890-	Emma Cons
1913-	Lilian Baylis
1938-	Ernest Bruce Digby-Worsley i.e. Bruce Worsley
1941	Tyrone Guthrie
Nov. 1941	*Not relicensed owing to war damage.*

Lord Chamberlain:

31. 10. 1912-	Lilian Baylis (for variety, in 1934 as a theatre)
1.12.1938-	Ernest Bruce Digby Worsley
1.12.1940-	William Tyrone Guthrie (to 1941)
1941	*Not to be relicensed owing to war damage*
1.12.1950	George Thomas Chamberlaine

Literature

Official records:

G.L.C. Arch. Dpt. Mss. Index; G.L.C. Arch. Dpt. Th. case 291; L.C.C. Th. & M-H. Com. App. Nov. 1889-; LC7/13-16, 20-26, 89; L.C.O. 374 and 528; Sel. Com. 1866, 1877 and 1892; Sy. Mich. Q.S. 1880-1888.

Contemporary accounts:

1859 BUILDING NEWS. 1859, Jan. 7th. p. 5.—Report of accident and note on exits and stairs.
BUILDING NEWS. 1859, Feb. 18th. p. 161.— Stone stairs to be erected.

1871 MORNING POST. 1871, Sept. 5th. 'The last of the Victoria Palace'—report of auction
DAILY TELEGRAPH. 1871, Dec. 25th. 'The new Victoria'—Description and report of opening.
BUILDER. 1871, Dec. 30th. p. 1029-30. — Brief description of reconstruction of interior.

1873 ERA ALMANACK. 1873. p. 7-12.—'Old Vic' by E. Blanchard.

1874 ROYAL VICTORIA PALACE THEATRE Particulars and conditions of sale of the above property.
Messrs. Green and Sons. . . 25th March. 1874. 6p. plans. (Copy in Enthoven Collection)

1880-7 BRITISH MUSEUM Collection of reports and pamphlets (10384 f. 1)

1888 BUILDER. 1888, April 21st. p. 291.—Proposed memorial to the late Samuel Morley. Appeal for money to buy freehold in order to turn it into a 'People's Palace' for South London.
BUILDER. 1888, Aug. 18th. p. 128.—Report of purchase of freehold and use of hall in connection with South London Polytechnic Schools. Ballad concerts and variety entertainment to continue. Class rooms to be added at the back.

1889 BUILDER. 1889, Aug. 31st. p. 161.—Report of opening as First People's Palace for South London.

1890 ILLUSTRATED LONDON NEWS. 1890, Feb. 22nd. p. 243.—Illus.

1918 GRAPHIC. 1918, Oct. 26th. p. 468. The Royal Victoria Theatre.—Illus.

1922 NATION. 1922, April 1st. p. 15-16, *and* May 20th. p. 256. 'The Old Vic as a Shakespeare Memorial Theatre'
LITERARY DIGEST. 1922, Sept. 2nd. p. 34-5. The saving of the 'Old Vic' for Shakespeare plays.

1923 DRAMA. 1923, April. p. 249-50. The saving of the 'Old Vic' by G. F. Reynolds.

1929 DRAMA. 1929, April. p. 197-8, 224. The Old Vic, the People's theatre of England, by A. G. Smaltz.

1949 TIMES. 1949, Dec. 3rd. Note of proposed re-opening.

1950 TIMES. 1950, July 15th. Note of proposed re-opening.

1950 TIMES. 1950, Sept. 15th. Note of proposed re-opening.
SPHERE. 1950, Nov. 11th.—illus. of building.
TIMES. 1950, Nov. 15th.—Report of re-opening.
ARCHITECTS JOURNAL. 1950. Nov. 23rd and 30th. p. 411-2, and 455-9.
DAILY TELEGRAPH. 1950, Nov. 15th.—Re-opening of the Old Vic.
SPHERE. 1950, Nov. 25th. —illus. of re-opening.
ARCHITECTURAL REVIEW. 1950, Dec. p. 419. New Old Vic.

Historical accounts:

1824 NIC-NAC, or Literary Cabinet, 1824, Sept. 25th. No. 95. 2p. illus.—A brief history of the Coburg Theatre.

1904 BAKER, H. Barton
History of the London stage and its players. p. 397-9.—Indexed under Victoria Theatre.

1917 BOOTH, John
A century of theatrical history, 1816-1916,
'The Old Vic'. Steads, 1917. 72 p. port. facsims.
1923 NEWTON, Henry Chance
The Old Vic and its associations: being my own
extraordinary experiences of 'Queen Victoria's
own theayter'. Fleetway Press, (1923). 86p.
plates.
1925 CHANCELLOR, E. B.
The pleasure haunts of London. p. 113-6.
1926 HAMILTON, Cicely, and BAYLIS, Lilian
The Old Vic. Jonathan Cape. 1926. 285 p.
c. 1930 MAYES, Ronald
The romance of London theatres, No. 13.
1935 WILLIAMS, E. G. Harcourt.
Four years at the Old Vic, 1929-1933. Putnam, 1935. 249p.
1936 FAGG, Edwin
The old 'Old Vic'...from its origin as 'The
Royal Coburg'...Henderson, 1936. 123p. ports.,
illus.
1938 WILLIAMS, E. G. Harcourt. editor.
Vic-Wells. The Work of Lilian Baylis. Cobden-
Sanderson, 1938. 106p.
1944 TIME, 1944, Sept. 18th. p. 70.
'The story of the Old Vic Theatre'.
1945 DENT, Edward J.
A theatre for everybody, the story of the Old
Vic and Sadlers Wells. Boardman, 1945. 167p.
1949 VICKERS, John
The Old Vic in photographs. Saturn, 1949
90p. col. illus.
WILLIAMS, E. G. Harcourt.
Old Vic saga. Winchester, 1949, 240 p.
1951 LONDON. County Council.
Survey of London. Vol XXIII. L.C.C. 1951.
p. 37-39.
1959 ENCICLOPEDIA dello spettacolo. Vol. 6,
Col. 1628-9.
1963 MANDER, Raymond, and MITCHENSON, Joe.
The theatres of London, 2nd ed. pp. 237-243.

Location of other material

The Vic-Wells Library, containing books, scrapbooks,
cuttings &c. is housed in the Old Vic Theatre.

Plans:

G.L.C. *Architects Department.*
Public Record Office, LC7/86 (9 sheets, 1870-1).

Programes and playbills and cuttings:

British Museum Library; Enthoven Collection;
Garrick Club; Lambeth Local Collection; London
Museum; Westminster Local Collection.

546

OLD WHITE HORSE PUBLIC HOUSE

Brixton Hill, Brixton.

Licensed: 1872-1874.

Management

Surrey justices:

Mich. 1872-	Hastings John Reeve	
" 1874	*No application.*	

Literature

Official records:

Sy. Mich. Q.S. 1872-1874.

547

OLD WILL SUMMERS PUBLIC HOUSE

Crispin Street, Stepney.

Licensed: 1851-1863

Also known as

Will Summers Public House (1862).

Management

Middlesex justices:

Mich. 1851-	John Farrington Peters	
" 1852-	Charles Widows	
" 1859-	William Smith Boult	
" 1861-	Samuel Robert Pether	
" 1862-	Charles William Britt	
" 1863	*No notice, no petition.*	

Literature

Official records:

Mx. Mich. Q.S. 1852-1863.

548

OLIVE BRANCH PUBLIC HOUSE

266, Southampton Street, Camberwell.

Licensed: 1874-1889.

Management

Surrey justices:

Mich. 1874-   George Sedgley
L.C.C. refused to renew licence in Nov. 1889.

Literature

Official records:

L.C.C. Th. & M-H. Com. App. Nov. 1889;
Sy. Mich. Q.S. 1874-1888.

549

OLYMPIC THEATRE

6-10, Wych Street, Strand.

Opened: 18th September, 1806. Demolished for
construction of the Aldwych, (1904).

Other names

Olympic Pavilion to Sept. 1853
New Olympic Theatre 27. 11. 1890-
Olympic Music Hall 1893-

Building details

1st building:

Erected: 1805

Built for: Philip Astley

Burnt Down: 29. 3. 1849

2nd building:

Erected: 1849

Architect: F. W. Bushill

Reconstructed 1869

Capacity: (seating) 889

Auditorium: S. 136; P. 161; D.C. 122; U.C. 87; G. 335; Bx. 48.

3rd building:

Erected: 1890

Architect: Bertie Crewe and W. G. R. Sprague

Capacity: 2, 150

—Finally used for services of the St. Giles's, Little Wild St. Mission.

Management

Lord Chamberlain:

29. 9. 1843-	George Wyld
1. 11. 1844-	Kate Howard
4. 4. 1846-	George Bolton
29. 9. 1847-	James McCann
27. 12. 1847-	William Davidson
26. 12. 1849-	Walter Watts (theatre rebuilt)
22. 7. 1850-	Henry Puckridge
29. 9. 1851-	William Farren
29. 9. 1853-	Alfred Wigan
10. 8. 1857-	Frederick Thomas Robson and William Samuel Emden
29. 9. 1864-	Horace Wigan
26. 12. 1866-	Benjamin Webster
29. 9. 1869-	William Henry Liston
29. 9. 1872-	Ada Cavendish
29. 9. 1873-	Henry Gartside Neville
12. 4. 1879-	Fanny Josephs
29. 9. 1880-	Charles Baker (to 30. 6. 1883)
29. 11. 1883-	Mrs. Anna Georgiana Harriet Conover
29. 9. 1886-	Grace Hawthorne
20. 6. 1887-	Agnes Hewitt
29. 9. 1889-	Charles Wilmot (to 28. 1. 1890)
27. 11. 1890-	Wilson Barrett
28. 9. 1891-	Charles Wilmot
25. 11. 1896-	Charlotte Wilmot
29. 9. 1899-	Theodor Rosenfeld (for one year)

London County Council:

1893-	Charles Wilmot
Nov. 1895	*Not licensed.*

Literature

Official records:

G.L.C. Arch. Dpt. Th. case 03;
L.C.C. Th. & M-H. Com. App. Nov. 1892-94;
LC1/507-712;
LC7/13-17, 20-42, 89;
M.B.W. Rpt. 1882, p. 205-217;
Sel. Com. 1866, 1877 and 1892.

Contemporary accounts:

1849 ILLUSTRATED LONDON NEWS. 1849, March 31st. illus.—Total destruction of the theatre by fire. Includes brief history of site.

BUILDER. 1849, Dec. 22nd and 29th. illus. —Description of new theatre.

1850 ILLUSTRATED LONDON NEWS. 1850, Jan. 12th.—Description and illus. of rebuilt theatre.

1879 DRAMATIC NOTES. 1879. p. 38-41.

1883 BUILDING NEWS. 1883, Nov. 30th. p. 872.—Note of internal structural alterations.

1887 SATURDAY REVIEW. 1887, June 18th. The site of the London theatres. . . No. 2.

1890 DAILY CHRONICLE. 1890, Dec. 5th. 'Opening of the new Olympic Theatre'.—report.
DAILY TELEGRAPH. 1890, Dec. 5th. 'New Olympic Theatre'.
BUILDER. 1890, Dec. 13th. p. 466.—Report of opening.
ILLUSTRATED SPORTING AND DRAMATIC NEWS. 1890, Dec. 13th.—Illus.

1893 BUILDER. 1893, March 18th. p. 213.—Report of proposal to convert it into music hall.

1894 BUILDER. 1894, July 7th. p. 9.—Report of court order for sale of theatre.

1898 BUILDER. 1898, June 4th. p. 551.—Report that New Italian Opera Syndicate formed to give lyric performances. Includes note on history.

1904 BUILDER. 1904, March 12th. p. 275.—Report of proposed demolition. Includes summary of history.

Historical accounts:

1879 ERA ALMANACK 1879. p. 31-34

1903 GORDON, C.
Old time Aldwych. . . p. 264-267. illus.

1904 BAKER, H. Barton
History of the London stage and its players. p. 247-273.

1923 PEARCE, C. E.
Madame Vestris and her times.
Stanley Paul, 1923.
—N.B. Mme Vestris was the best known as the manager of the theatre before 1850; she was at the Olympic from 1830-1839.

1925 CHANCELLOR, E. B.
The pleasure haunts of London. . . p. 126-128
SHERSON, Erroll
London's lost theatres. . . Chapter V. p. 77-120.

1930 CHANCELLOR, E. B.
The annals of Covent Garden and its neighbourhood. p. 222.

c. 1930 MAYES, Ronald.
The romance of London theatres, Nos. 6 and 211.

1933 WAITZKIN, L.
The witch of Wych Street: a study of the theatrical reforms of Madame Vestris.
(Harvard Honours Thesis in English No. 6, 1933)—*see note under* PEARCE, C. E.

1946 SCOTT, Harold
Early doors. . . p. 67+

1952 PULLING, Christopher
They were singing. . . Various refs.

1959 ENCICLOPEDIA dello spettacolo. Vol. 6, Col. 1629
THEATRE WORLD. 1959, May and Oct.
Lost London Theatres, by N. M. Bligh, No. 13. The story of the Olympic, 1806-1899. 6p.

1968 MANDER, Raymond *and* MITCHENSON, Joe
The lost theatres of London p. 253-287. 9 illus.

Location of other material

Plans: Public Record Office LC7/70. 7 sheets (1890)

Programmes and Playbills:

British Museum Library; Enthoven Collection;
Garrick Club; Guildhall Library (100 items); London
Museum; Westminster Local Collection.

550

OPERA COMIQUE THEATRE

Holywell Street, and 299, Strand.

Opened: 29th October, 1870. *Closed:* 1899.
Demolished for Aldwych rebuilding.

Building details

Architect: Francis H. Fowler

Builder: M. Reid, of Hammersmith

Capacity: (seating) 862

Auditorium: S. 140; L.C. 120; U.C. 200; G. 330; Bx. 72.

Reconstruction 1895

Architect: Fowler & Hall

Contractor: Patman & Fotheringham

Management

Lord Chamberlain:

27. 10. 1870-	Henry Leslie, Charles Steele and Washington Norton
1. 5. 1871-	Prospere Got
1. 11. 1871-	Camile Montelli
29. 9. 1872-	Edward Peron Hingston
5. 6. 1874-	Richard D'Oyly Carte
2. 11. 1874-	Ann Sheridan (cancelled 28. 3. 1875)
19. 1. 1875-	John Hollingshead
29. 3. 1875-	Alexis Pitron (to 6. 6. 1875)
1. 8. 1875	Charles Morton (not taken up)
29. 9. 1875-	Frederick C. Burnaud
13. 1. 1876-	Charles Morton
15. 4. 1876-	Horace Wigan
9. 8. 1876-	Richard Barker
1. 4. 1885-	David James
7. 10. 1885-	Frederick James Harris
29. 9. 1886-	William Duck
28. 12. 1886-	Frederick James Harris
29. 9. 1890-	Cissie Grahame
29. 9. 1891-	Edward Compton
29. 9. 1892-	Francis Fowler

Not relicensed in 1900

Literature

Official records:

G.L.C. Arch. Dpt. Th. case 02;
LC1/508-712; LC7/15-17, 24-33, 89.
M.B.W. Rpt. 1882, p. 62-82.
Sel. Com. 1877 and 1892.

Contemporary accounts:

1870　BUILDER. 1870, Oct. 8th. p. 803.—Brief report
　　　on 'last new theatre in Strand'.
　　　DAILY TELEGRAPH. 1870, Oct. 29th. 'The new
　　　Opera Comique'.—Description.
1870　ERA 1870. Oct. 29.—Description and report
　　　of opening
　　　BUILDER. 1870, Nov. 5th. p. 881-2.
　　　—Description.
1879　DRAMATIC NOTES, 1879. p. 49-51.

1885　ERA 1885 April 4. Description of redecoration
1887　SATURDAY REVIEW. 1887, June 18th. 'The
　　　state of the London theatres... No. 2'.
1895　BUILDING NEWS. 1895, Nov. 22nd. p. 758.—Brief
　　　description of reconstruction.
　　　BUILDER. 1895, Nov. 23rd. p. 385.—Report of
　　　internal structural alterations; balcony removed
　　　and pit extended.

Historical accounts:

1904　BAKER, H. Barton
　　　History of the London stage and its players.
　　　p. 334-5.
1925　SHERSON, Erroll
　　　London's lost theatres... p. 253-261.
c. 1930　MAYES, Ronald
　　　The romance of London theatres, No. 154.
1958　THEATRE WORLD, 1958 June.
　　　Lost London theatres, by N. M. Bligh. No. 11.
　　　The story of the Opera Comique. 3p.
1959　ENCICLOPEDIA dello spettacolo. Vol. 6, Col.
　　　1629.
1968　MANDER, Raymond *and* MITCHENSON, Joe
　　　The lost theatres of London. pp. 288-298

Location of other material

Plans: G.L.C. *Architects Department.*
Public Record Office. LC7/71. 6 sheets

Programmes:

British Museum Library; Enthoven Collection;
Garrick Club; London Museum; Westminster Local
Collection.

551

ORDNANCE ARMS PUBLIC HOUSE

37, Lewisham Road, Lewisham.

Licensed: 1866-1891

Building details

The concert room was on the first floor over the bar
of the public house. It measures 28' 8" × 15'. The
hall was closed as a result of the 1878 Act.

Management

West Kent justices:

Mich.	1866	Frederick Barnett
"	1867	Easter Holley Barnett
"	1868	George Emberson Fairchild
"	1869-	George Nevard
"	1877-	John Harris

London County Council:

1890-	John Harris
Nov. 1891	*Not licensed.*

Literature

Official records:

G.L.C. Arch. Dpt. Th. case 040/106;
L.C.C. Th. & M-H. Com. App. Nov. 1889-90;
W. Kt. Mich. Q.S. 1866-88.

OXFORD THEATRE

26-32, Oxford Street, St. Marylebone.

First licensed: 1859   *Closed:* May 1926
Demolished: 1927/8

Former names

Boar and Castle Public House to 1861
Oxford Music Hall
New Oxford Theatre

Building details

1st building:
First purpose—built music hall opened 26.3.1861

Architect: Messrs. Finch, Hill & Paraire

Decor: Messrs. White and Palby

Contractors: Messrs. Holland and Hannen

Destroyed: 11.2.1868.

2nd building:

Opened: 9.8.1869

Destroyed: 1.11.1872

3rd building:

Opened: 17.3.1873

Architect: E. L. Paraire

Builders: Messrs. Holland and Hannen

Closed: 4.6.1892

4th building:

Opened: 31.1.1893

Architect: Messrs. Wylson & Long

Builder: Frank Kirk

Capacity: (seating) 1,047

Auditorium: S. 375; P. 153; C. 154; G. 365.

Management

Middlesex justices:

Mich.	1859	Jules Wanthier
"	1860-	Charles Morton
"	1869	Edwin Taylor
"	1870-	Morris Robert Syers
"	1876-	John Henry Jennings.

London County Council:

1890-	John Henry Jennings
1892	James Kirk
1893-	Charles Richard Brighten
1895-	Ilford Ibbetson
1925-	Oxford Ltd.
1927	J. Lyons and Co. Ltd.
Nov. 1927	*Not licensed.*

Lord Chamberlain:

10. 1.1912-	Ilford Ibbetson
1.12.1922-	Walter Payne (to Nov. 1927)

Literature

Official records:

G.L.C. Arch. Dpt. Mss. Index;
G.L.C. Arch. Dpt. Th. case 242;
L.C.C. Th. & M-H. Com. App. Nov. 1889-27;
L.C.O. 374 and 503; Mx. Mich. Q.S. 1859-88;
Sel. Com. 1866, 1877 and 1892.

Contemporary accounts:

1861	BUILDING NEWS. 1861, March 22nd. p. 241. —Description. ERA, 1861, March 31st—Description.
1868	BUILDING NEWS. 1868, Feb. 14th. p. 110. —Report of destruction by fire. ERA, 1868, Feb. 11th.—Report of fire
1869	ERA, 1869. Aug. 15th.—Report of rebuilding & reopening.
1872	ERA, 1872, Nov. 3rd.—Report of fire
1873	ERA, 1873, March 23rd.—Report of reopening.
1887	SATURDAY REVIEW. 1887, Aug. 6th. 'The state of the London. . . music halls. . . No. 1.'
1890	BUILDER. 1890, Oct. 4th. p. 276. Report of order of sale under provisions of late Morris Robert Syer's will.
1893	BUILDER. 1893, Jan. 28th. p. 74.—Report of reconstruction. STAGE. 1893, Jan. 21st. ERA. 1893, Jan. 21st and Feb. 4th.
1893	OXFORD MUSIC HALL The Oxford: annals of old and new. The theatre 1893. 22p., illus.—Souvenir of the opening.
1897	SACHS, E. O., *and* WOODROW, E. A. E. Modern opera houses and theatres. Vols. 2 and 3 —Textual references and plates. Dates, dimensions, plans, section and elevations.

Historical accounts:

c. 1930	MAYES, Ronald, The romance of London theatres, Nos. 50 and 131.
1935	HADDON, Archibald The story of the music hall. p. 36, 48-51, and 130. illus.
1938	DISHER, M. W. Winkles and champagne. various refs.
1946	SCOTT, Harold Early doors, . . . p. 146-.
1952	PULLING, Christopher They were singing. . . various refs.
1959	ENCICLOPEDIA dello spettacolo. Vol. 6. Col. 1629.
1968	MANDER, Raymond *and* MITCHENSON, Joe The lost theatres of London. pp. 299-321, 6 illus.

Location of other material

Plans: G.L.C. *Architects Department;*
British Music Hall Society.

Programmes:

British Museum Library; Enthoven Collection;
London Museum; St. Marylebone Local Collection;
Westminster Local Collection.

PAKENHAM PUBLIC HOUSE

Knightsbridge Green, St. Margaret's, Westminster.

Licensed: 1862-1863

Management

Middlesex justices:

Mich. 1862-   William Stockley
   "   1863   *No notice, no petition.*

Literature

Official records:

Mx. Mich. Q.S. 1862-1863.

554

PALACE THEATRE

Cambridge Circus, Westminster.

Oxford Music Hall   (552)

(Ellis Ashton Collection, British Music Hall Society)

Opened: 31st January, 1891

Former names

D'Oyly Carte's New Theatre. Before opening
Royal English Opera House to 1893
Palace Theatre of Varieties

Building details

Built for: Richard D'Oyly Carte

Architects: T. E. Collcutt and G. H. Holloway

Capacity: 1,697

Auditorium: S. & Bx. 358; R.C. 235; 1st C. 236; A. 189;
G. 227.

Gallery reconstructed 1908:

Architect: J. Emblin Walker

Builder: Henry Lovatt, Wolverhampton

Management

Lord Chamberlain:

12. 1.1891-	Richard D'Oyly Carte
28.11.1892-	Sir Augustus Harris (surrendered 1.6.1893)
12. 1.1912-	Alfred Butt
1.12.1923-	Charles B. Cochran
1.12.1946-	Tom Arnold
1.12.1947-	Tom Arnold and Emile Littler

London County Council:

1893-	Thomas Ernest Polden
1918-	Alfred Butt
1924-	Charles B. Cochran
1925-	London Palace (1921) Ltd. (through 1950)

Literature

G.L.C. Arch. Dpt. Mss. Index.
L.C.C. Th. & M-H. Com. App. Nov. 1892-;
L.C.C. Th. & M-H. Com. Papers 1888-;
LC1/564-601; LC7/37; L.C.O. 374 and 510.

Royal English Opera House 1891   (554)

(The Builder)

Contemporary accounts:

1889 BUILDING NEWS. 1889, April 26th. p. 582.—Note.
Plate of front elevation.
1890 BUILDER. 1890, Feb. 15th. p. 118.—Description
of new theatre under construction.
DAILY NEWS. 1890, Nov. 3rd. 'The architecture
of London: Mr. D'Oyly Carte's new theatre'.
—Detailed report.
1891 BUILDER. 1891, Jan. 3rd. p. 10.—Report of name.
illus.
BUILDING NEWS. 1891, Jan. 9th. p. 64.—Descrip-
tion of Royal English Opera House. 2 plates of
interior.
DAILY GRAPHIC. 1891, Jan. 27th. The Royal
English Opera: Mr. D'Oyly Carte's new theatre.
—Description and illus.
BUILDER. 1891, Jan. 31st. p. 93.
ROYAL ENGLISH OPERA.
Monograph of the Royal English Opera...n.d.
16p. illus. (Copy in Enthoven Collection).
SUNDAY TIMES. 1891, Feb. 1st. 'Royal English
Opera: the opening night'.
BUILDING NEWS. 1891, Feb. 6th. p. 194-5.
—Detailed description.—Correction 13. 2. 1891,
p. 252.
BUILDER. 1891, Feb. 7th. p. 115.
BUILDER. 1891, Feb. 14th. p. 122, 126-6.
—Description.
BUILDER. 1891, Feb. 21st. p. 156.
BUILDER. 1891, Feb. 28th. p. 174. Correction.
1892 The PLAYERS. 1892, Aug. 5th. 'The Palace
Theatre Ltd.'.—Report on plan to turn the
English Opera House into a music hall, covering
financial question.
1896 SACHS, E. O. *and* WOODROW, E. A. E.
Modern opera houses and theatres. Vol. 1.
p. 35-37., and Vol. 3. p. 30-32, and other refs.
—Description, plans, sections and elevations.
1898 SACHS, E. O.
Stage construction... p. 30-33. illus.
1908 BUILDER. 1908, Oct. 10th. p. 379-380.—Detailed
report of rebuilding of gallery.

Historical accounts:

1895 RIMBAULT, E. F.
Soho and its associations... edited by George
Clinch. Delau, 1895. p. 185.
1904 BAKER, H. Barton
History of the London stage and its players.
p. 345-6. (as English Opera House).
c. 1930 MAYES, Ronald
The romance of London theatres, No. 1. and
179.
1935 DISHER, M. W.
Winkles and champagne. Various refs. and illus.
1938 HADDON, Archibald
The story of the music hall. p. 24, 26, 104-107.
1952 PULLING, Christopher
They were singing... p. 197-8, and other refs.
1959 ENCICLOPEDIA dello spettacolo. Vol. 6. Col.
1629.
1963 MANDER, Raymond *and* MITCHENSON, Joe
The theatres of London. 2nd ed. p. 122-125.
1966 GREATER LONDON COUNCIL
Survey of London, Vols. 33-34, 1966. pp. 300-305.
plans, plates.

Location of other material

Plans: G.L.C. *Architects Department;*
Enthoven Collection, 1947 (2 sheets).

Programmes:

British Museum Library; Enthoven Collection;
Garrick Club; Guildhall Library; London Museum;
Westminster Local Collection.

555

PALASEUM

226, Commercial Road, Stepney.

Opened: March 1912

Formerly

Fienman Yiddish Theatre

Literature

Official records:

G.L.C. Arch. Dpt. Mss. Index;
G.L.C. Arch. Dpt. Th. case 1485.

Contemporary accounts:

1911 BUILDER. 1911, May 26th. p. 653.—Brief
report of theatre under erection. Architect:
Messrs. Geo. Billings, Wright & Co.
1960 EAST LONDON ADVERTISER. 1960, Oct. 28th.
p. 14. 'Troxy to close'.—Formerly Palaseum.

Location of other material

Plans: G.L.C. *Architects Department*

556

PARK PUBLIC HOUSE

Lower Wandsworth Road, Battersea.

Licensed: 1870-1873

Management

Surrey justices:

| Mich. 1870- | John Sampson Litkey |
| " 1873 | *No application.* |

Literature

Official records:

Sy. Mich. Q.S. 1870-1873.

557

PARK THEATRE

Park Street, Camden Town.

Opened: 31st May, 1873.
Burnt Down: 11th September, 1881.

Former names

Alexandra Theatre	
Royal Alexandra Theatre	} to 1875
Regents Park Theatre	before opening
Royal Park Theatre	1890

Later

| Royal Park Hall | 1890- |

was erected on the site.

Building details

Architect: G. T. Robinson

Contractor: Edward Vaughan

Decorators: Messrs. Pashley, Newton, Young & Co.

Management

Lord Chamberlain:

31. 5.1873-	Thomas Thorpe Pede
29. 9.1875-	Stefano Arroni Parravincini and Wardle Corbyn
17. 4.1876-	Thomas Thorpe Pede
1. 7.1876-	Mrs. Mary Anne St. Claire
18.12.1878-	John Thomas Douglas, and Samuel Richard Douglas (to Sept. 1881)

A letter to the Lord Chamberlain LC 1/547 following the application of Joseph Bangs and Herbert Farraud Bangs 29. 9. 1890, for a licence for the *Royal Park Hall*, states that although licence refused, that for the past five years they had performed plays and would continue to do so.

Literature

Official records:

LC 7/16, 24-30, 89.

Contemporary accounts:

1873   BUILDER. 1873, Jan. 11th. p. 26.—Brief description of new theatre under construction.
BUILDING NEWS. 1873, Jan 17th. p. 88. 'Regents Park Theatre'—Description.
BUILDER. 1873, May 17th. p. 386-7.—Brief report and illus. of auditorium.
1879   DRAMATIC NOTES. 1879, p. 73.
1881   DAILY NEWS. 1881, Sept. 12th. 'Burning of the Park Theatre' report.
BUILDING NEWS. 1881, Sept. 16th. p. 349. 'Destruction of the Park Theatre and its lessons'.—Article.
PENNY ILLUSTRATED PAPER. 1881, Sept. 17th. p. 182. illus. of theatre.

Historical accounts:

1925   SHERSON, Erroll
London's lost theatres...p. 291-294.
1961   REYNOLDS, E.
Recreations and leisure in St. Pancras...1961. p. 39.

Location of other material

Programmes:

British Museum Library; Enthoven Collection; Garrick Club; Guildhall Library; Westminster Local Collection.

558

PARKHURST THEATRE

401, Holloway Road, Islington.

Opened: 24th May, 1890.   *Closed as theatre:* 1909.

Former names

Parkhurst Hall
Parkhurst Grand Hall and Theatre

Building details

Builder: Messrs. Driver and J. R. Perfect.

Capacity: 600

Management

Lord Chamberlain:

30. 4.1890-	James Robert Perfect
29. 9.1898-	Philip Ben Greet and Henry John Wilde (to 1902)

Literature

Official records:

L.C.C. Th. & M-H. Com. Papers 1889-99;
LC 1/546-692; LC 7/37.

Contemporary accounts:

1890   ERA. 1890, May 5th.—Description of building.

Historical accounts:

1898   PARKHURST THEATRE
Programme. 4. 6. 1898.—gives retrospective history.
1955   ISLINGTON. Public Libraries.
Islington and the theatre: exhibition catalogue.

Location of other material

Programmes:

Enthoven Collection; Islington Local Collection; Westminster Local Collection.

559

PAUL'S HEAD PUBLIC HOUSE

104, Paul Street, St. Leonard, Shoreditch.

Licensed: 1859-1865.

Management

Middlesex justices:

Mich.	1859	Charles Rooke Smallbone
"	1860	Thomas Power
"	1861-	Henry Alexander Goff
"	1865	*No notice, no petition.*

Literature

Official records:

Mx. Mich. Q.S. 1859-1864.

560

PAVILION THEATRE

191-193, Whitechapel Road, Stepney.

Opened: 10th November, 1828.   *Ceased to be used for entertainment:* 1934

Also known as

Eastern Opera House, Pavilion Theatre

Building details

1st building:
Burnt down: 13. 2. 1856.

2nd building:

Developer: Miss Conaughton

Architect: G. H. Simmonds

Contractor: Temple G. Tenney

Capacity: (1865) 3,500 with 2,000 in pit

Stage: 70' × 58'

Reconstructed 1874:

Architect: J. T. Robinson

Capacity: (1892) 2,650

Auditorium: S. 174; P. 436; D.C. 417; G. 690; Bx. 85.

Large alterations 1894:

Architect: Ernest Runtz

Management

Lord Chamberlain:

29. 9.1843-	John Johnson and Richard Nelson Lee
26.12.1844-	Thomas Richardson and Richard Samuel Thorne
29. 9.1845-	Richard Samuel Thorne
29. 9.1848-	Edwin Yarnold
6. 1.1849-	Emma Yarnold (widow)
29. 9.1849-	Richard Samuel Thorne
24.12.1852-	James Walker Elphinstone and Frederick Neale (destroyed by fire 9. 2. 1856)
28.10.1858-	John Douglass
29. 9.1864-	Henry Powell and Charles Harrison
29. 9.1865-	Henry Powell
29. 9.1868-	James Harwood
24. 4.1869-	John Thomas Douglass
4. 9.1871-	Morris Abrahams
28. 9.1894-	Isaac Cohen
15. 8.1905-	Donald Munro
1. 8.1907-	Max Merton (for Jewish plays)
25. 3.1908-	Edward Lancelot Lynd-Martin
28. 3.1908-	Edward King
24.12.1908-	Joseph Gordon
24. 5.1909-	Lawrence Cowen
1.11.1910-	Jacob Woolf Rosenthal
28. 1.1911-	Lawrence Cowen
27. 3.1911-	Jacob Woolf Rosenthal
16. 7.1912-	Harry Steinwoolf
(1.12.1920 undated)-	Frank Joseph Woollard
20. 4.1921-	William Russell
20. 6.1922-	Jacob Woolf Rosenthal (to Nov. 1934)

London County Council:

1923-1934	Jacob Woolf Rosenthal

Literature

Official records:

G.L.C. Arch. Dpt. Mss. Index; L.C.C. Th. & M-H. Com. App. Nov. 1922-33; L.C.C. Th. & M-H. Com. Papers. 1888-; LC 1/507-752; LC 7/13-17, 20-48, 89; L.C.O. 354 and 374; M.B.W. Rpt. 1882. p. 217-231; Sel. Com. 1866, 1877 and 1892.

Contemporary accounts:

1850 TALLIS'S DRAMATIC MAGAZINE, Nov. 1850-June 1851. p. 90.

172

1856 BUILDER. 1856, Feb. 16th.—Destruction of the Pavilion Theatre, Whitechapel.
ILLUSTRATED LONDON NEWS. 1856, Feb. 16th —Report of fire on 13th Feb. illus.
1858 BUILDER. 1858, May 15th.—Paragraph announcing erection of new theatre.
BUILDING NEWS. 1858. July 2nd. p. 681. —Rebuilding.
BUILDING NEWS. 1858, Aug. 13th. p. 808. —Description.
BUILDING NEWS. 1858, Aug. 20th. p. 840. —Correction.
BUILDER. 1858, Oct. 2nd. p. 654-5. —Detailed description.
BUILDING NEWS. 1858, Nov. 5th. p. 1107-8. —Detailed description.
ILLUSTRATED LONDON NEWS. 1858, Nov. 6th. 'New Royal Pavilion Theatre'.—Description and illus. of auditorium.
1887 SATURDAY REVIEW. 1887, July 23rd. The state of the London theatres...No. 6.
1895 ARCHITECT. 1895, Feb. 15th.—Description and illus. of auditorium, bars &c., and of terracotta figures of 'Comedy' and 'Tragedy' by W.J. Neatby.
1908 PALL MALL MAGAZINE. 1908. p. 173-179. 'The East-end Jew at his playhouse' by Anthony L. Ellis.
1961 DAILY EXPRESS. 1961, Aug. 18th.—Report on demolition by Alan Hunter. Illus.

Historical accounts:

1893 EDWARDS, Francis
Catalogue of playbills offered for sale, 1893. —Contains history. (Copy in Stepney Local Collection)
1895 SKETCH, 1895, Jan. 16th.
'Old Whitechapel and its theatres'. 1p.
BUILDER. 1895, Feb. 23rd. p. 145.
Report of Architectural Association visit, containing history.
1904 BAKER, H. Barton
History of the London stage and its players. p. 406.
c. 1930 MAYES, Ronald
The romance of London theatres, No. 43.
1954 WILSON, A. E.
East end entertainment. Chapters VI and VII.
1967 EAST, John M.
'Neath the Mask'. pp. 86-88, 233-236

Location of other materials

Plans:

G.L.C. *Architects Department.*
Public Record Office LC 7/72. 4 sheets. 19. 9. 1874.

Programmes and Playbills:

British Museum Library; Enthoven Collection; Garrick Club; Guildhall Library; London Museum; Stepney Local Collection; Westminster Local Collection.

561

PEABODY ARMS PUBLIC HOUSE

140, Shadwell High Street, Shadwell.

Licensed: 1855-1869

Former name

Globe and Pigeons Public House (to 1867)

Management

Middlesex justices:

Mich. 1855	George Lindsay Ormsby
" 1856-	John Cults
" 1861-	Priscilla Turnbull
" 1864-	Thomas Thompson
" 1867-	James Barney
" 1869	*Licence refused after two court cases.*

Literature

Official records:

Mx. Mich. Q.S. 1855-1869.

562

PEACOCK PUBLIC HOUSE

325, Cambridge Road, Bethnal Green.

Licensed: 1859-1883

Management

Middlesex justices:

Mich. 1859-	Thomas Gooding
" 1861-	Stephen Ballinger Medcalf
" 1865-	Edward Porter
" 1870-	Joseph Waller
" 1877-	Charles Wilson
" 1880	Helen Eliza Wilson
" 1881	George James Older
" 1882	Walter John Gear
" 1883	*Licence refused as it was seldom used.*

Literature

Official records:

Mx. Mich. Q.S. 1859-1883.

Location of other material

Playbills:

Bethnal Green Library has a playbill for the Peacock Tavern, Cambridge Heath Road, dated 27th November, 1860.

563

PECKHAM HIPPODROME

Peckham High Street, Peckham.

Opened: 31st October, 1898. *In use as a cinema* after 1912.

Former name

Crown Theatre

Later known as

Gaumont Cinema

Building details

Architect: Ernest Runtz

Contractor: Messrs. Colls & Sons

Decorator (Paintings): Charles Buchel

Capacity: 2, 600

Auditorium: S. 356; P. 259; B. 263; G. 358.

Stage: 138' wide × 40' deep.

Pavilion Theatre 1858 (560)

(Victoria & Albert Museum, Crown copyright)

Peckham Hippodrome 1898 (563)

(The Builder)

Management

Lord Chamberlain:

29. 9.1899-	Isaac Cohen
29. 9.1901-	Robert Arthur
18.12.1905-	Cecil Paget (to Sept. 1908)

London County Council:

1901-	Cecil Paget
1912-	Harry Thomas Underwood
Nov. 1924	*Not listed as a theatre or music hall.*

Literature

Official records:

G.L.C. Arch. Dpt. Mss. Index; G.L.C. Arch. Dpt. Th. case 251; L.C.C. Th. & M-H. Com. App. Nov. 1909-1924; L.C.C. Th. & M-H, Com. Papers 1897-; LC 1/-712-752; LC 7/45-48; L.C.O. 349 and 374.

Contemporary accounts:

1898 BUILDER. 1898, May 14th. p. 469.—Description and report of visit by members of Architectural Association.
BUILDING NEWS. 1898, Nov. 4th. p. 658. —Detailed description.
BUILDER. 1898, Nov. 5th. p. 408.—Description, plan and exterior elevation.
SACHS, E. O. *and* WOODROW, E. A. E.
Modern opera houses... Vol. 3.—Description, illus., plans.
1899 BUILDING NEWS. 1899, March 10th. p. 339. —Description. illus. of grand circle foyer and painted panels representing Colonies.
BUILDER. 1899, May 20th. p. 498.—Description.

Historical accounts:

c. 1930 MAYES, Ronald
The romance of London theatres.

Location of other material

Plans: G.L.C. *Architects Department.*

Programmes: Enthoven Collection.

Illustrations: Camberwell Local Collection

564

PECKHAM THEATRE OF VARIETIES

263, Southampton Street, Camberwell.

Licensed: 1849-1897

Former names

Rosemary Branch Music Hall and Public House
People's Palace of Varieties
Lovejoy's Music Hall

Later name

Cornwall Hall

Building details

Capacity: 430

Management

Surrey justices:

Mich.	1849-	James Smith
"	1863-	Thomas Garniss
"	1867-	William Udell
"	1872-	Thomas Garniss
"	1876-	James Whisson Morgan
"	1878-	Alexander Frederick Lovejoy

London County Council:

1890-	Alexander Frederick Lovejoy
1897-	Walter Alfred Lovejoy
Nov. 1897	*Not licensed.*

Literature

Official records:

G.L.C. Arch. Dpt. Th. case 031; L.C.C. Th. & M-H. Com. App. Nov. 1889-1897; Sel. Com. 1892; Sy. Mich. Q.S. 1849-1888.

Historical accounts:

n.d. The PLEASURE gardens of South London. Vol. II. pp. 239-240 (scrapbook in London Museum Library.)

Location of other material

Plans: G.L.C. *Architects Department.*

Programmes &c: Camberwell Local Collection.

565

PECKHAM GROVE PUBLIC HOUSE

Camberwell.

Licensed: 1850-1873

Also known as

Grove Public House

Management

Surrey justices:

Mich.	1850-	Michael Felix Horsley
"	1854-	Christopher Cayley
"	1857-	Charles Stray
"	1959-	James Welch
"	1873	*No application.*

Literature

Official records:

Sy. Mich. Q.S. 1850-1872.

566

PEGASUS PUBLIC HOUSE

Green Lanes, Stoke Newington.

Licensed: 1852-1874

Management

Middlesex justices:

Mich.	1852-	Thomas Wells
"	1856-	James Holleck Davis
"	1872	Peter McLean
"	1873	Henry Bales
"	1874	Thomas Morris *refused licence.*

Literature

Official records:

Mx. Mich. Q.S. 1852-1874.

567

PEMBROKE ARMS COFFEE PALACE

287, City Road, St. Lukes, Finsbury.

Licensed: 1878-1890

Former name

Pembroke Club

Management

Middlesex justices:

| Mich. 1878 | William Panckridge |
| " 1879- | William John Alland |

London County Council:

| 1890 | William John Alland |
| Nov. 1890 | *Not licensed.* |

Literature

Official records:

L.C.C. Th. & M-H. Com. App. Nov. 1889;
Mx. Mich. Q.S. 1878-1888.

568

PERCY ARMS PUBLIC HOUSE

26, Great Percy Street, Clerkenwell.

Licensed: 1864-1882

Management

Middlesex justices:

Mich. 1864-	William Pontin Mitchell
" 1868	Sarah Miller
" 1869	Joseph Horner
" 1870-	Charles Thomas Nunn(e)
" 1875-	John William Webster
" 1879	John Edward Smith
" 1880-	Arthur Goode
" 1882	*Licence not renewed.*

Literature

Official records:

Mx. Mich. Q.S. 1864-1881.

569

PERSEVERANCE PUBLIC HOUSE

Southgate Road, Balls Pond, St. John, Hackney.

Licensed: 1852-1863

Management

Middlesex justices:

| Mich. 1852- | John Gibson |
| " 1863 | *No notice, no petition.* |

Literature

Official records:

Mx. Mich. Q.S. 1852-1863.

570

PEWTER PLATTER PUBLIC HOUSE

Charles Street, Holborn.

Licensed: 1854-1861

Management

Middlesex justices:

| Mich. 1854- | John George Andrews |
| " 1861 | *House reported closed.* |

Literature

Official records:

Mx. Mich. Q.S. 1854-1861.

571

PEWTER PLATTER PUBLIC HOUSE

77, St. John Street, Finsbury.

Licensed: 1862-1870

Management

Middlesex justices:

Mich. 1862-	Samuel Thinpenny
" 1869-	William Pepper
" 1870	*No notice, no petition.*

Literature

Official records:

Mx. Mich. Q.S. 1862-1870.

572

PEWTER PLATTER PUBLIC HOUSE

White Lion Street, Norton Folgate.

Licensed: 1855-1859

Management

Middlesex justices:

| Mich. 1855- | Thomas Streacy |
| " 1859 | *No notice, no petition.* |

Literature

Official records:

Mx. Mich. Q.S. 1855-1859.

573

PHENE ARMS PUBLIC HOUSE

Phene Street, Chelsea.

Licensed: 1855-1877

Management

Middlesex justices:

Mich. 1855-   Marmaduke William Baxter
"   1864-   Hannah Baxter
"   1866-   Henry Druggan
"   1876   Alfred Sears
"   1877   *No notice, no petition.*

Literature

Official records:

Mx. Mich. Q.S. 1855-1877.

574

PHILHARMONIC ROOMS

Newman Street, St. Marylebone.

Licensed: 1854-1858

Management

Middlesex justices:

Mich. 1854   Charles Cotton
"   1855-   George Hetherington
"   1857   Henry Laurent
"   1858   *No notice, no petition.*

Literature

Official records:

Mx. Mich. Q.S. 1854-1857.

575

PHOENIX COFFEE TAVERN

254, Harrow Road, Paddington.

Licensed: 1890-1892

Building details

The coffee tavern included a music hall, which had a stage at its north end.

Capacity: 110

Closed as a result of the 1878 Act.

Management

London County Council:

1890-   Charles Leonard
Nov. 1892   *Not licensed.*

Literature

Official records:

G.L.C. Arch. Dpt. Th. case 040/108; L.C.C. Th. & M-H. Com. App. Nov. 1889-1891; Sel. Com. 1892.

576

PHOENIX HALL

34, Goldsmith's Row, Shoreditch.

Licensed: 1859-1864.

Formerly

Phoenix Temperance Hotel

Management

Middlesex justices:

Mich. 1859-   John Edward Molloy
"   1863   John Henry Giles
"   1864   *No notice, no petition.*

Literature

Official records:

Mx. Mich. Q.S. 1859-1863.

577

PHOENIX MUSIC HALL

8, Waterloo Street, Camberwell.

In use: c. 1887

Building details

An L.C.C. report dated 15.3.1887 states 'This hall... appears to have been recently built'. It accommodated 200 and was open nightly. It was not licensed, the tenancy being held by David Harris. Admission to the hall was obtained by purchasing a programme. It was closed as a result of the 1878 Act.

Literature

Official records:

G.L.C. Arch. Dpt. Th. case 040/109;

Location of other material

Plans: G.L.C *Architects Department.*

578

PHOENIX PUBLIC HOUSE

Phoenix Place, Ratcliff Cross, Ratcliff.

Licensed: 1853-1860, and 1862-1876

Management

Middlesex justices:

Mich. 1853   Robert Carr
"   1854   Henry Harding
"   1855-   Thomas Gale
"   1859   Thomas Brooks
"   1860   (No application)
"   1862   William Alexander Platt
"   1863-   Stanley Robinson
"   1868-   John Atcheson
"   1874-   John Middleton Reed
"   1876   *No application.*

Literature

Official records:

Mx. Mich. Q.S. 1853-59, 1862-76.

579

PHOENIX TEMPERANCE HALL

66, Bunhill Row, Finsbury.

Licensed: 1868-1870

Management

Middlesex justices:

Mich. 1868-	William Naismith
" 1870	*No application.*

Literature

Official records:

Mx. Mich. Q.S. 1868-1870.

580

PHOENIX THEATRE

Charing Cross Road, Holborn.

Opened: 24th September, 1930.

Building details

The theatre was built on the site of the *Alcazar,* an apparently unlicensed 'music hall', active in the 1920s.

Architects: Bertie Crewe, Sir Giles Gilbert Scott and Cecil Masey.

Art Director: Theodore Komisarjevsky

Constructed by: Bovis Ltd.

Capacity: 1,011

Auditorium: (1930) S. 478; C. 280; G. 252.

Stage: 31' 3" wide × 27' 2" deep.

Management

Lord Chamberlain:

Sept. 1930-	Sidney Lewis Bernstein
1.12.1932-	Victor Luxenburg
1.12.1939-	Jack Bartholomew
1.12.1942-	Thomas Charles Arnold
1.12.1944-	Prince Littler

London County Council:

1931-	Charing Cross Road Theatre Ltd.
1936-	Lux Estates Ltd.
1940	Unicos Property Corporation Ltd.
1941-	Phoenix Theatre (London) Ltd.
1943-	Julian Wylie Productions Ltd.
1945-	H.M. and S. Ltd.

Literature

Official records:

G.L.C. Arch. Dpt. Mss. Index; L.C.C. Th. & M-H. Com. App. Nov. 1930-; L.C.O. 169 and 374.

Contemporary accounts:

1930 PHOENIX THEATRE (Publicity pamphlet). 28p. photos.—(Copy in Enthoven Collection).
BUILDER. 1930.
STAGE. 1930, Sept. 25th.—Description.
BUILDING. 1930, Oct.
c.1930 MAYES, Ronald
The romance of London theatres, No. 156.
1932 HAMPTON & SONS LTD. The Phoenix Theatre... together with an important investment in shop property...for sale by auction on 6th December, 1932. (Copy in Enthoven Collection)
1950 THEATRE ownership...p. 59 and 91.

Historical accounts:

1959 ENCICLOPEDIA dello spettacolo. Vol. 6. Col. 1630
1963 MANDER, Raymond *and* MITCHENSON, Joe
The theatres of London. 2nd ed. p. 130-133.

Location of other material

Plans: G.L.C. *Architects Department.*

Programmes &c:

British Museum Library; Enthoven Collection; Garrick Club; Holborn Local Collection; London Museum; Westminster Local Collection.

581

PICCADILLY THEATRE

Denman Street, Westminster.

Opened: 27th April, 1928.

Building details

Built on site of derelict stables for the Piccadilly Theatre Co.

Architects: Bertie Crewe and Edward A. Stone

Contractors: Griggs and Sons

Decorator: Marc-Henri

Capacity: 1,395; (1950) 1,160

Auditorium: S. 538; D.C. 308; U.C. 340; Bx. 14.

Stage: 29' 10" wide × 35' deep.

After the opening play, the building was used as a cinema until November 1929.

Management

Lord Chamberlain:

April 1928-	Edward Laurillard
1.12.1932-	John Dowding Brown
1.12.1935-	Alfred Esdaile
1.12.1936-	John Dowding Brown
1.12.1937-	Pinero Brickwell
1.12.1939-	Albert Henry Billings
1.12.1944-	John Allison Webb

London County Council:

1936	Piccadilly (Vaudeville) Ltd.
1937	John Dowding Brown
1938-	A.S. & W. Ltd.
1945-	Piccadilly Theatre Ltd.

Literature

Official records:

G.L.C. Arch. Dpt. Mss. Index; L.C.C. Th. & M-H. Com. App. Nov. 1935-; L.C.O. 7 and 374.

Contemporary accounts:

1928 BUILDER. 1928, May 4th. p. 760, 772-4 and 780.
—Description of new theatre. Photos, sections & plans.
PICCADILLY THEATRE
(Descriptive publicity leaflet) 47p. illus. of building and ports.
(Copy in Enthoven Collection).

The Piccadilly Theatre: souvenir programme (of opening performance).
(B.M. 11795 r: 7)
1950 THEATRE ownership. p. 63-4 and 94-5.

Historical accounts:

c. 1930 MAYES, Ronald
The romance of London theatres, No. 141.
1959 ENCICLOPEDIA dello spettacolo. Vol. 6. Col. 1630.
LONDON. County Council.
Survey of London. St. James. Vol. 31. p. 17, 53-4.
1963 MANDER, Raymond *and* MITCHENSEON, Joe
The theatres of London, 2nd ed. p. 134-136.

Location of other material

Plans: G.L.C. *Architects Department.*

Programmes:

Enthoven Collection; London Museum; Westminster Local Collection.

582

PIED BULL PUBLIC HOUSE

Holloway Road, Islington.

Licensed: 1868-1871, and 1885-1887

Management

Middlesex justices:

Mich. 1868	Andrew Benjamin Penny	
" 1869	Executors of above.	
" 1870	Arthur Kelday and William Davies	
" 1871	*No notice, no petition.*	
" 1885-	William Newholm	
" 1887	*No notice, no petition.*	

Literature

Official records:

Mx. Mich. Q.S. 1868-70, 1885-7.

583

PIED HORSE PUBLIC HOUSE

3, Chiswell Street, Finsbury.

Licensed: 1851-1890

Management

Middlesex justices:

Mich. 1851	George Rook
" 1852-	Nicholas Joseph Carmon
" 1865-	Augustine Albertine Libert
" 1867-	John Hammond
" 1872-	Charles Mees
" 1874	Samuel Middleton
" 1875	Samuel Pike
" 1876-	William Heath

London County Council:

1890	William Heath
Nov. 1890	*Not licensed.*

Literature

Official records:

L.C.C. Th. & M-H. Com. App. Nov. 1889;
Mx. Mich. Q.S. 1851-1888.

584

PIER PUBLIC HOUSE

Woolwich High Street, Woolwich.

Licensed: 1848-1886

Also known as

Willis's Pier Music Hall

Management

West Kent justices:

Mich. 1848-	Ebenezer Brown (to Michaelmas 1851)
(Records for 1861-5 missing)	
Mich. 1866-	Henry Trimble
" 1873-	Edward Willis (to Michaelmas 1886)

Literature

Official records:

W. Kt. Mich. Q.S. 1848-1885.

Location of other materials

Bills: Guildhall Library (1 item)

585

PITMAN'S ARMS PUBLIC HOUSE

1 and 2, Pitman Buildings, York Road, St. Luke's, Finsbury.

Licensed: 1851-1879

Management

Middlesex justices:

Mich. 1851-	John Collinson
" 1857-	John Homewood
" 1867-	John Hasleden and G. S. Clement
" 1869	George Spencer Clement
" 1870-	Benjamin Broome
" 1873	John Wakelin
" 1874-	George Lovell
" 1876	James Beard
" 1877	Alfred Dobson
" 1878	Cornelius Redgrave
" 1879	*Licence not granted* to Jacob Beard.

Literature

Official records:

Mx. Mich. Q.S. 1851-1879.

586

PITT'S HEAD PUBLIC HOUSE

Henry Street, St. Marylebone.

Licensed: 1856-1871

Management

Middlesex justices:

Mich. 1856–   Joseph Pitt
  " 1871   *No application.*

Literature

Official records:

Mx. Mich. Q.S. 1856–1871.

587

PLAYER'S THEATRE

173–4, Villier's Street, Westminster.

Opened: 1866

Former names

The Arches 1867–
Hungerford Music Hall 1883
'Gatti's under the Arches'
Charing Cross Music Hall   } c. 1887
Gatti's Charing Cross Music Hall)
Arena Cinema 1910–1923
Forum Cinema 1928–1939
[Fire station 1939–1945]

Building details

Music hall constructed in two of the arches formed
by the Charing Cross Station, which was constructed
in 1863, on the site of the old Hungerford Market.
In 1910 it became a cinema, and was not used again
for live entertainment until 14th Jan. 1946 when the
Player's Theatre company (a theatre club) moved
there from 30 Albemarle Street, having previously
been at 43, King Street (Evans Song and Supper Rooms,
q.v.) and 6, New Compton Street.

Management

Middlesex justices:

Mich. 1867–   Carlo Gatti
  " 1878   Rosa Carazza Gatti
  " 1879–   Giacomo Corazza, and Luigi Corazza

London County Council:

1890–1904   Giacomo Corazza and Luigi Corazza
Nov. 1904–   *Not licensed as theatre or music hall.*

Literature

Official records:

G.L.C. Arch. Dpt. Th. case 566; L.C.C. Th. & M-H.
Com. App. Nov. 1889–1903; Mx. Mich. Q.S. 1867–88;
Sel. Com. 1877 and 1892.

Contemporary accounts:

1887 SATURDAY REVIEW. 1887, Aug. 20th. The state
of the London... music halls. No. 2.

Historical accounts:

c. 1930 MAYES, Ronald
The romance of London theatres, No. 202 and 210.
1943 ANDERSON, Jean
Late joys at the Players Theatre. T.V. Boardman, 1943. (N.B. this refers to the company, *not*
the theatre).

1951 PLAYERS THEATRE 'Late Joy's' past and
present, including special photographs repro-
duced by kind permission of Picture Post.
(1951) 20p.
1952 PULLING, Christopher
They were singing... (Various references).
SHERIDAN, P.
Late and early joys at the Players Theatre.
1952.
1962 STEWART, Hal D.
Player's Joys: a record of the first twenty five
years of the Player's Theatre Club. The
Theatre, 1962. 67p. illus.
1963 MANDER, Raymond *and* MITCHENSON, Joe
The theatres of London. 2nd ed. p. 260–264.

Location of other material

Plans: G.L.C. *Architects Department.*

Programmes: Enthoven Collection.

Cuttings, playbills &c. on Gatti's, Villiers St. in
Enthoven Collection folder on Gatti's, Westminster
Bridge.

588

PLAYHOUSE

Northumberland Avenue, Westminster.

Opened: 11th March, 1882. *Closed as theatre:* 1951

Former names

Royal Avenue Theatre 1882–
Avenue Theatre
Playhouse Theatre 1933–

Building details

1st building:

Architect: F.H. Fowler

Contractor: Kirk and Randall

Playhouse, Northumberland Avenue (588)

(Greater London Council Photograph Library)

Decorations: J. M. Boekbinder

Paintings: H. Verbuecken

Capacity: c. 1, 500

Auditorium: S. 147; P. 235; D.C. 191; U.C. 84; G. 636; Bx. 64.

5. 12. 1905 theatre crushed by the collapse of part of Charing Cross Station. Cyril Maude given £20,000 compensation by S. E. Railway.

2nd building:

Opened: 28. 1. 1907

Architect: Detmar Blow and Fernand Billeney

Builders: Portmand and Fotheringham

Capacity: (1950) 679

Auditorium: S. 224; D.C. & Bx. 194; U.C. & Bx. 259.

Stage: 24' 6" wide × 25' deep.

1951 taken over by B.B.C. as studio.

Management

Lord Chamberlain:

11. 3. 1882-	Edmund Burke
3. 6. 1882-	George Wood
24. 12. 1887-	Henry Watkins
8. 7. 1889-	George Thomas Cavendish Paget
29. 3. 1894-	Florence Emery
29. 9. 1894-	William Greet
29. 9. 1896-	Charles Henry Hawtrey
29. 9. 1901-	Frank Curzon (to 1905)
28. 1. 1907-	Cyril Francis Maude
7. 10. 1915-	Frank Curzon
1. 12. 1927-	Tom Benjamin Vaughan
1. 12. 1928-	Gladys Constance, Lady Pearson (i.e. Gladys Cooper)
1. 12. 1933-	Leon Marks Lion
1. 12. 1935-	Charles Egerton Killick
1. 12. 1942-	Claude David Soman

In 1917 licensed also by the L.C.C.

Literature

Official records:

G.L.C. Arch. Dpt. Mss. Index; G.L.C. Arch. Dpt. Th. case 440; L.C.C. Th. & M-H. Com. App. Nov. 1916; L.C.C. Th. & M-H. Com. Papers 1880-; LC 1/508-752; LC 7/17, 30-48; L.C.O. 347 and 374; M.B.W. Rpt. 1882. p. 23-35.

Contemporary accounts:

1881 BUILDER. 1881, Jan. 8th. p. 57.—Report of proposal to build theatre: brief description. BUILDING NEW. 1881, Sept. 9th. p. 341.—Note of construction of 'Avenue'.
1882 BUILDER. 1882, Feb. 4th. p. 146.—Site scheduled by S. E. Railway Co. for purpose of widening terminus. BUILDER. 1882, March 11th. p. 282.—Description. ROYAL AVENUE THEATRE (Descriptive publicity pamphlet) 11th March, 1882.—Copy in Enthoven Collection. BUILDER. 1882, March 25th. p. 374.—Description of interior decorations. ILLUSTRATED SPORTING AND DRAMATIC NEWS. 1882, March 25th.—Illus. of interior of auditorium.

1887 SATURDAY REVIEW. 1887, July 9th. The state of the London theatres... No. 4.
1905 BUILDER. 1905, Sept. 16th. p. 303.—Brief report that interior to be remodelled. BUILDER. 1905, Dec. 16th. p. 654.—Report of order for taking down certain external walls and roof after collapse of part of station.
1907 SKETCH. 1907, Jan. 30th. 'London's new theatre and its manager'. illus. BUILDING NEWS. 1907, Feb. 1st. p. 186.—Brief report of opening.

Historical accounts:

1904 BAKER, H. Barton
History of the London stage and its players. p. 516-8.
c. 1907? PLAYHOUSE. Souvenir of the Playhouse... 8 p illus. (Copy in Enthoven Collection).
c. 1930 MAYES, Ronald
The romance of London theatres. No. 26 and 108.
1959 ENCICLOPEDIA dello spettacolo. Vol. 6. Col. 1630.
1963 MANDER, Raymond *and* MITCHENSON, Joe
The theatres of London, 2nd ed. p. 279-281.

Location of other material

Plans:

G.L.C. *Architects Department.*
Enthoven Collection (2 sheets)
Public Record Office. LC 7/52. 3 sheets.

Programmes and Playbills:

British Museum Library; Enthoven Collection; Garrick Club; Guildhall Library; London Museum; Westminster Local Collection.

589

POPLAR HIPPODROME

East India Dock Road, Poplar.

Opened: Boxing Day, 1905. *Cinema by* 1925.

Former names

New Eldorado before opening
New Prince's Theatre 1905
Prince's Theatre
Hippodrome, Poplar 1907

Building details

Architect: Messrs. Owen and Ward

Builder: Messrs. Kirk and Kirk

Capacity: (1905) 2, 500

Auditorium: S. 89; P. 734; C. 95; B. 316; G. 610.

Stage: 60' wide × 41' deep.

Bombed 1939-45 war, and demolished 1950.

Management

Lord Chamberlain:

9. 11. 1905-	Clarence Sonnes
13. 6. 1907-	Walter Gibbons
31. 10. 1907-	Albert George Maxstead
4. 12. 1911-	Walter Gibbons
2. 7. 1912-	Charles Gulliver

After 1925 continued to have Lord Chamberlain's licence, but this was subsidiary to the L.C.C.'s cinema licence.

London County Council:

1908-	Walter Gibbons
1913-	Charles Gulliver
1925-	Empire Palace (Poplar) Ltd.
Nov. 1925	*Cinema licence only.*

Literature

Official records:

G.L.C Arch. Dpt. Mss. Index; G.L.C. Arch. Dpt. Th. case 257; L.C.C. Th. & M-H. Com. App. Nov. 1907-1925; L.C.C. Th. & M-H. Com. Papers 1901-1925; L.C.O. 374 and 492.

Contemporary accounts:

1905	EAST END NEWS. 1905, Dec. 15th. 'Poplar's new theatre'.—Detailed Description. BUILDING NEWS. 1905, Dec. 29th. p. 918.—Brief description.
1906	BUILDER. 1906, Jan. 6th. p. 25.—Report of opening. Brief description.

Historical accounts:

1954	WILSON, A. E. East end entertainment. p. 228.

Location of other material

Plans: G.L.C. *Architects Department.*

Programmes, Cuttings &c:

Enthoven Collection (1 bill); Poplar Local Collection.

590

PRENDERGAST ARMS PUBLIC HOUSE

St. Leonard's Road, Bromley.

Licensed: 1861-1883

Management

Middlesex justices:

Mich. 1861-		Abraham Hudson
"	1873	Charles Robert Baker
"	1874	Samuel Hadley
"	1875-	Robert Barrett
"	1877	Zachariah Fenning
"	1878	Henry Joseph Pounds
"	1879-	Edward Petty
"	1883	*Licence refused.*

Literature

Official records:

Mx. Mich. Q.S. 1861-1883.

591

PRINCE ALBERT PUBLIC HOUSE

Durnford Terrace, St. Pancras.

Licensed: 1856-1863

Management

Middlesex justices:

Mich. 1856-		Alfred Probyn
"	1863	*No notice, no petition.*

Literature

Official records:

Mx. Mich. Q.S. 1856-1863.

592

PRINCE ALBERT PUBLIC HOUSE

11, Hollingsworth St., Holloway, St. Mary, Islington.

Licensed: 1865-1866

Management

Middlesex justices:

Mich. 1865-		Thomas Rogers
"	1866	*No notice, no petition.*

Literature

Official records:

Mx. Mich. Q.S. 1865-1866.

593

PRINCE ALBERT PUBLIC HOUSE

Oxford Road, Islington.

Licensed: 1868-1869

Management

Middlesex justices:

Mich. 1868-		John Henry Maycock
"	1869	*No application.*

Literature

Official records:

Mx. Mich. Q.S. 1868-1869.

594

PRINCE ALBERT PUBLIC HOUSE

York Street, Kingsland Road, St. Leonard, Shoreditch.

Licensed: 1852-1864

Management

Middlesex justices:

Mich. 1852-		Edwin Charles White
"	1858-	Richard Newman
"	1861	Thomas How Bromley
"	1862-	George Westover
"	1864	*No notice, no petition.*

Literature

Official records:

Mx. Mich. Q.S. 1852-1863.

595

PRINCE ALFRED PUBLIC HOUSE

89, Raglan Road (*later* Pattison Road), Plumstead.

Licensed: 1867-1890

Building details

The concert room was on the first floor over the bar, 15′ × 33′ 6″; it was closed as a result of the 1878 Act.

Management

West Kent justices:

Mich. 1867-		James Young
"	1872-	Thomas Smith
"	1875-	Daniel Christopher Capon
"	1880-	Henry George Warren
"	1883-	William Henry Hebble
"	1886-	Ferdinand Robert Chapman

London County Council:

1890	Ferdinand Robert Chapman
Nov. 1890	*No application.*

Literature

Official records:

G.L.C. Arch. Dpt. Th. case 040/111; L.C.C. Th. & M-H. Com. App. Nov. 1889; W. Kt. Mich. Q.S. 1867-1888.

Location of other material

Plans: G.L.C. *Architects Department.*

596

PRINCE ARTHUR PUBLIC HOUSE

Boundary Road, Hampstead.

Licensed: 1868-1871

Management

Middlesex justices:

Mich. 1868-		John James Harris
"	1871	*Licence refused.*

Literature

Official records:

Mx. Mich. Q.S. 1868-1871.

597

PRINCE EDWARD PUBLIC HOUSE

West Terrace, Park Road, Holloway, St. Mary, Islington.

Licensed: 1854-1862

Management

Middlesex justices:

Mich. 1854-		Walter Swift Walford
"	1862	*Licence not renewed owing to death of Walford*

Literature

Official records:

Mx. Mich. Q.S. 1854-1862.

598

PRINCE GEORGE PUBLIC HOUSE

Park Road, Dalston, St. John at Hackney.

Licensed: 1856-1862

Management

Middlesex justices:

Mich. 1856-		Thomas Harford Cox
"	1862	*No petition, no application.*

Literature

Official records:

Mx. Mich. Q.S. 1856-1862.

599

PRINCE OF BRUNSWICK PUBLIC HOUSE

127, Barnsbury Road, Islington.

Licensed: 1858-1891

Building details

The concert room was on the first floor over the bar and bar parlour, and measured 26′3″ × 17′. It was closed as a result of the 1878 Act.

Management

Middlesex justices

Mich. 1858-		William Masters
"	1875-	Henry Scatchard
"	1882-	Alfred Wilson

London County Council:

1890-	Alfred Wilson
Nov. 1891	*No application*

Literature

Official records:

G.L.C. Arch. Dpt. Th. case 040/113; L.C.C. Th. & M-H. App. Nov. 1889-1890; Mx. Mich. Q.S. 1858-1888.

Location of other material

Plans: G.L.C. *Architects Department.*

600

PRINCE OF ORANGE PUBLIC HOUSE

Fieldgate Street, St. Mary, Whitechapel.

Licensed: 1852-1862

Management

Middlesex justices:

Mich. 1852-		John Gerhold
"	1854-	Jacob Kisler
"	1856-	Ludwig Meier
"	1862	*No petition, no application.*

Literature

Official records:

Mx. Mich. Q.S. 1852–1861.

601

PRINCE OF WALES MUSIC HALL AND PUBLIC HOUSE

1, Kensington Grove, Lambeth.

Licensed: 1870–1891

Building details

The concert room was on the first floor of the public house and measured 37′ to 47′ long, and 9′6″ to 16′ wide (irregular shape). It had a capacity of 100. It was closed as a result of the 1878 Act.

Management

Surrey justices:

Mich.	1870–	William Kirchhoff
"	1872	Sidney Augustus Hill
"	1873	Henry Donaghue
"	1875	Daniel Pinnock
"	1876–	Livingstone Walk
"	1878–	William Henry Martyn
"	1880	George Burling
"	1881	Henry Charles Corry
"	1882–	James Betts

London County Council:

1890–	Robert William Gray (licence retained)
Nov. 1891	*No application.*

Literature

Official records:

G.L.C. Arch. Dpt. Th. case 040/114; L.C.C. Th. & M-H. Com. App. Nov. 1889–90; Sel. Com. 1892; Sy. Mich. Q.S. 1870–1888.

Location of other material

Plans: G.L.C. *Architects Department.*

602

PRINCE OF WALES PUBLIC HOUSE

52, Banner Street, St. Lukes, Finsbury.

Licensed: 1851–1880

Management

Middlesex justices:

Mich.	1851–	Samuel Wickens
"	1866	Frances Sinclair
"	1867–	Samuel Dillon
"	1871–	Robert Benttell
"	1877	Charles Pay
"	1878–	Jane Armstrong
"	1880	John Hutton *refused licence.*

Literature

Official records:

Mx. Mich. Q.S. 1851–1880.

603

PRINCE OF WALES PUBLIC HOUSE

Bonner's Road, Victoria Park, St. Matthew, Bethnal Green.

Licensed: 1857–1865

Management

Middlesex justices:

Mich.	1857–	William Frederick Fearn
"	1865	*No notice, no petition.*

Literature

Official records:

Mx. Mich. Q.S. 1857–1865.

604

PRINCE OF WALES PUBLIC HOUSE

Caledonian Road, St. Mary, Islington.

Licensed: 1854–1876

Management

Middlesex justices:

Mich.	1854–	George Price
"	1856–	Ann Price
"	1869–	George Price
"	1876	*Licence refused* to George Francis Saunders.

Literature

Official records:

Mx. Mich. Q.S. 1854–1876.

605

PRINCE OF WALES PUBLIC HOUSE

Prince of Wales Road, St. Pancras.

Licensed: 1854–1878

Management

Middlesex justices:

Mich.	1854–	William Suter
"	1874–	Thomas Edward Cross
"	1876–	John Pinn
"	1878	*No application.*

Literature

Official records:

Mx. Mich. Q.S. 1854–1877.

606

PRINCE OF WALES PUBLIC HOUSE

Wellesley Road, St. Pancras.

Licensed: 1854–1860

Management

Middlesex justices:

Mich. 1854-		George Smith Howell
"	1857-	William Callaway
"	1860	*No petition, no application.*

Literature

Official records:

Mx. Mich. Q.S. 1857-1860.

607

PRINCE OF WALES THEATRE

Coventry Street, Piccadilly.

Opened: 18th January, 1884

Former name

Prince's Theatre to 1886

Building details

1st building:

Built by: Edgar Bruce, from the Scala q.v.

Architect: C. J. Phipps

Builder: Messrs. W. and D. M'gregor

Capacity: 960

2nd building:

Opened: 27th October, 1937

Architect: Robert Cromie

Builders: Marfix Ltd.

Capacity: 1, 357

Auditorium: S. 719; C. 400

State: 43' wide × 22'6" deep.

Management

Lord Chamberlain:

18. 1.1884-	Edgar Bruce
29. 9.1887-	Horace Sedger
29. 9.1892-	George Edwardes
29. 9.1893-	Henry Lowenfeld
24.12.1898-	Robert Arthur
29.12.1899-	John Highfield Leigh
29.12.1900-	Frank Curzon
3. 9.1915-	Edward Laurillard
1.12.1915-	John Highfield Leigh
1.12.1917-	Andre Charlot
1.12.1931-	Morris Edgar Benjamin
1.12.1932-	Charles Clore
1.12.1934-	Aflred Esdaile
1.12.1942-	Horace Stanley White
1.12.1947-	Valentine Charles Parnell

London County Council:

1938-	West End Attractions Ltd.
1942-	General Theatre Corporation Ltd.
1947-	Moss' Empires, Ltd.

Literature

Official records:

G.L.C. Arch. Dpt. Mss. Index; L.C.C. Th. & M-H.
Com. App. Nov. 1937-; L.C.C. Th. & M-H. Com. Papers

1887-; LC 1/508-752; LC 7/17, 31-48; L.C.O. 355 and
374; Sel. Com. 1892.

Contemporary accounts:

1883 BUILDER. 1883, Nov. 24th. p. 684.—'The Prince's
Hotel'—description and illus. of new block
including hotel, shops and theatre.—In course of
erection.

1884 BUILDER. 1884, Jan. 5th. p. 10.—Description of
iron curtain and other fire precautions.
BUILDING NEWS. 1884, Jan. 11th. p. 42-3.
'The Prince's Hotel and theatre'—Description.
ERA. 1884, Jan. 12th.—Description.
DAILY TELEGRAPH. 1884, Jan. 15th. 'The
Prince's Theatre'—description.
PRINCE'S THEATRE
(leaflet) 4p.—Description of construction and
arrangement. (Copy in Enthoven Collection).
TIMES. 1884, Jan. 19th. 'Opening of the Prince's
Theatre'.—Description and report.
ILLUSTRATED LONDON NEWS. 1884, Jan.
26th. p. 94.—Description of new theatre. Illus.
of interior and exterior.
ILLUSTRATED SPORTING AND DRAMATIC
NEWS. 1884, Jan. 26th.—Description of 1st
production, illus. of interior.

1884 PICTORIAL WORLD. 1884, Jan. 31st.—Illus.
interior.
BUILDER 1884, Feb. 9th. p. 219. Report of
important experiments in electric lighting for
theatre.

1886 BUILDER. 1886, Oct. 2nd. p. 507. Report that
permission given to call theatre 'Prince of
Wales'.

1887 SATURDAY REVIEW. 1887, July 23rd. The
state of the London theatres. . . No. 6.

1898 SACHS, E. O *and* WOODROW, E.A.E
Modern opera houses and theatres. . . Vol. III.
Plans.

1931 The PRINCE of Wales Theatre. . . For sale by
auction. April 22nd. 1931. 9p. illus. (Auction
catalogue).—Copy in Enthoven Collection
The PRINCE of Wales Theatre. . . For sale by
auction. Oct. 15th. 1931. 6p. (Auction catalogue).
—Copy in Enthoven Collection.

1937 BUILDING. 1937, Nov. Article on new building.
BUILDER. 1937, Nov. 5th. p. 835
ARCHITECT AND BUILDING NEWS. 1937,
Nov. 26th.
ARCHITECTURE ILLUSTRATED. 1937, Dec.

1950 THEATRE ownership. p. 60-1, 96-8.

Historical accounts:

1904 BAKER, H. Barton
History of the London stage and its players.
p. 519-521.

c. 1930 MAYES, Ronald
The romance of London's theatres. No. 14.

1959 ENCICLOPEDIA dello spettacolo. Vol. 6.
Col. 1630-31.

1963 MANDER, Raymond *and* MITCHENSON, Joe
The theatres of London. 2nd ed. p. 137-142.

Location of other material

Plans:

G.L.C. *Architects Department.*
Public Record Office. LC/7/73. 7 sheets of 1884
building.
Enthoven Collection, 1935 (2 sheets)

Programmes &c:

British Museum Library; Enthoven Collection;
Garrick Club; Guildhall Library; Westminster
Local Collection.

608

PRINCE OF WALES' FEATHERS PUBLIC HOUSE

Warren Street, St. Pancras.

Licensed: 1854–1856, and 1863–1870

Also known as

The Feathers Public House

Management

Middlesex justices:

Mich. 1854–	Charles Payne—to Michaelmas 1856
" 1863	William Moorton
" 1866–	George Robinson
" 1870	*Licence refused* to John Scully.

Literature

Official records:

Mx. Mich. Q.S. 1854–1856, 1863–1870.

609

PRINCE REGENT PUBLIC HOUSE

New Court, Goswell Street, St. Luke, Finsbury.

Licensed: 1862–1866

Management

Middlesex justices:

Mich. 1862–	Henry Hurst
" 1864	Samuel Hurst, executor of Henry Hurst
" 1865	Sarah Hurst
" 1866	*Refused* to James Hicks.

Literature

Official records:

Mx. Mich. Q.S. 1862–1866.

610

PRINCE REGENT PUBLIC HOUSE

8, St. George Street, St. George in the East.

Licensed: 1854–1889

Building details

The concert room was in the rear of the public house
on the ground floor level. It had a raised stage at the
southern end, and fixed seating round three sides.
It was 50′ long, including stage, and 16′2″ wide. It
was lit from above by a large lantern light. It was
finally closed as a result of the 1878 Act.

Management

Middlesex justices:

Mich. 1854–	William Newman
" 1862–	Christian Diederich Friederichs
" 1865–	Albert D. H. Behning
" 1885–	William Cleaver, and Henry Claus
" 1887–	John Roselios

London County Council:

Nov. 1889 Application for licence was withdrawn.

Literature

Official records:

G.L.C. Arch. Dpt. Th. case 040/112; L.C.C. Th. & M-H.
Com. App. Nov. 1889; Mx. Mich. Q.S. 1854–1888.

Location of other material

Plans: G.L.C. *Architects Department.*

611

PRINCE'S HALL OF VARIETIES

Rodney's Head Public House, 138, Whitechapel Road,
Stepney.

Licensed: 1854–1885

Building details

Cost: £3,000

Capacity: 240 (1866 given as 600)

Management

Middlesex justices:

Mich. 1854–	Robert Elliott
" 1860–	Thomas Turner
" 1871–	Cornelius Young
" 1874–	Treyer Fellice Evans
" 1876–	Mary White Evans
" 1877–	Samuel Emanuels
" 1885	*Application withdrawn.*

Literature

Official records:

G.L.C. Arch. Dpt. Th. case 3962; Mx. Mich. Q.S. 1854–
1885; Sel. Com. 1892.

Location of other material

Plans: G.L.C. *Architects Department.*

612

PRINCE'S THEATRE

Shaftesbury Avenue, Holborn.

Opened: 26th December, 1911.

Later name

Shaftesbury Theatre

Building details

Architect: Bertie Crewe

Capacity: 2392, (1950) 1726.

Auditorium: S. 231; P. 582; C. & Bx. 409; G. 500.

Stage: 31'10" wide × approx. 31' deep.

Management

Lord Chamberlain:

26.12.1911-	Walter Melville
1. 1.1919-	Seymour Hicks
1.12.1919-	C. B. Cochran
30.11.1922-	Walter and Frederick Melville
1.12.1934-	Harold James Pilbrow
1.12.1936-	Walter and Frederick Melville
1.12.1937-	Frederick Melville
1.12.1938-	Bert Ernest Hammond

London County Council:

1914-	Walter Melville (to Dec. 1916)

Literature

Official records:

G.L.C. Arch. Dpt. Mss. Index; L.C.C. Th. & M-H. Com. App. Nov. 1913-1915; L.C.C. Th. & M-H. Com. Papers 1911-; L.C.O. 374 and 474.

Contemporary accounts:

1911   BUILDING NEWS. 1911, Dec. 22nd. p. 870.
       —Brief description.
       ERA. 1911, Dec. 23rd.—Report and description
       of the new theatre.
1950   THEATRE ownership. . . p. 74.

Historical accounts:

c. 1930 MAYES, Ronald
        The romance of London theatres, No. 42.
1959   ENCICLOPEDIA dello spettacolo. Vol. 6, Col.
       1631.
1963   MANDER, Raymond *and* MITCHENSON, Joe
       The theatres of London, 2nd ed. p. 143-146.

Location of other material

Plans: G.L.C. *Architects Department.*

Programmes:

Enthoven Collection; Holborn Local Collection; Westminster Local Collection.

613

PRINCE'S HEAD PUBLIC HOUSE

Prince's Street, Westminster.

Licensed: pre 1850-1854

Management

Middlesex justices:

Mich. 1850-	Edward Taylor
" 1854	*No petition, no application.*

Literature

Official records:

Mx. Mich. Q.S. 1850-1854.

614

PRINCESS CONCERT ROOM

55, Castle Street, Oxford Street, St. Marylebone.

Licensed: pre 1850-1870

Management

Middlesex justices:

Mich. 1848-	John Turner
" 1851-	David Montague and William Wood
" 1863-	Thomas Shambler
" 1870	*No notice.*

Literature

Official records:

Mx. Mich. Q.S. 1840-1869.

615

PRINCESS ROYAL PUBLIC HOUSE

Johnson Street, Commercial Road, St. George in the East.

Licensed: 1854-1862

Management

Middlesex justices:

Mich. 1854-	James Flint
" 1856-	Thomas Denchfield
" 1862	*No petition, no application:* Denchfield reported to have left the house

Literature

Official records:

Mx. Mich. Q.S. 1854-1862.

616

PRINCESS'S THEATRE

73, Oxford Street, St. Marylebone.

Opened as a theatre: 30th September, 1840.
Closed: 1902. *Finally demolished:* 1931

Building details

1st building:

The theatre was built on the site of the Queen's Bazaar, previously the Royal Bazaar, British Diorama, and Exhibition of Works of Art, which had been opened by a Mr. Hamlet in 1828.

Designed by: T. M. Nelson

Decoration by: Messrs. Crace & Son

There were four tiers of boxes. 'The size was somewhere between the English Opera House and the Haymarket'.

2nd building:

Reopened: 2.8.1869.

In 1869 theatre redecorated by J. Macintosh of Langham Street, and new footlights and drop curtain were installed.

Closed: 19th May, 1880.

3rd building:

Opened: 6th November, 1880

Developer: Walter Gooch

Architect: C. J. Phipps

Builder: Mark Manley

Capacity: c. 1750

Auditorium: P. 554; S. 54; D.C. 207; U.C. 269; G. 511; Bx. 92.

Management

Lord Chamberlain:

29. 9.1843-	John Meddex Maddox
29. 9.1850-	Charles Kean and Robert Keeley
29. 9.1852-	Charles Kean
29. 9.1859-	Augustus Harris
29. 9.1862-	Henry William Lindus
14. 5.1863-	George James Vining
18. 1.1870-	Benjamin Webster
29. 9.1873-	James Guiver
6. 4.1874-	Ernest Valuay and Alexis Pitrou
7. 8.1874-	Frederick Balsir Chatterton
1. 5.1876-	Horace Wigan
10. 9.1877-	Walter Gooch
4. 6.1881-	Wilson Barrett
29. 9.1887-	Miss Grace Hawthorne
27. 7.1891-	Sidney Basing
29. 9.1892-	William Wallace Kelly
29.10.1892-	Rollo Balmain
29. 9.1893-	Walter Gooch
1. 1.1896-	James Crowdy
29. 9.1896-	Albert Augustus Gilmer
29. 9.1898-	Ernest Harley Peacock
29. 9.1899-	Robert Arthur
29. 9.1900-	John Moffitt
29. 9.1901-	Frank de Jong (to 28. 9.1902)

Note: Prior to 1843 the theatre had been licensed by the Middlesex justices.

Literature

Official records:

LC 1/507-752; LC 7/13-17, 20-48, 89; M.B.W. Rpt. 1882. p. 251-261; Mx. Mich. Q.S. (Miscellaneous papers). Sel. Com. 1866-1892.

Contemporary accounts:

1841 The MIRROR OF LITERATURE, AMUSEMENT & INSTRUCTION 1841, Jan. 16th. p. 34. Illus. and description.

1869 BUILDER. 1869, Aug. 7th. p. 620.—Description of redecoration. *see also* BUILDER, 1869, Aug. 14th. p. 651 for correction.

1880 DAILY NEWS. 1880, Oct. 4th. 'The Theatres' column. (Report on progress of rebuilding). ERA. 1880, Oct. 17th. The new Princess's Theatre.—report and description. BUILDING NEWS. 1880, Oct. 29th. p. 513. —Description of rebuilding. DAILY NEWS. 1880, Nov. 6th. 'The new Princess's Theatre'—Description. ERA. 1880. Nov. 7th.—Description. ILLUSTRATED SPORTING AND DRAMATIC NEWS. 1880, Nov. 13th.—Illus. of interior.

1881 BUILDING NEWS. 1881, April 1st. after p. 360. plate of front elevation.

1887 SATURDAY REVIEW. 1887, July 2nd. The state of the London theatres... No. 3.

1896 BUILDER. 1896, Feb. 22nd. p. 157.—Report that theatre for sale.

1902 BUILDER. 1902, Dec. 6th. p. 535.—Report of closure because of L.C.C. requirements. Includes description and brief history.

1905 BUILDER. 1905, Dec. 2nd. p. 582. Report of proposed rebuilding.

1907 BUILDER. 1907, July 27th. p. 119-120.—Report that structural alterations to be carried out under W.G.R. Sprague's direction.

1908 BUILDER. 1908, Aug. 1st. p. 124.—Report that syndicate formed to rebuild theatre.

1912 BUILDER. 1912, Aug. 16th. p. 201.—Report of proposed demolition.

Historical accounts:

1859 COLE, John William The life and theatrical times of Charles Kean... the English stage for the last fifty years, and... the management of the Princess's Theatre, from 1850-1869. Bentley, 1859. 2v. in one.

1876 ERA ALMANACK, 1876 History of the Princess's Theatre. p. 1-6.

1879 DRAMATIC NOTES. 1879. p. 28-31.

1880 SUNDAY TIMES. 1880, May 23rd. —Report of last performance includes brief history.

1904 BAKER, H. Barton History of the London stage and its players. p. 474-97.

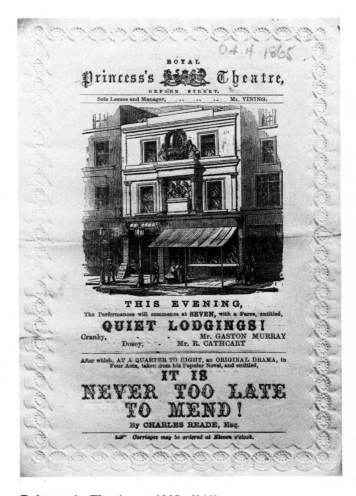

Princess's Theatre c. 1865 (616)

(Victoria & Albert Museum, Crown copyright)

1925 CHANCELLOR, E.B.
The pleasure haunts of London. p. 134.
SHERSON, Erroll
London's lost theatres... Chapters VI & VII,
p. 121-184.
c. 1930 MAYES, Ronald
The romance of London's theatres, Nos. 11 and
153.
1959 ENCICLOPEDIA dello spettacolo. Vol. 6. Col.
1631.
1962 THEATRE WORLD. 1962, Sept., Nov., and Dec.
Lost London theatres, by N.M. Bligh, No. 18
The Princess's, Oxford Street
1968 MANDER, Raymond *and* MITCHENSON, Joe.
The Lost Theatres of London. pp. 335-357
5 illus.

Location of other material

Programmes and playbills:

British Museum Library; Enthoven Collection;
Garrick Club; Guildhall Library (over 500 items);
London Museum; St. Marylebone Local Collection;
Westminster Local Collection.

Newscuttings (&c):

St. Marylebone Local Collection.

617

PRIORY PUBLIC HOUSE
St. Leonards Street, Bow.

Licensed: 1868-1883

Management

Middlesex justices:

Mich. 1868-	Rowland Henry Wallace (1871 as 'Wallis')
" 1872	Richard Agate
" 1873-	Richard Brown
" 1877-	Sidney Smith
" 1883	*Refused as hall rarely used for entertainments.*

Literature

Official records:

Mx. Mich. Q.S. 1868-1883.

618

PRINTER'S ARMS PUBLIC HOUSE
23, New Church Court, St. Mary-le-Strand.

Licensed: 1854-1862

Management

Middlesex justices:

Mich. 1854-	John Power Rivers
" 1855-	Charles Clark
" 1857-	John Ediker
" 1860-	William Weston
" 1862	*House closed.*

Literature

Official records:

Mx. Mich. Q.S. 1855-1861.

619

PUTNEY HIPPODROME

Gardener's Lane, (*later* Felsham Road) Putney.

Licensed: 1906-1924

Also known as

Putney Empire and Palace of Varieties

Building details

Built by: Hingston, on corporate ground.

Capacity: 1975

Auditorium: S. 117; P. 480; C. 403; G. 625; Bx. 16.

Management

London County Council:

1906	Walter Stephens
1907-	William John Grimes
1910-	Thomas Henry Masters
1913-	Charles Gulliver
Nov. 1924	*Not Listed as theatre or music hall.*

Literature

Official records:

G.L.C. Arch. Dpt. Mss. Index;
G.L.C. Arch. Dpt. Th. case 268;
L.C.C. Th. & M-H. Com. App. Nov. 1905-1923.

Location of other material

Plans: G.L.C. *Architects Department.*

620

QUEEN ELEANOR PUBLIC HOUSE

Church Path, Hackney.

Licensed: 1863-1891

Management

Middlesex justices:

Mich. 1863-	Charles Glassborow
" 1873-	Ann Matilda Glassborow
" 1878-	James Hanney
" 1880-	Joseph Bracey
" 1885-	Thomas John Gage
" 1888	Caroline Major Gage, and William Major Gage

London County Council:

1890	Catherine Major Gage and William Major Gage
1891	Catherine Major Gage
Nov. 1891	*No application.*

Literature

Official records:

L.C.C. Th. & M-H. Com. App. Nov. 1889-1890;
Mx. Mich. Q.S. 1863-1888.

621

QUEEN VICTORIA PUBLIC HOUSE

Barnet Grove, St. Matthew, Bethnal Green.

Licensed: 1865-1870

Management

Middlesex justices:

Mich. 1865-	Daniel Bushell
" 1870	*Licence refused.*

Literature

Official records:

Mx. Mich. Q.S. 1865-1870.

622

QUEEN VICTORIA PUBLIC HOUSE

82, Falcon Road, Battersea.

Licensed: 1868-1885

Management

Surrey Justices:

Mich. 1868-	William George Sayer
" 1874	Edward Petty
. " 1875-	Morria Padley
" 1881-	Thomas Richards
" 1884	Mary Ann Allatt
" 1885	*No application.*

Literature

Official records:

Sy. Mich. Q.S. 1868-1883.

623

QUEEN'S THEATRE

Long Acre.

Opened as place of entertainment: 1850.
Closed: 1879.

Former names

St. Martin's Hall
St. Martin's Music Hall
National Theatre

Building details

St. Martin's Hall was built at a cost of £50,000

Capacity: 4000

Building converted: Opened May 1867

Architect: C. J. Phipps

Contractors: Samuel Simpson

Management

Middlesex justices:

Mich. 1850-	John Hullah
" 1861-	Anne Dumergue
" 1867	*No application.*

Lord Chamberlain:

9. 10. 1867-	Alfred Wigan
18. 5. 1868-	William Henry Liston
29. 3. 1869-	Edward John Young
7. 9. 1870-	Ernest Clifton
29. 9. 1873-	George Everett
5. 5. 1876-	John Coleman
27. 10. 1877-	Alexander Henderson (as National Theatre)
20. 11. 1877-	George Everett (Closed 1879)

Literature

Official records:

LC7/15-16, 23-25, 89;
Mx. Mich. Q.S. 1850-67; Sel. Com. 1866 and 1892.

Contemporary accounts:

1850	BUILDER. 1850, Feb. 9th. p. 71.—Paragraph on Mr. Hullah's Music Hall. ILLUSTRATED LONDON NEWS—1850, Feb. 16th.—Report of opening. BUILDER. 1850, Feb. 16th. p. 75.—Description of 'St. Martin's Music Hall'.
1853	BUILDER. 1853, Nov. 26th. p. 714-5.—Description. illus. ST. MARTIN'S HALL —Description of St. Martin's Hall (&c) 4p. (B.M. 1879 c. 13 (50-)
1867	BUILDER 1867, Oct. 5th. p. 728-9.—Description of converted theatre BUILDING NEWS. 1867, Oct. 18th. p. 719-720. —plans & illus. of interior. MORNING ADVERTISER—1867 Oct. 24th. —Report of opening. ILLUSTRATED LONDON NEWS. 1867, Oct. 26th. p. 457.—Illus. of interior and description.
1879	ILLUSTRATED LONDON NEWS. 1879, Feb. 8th. —Illus. of demolition.

St. Martin's Music Hall 1855 (623)

(The Builder)

BUILDER. 1879, May 17th. p. 551,—Universal
Co-operative Stores: conversion of Queen's.
ILLUSTRATED SPORTING AND DRAMATIC
NEWS. 1879, Sept. 20th.—Illus of building and
description after Stores had opened on 1.9.1879.

Historical accounts:

1897 NEWS OF THE WORLD. 1879, Jan. 19th.
'The last of the Queen's Theatre'.—Summary of
history.
1904 BAKER, H. Barton
History of the London stage and its players...
p. 328-30.
1925 SHERSON, Erroll
London's lost theatres... Chapter IX. p. 201-210.
c. 1930 MAYES, Ronald
The romance of London theatres. No. 94.
1952 PULLING, Christopher
They were singing;...p. 137-9.
1956 THEATRE WORLD, 1956, Feb.
Lost London theatres, by N. M. Bligh.
No. 5. The story of the Queen's, Long Acre.
1968 MANDER, Raymond *and* MITCHENSON, Joe
The lost Theatres of London. pp. 358-379.
4 illus.

Location of other material

Programmes and plyabills:

British Museum Library; Enthoven Collection;
Garrick Club; Guildhall Library; London Museum.

Prints: London Museum.

624

QUEEN'S THEATRE

275-279, Poplar High Street, Poplar.

Licensed: 1856-

Former names

Queen's Arms Palace of Varieties and Public House
Apollo Music Hall
Albion Theatre
Oriental Theatre
Queen's Music Hall
Queen's Theatre of Varieties.

Building details

Original Hall:

Capacity: 800

Cost: £7,000

Reconstructed, 1898

Architect: Bertie Crewe

Capacity: 1,360

Auditorium: S. 391; C. 271; G. 279.

Management

Middlesex justices:

Mich. 1856-	Robert Green Grimes
" 1861-	William Davis
" 1863-	Frederick Abrahams
" 1884-	Frederick Abrahams, and Michael Abrahams
" 1887-	Michael Abrahams

London County Council:

1890-	James Chappell
1898-	Thomas Robert Salter Maltby
1900-	Thomas Flower Maltby
1906-	Michael Abrahams
1922-	Morris Abrahams
1927-	Queen's Theatre (Poplar) Ltd.

Lord Chamberlain:

4.10.1867-	Frederick Abrahams (to Sept. 1880)
24.12.1912-	Michael Abrahams
1.10.1922-	Morris Abrahams (until after 1950)

Literature

Official records:

G.L.C. Arch. Dpt. Mss. Index;
L.C.C. Th. & M-H. Com. App. Nov. 1889-;
L.C.O. 7/15-16, 23-26, 89; L.C.O. 374 and 517;
Mx. Mich. Q.S. 1856-1888; Sel. Com. 1866 and 1892.

Contemporary accounts:

1899 The MUSIC HALL AND THEATRE REVIEW,
1899, Jan. 27th.—Report on alterations...
1950 THEATRE ownership...p. 128.

Historical accounts:

1925 SHERSON, Erroll
London's lost theatres...p. 48.
1950 TIMES. 1850, Jan. 3rd.
'The Queen's Theatre, Poplar: a Victorian
music hall'.—Report.
1951 ROSE, Millicent
The east end of London. Cresset Press. 1951.
p. 271-2.—Description of music hall.
1954 WILSON, A. E.
East end entertainment...p. 226-8.
1955 TIMES. 1955, Aug. 24th.
'Managing the Queen's Theatre, Poplar.'—Report
on Morris Abrahams who had managed the
theatre for 49 years.

Location of other material

Plans:

G.L.C. *Architects Department;*
Public Record Office LC7/87, 5 plans dated 2.1.1874.
British Music Hall Society.

Programmes, newscuttings &c:
Poplar Local Collection.

625

QUEEN'S THEATRE

Queen's Road, Battersea.

c. 1890-1897.

Formerly

Park Town Hall and Theatre.
Park Town Theatre of Varieties.

Management

London County Council

1890-	John Thomas Virgo
1896	*Not licensed.*
1897	Alice Melville
Nov. 1897	*Licence refused as theatre not in use.*

Literature

Official records:

L.C.C Th. & M-H. Com. App. Nov. 1889-1897.

Location of other material

Playbill, cuttings &c. Enthoven Collection.

626

QUEEN'S THEATRE

Shaftesbury Avenue, Westminster.

Opened: 8th October, 1908.

Proposed name

Wardour Street Theatre.

Building details

Architect: W. G. R. Sprague

Capacity: (1917) 1,160; (1940) 1,043.

Auditorium: S. 410; D.C. 164; U.C. 150; G. 172.

Stage: 32′ wide × 40′ deep.

Letter dated 6th Sept. 1907 states J. E. Vedrenne applied for permission to name new theatre 'The Queen's'. Queen Alexandra's permission sought and granted. (Lord Chamberlain's Office)
Severely damaged by bombing, 24.9.1940. Reopened 1959.

Management

Lord Chamberlain:

1.11.1907-	John Eugene Vedrenne
1.11.1908-	William Greet
22.9.1909-	Henry Brodribb Irving
20.3.1911-	Herbert Sleath
25.9.1911-	Alfred Cyril Smyth-Pigott
6.4.1912-	Alfred Butt
1.12.1930-	Maurice Browne
1.12.1933-	Harold Gosling (to 1940)

Literature

Official records:

L.C.C. Th. & M-H. Com. Papers 1905-;
L.C.O. 56 and 374.

Contemporary accounts:

1904 BUILDER. 1904, April 23rd. p. 445.—Report that almoners of Christs Hospital have let 35-49 to Mr. Jacobus. Theatre to be erected on part of site.
1907 BUILDER. 1907, Sept. 21st. p. 319.—Brief report of recently constructed theatre to be called 'Wardour St. Theatre'.
STAGE. 1907, Oct. 10th.—Description.
1913 SPHERE. 1913, Oct. 11th.'Tango teas at the Queen's Theatre'.

Historical accounts:

c. 1930 MAYES, Ronald
The romance of London theatres, No. 77.
1959 ENCICLOPEDIA dello spettacolo, Vol. 6. Col. 1631.

1963 MANDER, Raymond *and* MITCHENSON, Joe
The theatres of London, 2nd ed. p. 147-150.
LONDON. County Council.
Survey of London. St. James', Vol. 31-32. p. 71 and 78-81. illus., plates.

Location of other material

Plans: G.L.C. *Architects Department.*
Enthoven Collection, 1935 (2 sheets)

Programmes:

British Museum Library; Enthoven Collection; Garrick Club; Guildhall Library; Westminster Local Collection.

627

QUEEN'S ARMS PUBLIC HOUSE

Burrage Road, Plumstead.

Licensed: 1875-1890

Management

West Kent justices:

Mich. 1875-		Frances Murphy
"	1881-	Charles Gordon
"	1885-	Thomas Lambert Emms
"	1888	Henry George

London County Council:

1890	Henry George
Nov. 1890	*No application.*

Literature

Official records:

L.C.C. Th. & M-H. Com. App. Nov. 1889;
W.Kt. Mich. Q.S. 1875-1888.

Queen's Theatre Poplar (624)
(Greater London Council Photograph Library)

628

QUEEN'S ARMS PUBLIC HOUSE

Caledonia Place, Caledonian Road, Islington.

Licensed: 1854-1856

Management

Middlesex justices:

Mich. 1854-   William Wheeler
"   1856   *No application.*

Literature

Official records:

Mx. Mich. Q.S. 1854-1856.

629

QUEEN'S ARMS PUBLIC HOUSE,

London Terrace, 288, Hackney Road, St. Matthew,
Bethnal Green.

Licensed: 1861-1883

Management

Middlesex justices:

Mich. 1861-   Ann Matthew
"   1865-   John Nicholas
"   1969   James Lewis Beech
"   1870-   Richard Buckley
"   1874-   Benjamin Phillips
"   1878-   William Buckley
"   1883   *Licence refused, hall seldom used.*

Literature

Official records:

Mx. Mich. Q.S. 1861-1883.

630

QUEEN'S ARMS PUBLIC HOUSE

Pine Apple Place, Edgeware Road (sic), Paddington.

Licensed: pre 1850-1864

Management

Middlesex justices:

Mich. 1848-   William Clark Child
"   1851-   John Kempshall
"   1863   William Hubble
"   1864   *No application.*

Literature

Offical records:

Mx. Mich. Q.S. 1848-1864.

631

QUEEN'S ARMS PUBLIC HOUSE

2, Queen's Crescent, Haverstock Hill, St. Pancras.

Licensed: 1864-1890

Management

Middlesex justices:

Mich. 1864-   John Hughes
"   1866-   William Stevens
"   1871   William Rider
"   1873-   George Coxen
"   1878-   Henry Flower
"   1887-   William George Pearce

London County Council:

1890   William George Pearce
Nov. 1890   *No application.*

Literature

Official records:

L.C.C. Th. & M-H. Com. App. Nov. 1889;
Mx. Mich. Q.S. 1864-1888.

632

QUEEN'S ARMS PUBLIC HOUSE

Warwick Street, Pimlico, St. George, Hanover Square.

Licensed: 1867-1882

Management

Middlesex justices:

Mich. 1867-   Henry Kingsland Harris
"   1876-   John Kirk Burch
"   1882   *No application.*

Literature

Official records:

Mx. Mich. Q.S. 1867-1882.

633

QUEEN'S HEAD PUBLIC HOUSE

Dog Row, (*later* 98, Cambridge Road) Bethnal Green.

Licensed: 1861-1891

Management

Middlesex justices:

Mich. 1861-   Cornelius David Watkins
"   1863   George Alfred Page
"   1864   John Gibbs
"   1866-   Charlotte Phillis Gibbs
"   1872-   Walter Garland
"   1875   George Wells
"   1876   Francis Whiter
"   1877   John Bond
"   1888   William Harwood

London County Council:

1890   William Harwood
1891   Abraham Abrahams
Nov. 1891   *Licence not renewed.*

Literature

Official records:

L.C.C. Th. & M-H. Com. App. Nov. 1889-1890;
Mx. Mich. Q.S. 1861-1888.

634

QUEEN'S PARK HALL

First Avenue, Harrow Road, Paddington.

Licensed: 1884-1903

Building details

Hall on the first floor.

Capacity: 400

Auditorium: A. 300; G. 100.

Management

Middlesex justices:

Mich. 1884-   Walter Jackson

London County Council:

1890-   Walter Jackson
1896-   George Whichelo
Nov. 1903   *Not listed as theatre or music hall.*

Literature

Official records:

G.L.C. Arch. Dpt. Mss. Index;
L.C.C. Th. & M-H. Com. App. Nov. 1889-1903;
Mx. Mich. Q.S. 1884-1888; Sel. Com. 1892.

635

RAGLAN MUSIC HALL

172, Union Street, Southwark.

Licensed: 1890-1892

Management

London County Council:

1890-   Catherine Grouse
1892   Solomon Barnett
Nov. 1892   *Refused as Barnett neither owner nor lessee.*

Literature

Official records:

L.C C. Th. & M-H. Com. App. Nov. 1890-1892.

636

RAILWAY HOTEL

Hanley Road, Islington.

Licensed: 1870-1890

Management

Middlesex justices:

Mich. 1870-   William Harling Baylis
 "   1874   Alfred Edmund Spalding Williams
 "   1875-   Andrew Charles Duggan
 "   1880-   George Edward Fritche
 "   1883   Richard Miller
 "   1884-   George Jackson
 "   1886-   Katherine Grace Abrams

London County Council:

1890   James Buxley Ponsford
Nov. 1890   *No application.*

Literature

Official records:

L.C.C. Th. & M-H. Com. App. Nov. 1889;
Mx. Mich. Q.S. 1870-1888.

637

RAILWAY HOTEL AND PUBLIC HOUSE

Putney High Street, (*later* 34 Upper Richmond Road) Wandsworth.

Licensed: 1869-1889

Building details

The concert hall was at the rear of the public house at ground floor level. 37' 6" × 20', it seated 100 persons, and was used two to three times a week. It was closed as a result of the 1878 Act.

Management

Surrey justices:

Mich. 1869-   James Yeoman Clipson
 "   1878-   William Henry Price
 "   1882-   Robert Crossley
 "   1884-   William Webb
 "   1888   Harry Dobbin

Literature

Official records:

G.L.C. Arch. Dpt. Th. case 040/124;
Sy. Mich. Q.S. 1869-1888.

638

RAILWAY PUBLIC HOUSE

King Henry's Walk, Balls Pond, St. Mary, Islington.

Licensed: 1870-1890

Management

Middlesex justices:

Mich. 1870-   Robert Robinson
 "   1874   Horace Hunt
 "   1875-   William Evans
 "   1878-   William Simms Cobb

London County Council:

1890   William Simms Cobb
Nov. 1890   *No application.*

Literature

Official records:

L.C.C. Th. & M-H. Com. App. Nov. 1889;
Mx. Mich. Q.S 1870-1888.

639

RAILWAY PUBLIC HOUSE

Laussane Road, (*later* Gibbon Road) Nunhead.

Licensed: 1874-1891

Management

Surrey justices:

Mich. 1874- Charles Brown
   " 1886- Thomas Conrad Simmons Brown

London County Council:

1890- Thomas Conrad Simmons Brown
Nov. 1891 *No application.*

Literature

Official records:

L.C.C. Th. & M-H. Com. App. Nov. 1889-1890;
Sy. Mich. Q.S. 1874-1888.

640

RAILWAY PUBLIC HOUSE

123, North Street, Wandsworth.

Licensed: 1861-1885

Building details

The hall was on the first floor over the bar.

Capacity: 80-100

Used twice a week. Closed by the 1878 Act.

Management

Surrey justices:

Mich. 1861- Harry Sheppard
   " 1864- Edward Blackman
   " 1866- Sarah Blackman
   " 1873- Edward Blackman
   " 1882- Rebecca Blackman
   " 1883- Charles William Gray
   " 1886- Jane Ann Ruddick
   " 1888 *No application.*

Literature

Official records:

G.L.C. Arch. Dpt. Th. case 040/122;
Sy. Mich. Q.S. 1861-1887.

641

RAILWAY PUBLIC HOUSE

131, Plumstead Road, Woolwich.

Licensed: 1867-1891; 1894-1903

Building details

Capacity: 140

Management

West Kent justices:

Mich. 1867- Thomas Neyler
   " 1885- Thomas Hastings

London County Council:

1890 Thomas Hastings (licence retained)
1891 John Edward Swanson
Nov. 1891 *Licence refused.*
1894 Henry Garland
Nov. 1903 *Not listed as theatre or music hall.*

194

Literature

Official records:

L.C.C. Th. & M-H. Com. App. Nov. 1889-1903;
Sel. Com. 1892; W. Kt. Mich. Q.S. 1867-1888.

642

RED BOOT COFFEE TAVERN

259 and 261, Camden Town High Street, St. Pancras

Licensed: 1879-1883

Management

Middlesex justices:

Mich. 1879- George Curtis
   " 1881 William Morgan
   " 1882 Charles Leonard
   " 1883 *No application.*

Literature

Official records:

Mx. Mich. Q.S. 1873-1883.

643

RED COW PUBLIC HOUSE

69, King Street, Deptford.

Licensed: 1846-1853

Management

West Kent justices:

Mich. 1846- George Henry Smith
   " 1853 *No application.*

Literature

Official records:

W. Kt. Mich. Q.S. 1846-1852.

644

RED COW PUBLIC HOUSE

Dalston.

Licensed: 1855-1856

Management

Middlesex justices:

Mich. 1855- Charles Birch
   " 1856 *No application.*

Literature

Official records:

Mx. Mich. Q.S. 1855-1856.

645

RED DEER PUBLIC HOUSE

Cambridge Heath, (*later* 393 Cambridge Road)
Bethnal Green.

Licensed: 1855-1883

Management

Middlesex justices:

Mich.	1855-	James Hunter
"	1861	Jasper Smith
"	1862	Mary Smith
"	1863-	John Smith
"	1865	William Alfred Clark
"	1866-	Robert Horn
"	1871-	George Thomas Plumb
"	1873-	Alfred Paine
"	1878	Alfred Coote
"	1879	Susannah Charles Cakebread
"	1881-	George Cakebread
"	1883	*Licence refused as it was seldom used.*

Literature

Official records:

Mx. Mich. Q.S. 1855-1883

646

RED LION PUBLIC HOUSE

Dockhead, Bermondsey.

Licensed: 1874-1875

Management

Surrey justices:

Mich.	1874-	Emma Porter
"	1875	*No application.*

Literature

Official records:

Sy. Mich. Q.S. 1874-1875.

647

RED LION PUBLIC HOUSE

East Street, Greenwich.

Licensed: 1877-1886

Management

West Kent justices:

Mich.	1877-	Benjamin George Phillips
"	1882-	Thomas Skinner
"	1884-	John Church
"	1886	*No application.*

Literature

Official records:

W. Kt. Mich. Q.S. 1877-1885.

648

RED LION PUBLIC HOUSE

Green Street, Theobalds Road, St. Andrew, Holborn.

Licensed: 1855-1863

Management

Middlesex justices:

Mich.	1855-	Joseph Saxl
"	1857-	George Loveluck
"	1861	Alfred Smith
"	1862	Isabella Smith, later transferred to James Glover.
"	1863	*No petition, no application.*

Literature

Official records:

Mx. Mich. Q.S. 1851-1863.

649

RED LION PUBLIC HOUSE

Pennington Street, Stepney.

Licensed: 1856-1868

Management

Middlesex justices:

Mich.	1856-	Mary Matilda Blinkham
"	1868	*Licence refused owing to Sunday opening.*

Literature

Official records:

Mx. Mich. Q.S. 1856-1868.

650

RED LION PUBLIC HOUSE

Rosoman Street, Clerkenwell.

Licensed: 1862-1863

Management

Middlesex justices:

Mich.	1862-	Maria Rountree
"	1863	*No notice, no petition.*

Literature

Official records

Mx. Mich. Q.S. 1862-1863.

651

RED LION PUBLIC HOUSE

Wilson Street, Finsbury, St. Leonard, Shoreditch.

Licensed: 1864-1867

Management

Middlesex justices:

Mich.	1864-	William Young
"	1867	*No notice, no petition.*

Literature

Official records:

Mx. Mich. Q.S. 1864-1867.

RED LION AND PUNCH BOWL PUBLIC HOUSE

51, St. John Street, Clerkenwell.

Licensed: 1859-1862

Management

Middlesex justices:

Mich. 1859-	George Clements	
" 1862	*Licence refused to Matilda Clements.*	

Literature

Official records:

Mx. Mich. Q.S. 1859-1862.

653

RED LION AND SPREAD EAGLE PUBLIC HOUSE

Whitechapel High Street, Stepney.

Licensed: 1859-1869

Management

Middlesex justices:

Mich. 1859	Thomas Bland
" 1860-	John Harris and Nicholas Collins
" 1863-	John Harris
" 1867	Charles William Langenscheid
" 1868	William Cooper, later Horatio Mearing
" 1869	*No application.*

Literature

Official records:

Mx. Mich. Q.S. 1859-1869.

654

REGENT MUSIC HALL AND PUBLIC HOUSE

21, Regent Street (*later* Regency Street) St. John The Evangelist, Westminster.

Licensed: 1861-1879

Former name

The Telegraph Public House

Management

Middlesex justices:

Mich. 1861-	Alfred Henry Fowler
" 1865-	Harry Frank Margatts
" 1867	Edward Garcia (application later withdrawn)
" 1868	John Newing
" 1869-	George Alison
" 1872	George Donnison
" 1873	Louis Levite
" 1874	George Titterton
" 1875-	William Plank Kesterton
" 1878	Alfred Frederick Marchment
" 1879	*No application.*

Literature

Official records:

Mx. Mich. Q.S. 1861-1879.

Contemporary advertisement:

1875 The Entr'acte and limelight... 1875, May 22nd No. 308.

655

REGENT GALLERY

Upper Hall, Regent Street, Westminster.

Licensed by the Lord Chamberlain during 1854 to legalise the performance of 'Mr. Woodin's Carpet bag and sketch book'. c.f. LC7/13.

656

REGENT THEATRE

Euston Road and Tonbridge Street, Kings Cross.

Opened: 26th December, 1900. Used as a cinema c. 1932-50.

Formerly

Euston Palace of Varieties
Euston Theatre
Euston Musical Hall.

Building details

Architect: Bertie Crewe & Wylson and Long

Capacity: 1, 310

Auditorium: S. 78; P. 495; C. 237; C. 490; Bx. 10.

Management

London County Council:

1899-	George Adney Payne (provision to 1901)
1911-	Ilford Ibbetson
1925-	Variety Theatres Consolidated Ltd.
1933-	King's Cross Cinemas Ltd.
1936-	Associated Cinema Properties Ltd.
1950	Park Theatrical Productions Ltd.

Lord Chamberlain:

10. 1.1912-	Ilford Ibbetson
1.12.1923-	W. Payne
1.12.1932-	Ernest William Pashley Peall (to Nov. 1937)

Literature

Official records:

G.L.C. Arch. Dpt. Mss. Index; G.L.C. Arch. Dpt. Th. case 105; L.C.C. Th. & M-H. Com. App. Nov. 1898-; L.C.C. Th. & M-H. Com. Papers 1896-; L.C.O. 374 and 504.

Contemporary accounts:

1901 BUILDER. 1901, Jan. 5th. p. 23. —Brief report of opening.

Historical accounts:

c. 1930 MAYES, Ronald
    The romance of London theatres. No. 97 and 170.

Location of other material:

Plans: G.L.C. *Architects Department.*

Programmes &c.

British Museum Library; Enthoven Collection; Garrick Club; Westminster Local Collection.

657

REGENT THEATRE

St. Anne, Westminster.

Licensed by the Lord Chamberlain to Edward Tyrrel Smith 23.12.1871 to 28.9.1872.

It was built before 1866 at a cost of £25,000 and had a capacity of 1,500.

Mentioned in: SELECT COMMITTEE ON THEATRICAL LICENSING AND REGULATIONS. Report 1866. *and* SELECT COMMITTEE ON THE METROPOLITAN FIRE BRIGADE. Report 1877.

It has not been possible to find out any further information about this building.

658

RIDLEY ARMS PUBLIC HOUSE

6, Ridley Road, Hackney.

Licensed: 1861-1890

Management

Middlesex justices:

Mich. 1861-	William and Richard Barlow
" 1864-	Edward Peter Barlow
" 1877-	William Scott
" 1878-	Edmund Simkins
" 1887	William Alfred Lynn
" 1888	William Katen Woodley

London County Council:

| 1890 | Ernest William Osborne Hodges |
| Nov. 1890 | *Licence refused.* |

Literature

Official records:

L.C.C. Th. & M-H. Com. App. Nov. 1889-1890; Mx. Mich. Q.S. 1861-1888.

659

RISING SUN PUBLIC HOUSE

46, Commercial Road, Pimlico.

Building details

Concert room was on the first floor. It could be divided by a movable partition. It was closed as a result of the 1878 Act.

Literature

Official records:

G.L.C. Arch. Dpt. Th. case O40/126. —includes plan.

660

RISING SUN PUBLIC HOUSE

New Road, and Chalton Street, Somers Town, St. Pancras.

Licensed: 1852-1861

Management

Middlesex justices:

| Mich. 1852- | Nathan Mare |
| " 1861 | *Licence refused to Joseph Turnham House burnt down.* |

Literature

Official records:

Mx. Mich. Q.S. 1852-1861.

661

RISING SUN PUBLIC HOUSE

Vernon Street, Fulham.

Licensed: 1855-1889

Management

Middlesex justices:

Mich. 1855-	John Newton
" 1859-	Alexandra Matthew Jackson
" 1863-	Thomas William Wilkinson
" 1866-	John Robertson
" 1877-	Henry Payne
" 1881-	Emma Payne.

Literature

Official records:

Mx. Mich. Q.S. 1855-1888.

662

ROBIN HOOD PUBLIC HOUSE

High Hill Ferry, Upper Clapton, Hackney.

Licensed: 1852-1861

Management

Middlesex justices:

| Mich. 1852- | Matthew Barrett |
| " 1861 | *No petition. House closed.* |

Literature

Official records:

Mx. Mich. Q.S. 1852-1861.

663

ROCK OF GIBRALTAR PUBLIC HOUSE

Evelyn Street, (*formerly* Gibraltar Row) Deptford.

Licensed: 1869-1882

Former name

The Gibraltar Public House

Management

West Kent justices:

Mich. 1869-	Frederick Smee
" 1875-	Frank Barnes
" 1880-	William Henry Burney (to 1882).

Literature

Official records:

W. Kt. Mich. Q.S. 1869-1881

664

ROSE PUBLIC HOUSE

58, Hatton Garden, Holborn.

Licensed: 1854-1858

Management

Middlesex justices:

Mich. 1854-	Charles Clarke
" 1858	*No application.*

Literature

Official records:

Mc. Mich. Q.S. 1854-1858.

665

ROSE AND CROWN PUBLIC HOUSE

Bromley High Street, (*formerly* Devon Lane) Bromley, St. Leonard.

Licensed: 1851-1874

Management

Middlesex justices:

Mich. 1851	Joseph Sacker
" 1852-	John William Bacon
" 1854-	Richard Everard
" 1859	Ellen Everard
" 1860-	Joseph Aslun
" 1869-	William Charles Wright
" 1871	Bejamin Beach
" 1872-	Samuel Spill
" 1874	*No application.*

Literature

Official records:

Mx. Mich. Q.S. 1851-1874.

666

ROSE AND CROWN PUBLIC HOUSE

83, Bunhill Row, Finsbury.

Licensed: 1860-1890

Management

Middlesex justices:

Mich. 1860-	Alexander Shaw
" 1874	William George Sayer
" 1875	Arthur Medworth
" 1876	William Ishmael Quinton
" 1877-	George Meyer Maxwell

London County Council:

1890	George Meyer Maxwell
Nov. 1890	*No application.*

Literature

Official records:

L.C.C. Th. & M-H. Com. App. Nov. 1889;
Mx. Mich. Q.S. 1860-1888.

667

ROSE AND CROWN PUBLIC HOUSE

20, Colville Place, St. Pancras.

Licensed: 1851-1864

Management

Middlesex justices:

Mich. 1851	Charles Abbott
" 1852	James Mayne Homewood
" 1853	William Dwelly
" 1854	John Kift
" 1863	John Hayward
" 1864	*Licence refused to Magdalene Pulford.*

Literature

Official records:

Mx. Mich. Q.S. 1852-1864.

668

ROSE AND CROWN PUBLIC HOUSE

57, Drury Lane.

Licensed: 1854-1858

Management

Middlesex justices:

Mich. 1854-	Thomas Matthews
" 1858	*No application.*

Literature

Official records:

Mx. Mich. Q.S. 1854-1858.

669

ROSE AND CROWN PUBLIC HOUSE

24, Fort Street, Old Artillery Ground, Tower.

Licensed: 1890-1891

Management

London County Council:

1890 Frederick James Pilliner
Nov. 1891 *Not licensed.*

Literature

Official records:

L.C.C. Th. & M-H. Com. App. Nov. 1889-1890.

670

ROSE AND CROWN PUBLIC HOUSE

26, Knightsbridge High Road, St. Margarets, Knightsbridge.

Licensed: 1852-1876

Management

Middlesex justices:

Mich. 1852- James Rennell
 " 1862- Charles Norman
 " 1876 *No application.*

Literature

Official records:

Mx. Mich. Q.S. 1852-1876.

671

ROSE AND CROWN PUBLIC HOUSE

203, St. George Street, Tower.

Licensed: 1890-1891

Management

London County Council:

1890 Jacob Schaumloeffel
1891 Pedro Femenia
Nov. 1891 *Licence refused.*

Literature

Official records:

L.C.C. Th. & M-H. Com. App. Nov. 1889-1891.

672

ROSE AND SHAMROCK PUBLIC HOUSE

222, Shadwell High Street, Shadwell.

Licensed: 1856-1861

Management

Middlesex justices:

Mich. 1856 James Ward
 " 1857- Benjamin Mitchell
 " 1861 *No application, no petition.*

Literature

Official records:

Mx. Mich. Q.S. 1856-1861.

673

ROSEMARY BRANCH MUSIC HALL AND PUBLIC HOUSE

18, Aberystwith Terrace, Shepperton Street, Islington.

Licensed: 1851-1855; 1857-1887

Building details

Capacity: 250

Management

Middlesex justices:

Mich. 1851- William Barton
 " 1854- William Barton, Henry Dodd and John Jay
 " 1855 *No application.*
 " 1857- Thomas Matthews
 " 1860- William Blake Stannard
 " 1863- Henry Mills
 " 1864 *Licence refused* to Henry John Lee
 " 1865- Henry Gabb
 " 1877- Edward Adams Pocock
 " 1878- Charles Leach
 " 1886- Charles William Nobbs
 " 1887 *Licence refused* as owner convicted for non compliance with requirements of M.B.W.

Literature

Official records:

Mx. Mich. Q.S. 1851-5, 1857-87; Sel. Com. 1892.

Contemporary accounts:

1852 THEATRICAL JOURNAL. 1852 —Description.
1871 ERA ALMANACK. 1871. p. 6. —Description.

Historical accounts:

1835 CROMWELL, Thomas
   Walks through Islington. p. 108—Description.
1858 TOMLIN, Thomas Edlyne.
   A perambulation of Islington. . 1858
   Various refs.—Description.
1907 WROTH, Warwick
   Cremorne and the later London gardens. . . .
   p. 48-51.

674

ROTHERHITHE HIPPODROME

34 and 36, Lower Road, Rotherhithe.

Opened: 16. 10. 1899

Formerly

Terriss' Theatre (to 1908)

Building details

Architect: W. G. R. Sprague

Builder: Messrs. Walter Wallis & Co.

Capacity: 2,087

Auditorium: S. 754; C. 349; G. 648; Bx. 60.

Stage: 70' × 32'

Management

Lord Chamberlain:

25. 10. 1899-	Edward George Saunders
20. 8. 1900-	George Conquest Jnr. and Herbert Leonard
2. 9. 1901-	Walter and Frederick Melville (to 2. 12. 1907)
4. 12. 1911-	Walter Gibbons
2. 7. 1912-	Charles Gulliver
25. 3. 1918-	Edward Walter Rice
Feb. 1922-	Alexander Share
1. 12. 1922-	Harry Eckstein
1. 12. 1923-	Charles Gulliver (to Nov. 1927)
1. 12. 1928-	David Albert Abrahams
1. 12. 1930-	Ralph Sidney Bromhead (A.B.C. Ltd.)
1. 12. 1934-	Arthur Stanley Moss (to Nov. 1939)
1. 12. 1943	(for one year) Archie Allerton Shenburn.

London County Council:

1908-	Walter Gibbons
1913-	Charles Gulliver
1919-	Edward Walter Rice
1923	Alexander Share
1924-	Charles Gulliver
1926-	London Theatres of Varieties Ltd.
1928-	Rotherhithe Hippodrome Ltd.
Nov. 1930	*Not licensed as theatre or music hall.*

Literature

Official records:

G.L.C. Arch. Dpt. Mss. Index;
G.L.C. Arch. Dpt. Th. case 278;
L.C.C. Th. & M-H. Com. App. Nov. 1907-1929;
L.C.C. Th. & M-H. Com. Papers 1898-;
LC1/712-752; LC7/46-48; L.C.O. 374 and 495.

Contemporary accounts:

1899 BUILDING NEWS. 1899, April 21st. p. 539.
—Description & plate of front elevation.
BUILDER. 1899, Sept. 2nd. p. 224. —Brief report
of new theatre in course of erection.
BUILDER. 1899, Oct. 21st. p. 378. —Report of
opening.

Historical accounts:

1961 THEATRE WORLD. 1961, Sept. Lost London
theatres, by N. M. Bligh. No. 16. The story of the
Terriss Theatre, Rotherhithe. 3p.

Location of other material

Plans: G.L.C. *Architects Department.*

Newscuttings: Bermondsey Local Collection.

Cuttings, playbills etc. Enthoven Collection.

675

ROYAL ALBERT PUBLIC HOUSE
Wandsworth Road.

Licensed: 1857-1863

Management

Surrey justices:

Mich. 1857-	James Heritage
" 1861-	Richard Vickery
" 1863	*No application.*

Literature

Official records:

Sy. Mich. Q.S. 1857-1862.

676

ROYAL ARTILLERY THEATRE AND OPERA HOUSE
Woolwich.

A place of entertainment from 1863. Theatre opened
21. 12. 1905 by Lord Roberts.

Formerly

Royal Artillery Recreation Rooms.

Building details

1863 Old Garrison church was converted into a theatre
and recreation rooms.

1903 This building burnt down.

1904 Rebuilt

Architect: W. G. R. Sprague

Capacity: c. 1000

Management

London County Council:

1905-1909	Government leased building to a number of managements.
1909-1939	to Mrs. Agnes Mary Littler
1st licence appears to have been granted Nov. 1926.	
1927-	Mrs Agnes Mary Littler
1940	Navy, Army & Air Force Institute and Charles Benjamin
1948	Swift Productions Ltd., and Robert Brighten Salisbury
1949-	Swift Productions Ltd., and James Noel Scott Green.

Literature

Official records:

L.C.C. Th. & M-H. Com. App. Nov. 1926-39, 1948-.

Contemporary accounts:

1905 BUILDER. 1905, Dec. 23rd. p. 684. —Note on
erection.
1906 BUILDER. 1906, Jan. 6th. p. 27. —Brief report on
opening.
1950 THEATRE ownership... p. 129.

Historical accounts:

c. 1930   MAYES, Ronald
Romance of London theatres, No. 124.

Location of other material

Plans: G.L.C. *Architects Department;* Enthoven Collection 1927 2 sheets.

Newscuttings &c: Woolwich Local Collection.

Playbills: Guildhall Library (1 item for 1883)

677

ROYAL CAMBRIDGE MUSIC HALL

136, Commercial Street, Shoreditch.

Opened: 1864. *Demolished:* 1936 for extension of tobacco factory.

Also known as

Cambridge Music Hall

Building details

Originally built at a cost of £16,000 with a capacity of 2000. By 1892 the capacity had been limited to 1488. Destroyed by fire, 1896.

1897-8 Rebuilt:

Architect: D. H. Percival

Builder: R. S. Lambe

Capacity: 926

Auditorium: P. & S. 309; C. 280; G. 313; Bx. 24.

Stage: 41' wide × 30' deep.

Management

Middlesex justices:

Mich. 1864-	George William Nugent
" 1867-	George Jones Sagin Page
" 1871-	George William Nugent
" 1880-	William Riley

London County Council:

1890-	William Riley
1897-	Charles Ambrose Wilkes
1903-	John Coveney
1906-	Charles Hector
1909-	Thomas Greenhill Richards
1923-4	Stanley Leyton
Nov. 1924	Not listed as theatre or music hall.

Literature

Official records:

G.L.C. Arch. Dpt. Mss. Index;
G.L.C. Arch. Dpt. Th. case 283;
L.C.C. Th. & M-H. Com. App. Nov. 1889-1924;
Mx. Mich. Q.S. 1864-1888; Sel. Com. 1866 and 1892.

Contemporary accounts:

1887   SATURDAY REVIEW. 1887, Aug. 27th. The state of the London... music halls... No. 3.
1897   BUILDER. 1897, Jan. 23rd. p. 83. Report of tender of Lambe for rebuilding.

BUILDER. 1897, April 10th. p. 344. —Report of foundation stone laying and description of building.
BUILDER. 1897, Dec. 4th. p. 476. —Report that building nearing completion.
1898   BUILDER. 1898, Jan. 15th. p. 65. —Report of re-opening with brief description.
ARCHITECT. 1899, Jan. 20th. —Double page illus. of frontage.

Historical accounts:

1952   PULLING, Christopher
They were singing... p. 237
1954   WILSON, A. E.
East end entertainment... p. 219.
1957   LONDON. County Council.
Survey of London. Vol. XXVII. p. 263-4. Plate.

Location of other material

Plans: G.L.C. *Architects Department.*

Programmes &c:

Enthoven Collection; Guildhall Library; London Museum.

678

ROYAL CLARENCE MUSIC HALL

Admiral Hardy Public House, Clarence Street, (*later* College Approach) Greenwich.

Licensed: c. 1839-1891

Also known as

Clarence Music Hall

Royal Clarence Music Hall   (678)

(Ellis Ashton Collection, British Music Hall Society)

Building details

The hall is (1964) situated over the northern entrance to Greenwich Market. It communicated by a doorway with the first floor of the Admiral Hardy. The hall was 46' × c. 24', with a small stage at the eastern end, and a balcony at the west end which was reached by a small steep staircase. It was closed as a result of the 1878 Act.

Capacity: 250

Management

West Kent justices:

Mich. 1839-		Henry Mitchell and Henry Richard Mitchell
"	1848-	Henry Richard Mitchell
"	1860	Louisa Mitchell
(Records from 1861-1865 missing)		
"	1866-	Robert Lauder
"	1868	James Lauder
"	1869-	Horatio James Wright
"	1874-	John Smith
"	1879-	Edward Deekes
"	1883	Rebecca Deekes
"	1884-	Benjamin George Phillips
"	1887-	William Lewis

London County Council:

1890-	William Lewis
Nov. 1891	*No application.*

Literature

Official records:

L.C.C. Th. & M-H. Com. App. Nov. 1889-90; W. Kt. Mich. Q.S. 1839-1888.

679

ROYAL COURT THEATRE

Sloane Square, Chelsea.

Opened: 24th September, 1888.

Formerly: Court Theatre

Building details

Rebuilding of the Court Theatre, Lower George St.q.v.

Architects: Walter Emden and W. R. Crewe

Capacity: 841

Auditorium: S. 148; P. 611; D.C. 121; Amphi. 84; G. 146.

The theatre was bombed in 1940, and was not reconstructed until after 1950. It had, however, not been used as a theatre from 1932.

Management

London County Council:

1890-	Matilda Caroline Wood, and Arthur Chudleigh
1893-	Arthur Chudleigh
1902	Henry Thomas Brickwell
1903-	Matilda Charlotte Wood
1905-	John Highfield Leigh
1916-	Otto Stuart Andreae
1918	Alfred Smyth-Piggott
1919-	Percival Keitley
1921-	James Bernard Fagan
1923-	Alfred Turner
1935-	Lux Estates Ltd, and Victor Luxembourg
1936-40	Royal Court Cinema Ltd., and Noel Pemberton-Billing.

Literature

Official records:

L.C.C. Th. & M-H. Com. App. Nov. 1889-.

Contemporary accounts:

1887 BUILDER. 1887, Aug. 13th. p. 256. —Report of proposed new theatre.
1888 BUILDING NEWS. 1888, Jan. 27th. p. 143. —Description.
1888 BUILDING NEWS. 1888, March 30th, p. 480. —Description.
BUILDER. 1888, Sept. 29th. Oct. 6th. and Nov. 29th. p. 225-6, 254. —Description of theatre.
1904 BUILDER. 1904, June 18th. p. 656. —Report of proposed alteration for amateur theatre.
1907 McCARTHY, Desmond
The Court Theatre.1904-1907: a commentary and criticism. London 1907. 169p.

Historical accounts:

1904 BRERETON, Austin
A short history of the Court Theatre. The Theatres, (1904) 6p.
c. 1930 MAYES, Ronald
The romance of London theatres. No. 40.
1952 PULLING, Christopher
They were singing.... —Various refs.
1959 ENCICLOPEDIA dello spettacolo. Vol. 6. col. 1618.

Location of other material:

Plans: G.L.C. *Architects Department.*

Programmes and playbills:
British Museum Library; Enthoven Collection; Garrick Club; Guildhall Library; London Museum; Westminster Local Collection.

Newscuttings, souvenirs, programmes etc.
Chelsea Local Collection.

680

ROYAL CRICKETERS PUBLIC HOUSE

211, Old Ford Road, Bethnal Green.

Licensed: 1858-1890

Former name

Hosford Arms Public House

Management

Middlesex justices:

Mich. 1858		James Roffway
"	1859	James Rowe
"	1863-	Cornelius Sutton
"	1867-	Edward Baker
"	1870-	Phillis Bass
"	1874-	George Oliver Jones
"	1880-	John Westgarth
"	1884-	John Dexter Birlein
"	1887-	William Marcus Critchfield

1890   William Marcus Critchfield
Nov. 1890   *Not licensed.*

Literature

Official records:

L.C.C. Th. & M-H. Com. App. Nov. 1889;
Mx. Mich. Q.S. 1858-1888.

681

ROYAL CROWN PUBLIC HOUSE

131, St. George Street, St. George in the East.

Licensed: 1851-1862, 1865-1872

Management

Middlesex justices:

Mich. 1851   Stephen Mercer
"   1852-   Henry Michell
"   1862   *Licence refused* to Philip Werner
"   1865-   William Meyer
"   1867-   Henry George Groh
"   1872   *Licence refused as dancing had been
               allowed.*

Literature

Official records:

Mx. Mich. Q.S. 1851-62, 1865-72.

682

ROYAL EDWARD PUBLIC HOUSE

King Edward's Road, Hackney.

Licensed: 1866-1891

Management

Middlesex justices:

Mich. 1866   William Bristo
"   1867-   Charles Ireland
"   1870-   George Charles Busby
"   1874-   Frederick Allen
"   1877-   Frederick Richardson
"   1888   Charles Steel

London County Council:

1890   Charles Steel
1891   William Provost (licence retained)
Nov. 1891   *No application.*

Literature

Official records:

L.C.C. Th. & M-H. Com. App. Nov. 1889-90;
Mx. Mich. Q.S. 1866-1888.

683

ROYAL GEORGE PUBLIC HOUSE

George Street, Chelsea.

Licensed: 1853-1864

Management

Middlesex justices:

Mich. 1853   Henry Briggs
"   1854-   Elizabeth Briggs
"   1863   Henry Smith
"   1864   *No notice, no petition.*

Literature

Official records:

Mx. Mich. Q.S. 1854-1864.

684

ROYAL HOTEL (Public House)

Lauriston Road (*formerly* Grove Road) Hackney.

Licensed: 1862-1889

Building details

The concert room was on the 1st floor with an area of
966′ 6″ exclusive of stage. It was closed as a result of
the 1878 Act.

Management

Middlesex justices:

Mich. 1862-   John Miles
"   1866-   William Ratcliff
"   1868-   James Simmons (to 1889)

Literature

Official records:

G.L.C. Arch. Dpt. Th. case 040/135;
Mx. Mich. Q.S. 1862-1888.

685

ROYAL HOTEL

560, Mile End Road, Stepney.

Licensed: 1865-1891

Management

Middlesex justices:

Mich. 1865-   Joseph Myerscough
"   1875-   Alfred Yates
"   1886   William James Goddard
"   1887-   Francis Newport

London County Council:

1890   Francis Newport
1891   Robert Marshall Rhodes (licence retained)
Nov. 1891   *Application withdrawn.*

Literature

Official records:

L.C.C. Th. & M-H. Com. App. Nov. 1889-1891;
Mx. Mich. Q.S. 1865-1888.

686

ROYAL KENT THEATRE

Kensington.

Opened: 1831. *Closed:* 1845. *Demolished:* 1851.

Literature

Historical accounts:

1958 THEATRE WORLD. 1958, Feb.
      Lost theatres of London, by N. M. Bligh. No. 10.
      The story of the Royal Kent Theatre, Kensington.

Location of other material

Playbills, prints, cuttings and watercolours:

Enthoven Collection;
Kensington Local Collection. (all pre-1850)

687

ROYAL OAK PUBLIC HOUSE

Barking Road.

Select Committee in 1892 states that this hall was
destroyed by fire 29.10.1867.

688

ROYAL OAK PUBLIC HOUSE

62, Glenthorne Road, Hammersmith.

Licensed: 1897-1899

Building details

Concert room on ground floor attached to public house.

Capacity: 100

Management

London County Council:

1897-   Edward Thomas Spurr
Nov. 1899   *No application.*

Literature

Official records:

G.L.C. Arch. Dpt. Mss. Index;
L.C.C. Th. & M-H. Com. App. Nov. 1896-1898.

689

ROYAL OAK PUBLIC HOUSE

Margaret Street, Hackney Fields.

Licensed: 1854-1882

Management

Middlesex justices:

Mich.	1854-	Mary Adkins
"	1859-	John Alexander Curel
"	1871-	Albert Norris
"	1882	*No application.*

Literature

Official records:

Mx. Mich. Q.S. 1854-1881.

204

690

ROYAL OAK PUBLIC HOUSE

220, Whitechapel Road, Stepney.

Licensed: 1851-1888

Management

Middlesex justices:

Mich.	1851-	Richard Riley Cragg
"	1854-	James Bloomfield
"	1856-	Alfred Jackson
"	1857-	James Isaac Dannit
"	1863	William Windett, executor to J. I. Dannit
"	1864-	James Grubb
"	1866-	William Young
"	1869-	Zebedee Wilcox
"	1873	George Robinson
"	1874	Clarence T. Smith
"	1875-	John William Greeves
"	1888	*Licence refused.*

Literature

Official records:

Mx. Mich. Q.S. 1851-1888.

691

ROYAL PAVILION

North Woolwich.

Licensed: 1851-1890

Former Names

Royal Pavilion Hotel   1853
Pavilion Gardens   1852
Royal Pavilion Gardens

Also known as

North Woolwich Gardens and Theatre

Management

West Kent justices:

Mich.	1851	Henry Churchill Lovegrove
"	1852-	Isaac Churchyard Dowsing
"	1857-	Edward McNamara
"	1868	Charles Morton
"	1869-	William Holland
"	1882	Richard Bosley
"	1883-	Walter Davenport
"	1885-	Richard Bosley
"	1888	Benjamin Carter

London County Council:

1890   Benjamin Carter
Nov. 1890   *Application withdrawn.*

Literature

Official records:

L.C.C. Th. & M-H. Com. App. Nov. 1889-90;
Sel. Com. 1877; W. Kt. Mich. Q.S. 1851-1888.

Historical accounts:

Alladyce Nicholl lists the 'North Woolwich Gardens
and Theatre' in 'Later Nineteenth Century Drama'.

692

ROYAL SOVEREIGN PUBLIC HOUSE

Blue Gate Fields, St. George in the East.

Licensed: 1855-1860

Management

Middlesex justices:

Mich. 1855-   Johan Bruns
  " 1860   *No petition, no application.*

Literature

Official records:

Mx. Mich. Q. S. 1855-1860.

693

ROYAL STANDARD PUBLIC HOUSE

Albion Street, Bethnal Green.

Licensed: 1853-1858

Management

Middlesex justices:

Mich. 1853   William Austin
  " 1854-   George Alexander King
  " 1858   *No application.*

Literature

Official records:

Mx. Mich. Q. S. 1854-1857.

694

ROYAL STANDARD PUBLIC HOUSE

Fleming Street, Kingsland Road.

Licensed: 1854-1856

Management

Middlesex justices:

Mich. 1854-   Thomas Alexander Wesley
  " 1856   George Alexander King
  " 1858   *No application.*

Literature

Official records:

Mx. Mich. Q. S. 1854-1858.

695

ROYAL STANDARD MUSIC HALL

112, Albert Road, (*later* High Street), North Woolwich.

Licensed: 1866-1898.

Building details

The hall had a capacity of 200.

Management

West Kent justices:

Mich. 1866-   Charles Tyson
  " 1872-   George Clamp

London County Council:

1890-   George Clamp
1893-   Frank Neville Clamp
1895   Emma Jane Clamp
1896-   Arthur John Clamp
Nov. 1898 *No application.*

Literature

Official records:

G.L.C. Arch. Dpt. Th. case 034;
L.C.C. Th. & M-H. Com. App. Nov. 1889-1897;
Sel. Com. 1892; W. Kt. Mich. Q. S. 1866-1888.

Location of other material

Plans: G.L.C. *Architects Department.*

696

ROYAL SURREY GARDENS

Walworth, Newington.

Licensed: 1849-62, 1873-4 and 1876-78

Management

Surrey justices:

Mich. 1849-   William Tyler
  " 1856-   Royal Surrey Gardens Co. Ltd.
  " 1859   Thomas Bartlett Simpson
  " 1860-   Charles Bishop
  " 1862   *No application.*
  " 1873   Reginald Claude Poole
  " 1876-   Thomas Simpson
  " 1878   *No application.*

Literature

Official records:

Sy. Mich. Q. S. 1849-61, 1873, 1876-7.

697

ROYAL VICTORIA MUSIC HALL

Royal Victoria Public House, 234, Old Ford Road, Bethnal Green.

Licensed: 1867-87 and 1891-1903

Building details

The concert hall was on the ground floor attached to the public house, accommodating c. 300. In 1890 the hall was reconstructed.

Management

Middlesex justices:

Mich. 1867-   William Scaddan
  " 1879-   Joseph Bruton
  " 1887   *Licence refused.*

1891	Constant Van Hoydonck
1892-	Jonathan Saul Waterhouse
1897	John George Wyatt
1898	Charles Pennell Sutton
1899	Charles James Hollingsworth
1900-	Francis Christopher Hill
1902	Edward Cecil Moore
1903	Edward Bessell
Nov. 1903	*Not listed as a theatre or music hall.*

Literature

Official records:

G.L.C. Arch. Dpt. Th. case 290;
L.C.C. Th. & M-H. Com. App. Nov. 1889-1903;
Mx. Mich. Q. S. 1867-1887.

Location of other material

Plans: G.L.C. *Architects Department.*

698

ROYAL YORK PUBLIC HOUSE

19, Weston Place, Pancras Road, St. Pancras.

Licensed: 1854-1864

Management

Middlesex justices:

Mich. 1854-	Joseph Grose
" 1861	William Thomas Purkiss
" 1862-	Thomas Goswell
" 1864	*No notice, no petition.*

Literature

Official records:

Mx. Mich. Q. S. 1854-1864.

699

ROYALTY THEATRE

73, Dean Street, Soho.

Opened: 25. 3. 1840. *Closed:* 25. 11. 1938, and later damaged by bombing. Replaced by 'Royalty House' (Office block).

Formerly

Miss Kelly's Theatre
Royal Soho Theatre
Soho Theatre (1850-)
New English Opera House (1850)
New Royalty Theatre
Théatre Francais

Building Details

Opened 1840, but owing to elaborate stage machinery causing vibration it closed again after five days.

1850 Reopened.

1861 Reconstructed.

Foyer one building, theatre proper in another.
Auditorium: S. 112: P. 88; D.C. 123; G. 295; Bx. 27.

1883 Reconstructed.

Architect: T. Verity Senior

Capacity: 657

Auditorium: S. 171; P. 150; C. 153; U.C. 51; G. 100; Bx. 32.

Stage: 24' wide × 24' deep.

Management

Lord Chamberlain:

2. 6. 1845-	Miss Frances Maria Kelly
21. 1. 1850-	Charles Gould Gilbert
29. 9. 1852-	Thomas Pratt Mowbray
21. 1. 1860-	Thomas Thurling
29. 9. 1860-	Thomas Pratt Mowbray
29. 9. 1867-	Martha Oliver
8. 6. 1870-	Thomas Pratt Mowbray
5. 9. 1870-	Ernest Clifton
29. 9. 1872-	Henrietta Hodson (or Hodgson)
29. 9. 1877-	Kate Santley
29. 11. 1879-	Edgar Bruce
24. 2. 1881-	Kate Santley (1904-06 much correspondence and lawsuit on state of building)
23. 10. 1906-	Thomas Buffen Davis
10. 4. 1911-	John Eugene Vedrenne
1. 12. 1919-	Dennis Eadie
1. 12. 1928-	Arthur Handel Elliott Gibbons
1. 12. 1935-	Frederick Dudman Bromwich (to 1938)

London County Council:

1946-1950	Seventy Sixth Trust Ltd.

Literature

Official records:

G.L.C. Arch. Dpt. Mss. Index;
G.L.C. Arch. Dpt. Th. case 444;
L.C.C. Th. & M-H. Com. App. Nov. 1945- ;
L.C.C. Th. & M-H. Com. Papers 1889-; LC 1/507-752;
LC 7/13-17, 20-48, 89; L.C.O. 357 and 374;
M.B.W. Rpt. 1882. p. 261-271;
Mx. Mich. Q. S. Papers; Sel. Com. 1866, 1877 and 1892.

Contemporary accounts:

1861 ERA. 1861 Nov 17th. Report of opening.
1877 ROYALTY THEATRE Programme, 11th October 1877. Notes redecoration.
1883 ERA. 1883 April 28th. Description of rebuilding.
1895 BUILDING NEWS. 1895, Aug. 30th. p. 318—Note of reconstruction.
1906 BUILDING NEWS. 1906, Jan. 5th. p. 50—Description of reconstruction.

Historical accounts:

1879 DRAMATIC NOTES. 1879, p. 62-3.
1893 EDWARDS, Francis. bookseller.
Playbills: a collection and some comments ... p. 14-19.
1895 RIMBAULT, E. F.
Soho and its associations ... p. 185-6.
1904 BAKER, H. Barton,
History of the London stage and its players. p. 451-5.
1925 CHANCELLOR, E. B.
The pleasure haunts of London ... p. 133.

c. 1930 MAYES, Ronald
The romance of London theatres, No. 58.
1931 CHANCELLOR, E. B.
The romance of Soho . . . p. 244-5.
1950 FRANCIS, Basil
Fanny Kelly of Drury Lane, Rockliff. 1950. 207p.
illus.
1955 THEATRE WORLD, 1955, May.
Lost London theatres, by N. M. Bligh. No. 4.
The story of the Royalty, Soho. 2p.
1959 ENCICLOPEDIA dello spettacolo. Vol. 6, Col.
1632.
1966 GREATER LONDON COUNCIL
Survey of London, Vol. 33, 1966, pp. 215-21
plans, plates.
1968 MANDER, Raymond *and* MITCHENSON, Joe
The lost theatres of London. pp 402-429.
7 illus.

Location of other material

Plans: G.L.C. *Architects Department,*
Enthoven Collection, 1912 (6 sheets)
Public Record Office. LC 7/75. 5 sheets, 1882.

Programmes and playbills: British Museum Library;
Enthoven Collection; Garrick Club; Guildhall Library;
London Museum; Westminster Local Colléction.

700

RUNNING HORSE PUBLIC HOUSE

82, Harrow Road, Paddington.

Licensed: 1855-1881

Management

Middlesex justices:

Mich.	1855	John Malchar
"	1856-	Ann Malchar
"	1860-	Edmund Furley
"	1863-	Richard Green
"	1864-	Robert Hammond
"	1872-	James Alfred Lee
"	1874-	Lewis Ascott
"	1877-	John Holmes
"	1879-	Thomas Morris
"	1881	*Licence not renewed.*

Literature

Official records:

Mx. Mich. Q. S. 1855-1881.

701

SABERTON ARMS PUBLIC HOUSE

99, Upper North Street, Poplar.

Licensed: 1861-1884

Management

Middlesex justices:

Mich.	1861-	William D. Carrington
"	1871-	Henry Edward Wilson
"	1874	John Baker
"	1875	James Freeman Randall
"	1876-	William Jordan Cairns
"	1884	*Licence refused as it had not been used for 4 years.*

Literature

Official records:

Mx. Mich. Q. S. 1861-1884.

702

SADLER'S WELLS THEATRE

Rosebery Avenue, Finsbury.

First opened as place of entertainment: 3rd June,
1683.

Royalty Theatre, Dean Street   (699)

(Victoria & Albert Museum, Crown copyright)

Royalty Theatre, Dean Street   (699)

(Victoria & Albert Museum, Crown copyright)

Building details

1st building:

Wooden construction with stage.

Demolished 1765.

2nd building:

Stone building erected.

Opened: 8.4.1765

Developer: Thomas Rosoman.

3rd building: (Reconstruction) 1879.

Architect: C.J. Phipps

Capacity: approx. 1,600.

Auditorium: (1882) S. 293; P. 216; D.C. 155; U.C. 256; G. 600; Bx. 48.
Closed as theatre 1906. Stood derelict after 1918.

4th building:

Opened: 6.1.1931.

Architect: F.G.M. Chancellor

Capacity: 1,650.

Auditorium: S. 210; P. 408; C. 414; G. 428.

Stage: 29′ 6″ wide × 38′ deep.

Extension: 1938.

Architects: Stanley Hall and Easton & Roberts.

Management

Lord Chamberlain:

29. 9.1843–	Thomas Longden Greenwood
29. 9.1845–	T.L. Greenwood, Samuel Phelps, and Robert Warner
29. 9.1846–	T.L. Greenwood and Samuel Phelps
29. 9.1862–	Catherine Lucette
29. 9.1863–	Robert Edgar
14.10.1871–	Frederick Belton (licence returned 27.4.1872)
30. 8.1872–	Romaine Delatorre
3.11.1873–	Henry Powell
29. 9.1879–	Sidney Francis Bateman
13. 1.1881–	Isabella Bateman
29. 9.1881–	Frederick Balsin Chatterton
4. 2.1882–	Matthew Robson
1. 8.1885–	John Ward
29. 9.1886–	James Deacon
5.11.1887–	Joseph Arnold Cave
28. 9.1888	George Tooke Robert
17. 8.1889–	George Neagherson and Michael Byrmes
19.10.1889–	Todd Angell
6.11.1889–	Charles Smith
28. 9.1890–	Charles Wilmot and Henry A. Freeman
29. 9.1892–	Henry A. Freeman
26. 1.1895–	Charles Wilmot
29. 9.1896–	Henry A. Freeman (to 28.9.1902)
8. 1.1910–	Henry A. Freeman (to 31.10.1911)
30.12.1912–	Frederick Baugh (to 30.11.1914)
1.12.1931–	Lilian Mary Baylis
1.12.1938–	Ernest Bruce Digby Worsley
1.12.1939–	William Tyrone Guthrie (to Nov.1942)
1.12.1945–	George Thomas Chamberlain

London County Council:

1891-2	Charles Wilmot, and Henry A. Freeman
Nov.1892	*Licence refused:*
1904-1910	Henry A. Freeman
1912	Frederick Baugh
1915-1918	Harry Thomas Underwood
1932-1937	Lilian Mary Baylis
1938-1939	'Bruce' Worsley
1940-1942	Tyrone Guthrie
1946-	The Governors of Sadler's Wells Foundation.

Literature

Official records:

G.L.C. Arch. Dpt. Mss. Index; G.L.C. Arch. Dpt. Th. case 293; L.C.C. Th. & M-H. Com. App. Nov. 1890–1918; 1931-41; 46–; LC 1/508-752; LC 7/13-17, 20-48; L.C.O. 374 and 455; M.B.W. Rpt. 1882. p. 295-305; Sel. Com. 1892.

Contemporary accounts:

1862 BUILDING NEWS. 1862, Feb. 7th. p. 86.—Note of forthcoming auction.

1872 DAILY TELEGRAPH. 1872, Sept. 5th.—Report that theatre under same management as the Victoria.

1877 BUILDER. 1877, March 3rd. p. 216.—Report of dismantling interior for construction of rink, and work in compliance with Lord Chamberlain's requirements.

1878 BUILDER. 1878, Sept. 28th. p. 1022.—Report that Mrs. Bateman new lessee.

1879 BUILDER. 1879, March 29th and April 5th, p. 354 and 379.—Report of rebuilding. BUILDING NEWS. 1879, Oct. 17th. p. 476.—Description of new theatre. Correction 24.10. 1879, p. 509.

1901 BUILDER. 1901, June 1st. p. 536.—Brief report of renovations.

1902 DAILY GRAPHIC. 1902, July 22nd. 'Merry old Sads' —Report that theatre to be reopened.

1925 DAILY CHRONICLE. 1925, March 30th. 'An 'Old Vic' for North London.
DAILY TELEGRAPH. 1925, March 30th. 'Sadler's Wells Theatre: Old Vic for North London'
MORNING POST. 1925, March 30th. 'Sadler's Wells Theatre: Duke of Devonshire's scheme. and Old Vic for North London. A £60,000 appeal'. *Also* letter from the Duke.
ISLINGTON GAZETTE. 1925, April 1st. North London's Old Vic: Miss L. Baylis welcomes Duke's scheme.
ESTATES GAZETTE. 1925, April 18th. Sadler's Wells sold: report of transaction.
DAILY TELEGRAPH. 1925, April 31st *and foll. weeks.* —Saving Sadler's Wells: lists of subscribers.
JOHN O'LONDON'S WEEKLY. 1925, May 2nd. 'Letters to Gog and Magog: Sadler's Wells'. —Report of fund and note of history.
ISLINGTON GAZETTE. 1925, July 9th. Sadler's Wells Fund: grant of £14,200 by Carnegie Trust'.
TIMES. 1925, Oct. 26th. Sadler's Wells: progress of the fund: letter from Duke of Devonshire.

1926 SADLER'S WELLS THEATRE Sadler's Wells subscription fund: report and appeal. 1926. (Copy in B.M. 11805, m. 44.)

1929 ISLINGTON GAZETTE. 1929, Oct. 22nd. 'A regrettable decision'. —Report of Islington Borough Council's failure to support fund. ISLINGTON GAZETTE. 1929, Nov. 1st. '£10,000'. Dependent upon 'Gazette' raising 20,000 shillings'. —Article on scheme for converting theatre into a People's Theatre.

1930 ISLINGTON GAZETTE. 1930, Aug. 29th. 'Sadler's Wells Theatre: probable re-opening on Boxing Day'. ISLINGTON GAZETTE. 1930, Dec. 24th. 'Opening of Sadler's Wells' —report. STAR. 1930, Dec. 31st. 'Sadler's Wells reopening, by A. E. Wilson'.

1931 BUILDING. 1931, Jan. p. 51-2. GRAPHIC. 1931, Jan. 3rd. and Jan. 17th. p. 18 and 94. DAILY TELEGRAPH. 1931, Jan. 7th. —Report of opening. TIMES. 1931, Jan. 7th. —Report of opening. ARCHITECT AND BUILDING NEWS. 1931, Jan. 9th. p. 55-59. The new Sadler's Wells. illus., plans. ILLUSTRATED LONDON NEWS. 1931, Jan. 24th. p. 128. —Report. The OLD VIC AND SADLER'S WELLS MAGAZINE. No. 1. Jan. 1931—

Historical accounts:

1813 GENTLEMAN'S MAGAZINE. 1813, Dec. The Old London Theatres: No. 5. p. 553-563. -reprinted in 'The Gentleman's Magazine' Topographical history... Vol. 1. p. 100-112.

1828 CROMWELL, T. History of Clerkenwell...p. 306-378.

? MIRROR. No. 971, Vol. XXXIV, p. 218.

1872 ERA ALMANACK, 1872. —The playgoer's portfolio by E. L. Blanchard. p. 1-6. —History of Sadler's Wells.

1879 DRAMATIC NOTES. 1879, p. 65-7.

1880 PINKS, William J. History of Clerkenwell...p. 409-436.

1881 THEATRE. 1881, April 1st. p. 229-31. —Recollections of Sadler's Wells, by G.L.C.

1883 WILLIAMS, Michael Some London theatres...p. 1-32.

1902 ISLINGTON DAILY GAZETTE AND NORTH LONDON TRIBUNE, 1902, Nov. 21st. 'Ye old Sadler's Wells'.

1904 BAKER, H. Barton. History of the London stage and its players. p. 351-75.

1925 CHANCELLOR, E. B. Pleasure haunts of London...p. 392-395. FOSTER, Ardeen The romance of the Sadler's Wells Theatre. Sadler's Wells Theatre Fund, (1925?). EVENING NEWS. 1925, June 19th. 'Magic nights at old Sadler's Wells...by Sir Arthur Pinero'.

c.1930 MAYES, Ronald The romance of London theatres, No. 3. and 190. PARKER, John Sadler's Wells. The Theatre (193-). 7p.

c.1903 SADLER'S WELLS SOCIETY. The Sadler's Wells book: a souvenir of the Sadler's Wells Theatres, past, present and future, n.d. 44p. illus., plates.

1935 FAGG, Edwin Old 'Sadler's Wells'. Vic-Wells Assoc. 1935. 16p.

1938 DISHER, M. W. Winkles and champagne... —Various refs.

194- WILSON, A. E. Pantomime pageant... —Various refs.

1944 THEATRE ARTS. 1944, Oct. p. 598-604. Sadler's Wells Theatre under the management of Samuel Phelps. 1844-62. by Shirley Allen.

1945 DENT, Edward J. A theatre for everybody.

1952 PULLING, Christopher They were singing...p. 168.

1954 THEATRE WORLD. 1954, Feb. Sadler's Wells—Yesterday and today. 2p.

1956 SPEAIGHT, George The memoirs of Charles Dibdin, the younger.

1959 ENCICLOPEDIA dello Spettacolo. Vol 6, Col. 1932-3.

1963 MANDER, Raymond *and* MITCHENSON, Joe The theatres of London, 2nd ed. p. 245-249.

Location of other material

Finsbury Local Collection contains a very large collection of cuttings, playbills etc., relating to this theatre.

Other sources

Plans:

G.L.C. *Architects Department.*
Enthoven Collection, 1947 (4 sheets)
Public Record Office, LC 7/76. 17 sheets (1877, 1878 and 1901)

Scrapbooks:

British Museum Library (Th. Cts. 49) 'Collection of plates, cuttings... relating to Sadler's Wells Theatre from c. 1740-1866'.

Programmes, playbills &c:

British Museum Library; Enthoven Collection; Garrick Club; Guildhall Library; London Museum; Westminster Local Collection.

Prints:

British Museum; Enthoven Collection; Finsbury Local Collection; Guildhall; London Museum; Westminster Local Collection.

703

ST. GEORGE'S HALL

4, Langham Place, St. Marylebone

Opened: 22nd April, 1867. *Bombed:* during World War II.

Also known as

Matinee Theatre
St. George's Theatre
Maskelyne's Theatre

Building details

Built as a large concert hall.

Architect: John Taylor, Jnr.

Alterations: 1881

Architect: J. R. Tasker

Capacity: c.1,000

Auditorium: (1882) S. 692; B.S.&C. 276; Bx. 44.

Stage: 50' wide × 49' deep.

Management

Lord Chamberlain:

22. 4.1867-	Dr. Henry Wylde.
29. 9.1871-	Gilbert Robinson Wilkinson
29. 9.1872-	Thomas Edward Evans
29.12.1877-	Alfred Reed and Richard Corney Grain
27. 6.1895-	Henry Dore Reed
29. 9.1897-	Philip Yorke
5. 4.1898-	Mayrick-Beaufoy Held Milton
29. 9.1899-	William Gerald Elliot (to Oct.1902?)
1.12.1904-	John Nevil Maskelyne
31.10.1911-	David Devant
1.12.1915-	J.N. Maskelyne
18. 5.1917-	Nevil Maskelyne
1.12.1924-	Edmund Clive Maskelyne
1.12.1926-	Jasper Maskelyne
1.12.1930-	Noel Maskelyne
1.12.1931-	Jasper Maskelyne (to 1933)

Middlesex justices:

Mich.1873-	Thomas Edward Evans
" 1878-	Alfred Reed and Richard Corney Grain (to 1889)

London County Council:

1890-	Alfred Reed and Richard Corney Grain
1896-	Henry Dore Reed
1898	Philip Yorke
1899	Mayrick Beaufoy Field Milton
1900-	William Gerald Elliott
Nov.1902	*Not licensed as theatre or music hall.*

Literature

Official records:

G.L.C. Arch. Dpt. Mss. Index;
G.L.C. Arch. Dpt. Th. case 445;
L.C.C. Th.& M-H. Com. App. Nov. 1889-1902;
LC 1/507-752; LC 7/15, 23-48, 89;
L.C.O. 372 and 374;
M.B.W. Rpt. 1882, p. 271-281; Mx. Mich. Q.S. 1873-1888.

Contemporary Accounts:

1867 ERA 1867 April 28th. —Report of opening.
1905 ERA. 1905 Jan. 7th. —Report of alterations.

Historical accounts:

c. 1930 MAYES, Ronald
The romance of London theatres, No. 103.
'Maskelyne's Theatre'.
1952 PULLING, Christopher
They were singing...p. 139-141.
1968 MANDER, Raymond *and* MITCHENSON, Joe
The Lost Theatres of London. pp. 430-450
4 illus.

Location of other material

Plans:

G.L.C. *Architects Department.*
Public Record Office: LC 7/77 4 sheets for 1867
1 sheet for 1881.

210

Programmes:

British Museum Library;
Enthoven Collection; Guildhall Library;
Westminster Local Collection.

704

ST. HELENA MUSIC HALL, GARDENS AND PUBLIC HOUSE

Corbett's Lane, Rotherhithe.

Licensed: 1849-1878.

Management

Surrey justices:

Mich. 1849-	Richard Edgington
" 1855-	Richard Preece the Younger
" 1866-	Frederick Preece
" 1874-	John Richard Carter
" 1876-	Thomas Porter
" 1878	*No application.*

Literature

Official records:

Sy. Mich. Q.S. 1849-1877.

Contemporary accounts:

GLASIER & SONS. *Auctioneers.* Particulars and conditions of sale...at the Mart, Tokenhouse Yard, 28th July, 1881. —Gives plan of building— one side being the tavern, the other the music hall with gallery and stage— all made of wood. The music hall was 113' × 29' 6".

Location of other material

Illustrations, playbills, newscuttings:

London Museum Library. —The Pleasure gardens of South London, Vol. II. pp. 140-150.

705

ST. JAMES'S THEATRE

King Street, Piccadilly.

Opened: 14th December, 1935. *Demolished:* 1957.

Also known as

Prince's Theatre

Building details

Architect: Samuel Beazley

Builders: Grissel and Peto

1879 Alterations:

Architect: Thomas Verity

Capacity: c.1,200

Auditorium: S. 222; P. 180; D.C. 181; U.C. 153; G. 311; Bx. 58.

1900 Reconstruction:

Architect: A. Blomfield Jackson

Capacity: 1,099, (1950) 950.

Auditorium: S. 242; P. 111; D.C. 174; U.C. 150; G. 334.

Stage: 26′ wide × 42′ 6″ to 60′ deep.

Management

Lord Chamberlain:

29. 9.1843-	John Mitchell
28. 1.1851-	John Henry Anderson
29. 9.1851-	John Mitchell
29. 9.1854-	Jzmes Bunce Curling
29. 9.1855-	John Hamilton Braham
29. 9.1857-	Charles Braham
29. 9.1859-	Frederick Balsir Chatterton
29. 9.1860-	Alfred Wigan
26.12.1862-	Frank Matthews
10.12.1863-	Frederick Acclon Milbank
30. 1.1864-	Benjamin Webster
26.12.1864-	Ruth Herbert
2.11.1868-	William Emden
18. 5.1869-	John Mitchell
29. 9.1869-	Mrs. John Wood
29. 9.1874-	Stephen Fiske
20. 1.1875-	Mrs. John Wood
24. 3.1875-	Marie Litton
8. 1.1876-	Horace Wigan
10. 4.1876-	Mrs. John Wood
27.10.1877-	Henry Laurance (to 30.10.1877)
3.11.1877 *only*	William Clarke
28.12.1877-	Samuel Hayes (to 25.5.1878)
29. 9.1879-	John Hare, and William Hunter Kendal
28. 9.1888-	Rutland Barrington
28. 9.1889-	Romer Williams
13. 1.1890-	Lily Langtry
27.10.1890-	Michael Leopold Mayer
Feb. 1891-	George Alexander
9. 4.1918-	Charles Thomas Hunt-Helmsley
1. 1.1919-	Gilbert Heron Miller
1.12.1926-	Tom Benjamin Vaughan
1.12.1928-	Gerald du Maurier
1.12.1929-	Stanley Joseph Passmore
1.12.1932-	James Ernest Sharpe
1.12.1933-	Thomas Henry Bostock
1.12.1943-	Prince Littler (through 1950)

Literature

Official records:

G.L.C. Arch. Dpt. Mss. Index;
G.L.C. Arch. Dpt. Th. case 446;
L.C.C. Th. & M-H. Com. Papers 1888-;
LC 1/507-752; LC 7/13-17, 20-48, 89;
L.C.O. 358 and 374;
M.B.W. Rpt. 1882, p. 281-295; Sel. Com. 1866 and 1892.

Contemporary accounts:

1836 MIRROR OF LITERATURE, AMUSEMENT
& INSTRUCTION. 1836, Oct. 29th. p. 274-5.
—Description of new building.

1887 OBSERVER. 1877, Dec. 30th. —Report of opening
under S. Hayes' management.

1879 ERA, 1879 Oct. 5th. —Description of
reconstruction.
BUILDER. 1879, Oct. 25th. p. 1184. —Description
of redecoration.

1887 SATURDAY REVIEW. 1887, June 11th. The
state of the London theatres. . . No. 1.

1888 The THEATRE, 1888. Sept. —Report of Hove-
Kendal partnership.

1889 BUILDER. 1889, Nov. 25th. p. 496. —Brief report
that A. Blomfield Jackson is appointed architect
for rebuilding.

1900 ERA 1900, Jan 13th. —Report of major
alterations.
SKETCH. 1900, Feb. 7th. p. 103. —Brief description and illus. of interior as renovated by
George Alexander.

1906 THRONE. 1906. Nov. 24th. p. 119. —Brief history
with seating plan.

1950 THEATRE ownership. . . p. 59 and 90.

Historical accounts:

1897 DRAMATIC Notes, 1879, p. 31-2.

c.1900 A CHRONICLE of the St. James's Theatre
from its origin in 1835. (Guild of Women
Binders). 87p.

1904 BAKER, H. Barton
History of the London stage and its players. . .
p. 456-73.

c.1930 MAYES, Ronald
The romance of London theatres, No. 54 and 184.

1935 MASON, Albert Edward Woodley
Sir George Alexander and the St. James'
Theatre. . . Macmillan, 1935. 247p. plates.

1950 COMING EVENTS. 1950. Feb. p. 11. illus.
—Brief summary of history.

1955 ILLUSTRATED. 1957, Nov. 16th. p. 11-13. illus
5th. illus. 'Ghosts in St. James's' by J. C. Trewin.
SPHERE, 1955, Jan. 29th.
'St. James's Theatre, 1835-1955: memories of
the personalities who grew fame in the. .theatre'
by Macqueen Pope.

1957 ILLUSTRATED. 1957, Nov. 16th. p. 11-13. illus
of performance: 'My memories of the St. James's
by Laurence Olivier.

1958 POPE, Walter James Macqueen
St. James's: theatre of distinction.
W H. Allen, 1958.

1959 ENCICLOPEDIA dello spettacolo. Vol. 6.,
Col. 1633.

1960 LONDON. County Council
Survey of London. Vol. 29, 1960. p. 299-304.
plates, plans.

1964 DUNCAN, Barry
The St. James Theatre: its strange and complete
history. 1835-1957.
Barrie and Rockliff, 1964. 407p. illus., plates.
facsims, tables.

1968 MANDER, Raymond *and* MITCHENSON, Joe
The Lost theatres of London. pp. 451-484 4 illus.

Location of other material

Plans: G.L.C. *Architects Department;* Enthoven Collection, 1900 (3 sheets); Public Record Office LC 7/78
6 sheets for 1878. 6 sheets for 1899.

Programmes, playbills & c:

British Museum Library; Enthoven Collection;
Garrick Club; Guildhall Library; London Museum;
Westminster Local Collection.

706

ST. JOHN OF JERUSALEM PUBLIC HOUSE

164, St. John Street, Clerkenwell.

Licensed: 1859-1862

Building details

Music room on 1st floor. Closed as a result of the 1878 Act.

Management

Middlesex justices:

Mich. 1859–	William Weatherly
" 1861	Charles Duddridge
" 1862	*No application as Duddridge dead.*

Literature

Official records:

G.L.C. Arch. Dpt. Th. case 040/137;
Mx. Mich. Q.S. 1859-1861.

Location of other material

Plans: G.L.C. *Architects Department.*

707

ST. JOHN'S WOOD PUBLIC HOUSE

Lords, St. Marylebone.

Licensed: pre 1850-1889

Management

Middlesex justices:

Mich. 1848	Peter Snow
" 1849–	William Holt
" 1857–	John Day
" 1872–	William Crick
" 1878	George Parsons
" 1879–	Frederick William Butterworth
" 1882–	Robert Reader (to 1889)

Literature

Official records:

Mx. Mich. Q.S. pre 1850-1888.

708

ST. LEONARD'S HALL

153, Shoreditch High Street, Shoreditch.

Licensed: 1854-1870

Management

Middlesex justices:

Mich. 1854–	Thomas Harwood
" 1865–	Sarah Harwood
" 1867–	George Harwood
" 1870	*Not licensed as building destroyed by fire 28.4.1870.*

Literature

Official records:

Mx. Mich. Q.S. 1854-1869; Sel. Com. 1892.

709

ST. MARTIN'S THEATRE

West Street, Holborn.

Opened: 23rd Nov. 1916.

Proposed name

Irving Theatre (Proposed theatre 1912)

Building details

Architect: W. G. R. Sprague

Builders: Lenn Thornton & Co.

Capacity: 600, (1950) 550

Auditorium: S. 221; P. 44; D.C. 125; U.C. 153; Bx. 19.

Stage: 26′ wide × 23′ to 25′ deep.

Management

Lord Chamberlain:

15.11.1916–	Bertie Alexander Meyer
3. 2.1919–	Charles B. Cochran
1. 7.1920–	Alec Lionel Rea
1.12.1937–	William Foster Horsfield
1.12.1942–	W. G. Curtis
1.12.1943–	Ronald Harry Shipley (through 1950)

Literature

Official records:

G.L.C. Arch. Dpt. Th. case 2578; L.C.C. Th. & M-H. Com. Papers 1912-; L.C.O. 68 and 374.

Contemporary accounts:

1912 BUILDING NEWS. 1912, Nov. 15th. p. 705.
'Irving Theatre—Wallrock & Co. v. Hoffman'.
—Case following proposal to build new theatre.
1916 ARCHITECTURAL REVIEW. 1916, Nov.
—Description.
1950 THEATRE ownership...p. 75, 111.

Historical accounts:

c. 1930 MAYES, Ronald
The romance of London theatres, No. 34.
1959 ENCICLOPEDIA dello spettacolo, Vol. 6, Col. 1633.
1963 MANDER, Raymond *and* MITCHENSON, Joe.
The theatres of London. 2nd ed. pp. 165-169.

Location of other material

Plans: G.L.C. *Architects Department.*
Enthoven Collection.

Programmes &c.

Enthoven Collection; Holborn Local Collection;
London Museum; Westminster Local Collection.

710

ST. PANCRAS ATHENAEUM

George Street, New Road, St. Pancras.

Licensed: 1855-1857

Management

Middlesex justices:

| Mich. 1855– | Daniel William Ruffy |
| " 1857 | *No petition, no application.* |

Literature

Official records:

Mx. Mich. Q.S. 1855-1857.

711

ST. PANCRAS COFFEE TAVERN

122, Euston Road, St. Pancras.

Licensed: 1881-1882

Management

Middlesex justices:

Mich. 1881   William Taylor
" 1882   *No application.*

Literature

Official records:

Mx. Mich. Q.S. 1881-1882.

712

ST. PANCRAS PEOPLES THEATRE

Charrington Hall, Charrington Street, St. Pancras.

Licensed: 1926-1940

Also known as

Tavistock Little Theatre

Later

Mary Ward Settlement

Building details

Capacity: 419

Auditorium: S. 393; G. 26.

Management

Lord Chamberlain:

1. 12. 1926-1. 12. 1940   Edith Neville

Literature

Official records:

G.L.C. Arch. Dpt. Th. case 249; L.C.O. 363 and 374.

Contemporary accounts:

1928-   St. Pancras People's Theatre Magazine.
(B.M. P.P. 5224. dbh).

Location of other material

Plans: G.L.C. *Architects Department.*

Programmes: Enthoven Collection.

Note: This hall continued to hold a licence as an education establishment.

713

SALMON AND BALL PUBLIC HOUSE

Bethnal Green Road.

Licensed: pre 1850-1853

Management

Middlesex justices:

Mich. 1848-   Charles Lord
" 1851-   John Warne Cathie
" 1853   *No petition, no answer.*

Literature

Official records:

Mx. Mich. Q.S. 1848-1852.

Historical accounts:

POPE, Walter Macqueen
The melodies linger on.—Mention only.

Location of other material

Bills: Guildhall Library (1 item for 1836)

714

SALMON AND COMPASSES PUBLIC HOUSE

33, Penton Street, Clerkenwell.

Licensed: pre 1850-1862

Management

Middlesex justices:

Mich. 1848-   James William Jolliffe
" 1850-   Frederick Rountree
" 1860   Robert Hart
" 1861   William Henry Davis
" 1862   *No petition, no application.*

Literature

Official records:

Mx. Mich. Q.S. 1848-1862.

715

SAVILLE THEATRE

135-49, Shaftesbury Avenue, Holborn.

Opened: 8th October, 1931.

Building details

Consulting Architect: Bertie Crewe

Builder: Messrs. Gee, Walker and Slater

Designed by: T. P. Bennett & Sons

Capacity: 1, 426; (1950) 1, 250

Auditorium: S. 646; D.C. 261; U.C. 319; Bx. 8.

Stage: 31' 6" wide × 27' 6" to 30' 6" deep.

Management

Lord Chamberlain:

1. 12. 1931-   Albert Edward Fournier
1. 12. 1946-   Edward Ramsden Hall
1. 12. 1947-   Leonard Frank Ridgley
1. 12. 1950-   Marianne Davis

London County Council:

1931-   Saville Theatre Ltd.
1947-   Delhall Ltd.

Literature

Official records:

G.L.C. Arch. Dpt. Th. case. 4172; L.C.C. Th. & M-H. Com. App. Nov. 1930-; LCO 255 and 374.

Contemporary accounts:

1930 BUILDER, 1930. Vol. 138, p. 888, 914.
c. 1930 MAYES, Ronald
The romance of London theatres, No. 171.
1931 ARCHITECTURE ILLUSTRATED. 1931, Nov.
BUILDER. 1931. Vol. 141. p. 381-83 &c. illus.
BUILDING. 1931. Sept.
THEATRE WORLD. 1931, Oct. p. 188-9. illus.
STAGE. 1931, Oct. 8th.—Description.
1950 THEATRE ownership.

Historical accounts:

1963 MANDER, Raymond *and* MITCHENSON, Joe
The theatres of London. 2nd ed. p. 170-3.

Location of other material

Plans: G.L.C. *Architects Department.*
Enthoven Collection, 1930 (3 sheets)

Programmes:

Enthoven Collection; Garrick Club; Holborn Local Collection; Westminster Local Collection.

716

SAVOY THEATRE

Beaufort Buildings, Strand.

Opened: 10th October, 1881.

Proposed name

Beaufort Theatre (Before opening).

Building details

1st building:

Architect: C. J. Phipps

Builder: Messrs. Patman and Fotheringham

Capacity: c. 1, 300

Auditorium: S. 175; P. 165; B. 187; C. 178; A. 118; G. 373; Bx. 78.

Stage: 60′ wide × 52′ deep.

2nd building:

Opened: 21. 10. 1929.

Architect: Frank A. Tugwell

Builder: Pitcher Construction Company

Decorator: Basil Ionides

Capacity: 1, 138

Auditorium: S. 500; D.C. 371; U.C. 271.

Stage: 29′ 4″ wide × 29′ 6″ deep.

Management

Lord Chamberlain:

29. 9.1881-   Richard D'Oyly Carte
29. 9.1901-   William Greet

June 1903-   Mrs. Helen D'Oyly Carte
4. 2.1904-   John Highfield Leigh
8. 12.1906-   Helen D'Oyly Carte
1. 11.1911-   George Augustus Richardson
22. 2.1915-   Rupert D'Oyly Carte
1. 12.1948-   High Walter Kingwell Wontner

Literature

Official records:

G.L.C. Arch. Dpt. Mss. Index; G.L.C. Arch. Dpt. Th. case 447; L.C.C. Th. & M-H. Com. Papers. 1888-; LC 1/507-752; LC 7/17, 28-48; L.C.O. 87 and 374; M.B.W. Rpt. 1882. p. 305-314; Sel. Com. 1892.

Contemporary accounts:

1881 BUILDING NEWS. 1881, April 1st. plate after p. 360.—Victoria Embankment frontage.
BUILDING NEWS. 1881, Sept. 9th. p. 341.—Brief description of 'Beaufort'.
BUILDING NEWS. 1881, Sept. 23rd. p. 389. —Detailed description.
BUILDER. 1881, Sept. 24th. p. 402-3.—Description.
DAILY TELEGRAPH. 1881. Sept. 30th.—Report.
DAILY TELEGRAPH. 1881, Oct. 10th.—Report of stage illumination and use of electric lighting.
TIMES. 1881, Oct. 10th.—Description.
DAILY NEWS. 1881, Oct. 11th.—Report of opening.
MORNING POST. 1881, Oct. 11th.—Report of lighting.
ILLUSTRATED SPORTING AND DRAMATIC NEWS. 1881, Oct. 29th. illus.
1882 ENGINEERING. 1882, March 3rd. 'Lighting of the Savoy Theatre'. *Reprinted in* TABS, 1962, Sept. p. 29-32.
1887 SATURDAY REVIEW. 1887, July 16th. The state of the London theatres. . . No. 5.
1902 BUILDER. 1902, April 26th. p. 421.—Note on erection of iron and glass covered way.
1903 BUILDER. 1903, Aug. 29th. p. 233.—Brief report of redecorations and repairs.
1929 BUILDER. 1929, Nov. 1st. p. 723, 741, 742. —Photos. of reconstruction.
BUILDING. 1929, Nov.—Description.
1930 ARCHITECTURAL REVIEW. 1930, Jan. p. 21-9, 41-2. Light opera: Savoy Theatre, by R. McGrath. illus. plates, plans.
1950 THEATRE ownership. . . p. 75 and 110.

Historical accounts:

1894 FITZGERALD, P.
The Savoy opera and the Savoyards. 1894.
1904 BAKER, H. Barton
History of the London stage and its players. p. 512-4.
1924 FITZGERALD, S. J. A.
The story of the Savoy opera. Stanley Paul, 1924.
1929 COUNTRY LIFE. 1929, Nov. 16th.
Article by Christopher Hussey.
The ROMANCE of the famous London theatre: the old Savoy Theatre and the new. Curwen Press, 1929. 12p. (B.M. 11795 p. 20).
c. 1930 MAYES, Ronald
The romance of London theatres, No. 28.
1959 ENCICLOPEDIA dello spettacolo. Vol. 6, Col. 1634.

1963 MANDER, Raymond *and* MITCHENSON, Joe.
The theatres of London, 2nd ed. p. 174-179.

Location of other material

Plans:

G.L.C. *Architects Department.*
Public Record Office LC 7/79 9 sheets for 1881.

Programmes:

British Museum Library; Enthoven Collection;
Garrick Club; Guildhall Library; London Museum;
Westminster Local Collection.

717

SCALA THEATRE

Charlotte Street, St. Pancras.

Opened as a place of entertainment: 1772

Closed for demolition 1969

Former names

1772 The New Rooms in Tottenham Street
1780 King's Concert Rooms
1786 Rooms for Concerts of Ancient Music
  -   Hyde's Rooms
1802 Cognoscenti Theatre
1808 New Theatre in Tottenham Street
      Tottenham St. Theatre
1815 Regency Theatre
1820 West London Theatre
1831 Queen's Theatre
1833 Fitzroy Theatre
1835 Queen's Theatre
1837 Fitzroy Theatre
1839 Queen's Theatre knows as 'The Dust Hole'
1865 Prince of Wales Theatre (Prince of Wales'
      Royal Theatre)
(1904 F. Verity asked permission to name theatre
      'Royal Sovereign Playhouse'—The King
      refused permission.)
1905 The Scala
1923 New Scala

Savoy Theatre 1881 (716)

(Victoria & Albert Museum, Crown copyright)

Scala Theatre (717)

(Greater London Council Photograph Library)

Building details

1810 Music rooms converted into theatre.
Altered and redecorated a number of times.

1865 Reconditioned:

Capacity: c. 600

Auditorium: S. 143; P. 85; G. 134; Bx. 142.

1882 Building reported as unsafe.

1884-1886 Empty.

1886-1903 Salvation Army Hostel.

1904 Rebuilding:

Opened: 23. 9. 1905.

Architect: Frank T. Verity

Builder: Messrs. Allen & Sons

Capacity: 1, 139

Auditorium: S. 192; P. 283; D. C. 208; U. C. 242; G. 223.

Stage: 30' 6" wide × 54' deep.

Management

Lord Chamberlain:

29. 9. 1843-	Charles James James
29. 9. 1869-	Marie Wilton and Charles James James
29. 9. 1871-	Squire Bancroft Bancroft, and C. J. James
29. 9. 1875-	Squire Bancroft Bancroft
21. 2. 1880-	Edgar Bruce (to 28. 9. 1872)
1. 3. 1905-	Edmund Distin Maddick
23. 3. 1922-	Cecil Russell Snape
2. 10. 1922-	Frank Daniel Kendrill
1. 12. 1923-	D. A. Abrahams (to after 1950)

Literature

Official records:

G. L. C. Arch. Dpt. Mss. Index; G. L. C. Arch. Dpt. Th. case 448; L. C. C. Th. & M-H. Com. Papers. 1888-; LC 7/15-17, 20-29, 89; M. B. W. Rpt. 1882. p. 241-251; Sel. Com. 1866 and 1892.

Contemporary accounts:

1896 BUILDER. 1896, Jan. 25th. p. 70.—Report that theatre to let. Brief history.
1899 BUILDER. 1899, Oct. 28th. p. 400.—Report of Mr. Greatbach's plans for rebuilding.
1901 BUILDER. 1901, Oct. 26th. p. 360.—Report of auction (withdrawn).
1902 DAILY GRAPHIC. 1902, Aug. 22nd.—Illus. of exterior and brief history.
1904 BUILDER. 1904, Dec. 17th. p. 636. (Correction in issue of 7. 1. '05 p. 3.)—Report of Architectural Association visit: detailed description.
BUILDING NEWS. 1904, Dec. 23rd. p. 920. —Brief description.
SKETCH. 1904, Dec. 28th.—Illus. description.
1905 SOUVENIR brochure. 1905 to celebrate opening. —A pictorial and historical guide. Text by Distin Maddick.
BUILDING NEWS. 1905, July 7th. p. 13.—Brief description. Plate-section.
BUILDER. 1905, Dec. 2nd. p. 590.—Description. illus. of interior.

Historical accounts:

1874 ERA ALMANACK. 1874. p. 1-6.
—History of the Prince of Wales Theatre.
1879 DRAMATIC notes. 1879. p. 33-7.
1893 EDWARDS, Francis. bookseller.
Playbills: a collection and some comments. p. 1-6.
1899 ST. PANCRAS NOTES AND QUERIES.
March 3rd. No. 100. April 7th. 106
SCOTT, Clement
The drama of yesterday and today. . . p. 479, 482-3, 596.
1900 ST. PANCRAS NOTES AND QUERIES. 1900, Feb. 2nd. No. 138.
1901 ST. PANCRAS NOTES AND QUERIES. 1901, Nov. 1st. No. 223
1902 ST. PANCRAS NOTES AND QUERIES. 1902. Feb. 7th. No. 232
Aug. 1st. No. 285
Oct. 3rd. No. 296
Nov. 7th. No. 301
1903 TATLER. 1903, Sept. 9th.
—Illus. of interior: history.
1904 BAKER, H. Barton
History of the London stage and its players. . . p. 311-328.
1911 WINDSOR, 1911, Dec. p. 74.
'Prince of Wales' (1870). illus.
1913 WORLD'S WORK, 1913, Sept. p. 245, 296-305.
The Scala (1904), by R. R. Buckley.
1925 CHANCELLOR, E. B.
The pleasure haunts of London. . . p. 129-132.
CHANCELLOR, E. B.
London's Old Latin quarter. . . p. 108-16.
c. 1930 MAYES, Ronald
The romance of London theatres, Nos. 53, 74, 163.
1936 NICOLL, Allardyce
The English Theatre. . . p. 219-20.
1949 LONDON. County Council.
Survey of London. Vol. 21, 1949. p. 38-9.
1952 PULLING, Christopher
They were singing. . . p. 176, 210, 221, 227.
1959 ENCICLOPEDIA dello spettacolo. Vol. 6. Col. 1634.
1961 REYNOLDS, E.
Recreations and leisure in St. Pancras. Chapter VI, p. 44-52.
1963 MANDER, Raymond *and* MITCHENSON, Joe
The theatres of London. 2nd ed. p. 180-185.

Location of other material

Plans: G. L. C. *Architects Department.*

Programmes, playbills &c.

British Museum Library; Enthoven Collection; Garrick Club; Guildhall Library; London Museum; Hampstead Local Collection (Heal Collection); Westminster Local Collection.

718

SCARBOROUGH ARMS PUBLIC HOUSE

St. Mark's St., Goodman's Fields.

Licensed: 1854-1856.

Management

Middlesex justices:

Mich. 1854-		Robert Green Grimes
"	1856	*No petition, no answer.*

Literature

Official records:

Mx. Mich. Q.S. 1854-1856.

719

SEBRIGHT MUSIC HALL

Coate Street, (*formerly* 2, Hill Street) Hackney.

Opened: 1865

Former names

Sebright Arms Public House
Belmont's Sebright
Regent Theatre of Varieties
English's (Sebright) Musichall

Building details

1885 Premises reconstructed.

Capacity: 704

Auditorium: P. 274; G. 150

Management

Middlesex justices:

Mich.	1865	Julius Simon
"	1866-	George Cunnington
"	1869-	George Barrow
"	1874-	William Turnham
"	1880-	Richard James Ames
"	1883-	John Keeble
"	1885-	George Archer Blanchett

London County Council:

1890-	George Archer Blanchett
1892-	George Edwin English
1904-	George Archer Blanchett
(Nov. 1904	*Not licensed as theatre or music hall.*
Nov. 1910	Licensed as Sebright Picture Palace)
1912	Francis John Bliss
1913-	Frank Stebbings
1919-	Herbert Tankard (to Dec. 1920)

Literature

Official records:

G.L.C. Arch. Dpt. Mss. Index; L.C.C. Th. & M-H. Com. App. 1889-1903, 1911-1919; Mx. Mich. Q.S. 1865-1888.

Contemporary accounts:

1887 SATURDAY REVIEW. 1887, Aug. 27th. The state of the London... music halls... No. 3.

Historical accounts:

1938 DISHER, M. W.
Winkles and Champagne... p. 39.
1954 WILSON, A. E.
East end entertainment... p. 217-8.
1952 HACKNEY GAZETTE. 1952, Sept. 19th.
Correspondence—2 letters on the history of the Sebright.

Location of other material

Playbills, cuttings &c.: Bethnal Green Local Collection.

720

SEKFORDE ARMS PUBLIC HOUSE

34, Sekforde Street, Clerkenwell.

Licensed: 1851-1862, 1866-1891

Building details

The concert room was situated on the 1st floor, and was 29′ 6″ × 19′ 2″. It was closed as a result of the 1878 Act.

Management

Middlesex justices:

Mich.	1851-	Edward Parfitt
"	1855-	Boyfield Wortley
"	1861	Alice O'Connell
"	1862	*Licence refused to Thomas Smith.*
"	1866-	George Masters
"	1871-	Harriet James
"	1874-	Frederick Backlof
"	1879-	George Reuter
"	1882-	Sarah Ann Reuter
"	1888	Sarah Ann Fenwick

London County Council:

1890-1891	Sarah Ann Fenwick
Nov. 1891	*No application.*

Literature

Official records:

G.L.C. Arch. Dpt. Th. case 040/140;
L.C.C. Th. & M-H. Com. App. Nov. 1889-1890;
Mx. Mich. Q.S. 1851-62, 1866-88.

Location of other material

Plans: G.L.C. *Architects Department.*

721

SESSIONS HOUSE HOTEL

Turnmill Street, Clerkenwell.

Licensed: 1866-1877

Management

Middlesex justices:

Mich.	1866-	William House
"	1876-	Charles Smith
"	1877	*House destroyed, no notice served.*

Literature

Official records:

Mx. Mich. Q.S. 1866-1877.

722

SEVEN STARS PUBLIC HOUSE

Brick Lane, Christchurch.

Licensed: 1852-1884

Management

Middlesex justices:

Mich. 1852 - John Robert Bowen
" 1862 - David Charles Bansback
" 1866 - William Lindsay
" 1871 - Hubert Rowe
" 1874 Thomas Bridge
" 1875 - John Harris
" 1877 - George Ratcliff
" 1880 - William Lovesay (Lovesy)
" 1884 *Licence refused.*

Literature

Official records:

Mx. Mich. Q.S. 1852-1884.

723

SEYMOUR ARMS PUBLIC HOUSE

42, Upper Seymour Street.

Licensed: 1855-1857

Management

Middlesex justices:

Mich. 1855 - Thomas Willes
" 1857 *No answer.*

Literature

Official records:

Mx. Mich. Q.S. 1855-1857.

724

SHADWELL DOCK COFFEE HOUSE

Griffin Street, Lower Shadwell.

Licensed: pre 1850-1854

Management

Middlesex justices:

Mich. 1848 - James Thomson
" 1850 - Daniel Ross
" 1854 *No petition, no application.*

Literature

Official records:

Mx. Mich. Q.S. 1848-1854.

725

SHAFTESBURY THEATRE

Shaftesbury Avenue, Westminster.

Opened: 20.10.1888. *Destroyed by bombing:* 17.4.1941.

Building details

Architect: C. J. Phipps

Capacity: 1,196

Auditorium: S. 177; P. 278; D.C. 187; U.C. 189; G. 355.

218

Stage: 28' 6" wide × 28' 6" deep.

Site still vacant 1969.

Management

Lord Chamberlain:

20.10.1888 - John Lancaster
28. 9.1889 - Edward Willard and John Lart
28. 9.1890 - John Lancaster
28. 9.1891 - George Edwardes
28. 9.1892 - Ada Rosalind Bennett Edwardes
7. 1.1893 - Marie Halton (Mrs. Richard Foster)
29. 9.1893 - Herbert J. Pearson
16.10.1895 - Lewis Waller and Henry Harvey Morell
29. 9.1896 - Adolph Henri Chamberlyn
1898 - (undated app.) George Musgrove
8. 4.1905 - Tita Brand
7. 6.1905 - Alfred Herbert Briggs and George Kirkham —Trustees of will of late John Lancaster.
26. 9.1905 - Thomas William Ryley (new lessee) —22. 5.1906 licence withdrawn through failure to do building work required. Ryley defaulted and theatre reclaimed by owners.
22.12.1906 - Alfred Henry Briggs and G. W. C. Kirkham
31.10.1907 - Ells Dagnall
1.11.1908 - Henry Brodrib Irving
20. 4.1909 - Robert Courtneidge
20. 6.1917 - Edward Laurillard
23.10.1920 - George Grossmith and Edward Laurillard
1. 7.1921 - George Grossmith and Joseph Archibald Edward Malone
1.12.1926 - William Clifford Gaunt
1.12.1931 - George Brunton McLallan
1.12.1932 - James Ernest Sharpe
1.12.1933 - Thomas Henry Bostock
1.12.1940 - William Foster Horsfield (Bombed April 1941)

Literature

Official records:

G.L.C. Arch. Dpt. Mss. Index;
G.L.C. Arch. Dpt. Th. case 449;
L.C.C. Th. & M-H. Com. Papers. 1888-;
LC 1/508-752; LC 7/35-48; L.C.O. 320 and 374.

Contemporary accounts:

1888 ERA 1888 Sept. —Description
PALL MALL BUDGET. 1888, Oct. 18th. p.15. —Drawing of exterior.
1897 ERA 1888 Oct. 20th. —Description
1897 SACHS, E. *and* WOODROW, E.
Modern opera houses and theatres. Vol. III. Various refs. plans and plates.
1941 SPHERE. 1941, Sept. 27th. —Illus. of theatre after bombing.

Historical accounts:

c. 1930 MAYES, Ronald
The romance of London theatres. No. 38.
1959 ENCICLOPEDIA dello spettacolo. Vol 6, Col. 1634.
1966 GREATER LONDON COUNCIL
Survey of London, Vol. 33, 1966. pp. 304-306. plans.

1968 MANDER, Raymond *and* MITCHENSON, Joe.
The lost theatres of London. pp. 492-505 2 illus.

Location of other material

Plans: G.L.C. *Architects Department.*

Programmes:

British Museum Library; Enthoven Collection;
Garrick Club; Guildhall Library; London Museum;
Westminster Local Collection.

726

SHAKESPEARE PUBLIC HOUSE

Downs Park Road, Hackney.

Licensed: 1867-1884

Management

Middlesex justices:

Mich. 1867-	Frank Luke Ridge
" 1873-	John W. F. Cox
" 1875-	William Henry Bedding
" 1884	*Application withdrawn.*

Literature

Official records:

Mx. Mich. Q.S. 1867-1884.

727

SHAKESPEARE THEATRE AND OPERA HOUSE

Lavender Hill, Battersea.

Opened: 16th November, 1896. *Cinema by* Nov. 1923
Demolished: 1956/7

Building details

Architect: W.G.R. Sprague

Contractor: Charles Gray Hill

Capacity: 1, 205

Auditorium: S. 74; P. 475; D.C. 90; B. 150; G. 400; Bx. 16.

Management

London County Council:

1896-	William Bennett
1907	Henry George Dudley Bennett
1909-	William Bennett
1912	Henry George Dudley Bennett
1913	Frederic Nevile Baildon
1914-	Thomas Edwin Baxter
1916	Joseph Clozenberg
1917-	Joseph Charles Clavering
Nov. 1923	*Listed as cinema.*

Literature

Official records:

G.L.C. Arch. Dpt. Mss. Index;
G.L.C. Arch. Dpt. Th. case 330;
G.L.C. Th. & M-H. Com. App. Nov. 1896-1923.

Contemporary accounts:

1896 BUILDER. 1896, Jan. 4th. p. 20. —Description
of plans of new theatre.
LONDON. 1896, Feb. 20th. p. 170. —Report and
description. Illus. of front elevation.
BUILDER. 1896, June 27th. p. 563. —Report of
laying of commemoration stone by Forbes
Robertson. —Description.
SKETCH. 1896, Nov. 25th. —Description. Illus.

Historical accounts:

c.1930 MAYES, Ronald
The romance of London theatres, No. 196.

Location of other material

Plans: G.L.C. *Architects Department.*

Programmes:

Enthoven Collection; Garrick Club; Guildhall Library.

728

SHAKESPEARE'S HEAD PUBLIC HOUSE

46, Percival Street, Clerkenwell.

Licensed: 1861-1889

Management

Middlesex justices:

| Mich. 1861- | William Stebbing |
| " 1863- | Henry Boyce (to 1889) |

Literature

Official records:

Mx. Mich. Q.S. 1861-1888.

729

SHELLEY THEATRE

Tite Street, Chelsea.

In use: 1882

A private theatre belonging to Sir Percy F. Shelley,
seating 250 people.

Literature

Contemporary accounts:

1879 BUILDING NEWS. 1879, May 16th. p. 535.
—Private theatre.
1882 BUILDER. 1882, June 3rd. p. 690. —Report of
performance.
1896 BUILDER. 1896, March 7th. p. 210. —Report of
proposed demolition & auction of site.

730

SHEPHERDS BUSH EMPIRE

Shepherds Bush, Hammersmith.

Opened: 17th. Aug. 1903

Building details

Architect: Frank Matcham

Capacity: 2,332

Auditorium: S. 471; P. 396; D.C. & Bx. 299; U.C. 270; G. 419.

Management

London County Council:

1905-	Oswald Stoll
1925-	Hackney and Shepherds Bush Empires Ltd. (through 1950)

Literature

Official records:

G.L.C. Arch. Dpt. Mss. Index;
G.L.C. Arch. Dpt. Th. case 331;
L.C.C. Th. & M-H. Com. App. Nov. 1904-;

Contemporary accounts:

1950 THEATRE ownership...p. 128.

Location of other material

Plans: G.L.C. *Architects Department.*

Cuttings, programmes &c: Enthoven Collection.

731

SHIP PUBLIC HOUSE

Camden Street, St. Mary, Islington.

Licensed: 1852-1854

Management

Middlesex justices:

Mich. 1852-	William Webb
" 1854	Petition sent in the name of John Latham Canish. No notice of transfer. Opposition petitions. *Licence refused.*

Literature

Official records:

Mx. Mich. Q.S. 1852-1854.

732

SHIP PUBLIC HOUSE

Fore Street, Lambeth.

Licensed: 1850-1867

Management

Surrey justices:

Mich. 1850-	Andrew Wentzell
" 1867	*No application.*

Literature

Official records:

Sy. Mich. Q.S. 1850-1866.

733

SHIP PUBLIC HOUSE

George Street, Woolwich.

Licensed: 1867-1887

Management

West Kent justices:

Mich. 1867-	Ellen Sloman
" 1885-	Clarence Thomas Curtis
" 1887	*No application.*

Literature

Official records:

W. Kt. Mich. Q.S. 1867-1887.

734

SHIP PUBLIC HOUSE

High Street, Mile End, New Town.

Licensed: 1855-1861

Management

Middlesex justices:

Mich. 1855-	Henry Peter Geils
" 1857-	George Brice Sainsbury
" 1860	William Edmonds Lambert
" 1861	*No application, no petition.*

Literature

Official records:

Mx. Mich. Q.S. 1855-1861.

735

SHIP PUBLIC HOUSE

25, Vauxhall Bridge Road, Westminster.

Licensed: 1854-55, 1869-1889

Management

Middlesex justices:

Mich. 1854	Robert Clayton
" 1855	*No application.*
" 1869-	James Edward Miles
" 1872-	William Purchase (except Michaelmas 1882)

Literature

Official records:

Mx. Mich. Q.S. 1854, 1869-1888.

736

SHIP AND BLUE COAT BOY PUBLIC HOUSE

286, Walworth Road, Camberwell.

Licensed: 1876-1888

Management

Surrey justices:

Mich.	1876-	Mannas Rantzon
"	1879-	Edward Smith
"	1881-	Annie Maria Smith
"	1882-	George Cooper
"	1884-	Edgard Guess
"	1888	*No application.*

Literature

Official records:

Sy. Mich. Q.S. 1876-1887.

737

SHIP AND CAMEL PUBLIC HOUSE

Bermondsey.

Licensed: 1854-1855

Management

Surrey justices:

Mich.	1854-	Henry Plimmer
"	1855	*No application.*

Literature

Official records:

Sy. Mich. Q.S. 1854-1855.

738

SHIP AND STAR PUBLIC HOUSE

112, Shadwell High Street, Shadwell.

Licensed: 1855-1869

Management

Middlesex justices:

Mich.	1855-	Alfred James Crawley
"	1856-	Robert James Feather
"	1858-	Elizabeth Feather
"	1861-	Robert James Feather
"	1867-	Isaac John Hilldrup
"	1869	*Licence refused following a court case.*

Literature

Official records:

Mx. Mich. Q.S. 1856-1869.

739

SHOREDITCH EMPIRE

95-99, Shoreditch High Street, (*formerly* Holywell Street), Shoreditch.

Opened as a place of entertainment: 1856. *Closed as theatre:* 1934

Former names

Griffin Music Hall and Public House to 1896
London Music Hall 1896-1916 and occasionally after.
London Theatre of Varieties 1895

Building details

Griffin Music Hall

Capacity: (1892) 250

Shepherds Bush Empire (730)

(Hammersmith Public Libraries)

The London Music Hall (739)

(John R. Freeman & Co.)

1894 Reconstruction:

Architect: Frank Matcham

Auditorium: P. 320; B. 258; G. 323.

Capacity: approx. 1, 000

Management

Middlesex justices:

Mich.	1856-	William Smith
"	1866-	John Hamlin
"	1876	James Blumson
"	1877-	George Neary
"	1882-	Mary Catherine Walsh
"	1884	John Henry Williams
"	1885-	Alfred Neary

London County Council:

1890	Alfred Neary
1891-	Barney Morris
1893-	Edward Arpthorp
1895-	Edwin Samuel Barnes (London Theatre of Varieties)
1901-	William Henry Burney
1916-	John McMullen Brooks
1921-	Victor Sylvester Peel
1923	Percy Weiller Straus
1924	Frederick Thomas Peel
1925-	Shoreditch Theatre (London) Ltd.
Nov. 1934	*Not licensed as theatre or music hall.*

Lord Chamberlain:

1.12.1919-	John McMullan Brooks
20. 3.1920-	Victor Sylvester Peel
8. 4.1922-	Percy Weiller Straus. *Receiver.*
1.12.1923-	Frederick Thomas Peel (to 30.11. 1934)

Literature

Official records:

G.L.C. Arch. Dpt. Mss. Index; G.L.C. Arch. Dpt. Th. case 201; L.C.C. Th. & M-H. Com. App. Nov. 1889-1934; L.C.O. 69 and 374; Mx. Mich. Q.S. 1856-1888; Sel. Com. 1892.

Contemporary accounts:

1893 BUILDER. 1893, Dec. 16th. p. 455.—Company formed to buy theatre.

1934 HACKNEY GAZETTE. 1934, June 6th. 'Future of the old London Music Hall'—Bought by Jeremiah Rotherham & Co., Drapery ware housemen.

1935 SUNDAY DESPATCH. 1935, Mar. 17th.—Illus. of demolition work.

Historical accounts:

1952 HACKNEY GAZETTE, 1952, Jan. 19th. 'Echos of the past'—Opening of the London Theatre of Varieties.

1954 WILSON, A. E. East End entertainment...p. 219-220.

Location of other material

Plans: G.L.C. *Architects Department.*

Newscuttings, playbills &c:

Enthoven Collection; Guildhall Library (1 item for 1896)

222

740

SHOREDITCH OLYMPIA

203-4, Shoreditch High Street, Shoreditch.

Opened as a place of entertainment: 1837
In use as cinema: Nov. 1926

Former names

Royal Standard Public House and Pleasure Gardens
Royal Standard Theatre
New Standard Theatre
Standard Theatre
National Standard Theatre
Olympia, Shoreditch.

Building details

1st building:

Interior in horse shoe form.
Proscenium 30' wide × 30' high.
Stage could be removed for circus performances.

Capacity: 3, 400

Destroyed by fire: 21.10.1866.

2nd building:

Opened: Dec. 1867

Capacity: approx. 3, 000

Auditorium: S. & P. 670; B.C. 579; L.C. 405; U. Bx. 485; G. 719.

3rd building:

Architect: Bertie Crewe

Capacity: 2, 463

Auditorium: S. & P. 903; 1st C. 397; 2nd C. 354; G. 480; Bx. 36.

Management

Lord Chamberlain:

29. 9.1843-	John Grundy
29. 9.1844-	John Johnson and Richard Nelson Lee
29. 9.1848-	John Douglass
29. 9.1861-	Robert Edgar
29. 9.1864-	John Douglass
26. 2.1874-	John T. Douglass and Samuel Richard Douglass
1. 7.1884-	John (T. ?) Douglass
29. 9.1885-	John Thomas Douglass
28. 9.1888-	Richard Douglass
13. 4.1889-	Andrew Melville
3. 8.1896-	Alice Melville
29. 9.1904-	Walter Melville and Frederick Melville (to 31.10.1907)
4.12.1911-	Walter Gibbons
2. 7.1912-	Charles Gulliver
1.12.1926	*Licensed to Arthur Gilbert as New Olympia Picturedrome* Continued to have Lord Chamberlain's licence until 1939.

London County Council:

1908-	Walter Gibbons
1913-	Charles Gulliver
1925-	London Theatres of Varieties
Nov. 1926	*Not listed as theatre or music hall.*

Literature

Official records:

G.L.C. Arch. Dpt. Mss. Index; G.L.C. Arch. Dpt. Th. case 241; L.C.C. Th. & M-H. Com. App. Nov. 1907-25; LC 1/508-752; LC 7/13-17; 20-48; 89. M.B.W. Rpt. 1882, p. 315-333; Sel. Com. 1866, 1877 and 1892.

Contemporary accounts:

1845 ILLUSTRATED LONDON NEWS. 1845, May. 'New Standard Theatre'.

1849 DAVIS & VICERS. *Auctioneers*. Particulars and conditions of sale... Royal Standard Theatre (to be) sold by auction... at the Auction Mart... on Thursday, 15th November, 1849. (Copy in Shoreditch Local Collection.)

1866 BUILDER. 1866, Oct. 27th. p. 800.—Report of fire on previous Sunday.
ILLUSTRATED SPORTING AND DRAMATIC NEWS. 1866, Oct. 27th. 'Destruction by fire of the Standard Theatre'.

1867 BUILDER. 1867, Dec. 28th. p. 941-2.—Description of new building. Illus. of auditorium.

1868 BUILDER. 1868, Nov. 14th. p. 846.—Report of rating case Douglass v. St. Leonard, Shoreditch, at the Middlesex Sessions.

1876 BUILDER. 1876, Jan. 1st. p. 4.—Report of rebuilding with description of new front elevation. (+correction 15. 1. 1876, p. 64)

1879 ILLUSTRATED SPORTING AND DRAMATIC NEWS. 1879, July 5th. 'Our captious critic'— Questioning of right to call it 'the largest and most magnificat theatre in the world.'

1882 FAREBROTHER & CO.
Particulars and conditions of sale... comprising the National Standard Theatre... Bishopsgate Hall adjoining... which will be auctioned... Thursday, Nov. 16th. 1882.—Includes large ground plan. (Copy in Shoreditch Local Collection).
BUILDER. 1882, Nov. 25th. p. 682.—Report of sale.

1884 BUILDER. 1884, March 29th and April 12th. p. 434, 459-60, 528.—Reports of inquiry and M.B.W. requirements of alterations.

1887 SATURDAY REVIEW. 1887, July 23rd. The state of the London theatres... No. 6.

1888 BUILDER. 1888, Aug. 25th. p. 134.—Report of proposed sale following court order.
BUILDER. 1888, Oct. 13th. p. 271.—Report of auction.

1940 HACKNEY GAZETTE. 1940, Jan. 24th.—Demolition report.

Historical accounts:

1879 DRAMATIC NOTES. 1879, p. 68-9.

1898 SHOREDITCH OBSERVER. 1898, Feb. 12th. 'Correspondence on Old Shoreditch No. X' 1 paragraph.

1904 BAKER, H. Barton.
History of the London stage and its players... pp. 408-409.

1925 DOUGLASS, Albert.
Memories of mummers and the old Standard Theatre. Era, 1925. 138 p.

1927 HACKNEY GAZETTE, 1927 June 20th. '100 years of Shoreditch history, 1854'.—Note of erection.

c. 1930 MAYES, Ronald.
The romance of London theatres, No. 39 and 147.

National Standard Theatre (740)

(Victoria & Albert Museum, Crown copyright)

National Standard Theatre (740)

(Victoria & Albert Museum, Crown copyright)

1946 SCOTT, Harold.
Early doors...p. 71 et seq.
1954 WILSON, A. E.
East end entertainment... Chapters X and XI.
1959 ENCICLOPEDIA dello spettacolo. Vol. 6, Col. 1635.

Location of other material

Plans: G.L.C. *Architects Department;*

Enthoven Collection; Public Record Office, LC7/80 5 sheets dated 9.12.1897.

Programmes and playbills:

British Museum Library; Enthoven Collection; Garrick Club; Guildhall Library.

741

SILVER CUP PUBLIC HOUSE

17, Cromer Street, Grays Inn Road, St. Pancras.

Building details

Concert room on the 1st floor, 40′ × 13′ with platform 10′ × 7′ 4″. The hall was closed as a result of the 1878 Act.

Literature

Official records:

G.L.C. Arch. Dpt. Th. case 040/147.

742

SIR JOHN BARLEYCORN PUBLIC HOUSE

Thomas Street, Whitechapel Road, Whitechapel.

Licensed: 1853-1860

Management

Middlesex justices:

Mich. 1853	Thomas Hastilow
" 1854-	John Smith
" 1859	Thomas Adams
" 1860	*Police complaint. Licence refused.*

Literature

Official records:

Mx. Mich. Q.S. 1854-1860.

743

SIR JOHN CASS PUBLIC HOUSE

52, Victoria Park Road, Hackney.

Licensed: 1855-1863, 1870-1890.

Management

Middlesex justices:

| Mich. 1855 | Joseph Collins |
| " 1856- | Richard George Steib (except 1863-70). |

London County Council:

| 1890 | Richard George Steib |
| Nov. 1890 | *Licence refused.* |

Literature

Official records:

L.C.C. Th. & M-H. Com. App. Nov. 1889-90; Mx. Mich. Q.S. 1855-63, 1870-88.

744

SIR JOHN FALSTAFF MUSIC HALL AND PUBLIC HOUSE

53 (formerly 126) Old Street, St. Luke, Finsbury.

Licensed: 1852-1899

Former name

Falstaff Music Hall and Public House

Building details

Capacity: 250

Management

Middlesex justices:

Mich. 1852-	Luke James Marshall
" 1868-	James Short
" 1871-	Thomas Smith
" 1878-	Alfred Smith
" 1880-	William Hall
" 1884	Alfred Robert Vallance
" 1885-	Louisa Mary Ann Vallance
" 1888	Frederick Naylor

London County Council:

1890	Frederick Naylor
1891-	Lionel Fairweather
1893-	David John Barnard
1896-	Henry William Parker
Nov. 1899	*Licence refused.*

Literature

Official records:

G.L.C. Arch. Dpt. Th. case 1345; L.C.C. Th. & M-H. Com. App. Nov. 1889-1899; Mx. Mich. Q.S. 1852-1888; Sel. Com. 1892.

Historical accounts:

1938 DISHER, M. W.
Winkles and champagne...p. 39.—Mentions Marie Lloyd sang at the Falstaff.

Location of other material

Plans: G.L.C. *Architects Department.*

Playbills: Guildhall Library (1 item)

745

SIR JOHN FALSTAFF PUBLIC HOUSE

Deptford.

Licensed: 1847-1853

Management

West Kent justices:

Mich. 1847-	William Brooks
" 1851-	William Henry Mussett
" 1853	*No application.*

Literature

Official records:

W. Kt. Mich. Q.S. 1847-1852.

746

SIR JOHN FRANKLIN PUBLIC HOUSE

St. Leonard's Road, Bromley.

Licensed: 1862-1863

Management

Middlesex justices:

| Mich. 1862- | Francis Rogers |
| " 1863 | *No answer, but would not have been renewed as it was a beer house.* |

Literature

Official records:

Mx. Mich. Q.S. 1862-1863.

747

SIR ROBERT PEEL PUBLIC HOUSE

Eagle Wharf Road, Shoreditch.

Licensed: 1852-1858

Management

Middlesex justices:

| Mich. 1852- | Henry Brading |
| " 1858 | *No petition.* |

Literature

Official records:

Mx. Mich. Q.S. 1852-1858.

748

SIR SIDNEY SMITH PUBLIC HOUSE

11, Dock Street, Whitechapel.

Licensed: 1855-1869.

Management

Middlesex justices:

Mich. 1855-	Henry Mogge
" 1863	Nicholas Pollybank
" 1864-	James Richard Andrews
" 1867-	Thomas Gooding
" 1869	*Licence refused, no notice served.*

Literature

Official records:

Mx. Mich. Q.S. 1855-1869.

749

SKINNER'S ARMS PUBLIC HOUSE

Coburg Street, Clerkenwell.

Licensed: 1858-1862

Management

Middlesex justices:

Mich. 1858	Charles Wright
" 1859	Robert Woodward
" 1860-	William Saunders
" 1862	*George Soole's application withdrawn.*

Literature

Official records:

Mx. Mich. Q.S. 1858-1862.

750

SOMERSET ARMS PUBLIC HOUSE

Someset Place, New Road, Mile End.

Licensed: 1855-1862

Management

Middlesex justices:

| Mich. 1855- | Henry Thomas Clubb |
| " 1862 | *Licence refused owing to sale of spirits.* |

Literature

Official records:

Mx. Mich. Q.S. 1855-1862.

751

SOUTH LONDON PALACE OF VARIETIES

92, London Road, Lambeth.

Opened: 30th December, 1860.

Former name

South London Music Hall

Building details

1st building

Cost: £8, 000

Capacity: 1, 200

Destroyed by fire: 28.3.1869.

2nd building:

Opened: 19.12.1869

Architect: William Paice

Builder: Messrs. Langmeed & Way.

Capacity: c. 4, 000

Auditorium: P. 287; S. 386; B. 240; G. 390.

Management

Surrey justices:

Mich. 1860-	James Frederick Tindall and Robert Edwin Villiers
" 1862-	Robert Edwin Villiers
" 1873-	Henry Speedy and John Poole
" 1880-	John Joshua Poole
" 1882-	Ellen Poole

London County Council:

1890-	Ellen Poole
1896-	Acton Phillips Jnr.
1897-	Frank Egerton
1898-	Frederick Walace McAvoy
1900-	Gilbert Hastings Macdermott
1902-	Frank Weeks
1907-	William Payne
1908-	Ilford Ibbetson
1925-	Variety Theatres Consolidated Ltd.
Nov. 1940	*Not listed as theatre or music hall.*

Lord Chamberlain:

10. 1.1912-	Ilford Ibbetson
1.12.1932-	Walter Payne

(Until 1941 when theatre was closed by war damage).

Literature

Official records:

G.L.C. Arch. Dpt. Mss. Index; G.L.C. Arch. Dpt. Th. case 333; L.C.C. Th. & M-H. Com. App. Nov. 1889-1939; L.C.O. 374 and 509; Sel. Com. 1866, 1877 and 1892; Sy. Mich. Q.S. 1860-88.

Contemporary accounts:

1860 SOUTH LONDON CHRONICLE. 1860, March 17th. 'Refusal of licence to the proposed music hall in the London Road at the General Licensing Meeting.'
1869 BUILDER. 1869, Sept. 18th.—Report of foundation stone ceremony.
1870 BUILDING NEWS. 1870, May 13th. p. 361.— Report and description.
1870 SOUTH LONDON PALACE JOURNAL. 1870, Oct. 3rd.+
1875 ORGILL, J. J., SWANN & ORGILL. *Auctioneers.* Particulars and conditions of sale of the exceedingly valuable lease with possession of the South London Palace... for sale by auction ... 11th Jan. 1875. (Copies in Southwark Local Collection).
1887 SATURDAY REVIEW. 1887, Aug. 27th. The state of the London... music halls... No. 3.
1955 EVENING NEWS. 1955, Jan. 21st. 'Palace where a "Baron" glittered is coming down for shops'.
SOUTH LONDON PRESS. 1955, Jan. 21st.— Report of demolition.

Historical accounts:

c.1930 MAYES, Ronald
The romance of London theatres, No. 194.
1935 HADDON, Archibald
The story of the Music Hall... p. 43-47, 53, 130. Illus.
1938 RADIO TIMES. 1938, Oct. 7th. illus. of interior.— Broadcast on Fri. 14th Oct. 1938, by Leslie Bailey. Transcript in Lambeth Local Collection.
1959 ENCICLOPEDIA dello spettacolo. Vol. 6., Col. 1634.

Location of other material

Plans: G.L.C. Architects Department.
Enthoven Collection 1925 (2 sheets)

Programmes: London Museum

Playbills: Guildhall Library

752

SOUTH METROPOLITAN TEMPERANCE HALL

115, Blackfriars Road, Southwark.

Licensed: 1877-1896

Management

Surrey justices:

Mich. 1877-	John Mann

London County Council:

1890-	John Mann
Nov. 1896	*Licence refused.*

Literature

Official records:

L.C.C. Th. & M-H. Com. App. Nov. 1889-1896; Sy. Mich. Q.S. 1877-1888.

753

SOUTHWARK PARK MUSIC HALL AND PUBLIC HOUSE

Southwark Park Road, (*formerly* 138, Jamaica Level), Bermondsey.

Licensed: 1874-1889.

Building details

The music hall was situated on the first floor, 39'10"× 18'3"; it had a small movable platform and could seat 150 people.
It was closed as a result of the 1878 Act.

Management

Surrey justices:

Mich. 1874-		George Freeland
"	1878-	George Page
"	1883	William Ellis
"	1884	Thomas Foster
"	1885	Arthur Emmett and George Wyatt
"	1886-	William Henry Jacks
"	1888	James Lee

London County Council:

Nov. 1889	*Licence refused.*

Literature

Official records:

G.L.C. Arch. Dpt. Th. case 040/151; L.C.C. Th. & M-H. Com. App. Nov. 1889; Sy. Mich. Q.S. 1874-1888.

754

SOUTHWARK MUSIC HALL

Flourishing c. 1856.

RITCHIE, J. Ewing
The Night side of London... p. 221-226.

755

SPORTSMAN PUBLIC HOUSE

315, City Road, (*formerly* Oakley Crescent, City Road) St. Luke, Finsbury.

Licensed: 1852-1889

Management

Middlesex justices:

Mich. 1852-	William Michael Chamberlain	
" 1854-	George Chamberlain	
" 1857-	James Drewry	
" 1860-	Alexander Macdonald	
" 1862	James Drewry	
" 1863-	Thomas Bray	
" 1869-	Adolphus Frederick Esse	
" 1873-	John Bayes	
" 1876-	Thomas Daniel Spurgin	
" 1884-	Arthur Jones (to 1889).	

Literature

Official records:

Mx. Mich. Q.S. 1852-1888.

756

SPREAD EAGLE PUBLIC HOUSE

1, Kingsland Road, Shoreditch.

Licensed: 1848-64, 1867-1889

Building details

The hall was on the first floor, and had a small plat-
form. It was closed as a result of the 1878 Act.
The public house was later demolished for North
London Railway.

Management

Middlesex justices:

Mich. 1848-	William Grove
" 1861-	George John Graham
" 1862-	Thomas Sell
" 1864-	*Licence refused* to James Bonney.
" 1867-	Samuel Keable
" 1872-	James Frederick Gibbs
" 1882-	Harry Thomas Brown
" 1883-	James Collins
" 1885-	Charles William Bates
" 1888	August Haitsch.

London County Council:

Nov. 1889 *Licence refused.*

Literature

Official records:

G.L.C. Arch. Dpt. Th. case 040/153;
L.C.C. Th. & M-H. Com. App. Nov. 1889;
Mx. Mich. Q.S. 1848-64, 1867-88.

Historical accounts:

1898 SHOREDITCH OBSERVER. 1898, Feb. 12th.
Correspondence: Chapters on Old Shoreditch
No. X.

757

SPREAD EAGLE ASSEMBLY ROOMS AND HOTEL

Wandsworth High Street, Wandsworth.

Licensed: 1859, 1864-1903.

Building details

Capacity: 323

Management

Surrey justices:

Mich. 1859	James Henry Dea
" 1864-	James Philip Brown
" 1866-	Joseph Bridge Bell
" 1869-	Thomas Hammond
" 1874-	Henry Dougherty
" 1888	John Lakin Maple

London County Council:

1890-	John La(r)kin Maple
1895	Eliza Maple
1896-	Annie Marie Mudd
1898	Zachariah Chaplin
1899-	Henry Paice Stuart
Nov. 1903	*Not listed as a theatre or music hall.*

Literature

Official records:

L.C.C. Th. & M-H. Com. App. Nov. 1889-1903;
Sel. Com. 1892; Sy. Mich. Q.S. 1859, 1864-88.

Contemporary accounts:

1859 SUNDAY TIMES. 1859, April 17th.—Review of
'The Juvenile Comedians'.

South London Palace (751)

(Ellis Ashton Collection, British Music Hall Society)

STAG PUBLIC HOUSE

Brooksby Walk, Homerton, Hackney.

Licensed: 1860-1867

Management:

Middlesex justices:

Mich. 1860-   Edwin Hedges
"   1863-   James Frederick Munro
"   1867   *No notice, no petition.*

Literature

Official records:

Mx. Mich. Q.S. 1860-1867.

759

STANDARD MUSIC HALL

32, Stockbridge Terrace, Pimlico.

The Select Committee on Theatres and Places of Entertainment says it had a capacity of 400.

It existed prior to 1871 to after 1886.

760

STANHOPE ARMS PUBLIC HOUSE

Oval Road, Camden Town.

Licensed: 1850-1864, 1868-1882

Management

Middlesex justices:

Mich. 1850-   George Freeborn
"   1864   *No notice, no petition.*
"   1868-   George Freeborn
"   1882   *Not licenced:*

Literature

Official records:

Mx. Mich. Q.S. 1850-64, 1868-82.

761

STAR MUSIC HALL

Star and Garter Public House, 189, Abbey Street, (*formerly* Neckinger Rd.) Bermondsey.

Licensed: 1867-1919 *Demolished:* 1963

Building details

Capacity: 1, 395

Auditorium: Ar. 364; B. 233; G. 224.

Management

Surrey justices:

Mich. 1867-   Thomas Hayes
"   1879   Frederick William Evans
"   1880   Thomas Hayes
"   1881   Edward Bartholomew

"   1883-   Henry Hart
"   1885-   John Hart

London County Council:

1890-   John Hart
Nov. 1919   *Not licensed as theatre or music hall.*

Literature

Official records:

G.L.C. Arch. Dpt. Mss. Index;
L.C.C. Th. & M-H. Com. App. Nov. 1889-1918;
Sel. Com. 1892; Sy. Mich. Q.S. 1867-1888.

Historical accounts:

1952 PULLING, Christopher
    The were singing. . . p. 182.
1964 FLETCHER, Geoffrey S.
    London overlooked.—Illus. of exterior.

Location of other material

Playbill:

Bermondsey Local Collection *also* copy in Enthoven Collection; Guildhall Library (1 item for 1896).

762

STAR AND GARTER PUBLIC HOUSE

13, Green Street, Leicester Square, St. Martin in the Fields.

Licensed: 1858-1862.

Management

Middlesex justices:

Mich. 1858-   Richard Stevens
"   1859-   John Cook
"   1862   *Licence refused to John Wood.*

Literature

Official records:

Mx. Mich. Q.S. 1858-1862.

763

STAR AND GARTER PUBLIC HOUSE

Kingsland, Hackney.

Licensed: 1856-1859

Management

Middlesex justices:

Mich. 1856-   Matthew Hitchcock
"   1859   *No petition.*

Literature

Official records:

Mx. Mich. Q.S. 1856-1859.

764

STOLL THEATRE

Kingsway.

Opened: 13th November, 1911. *Closed:* 4th August, 1957.

Former names

London Opera House
National Theatre of England (1914-15)
Stoll Picture Theatre

Building details

Architect: Bertie Crewe

Built for: Oscar Hammerstein

Capacity: 2, 660 (2, 420 when theatre closed).

Auditorium: S. & Bx. 739; Bx. C. 140; C. & Bx. 678; L.C. 403; U.C. 344.

Stage: 44′8″ × 78′

Demolished and replaced by office block into which is incorporated the Royalty Theatre.

Management

Lord Chamberlain:

31. 10. 1911-	Oscar Hammerstein
26. 12. 1912-	Ben Nathan
17. 6. 1913-	Edward Arthur Vesey Stanley
17. 9. 1914-	Clarkes Blake Cochran
23. 11. 1914-	Henry Langley
5. 4. 1915-	Edmond Henry Wiley
15. 5. 1916-	Oswald Stoll
Letter 8. 4. 1919 no longer licensed by Lord Chamberlain: a cinema	
29. 9. 1928-	Oswald Stoll
29. 9. 1942-	Prince Littler

London County Council:

1913	Oscar Hammerstein
1914	Edward Arthur Vesey Stanley
1915-	Esmond Henry Wiley
1917-	Oswald Stoll
Nov. 1919	*Licensed as a cinema.*
1948-	Stoll Theatre, Kingsway, Ltd.

Literature

Official records:

G.L.C. Arch. Dpt. Mss. Index; G.L.C. Arch. Dpt. Th. case 1639; L.C.C. Th. & M-H. Com. App. Nov. 1913- 1919, 1947-; L.C.O. 374 and 562.

Contemporary accounts:

1910 BUILDER. 1910, Sept. 24th. p. 351.—'New Variety theatres. . .' Brief note of proposal to build opera house.
1950 THEATRE ownership. . . p. 58 and 86.
1955 ILLUSTRATED LONDON NEWS. 1955, Jan. 22nd.—Announcement of possible demolition.

Historical accounts:

c. 1930 MAYES, Ronald
The romance of London theatres, No. 66.
1959 ENCICLOPEDIA dello spettacolo, Vol. 6, Col. 1635.
1963 MANDER, Raymond *and* MITCHENSON, Joe
The theatres of London. 2nd ed. p. 158-161.

Location of other material

Plans: G.L.C. *Architects Department.*
Enthoven Collection., 1911 (4 sheets).

Programmes:

Enthoven Collection; Westminster Local Collection.

765

STRAND THEATRE

Aldwych.

Opened: 22nd May, 1905.

Former names

Waldorf Theatre 1905-9
Strand Theatre 1909-11
Whitney Theatre 1911-13

Building details

Architect: W. G. R. Sprague

Builder: S. & J. Waring

Capacity: 1, 193, (1950) 1, 210

Auditorium: S. 292; P. 230; D.C. 200; B. 196; G. 267; Bx. 8.

Stage: 31′ wide × 32′ deep
—Last three tier theatre to be built in London.

Management:

Lord Chamberlain:

4. 5. 1905-	Sam S. Shubert
15. 5. 1905-	Lee Shubert
31. 10. 1905-	George Brixton McLellan
1. 11. 1906-	Frederick James Turner
1. 11. 1907-	George Frederick Hughes Morgan
1. 11. 1908-	Henry Richard Smith
23. 10. 1909-	John Arthur Harrison
30. 4. 1910-	Austen Hurgon
1. 9. 1910-	Herbert Stanley Cooke
23. 1. 1911-	Arthur Frederick Hardy

London Opera House 1915 (764)

(Greater London Council Photograph Library)

13. 4.1911-	Frederick Clark Whitney
1. 9.1912-	Louis Meyer
1. 2.1915-	Edward Albert Pickering
1.12.1916-	Jose Gerald Levy, and Thomas Dett
30. 5.1919-	Jose Gerald Levy
1.12.1919-	Arthur Bouchier
1.12.1925-	Arthur Bouchier
1.12.1927-	George Grossmith
1.12.1931-	Violet Marion Beckett
1.12.1936-	Lionel Louis Falck

Literature

Official records:

G.L.C. Arch. Dpt. Mss. Index; G.L.C. Arch. Dpt. Th. case 452; L.C.C. Th. & M-H. Com. Papers 1905-; L.C.O. 374 and 385.

Contemporary accounts:

1904 BUILDER. 1904, Aug. 13th p. 185.—Brief report of building.
1905 ERA. 1905, May 20th.—Description.
BUILDING NEWS. 1905, May 12th. p. 675. —Brief description.
SKETCH. 1905, May 24th. p. 165.—Illus.
1950 THEATRE ownership. . . p. 75 and 110.

Historical accounts:

c. 1930 MAYES, Ronald
The romance of London theatres, No. 68.
1959 ENCICLOPEDIA dello spettacolo. Vo. 6., Col. 1635.
1963 MANDER, Raymond *and* MITCHENSON, Joe
The theatres of London. 2nd ed. p. 186-190.

Location of other material

Plans: G.L.C. *Architects Department;* Enthoven Collection. 1935 (2 sheets)

Programmes:
British Museum Library; Enthoven Collection; Garrick Club; Guildhall Library; London Museum; Westminster Local Collection.

766

STRAND THEATRE

168-9, Strand, Westminster.

Opened: 25th January, 1832. *Demolished:* 1905

Former names

New Strand (Subscription) Theatre
Punch's Playhouse and Marionette Theatre
Rayner's New Subscription Theatre in the Strand

Building details

Original cost: £30,000

Redecorated 1858

Architect: Samuel Field

Cost: £700

Enlarged: 1864

Architect: John Ellis

Builder: C. Foster

Capacity: 1,500

Reconstructed: 1882

Architect: C.J. Phipps

Builder: Messrs. Patman & Fotheringham

Decorators: Messrs. Jackson & Sons and E. Bell.

Management:

Lord Chamberlain:

29. 9.1843-	Richard Lawrence
12. 7.1844-	Henry Ball Roberts
12. 5.1845-	Coplestone Coward Hodges
29. 6.1845-	Jacques Phillippe
3.10.1846-	William Davidson
12.12.1846-	Benjamin Hurwith
21. 4.1847-	Frederick Fox Copper
29. 9.1848-	Edmund Hooper
16. 5.1849-	William Farren
2. 9.1850-	George Bolton
2.12.1850-	William Robert Copeland
27.12.1852-	Frederick William Allcroft
29. 9.1855-	Thomas Payne
5. 4.1858-	Louisa Swanborough
29. 9.1861-	Henry V. Swanborough
7. 6.1863-	William Henry Swanborough
29. 9.1864-	Mrs. Mary Ann Swanborough
29. 9.1885-	John Sleeper Clarke
29. 9.1899-	Thomas William Broadhurst and George Howells Broadhurst
29. 9.1900-	Frank Curzon (to 1904)

Literature

Official records:

G.L.C. Arch. Dpt. Th. case 05;
L.C.C. Th. & M-H. Com. Papers 1889-1905;
LC1/507-752; LC7/13-17, 20-33;
M.B.W. Rpt. 1882, p. 70-82.

Contemporary accounts:

1858 BUILDING NEWS. 1858, April 2nd. p. 348.— Note of repair and redecoration.
1865 BUILDER. 1865, Aug. 19th. p. 594.—Proposed reconstruction of roof.
ERA 1865, Nov. 12th.—Details of alterations
1882 BUILDING NEWS. 1882, Nov. 17th. p. 599. —Description of remodelling.
1887 SATURDAY REVIEW. 1887, June 18th. The state of London theatres. . . No. 2.
1905 BUILDER. 1905, Oct. 21st. p. 412.—Report of demolition for the building of the Aldwych Tube Station.

Historical accounts:

1872 ERA ALMANACK, 1872.
History of the Strand Theatre, by E. L. Blanchard
1879 DRAMATIC NOTES. 1879, p. 51-3.
1904 BAKER, H. Barton.
History of the London stage and its players. p. 43-50, 451.
1925 CHANCELLOR, E. B.
The pleasure haunts of London. . . p. 125-6.
SHERSON, Erroll
London's lost theatres. . . p. 211-236.
c. 1930 MAYES, Ronald
The romance of London theatres, No. 112.
1964 THEATRE WORLD. 1964, Oct. and Nov.
Lost London theatres, by N. M. Bligh. No. 20.
The (Old) Strand Theare. 5p. Illus.

1968 MANDER, Raymond *and* MITCHENSON, Joe
The Lost Theatres of London pp. 380-401
4 illus.

Location of other material

Plans:

G.L.C. *Architects Development.*
Public Record Office. LC 7/81. 8 sheets. 1882.

Programmes and playbills:

British Museum Library; Enthoven Collection;
Garrick Club; Guildhall Library; London Museum;
Westminster Local Collection.

767

STREATHAM HILL THEATRE

56-60, (or 100) Streatham Hill.

Opened: 18th November, 1929.

Management

London County Council:

1930-   Streatham Hill Playhouse, Ltd., and James
Walter Perry.

Literature

Official records:

G.L.C. Arch. Dpt. Th. case 4146;
L.C.C. Th. & M-H. Com. App. Nov. 1929-.

Contemporary accounts:

1929 BUILDER. 1929. Vol. 137, p. 908-912
STREATHAM HILL THEATRE (Publicity
pamphlet on opening) 32p.
c. 1930 MAYES, Ronald
The romance of London theatres, No. 150.

Location of other material

Plans: G.L.C. *Architects Department.*

Programmes:

British Museum Library; Enthoven Collection;
London Museum; Westminster Local Collection.

768

SUGAR LOAF HALL OF VARIETIES

187, Hanbury Street, Whitechapel.

Building details

The hall was situated at the back of the public house
on the ground floor. It held about 90 people, and was
closed as the result of the 1878 Act.

Literature

Official records:

G.L.C. Arch. Dpt. Th. case 040/154.—including plans.

769

SUGAR LOAF PUBLIC HOUSE

34, Betts Street, St. George in the East.

Licensed: 1854-1858, and 1861-1872

Management

Middlesex justices:

Mich. 1854-	James Owen
" 1856-	William Serjeant (to 1858)
" 1861-	Henry Sehrt
" 1866-	Peter Sehrt
" 1868-	Heinrich Schnacke
" 1872	*Licence refused as gambling was permitted.*

Literature

Official records:

Mx. Mich. Q.S. 1854-58, 1861-72.

770

SUGAR LOAF PUBLIC HOUSE

Church Street, Mile End New Town.

Licensed: 1859-1863

Management:

Middlesex justices:

Mich. 1859	Charles Frederick Rimbault
" 1860-	Alfred Greaves
" 1862	William John Tollady
" 1863	*No notice, no petition.*

Strand Theatre, Strand (766)

Literature

Official records:

Mx. Mich. Q.S. 1859-1862.

771

SUN MUSIC HALL

26, Knightsbridge High Street, Knightsbridge.

Licensed: 1851-1888, 1890

Former name

Rising Sun Public House

Later incorporated as the Shibays Concert Hall, into Humphreys Hall, q.v.

Building details

Capacity: 800

Cost: £5,000

Management

Middlesex justices:

Mich.	1851	William Wetherby
"	1852-	James MacKeeley
"	1854-	Edwin Williams
"	1881-	Henry Willson
"	1883	Ellen Dumain
"	1884	Henry Hart
"	1885-	James Charlton Humphreys.

London County Council:

	1890	James Charlton
Nov.	1890	*Licence refused.*

Literature

Official records:

G.L.C. Arch. Dpt. Th. case 028;
L.C.C. Th. & M-H. Com. App. Nov. 1889-90.
Mx. Mich. Q.S. 1851-1888

Historical accounts:

c. 1930 MAYES, Ronald
   The romance of London theatres, No. 221.
1935 HADDON, Archibald
   The story of the music hall...p. 36.
1938 DISHER, M.W.
   Winkles and champagne...p. 23.
1952 PULLING, Christopher
   They were singing...p. 178.

Location of other material

Plans: G.L.C. Architects Department.

Newscuttings and playbills; Enthoven Collection.

772

SUN PUBLIC HOUSE

Green Street, Bethnal Green.

Licensed: 1869-1903

Management

Middlesex justices:

Mich. 1869- William Yetton

London County Council:

	1890-	William Yetton
	1902-	William Yetton Junior
Nov.	1903	*Not listed as theatre or music hall.*

Literature

Official records:

L.C.C. Th. & M-H. Com. App. Nov. 1889-1903;
Mx. Mich. Q.S. 1869-1888.

773

SUN PUBLIC HOUSE

78, Gray's Inn Road, St. Andrew, Holborn.

Licensed: 1854-1871

Management

Middlesex justices:

Mich.	1854-	John Champion
"	1857-	John Newman
"	1859-	Charles Scott
"	1861	Thomas Friswell
"	1862-	George Gill
"	1865	Henry Webb
"	1866-	James Frederick Charles Crane
"	1869-	Charles James Lavers
"	1871	*No notice.*

Literature

Official records:

Mx. Mich. Q.S. 1854-1871.

774

SUN AND SAWYERS AND ROYAL EXCHANGE PUBLIC HOUSE

241, Poplar High Street, Poplar.

Licensed: 1866-1889

Former name

Sun and Sawyers Public House

Management

Middlesex justices:

Mich.	1866-	George West
"	1883-	John North
"	1886-	Henry Wickes

Literature

Official records:

Mx. Mich. Q.S. 1866-1888.

775

SURPRISE PUBLIC HOUSE

Caversham Square, Chelsea.

Licensed: 1856-1858

Management

Middlesex justices:

Mich. 1856-   John Willson
  " 1858   *No petition.*

Literature

Official records:

Mx. Mich. Q.S. 1856-1858.

776

SURPRISE PUBLIC HOUSE

6, Christchurch Terrace, Chelsea.

Licensed: 1869-1890

Management

Middlesex justices:

Mich. 1869   Benjamin Burkin
  " 1870   William Wharton
  " 1871   Charles Wilson
  " 1877-   Catherine Place

London County Council:

1890   Catherine Place

Literature

Official records:

L.C.C. Th. & M-H. Com. App. Nov. 1889;
Mx. Mich. Q.S. 1869-1888.

777

SURREY MUSIC HALL

Surrey Zoological Gardens, *Between* Kennington Park and Walworth Roads, Southwark.

Opened: 1831 as pleasure gardens. *Finally closed:* 1878.

Also known as:

Royal Surrey Gardens Music Hall

Later name

Surrey Gardens Theatre (1872-78).

Building details

Music hall built: 1856.   *Opened:* 15th July 1856.

Architect: Horace Jones.

Capacity: c. 10, 000.

Cost: £18, 200.

Destroyed by fire: June 1861.

Between 1861 and 1871 the hall was rebuilt and used by St. Thomas's Hospital until the hospital moved to the Albert Embankment.
1872: The music hall was remodelled as a theatre and used regularly until August 14th, 1877.

Management

Lord Chamberlain:

20. 5. 1861-   Charles Bishop to 1. 6. 1861.
11. 5. 1872-   Frederick Strange to 28. 9. 1873

8. 5. 1875-   Reginald Claude Poole and Walter
               Stacey to 28. 9. '75.

Literature

Official records:

LC7/14-16.

Contemporary accounts:

1856 BUILDER. 1856 July 19, pp. 395-6. 'The
      music hall at the Surrey Gardens'.—Detailed
      description.
1856 BUILDER. 1856 Oct. 25, p. 581.—Accident at
      the Surrey Music Hall during religious meeting:
      6 killed in panic.
1857 FACTS and documents relating to the reverses
      of the Surrey Gardens Company; by a pensive
      shareholder. London, 1857.
1861 ILLUSTRATED LONDON NEWS. 1861 June
      22. 'Destruction of the Surrey Music Hall by
      fire'.

Historical accounts:

1871 ERA ALMANACK, 1871, p. 4-5.
      'Surrey Zoological Gardens. '
1889 MONTGOMERY, Bishop H. H.
      Kennington. . . Chapter XI.
1907 WROTH, Warwick.
      Cremorne and later London gardens. . . pp. 83-
      92. illus.
c. 1930 MAYES, Ronald
      The romance of London theatres, No. 142.
1952 PULLING, Christopher.
      They were singing. . . pp. 177-178.
1955 LONDON. County Council.
      Survey of London. Vol. 25, 1955. p. 87. plate.

Location of other material

Playbills: British Museum Library; Guildhall
Library; London Museum.

Newscuttings: British Museum Library. Th. Cts.
51-58.

Illustrations, playbills and newscuttings:

London Museum Library *in* The PLEASURE gardens
of South London. Vol. II. pp. 151-204.

778

SURREY THEATRE

124, Blackfriars Road, Lambeth.

Opened: 14th November 1782. *Used as a cinema*
1920-4. *Demolished* 1934.

Also known as

Royal Circus (1782-1810).
Royal Surrey Theatre.
Surrey Vaudeville Theatre.
Surrey Theatre of Varieties.

Building details

1st building:

Destroyed by fire: 1799.

Interior rebuilt: 1800.

Burnt down: 12. 8. 1805

2nd building:

Rebuilt: 1805.

Architect: Mr. Cabanall Jnr.

Builder: Mr. Donaldson.

Foreman: Thomas Cubitt.

1809: Auditorium reconstructed.
1810: Amphitheatre and stables abolished.
1852: Interior redecorated by E. T. Archer.—Description in programme for 4. 10. 1852.

Burnt down: 30. 1. 1865.

3rd building:

Opened: 26. 12. 1865

Architect: John Ellis.

Contractor: C. M. Foster, of New Wharf, Whitefriars.

Cost: £25, 000

Capacity: 2161, plus standing.

Auditorium: S. 30; P. 601; D.C. 176; Bx. 264; G. 1090.

Stage: 70′ wide × 60′ deep.

1904: Converted into a music hall by Kirk and Kirk.

Demolished: 1934.

Management

Lord Chamberlain:

29. 9. 1843-		Mrs. Frances Davidge
"	1847-	Mrs. Frances Davidge and Alfred Bunn
"	1848-	Richard Shepherd
"	1850-	Richard Shepherd and William Creswick
"	1862-	Richard Shepherd
"	1863-	Richard Shepherd and James Robertson Anderson
"	1865-	Richard Shepherd
"	1866-	Richard Shepherd and William Creswick
"	1869-	Mrs. Ellen. Pitt. *Licence later withdrawn and theatre closed.*
"	1870-	Edward Tyrrell Smith
31. 8. 1871-		Edward Fisher Edgar
29. 9. 1872-		Miss Virginia Blackwood
24. 12. 1873-		William Holland (Cancelled 6. 7. 1881)
1. 8. 1881-		George Conquest and Paul Meritt
29. 9. 1885-		George Oliver Conquest
"	1886-	George Augustus Oliver Conquest
"	1901-	Frederick Oliver Conquest (to Nov. 1903).
10. 1. 1912-		Temple de la Pole Temple-West
26. 12. 1919-		William Hamilton Miln
30. 11. 1921-		Hubert Sillitoe Chambers (to 30. 11. 1923)

London County Council:

1905-	Temple de la Pole Temple West (to Dec. 1918).
1922-	Hubert Sillitoe Chambers
1924	David Roth
Nov. 1924	*Not licensed as theatre or music hall.*

Literature

Official records:

G.L.C. Arch. Dpt. Mss. Index;

234

G.L.C. Arch. Dpt. Th. case No. 348;
L.C.C. Th. & M-H. Com. App. Nov. 1904-1923;
L.C.C. Th. & M-H. Com. Papers 1889-;
LC1/507-752; LC7/13-17, 20-48, 89; L.C.O. 509.
M.B.W. Rpt. 1882, pp. 333-343;
Sel. Com. 1866 and 1877;
Sel. Com. 1892. Paras. 3070-78; 3079-83, 3279-86.
—Details of seating and standing capacity, and prices charged.

Contemporary accounts:

1782 UNIVERSAL MAGAZINE. 1872 Nov.—Account of opening of the Royal Circus, 4th Nov. 1782.
1849 ILLUSTRATED LONDON NEWS. 1849 Jan. 13. illus.—Description of redecoration.
1865 BUILDER. 1865 Feb. 4, p. 79. 'Destruction of the Surrey Theatre. '
 ILLUSTRATED LONDON NEWS. 1865 Feb. 4. illus. 'Burning of the Surrey Theatre. '
 BUILDER. 1865 April 1. p. 231.—Report that Lieut.-Col. Temple West has commissioned John Ellis as architect of new theatre.
 BUILDER. 1865 May 13.—Report of foundation stone ceremony.
 BUILDER. 1865 Dec. 16. pp. 889-890.—Description, longitudinal section.
1865 BUILDING NEWS. 1865 Dec. 29, p. 923.—Description.
 BUILDER. 1865 Dec. 30, pp. 917-918.—Detailed description, and history of previous theatres.
1866 ILLUSTRATED LONDON NEWS. 1866 Jan. 20. 'New Surrey Theatre'.—Report of architectural competition, and description.
1872 BUILDING NEWS. 1872 May 10, p. 387. 'Final closing of the Surrey Theatre'.—Brief report that property to be sold by auction.
1887 SATURDAY REVIEW. 1887 July 16. 'The state of the London theatres. . . No. 5.
1904 BUILDER. 1904 April 2, p. 358. Report of forthcoming sale, following the death of the owner. —Brief summary of history.
 BUILDER. 1904 Dec. 31. p. 705. Report of conversion into a music hall.
1932 DAILY TELEGRAPH. 1932 June 18. 'Surrey Theatre to be sold'.—Report that building tenantless for 5-6 years.
 MANCHESTER GUARDIAN. 1932 July 13. 'The old Surrey'.—Report that lessees had been found.
 DAILY TELEGRAPH. 1932 Sept. 9. 'Surrey Theatre to reopen: £30, 000 renovations'.—Report on negotiations.
1934 DAILY TELEGRAPH. 1934 July 12. 'Surrey Theatre in the market'—Note of sale.
 EVENING STANDARD. 1934 July 12. 'In the old Surrey Theatre'—Report.
 DAILY TELEGRAPH. 1934 Aug. 1. 'Surrey Theatre sold: site acquired by eye hospital'.
1935 DAILY TELEGRAPH. 1935 Jan. 1. 'Surrey Theatre: site bought by Royal Eye Hospital. ' —Completion of sale.

Historical accounts:

1824 NIC-NACS. 1824 March 27. —History up to the fire of 1805.
1865 BUILDER. 1865 Dec. 30, p. 917 —History of previous theatres.
1866 H.D.M.
 The two 'circuses' and the two 'Surrey Theatres': topographical, historical, dramatic and descriptive. Thomas Hailes Lacy, 1866. 16p.
1876 ERA ALMANACK. 1876. pp. 6-10.—History.

1879 DRAMATIC NOTES. 1879. pp. 69-70.
1904 ROYAL SURREY THEATRE
      A souvenir of George Conquest's farewell
      benefit, July 18-23, 1904. Souvenir booklet. 8p.
      —Contains history of the theatre from 'Sketches
      of Southwark' by Robert W. Burers.
      BAKER, H. Barton.
      History of the London stage and its players.
      pp. 389-96.
      SOUTHWARK RECORDER, 1904 July 30.
      'The passing of the Surrey Theatre: a sketch of
      its history.'
1910 SOUTH LONDON PRESS, 1910 June 24.
      'Annals of Surrey Theatre: home of transpontine
      drama to be reconstructed'.—Report of interview
      with Mr. Cochrane, manager.
1925 CHANCELLOR, E. B.
      The pleasure haunts of London... pp. 110-113.
c. 1930 MAYES, Ronald.
      The romance of London theatres. Nos. 29, 76
      and 188.
1934 EVENING STANDARD, 1934 July 12.
      'In the old Surrey Theatre: stage that knew all
      the stars: report by Ian Coster'.
194-? WILSON, A. E.
      Pantomime pageant... pp. 45 et seq., 53 et seq.
1946 SCOTT, Harold.
      Early doors... pp. 99 et seq.
1953 FLEETWOOD, Frances.
      Conquest: the story of a theatre family...
      pp. 135-176, 261-8.
1955 LONDON. County Council.
      Survey of London. Vol. XXV. p. 50, 57-58. plates.
1959 ENCICLOPEDIA dello spettacolo, Vol. 6, Col.
      1636.
1963 THEATRE WORLD, 1963 April, July, Sept. Lost
      London theatres, by N. M. Bligh. No. 19 The
      Royal Circus or the Surrey Theatre, 1782-1924.
      6p. illus.

Location of other material

Plans: G.L.C. *Architects Department.*
Enthoven Collection, 1918 (2 sheets).

Programmes and playbills:

British Museum Library; Enthoven Collection;
Garrick Club; Guildhall Library; Lambeth Local
Collection; London Museum; Southwark Local Collection;
Westminster Local Collection.

Scrapbook:

Scrapbook of newspaper cuttings on William Holland,
1876-1884. (In Southwark Location Collection.)

Prints:

British Museum; Enthoven Collection; Lambeth
Local Collection; London Museum.

779

SURREY CANAL PUBLIC HOUSE

Camberwell.

Licensed: 1853-1857.

Management

Surrey justices:

Mich. 1853-	Peter Kelly	
" 1854-	George Gilham	
" 1857	*Not licensed.*	

Literature

Official records:
Sy. Mich. Q.S. 1853-1856.

780

SURREY DOCK PUBLIC HOUSE

Rotherhithe Street, Rotherhithe.

Licensed: 1873-1888.

Management

Surrey justices:

Mich. 1873-	Edward Mark Sells	
" 1874-	John Swannell	
" 1876-	John Sparkes (through 1888).	

Literature

Official records:

Sel. Com. 1892.
Sy. Mich. Q.S. 1873-1887.

781

SUSSEX ARMS PUBLIC HOUSE,

107, Culford Road, Kingsland, Hackney.

Surrey Theatre (778)

(Lambeth Public Libraries)

Licensed: 1854-1903.

Building details

The concert room was on the ground floor, connected with the public house.

Capacity: 200

Management

Middlesex justices:

Mich.	1854-	James Davies
"	1863-	Robert Mann
"	1874-	William Magness
"	1875-	James Clayson
"	1877-	George Hough
"	1883-	William Henry Dodd.

London County Council:

1890	William Henry Dodd
1851	Edmund Clare
1892	Philip Brown Twentyman
1893-	James Barley
1898-	Alfred James Mitchell
1900	Albert Ernest Robinson
1901-	Frederick Richard
Nov. 1903	*Not listed as a theatre or music hall.*

Literature

Official records:

G.L.C. Arch. Dpt. Mss. Index.
L.C.C. Th. & M-H. Com. App. Nov. 1889-1903.
Mx. Mich. Q.S. 1854-1888.

782

SUSSEX ARMS PUBLIC HOUSE

Upper North Street, Poplar.

Licensed: 1860-1867.

Management

Middlesex justices:

Mich.	1860-	Alfred Edward Hubbard
"	1863-	John Holt
"	1865-	Rowland Henry Wallis
"	1867	*No notice, no petition.*

Literature

Official records:

Mx. Mich. Q.S. 1860-1867.

783

SWALLOW STREET MUSIC HALL

Goat and Star Public House, 6 Swallow Street, Piccadilly.

Licensed: pre 1850-1903.

Also known as

Swallow Public House.

Building details

Built prior to 1860. The concert room was on the first floor, attached to the public house.

236

Cost: £2000.

Capacity: 500.

Rebuilt: 1891.

Capacity: 180.

Management

Middlesex justices:

Mich.	1848-	William Jones
"	1857-	Henry Cockerell
"	1873-	John Frederick Brian
"	1875-	Miriam Ashton
"	1878-	Frank White
"	1879-	Henry James Munday
"	1880-	Arthur Harrison
"	1881-	Benjamin Henry Swallow
"	1884-	John Malsbury Dancer
"	1885-	Margaret Brigham
"	1886-	Edwin Bratt

London County Council:

1890-	Edwin Bratt
1897-	Nathanial George Workley
Nov. 1903	*Not listed as theatre or music hall.*

Literature

Official records:

G.L.C. Arch. Dpt. Mss. Index.
G.L.C. Arch. Dpt. Th. case 350.
L.C.C. Th. & M-H. Com. App. Nov. 1889-1903.
Mx. Mich. Q.S. 1850-1888.
Sel. Com. 1866.

Historical accounts:

1952 PULLING, Christopher.
They were singing...p. 182.

Location of other material

Plans: G.L.C. *Architects Department.*

784

SWAN PUBLIC HOUSE

Bethnal Green Road (*formerly* Swan Yard), Shoreditch.

Licensed: 1854-1891.

Management

Middlesex justices:

Mich.	1854-	Thomas George Watkinson (to Mich. 1858).
"	1859-	Mary Maria Venner (to Mich. 1860)
"	1863-	William George Murrey
"	1864-	Sidney Joseph Silver
"	1866-	Frederick Thomas Philo
"	1867-	Charles Buckenham Jnr.
"	1873-	Sarah Malet
"	1875-	Stewart James Robinson
"	1878-	John Grey
"	1887-	George Cox.

London County Council:

1890-	George Cox
Nov. 1891	*Not licensed.*

Literature

Official records:

L.C.C. Th. & M-H. Com. App. Nov. 1889-90.
Mx. Mich. Q.S. 1854-60, 1863-1888.

785

SWAN PUBLIC HOUSE

Hungerford Market, St. Martin-in-the-Fields.

Licensed: pre 1850-1862.

Former name

Swan Public House and Lord Drover's Hotel.

Building details

Stuart and Park (see below) note that the house stood next to the river, and was demolished for the building of the Charing Cross Station.

Management

Middlesex justices:

Mich. 1848-	John Buckmaster
" 1851-	Joseph Buckmaster
" 1854-	Richard Dawson
" 1858-	Thomas Corby Jnr.
" 1862	*Reported that house closed. No petition, no application.*

Literature

Official records:

Mx. Mich. Q.S. pre 1850-1861.

Historical accounts:

1895 STUART, C.D., *and* PARK, A.J.
The variety stage... (Mention only).

786

SWISS COTTAGE PUBLIC HOUSE

Stanstead Road, Forest Hill.

Licensed: 1872-1891.

Management

West Kent justices:

| Mich. 1872- | William James Edwards |
| " 1887- | Joseph George Stotem. |

London County Council:

| 1890- | Joseph Stotem |
| Nov. 1891 | *Not licensed.* |

Literature

Official records:

L.C.C. Th. & M-H. Com. App. Nov. 1889-1890.
W. Kt. Mich. Q.S. 1872-1888.

787

SWISS COTTAGE PUBLIC HOUSE

109, Lauriston Road (*formerly:* Grove Road), Hackney.

Licensed: 1865-1891.

Building details

The concert hall was on the first floor over the bar. It was closed by the 1878 Act.

Management

Middlesex justices:

Mich. 1865-	Thomas Gooding
" 1866-	James John Jackson
" 1867-	Elizabeth Emma Jackson
" 1871-	Sidney Smith (through 1888).

London County Council:

| 1890- | Sidney Smith |
| Nov. 1891 | *No application.* |

Literature

Official records:

G.L.C. Arch. Dpt. Th. case 040/157.
L.C.C. Th. & M-H. Com. App. Nov. 1889-1891.
Mx. Mich. Q.S. 1865-1888.

Historical accounts:

Mentioned in W. Macqueen Pope's 'Melodies linger on'.

788

TALBOT PUBLIC HOUSE

19, Lansdowne Terrace (*later* 97 Caledonian Road). Islington.

Licensed: 1854-1867.

Management

Middlesex justices:

Mich. 1854-	Arthur Stapley
" 1857-	Henry Joseph Cattell
" 1859-	Henry Samuel Love
" 1860-	Thomas Watson Francis
" 1865-	Henry Richard Speed
" 1866-	William Edward George
" 1867	*No notice, no petition.*

Literature

Official records:

Mx. Mich. Q.S. 1854-1867.

789

TALMA PUBLIC HOUSE

Lewisham.

Licensed: 1866-1871.

Management

West Kent justices:

Mich. 1866-	William Lee Jarvis
" 1868-	William Smith
" 1870-	John Mills
" 1872	*No petition.*

Literature

Official records:

W. Kt. Mich. Q.S. 1866-1871.

790

TAVISTOCK ARMS PUBLIC HOUSE

Stibbington Street, Oakley Square, St. Pancras.

Licensed: 1862-1863.

Management

Middlesex justices:

Mich. 1862-   Edwin Franklin Pickering
"   1863   *No notice, no petition.*

Literature

Official records:

Mx. Mich. Q.S. 1862-1863.

791

TEMPERANCE HALL

London Terrace, Hackney Road, Bethnal Green.

Licensed: 1861-1894.

Management

Middlesex justices:

Mich. 1861-   Thomas Penny
"   1878-   George Ferry
"   1881-   William Haywood.

London County Council:

1890-   William Haywood
Nov. 1894   *Not licensed.*

Literature

Official records:

L.C.C. Th. & M-H. Com. 1889-1894.
Mx. Mich. Q.S. 1861-1888.

792

TEMPERANCE HALL

Middlesex Street, St. Pancras.

Licensed: 1856-1859.

Management

Middlesex justices:

Mich. 1856-   James Tilbury
"   1859   *No petition, opposed.*

Literature

Official records:

Mx. Mich. Q.S. 1856-1859.

793

TEMPERANCE HALL

211, Shoreditch High Street, Shoreditch.

238

Opened: Dec. 1863   *Licensed until* 1875.

Former name

Eastern Alhambra Music Hall.

Building details

The hall was built at a cost of £2000.
Capacity: 1000.

Management

Middlesex justices:

Mich. 1864-   Robert Fort
"   1870-   George Parkes and William Tanner
"   1875-   *No notice, no petition.*

Literature

Official records:

Mx. Mich. Q.S. 1864-1875.

794

TEMPERANCE HALL

4 & 5, Weir's Passage, Somers Town, St. Pancras.

Licensed: 1856-1882.

Management

Middlesex justices:

Mich. 1856-   Robert Tackley
"   1882-   *No certificate returned, no application.*

Literature

Official records:

Mx. Mich. Q.S. 1856-1882.

795

TEMPLE ARMS COFFEE TAVERN

26, Great Earl Street, Seven Dials, St. Giles-in-the-Fields.

Licensed: 1879-1883.

Management

Middlesex justices:

Mich. 1879-   George Curtis
"   1881-   William Morgan
"   1882-   Charles Leonard
"   1883   *No notice of application, no certificate.*

Literature

Official records:

Mx. Mich. Q.S. 1879-1883.

796

TERRY'S THEATRE

105 and 106, Strand, Westminster.

Opened: 17th October 1887   *Closed as a theatre:* 8th October, 1910   *Demolished:* 1923.

Building details

Architect: Walter Emden.

Contractor: Messrs. Holliday and Greenwood.

Capacity: 888; plus standing.

Auditorium: P. & S. 370; D.C. 140; U.C. 90; G. 250;
Bx. 38.

1905: Alterations:

Architect: Frank Matcham.

—The theatre, built for Edward Terry, was near the
site of the *Coal Hole* q.v. It was built on the site of
the Occidental Tavern. In 1910 it became the Grand
Casino Cinema.

Management

Lord Chamberlain:

17. 10. 1887- Edward O'Connor Terry.

London County Council:

Cinema licence Nov. 1910 to Arthur Soden Maxwell.

Literature

Official records:

G.L.C. Arch. Dpt. Th. case 450;
L.C.C. Th. & M-H. Com. Papers 1885+;
LC1/507-752; LC7/17; LC7/34-48;
L.C.O. 182

Contemporary accounts:

1885 BUILDER, 1885 Aug. 8, p. 180.—Brief accounce-
      ment of new theatre, on site of Occidental
      Tavern.
1886 BUILDING NEWS, 1886 Aug. 27.—illus., plans.
1887 BUILDER, 1887 April 2, p. 494.—Reports
      collapse of Occidental Tavern.
      BUILDER, 1887 April 9, pp. 555-6.—Report of
      commencement of building and description.
      Details of subcontractors.
      ERA. 1887 Aug. 20th.—Report of interviews
      with Edward Terry.
      DAILY TELEGRAPH, 1887 Oct. 14 and 18.
      'Terry's Theatre'.—Report of new theatre to
      open on following Monday.
      DAILY TELEGRAPH, 1887 Oct. 18.—Report of
      opening.
      TIMES, 1887 Oct. 18—Report of opening.
      BUILDER, 1887 Oct. 22, p. 556.—Description.
      ERA. 1887. Oct. 22nd.—Report of opening.
      BUILDER, 1887 Oct. 29, p. 598, 605.—Architect's
      description. illus., plan., section.
      BUILDER, 1887 Nov. 5, p. 617, 652.—Comment on
      colour scheme and correction.
1905 BUILDER, 1905 July 22, p. 100.—Frank Matcham
      appointed to make alterations.

Historical accounts:

1883 BUILDER, 1883 June 16. pp. 803-4.
      —History of site.
1904 BAKER, H. Barton.
      History of the London stage and its players...
      pp. 521-2.
c. 1930 MAYES, Ronald.
      The romance of London theatres, No. 119 and
      181.
1968 MANDER, Raymond *and* MITCHENSON, Joe.
      The lost theatres of London. pp. 506-517. 2 illus.

Location of other material

Plans:

G.L.C. *Architects Department;* Enthoven Collection;
Public Record Office, LC7/49, 5 sheets 1887.

Programmes:

Enthoven Collection; London Museum.

797
THREE COLTS PUBLIC HOUSE

Dog Row, Bethnal Green.

Terry's Theatre 1886 (796)

(The Builder)

239

Licensed: 1858-1863.

Management

Middlesex justices:

| Mich. 1858- | William Richardson |
| " 1863 | *No notice, no petition.* |

Literature

Official records:

Mx. Mich. Q.S. 1858-1863.

798

THREE COLTS PUBLIC HOUSE

Grove Street (*later* Lauriston Road), Hackney.

Licensed: 1863-1875

Also known as

Scott's New Music Hall, (1867).

Management

Middlesex justices:

Mich. 1863-	Keable Smyth
" 1864-	John Johnson
" 1866-	John Walter Scott
" 1868-	Richard James Markham
" 1870-	James Frederick Munro
" 1872-	George Lovell
" 1875	*Not licensed. Police report that Lovell fined for keeping house open at prohibited hours.*

Literature

Official records:

Mx. Mich. Q.S. 1863-1874.

Historical accounts:

Mentioned in W. Macqueen Pope's 'Melodies linger on'.

799

THREE COLTS PUBLIC HOUSE

Old Ford Road, Stratford, Bow.

Licensed: 1865-1872

Management

Middlesex justices:

Mich. 1865-	James Lewis Beech
" 1866-	Edward Cross
" 1870-	Benjamin Farmer
" 1872	*Licence refused. Fined for illegal Sunday trading.*

Literature

Official records:

Mx. Mich. Q.S. 1865-1872.

800

THREE COMPASSES PUBLIC HOUSE

77, Mount Street, Grosvenor Square, St. George, Hanover Square.

240

Licensed: 1855-1862.

Management

Middlesex justices:

Mich. 1855-	Thomas Hammant
" 1856-	John Harper
" 1862	*No petition, no application.*

Literature

Official records:

Mx. Mich. Q.S. 1855-1862.

801

THREE COMPASSES PUBLIC HOUSE AND TEA GARDENS

Dalston, Hackney.

Licensed: 1858-1863.

Management

Middlesex justices:

Mich. 1858-	William Thomas Hamilton
" 1860-	John Hart
" 1863	*No notice, no petition.*

Literature

Official records:

Mx. Mich. Q.S. 1858-1863.

802

THREE CRANES PUBLIC HOUSE

Church Street, Hackney.

Licensed: 1853-1860.

Management

Middlesex justices:

Mich. 1853-	John English
" 1854-	James Butcher
" 1856-	Joseph Percival Pennington
" 1859-	Frances Pennington
" 1860	*Licence refused*

Literature

Official records:

Mx. Mich. Q.S. 1853-1860.

803

THREE CROWNS PUBLIC HOUSE

4, Queen's Road, Chelsea.

Licensed: 1853-1861

Management

Middlesex justices:

Mich. 1853-	Robert Edward Batley
" 1854-	Edward Smith
" 1855-	Robert Alfred Moore
" 1857-	Charles Tilling
" 1861	*No application, no petition.*

Literature

Official records:

Mx. Mich. Q.S. 1853-1861.

804

THREE CROWNS PUBLIC HOUSE

North Woolwich.

Licensed: 1866-1903.

Building details

The concert room was on the ground floor at the back of the public house.

Capacity: c. 200.

Management

West Kent justices:

Mich. 1866-   Edward West
"   1887-   Walter Edward Richardson.

London County Council:

1890-   Walter Edward Richardson
1901-   Emma West
Nov. 1903   *Not listed as theatre or music hall.*

Literature

Official records:

G.L.C. Arch. Dpt. Mss. Index.
L.C.C. Th. & M-H. Com. App. Nov. 1889-1903.
W.Kt. Mich. Q.S. 1866-1888.

805

THREE CROWNS PUBLIC HOUSE

Upper East Smithfield, Wapping.

Licensed: 1854-1866.

Management

Middlesex justices:

Mich. 1854-   Martin George
"   1866   *No application.*

Literature

Official records:

Mx. Mich. Q.S. 1854-1866.

806

THREE CUPS PUBLIC HOUSE

7, Matilda Place, Trafalgar Road, Greenwich.

Licensed: 1884-1890.

also known as

Three Cups Coffee Tavern

Building details

Capacity: 150.

Management

West Kent justices:

Mich. 1884-   Charles Stone

London County Council:

1890-   Charles Stone
Nov. 1890   *Not licensed.*

Literature

Official records:

L.C.C. Th. & M-H. Com. App. Nov. 1889.
Sel. Com. 1892.
W.Kt. Mich. Q.S. 1884-1888.

807

THREE CUPS PUBLIC HOUSE

20, Prince's Terrace, Fulham.

Licensed: 1881-1882

Management

Middlesex justices:

Mich. 1881-   William Morgan
"   1882   *No application, no certificate returned.*

Literature

Official records:

Mx. Mich. Q.S. 1881-1882.

808

THREE HORSE SHOES PUBLIC HOUSE

7, Milford Lane, St. Clement Danes.

Licensed: 1885-1859.

Management

Middlesex justices:

Mich. 1855-   George Wilson, *afterwards* William Thomas Kipling.
"   1856-   John Prescod Whitmore
"   1857-   Henry Stevenson
"   1859   *Reported closed.*

Literature

Official records:

Mx. Mich. Q.S. 1855-1859.

809

THREE JOLLY GARDENERS PUBLIC HOUSE

Rochester Row, Westminster.

Licensed: 1852-1857.

Management

Middlesex justices:

Mich. 1852-   John Jones
"   1857   *No application.*

Literature

Official records:

Mx. Mich. Q.S. 1852-1857.

810

THREE MARINERS HOTEL

Cassland Road, Hackney.

Licensed: 1867-1873

Management

Middlesex justices:

Mich. 1867-	George Davis	
"	1872-	Alfred Homer
"	1873	*Licence refused.*

Literature

Official records:

Mx. Mich. Q.S. 1867-1873.

811

THREE NEATS' TONGUES PUBLIC HOUSE

3, Great Pearl Street (*formerly* Pearl Street), Spitalfields.

Licensed: 1854-1865.

Management

Middlesex justices:

Mich. 1854-	James Abbott	
"	1856-	James Weston
"	1858-	Edward Cooke
"	1860-	James Shearman
"	1861-	Jules Wanthier
"	1864-	George William Nugent
"	1865	*No notice, no petition.*

Literature

Official records:

Mx. Mich. Q.S 1854-1865.

812

THREE WHEATSHEAVES PUBLIC HOUSE

Islington High Street, Islington.

Licensed: 1859-1868.

Management

Middlesex justices:

Mich. 1859-	James Deller	
"	1864-	Henry Davis
"	1866-	George Robert Linford
"	1868	*No application.*

813

TIVOLI MUSIC HALL

65-70½, Strand, Westminster.

Opened: 1890   *Rebuilt as cinema:* 1923
Demolished: 1957

Building details

Architect: C. J. Phipps.

Capacity: 1510.

Aduitorium: P. 305; S. 336; G. C. 132; U. C. 234.

Alterations, 1900.

Architect: Walter Emden.

Contractor: Kirk & Randall.

Capacity: c. 1000.

Management

Middlesex justices:

Mich. 1884-   Charles Hürter.

London County Council:

1890-	Charles Hürter
1893	Charles Morton
1894-	Vernon Dowsett
1903-	Philip Yorke
1905-	James Howell
1915-	Ilford Ibettson
Nov. 1923	*Listed as a cinema.*

Lord Chamberlain:

10. 1. 1912-   James Howell (to 30. 11. 1914)
—*Licensed on assumption that theatre was to be built.*

Literature

Official records:

G.L.C. Arch. Dpt. Mss. Index;
G L.C. Arch. Dpt. Th. case 360;
L.C.C. Th. & M-H. Com. App. Nov. 1889-1923;
Mx. Mich. Q.S. 1884-1888.

Contemporary accounts:

1888 BUILDING NEWS, 1888 Oct. 26, p. 538.—Description. Plate of facade & plans.
THEATRE 1888, Nov.—Report of new theatre.
1890 ERA. 1890. April 5th.—Description
BUILDING NEWS, 1890 May 30, p. 760, Col. 3. —Note of opening. Correction 6. 6. 1890, p. 819.
BUILDER, 1890 May 31st, p. 398.—Description of 'new concert hall and restaurant'.
ERA. 1890. May 31st.—Report of opening
1891 ERA—1891 May 2nd.—Report of auction.
1891 BUILDER, 1891 June 13, p. 472.—Report of sale.
1892 DAILY GRAPHIC, 1892 July 30.—Mention only.
1900 BUILDER, 1900 Sept. 1, p. 199.—Description of alterations done for 9th anniversary of opening.
1914 TIMES, 1914 Jan. 31. 'The art of the music hall'. —On closing of the Tivoli.

Historical accounts:

1938 DISHER, M. W.
Winkles and champagne. . . p. 26.
1946 SCOTT, Harold.
Early doors. . . p. 178 et seq.
1952 PULLING, Christopher.
They were singing. . . pp. 198-199, 227.
1959 ENCICLOPEDIA dello spettacolo, Vol. 6, Col. 1637.

1968 MANDER, Raymond *and* MITCHENSON, Joe
The lost theatres of London. pp. 518-529. 3 illus.

Location of other material

Plans: G.L.C. *Architects Department.*

Programmes:

British Museum Library; Enthoven Collection; London Museum.

814

TOOLE'S THEATRE

King William Street, Charing Cross.

Opened as a place of entertainment: 1854.
Demolished: 1895.

Former names

Polygraphic Hall 1854-1869
Charing Cross Theatre 1869-1876
Folly Theatre 1876-1882

Building details

The Polygraphic Hall was opened in 1854, in a building that had been used first as a cigar divan, and later as a chapel. Hall converted into a theatre: 1869.

Builder: Messrs. Bradwell & Field.

Reconstruction and redecoration: 1876

Theatre enlarged: 1881.

Opened: 16. 2. 1882

Architect: John I. Thomas

Builder: David Laing & Son.

Capacity: c. 600.

Auditorium: S. 102; P. 109; D.C. 150; U.C. 106; G. 85; Bx. 24.

New frontage on 404-5 Strand.

Architect: G. J. Phipps.

Demolished for an extension to the Charing Cross Hospital.

Management

Lord Chamberlain:

17.6.1869-	Edmund William Bradwell and William Riderwood Field
29.9.1872-	John S. Clarke
1.9.1873-	William Hamilton Codrinton Nation
12.9.1876-	William Ridewood Field
29.9.1876-	Alexander Henderson
29.9.1879-	John Lawrence Toole (to 28.9.1881)
16.2.1882-	John Lawrence Toole (to 28.9.1895)

Literature

Official records:

G.L.C. Arch. Dpt. Th. case 010;
LC1/507-617; LC7/15-17, 23-42;
M.B.W. Rpt. 1882. pp. 343-355;
Sel. Com. 1877 and 1892.

Contemporary accounts:

1869 BUILDER, 1869 June 19, p. 489.—Brief report on converted theatre.
ERA: 1869 June 20.—Report of opening
SUNDAY TIMES, 1869 June 20 'Opening of the new Charing Cross Theatre'.
1879 DAILY NEWS, 1879 Aug. 25. 'The theatres' column.—Report of Toole's problems of obtaining various properties on the site.
DRAMATIC NOTES, 1879, pp. 56-8.
BUILDER, 1879 Sept. 20, p. 1065.—Report of abandonment of plans.
1882 BUILDING NEWS, 1882 Feb. 17, pp. 195-6. —Detailed description of remodelling.
BUILDER, 1882 Feb. 18, p. 207.—Brief report.
ILLUSTRATED SPORTING AND DRAMATIC NEWS, 1882 March 4. illus.
1887 SATURDAY REVIEW, 1887 July 2. 'The state of London theatres... No. 3
1891 TOOLE'S THEATRE (Publicity handout). Jan. 13, 1891.

Tivoli Music Hall (813)

(Victoria & Albert Museum, Crown copyright)

Toole's Theatre 1882 (814)

(British Museum)

1892 BUILDER, 1892 April 2, p. 269.—Report of
L.C.C. finding that theatre was unsatisfactory,
but as lease has only 3 ½ years to run that they
do not propose to enforce alterations.
1896 BUILDER, 1896 May 16, p. 418.—Report of proposed demolition.

Historical accounts:

1904 BAKER, H. Barton.
History of the London stage and its players.
pp. 335-337.
1925 SHERSON, Erroll
London's lost theatres. . . pp. 305-313.
c. 1930 MAYES, Ronald.
The romance of London theatres, No. 102.
1952 PULLING, Christopher
They were singing. . . p. 139, 195, 214.
1955 THEATRE WORLD, 1955 Jan.
Lost London theatres, by N. M. Bligh. No. 3.
The story of Toole's Theatre, Charing Cross.
3p. illus.
1968 MANDER, Raymond *and* MITCHENSON, Joe
The Lost Theatres of London pp. 530-550.
2. illus.

Location of other material

Plans:

G.L.C. *Architects Department.*
Public Record Office. LC7/82. 5 sheets, dated
19.3.1869.

Programmes and playbills:

British Museum Library; Enthoven Collection;
Garrick Club; Guildhall Library; London Museum;
Westminster Local Collection.

815

TRAFALGAR BEER HOUSE

17, Remington Street, City Road.

Licensed: 1854-1890.

Management

Middlesex justices:

Mich.	1854-	James Cave Price
"	1859-	James Cooper
"	1864-	George Henry Taylor
"	1870-	Robert Scott
"	1877-	Robert Bedwell
"	1884-	Mary Ann Bedwell.

London County Council:

1890	Mary Ann Bedwell
Nov. 1890	*Licence refused.*

Literature

Official records:

L.C.C. Th. & M-H. Com. App. Nov. 1889-1890;
Mx. Mich. Q.S. 1854-1888.

816

TRAFALGAR PUBLIC HOUSE

45, Southgate Road, Hackney.

Licensed: 1870-1890.

Management

Middlesex justices:

Mich.	1870-	Thomas John Maidwell
"	1873-	Charles Kitching
"	1874-	Alfred Charles Stock
"	1878-	George Hill
"	1879-	John Elves.

London County Council:

1890	John Elves
Nov. 1890	*Application withdrawn.*

Literature

Official records:

L.C.C. Th. & M-H. Com. App. Nov. 1889-1890;
Mx. Mich. Q.S. 1870-1888.

817

TREVOR MUSIC HALL

Trevor Arms Public House, 4-5, Trevor Place,
Knightsbridge.

Licensed: 1854-1889.

Building details

The Select Committee of 1866 reported that the hall
was built at a cost of £5000, and had a capacity of 800.
The hall was situated at the rear of the public house.
It measured 64′ 3″ × 31′, with a stage at the southern
end, and a balcony on three sides. Two small dressing rooms were situated near the stage.
By 1889 the hall had been converted into a billiard hall.

Management

Middlesex justices:

Mich.	1854-	Robert Street
"	1863-	Henry Edward Street
"	1874-	Marion Street
"	1875-	William Vincent Hummerston
"	1885-	Alfred Reeve.

Not licensed by the L.C.C. in Nov. 1889.

Literature

Official records:

G.L.C. Arch. Dpt. Th. case 08;
Mx. Mich. Q.S. 1854-1888;
Sel. Com. 1866 and 1877.

Historical accounts:

1952 PULLING, Christopher
They were singing. . . p. 178.

Location of other material

Plans: G.L.C. *Architects Department.*

Playbills: Harry Beard Collection.

818

TRINITY ARMS PUBLIC HOUSE

Church Street, Deptford.

Licensed: 1866-1880.

Management

West Kent justices:

Mich. 1866-	Bartholomew Hockin
" 1880	*No application.*

Literature

Official records:

W. Kt. Mich. Q.S. 1866-1880.

819

TROCADERO MUSIC HALL

7-8, Great Windmill Street, Piccadilly.

Opened: 1820.   *Converted into a restaurant:* 1902.

Former names

Royal Albion Theatre 1832
New Queen's Theatre 1833-4
Theatre of the Arts 1834
New Queen's Theatre 1835
Royal Albion Subscription Theatre 1835
Dubourg's Theatre of Arts 1840-5
Ancient Hall of Rome 1846
Argyll Rooms to 1882
Royal Trocadero Palace of Varieties 1882-
Royal Trocadero Music Hall
Royal Trocadero and Eden Theatre 1884

Building details

The site was used from c. 1744, as a tennis court, and from 1820 the tennis court was used as a circus and theatre.

Management

Middlesex justices:

Mich. 1849-	George French Bryer
" 1850-	Charles Emile Laurent
" 1857-	Robert Richard Bignell
" 1879	*No application.*
" 1882-	Robert Richard Bignell
" 1888-	Emma Alice Chapman, Sarah Ann Squier and Henry Edward Herman.

London County Council:

1891-	Samuel Adams
1893-	Florence Dorling (executrix of above)
1894-	Augustus Edin Hibberd
Nov. 1894	*Reported closed.*

Literature

Official records:

L.C.C. Th. & M-H. Com. App. Nov. 1889-1894;
Mx. Mich. Q.S. 1849-1888.

Contemporary accounts:

1887 SATURDAY REVIEW, 1887 Aug. 6. 'The state of London... music halls... No. 1'

Historical accounts:

1904 The KING... 1904, Aug. 6.
   —The nights of other days: IV. The Argyll Rooms and the Middlesex.

1925 SHERSON, Erroll
   Lost London Theatres... p. 320.
c. 1930 MAYES, Ronald
   The romance of London theatres, No. 207.
1935 HADDON, Archibald
   The story of the music hall... p. 19.
1938 DISHER, M. W.
   Winkles and champagne... Various refs. illus.
1952 PULLING, Christopher
   They were singing... p. 33, 191, 228.
1946 SCOTT, Harold
   Early doors... pp. 163 et seq.
1959 ENCICLOPEDIA dello spettacolo. Vol. 6, Col. 1637.
1963 LONDON. County Council.
   Survey of London. St. James. Vols. 31-32. pp. 46-7, 83, 84. Plates. (exterior in Vol. 32).
1968 MANDER, Raymond *and* MITCHENSON, Joe
   The lost theatres of london. pp. 551-559. 4 illus.

Location of other material

Programmes: British Museum Library.

Playbills cuttings &c.

Enthoven Collection; Guildhall Library; Westminster Local Collection.

820

TRUNDLE ARMS PUBLIC HOUSE

Almack Road, Clapton Park.

Licensed: 1886-1890.

Management

Middlesex justices:

Mich. 1886-	Francis Trundle
" 1887-	Harriet Sarah Trundle.

London County Council:

1890	Harriet Sarah Trundle.
Nov. 1890	*No application.*

Literature

Official records:

L.C.C. Th. & M-H. Com. App. Nov. 1889-1890.
Mx. Mich. Q.S. 1886-1888.

821

TUFNELL ARMS PUBLIC HOUSE

162, Tufnell Park Road, Islington.

Licensed: 1870-1898.

Also known as

Tufnell Park Hotel 1890-1898.

Building details

Capacity: 200

Management

Middlesex justices:

Mich. 1870-	William James Page
" 1877-	Thomas Lloyd Morgan

" 1878- John Martin
" 1884- Joseph Knights
" 1886- Frederick James Meadwell.

London County Council:

1890-	Frank Lees
1898	John Charles Pratt
Nov. 1898	*No application.*

Literature

Official records:

L.C.C. Th. & M-H. Com. App. Nov. 1889-97;
Mx. Mich. Q.S. 1870-1888;
Sel. com. 1892

822

TURK'S HEAD AND METROPOLITAN HOTEL

74, Turnmill Street, Finsbury.

Licensed: 1867-1868.

Management

Middlesex justices:

| Mich. 1867- | James Marsden |
| " 1868 | *No notice, no petition.* |

Literature

Official records:

Mx. Mich. Q.S. 1867-1868.

823

TWENTIETH CENTURY THEATRE

21, Archer Street, Bayswater.

Opened: 1863.

Former names

Victoria Hall
Bijou Theatre
Century Theatre

Management

Middlesex justices:

Mich. 1863-	John Robert Burgoyne
" 1866-	William Trist Bailey
" 1871-	Samuel Thomas Wadham
" 1873	*No application*
" 1888-	Peter Joseph George.

London County Council:

1893-	Peter Joseph George
1897-	Ann Susanna George
Nov. 1903	*Not listed as theatre or music hall.*
1925-	Lena Ashwell Players Ltd.
1937-	Rudolf Steiner Association Ltd. and Vera Compton-Burnett. (through 1950).

Literature

Official records:

G.L.C. Arch. Dpt. Th. case 368;
L.C.C. Th. & M-H. Com. App. Nov. 1892-1903, 1925-1950;
Mx. Mich. Q.S. 1863-73, 1888.

Historical accounts:

| c. 1930 | MAYES, Ronald The romance of London theatres, No. 129. |
| 1950 | FERGUSON, Rachel Royal borough. J. Cape, p. 266. |

Location of other material

Plans: G.L.C. *Architects Department.*

Programmes & cuttings: Kensington Local Collection.

824

TWO BREWERS PUBLIC HOUSE

13, Buckingham Row (*later* 96 James Street),
Westminster.

Licensed: 1863-1885.

Management

Middlesex justices:

Mich. 1863-	George Vigurs
" 1866-	Benjamin King
" 1885	*No notice of application, no certificate.*

Literature

Official records:

Mx. Mich. Q.S. 1863-1885.

825

TWO BREWERS PUBLIC HOUSE

Vine Street, Saffron Hill, Holborn.

Licensed: 1860-1861.

Management

Middlesex justices:

| Mich. 1860- | Henry Underhill |
| " 1861 | *House closed, no application.* |

Literature

Official records:

Mx. Mich. Q.S. 1860-1861.

826

TYSSEN ARMS PUBLIC HOUSE

Dalston.

Licensed: 1848-1857.

Management

Middlesex justices:

| Mich. 1848- | Sarah Johnson |
| " 1857 | *No petition, no application.* |

Literature

Official records:

Mx. Mich. Q.S. 1848-1857.

827

UNION SALOON

Shoreditch.

Mentioned as being run by Samuel Lane before he went to the Britannia Theatre.

Literature

Historical accounts:

1895 STUART, C. D., *and* PARK, A. G.
      The variety stage. pp. 37-38.
1898 SHOREDITCH OBSERVER, 1898 Feb. 12.
      Correspondence: Chapters of Old Shoreditch,
      X. Theatres—music halls—baths.

828

UNITY THEATRE

Goldington Street, St. Pancras.

Opened: 1936. *Theatre closed for rebuilding:* 1966.

Management

Not licensed as run as a theatre club.

Literature

Official records:

G.L.C. Arch. Dpt. Th. case 3117.

Contemporary accounts:

1966 THEATRE WORLD, 1944 March, pp. 18-19
      Work of the Unity Theatre, by P. Noble.
1947 ST. PANCRAS JOURNAL, 1947 Nov., No. 7,
      pp. 101-102. That great little theatre at
      King's Cross.
1948 ST. PANCRAS JOURNAL, 1948 Jan./Feb. *and*
      April. Nos. 9, 11. pp. 134, 180-181. Theatre of
      aspirations; *and* reply to a critic.

829

VARIETY THEATRE

18-20, Pitfield Street, Hoxton, Shoreditch.

Opened: 13th March 1870. *Cinema after* 1910.

Also known as

Theatre of Varieties
Varieties Music Hall
Harwood's Music Hall 1870-89—not official.
New King's Theatre 1903-6—not official, and in 1906
forbidden by the Lord Chamberlain.
Bromwich Theatre 1. 11. 1906-7. 9. 1907
Mortimer's Theatre 7. 9. 1907-Nov. 1907.
but managers continually reverted to 'Variety
Theatre'.

Building details

Built: 1869.

Architect: C. J. Phipps.

Capacity: 830.

Auditorium: P. 292; Bx. 220; G. 328.

Theatre adjoined and communicated with the public

house. The back parts of the boxes and gallery were formerly the 1st and 2nd floor of the public house, and were added after the original construction.

Management

Lord Chamberlain:

12.	3. 1870-	Verrell Nunn
29.	9. 1870-	George Harwood
11.	2. 1889-	Augustus Leach
17.	5. 1896-	James Kirk
29.	9. 1896-	Gilbert Hastings Macdermott
30.	5. 1901-	William Henry Pannell
4.	9. 1906-	Frederick William Bromwich
7.	9. 1907-	Leonard Mortimer
8.	11. 1907-	John Edward Stubbs
1.	11. 1909-	Matthew Raymond (to 31. 3. 1910).

Literature

Official records:

G.L.C. Arch. Dpt. Mss. index;
G.L.C. Arch. Dpt. Th. case 438;
L.C.C. Th. & M-H. Com. Papers, 1887-;
LCI/507-752; LC7/15-17, 23-48, and 89;
L.C.O. 162;
M.B.W. Rpt. 1882, pp. 355-61;
Sel. Com. 1877 and 1892.

Contemporary accounts:

1870 BUILDING NEWS, 1870 March 18, p. 210.
1905 MERCURY, 1905 March 18.—'Mr. Leonard
      Mortimer...'. port.
      SHOREDITCH MAIL, 1905 Sept. 2. 'Mr. Will
      Thompson (acting manager)'. 2. cols. port.

Historical accounts:

1913 STAR, 1913 Nov. 29.
      'Tales of the old halls: Hoxton Varieties to
      make way for cinema shows'.—Brief history.
1923 STAR, 1923 Aug. 15.
      'Seat in the stalls for sixpence: recollections
      of Harwood's Music Hall. Building now for
      sale. '

Location of other materials

Plans: G.L.C. Architects Department.

Public Record Office. LC7/83. 1869, 1874 and 1882.

Programmes, playbills & newscuttings:

Shoreditch Local Collection.

830

VAUDEVILLE THEATRE

404, Strand, Westminster.

Opened: 16th April 1870.

Building details

1st building:

Architect: C. J. Phipps.

Builder: Mr. Hyde.

Capacity: 1000.

Auditorium: S. 90; P. 285; D.C. 67; U.Bx. 88; A. 76;
G. 186.

2nd building:

Opened: 13.1.1891.

Architect: C.J.Phipps.

Capacity: 740.

Auditorium: P. 228; S. 140; B. 74; C. 89; U.C. 83; G. 111; Bx. 16.

Stage: 21′ 8½″ wide × 22′ 8″ deep.

3rd building:

Opened: 23.2.1926.

Architect: Robert Atkinson.

Capacity: 650.

Auditorium: S. 334; D.C. 188; U.C.167; Bx. 16.

Stage: 21′ 10″ wide × 29′ deep.

The façade that had been reconstructed in 1891 on the frontage of 403-4 Strand, was retained in 1926.

Management

Lord Chamberlain:

16. 4.1870-	Henry James Montague, David James, Thomas Thorne.
29. 9.1871-	David James and Thomas Thorn (sic).
29. 9.1881-	Thomas Thorn
29. 9.1892-	Stefano Gatti
29. 9.1895-	Agostino Gatti
29. 9.1896-	Stefano Gatti
10. 1.1905-	Agostino and Stefano Gatti and Charles Frohman.
1.11.1905-	John Maria Gatti and Rocco Gatti
1.12.1929-	Rocco Gatti
1.12.1932-	Arthur Herbert Greville Earle
1.12.1933-	Rocco Gatti
1.12.1935-	Andre Charlot
1.12.1937-	Robert Henry Schofield
1.12.1939-	Rocco Gatti and John Austin Gatti
1.12.1950-	John Austin Gatti.

In 1934 the L.C.C. granted a licence to Arthur Earle.

Literature

Official records:

G.L.C. Arch. Dpt. Mss. index;
G.L.C. Arch. Dpt. Th. case 451;
L.C.C. Th. & M-H. Com. Papers 1888-;
LC1/507-752; LC7/15-17, 23-48, and 189;
L.C.O. 307 and 374;
M.B.W. Rpt. 1882. pp. 83-93;
Sel. Com. 1877 and 1892.

Contemporary accounts:

1870 BUILDING NEWS, 1870 March 18, p. 210.
—Announcement of name.
ERA, 1870 April 17.—Description of opening, and theatre.
SUNDAY TIMES, 1870 April 17.—Description.
BUILDING NEWS, 1870 April 22, p. 305.
—Description,
BUILDING NEWS, 1870 April 29, p. 331.
—Correction.
BUILDING NEWS, 1870 May 6, p. 348.—Reply.
BUILDER, 1870 April 23, p. 319.—Description.
1879 DRAMATIC NOTES, 1879, pp. 53-5.
1887 SATURDAY REVIEW, 1887 July 16. 'The state of the London theatres...No. 5'.

1890 BUILDER, 1890 July 12, p. 33.—Brief note of proposed remodelling of theatre.
1891 ERA, 1891 Jan. 10.—Description.
ILLUSTRATED SPORTING AND DRAMATIC NEWS, 1891 Jan. 24. illus.
1895 BUILDER, 1895 Feb. 2, p. 77.—Report of Messrs. Crompton & Co.'s heating of the Vaudeville by electricity.
1926 BUILDER, 1926, March 19, pp. 463, 472, 474-6.
—Description, photos., plans.
1950 THEATRE ownership...p. 76 (3 lines only).

Historical accounts:

1904 BAKER, H. Barton.
History of the London stage and its players. pp. 498-501.
1920 RENDLE, T. McDonald
Jubilee of the Vaudeville Theatre, 1870-1920.
Miles, (1920). 33p. illus., ports, facsims.
c. 1930 MAYES, Ronald
The romance of London theatres, No. 10.
1945 THEATRE WORLD, 1945 Nov. pp. 26-7.
History of the Vaudeville Theatre, 1870-1945; by A. F. M. Beales.
1959 ENCICLOPEDIA dello spettacolo, Vol. 6, Col. 1637.
1963 MANDER, Raymond, *and* MITCHENSON, Joe.
The theatres of London. 2nd ed. pp. 191-198.

Location of other material

Plans: G.L.C. *Architects Department;* Enthoven Collection 1927 (2 sheets); Public Record Office LC7/84. 5 sheets, 1870.

Programmes:

British Museum Library; Enthoven Collection; Garrick Club; Guildhall Library; London Museum; Westminster Local Collection.

831

VAUXHALL GARDENS

Lambeth.

Opened: during 17th century.
Closed: 25th July 1859.

Management (after 1850)

Surrey justices:

Mich. 1849-	William Fowler
" 1858-	Henry Ernest
" 1859	*No application.*

Literature

Official records:

Sy. Mich. Q.S. 1849-1858.

Contemporary accounts:

1850 ERA, 1850 Feb. 17, p. 10.—Bankruptcies of Cremorne and Vauxhall Gardens.
1862-5 PARTICULARS of sales in connection with the Vauxhall Gardens Estate. 22. Aug. 1862.
20. May 1864. 11th April 1865 (Copies in the Guildhall Library).

Historical accounts:

1870 ERA ALMANACK, 1870, pp. 9-16.

1908 DAILY TELEGRAPH, 1908, Jan. 25.
     The old gardens...—Brief history.
1925 CHANCELLOR, E.B.
     The pleasure haunts of London...pp. 205-227.
c. 1930 MAYES, Ronald
     The romance of London theatres, Nos. 81 and
     120.
1946 SCOTT, Harold
     The early doors..pp. 22-, pp. 62-.
1951 LONDON. County Council.
     Survey of London. Vol. 23, 1951. pp. 64, 123, 145,
     146-7. Plates 124-7.

Location of other material

Playbills (&c). British Museum Library; Enthoven Collection; Guildhall Library; Lambeth Local Collection.

Scrapbook:

HANDBILLS and programmes c. 1827-1859. (182 items—133 handbills—10 tickets—3 maps, 20 leaves of sale catalogues—10 illustrations &c.) *in* London Museum Library.

832

VICAR OF WAKEFIELD PUBLIC HOUSE

83, Coventry Street (*formerly* Suffolk Street), Bethnal Green.

Licensed: 1855-1890.

Management

Middlesex justices:

Mich.	1855-	John Goward
"	1861-	John Elves
"	1863-	William George
"	1865-	Alexander Smellie
"	1871-	Henry Blyther
"	1874-	Fulcher Johnson
"	1875-	George Leech
"	1877-	George Wells
"	1879-	Frederick Thomas Hillyard
"	1880-	Ellen Hillyard
"	1881-	George Alfred Page
"	1884-	Charles William Ewen
"	1886-	George Frederick Weige

London County Council:

1890   Frederick John Weige
Nov. 1890   *No application.*

Literature

Official records:

L.C.C. Th. & M-H. Com. App. Nov. 1889.
Mx. Mich. Q.S. 1855-1888.

833

VICTORIA HALL

118, Holywell Street, Shoreditch.

Licensed: 1854-1866.

Former name

Bianchi's Waxwork Exhibition Rooms to 1861.

Management

Middlesex justices:

Mich.	1854-	Peter Bianchi
"	1861-	William Griffiths
"	1864-	William Allsop
"	1866	*No notice, no petition.*

Literature

Official records:

Mx. Mich. Q.S. 1854-1865.

834

VICTORIA PALACE

126, Victoria Street, Victoria.

Opened as a place of entertainment c. 1840.

Former names

Royal Standard Hotel, Stockdale Terrace.
Moy's Music Hall (unofficial name)
Royal Standard Music Hall
Victoria Palace Theatre.

Building details

1832: Public house built.

1863: Hall redecorated.

Opened: 26. 12. 1863.

Capacity: 2440

Auditorium: S. 681; B. & Bx. 448; G. 399.

Vaudeville Theatre 1891 (830)

(British Museum)

1886: The Stockdale Terrace building demolished for the building of Victoria Station.
Royal Standard Music Hall erected.

1911: Hall rebuilt.

Opened: 6.11.1911.

Architect: Frank Matcham

Builder: Henry Lovatt, Ltd.

Capacity: 1500

Auditorium: S 700; D.C. 385; U.C. 400; 6 Bx.; G.

Stage: 35' wide × 25' deep.

Management

Middlesex justices:

Mich. 1848-	John Moy	
" 1864-	Robert Alfred Brown	
" 1869-	Alfred Elliott	
" 1873-	Robert Bunn	
" 1877-	Richard Wake.	

London County Council:

1890-	Richard Wake
1897-	Thomas Samuel Dickie
1912-	Alfred Butt
1925-	Victoria Palace, Ltd. (through 1950).

Lord Chamberlain:

12. 1.1912-	Alfred Butt
1.12.1930-	Richard Henry Gillespie
1.12.1948-	Val. Parnell.

Literature

Official records:

G.L.C. Arch. Dpt. Mss. index; G.L.C. Arch. Dpt. Th. case 289; L.C.C. Th. & M-H. Com. App. Nov. 1889-; L.C.O. 374 and 511;
Mx. Mich. Q.S. 1850-1888.

Contemporary accounts:

1901	ERA, 1901 Nov. 4.—Description.
1911	BUILDER, 1910, July 9, p. 51.—Report that company formed to acquire Royal Standard and an adjoining site in Allington St. to build new theatre.
1950	THEATRE ownership. . .p. 62 and p. 98.

Historical accounts:

1891	ERA ALMANACK, 1891 —Description of 1886 rebuilding.
c. 1930	MAYES, Ronald The romance of London theatres, No. 114.
1935	HADDON, Archibald The story of the music hall. . .—Various refs.
1959	ENCICLOPEDIA dello spettacolo, Vol. 6, Col. 1637.
1963	MANDER, Raymond, *and* MITCHENSON, Joe. The theatres of London. 2nd ed. pp. 199-202.
1965	MANDER, Raymond, *and* MITCHENSON, Joe. British Music Hall. . . Illus. nos. 54 and 223, with brief text.

Location of other material

Plans: G.L.C. *Architects Department.*

Programmes:

Enthoven Collection; Westminster Local Collection.

250

835

VICTORIA PUBLIC HOUSE

Boundary Road, Hampstead.

Licensed: 1856-1867.

Management

Middlesex justices:

Mich. 1856-	Charles Somers	
" 1857-	Edwin Charles White	
" 1866-	Andrew Weatherly	
" 1867	*No notice, no petition.*	

Literature

Official records:

Mx. Mich. Q.S. 1856-1867.

836

VICTORIA PUBLIC HOUSE

Gainsboro' Road, Hackney Wick.

Licensed: 1868-1891.

Management

Middlesex justices:

Mich. 1868-	John F. Battle	
" 1874-	Robert Croucher	
" 1879-	George Denton	
" 1881-	Alexander Smellie	

London County Council:

1890-	Alexander Smellie
Nov. 1891	*No application.*

Literature

Official records:

L.C.C. Th. & M-H. Com. App. Nov. 1889-1890; Mx. Mich. Q.S. 1868-1888.

837

VICTORIA PUBLIC HOUSE AND TEA GARDEN

110, Grove Road, Bethnal Green.

Licensed: 1857-1890.

Management

Middlesex justices:

Mich. 1857-	George Healey	
" 1860-	James Withers	
" 1861-	Thomas Adams	
" 1863-	Sarah Coppen	
" 1865-	Thomas Swindell	
" 1867-	George Chamberlain	
" 1868-	John Davis	
" 1871-	Cord Campe	
" 1875-	Henry Phillips	
" 1883-	William George Bradly	

London County Council:

1890-	Edward James Bradley
Nov. 1890	*Licence refused.*

Literature

Official records:

L.C.C. Th. & M-H. Com. App. Nov. 1889-1890;
Mx. Mich. Q.S. 1857-1888.

838

VICTORIA PUBLIC HOUSE

21, Morpeth Road, Bethnal Green.

Licensed: 1854-1890.

Building details

The music hall was on the first floor, and measured
13′ 6″ × 29′ 9″. It was closed as a result of the 1878
Act.

Management

Middlesex justices:

Mich. 1854-	Richard Coleman Nunn	
"	1855-	Christopher George Poole
"	1856-	Robert Carr
"	1860-	Charles Johnson
"	1865-	Sharp Tugby
"	1876-	Joseph Coveney
"	1877-	William Wilse Key
"	1878-	Walter Hammond
"	1879-	Samuel Scarf

London County Council:

1890   Samuel Scarf
Nov. 1890   *No application.*

Literature

Official records:

G.L.C. Arch. Dpt. Th. case 040/166; L.C.C. Th. & M-H.
Com. App. Nov. 1889; Mx. Mich. Q.S. 1854-1888.

839

VICTORIA PUBLIC HOUSE

Queen's Road, Dalston.

Licensed: 1870-1891.

Management

Middlesex justices:

Mich. 1870-	William Harris Johns	
"	1872-	Henry Guillam Worlock
"	1873-	Charles Tubb
"	1874-	Andrew Price
"	1876-	William Moore
"	1878-	Charles John Glassborow
"	1886-	Alfred William Grimes

London County Council:

1890-   Alfred William Grimes
Nov. 1891   *Transfer of licence refused.*

Literature

Official records:

L.C.C. Th. & M-H. Com. App. Nov. 1889-1891;
Mx. Mich. Q.S. 1870-1888.

840

VICTORIA THEATRE OF VARIETIES

Marsham Street, Westminster.

Licensed: 1887-1890.

Also known as

Blue Ribbon Hall.

Building details

The music hall was situated at the rear of premises
fronting on the Marsham Street. The hall was fitted
up as a theatre. It had a small stage, proscenium
wall, footlights and a drop curtain.

Capacity: 175

Auditorium: Ar. 150; G. 25.

It was closed as a result of the 1878 Act.

Management

Middlesex justices:

Mich. 1887-   James Sanderson

London County Council:

1890   James Sanderson
Nov. 1890   *Licence refused.*

Literature

Official records:

G.L.C. Arch. Dpt. Th. case 040/16; L.C.C. Th. & M-H.
Com. App. Nov. 1889-1890; Mx. Mich. Q.S. 1887-1888.

Location of other materials

Plans: G.L.C. *Architects Department.*

841

VICTORY PUBLIC HOUSE

Rotherhithe New Road.

Licensed: 1873-1889.

Management

Surrey justices:

Mich. 1873-	John Parsons	
"	1874-	Alfred George Sibun
"	1875-	William David Butler
"	1879-	John Parker
"	1888	William Blackmore Salter.

The hall was not licensed by the L.C.C. in 1889.

Literature

Official records:

Sy. Mich. Q.S. 1873-1888.

842

VOLUNTEER PUBLIC HOUSE

Mill Place, Commercial Road, Limehouse.

Licensed: 1869-1879.

Management

Middlesex justices:

Mich.	1869-	Thomas Holmes
"	1874-	Thomas Napier Beach
"	1876-	Joseph Myerscough
"	1879	*Application withdrawn.*

Literature

Official records:

Mx. Mich. Q.S. 1869-1879.

843

WAGGON AND HORSE PUBLIC HOUSE

10, Hertford Road, Kingsland, Hackney.

Licensed: 1862-1875.

Management

Middlesex justices:

Mich.	1862-	Joseph Horner
"	1863-	Henry Raybould
"	1866-	Joseph Octavius Sanders
"	1868-	John Jones
"	1869-	Cornelius Young
"	1871-	George Whowell
"	1872-	John Jones
"	1875	*No formal application* by Esther Stratford.

Literature

Official records:

Mx. Mich. Q.S. 1862-1875.

844

WALLACE ARMS PUBLIC HOUSE

Bethnal Green Road, Bethnal Green.

Licensed: 1880-1883.

Management

Middlesex justices:

Mich.	1880-	George Curtis
"	1881-	William Morgan
"	1882-	Charles Leonard
"	1883	*No application, no certificate.*

Literature:

Official records:

Mx. Mich, Q.S. 1880-1882.

848

WALPOLE ARMS PUBLIC HOUSE

Sandy Hill, Woolwich.

Licensed: 1867-1891.

Management

West Kent justices:

Mich.	1867-	William Nowlan
"	1870-	Edmund Biddick Jnr.
"	1873-	William Phillips

252

London County Council:

1890-	William Phillips
Nov. 1891	*No application.*

Literature

Official records:

L.C.C. Th. & M-H. Com. App. Nov. 1889-1890;
W. Kt. Mich. Q.S. 1867-1888.

846

WATERLOO HERO PUBLIC HOUSE

Gough Street, Poplar.

Licensed: 1861-1884

Management

Middlesex justices:

Mich.	1861-	Henry Holt, Jnr.
"	1863-	Joshua Holt.
"	1867-	James Royner
"	1877-	James Finch
"	1880-	George Henry Hake
"	1882-	John Flower
"	1883-	George Kirkley
"	1884	*Licence refused as it had not been used for two years.*

Literature

Official records:

Mx. Mich. Q.S. 1861-1884.

847

WATERMAN'S ARMS PUBLIC HOUSE

Castle Street (later 43 Virginia Road), Bethnal Green.

Licensed: 1855-63, and 1865-1890.

Management

Middlesex justices:

Mich.	1855-	William Godier
"	1860-	George Coe
"	1863	*No application*
"	1865-	John Quaintrell
"	1868-	George English
"	1877-	William Frederick Norton
"	1880-	Arthur Leonard Lawrence
"	1881-	James Hart
"	1888	Emily Hart

London County Council:

1890	Emily Hart
Nov. 1890	*Licence refused.*

Literature

Official records:

L.C.C. Th. & M-H. Com. App. Nov. 1889-1890;
Mx. Mich. Q.S. 1855-1863, 1865-1888.

848

WATERMAN'S ARMS PUBLIC HOUSE

Waterman's Fields, Woolwich.

Licensed: 1866-1867.

Management

West Kent justices:

Mich. 1866-   William Nowlan
"   1867   *No application.*

Literature

Official records:

W. Kt. Mich. Q.S. 1866-1867.

849

WEAVER'S ARMS PUBLIC HOUSE

Baker's Row, Whitechapel.

Licensed: 1854-1859.

Management

Middlesex justices:

Mich. 1854-   William Brown
"   1855-   John West
"   1859   *Application opposed.*

Literature

Official records:

Mx. Mich. Q.S. 1854-1859.

850

WELLINGTON HALL

Wellington Street (*later* Almeida Street), Islington.

Licensed: 1871-1903.

Management

Middlesex justices:

Mich. 1871-   John Grover

London County Council:

1890-   John Grover
1896-   Charles Smith
1898-   Albert James Morgan
Nov. 1903   *Not listed as a theatre or music hall.*

Literature

Official records:

L.C.C. Th. & M-H. Com. App. Nov. 1889-1903;
Mx. Mich, Q.S. 1871-1888;
Sel. Com. 1892.

851

WELLINGTON MUSIC HALL

28 and 29, Brooke Street, St. Andrew, Holborn.

Licensed: 1856-1858, and 1865-1879.

Former names

Greyhound Public House
Wellington Public House.

Management

Middlesex justices:

Mich. 1856-   Henry Philip Lyon
"   1857-   Thomas Mansfield (to Mich. 1858)
"   1865-   Edward Scales
"   1866-   Annie Maria Scales
"   1867-   John Randall
"   1874-   William Athole Robertson
"   1876-   John Baker
"   1877-   Frederick William May
"   1878-   Charles Guttman
"   1879   William Braithwaite Feethan reported
               to have absconded.

Literature

Official records:

Mx. Mich. Q.S. 1856-7, 1865-79.

852

WEST KENT YEOMAN PUBLIC HOUSE

63, Edward Street, Deptford.

Licensed: 1868-1890.

Building details

The concert hall on the 1st floor, 30'6" × 23'6", with
a raised platform. It was used on Monday and Saturday evenings, averaging 80 visitors.
The hall was closed as a result of the 1878 Act.

Management

West Kent justices:

Mich. 1868-   George Henry Boncey
"   1869-   Frederick Malyon
"   1877-   Richard John Poole
"   1878-   Alfred James Arnold
"   1879-   Thomas Foster
"   1884-   Charles Spurgin
"   1886-   William Thomas Bird.

London County Council:

1890-   Alexander Cavender
Nov. 1890   *Licence refused.*

Literature

Official records:

G.L.C. Arch. Dpt. Th. case 040/169;
L.C.C. Th. & M-H. Com. App. Nov. 1889-1890;
W. Kt. Mich. Q.S. 1868-1888.

Location of other material

Plans: G.L.C. *Architects Department.*

853

WEST LONDON THEATRE

69, Church Street, Edgware Road, St. Marylebone.

Opened: 1832.   *Cinema:* 1932.   *Damaged by bombing:*
1941.

Former names

Royal Pavilion West 1832-35
Portman Theatre 1835-37

Royal Mary-le-bone Theatre 1837
Royal Marylebone Theatre 1837-68
Theatre Royal, Marylebone—used occasionally
Royal Alfred Theatre 1868-73
Alfred Theatre—used occasionally
Royal Marylebone Theatre 1873-1893
Royal West London Theatre
West London Stadium 1916-17.

Building details

1831: Erected.

1842: Rebuilt.

1854: Enlarged.

Capacity: (1882) c. 1500.

Auditorium: S. 148; P. 441; Bx. 218; G. 564; Bx. 70.

1914: Stage altered and provided with seating and a boxing ring.

Management

Lord Chamberlain:

29. 9. 1843-	John Douglass
8. 9. 1847-	Robert William Warner
29. 9. 1848-	Walter Watts
8. 4. 1850-	John Loveridge
18. 11. 1850-	Joseph Stammers
29. 9. 1851-	Edward Tyrrell Smith
29. 9. 1853-	James William Wallack
29. 9. 1855-	John Douglass
29. 9. 1856-	Samuel Anderson Emery
29. 9. 1857-	Joseph Clarence Holt
29. 9. 1858-	Joseph Henry Arnold Cave
29. 9. 1868-	Henry Richard Lacey
31. 2. 1869-	Marian Henrade
27. 7. 1869-	Charles Harcourt, and George Frederick Sydney
29. 9. 1869-	George Frederick Sydney (later wanted for forgery).
29. 3. 1870-	Mrs. Ellen Sydney
29. 9. 1870-	Robert Hale
21. 11. 1870-	Edward Giovanelli
8. 4. 1871-	Charles Harcourt
16. 11. 1872-	James Frederick McFadyen
24. 5. 1873-	Joseph Cave
29. 9. 1878-	John (sic) Cave, and Albert West
2. 7. 1883-	George Augustus Loveridge, and Alfred Loveridge
31. 3. 1885-	Thomas George Clark
23. 5. 1885-	Alfred Loveridge
29. 9. 1886-	Henry Gascoigne
9. 3. 1889-	Enrique Colchester
28. 9. 1891-	Henry Gascoigne
29. 3. 1893-	William Bailey
25. 4. 1910-	Frederick Richard Griffiths (theatre purchase by New Bioscope Trading Co.)
21. 8. 1911-	George Robson Beaumont
24. 2. 1913-	Henry John Goldberg
3. 3. 1913-	Henry John Goldberg and John George Bartleman
30. 11. 1913-	John George Bartleman
1. 5. 1914-	John Stewart Percy

Letter dated 4. 6. 1914 states licence no longer required as building now used exclusively as a cinema.

1. 12. 1915-	Arthur Frederick Bettinson (to 30. 11. 1916)

London County Council:

1915-	Sidney James Steel
1916-	Arthur Frederick Bettinson
1918-	William Herbert Percy
Nov. 1923	*Listed as a cinema.*

Literature

Official records:

G.L.C. Arch. Dpt. Mss. index;
G.L.C. Arch. Dpt. Th. case 453;
L.C.C. Th. & M-H. Com. App. Nov. 1915-1923; Papers, 1888-;
L.C.O. 359; LC1/508-752; LC7/13-17, 20-48, and 89;
M.B.W. Rpt. 1182, pp. 193-205;
Sel. Com. 1866, 1877 and 1892.

Contemporary accounts:

1864 ROYAL MARYLEBONE THEATRE
7th year of an uninterrupted season: address to the public (by Joseph Cave). 10th May, 1864.

1868 BUILDING NEWS, 1868 Sept. 4, pp. 598-9. —Report of lawsuit following builders failure to meet M.B.W.'s requirements.

1879 DRAMATIC NOTES, 1879, pp. 73-4.

1884 BUILDER, 1884 Oct. 25, p. 575. —Report of summons.

1885 BUILDER, 1885 March 7, p. 329. —Report of fine for neglecting state of building.

1887 SATURDAY REVIEW, 1887 July 30. 'The state of the London theatres. . . . No. 7'.

1890 BUILDER, 1890 March 15, p. 188. —Report of auction.

1908 BUILDER, 1908 Oct. 31, p. 471. —Report that property up for sale. Summary of history.

Historical accounts:

1883 WILLIAMS, Michael
Some London theatres. . . pp. 80-116.

1893 EDWARDS, Francis, *Bookseller.*
Playbills: a collection and some comments. . . pp. 7-13.

1904 BAKER, H. Barton.
History of the London stage and its players. . . p. 438.

1925 SHERSON, Erroll
London's lost theatres. . . pp. 278-289.

c. 1930 MAYES, Ronald
The romance of London theatres, Nos. 117 and 218.

c. 1940 WILSON, A. E.
Pantomine pageant. . . Various refs.

1954 THEATRE WORLD, 1954 June.
Lost London theatres, by N. M. Bligh. No. 2. The story of the Marylebone Theatre. 2p. illus.

1959 ENCICLOPEDIA dello spettacolo. Vol. 6, Col. 1637.
STAGE, 1959 Sept. 17,
—Article on history by Stewart Valdar.

1960 MORLEY, Malcolm
The old Marylebone Theatre. St. Marylebone Society, 1960. 40p. (Publication No. 2).

1962 MORLEY, Malcolm
Royal West London Theatre. St. Marylebone Society, 1962. 44p. (Publication No. 6).

Location of other material

Plans:

G.L.C. *Architects Department.*

Enthoven Collection., 1936 (3 sheets)—cinema.
Public Record Office. LC7/67. 1 sheet. 1863.

Programmes and playbills:

British Museum Library, Enthoven Collection;
Garrick Club; Guildhall Library; St. Marlebone
Local Collection; Westminster Local Collection.

854

WESTMINSTER THEATRE

12, Palace Street, Buckingham Palace Road,
Westminster.

Opened: 7th October 1931.

Building details

In 1830 a chapel of ease was built.
In 1924 the chapel was converted into a cinema, a new
frontage was also added. (St. James' Picture Theatre).
In 1931 the building was converted into a theatre.

Capacity: 650.

Auditorium: S. 480; B. & Bx.

Stage: 27' 6" wide × 17' deep at centre.

Management

Lord Chamberlain:

1.12.1931-	Alderson Burrell Horne (i.e. Amner Hall. pseud.)
1.12.1946-	James Kenneth Lindsay.

London County Council:

1936-	Alderson Burrell Horne
1947-	Robert Stuart Sanderson.

Literature

Official records:

L.C.C. Th. & M-H. Com. App. Nov. 1935-;
L.C.O. 256 and 374.

Contemporary accounts:

c.1930 MAYES, Ronald
      The romance of London theatres, No. 174.
1931 THEATRE WORLD, 1931 Nov. 'Westminster's
      triumph'.
1950 THEATRE ownership...p. 76.

Historical accounts:

1959 ENCICLOPEDIA dello spettacolo.Vol. 6,
      Col. 1637.
1963 MANDER, Raymond, *and* MITCHENSON, Joe.
      The theatres of London. 2nd ed. pp. 203-206.
1965 BELDEN, K. D.
      The story of the Westminster Theatre. West-
      minster Productions Ltd., 1965. 56p. plates.

Location of other material

Plans: G.L.C. *Architects Department.*

Programmes:

Enthoven Collection; London Museum;
Westminster Local Collection.

855

WESTMINSTER ARMS PUBLIC HOUSE

Warner Place South, Bethnal Green.

Licensed: 1861-1890.

Management

Middlesex justices:

Mich.	1861-	John Everard
"	1866-	Frederick Lock
"	1874-	John Wilson
"	1877-	Thomas John Buxley
"	1885-	William Marcus Critchfield
"	1887-	Raffaelle Critchfield

London County Council:

1890	Raffaelle Critchfield
Nov. 1890	*Licence refused.*

Literature

Official records:

L.C.C. Th. & M-H. Com. App. Nov. 1889-1890;
Mx. Mich. Q.S. 1861-1888.

856

WESTMINSTER TEMPERANCE HALL

93, Regent Street (*later* Regency Street), St. John the
Evangelist, Pimlico, Westminster.

Licensed: 1875-1886.

Managment

Middlesex justices:

Mich.	1875-	John Thomas Wadham
"	1876-	Edward Curtice
"	1882-	Henry Longden
"	1883-	Thomas John Jennings
"	1886	*No notice of application, no petition, no certificate.*

Literature

Official records:

Mx. Mich. Q.S. 1875-1886.

Note

In the Select Committee report of 1866, the *Westminster*, Pimlico is reported to have been built at
a cost of £3000, and to have a capacity of 800.
Mention is also made of the hall in the 1877 report,
but there are no licensing records for a hall of that
name in the 1860's, and no information to link it
definitely with the Westminster Temperance Hall.

857

WESTON'S RETREAT

Rear of 93-97, Highgate Road, St. Pancras.

Opened: June 1863. *Closed:* October 1866.

Literature

Contemporary accounts:

1863   ERA, 1863 April 19. —Announcement of opening.
ERA, 1863 May 24. —Announcement of postponement and final opening.

Historical accounts:

1902   ST. PANCRAS NOTES AND QUERIES, 1902
Jan. 3. No. 228. pp. 177-180.
ST. PANCRAS GUARDIAN. 1902 Jan. 3.
Article by 'P' (Mr. R. B. Prosser).
1907   WROTH, Warwick
Cremorne and the later London gardens...
pp. 44-5.
1938   LONDON County Council
Survey of London... Vol. 19. p. 57.
1961   REYNOLDS, E.
Recreations and leisure in St. Pancras...
pp. 19-20.

858

WHEATSHEAF PUBLIC HOUSE AND MUSIC HALL

Hand Court, Holborn.

Licensed: 1855-1858.

Management

Middlesex justices:

Mich. 1855-	Henry George Oliver
" 1856-	William Burton
" 1858	*No petition.*

Literature

Official records:

Mx. Mich. Q.S. 1855-1858.

859

WHEATSHEAF PUBLIC HOUSE

Upper Marylebone Street, St. Marylebone.

Licensed: 1851-1860.

Management

Middlesex justices:

Mich. 1851-	Thomas Newell Newton
" 1853-	George Gaze
" 1860	*Licence refused. Petition lodged in the name of John Ellen. No notice of transfer.*

Literature

Official records:

Mx. Mich. Q.S. 1851-1860.

860

WHITE BEAR PUBLIC HOUSE

1, St. George Street (*formerly* Ratcliff Highway),
St. George in the East.

Licensed: 1854-1887.

Management

Middlesex justices:

Mich. 1854-	Herman Gerdes
" 1860-	Hinrich Brandes
" 1864-	John Bonken
" 1873-	Hans G. Siert
" 1882-	Justine Wilhelmine Siert
" 1884-	Paul Carl Richard Gross
" 1886-	George James Jones
" 1887	*No notice, no certificate.*

Literature

Official records:

Mx. Mich. Q.S. 1854-1886.

861

WHITE CONDUIT HOUSE

1, Queen's Terrace, Islington.

Licensed: 1850-1853.

Management

Middlesex justices:

Mich. 1847-	Richard Rouse
" 1848-	John William Read
" 1851-	Benjamin Hudson
" 1854	*No petition, no application.*

Literature

Official records:

Mx. Mich. Q.S. 1850-1852.

Historical accounts:

1896   WROTH, Warwick.
The London pleasure gardens...

862

WHITE HART PUBLIC HOUSE

Bethnal Green Road, Bethnal Green.

Licensed: 1860-1866.

Management

Middlesex justices:

Mich. 1860-	Thomas George Jones
" 1862-	Henry Quaintrell
" 1866	*No notice, no petition.*

Literature

Official records:

Mx. Mich. Q.S. 1860-1865.

863

WHITE HART PUBLIC HOUSE

191, Drury Lane, Holborn.

Licensed: 1852-1891.

Management

Middlesex justices:

Mich. 1852-   Henry George Oliver
"   1855-   William Daniel Haines
"   1856-   Frederic Ludby
"   1863-   Thomas Groves
"   1877-   Emilia Ann Hitchen
"   1878-   George Greenfield
"   1880-   George May
"   1887-   James Leftwich Warner

London County Council:

1890-   James Leftwich Warner
Nov. 1891   *No application.*

Literature

Official records:

L.C.C. Th. & M-H. Com. App. Nov. 1889-1890;
Mx. Mich. Q.S. 1852-1888.

864

WHITE HART PUBLIC HOUSE

Gray's Place, Roadside, Mile End, Old Town.

Licensed: 1856-1865.

Management

Middlesex justices:

Mich. 1856-   Charles Gurney
"   1861-   Frederick Stubbs
"   1864-   Nicholas Pollybank
"   1865   *No notice, no petition.*

Literature

Official records:

Mx. Mich. Q.S. 1856-1864.

865

WHITE HART PUBLIC HOUSE

49, King's Road, Chelsea.

Licensed: Pre 1850-1890.

Management

Middlesex justices:

Mich. 1848-   Francis Ward
"   1869-   William Woodcock Pitt
"   1875-   Thomas Clifford
"   1878-   Matilda Jemina Potter
"   1881-   James John Pope
"   1887-   George Perugia

London County Council:

1890   George Perugia.
Nov. 1890.   *Licence refused as work required had
not been completed.*

Literature

Official records:

L.C.C. Th. & M-H. Com. App. Nov. 1889-1890;
Mx. Mich. Q.S. 1848-1888.

866

WHITE HART PUBLIC HOUSE

43, Leman Street, Whitechapel.

Licensed: 1853-1864.

Management

Middlesex justices:

Mich. 1853-   Adolphus Alexander
"   1854-   Isaac Levy
"   1858-   Henry Dittman
"   1859-   Elizabeth Kisler
"   1861-   Melchior Bamm
"   1864   *Licence refused following police
report.*

Applications to the L.C.C. in Nov. 1890 were refused.

Literature

Official records:

L.C.C. Th. & M-H. Com. App. Nov. 1889-1890.
Mx. Mich. Q.S. 1853-1890.

867

WHITE HART PUBLIC HOUSE

New Cross Road, Hatcham.

Licensed: 1876-1889.

Management

Surrey justices:

Mich. 1876-   James Veysey Southcott
"   1880-   *Executors of above.*
"   1881-   Frederick Alexander. (through 1888).

Not relicensed by the L.C.C.

Literature

Official records:

Sy. Mich. Q.S. 1876-1888.

868

WHITE HORSE PUBLIC HOUSE

Baldwin's Gardens, Holborn.

Licensed: 1855-1856.

Management

Middlesex justices:

Mich. 1855-   Thomas Grogan
"   1856   *No petition.*

Literature

Official records:

Mx. Mich. Q.S. 1855-1856.

869

WHITE HORSE PUBLIC HOUSE

21, Castle Street East, Oxford Market, St. Marylebone.

Licensed: 1862-1885.

Management

Middlesex justices:

Mich.	1862–	Henry Thomas Turner
"	1863–	Alexander Matthew Jackson
"	1864–	Samuel Crago
"	1865–	John Kinggett
"	1867–	John Clapham
"	1868–	Joseph Brown
"	1869–	Walter Maiden
"	1873–	William Simmons
"	1874–	Thomas Ming
"	1875–	John Rumsey, Jnr.
"	1876–	John Alfred Avey
"	1877–	Henry James Maisey
"	1879–	Walter John Batchelor
"	1880–	William John Hutchins
"	1881–	Albert Berg
"	1885	*No notice of application, no certificate.*

Literature

Official records:

Mx. Mich. Q.S. 1862–1885.

870

WHITE HORSE PUBLIC HOUSE

12, Fann Street, Aldersgate.

In the theatre case (see below) it is stated that a small music hall existed on the first floor in the rear of the premises. The hall, which seated 130 persons, had a small stage.
It was closed as a result of the 1878 Act.

Literature

Official records:

G.L.C. Arch. Dpt. Th. case 040/173, including plans.

871

WHITE HORSE PUBLIC HOUSE

21, Finsbury Street, St. Luke, Finsbury.

Licensed: 1862–1865.

Management

Middlesex justices:

Mich.	1862–	Henry Eager
"	1863–	William Mills
"	1864–	Joseph Radburn
"	1865	*No notice, no petition.*

Literature

Official records:

Mx. Mich. Q.S. 1862–1865.

872

WHITE HORSE PUBLIC HOUSE

Hare Street, Bethnal Green.

Licensed: 1861–1890.

Management

Middlesex justices:

Mich.	1861–	Thomas Blake
"	1876–	John Elves
"	1877–	Ebenezer Ferry
"	1884–	John Thomas Grinonneau

London County Council:

1890   John Thomas Grinonneau
Nov. 1890   *Licence refused.*

Literature

Official records:

L.C.C. Th. & M-H. Com. App. Nov. 1889–1890;
Mx Mich. Q.S. 1861–1888.

873

WHITE HORSE PUBLIC HOUSE

100, Holborn, St. Andrew, Holborn.

Licensed: 1854–1859.

Management

Middlesex justices:

Mich.	1854–	Robert Collons
"	1857–	Henry Phillips
"	1859	*No petition. Said to have left house.*

Literature

Official records:

Mx. Mich. Q.S. 1854–1859.

874

WHITE HORSE PUBLIC HOUSE

Roman Road, Stratford, Bow.

Licensed: 1865–1883.

Management

Mich.	1865–	William Veale
"	1869–	George Hillyer
"	1883	*Licence refused as it was seldom used.*

Literature

Official records:

Mx. Mich. Q.S. 1865–1883.

875

WHITE LION PUBLIC HOUSE

Church Street, Woolwich.

Licensed: 1848–1854, and 1872–1884.

Management

West Kent justices:

Mich.	1848–	Thomas Selves
"	1853–	William Hare
"	1854	*No application.*
"	1872–	George Robert Lomax

	1874-	Arthur Culver
"	1877-	William Asher Kirby
"	1880-	Richard Shaw Bell
"	1885	*No application.*

Literature

Official records:

W. Kt. Mich. Q.S. 1848-1853, and 1872-1884.

876

WHITE LION PUBLIC HOUSE

49, Green Bank, Wapping.

Licensed: 1856-1890.

Management

Middlesex justices:

Mich.	1856-	Robert Daniel Upson
"	1857-	Alfred Smeeton
"	1859-	Charles Nicholls
"	1861-	Charles Bannister
"	1870-	William Bartholomew
"	1873-	Joseph Bannister
"	1879-	William Lawrence

London County Council:

1890	William Lawrence
Nov. 1890	*No application.*

Literature

Official records:

L.C.C. Th. & M-H. Com. App. Nov. 1889;
Mx. Mich. Q.S. 1856-1888.

877

WHITE LION PUBLIC HOUSE

Hackney Wick.

Licensed: 1851-1891.

Building details

The music hall was on the ground floor and measured 19' 6" × 19' 5". It was closed as a result of the 1878 Act.

Management

Middlesex justices:

Mich.	1851-	John Baum
"	1854-	Elizabeth and James Baum
"	1858-	James Collins Baum
"	1869-	James Strutt
"	1872-	Alexander James Baxter
"	1875-	Joseph Elves
"	1876-	Alfred Henry Coltman
"	1880-	Joseph B. Sherwin and James B. Sherwin
"	1881-	Jospeh B. Sherwin
"	1886-	Alfred Yates
"	1888	George Gravely and Joseph Holland.

London County Council:

1890	John Jennings, and later Harriet Lucy Jennings

1891	William George Newman
Nov. 1891	*No application.*

Literature

Official records:

G.L.C. Arch. Dpt. Th. case 040/174;
L.C.C. Th. & M-H. Com. App. Nov. 1889-90;
Mx Mich. Q.S. 1851-1888.

878

WHITE LION PUBLIC HOUSE

68, Shadwell High Street, Shadwell.

Licensed: 1859-1884.

Management

Middlesex justices:

Mich.	1859-	Matthew Mills
"	1862-	Thomas Husselbee
"	1865-	Joseph Timms
"	1867-	Thomas Barlow Lovell
"	1868-	James Hams
"	1869-	William Creighton
"	1880-	John Dear
"	1881-	Henry Collard
"	1882-	Charles Archibald Johnston
"	1884	*Licence refused.*

Literature

Official records:

Mx. Mich. Q.S. 1859-1884.

879

WHITE RAVEN PUBLIC HOUSE

Raven Street, Whitechapel.

Licensed: 1850-1863.

Management

Middlesex justices:

Mich.	1850-	George Kerridge
"	1851-	Catherine Kerridge
"	1860-	Anne Pitcher
"	1863	*Licence refused.*

Literature

Official records:

Mx. Mich. Q.S. 1850-1863.

880

WHITE SWAN PUBLIC HOUSE

Deptford High Street, Deptford.

Licensed: 1846-1891.

Management

West Kent justices:

Mich.	1846-	William Henry Bragger
"	1850-	John Porter
"	1868-	Elizabeth Porter
"	1878-	Frederick Morgan
"	1888-	St. John Winne

London County Council:

1890	St. John Winne
1891	Will Harold Vint
Nov. 1891	*No application.*

Literature

Official records:

L.C.C. Th. & M-H. Com. App. Nov. 1889-1890;
W. Kt. Mich. Q.S. 1848-1888.

881

WHITE SWAN PUBLIC HOUSE

229, Mile End Road (*formerly* Roadside), Mile End Old Town.

Licensed: 1859-1884.

Management

Middlesex justices:

Mich. 1859-	William Woodward
" 1860-	Alfred Paine
" 1864-	Thomas Marshall
" 1866-	Harry Tucker
" 1875-	Richard William Motion
" 1877-	William Rose
" 1884	*No application.*

Literature

Official records:

Mx. Mich. Q.S. 1859-1883.

882

WHITE SWAN PUBLIC HOUSE

225, Shadwell High Street, Shadwell.

Licensed: 1851-1886.

Management

Middlesex justices:

Mich. 1851-	George Matthews
" 1875-	John Kersten
" 1880-	Charles Krumm
" 1882-	Charles Reed
" 1886	*No application, no certificate.*

Literature

Official records:

Mx. Mich. Q.S. 1851-1885.

883

WHITE SWAN PUBLIC HOUSE

Steyman's Row, Holloway Road, Islington.

Licensed: 1859-1864.

Management

Middlesex justices:

| Mich. 1859- | Henry Burnard |
| " 1864 | *No notice, no petition.* |

260

Literature

Official records:

Mx. Mich. Q.S. 1859-1864.

884

WHITEHALL THEATRE

Whitehall, Westminster.

Opened: 29th September 1930.

Building details

Architect: Edward A. Stone

Capacity: 620

Auditorium: S. 380; D.C. 255; Bx. 25.

Stage: 27' 7" wide × 12' to 15' 6" deep.

Management

Lord Chamberlain:

1.12.1930-	Walter Hackett
" 1934-	Henry Thomas Richardson
" 1935-	Edward Albert Stone
" 1937-	Thomas William Bowyer
" 1939-	Alfred Staines (to 1.12.1940)

(8.8.1941 Theatre unlet and receiver appointed).

| 1.12.1942- | Harold Moore |
| " 1944- | Louis Cooper. |

London County Council:

1943-	Harold Meed Moore
1945-	Phyllis Dixey, Ltd.
1948-	Louis Cooper.
1950-	Mrs. Louis Cooper.

Literature

Official records:

G.L.C. Arch. Dpt. Mss. Index;
L.C.C. Th. & M-H. Com. App. Nov. 1942-;
L.C.O. 229 and 374.

Contemporary accounts:

1930 TIMES, 1930 Sept. 29.—Report of opening.
ARCHITECT AND BUILDING NEWS, 1930 Oct. 3, pp. 453, 457-62.—Description, plates and plans.
BUILDER, 1930 Oct. 3, pp. 554-7, plates, plans.
ARCHITECTURE ILLUSTRATED, 1930 Nov.—Description.
TIMES, 1930 Nov. 29.—Illus.
1931 ARCHITECTS' JOURNAL, 1931 Jan. 14.
c. 1931 MAYES, Ronald. The romance of London theatres, No. 139.
1950 THEATRE ownership. . . p. 76 and p. 111.

Historical accounts:

1959 ENCICLOPEDIA dello spettacolo. Vol. 6, Col. 1637.
1963 MANDER, Raymond, *and* MITCHENSON, Joe. The theatres of London. 2nd ed. pp. 206-208.

Location of other material

Plans:

G.L.C. *Architects Department.*
Enthoven Collection, 1930 (2 sheets).

Programmes:

Enthoven Collection; London Museum; Westminster
Local Collection.

885

WILLIAM THE FOURTH PUBLIC HOUSE

New Gravel Lane, Shadwell.

Licensed: 1851-1852

Management

Middlesex justices:

Mich. 1851-   Richard Morris
" 1852   *No petition, no application.*

Literature

Official records:

Mx. Mich. Q.S. 1851-1852.

886

WILTON'S MUSIC HALL

Prince of Denmark Public House, 1, Grace's Alley,
Wellclose Square.

Opened: c. 1850. *Closed by fire:* 30th August 1877.

Other names

Albion Saloon
Old Mahogany Bar
Frederick's Royal Palace of Varieties.

Building details

New hall opened: 28. 3. 1858.

Architect: Jacob Maggs.

Builder: Thomas Ennor.

Decorators: Messrs. White and Parlby.

Cost: £20,000

Capacity: 1500

'Mr. Wilton... having found his old music-room totally
inadequate to accommodate his great influx of visitors
has been compelled to erect a hall on a more extended scale.' (Building News, 15. 4. 1859)

Management

No licensing records at Middlesex Record Office.

From London Directories: to 1869   John Wilton
1870-   George Robinson
1874-   George Fredericks
1877   Henry Hodkinson

Literature

Official records:

Sel. Com. 1866, 1877 and 1892.

Contemporary accounts:

1857 RITCHIE, Ewing. Night side of London...
—Description.
1859 ERA. 1859 April 3.—Report of opening.
BUILDING NEWS, 1859 April 15, p. 348.
—Detailed description.

BUILDING NEWS, 1859 April 22, p. 388.
—Correction
PEEPING TOM: a journal of town life No. 5.
'Wilton's New Music Hall.'
1877 METROPOLITAN BOARD OF WORKS
Fire report, 1877.
1878 BUILDER, 1878 May 5. Tender list for rebuild-
ing.

Historical accounts:

1938 EAST END STAR, 1938, Feb.—Interior in 1871.
1954 WILSON, A. E.
East end entertainment... pp. 212-214.
1955 LONDON ELECTRICITY, 1955 Spring. pp. 15-.
1964 ELAM (East London Arts Magazine) Vol. 1,
No. 2, July.—Article by Ellis Ashton on East
End music halls. *(also in* CALL-BOY, 1964,
Aug. *)*
DAILY TELEGRAPH, 1964 Sept. 24.
—Report on preservation fight. Note of history.
FINANCIAL TIMES, 1964 Oct. 6.
FLETCHER, Geoffrey S.
London overlooked.—Illus of balcony.
1965 MANDER, Raymond, *and* MITCHENSON, Joe.
British music hall... Illus. no. 15, with text.

Location of other material

Photographs: Enthoven Collection.

887

WINCHESTER MUSIC HALL

Southwark Bridge Road (*formerly* Great Suffolk
Street), Southwark.

Opened: 1830's ? *Closed:* 1878

Former names

Grapes Public House
British Saloon (Grapes Tavern)

Wilton's Music Hall (886)

(Greater London Council Photograph Library)

Grand Harmonic Hall
Surrey Music Hall

Building details

Cost: £15,000

Capacity: 2000

Management

Surrey justices:

Mich. 1849–	Richard Preece, the Elder.
" 1866–	Richard Preece, Jnr.
" 1878–	William Burnham Fair
" 1880–	Joseph Knights (theatre not in use.)
" 1882	*No application.*

Literature

Official records:

Sel. Com. 1866 and 1877; Sy. Mich. Q.S. 1849–1881.

Contemporary accounts:

1843 Newscutting in Southwark Local Collection reports on performance at British Saloon.

Historical accounts:

1938 DISHER, M.W.
Winkles and champagne...p.26.
1946 SCOTT, Harold.
Early doors...pp.55–
1952 PULLING, Christopher
They were singing...p.177 and 186.
1965 MANDER, Raymond, *and* MITCHENSON, Joe.
British music hall...Illus. No.4. (playbill), brief text.

Location of other material

Cuttings, playbills &c: Enthoven Collection

888

WINDMILL PUBLIC HOUSE

20, Windmill Street (*later* Tabernacle Street), St. Luke, Finsbury.

Licensed: 1862–1890.

Building details

The hall was on the first floor, and had a platform at one end. It was closed as a result of the 1878 Act.

Management

Middlesex justices:

Mich. 1862–	Henry James
" 1863–	Phoebe Ann James
" 1875–	Henry Robert James
" 1876–	Joseph Henry Ferrar
" 1883–	Alfred Brearey White
" 1884–	William Henry Birch
" 1885–	Charles Septimus Speed Andrews
" 1888	Samuel Briscoe

London County Council:

1890 Samuel Briscoe
Nov. 1890 *No application.*

Literature

Official records:

G.L.C. Arch. Dpt. Th. case 040/177; L.C.C. Th. & M-H. Com. App. Nov. 1889; Mx. Mich. Q.S. 1862–1888.

889

WINDMILL THEATRE

17-19, Great Windmill Street, Piccadilly.

Opened: 22nd June 1931.   *Cinema:* 1964.

Building details

1910: Built as a cinema.
1931: Converted into a theatre.

Architect: Howard Jones.

Accommodation: Ar. 213; C. 113.

Management

Lord Chamberlain:

1.12.1931–   Laura Henderson
1.12.1944–   Vivian Van Damm.

London County Council:

1931–   Windmill Theatre Co. Ltd.

Literature

Official records:

G.L.C. Arch. Dpt. Mss. Index; L.C.C. Th. & M-H. Com. App. Nov. 1930–; L.C.O. 248 and 374.

Contemporary accounts:

1950 THEATRE ownership...p.76 and p.111.

Historical accounts:

c.1933 MAYES, Ronald
The romance of London theatres, No. 185.
1942 NEWSWEEK, 1942 Feb. 23, p. 55.
LIFE, 1942 March 16, pp. 57-60.
1952 PULLING, Christopher
They were singing...p. 227.
VAN DAMM, Vivian.
Tonight and every night...S. Paul, (1952), 206p. plates.
1963 LONDON. County Council.
Survey of London. St. James, Vol. 31.
pp. 45, 50-1, 52. plan.
MANDER, Raymond, *and* MITCHENSON, Joe.
The theatres of London. 2nd ed. pp. 209-211.

Location of other material

Plans: G.L.C. *Architects Department.*
Enthoven Collection (1 sheet)

Programmes:

Enthoven Collection; Westminster Local Collection.

890

WINDSOR CASTLE MUSIC HALL AND PUBLIC HOUSE

Coopers Road, Camberwell.

Licensed: 1862-1864, and 1873-1889.

Also known as

'Turners's Music Hall'.

Building details

The concert room was on the first floor, and measured 40' × 15', excluding the platform at the southern end of the room.
It was closed as a result of the 1878 Act.

Management

Surrey justices:

Mich. 1862-		Andrew Weatherly
"	1864	*No application.*
"	1873-	Samuel Turner
"	1880-	Thomas Cason
"	1888	Edwin Osment.

Literature

Official records:

G.L.C. Arch. Dpt. Th. case 040/178; Sel. Com. 1892; Sy. Mich. Q.S. 1862-3, and 1875-88.

Historical accounts:

1895 STUART, C.D., *and* PARK, A.G.
The variety stage...
—Mention of Turner's Music Hall.

891

WINDSOR CASTLE PUBLIC HOUSE

119, Bishop's Road, Bethnal Green.

Licensed: 1858-1891

Management

Middlesex justices:

Mich. 1858-		Charles Frederick Watkins
"	1872-	Thomas Cusson
"	1876-	William Spong
"	1878-	John Perkins
"	1880-	William Millar
"	1882-	Charles Malone Merritt
"	1883-	James Hildreth

London County Council:

1890-	James Hildreth
Nov. 1891	*No application.*

Literature

Official records:

L.C.C. Th. & M-H. Com. App. Nov. 1889-90; Mx. Mich. Q.S. 1858-1888.

892

WINDSOR CASTLE PUBLIC HOUSE

10, Regent Street, City Road, St. Luke, Finsbury.

Licensed: 1856-1863, and 1865-1877.

Management

Middlesex justices:

Mich. 1856-		George King
"	1861-	Thomas Coles
"	1862	*Licence refused as Coles reported dead.*
"	1865-	William Lamprey James
"	1869-	Lewis James
"	1877	*No appearance at licensing meeting.*

Literature

Official records:

Mx. Mich. Q.S. 1856-62, and 1865-77.

893

WINDSOR CASTLE PUBLIC HOUSE

27, Long Acre, St. Martin in the Fields.

Licensed: 1850-1859.

Management

Middlesex justices:

Mich. 1850-		Augustus Ferdinand Seharttner
"	1859	*No petition. Licensee reported dead.*

Literature

Official records:

Mx. Mich. Q.S. 1850-1859.

894

WINDSOR CASTLE PUBLIC HOUSE

Vauxhall Bridge Road, St. George, Hanover Square.

Licensed: 1850-1864.

Management

Middlesex justices:

Mich. 1848-		Thomas Couchman
"	1861-	Joseph Willing Willcocks
"	1864	*No notice, no application, no petition.*

Literature

Official records:

Mx. Mich. Q.S. 1848-1864.

895

WINDSOR CASTLE PUBLIC HOUSE

36, Maxey Street, Plumstead, Woolwich.

Licensed: 1867-1899.

Also known as

Windsor Castle Music Hall.

Building details

Capacity: 300.

In 1909 Messrs. Whitelock and Storr submitted drawings of alterations proposed for the public house, and stated that a music and dancing licence would be requested for the Windsor Castle Music Hall.

Management

West Kent justices:

Mich. 1867- Thomas Hopperton
" 1873- William Thomas Beaver
" 1877- John James Elliott
" 1879- Henry Gigney.

London County Council:

1890   Henry Gigney
1891- Thomas Primus Moore
1895- John Parry Dipple
1897- Alfred Edgar Gladwin
Nov. 1898 *No application*

Literature

Official records:

L.C.C. Th. & M-H. Com. App. Nov. 1889-1898;
Sel. Com. 1892; W. Kt. Mich. Q.S. 1867-1888.

896

WINTER GARDEN THEATRE

167, Drury Lane, Holborn.

Opened as a place of entertainment: 17th century.

Closed: 1960. *Demolished:* 1965.

Former names

Great Mogul
Mogul Saloon 1847-1851
Turkish Saloon occasionally
Mogul Music Hall occasionally
Middlesex Music Hall 1851-1911
New Middlesex Theatre of Varieties 1911-1919
Winter Garden Theatre 1919-

Building details

167 Drury Lane was a place of public entertainment
from Elizabethan times. .
1847: Mogul Saloon opened on 27th December 1847.

Cost: £12,000

Capacity: 1,200

1872 and 1891 reconstructed.

1911 Rebuilt.

Architect: Frank Matcham

Capacity: 1800

Auditorium: S. & Bx. 823; B. 476; G. 601.

Stage: 33' wide × 26' deep.

1966 Reported that new theatre to be designed by
Sean Kenny.

Management

Middlesex justices:

Mich. 1851- Edwin Winder
" 1864- Edward Wood
" 1866- George Richard Speedy
" 1867- Henry George Lake
" 1875- James Laurence Graydon

London County Council:

1890- James Lawrence Graydon
1918- Oswald Stoll

1920- George Grossmith and Edward Laurillard
1922- George Grossmith and Joseph Edward
Malone
Nov. 1922 *No application*
1946- Millenium Productions Ltd.
1949- Winter Garden Theatre (London) Ltd.

Lord Chamberlain:

27.11.1911- Oswald Stoll
22. 1.1912- James Laurence Graydon
1.12.1916- Oswald Stoll
28. 2.1919- George Grossmith and Edward
Laurillard
30.11.1921- George Grossmith and Joseph Malone
1.12.1926- William Clifford Gaunt
1.12.1928- William Cooper
1.12.1945- Richard Herbert Dewes.

Literature

Official records:

G.L.C. Arch. Dpt. Mss. index; G.L.C. Arch. Dpt. Th.
case 214; L.C.C. Th. & M-H. Com. App. Nov. 1889-21,
1945-; L.C.C. Th. & M-H. Com. Papers 1889-;
L.C.O. 374 and 489; Mx. Mich. Q.S. 1851-1888;
Sel. Com. 1866, 1877 and 1892.

Contemporary accounts:

1857 RITCHIE, J. Ewing. The night side of London...
pp. 165-171
1887 SATURDAY REVIEW, 1887 Aug. 6. The state of
the London... music halls... No. 1.
1902 MIDDLESEX MUSIC HALL The Middlesex:
Drury Lane: souvenir of the 31st anniversary.
Artistic Stationery Co. (1902). 27p. illus.
1909 GLOBE, 1909, Nov. 6. 'Under the hammer: sale
of the Middlesex Music Hall.'
1911 ERA, October 28.—Description.
EVENING STANDARD, 1911 Oct. 30. 'The Old
Mogul' a famous music hall in a new guise:
Mr. Stoll's scheme.
MORNING POST, 1911 Oct. 30. 'The new
Middlesex'.
1919 WINTER GARDEN THEATRE Winter Garden
Theatre, Drury Lane. Opened on the 20th day
of May MDCCCCXIX...
1950 THEATRE ownership... p. 76 and 112.

Historical accounts:

1904 KING, ... 1904, Aug. 6.
The nights of other days IV. The Argyll Rooms
and the Middlesex.
1906 PALL MALL GAZETTE, 1906 Oct. 18.
London's oldest music hall: some Middlesex
reminiscences.
c. 1930 MAYES, Ronald
The romance of London theatres, Nos. 69, 101
and 187.
1935 HADDON, Archibald
The story of the music hall... p. 39, pp. 65-70,
76, 148.
1938 DISHER, M. W.
Winkles and champagne... p. 39 and 114.
1959 ENCICLOPEDIA dello spettacolo, Vol. 6, Col.
1637.
1963 MANDER, Raymond, *and* MITCHENSON, Joe.
The theatres of London. 2nd ed. pp. 211-216.
1965 MANDER, Raymond, *and* MITCHENSON, Joe.
British music hall... Illus. nos. 10 and 52, with
brief text.

Location of other material

Plans: G.L.C. *Architects Department.*
Enthoven Collection, 1931 (2 sheets)

Programmes and playbills:

British Museum Library; Enthoven Collection;
Holborn Local Collection; London Museum;
Westminster Local Collection.

897

WOLVERLEY ARMS PUBLIC HOUSE

South Conduit Street, Bethnal Green.

Licensed: 1856-1862.

Management

Middlesex justices:

Mich.	1856-	Elizabeth Newton
"	1857-	Thomas George Watkinson
"	1860-	Edwin Jarman
"	1862	*Licence refused.*

Literature

Official records:

Mx. Mich. Q.S. 1856-1862.

898

WOODMAN PUBLIC HOUSE

11, D'Oyley Street, Chelsea.

Licensed: 1853-1865, and 1869-1888.

Management

Middlesex justices:

Mich.	1853-	Thomas Franklin
"	1854-	Henry Wilkins
"	1855-	Conrad Stenhardt
"	1856-	Richard Cook
"	1865	*No application.*
"	1869-	Robert Bunn
"	1872-	Henry John Nind
"	1875-	Job Higgins. (through 1889).

Literature

Official records:

Mx. Mich. Q.S. 1853-65, 1869-88.

899

WOODMAN PUBLIC HOUSE

26, Queen Street and Charles Square, Hoxton,
Shoreditch.

Licensed: 1858-1870.

Building details

Cost: £2,000..

Capacity: 500.

Management

Middlesex justices:

| Mich. | 1858- | Henry Hellyer Miller |
| " | 1867- | Mary Miller |

| " | 1869- | Barker Woolhouse |
| " | 1870 | *Licence refused following police report.* |

Literature

Official records:

Mx. Mich. Q.S. 1858-1870;
Sel. Com. 1866.

900

WOODMAN PUBLIC HOUSE

Winchester Street, Bethnal Green.

Licensed: 1851-1871.

Management

Middlesex justices:

Mich.	1851-	Henry Gould Haywood
"	1852-	James King
"	1856-	William George Bunn
"	1862	*Licence refused.*
"	1864-	William Bunn
"	1871	*No application.*

Winter Garden Theatre (896)

(Greater London Council Photograph Library)

Literature

Official records:

Mx. Mich. Q.S. 1851-62, and 1864-71.

901

WOODVILLE ARMS PUBLIC HOUSE

Mildmay Road, Islington.

Licensed: 1865-1869.

Management

Middlesex justices:

Mich. 1865- Thomas Meecham
   " 1869 *No notice served.*

Literature

Official records:

Mx. Mich. Q.S. 1865-1869.

902

WOOLWICH EMPIRE

Beresford Street, Woolwich.

Opened: 3rd January 1835.

Former names

New Portable Theatre, Woolwich. 1834
West Kent Theatre. 1835
Duchess of Kent's Theatre. 1837
Barnard's Theatre. 1892-
Woolwich, Theatre Royal. -Occasionally
Empire Theatre, Woolwich. 1932-

Building details

1835: Permanent theatre built.

1899: Building reconstructed:

Architect: Frank Matcham.

Capacity: 1450.

Auditorium: Ar. 750; B. 300; G. 400.

Management

The records of the stage play licences issued by the West Kent justices do not appear to have survived.

London County Council:

1890 Henry Jones Borley and Sarah Elizabeth Monro.
1891 John Frederick Brian.
1892- Samuel Barnard.
1930- David Barnard.
1932- Woolwich Empire Ltd.
1939 South London Theatres Ltd.
1940- Mrs. Sarah Rothstein and Woolwich Empire Ltd.

Literature

Official records:

G.L.C. Arch. Dpt. Mss. index;
G.L.C. Arch. Dpt. Th. case 357;
L.C.C. Th. & M-H. Com. App. Nov. 1889-.

Contemporary accounts:

1950 THEATRE ownership. . . p. 129 and 147.
1958 DAILY MAIL, 1958 March 31.
   'I was there when a music hall died.'

Historical accounts:

18— VINCENT, W. T.
   The records of the Woolwich district.
   Virtue, n.d. p. 76. illus, (1837).
c. 1930 MAYES, Ronald.
   Romance of London theatres, No. 168.

Location of other material

Plans: G.L.C. *Architects Department.*

Programmes and playbills:

Enthoven Collection; Guildhall Library (2 items); Woolwich Local Collection.

903

WOOLWICH HIPPODROME

Wellington Street, Woolwich.

Opened: 18th October 1900. *In use as cinema by* 1924.

Former name

Grand Theatre and Opera House To 1908.

Building details

Architect: Bertie Crewe.

Builder: Messrs. W. Johnson & Co.

Capacity: 1680.

Auditorium: S. 95; P. 659; C. 362; G. 532; Bx. 32.

Management:

London County Council:

1900- Clarence Sounes
1908- Walter Gibbons
1913- Charles Gulliver (to Dec. 1924).
Nov. 1924 *No longer listed as theatre or music hall.*

Literature

Official records:

G.L C. Arch. Dpt. Mss. index;
G.L.C. Arch. Dpt. Th. case 380;
L.C.C. Th. & M-H. Com. App. Nov. 1900.

Contemporary accounts:

1900 BUILDER, 1900 Oct. 27, p. 371.—Description.

Location of other material

Plans: G.L.C. *Architects Department*

Programmes: Enthoven Collection.

904

WORLD'S END PUBLIC HOUSE

Rhodeswell Street (*later* 47 Ben Jonson Road), Mile End, Old Town.

Licensed: 1856-1883.

Management

Middlesex justices:

Mich. 1856-	Edmund Roberts
"	1864-	David Drysdale
"	1866-	William Hunt
"	1872-	Edward Bradley
"	1873-	George Wells
"	1874-	Henry Thwaites
"	1876-	Richard Raynard Stearns
"	1880-	James Nicholson
"	1881-	James Whitehead
"	1883	*No application, no certificate.*

Literature:

Official records:

Mx. Mich. Q S. 1856-1882.

905

WYNDHAM'S THEATRE

Charing Cross Road, Westminster.

Opened: 16th November 1899.

Building details

Architect: W. G. R. Sprague.

Cost: £30,000.

Capacity: (1897) 1200. (1950) 730.

Auditorium: P. & S. 320; D.C. 167; U.C. 111; G. 142; Ex. 48.

Stage: 60' wide × 30' deep.

Management

Lord Chamberlain:

16.11.1899-	Charles Wyndham
1.10.1903-	Frank Curzon
1.12.1927-	Leon Marks Lion
1.12.1931-	Violet Ethel Wallace
1.12.1932-	Howard James Wyndham
1.12.1945-	Howard James Wyndham and Bronson James Albery
1.12.1947-	Bronson James Albery

Literature

Official records:

G.L.C. Arch. Dpt. Mss. index;
G L.C. Arch. Dpt. Th. Case 454;
L.C.C. Th. & M-H. Com. Papers, 1898-.
LC1/712-752; L.C.O. 239 and 374.

Contemporary accounts:

1897 BUILDING NEWS, 1897 Dec. 24, p. 903.—Brief description.
1898 BUILDER, 1898 Aug. 27, p. 196.—Report that Charles Wyndham is to build theatre.
1899 BUILDING NEWS, 1899 Aug. 4, p. 150.—Application to construct roof garden over the auditorium.
1899 WYNDHAM'S THEATRE (Souvenir of opening). 14p. —Gives plan, interior and exterior view.
1899 BUILDER, 1899 Nov. 25, p. 496.—Report of opening: brief description.

Historical accounts:

c.1930 MAYES, Ronald.
The romance of London theatres, No. 18.

1949 STAGE, 1949 Nov. 17.
'Fifty years at famous theatre: Wyndham's celebrates its jubilee', by W. Macqueen Pope.
1959 ENCICLOPEDIA dello spettacolo. Vol. 6, Col. 1637.
1963 MANDER, Raymond *and* MITCHENSON, Joe. The theatres of London. 2nd ed. pp. 217-221.

Location of other material

Plans: G.L.C. *Architects Department.*
Enthoven Collection (2 sheets)

Programmes:

British Museum Library; Enthoven Collection; Garrick Club; Guildhall Library; London Museum; Westminster Local Collection.

906

YE OLDE GREEN DRAGON PUBLIC HOUSE

Beast Lane (*later* Spring Garden Place), Stepney.

Licensed: 1848-1903.

Also known as

Green Dragon Music Hall.

Building details

Concert room on the ground floor attached to the public house.

Woolwich Empire (902)

(Greater London Council Photograph Library)

Capacity: 200.

Management

Middlesex justices:

Mich. 1848-   Thomas Walter
" 1879-   Alfred Walter
" 1887-   Septimus Phillips.

London County Council:

1893-   Emma Simmons
1897-   Elizabeth Cole
1899-   Walter Pinn
1900-   John Marchant
Nov. 1903   *Not licensed as a theatre or music hall.*

Literature

Official records:

G.L.C. Arch. Dpt. Mss. index.
L.C.C. Th. & M-H. Com. App. Nov. 1892-1903.
Mx. Mich. Q.S. 1848-1888.
Sel. Com. 1892

907

YORK AND ALBANY PUBLIC HOUSE

Stanhope Terrace, Regents Park, St. Pancras.

Licensed: 1854-1877.

Management

Middlesex justices:

Mich. 1854-   Thomas Stevens
" 1860-   William Edward Stevens
" 1862-   George Lancefield
" 1869-   John Reed
" 1877   *Licence refused to Charles Horner.*

908

YORK MINSTER MUSIC HALL AND PUBLIC HOUSE

44, Philpot Street, Stepney.

Licensed: 1858-1903.

Building details

The room was on the first floor of the public house.

Capacity: 230.

Management

Middlesex justices:

Mich. 1858-   Elizabeth Newton
" 1863-   Henry Holt
" 1866-   William Thomas Backham
" 1873-   Charles Ogden
" 1877-   Joseph Thomas Curzey
" 1881-   Maria Mary Curzey
" 1884-   Joseph Hamann
" 1888   Thomas Billing

London County Council:

1890   Thomas Billing
1891   Sarah Billing

1892-   Edward Wilshear
1897-   Henry Thomas Hollington
1898   James Polson Macleod
1899   Adam Smith
1900   Mark Goldstein
1901-   Henry George Gill
Nov. 1903   *Not listed as a theatre or music hall.*

Literature

Official records:

G.L.C. Arch. Dpt. Mss. Index;
G.L.C. Arch. Dpt. Th. case 385;
L.C.C. Th. & M-H. Com. App. Nov. 1889-1903;
Mx. Mich. Q.S. 1858-1888.

Location of other material:

Plans: G.L.C. *Architects Department.*

909

YORKSHIRE GREY PUBLIC HOUSE

Yorkshire Grey Yard, Hampstead.

Licensed: 1855-1885.

Management

Middlesex justices:

Mich. 1855-   James Joseph Jordan
" 1858-   Philip White
" 1861-   Henry Hawksley
" 1883-   Harriet Richardson and
                Eliza Richmond.
" 1885   *No application, no certificate.*

Literature

Official records:

Mx. Mich. Q.S. 1855-1885.

910

YORKSHIRE STINGO PUBLIC HOUSE

New Road, St. Marylebone.

Licensed: Pre 1850-1855.

Also known as:

Albion Saloon.

Management

Middlesex justices:

Mich. 1848-   William Allen
" 1854-   Lewis Sulsh
" 1855   *No application, no petition.*

Literature

Official records:

Mx. Mich. Q.S. pre 1850-1855.

Location of other material

Playbills: Enthoven Collection; Guildhall Library.

PART II

Bibliography of General Works

i. BIBLIOGRAPHIES

BAKER, Blanch Merritt.
  Dramatic bibliography. New York, 1933.
BAKER, Blanch Merritt.
  Theatre and allied arts. New York, 1952.
BOSTON. PUBLIC LIBRARY. *Allen A. Brown Collection.*
  Catalogue of the Allen A. Brown Collection of books
  relating to the stage. The Library, 1919. —Major source.
CHESHIRE, David.
  Theatre: history, criticism and reference.
  Clive Bingley, 1967. (The readers guide series)
FLETCHER, Ivan Kyrle.
  British theatre, 1530-1900. An exhibition of books...
  National Book League, 1950.
GILDER, Rosamond.
  A theatre library. National Theatre Conference.
  New York, 1932.
LIST of references on the theatre and show business: its
  management and finance. Library of Congress,
  Washington, 1915.
LIST of selected books on theatre and drama.
  Glasgow Corporation. Public Libraries, 1950.
LOWE, Robert William.
  A bibliographical account of English theatrical literature
  from the earliest times to the present day. Nimmo, 1888.
  -Standard work; the publication of the new edition
  extending the work to 1900 is announced for 1969.
NORTH-WESTERN POLYTECHNIC. School of Librarian-
  ship.
  Occasional paper No. 5. The British Theatre: a select
  list; by A. M. C. Kahn. —A guide to the literature.
PAWLEY, Frederic Anden.
  Theatre architecture: a brief bibliography... New York,
  1932.
SCOTT, Clement.
  The drama of yesterday and today. 1899. ii. 479-558.
  —Continues lists given in John Genest 'Some account of
  the English stage, 1660-1830' from 1830 to end of 19th
  century.
STOTT, Raymond Toole.
  Circus and allied arts. A world bibliography 1500-1957.
  Derby, 1958 and 1960. 2v.
SOBEL, Bernard.
  The theatre handbook. New York, 1940.

ii. OFFICIAL RECORDS AND PUBLICATIONS

(a) Acts of Parliament
(b) Bills
(c) Reports
(d) Official records

(a) Acts of Parliament

1751 The Disorderly Houses Act, 1751 (25 Geo. 2 c. 36)
      An act... for regulating places of publick entertain-
      ment, and punishing people keeping disorderly houses.
1839 The Metropolitan Police Act, 1839 (2 & 3 Vict. c. 47)
      An act... authorising superintendents to enter unlicen-
      sed theatres and apprehend persons found there.
1843 The Theatres Act, 1843 (6 & 7 Vict. c. 68)
      An act for regulating theatres.
1860 The Refreshment Houses Act, 1860 (23 Vict. c. 27)
      An act... for regulating the licensing of refreshment
      houses...
1875 The Public Entertainments Act, 1875 (38 & 39 Vict. c. 21)
      An act for amending the law relating to houses of
      public dancing, music, or other public entertainment of
      the kind, in the Cities of London and Westminster.

1878 The Metropolis Management and Building Acts
      Amendment Act, 1878 (41 & 42 Vict. c. 32)
      An act to amend the Metropolis Management Act, 1855,
      and the Acts amending the same respectively.
1882 The Metropolitan Board of Works (Various Powers)
      Act, 1882 (45 Vict. c. 56).
1888 The Local Government Act, 1888 (51 & 52 Vict. c. 41).
      An act to amend the laws relating to local government
      in England and Wales, and for other purposes connec-
      ted therewith.
1890 The Public Health Acts Amendment Act, 1890 (53 &
      54 Vict. c. 59).
      An act to amend the Public Health Acts.
1909 The Cinematograph Act, 1909 (9 Edw. 7. c. 30).
      An act to make better provision for securing safety
      at cinematograph and other exhibitions.
1915 London County Council (Parks, etc.) Act, 1915 (5 & 6
      Geo. 5. c. lxxvi).
      An act to confer further powers upon the London
      County Council with regard to parks and open spaces
      and other matters...
      —Part IV Section 8: Royal Albert Hall to be subject to
      certain existing enactments.
1932 Sunday Entertainments Act, 1932 (22 & 23 Geo. 5. c. 51).
      An act to permit and regulate the opening and use of
      places on Sunday for certain entertainments...

The London County Council (General Powers) Acts also
contain regulations relating to theatres and other places of
entertainment...

1915 (5 & 6 Geo. 5 c. iii) An act to make provision with
      regard to high-pressure gas meters, music and
      dancing licences... (&c).
      Part III: music and dancing licences.
1923 (13 & 14 Geo. 5 c. vii) An act to confer further powers
      upon the London County Council...
      Part I Section 16: Council may vary conditions atta-
      ched to licences for stage plays etc.
1924 (14 & 15 Geo. 5 c. lvii)...
      Part III. Places of entertainment.
1930 (21 & 22 Geo. 5 c. clix)...
      Part III. Control of public boxing.
1935 (25 & 26 Geo. 5 c. xxxiii)...
      Part IV. Public entertainments (Occasional use of
      premises).
1936 (26 Geo. 5 & 1 Edw. 8 c. lx)...
      Part VII. Public entertainments. (Fees on application
      for music and dancing licences).
1937 (1 Edw. 8 & 1 Geo. 6 c. xci)...
      Part XII. Miscellaneous. Para. 121-138.
      (Dispensing with certificates of suitability—introduced
      by 1878 Act).
      (Dispensation by Council with bonds by theatre
      managers—introduced by 1843 Act).
1938 (1 & 2 Geo. 6 c. xxxviii)...
      Para. 5. (Control of public wrestling).

The above acts, giving the law relating to theatres and places
of entertainment as it stood in 1950, are collected together
in...
      Halsbury's Statutes of England. 2nd edition. Volume 25.
      —Theatres and other places of entertainment.

(b) Bills (Proposed legislation that did not receive the royal assent)

1860 A bill to amend the Acts concerning Theatres and
      public houses.
      (Public Bills 1860 VI, 521 (266)).
1865 A bill to amend the law relating to Theatres and other
      Places of Public Amusement.
      (Public Bills 1865 IV, 521 (64)).

1875 A Bill intituled An Act to amend the Law relating to Musical and other Entertainments in the Metropolis and Neighbourhood.
(House of Lords Sessional Papers 1875 (49)).

1883 A Bill For the better Regulation of Theatres and other places of Public Entertainment.
(Public Bills 1883 X, 1 (81)).

1883 A Bill intituled An Act to amend the Law for regulating Theatres.
(House of Lords Bills 1883 (32) Stage plays in aid of Charities (H. L.)).

1884 A Bill For the better Regulation of Theatres and Music Halls within the Metropolitan Area.
(Public Bills 1884 VII, 257 (61)).

1886 A Bill For the better Regulation of Theatres and Music Halls in the Metropolis.
(Public Bills 1886 VI, 35 (69 sess. 1)).

1886 A Bill to confer further powers upon the Metropolitan Board of Works for inspecting Theatres and Music Halls and granting certificates.
(Public Bills 1886 IV, 119 (44 sess. 1)).

1887 A Bill to confer further powers upon the Metropolitan Board of Works for inspecting Theatres and Music Halls and granting certificates.
(Public Bills 1887 IV, 227 (117)).

1887 A Bill for the better regulation of Theatres and Music Halls in the Metropolitan Area.
(Public Bills 1887 VI, 327 (15)).

1883 A Bill for the better regulation of Theatres and Music Halls in the Metropolis.
(Public Bills 1888 VII, 415 (37)).

1890 A Bill to make better Provision for the Regulation of Theatres in London (Not Printed).
(Public Bills 1890 IX, 93 (133)).

1890 A Bill to amend and extend the Law relating to Theatres, Music Halls, and Places of Public Entertainment or Resort in the Administrative County of London (Not Printed).
(Public Bills, 1890 IX, 95 (159)).

1891 A Bill to provide for the control and regulation of Theatres, Music Halls, and Places of Public Entertainment in the Administrative County of London; and for other purposes.
(Public Bills 1890-91 X, 329 (106)).

1948 A Bill to amend the law relating to the censorship of plays and the licensing of theatres so as to exempt the theatre from restrictions upon the freedom of expression in excess of those applicable to other forms of literature; and for purposes connected therewith.
(Public Bills 1948-49 I, 361 (56)).

(c) Reports

1852-3 Select Committee appointed to examine into the system under which public houses, hotels, beershops, dancing saloons, coffee houses, theatres, temperance hotels, and places of public entertainment are sanctioned and regulated, with a view of reporting whether any alteration of the law can be made for the better preservation of public morals, the protection of the revenue, and for the proper accommodation of the public.
—Report, with proceedings, minutes of evidence, appendix and index. 1852-53 (855) xxxvii. 1.
(as above)—Report with the proceedings minutes of evidence, appendix and index. 1854 (367) xiv. 231.
—(Short title: Select Committee on Public Houses).

1858 Return of the number of the Metropolitan Police Force employed on Special Duty and not in the ordinary duties of the Public... and the number employed at the several Docks, Dockyards, Public Buildings, Museums, Institutions and Theatres...
1857-8, XLVII, 653 (384). (Accounts and papers).

1864 Copies of a letter relating to precautions against fire addressed by the Lord Chamberlain to the Managers of Theatres, dated 7th February 1864; and, of a Memorandum by the Lord Chamberlain, dated 5th February 1864, and transmitted by him to Managers of Theatres; together with a copy of regulations for better protection against accidents by fire.
1864, L, 489 (64). (Accounts and papers).

1866 Select Committee appointed to inquire into the working of the Acts of Parliament for licensing and regulating theatres and places of entertainment in Great Britain. Report... together with the proceedings of the Committee, minutes of evidence, and appendix.
1866, XVI, 1. (375). (Reports of Committees).
Includes: Appendix G. Licences granted by the Lord Chamberlain in 1843 after the passing of 6 & 7 Vict., 68.
Appendix H. Licences granted for stage plays by Lord Chamberlain, 1865.
also: Capacities of various parts of house, p. 295; estimated cost of buildings and fittings and number of people accommodated daily in London concert halls, music halls and entertainment galleries.
(Short title: Select Committee on Theatrical Licences and Regulations).

1876-7 Select Committee appointed to inquire into the constitution, efficiency, emoluments, and finances of the Metropolitan Fire Brigade, and into the most efficient means of providing for security from loss of life and property by fire in the metropolis.
—Report... with proceedings, evidence, appendix and index.
1876 (Sessional papers, Vol. 11, p. 53).
(as above)—Report... (&c).
1877 (Sessional papers, Vol. 14, p. 37).
Includes: Appendix 3-Metropolitan theatres licensed by the Lord Chamberlain.
Appendix 4-List of music halls (&c) licensed by the magistrates, and lists of theatres licensed by the Lord Chamberlain (and)... by the magistrates.
(Short title: Select Committee on the Metropolitan Fire Brigade).

1881 Return (Pursuant to an Order of the House of Lords, dated 5th April 1881,) showing the various Modes of Exit for Theatres licensed by the Lord Chamberlain.
(House of Lords Sessional Papers 1881 (80)).

1882 Metropolitan Board of Works.
Prevention of fires in theatres: report by the Chief Officer of the Fire Brigade on the condition of various theatres in London.
(No. 1, 035) 1882, March & July. (Bound together).
(Cover title: Prevention of fire in theatres: reports by Captain Shaw).
Contains: detailed description of layout, as well as fire prevention details and recommendations for improvements. Seating figures given in the report are based on safety requirements, and are recommended rather than actual seating capacities.

1887 London. County Council.
Music, dancing, theatre and other licences: list of places now within the jurisdiction of the Council as the licensing authority, in respect of which licences were granted or refused at the Michaelmas Sessions 1888 by the Justices of the City of London, Kent, Middlesex and Surrey.
Printed by Judd & Co. 1887. 23p. (No. 30)

1889 Conference between the Theatres and Music Halls Committee of the London County Council and a deputation of managers of theatres and music halls. *Vestry Hall. St. Martin's-in-the-Fields, 20th November, 1889.*
Transcript of proceedings from shorthand notes.
The Council, 1889.
30p.

1892 Select Committee appointed to inquire into the operations of Acts of Parliament relating to the licensing and regulation of theatres and places of public entertainment, and to consider and report any alterations in the law which may appear desirable. —Report... together with proceedings of the committee, minutes of evidence, appendix and index. 1892, XVIII, 1, (240).
(Reports of committees). *Includes:* lists of theatres
Includes: lists of theatres and music halls in existence at passing of the 1882 Act. 260 places surveyed, another 101 being outside the control of the Metropolitan Board of Works being under 500 sq'.
Also: lists new theatres and music halls erected since the passing of the act. —(Short title: Select Committee on Theatres and Places of Entertainment).

1892 London. County Council.
Return of the theatres and music halls in the County

of London, showing the number of seats in each theatre or music hall, the date when the works required by the Metropolitan Board or the London County Council were completed or the certificate granted, and other particulars. Compiled from the evidence given by T. G. Fardell...before the Select Committee of the House of Commons on Theatres and Places of Entertainment, 28th March 1892 and other dates, and from subsequent information supplied by the Theatres Branch of the Clerks Department of the Council. May 1892. 22p.

(d) Official records

GREATER LONDON. Record Office. *London Records*

The 1878 Act gave the Metropolitan Board of Works considerable powers over the theatres and music halls of London. Records relating to the Board's building requirements appear in:—

Metropolitan Board of Works. *Building Act Committee. Sub-Committee on Theatres and Music Halls.*
Minutes, 1882-1889. 8 vols.
Papers, 1882-1889. 6 vols.

Metropolitan Board of Works. *Works and General Purposes Committee. Theatres and Sub-Committee.*
Minutes.
(Bound in volumes of special committees).

Reports of fires, and requirements and recommendations appear in:—

Metropolitan Board of Works. *Metropolitan Fire Brigade.*
Reports of the Chief Officer, for the years 1866-1888.

The London County Council was responsible for the licensing of theatres and music halls in the London area (with the exception of those licensed by the Lord Chamberlain). The Council retained the powers that had been granted to the Metropolitan Board of Works by the 1878 and 1882 Acts, and acted as adviser to the Lord Chamberlain on building and safety matters. This work was recorded in the minutes and papers of a series of committees:-

Theatres and Music Halls Committee (March 1889-March 1931)
Minutes. 55 vols. (these contain minutes of such sub committees as *Inspection Sub-Committee*).
Presented papers, 1889-1909. (The papers relating to each building, or subject, were gathered together and bound alphabetically).
Presented papers, 1909-1931. (Papers bound chronologically, in one sequence, in 229 vols.)
Printed papers, 1889-1928. (Breakdown of printed papers given below)

In 1931 the functions of the above committee were taken over by:-

Entertainments (Licensing) Committee (March 1931-Dec. 1940)
Minutes. 20 vols.
Presented papers. 161 vols.

At the end of 1940 the work of this committee was handed over to another committee that had already been in existence some time:—

Public Control Committee (1941-   )
Minutes (contain theatre material) Vol. 54+
Presented papers   "   Vol. 209+

Reports of all these committees appear in
London. County Council. Minutes, 1889+.

The following is a breakdown of a typical year's (i.e. 1915) printed papers issued by the Theatres and Music Halls Committee between 1889 and 1928.

London. County Council.
Music, music and dancing and stage licences, rules and regulations.

Internal.

London. County Council. *Theatres and Music Halls Committee*...List of applications for licences to be heard by the...Committee of the London County Council at the Clerkenwell Sessions House on...November... No... *Published.*
(Divided north and south of the Thames).
i.   Applications for renewals, (subdivided by electoral divisions)
ii.   "   for transfers   "
iii.   "   for the removal or modification of restrictions "
iv.   "   for new licences.

London. County Council. *Theatres and Music Halls Committee*....Opposed applications. No... *Published.*
(Gives name of hall, name of person applying, name of opposer and reason.)

London. County Council. *Theatres and Music Halls Committee*...Meeting of the Committee...to consider applications for licences... *Internal.*
(Transcript of shorthand notes giving verbatim report of proceedings dealing with opposed applications. Representatives giving reasons for both application and opposition).

London. County Council. *Theatres and Music Halls Committee*...Report...Upon the applications for licences... *Internal.*
(Divided north an south of the Thames).
Part I. Unopposed.
i.   Licences recommended without undertakings.
ii. Licences recommended subject to undertakings without alteration of terms (which are given).
iii. Licences recommended in cases of application for transfer.
iv. Licences recommended in cases requiring special notices.
Part II. Opposed.
i.   Refusals
ii. Applications for the removal or modification of restrictions.
iii. Applications for new licences (describes purpose of building).
iv. Refusals recommended.
Part III. Preparation and sealing of licences...
Part IV. Applications withdrawn.

London. County Council.
...List of cases in which notice of opposition to the recommendations of the...Committee has been given. *Internal.*
Finally, two series of publications relating to the granting of licences appear in the series of London County Council publications. In the Greater London Record Office the publications of the Council are bound in running number order:-

London. County Council.
Applications for music, music and dancing, ...licences (Title varies), heard on...November...(1914-1937).
1716/30 (1914); 1796/8 (1915); 1850/5 (1916); 1912/14 (1917); 1936/9 (1918); 1985 (1919); 2055/8 (1920); 2118/21 (1921); 2182/6 (1922); 2263/5 (1923); 2335/40 (1924); 2408/10 (1925); 2469/73 (1926); 2530/1 (1927); 2597/2600 (1928); 2686/7 (1929); 2792/5 (1930); 2871/2 (1931); 2924 (1932); 3074 (1933); 3143/4 (1934); 3222/3 (1935); 3303/4 (1936); 3385/6 (1937).

London. County Council.
Music, music and dancing, cinematograph, stage plays... licences and permissions granted by the Council and in force on 1st January...3001/2 (1933); 3095 (1934); 3166 (1935); 3247 (1936); 3322 (1937); 3394 (1938); 3409 (1939); 3462 (1940); 3481 (1941); 3503 (1942); 1943-45 not published; 3565 (1946); 3581 (1947); 3614 (1948); 3640 (1949); 3679 (1950).
—Published from 1933 to 1965.

GREATER LONDON. Record Office. *Middlesex records.*

Records relating to theatres and music halls are in the *series M & D.* 1-4 relate almost exclusively to the period before 1850, but have been listed here in order that the calendar may be complete.

M & D 1. 1/1-39 Music and dancing licences 1752-1844.
In this group the following relate to the London area:-
1/1 The New Theatre Haymarket, 1763.
1/7 Long Room, Hampstead, 1769.
1/20 Hickford's Great Room, Brewer Street, 1770.
1/24 Marylebone Gardens, 1774.
1/38 "Draft of a lycense for publicke entertaining houses". Original music and dancing licence for Thomas Roseman and Ann Hough of St. James Clerkenwell. Unsigned.
Altered for John Whitehead and Mary Brayfield for music and dancing licence for the new theatre in the Haymarket. Unsigned.
1/39 Westminster licence as altered for Haymarket, 1752.
M & 2. Application for renewal of music and dancing licences, 1840.
M & D 3. Miscellaneous applications... 1841-1895.
M & D 4. 4/1-176 Applications for licences, 1849.
M & D 5. 5/1-8 Record of applications for music and dancing licences granted or refused 1850-1857.
M & D 6. 6/1-39 Argyll Rooms and Trocadero. 1850-1887, applications, petitions (&c).
   6/40a-d Argyll Rooms and Trocadero plans.
M & D 7. 7/1-48 Orders, reports, regulations and printed applications, 1851-3, 1855-8, 1861-4; 1866-8; 1870; 1874-7; 1881-2, 1886-8.
M & D 8. 8/1-26 Applications for licences and notices of intention to apply, 1855.
M & D 9. 9/1-400 Applications for licences, 1856, including police and justices returns.
M & D 10. 'The Regulations of music halls. A summary of the attempts made by the music hall proprietors to obtain an improvement in the law regulating places of public entertainment, 1883. With some opinions of the press'. (Printed booklet, refering to numerous licensed premises).
M & D 11. 11/1-25 Petitions to the justices against the granting of music and dancing licences, 1860.
11/1 Alhambra.
11/2-3 Chalk Farm Tavern and Tea Gardens
11/4-8 Board and Castle (Oxford Music Hall).
11/9-11 Cremorne Gardens.
11/12 Windsor Castle, 27 Long Acre.
11/13-8 Bessborough Arms, and other petitions.
11/19 Kings Arms, Holywell Street.
11/20-5 Other petitions.

Example of full title:-
(11/19) Petition by Benjamin Conquest, John Douglas, Samuel Lane, John Johnson and Nelson Lee, the individual proprietors of the Grecian Theatre, the Standard Theatre and the City of London Theatre William Grove, the proprietor of the Spread Eagle Tavern, Kingsland Street, Thomas Harwood of Shoreditch High Street; the parochial authorities and householders of Holywell Street... against a music licence for the Kings Arms, Holywell Street.
M & D 12. 12/1-380 Applications for licences for Uxbridge music licences, 1858.
M & D 13. 13/1-8 Plans (miscellaneous), 1857-1886.
Including: 13/5 Agricultural Hall, St. Mary's Hall. Proposed alterations to entrance.
   13/6 The Royal Music Hall, Holborn. Ground floor plan by Edward Clarke, 27th Sept. 1881.
M & D 14 14/1-32 Applications for licences for Uxbridge premises.
M & D 15. 15/1-21 Printed applications for licences, 1865-1888.
M & D 16. 16/1-3 Bound volumes of printed applications, 1859-1888.
16/1 1859-1868
16/2 1869-1878
16/3 1879-1888.
M & D 17. 17/1-15 Police reports, 1862-73.
M & D 18. 18/1-21 Miscellaneous papers.
Including: 18/1   Highbury Barn and Alexandra Theatre.
      Petition for licence, 1870
      Petition against licence, 1871,
   18/2   Islington Hall, Islington Green, Angel Coffee Tavern, 1881.
      Notice advertising benefit concert.

18/16   Eastern Alhambra and Grand Temperance Hall of Science, Shoreditch.
      Poster advertising music hall show.
18/17-21. Notice advertising performances at Royal Park hall, Camden Town, 1887.
M & D 19. 19/1-14 Cremorne Gardens: applications, letters, petitions.
M & D 20. 20/1-13 As above.
M & D 21. 21/1-20 Licences of music and dancing, 1880-1881.
M & D 22. 22/1-21 Reports from Metropolitan Board of Works, 1886.
M & D 23. 'The state of the London theatres and music halls, 1887'.
M & D 24. 24/1-7 The Empire, Leicester Square. Applications, petitions and plans.
M & D 25. 25/1-51 Justices and police reports, 1863, 1866 and 1867.
M & D 26. 26/1-316 Applications for licences, 1888.
M & D 27. 27/1-26 Letters from the Metropolitan Board of Works to the Clerk of the Peace, 1887-1888.
M & D 28. 28/1-27 Correspondence with the Clerk of the Peace, 1888
M & D 29. 29/1-16 Justices reports, 1888.
M & D 30. 30/1-5 Applications for 1837: St. James' Theatre, Duchess of Clarence Public House, Vauxhall, Swan Tavern, Hungerford Market.

A card index to the above papers has been compiled under the names of the individual halls. The index entries refer to the justices' and police reports, applications, and notices and petitions; they do not refer to individual entries in the lists of applications.

GREATER LONDON COUNCIL. *Architects Department.*

Theatre cases: Each site occupied by a theatre or music hall, or other place of entertainment has been given a separate file, with a serial number under which it is stored.

These files contain all the correspondence relating to the structure of the building, between the department and the architects, managers, and organisations and individuals concerned with the safety of the building.

Thus the history of the site is traced from the developers initial approaches to the Council, through the architects designs, the actual building and final certification, later alterations initiated either by the manager or by L.C.C. requirements, reconstruction and expansion, to the final demolition.

Plans: Plans showing the layout and elevations of halls are filed by the department. Besides those submitted by the architects of the building originally, the department itself has maintained the practice of redrawing the plans of each building at approximately ten year intervals, thus recording each structural change.

Manuscript index to cases: This is a two volumed work, known to the department as 'The bible', in which is recorded a brief history of each building extant between the years 1903 and circa 1940.

Card index to cases: The card index does not contain information, other than changes of name, but refers the searcher to the actual files.

KENT. Record Office.

West Kent. Michaelmas Quarter Sessions.
Order books, and related papers, 1850-1888.

—The records of the houses licensed for music, and music and dancing are included in the bound books of the Quarter Sessions. There are no printed lists of applications such as the Middlesex ones. The papers relate to notices and petitions with few reports surviving.

The stage play licences were not recorded in the same way, and the records of stage play licences granted after 1850 do not appear to have survived.

LORD CHAMBERLAIN'S OFFICE. Records.

Pre 1903 records are held by the Public Record Office.
  LC1/48-53 Letter books, 1843-1857.
  LC1/58-455 Letters, 1858-1885.
      Those relating to theatres are:-
      58, 70-71, 83-84, 98-99, 112-3, 127-8, 141-2, 153-4,
      166-8, 185-6, 200-2, 220-2, 232-4, 246-9, 263-4,
      275-7, 285-7, 297-9, 311-3, 325-7, 341-3, 357-8,
      367-9, 383-5, 398-401, 417-9, 435-7, 453-5.
  LC1/469-767 Letters, 1886-1902.
      This sequence includes licence applications:-
      469-70, 488-91, 507-9, 525-7, 546-7, 564-5, 582-3,
      601, 617-8, 638-9, 657, 675, 692, 711-2, 730-1, 751-2,
      767.
  LC7/13-17 (part) Licences, 1843-1887.
  LC7/20-23 Weekly account of bills, posters etc., 1861-1870.
      —Notes only that a bill has been received or if the
      theatre is closed; i.e. no details of performance unless
      unusual, such as amateurs, concerts, foreign companies
      etc.
  LC7/24-32 Inspection records, 1877-1885.
  LC7/35-48 Inspection records, 1886-1901.
  LC7/49-87 Theatre plans, 1870-1900.
  LC7/89   Night inspections (Safety precautions), 1876-7.
            —reports and correspondence including size of
            audience.
Records 1903 to date are retained by the Lord Chamberlain's
Office at St. James's Palace.

The theatres have each been allocated a serial number.
The material is filed in serial number order, separately,
each year. From 1903 to 1921 the licence applications are
filed with the correspondence relating to the theatre;
from 1922 the licensing records are gathered together in
File 374, under each year.

Much of the correspondence is duplicated by the files kept
by the Greater London Council. Licensing applications, and
all matters not relating to the physical condition of the
building, are not duplicated.

SURREY. Record Office.

Surrey. *Michaelmas Quarter Sessions.*
  Order books and working papers, 1850-1888.

  —As with the Kent records, the licensing records for
  Surrey appear in the bound books of the Quarter Sessions
  only.

iii. LIST OF LOCAL NEWSPAPERS

Balham and Tooting News	(1878-)
Chelsea News	(1857-)
Clapham Observer	(1865-)
East London Advertiser	(1865-)
East London Observer	(1857-)
Finsbury Weekly News	(1884-)
Fulham Chronicle	(1887-)
Hackney Gazette...	(1864-)
Hampstead and Highgate Express	(1860-)
Holborn Guardian	(1868-)
Islington Gazette	(1856-)
Islington Guardian...	(1884-)
Kensington News...	(1869-)
Kensington Post...	(1889-)
Kentish Independent	(1843-)
Kentish Mercury	(1833-)
Kilburn Times	(1868-)
Lewisham Borough News	(1889-)
Lewisham Journal	(1899-)
Marylebone Chronicle	(1919-)
Marylebone Mercury...	(1857-)
North London Press	(1943-)
Paddington Mercury	(1881-)
Paddington News	(1919-)
St. Marylebone and Paddington Record	(1914-)
St. Pancras Chronicle	(1857-)
Shepherd's Bush Gazette	(1868-)
South East London Mercury	(1833-)
South London Advertiser	(1895-)
South London Observer	(1868-)
South London Press	(1865-)
South Western Star	(1877-)
Stoke Newington and Hackney Observer	(1940-)
Streatham News	(1868-)
Westminster Chronicle	(1919-)

The British Museum Newspaper Library has comprehensive
files of the local London newspapers. The files in the public
libraries tend to be weak for the Nineteenth and early Twentieth Centuries.

iv. SELECT LIST OF THEATRICAL PERIODICALS

1828- The ATHENAEUM: a journal of literature, science,
    the fine arts music and the drama. London. 1828-1921.
1838- The ERA. London. 1838-1939.
1839- The THEATRICAL journal. London. 1839-1873.
1851- Dramatic register. 1851-1853. Annual.
1862- ILLUSTRATED sporting news. London. 1865-1870.
1868- DRAMATIC register. 1851-1853. Annual.
1868- ERA almanac. London. 1868-1919. Annual.
1869- LONDON Entr'acte. London. 1869-1907.
1873- The ENTRACTE almanack and theatrical and music
    hall annual. London. 1873-1906.
1874- ILLUSTRATED sporting and dramatic news. London
    1874-1945.
1877- The THEATRE. London. 1877-1897.
1879- DRAMATIC notes: an illustrated year-book... London.
    1879-1893.
1881- The STAGE. London. 1881-
1889- The MUSIC HALL and theatre review. London. 1889-
    1912.
1906- The GREEN room book. *then* WHO's who in the theatre.
    1906- Annual, later irregular.
1925- THEATRE world. London. 1925-

A detailed listing of theatrical periodicals is given in:-
  'A bibliography of British Dramatic Periodicals, 1720-
  1960', by Carl J. Stratman. New York Public Library, 1962.
  It should be noted however that the British Museum hold-
  ings that are quoted do not take the wartime losses into
  account.

v. OTHER PUBLICATIONS

ADAMS, John. A letter to the Justices of the Peace of the
    County of Middlesex on the subject of licenses for public
    music and dancing. 25 Geo. II. c. 36.
    James Ridgway, 1850. 23p.
    —Pamphlet traces the history of licensing from 1751 to
    1850.
AGATE, James Evershed. Immoment toys: a survey of ...
    entertainment on the London stage, 1920-1943.
    Cape, (1945). 264p.
BAKER, Henry Barton. The London stage: its history and
    traditions from 1576 to 1888...
    W. H. Allen, 1889, 2v.
BAKER, Henry Barton. History of the London stage and its
    famous players (1576-1903). 2nd edition (of The London
    stage). Routledge, 1904. 546p.
BANCROFT, *Sir* Squire, *and* BANCROFT, Marie Effie. *Lady
    Bancroft*. Mr. and Mrs. Bancroft on and off the stage...
    Bentley, 1868. 2v. ports.
BAXTER, *Sir* Arthur Beverley. First nights and footlights.
    Hutchinson, 1955. 256p. plates.
BEERBOHM, *Sir* Max. Around theatres. Rupert Hart Davis.
    1953. 2v. in 1.
BESANT, *Sir* Walter. London in the nineteenth century.
    Black, 1909.
    —Chapter VII. Theatres, by John Hollingshead, pp. 192-
    215. A general discussion about legislation and its effect
    on the growth of theatres.
BISHOP, George Walter. Barry Jackson and the London
    theatre... Barker, (1933). 215p. plates.
BLOW, Sydney. Through stage doors; or memories of two in
    the theatre. Chambers, 1960. 236p.
BOARDMAN, William H. ('Billy'). Vaudeville days.
    Jarrolds, 1935. 288p. illus.

BOOTH, John Bennion (also under pseudonymous name of 'Costs').
   The days we knew... Laurie, (1943). 256p. illus.
   —Anecdotes.
   Life, laughter and brass hats. Laurie, 1939. 350 p., illus.
   London town. Laurie, (1929). 324p. illus., ports.
   'Master' and men: Pink'un yesterdays. Laurie, 1926. 38p. illus.
   Palmy days. Richards Press, 1957. 17-232p. ports.
   —Covers years 1891-01
   Pink parade. Thornton Butterworth, (1933). 317p. plates.
   A Pink'un remembers. Laurie, (1937), 286p. illus.
BOURDON, Georges. Les theatres anglais...
   Paris, Bibliothèque-Charpentier, 1903. 329p.
   —Mainly London theatres. Appendix gives list of theatres and music halls active in 1903.
BRIDGES-ADAMS, William. British theatre, 3rd. edition.
   Longmans, 1947. 51p.
BROADBENT, R.J. Stage whispers. Simkin, 1901. 181p.
BROOK, Donald. The romance of the English theatre.
   Revised edition. Rockliff, 1947. 208p. Further edition published 1952. —Chapters VIII-XI on 19th and 20th centuries. The latter chapter covers theatre building and policy.
BROOKFIELD, C.H.E. Random reminiscences. E. Arnold, 1902. 318p.
BUCKLE, J.G. Theatre construction and maintenance.
   London, 1888. 157p.
The BUILDER. (General articles.)
   1858, June 5, pp. 385-6. —Penny theatres.
   1858, Sept. 25 and Oct. 2, pp. 644-5, 654-5. —'New theatres: Hoxton and Whitechapel'. General article on theatre buildings including comments on Surrey Music Hall, National Standard Theatre, Covent Garden, Drury Lane and Astley's.
   1867, June 1, pp. 381-2. —A French survey of English (i.e. London) theatres, by G. Davioud.
   1877, Jan. 27, pp. 74-6. —Theatres: the law and the Lord Chamberlain.
   1879, April 26, p. 467. —Brief report on new theatres.
   1879, May 10, pp. 524-5. —Theatres and the Metropolitan Board of Works. Regulations made under provisions of 1878 Act.
   1882, May 6, pp. 544-5. —London theatres: regulations by proposed new London County Council.
   1884, April 5, p. 493. —History of legislation for regulation of theatres and music halls.
   1884, Aug. 23, 30 and Nov. 15, pp. 248-50, 282-3, 652-3. '—The Metropolitan Board of Works and London theatres'.
   Article on report of Select Committee, passage of Metropolis Management and Building Act Amendment Act, &c.
   Action taken by the Metropolitan Board of Works; report of arbitration.
   1885, Oct. 24, p. 563. —Report of Home Secretary's offer to support bill giving the Metropolitan Board of Work's power to inspect theatres annually.
   1885, Nov. 28, p. 745. —Report of Metropolitan Board of Works' intention to bring in a bill to provide that before places of entertainment are licensed they should be given a certificate of structural efficiency.
   1887, Feb. 19, p. 280. —Report on bill for further regulation of theatres.
   1888, Jan. 21, p. 54. —Report of question at Paddington Vestry of why Captain Shaw's report on London theatres was being suppressed.
   1888, Sept. 1, p. 163. —Brief note of alteration of routine in award of certificates.
   1889, May 11, p. 349. —Report of withdrawal of Theatres (County of London) Bill, and need for legislation.
   1889, Aug. 10, p. 104. —Report that it would not be possible to put Theatre Bill through this session.
   1901, Aug. 3, p. 96. —Report of new L.C.C. regulations.
   1902, Oct. 25, p. 361. —L.C.C. and the theatres—effects of regulations.
   1904, Sept. 17, p. 288. —New theatre rules issued by Lord Chamberlain.
   1922, June 30, p. 1005. —New L.C.C. regulations.
BURKE, Thomas. English night-life from Norman curfew to present black-out. Batsford, 1941. 150p. plates.

BURRIS-MEYER, H. and COLE, E.C. Theatres and auditoriums. Chapman and Hall, 1949. 228p. illus.
BURTON, Ernest James. The British theatres: its repertory and practice, 1100-1900. Jenkins, 1960. 217p. illus.
CALTHROP, Dion Clayton. Music hall nights. John Lane, 1925. 147p. illus.
CHANCELLOR, Edwin Beresford. London's old Latin Quarter... J. Cape, 1930. 300p. —An account of the Tottenham Court Road area.
   The pleasure haunts of London during four centuries. Constable, 1925. 466p. plates.
   The romance of Soho... Country Life, 1931. 276p.
CHARLES, Jacques. Cent ans de music-hall... Paris, Genève, 1956.
   —Part I. Brief history of English music hall.
CHARQUES, Richard Dennis. ed. Footnotes to the theatres. Davies, 1938. 335p.
CHARRINGTON, Frederick Michelas. The battle of the music halls. Dyer Bros., (1885?), 15p. —Written to aid author's fight against the music halls.
COOK, Edward Dutton. Nights at the plays: a view of the English stage (1867-1881). Chatto, 1883. 2v.
DAILY NEWS, 1868, Dec. 18. 'Behind the scenes'. —Survey of costs.
DARBYSHIRE, A. Theatre exits: a paper.
   British Fire Prevention Committee, 1898. (Publication No. 4).
DARK, S. Stage silhouettes. London, 1901. 160p.
DAVEY, Peter, Mss. notes for 'Old country theatres'. 33v. (some in parts) with index (In Enthoven Collection).
DENT, Alan. Nocturnes and rhapsodies. Hamish Hamilton, 1950. 289p. plates.
DESMOND, Shaw. London nights long ago. Duckworth, 1927. 252p. illus.
   (Same) London nights in the gay nineties. N.Y.
DISHER, Maurice Willson.
   Fairs, circuses and music halls. Collins, 1942. 47p. 8 plates
   Music hall parade. see Winkles and champagne.
   Pleasures of London. Hales, (1950), 346p. illus., plates.
   Winkles and champagne: comedies and tragedies of the music hall. Batsford, 1938. 149p. plates.
   (Same) Music hall parade. N.Y.
DORAN, John. In and about Drury Lane and other papers. Bentley, 1881. 2v.
EAST, John M. 'Neath the mask: the story of the East family. George Allen and Unwin, 1967. 356p. illus.
ENCICLOPEDIA dello spettacolo. Fondata da Silvio d'Amico. Rome, Casa Editrice le Maschere. Vol VI Londra entry.
ERLE, Thomas William. Letters from a theatrical scene-painter; being sketches of the minor theatres of London... twenty years ago. Ward, 1880. 116p.
ERVINE, St. John G. Theatre in my time. Rich, 1933. 253p.
FEASEY, Lynette. On the playbill in old London. Harrap, (1948), 220p.
FILON, Augustin. The English stage: being an account of the Victorian drama; translated from the French by Frederic Whyte. John Milne, 1897. 519p. —General history of the drama and the theatre.
FINDLATER, Richard. The unholy trade. Gollancz. 1952. 224p.
FINSBURY. Borough Council. ...Theatres of north London: (an illustrated handbook to the exhibition held at the Finsbury Town Hall). The Council, 1951. (13p). 4 plates.
FITZGERALD, Percy. Music-Hall land. London, 1890.
FITZGERALD, Percy. The world behind the scenes. Chatto and Windus, 1881. 320p. —Stage illusions-spectacles-actors-theatres-authors.
FLEETWOOD, Frances. Conquest: the story of a theatre family. W.H. Allen, 1953. 282p. plates, bibliog.
FLETCHER, Geoffrey S. London overlooked. Hutchinson, 1964. 128p. illus.
FORSYTH, Gerald. Historical notes on London theatres, music halls and places of entertainment made (by permission) from L.C.C. records. October, 1948. (In Greater London Council. Architects Department.)
FOSTER, George. Spice of life: sixty-five years in the glamour world. Hurst and Blackett, 1939. 288p. illus.
FREEDLEY, George, and REEVES, J. A history of the theatre. New ed. Crown, 1941. 880p. illus.

The GENTLEMAN'S MAGAZINE. Topographical history of London: a classified collection of the chief contents of 'The Gentleman's Magazine' from 1731-1868, edited by George Lawrence Gomme. Elliot Stock, 1904.
—Vol. One. of London theatres. pp. 86-146.

GIBBS, Henry. Theatre tapestry. Jarrolds, (195?), 263p. Chapter entitled 'This site has been acquired for-' covers theatre building.

GODFREY, Philip. Back stage: a survey of the contemporary British theatre from behind the scenes. Harrap, 1933. 231p. illus.

GORDON, Charles. Old time Aldwych, Kingsway and neighbourhood. T. Fisher Unwin, 1903. 368p. illus.

GORELIK, Mordecai. New theatre for old. Dobson, 1948. 553p. illus.

GOSSET, A. Truite de la construction des théâtres. Paris, 1886.

GREIN, J. T. The world of the theatre: impressions and memories. Heinemann, 1921. 168p.

HADDON, Archibald. The story of the music hall from Cave of Harmony to cabaret. Fleetway Press, 1935. 203p. illus.

A HANDY book on the law of the drama and music. London, 1864.

HANLEY, Peter. A jubilee of playgoing... 3rd. edition. Tinkler, 1887. 113p. —Reminiscences of the London theatre.

HAXELL, Edward Nelson. A scramble through London and Brighton, with anecdotes of the stage past and present. 2nd. edition. Pitman, 1886. 186p. illus.

HAYS, Alfred. *publishers*. Plans of all the principal theatres in London. Hays, (188?), 35p.

HIBBERT, Henry George. Fifty years of a Londoner's life... Grant Richards, 1916. 303p. illus., ports. —A journalist's recollection chiefly of the stage, music hall and entertainment life in London, during the second half of the 19th century.

HIBBERT, Henry George. A playgoer's memories. Grant Richards, 1920. 303p.

HOLLINGSHEAD, John. My lifetime. 2nd. edition. Sampson, Low, Marston & Co., 1895. 2v.
The story of Leicester Square. Simpkin & Marshall, 1892. 76p. illus.

HOOPER, W. Eden. *compiler*. The stage in the year 1900, a souvenir... The history of the stage during the Victorian era, written by Joseph Knights. Spottiswoode, 1901. 184p. illus.

HOWARD, J. B. Fifty years of a showman. Hutchinson, 1938. 287p. illus.

HOWE, Percival Presland. Repertory theatre: a record and a criticism. Secker, 1910. 242p.

HUGHES, Patrick Cairns. Great opera houses: a traveller's guide to their history and traditions (by) Spike Hughes. Weidenfeld and Nicholson, 1956. 362p. illus.

HUDSON, Lytton Alfred. English stage, 1850-1950. Harrap, 1951. 223p. illus.

ISLINGTON. Public Libraries. ... Islington and the theatre: an exhibition. Islington Borough Council, 1955. 16p.

JOSEPH, Stephen. The story of the playhouse in England. Barrie and Bookliff, 1963. 156p. illus.

KENSINGTON. Borough Council. ... Some London theatres and Christmas entertainments... (An exhibition held from) 29th November 1951 (to)... 26th January 1952 (at) Leighton House. The Council, 1951. 20p.

KNIGHT, Charles. London. London, 1841-4. 6v. Vol. 5: Theatres of London.

LAWRENCE, W. J. Old theatre days and ways. (16th-19th centuries). Harrap, 1935. 255p. illus.

LEFEVRE, J. L'électricité au théâtre. Paris, 1894.

LIBRARY ASSOCIATION. *Reference and Special Libraries Section (South Eastern Group)*
Library resources in the London area, N.4. Theatre collections: a symposium edited by A. M. C. Kahn. L.A., 1955. 29p.

LITTLE, Charles P. London pleasure guide for 1898. Simpkin Marshall, 1898. 429p.

LONDON life as it is; or a handbook to all the attractions, wonders, and enjoyments of the great city; including the theatres... A new edition. Cradock & co., n.d. (c. 1850). 64p. —Theatres pp. 35-47 given brief history and description of each theatre, hours of performance and prices.

LONDON theatre diagrams. Hotel Publishing Co., 1908. 63p.

McKECHNIE, Samuel. Popular entertainments through the ages. Sampson Low, Marsten, n.d. (c. 1930). 240p.
—Music halls covered pp. 135-173.

MACOMBER, Philip Alan. The iconography of London theatre auditorium architecture, 1660-1900. Thesis presented at Ohio University, 1959.
Ann Arbor, Michigan, University Microfilms, (1959).

MACQUEEN-POPE, Walter James *see* POPE, Walter James Macqueen.

MANDER, Raymond, *and* MITCHENSON, Joe.
British music hall. Studio Vista, 1965. 208p. illus.
The British theatre, Hulton Press, 1957. 160p. illus., ports.
The lost theatres of London. Hart-Davis, 1968. 572p. illus., maps.
The theatres of London, 2nd. edition. Hart Davis, 1963. 292p. illus. (1st edition, 1961).

MAPLESON, James Henry. The Mapleson memoirs, 1848-1888. Remington, 1888. 2v. ports.
The Mapleson memoirs, the career of an operatic impresario; new edition edited by Harold Rosenthal. Putnam, 1966. 346p. plates.

MARRIOTT, J. W. The theatre. New edition revised. Harrap, 1945. 224p.

MARSHALL, Norman. The other theatre. Lehmann, 1947. 240p. illus.
—An account of the experimental and non-commercial theatre.

MASK, 1926 April. pp. 53-65. —A few facts and dates about theatres. plates 1-8

MAYES, Ronald. The romance of London theatres.
—Series of single page histories, printed in The Magazine Programme.
Bound set in Enthoven Collection.

The MICROCOSM of London, or London in miniature. Methuen, 1904.
—Originally published by R. Ackermann.

MORLEY, Henry. The journal of a London playgoer from 1851 to 1866. Routledge, 1866. 384p.

NATHAN, G. J. Encyclopaedia of the theatre. Knopf, 1940. 449p.

NEWTON, Henry Chance. Cries and curtain calls. John Lane, 1927. 306p.

NICOLL, Allardyce. Development of the theatre. 4th edition. Harrap, 1958. 318p. illus., plans.
A history of English drama, 1660-1900. Cambridge U.P., 1952-9. 6v.

OLIVER, D. E. English stage: its origins and modern developments. A critical and historical study. Cuseley, 1912. 168p.

OXFORD companion to the theatre, edited by Phyllis Hartnoll. 3rd. ed. O.U.P.. 1967. 1088p. plates.

PASCOE, Charles Eyre. Dramatic notes: an illustrated handbook of the London theatres, 1879, with... sketches of scenes and characters by T. Walter Wilson. London, 1879.

PAXTON, Sydney. Stage see-saws; or the ups and downs of an actor's life. Mills and Boon, 1917. 251p.

PEARSON, Hesketh.
Beerbohm Tree: his life and laughter. Methuen, (1956), 250p. illus.
Last actor managers. Methuen, 1950. xii, 83p. illus.

PEMBERTON, Thomas Edgar. The life and writings of T. W. Robertson... Bentley, 1893. 320p. illus.

PLANCHE, James Robinson. The recollections and reflections... a professional autobiography. Tinsley, 1872. 2v. illus.

POPE, Walter James Macqueen.
Carriages at eleven: the story of the Edwardian theatre... Hutchinson, (1947). 232p. illus.
The curtain rises: a story of the theatre. Nelson, 1961. 336p. illus.
The footlights flickered. Jenkins, (1959), 256p. illus. —The 1920s'.
Ghosts and greasepaint: a story of the days that were... Hale, (1951), 334p. illus.
An indiscreet guide to theatreland... Muse Arts Ltd. (1947). 135p.
Ladies first: the story of woman's conquest of the British stage. W. H. Allen, 1952. 384p., ports.
The melodies linger on: the story of the music hall. W. H. Allen, (1950). 459p. illus.
Nights of gladness. Hutchinson, 1956. 268p. illus.

POPE, Walter James Macqueen *cont*.
Shirt fronts and sables: a story of the days when money could be spent. Hale, 1953. 320p. illus.

POUGIN, A. Dictionnaire du Théâtre. Paris, 1885.

PULLING, Christopher. They were singing and the songs they sang about. Harrap, 1952. 276p. illus. —Includes the history of music hall.

RENDLE, T. McDonald. Swings and roundabouts. Chapman, 1919. 274p. illus.

RENTON, E. Vaudeville theatre, building, operation, management. N.Y., Gotham Press, 1918. —Few references to London.

REYNOLDS, Elizabeth. Recreations and leisure in St. Pancras, during the Nineteenth Century 1961. —Thesis (*Copy in* St. Pancras Local Collection).

REYNOLDS, Ernest. Modern English drama: a survey of the theatre from 1900. Harrap, 1949. 240p. plates, bibliog.

RICE, E. L. Living theatre. Heinemann, 1960. 306p.

RIMBAULT, E. F. Soho and its associations... edited by George Clinch. Dulau, 1895.

RITCHIE, J. Ewing. The night side of London. William Tweedie, 1857. 236p. —A condemnation of music halls, describing the audiences and entertainments at a number of them.

ROBINSON, Henry Crabbe. The London theatre 1811-1866: selections from the diary of Henry Crabbe Robinson. Society for Theatre Research, 1966. 227p.

ROTH, W. E. Theatre hygiene: a scheme for the study of a somewhat neglected department of public health. Bailliere, [1883]. 53p.

ROWELL, George. The Victorian theatre: a survey. Oxford U.P., 1956. 203p. illus. —pp. 159-189: Bibliography of the English theatre, 1792-1914.
The Victorian theatre... 1st edition, corrected, reprinted lithographically. Oxford, Clarendon Press, 1967. 209p. plates, bibliog.

SACHS, Edwin O.
Fires and public entertainments: a study of some 1100 notable fires... during the last 100 years. Layton, 1897. 58p. plans.
Stage constructions: examples of modern stages selected from playhouses recently erected in Europe, with descriptive and critical text. Batsford, 1898. 86p.

SACHS, Edwin O., *and* WOODROW, Ernest A. E.
Modern opera houses and theatres. Examples selected from playhouses recently erected in Europe, with descriptive text, a treatise on theatre planning and construction, and supplements on stage machinery, theatre fires and protective legislation. Batsford, 1896-1898. 3v. illus., tables.

ST. JAMES'S GAZETTE, 1885 Jan. 10-Feb. 27.
The theatrical business (by an old lessee). 6 parts. —Article on finances &c. of the theatre business.

ST. JAMES'S GAZETTE, 1892 April 21 and 27.
The music hall business. 2 parts. —Mentions Canterbury, Weston's, Pavilion, and Tivoli.

ST. PANCRAS. Arts Festival. The lost theatres of St. Pancras. An exhibition of playbills and other materials relating to the theatrical history of the borough from the Heal Collection of St. Pancras literature. 24th February-8th March 1958. St. Pancras Borough Council, 1958. 27p.

SANACHSON, Dorothy, *and* SANACHSON, Joseph. The dramatic story of the theatre. Abelard-Schuman, 1957. 168p. illus.

SCOTT, Harold. The early doors: origins of the music hall. Nicholson & Watson, 1946. 259p. illus. bibliog. —Index consistently one page forward, e.g. p.60 should read p.59 &c.

SCOTT, Margaret. 'Mrs. Clement Scott'.
Old days in Bohemian London (recollections of Clement Scott). Hutchinson, (1918). 272p. illus.

SHARP, R. Farquharson. A short history of the English stage from its beginnings to the summer of the year 1908. Walter Scott, 1909. 355p.

SHAW, *Captain* Eyre. Fires in theatres. 1st edition, London. 1876. 2nd ed, 1889. xx. 86p. E. & N. F. Spon.

SHEREK, Henry. Not in front of the children. Heinemann, 1959. 246p.

SHERSON, Erroll. London's lost theatres of the Nineteenth Century, with notes on plays and players seen there. John Lane, 1925. 392p. illus.

SHORT, Ernest Henry.
Fifty years of vaudeville. Eyre and Spottiswoode, (1946), 271p. illus.
Sixty years of theatre. Eyre and Spottiswoode, 1951. 402p. illus.

SHORT, Ernest Henry, *and* COMPTON-RICKETT, Arthur. Ring up the curtain: being a pageant of English entertainment covering half a century. Jenkins, 1938. 319p. illus.

SILLARD, H. M. Barry Sullivan and his contemporaries: a histrionic record. Unwin, 1901. 2v.

SNAITH, Stanley. Bethnal Green's music halls. 1951. *Typescript. (Copy in* Bethnal Green. Local Collection).

The STANDARD, 1894 Oct. 20, pp. 73+. The Music hall. —Mentions White Lion (Metropolitan); Salmon and Compasses, Penton St.; King's Head, Knightsbridge; Grapes (Winchester); Britannia Theatre; Yorkshire Stingo; Grecian; Canterbury; Weston's; Oxford; Marylebone; Collins; Raglan; Alhambra; Paragon and Empire.

The STATE of the London theatres and music halls, 1887. ... Reprinted from the 'Saturday Review'. Frederick Warne, 1887. 44p. —A series of articles following the fire at the Paris Opera Comique. Surveys of theatres and music halls with particular reference to their safety.

STUART, Charles Douglas, *and* PARK, A. J. The variety stage: a history of the music halls from the earliest period to the present time. T. Fisher Unwin, (1895). 255p. —Used as source book by many later writers.

STUDIES in English theatre history, in memory of Gabrielle Enthoven. Society for Theatre Research, 1952, 133p. illus. (Society for Theatre Research. Annual publication N. 3).

TAYLOR, Tom. The theatre in England: Some of its shortcomings and possibilities... British and Colonial Publishing Co., 1871. 11p. —Reprinted from 'The Dark Blue'. August 1871.

THEATRE ownership in Great Britain: a report prepared for the Federation of Theatre Unions. (The Federation), 1953. 281p. tables.

TITTERTON, W. E. From theatre to music hall. Stephen Swift, 1912. 242p.

TREWIN, John Courtney.
The gay twenties... Macdonald, 1958. 128p. illus.
The night has been unruly. Hale, 1957. 288p. plates., ports. —Covers the years 1769 to 1955.
Theatre since 1900. Dakers, 1951. 17-339p. plates, ports.
The turbulent thirties... Macdonald, 1960. 144p. illus.

WATSON, Ernest Bradlee. Sheridan to Robertson: a study of the 19th century London stage. Oxford U.P., 1926. 485p. plates —Reprinted by B. Blom in U.S.A. 1964.

WEALE, John. ed. London and its vicinity exhibited in 1851... John Weale, 1851. pp. 772-5 lists London's theatres and pleasure gardens.

WILLIAMS, Michael. Some London theatres, past and present. Sampson, Low, 1883. 215p.

WILLIAMSON, Audrey. Theatre of two decades. Rockliff, 1951 391p.

WILSON, Albert Edward.
East end entertainment. Arthur Barker, 1954. 240p. illus.
Edwardian theatre. Arthur Barker, 1951. 256p. plates.
Half a century of entertainment. Yates, 1951. 48p. illus.
Pantomine pageant: a procession of harlequins, clowns, comedians, principal boys, pantomine-writers, producers and playgoers. Stanley Paul, (194?). 136p. illus.

WROTH, Warwick. Cremorne and later London gardens. Eliot Stock, 1907. 102p. illus.

Location of Material: Directory of Collections

BATTERSEA. Local Collection.

Battersea District Library (London Borough of Wandsworth),
Lavender Hill, S. W. 11   01-228-3474

Hours: Mon. -Fri. 9-9;
            Sat. 9-5; Sun. 2-6.

BERMONDSEY. Local Collection.

Newington District Library (London Borough of Southwark),
155-157, Walworth Road, S. E. 17   01-703-3324

Hours: Mon. -Fri. 9. 30-8;
            Sat. 9. 30-5.

Small collection on Rotherhithe Hippodrome (Terriss's).

BETHNAL GREEN. Local Collection.

Tower Hamlets Central Library
(London Borough of Tower Hamlets),
277, Bancroft Road, E. 1   01-980-4366

Hours: Mon. -Fri. 9-8;
            Sat. 9-5.

BRITISH BROADCASTING CORPORATION.

B.B.C. Reference Library,
Broadcasting House,
Portland Place, W. 1   01-580-4468
                              Ext. 3746/7

Private collection. Scripts and illustrations.

BRITISH DRAMA LEAGUE.

British Drama League, The Library,
9-10, Fitzroy Square, W. 1   01-387-2666

Available to members only. Subscription: 4 gns. per annum.

Hours: Mon., Tues., Thurs., Fri. 10-5;
            Wed. 10-8; Sat. 10-12. 30.

Specializes in all subjects relating to drama, theatre and
allied subjects. Large collection of books and play sets.
Playbills dating from 1877 to date.

BRITISH MUSEUM.

British Museum, Great Russell Street, W. C. 1
                                01-636-1555

Department of Printed Books:
  Library hours: (Reading Room): Mon., Fri., Sat. 9-5.
                                Tues. -Thurs. 9-9.

National copyright library, with comprehensive collection
of British material; however a considerable number of
periodical files and other material was lost through war
damage. These items are still listed in the catalogue.
Stock includes miscellaneous collection of playbills; a list
of these is available at the enquiry desk.

Department of Manuscripts:
  Hours: Mon. -Fri. 10-4. 40;
            Sat. as above.

Collection includes account books, leases and agreements;
and letters and signatures of actors and managers.

Department of Prints and Drawings:
  Print room hours: Mon. -Fri. 10-4;
                        Sat. 10-12. 30.

Many theatrical engravings. Also six volumes of material
on Henry Irving and the Lyceum Theatre.

BRITISH MUSEUM (Newspaper Library).

British Museum Newspaper Library,
Colindale, N. W. 9   01-205-6039

Hours: Mon. -Sat. 10-4.

Comprehensive collection of local newspapers for the
London area, from 1850.

BRITISH MUSIC HALL SOCIETY

British Music Hall Society,
1, King Henry Street, N. 16   01-254-4209

Archives available to members of the society, and serious
researchers by appointment.
Collection of programmes, playbills, photographs and
gramophone records on the London music halls.

BRITISH THEATRE MUSEUM

British Theatre Museum,
Leighton House, 12 Holland Park Road, W. 14
                              01-937-3052

Hours: Tues., Thurs., Sat. 11-5.

Large collection of documents and letters in the Irving
Archive, and a number of plans from Sir Herbert Beerbohm Tree's collection.

CAMBERWELL. Local Collection.

Newington District Library (London Borough of Southwark).
155-157, Walworth Road, S. E. 17   01-703-3324

Hours: Mon. -Fri. 9. 30-8;
            Sat. 9. 30-5.

CHELSEA. Local Collection.

Chelsea Public Library (Royal Borough of Kensington and
Chelsea),
Manresa Road, S.W.3   01-352-6056

Hours: Mon. -Sat. 9-8.

Good collection of material on Royal Court Theatre,
Cremorne Gardens and Chelsea Palace; some other
material.

City of London. Local Collection. *see* GUILDHALL
LIBRARY

DEPTFORD. Local Collection.

Deptford Library (London Borough of Lewisham),
Lewisham Way, S.E.14   01-692-3649
The local history collection is in process of being
transferred to:-
Manor House Library, Old Ford Road, S.E.13
                              01-852-5050

All enquiries should be made to the archivist at the Manor
House Library before visiting the Deptford Library.

Hours: Mon. -Wed., and Sat. 10-6;
            Tues., Thurs., Fri. 10-7. 30.

ENTHOVEN COLLECTION.

Gabrielle Enthoven Collection,
Theatre Section, Department of Prints, and Engravings,
Victoria and Albert Museum,
South Kensington, S.W.7   01-589-6371

Hours: Mon. -Fri. 10-4. 50;
            Sat. By appointment only.

Major collection of playbills, prints, programmes and
other printed and manuscript material.
Indexes to plays, designers, producers, illustrations of
plays, portraits, posters, theatres, managements &c.

FINSBURY. Local Collection.

Finsbury Library (London Borough of Islington),
St. John St., E.C.1.   01-837-4161

Hours: Mon.-Fri. 9-8; Sat. 9-5

Large collection on Sadler's Wells Theatre.
Some material on local music halls.

FULHAM. Local Collection.

Fulham Library (London Borough of Hammersmith),
598, Fulham Road, S.W.6   01-736-1127

Hours: Mon.-Fri. 9. 15-8;
          Sat. 9. 15-5.

Small collection.

GARRICK CLUB

Garrick Club, Garrick Street, W.C.2   01-836-1737

This club is strictly private. Material may be seen only
on permission of the committee. Enquiries should be
made through the Secretary's Office.

GREATER LONDON COUNCIL

Greater London Council,
County Hall, Westminster Bridge, S.E.1 01-928-5000

Architects Department: Middlesex House, 20 Vauxhall Bridge
Rd.
Plans and files on all places of entertainment active in
London after 1888. Arrangements can be made for seri-
ous researchers to see non-current material. With appli-
cation or introduction through Record Office.

Members' Library: County Hall.
Large collection on London topography and administration.

Hours: Mon.-Fri. 9. 15-5. 15; Sat. 9. 30-12. 30.

Record Office. Room B 21, County Hall.

Hours: 9-4. 45 Mon.-Fri.

Reports, papers and publications relating to the work of
the committees and departments of the London County
Council. Prints and photographs, and non-current plans.

GREATER LONDON RECORD OFFICE (MIDDLESEX
RECORDS)

Middlesex Record Office,
1, Queen Anne's Buildings, Dartmouth St., S.W.1
                                   01-839-7799

Hours: 9. 30-5. 30 Mon.-Fri.

Reports, papers and publications relating to the work of
the Middlesex Sessions. These cover the County of
London, north of the Thames, until 1889.

GREENWICH. Local Collection.

Blackheath Branch Library (London Borough of Green-
wich)
St. John's Park, S.E.3   01-858-1131
Local material may be seen by appointment.

GUILDHALL LIBRARY

Guildhall Library, Basinghall Street, E.C.2
                                   01-606-3030

Hours: Mon.-Sat. 9. 30-5.

Over 15, 000 items relating to theatres- playbills, programmes, scrapbooks and prints. Special London Collection covers theatres, including standard histories.

HACKNEY. Local Collection.

Hackney Central Library (London Borough of Hackney)
Mare Street, E.8   01-985-8262

Hours: Mon.-Fri. 9-9;
          Sat. 9-6.

Small collection of cuttings.

278

HAMMERSMITH. Local Collection.

Hammersmith Central Library (London Borough of
Hammersmith),
Shepherds Bush Road, W.6   01-748-6032

Hours: Mon.-Fri. 9. 15-8;
          Sat. 9. 15-5.

Small collection of material on earlier theatres, and on
Lyric and King's Theatre from 1948.

HAMPSTEAD. Local Collection

Hampstead Central Library (London Borough of Camden),
Swiss Cottage, N.W.3   01-586-0061-6

Hours: Mon.-Fri. 9. 30-8;
          Sat. 9. 30-5.

HARRY R. BEARD THEATRE COLLECTION

Harry R. Beard, Esq.
Little Eversden, Cambridge.

Personal collection, but may be seen by serious researchers, by appointment only.
Very large collection of prints, engravings, playbills &c.
Mainly relating to periods before 1850, but some unique
material on later period.

HOLBORN. Local Collection.

Holborn Central Library (London Borough of Camden),
32-38, Theobalds Road, W.C.1   01-405-2705-6

Hours: Mon.-Fri. 9. 30-9;
          Sat. 9. 30-5.

Collection of playbills, a few programmes and prints.

ISLINGTON. Local Collection.

Islington Central Library (London Borough of Islington),
68, Holloway Road, N.7   01-607-4038

Hours: Mon.-Fri. 9-8;
          Sat. 9-5.

Collection on local music halls.

KENSINGTON. Local Collection.

Kensington Central Library
(Royal Borough of Kensington and Chelsea),
Phillimore Walk, W.8   01-937-2542

Hours: Mon., Tues., Thurs., Fri. 10-8;
          Wed., Sat. 10-5.

Small collection, mostly on Royal Kent Theatre.

KENT. Record Office.

The Record Office,
County Hall, Maidstone, Kent.   0622-4321

Hours: Mon.-Fri. 9-5. 15;
          Sat. By arrangement.

Sessional records.

LAMBETH. Local Collection.
Minet Library (London Borough of Lambeth),
Knatchbull Road, S.E.5   01-274-5325

Hours: Mon.-Fri. 9. 30-7;
          Sat. 9. 30-5.

Researchers are requested to make an appointment before
visiting the library.
Large collection of playbills, cuttings and prints.

LEWISHAM. Local Collection.
Manor House Library,
Old Road, S.E. 13   01-852-5050

Hours: Mon.-Wed., and Sat. 10-6;
          Tues., Thurs., Fri. 10-7. 30.

LONDON MUSEUM

London Museum,
Kensington Palace, W.8.   01-937-6325

Hours: Mon.-Fri. 10-6

Theatre material may be seen by appointment.
Prints, playbills and personal relics.

LORD CHAMBERLAIN'S OFFICE

Lord Chamberlain's Office,
St. James's Palace, S.W.1

Serious researchers may seek permission to see the
records relating to theatre licensing, by letter.

PADDINGTON. Local Collection.

Paddington District Library (City of Westminster),
Porchester Road, W.2   01-229-6611

POPLAR. Local Collection.

Tower Hamlets Central Library
(London Borough of Tower Hamlets),
277, Bancroft Road, E.1   01-980-4366

Hours: Mon.-Fri. 9-8;
　　　　 Sat. 9-5.

PUBLIC RECORD OFFICE

Public Record Office,
Chancery Lane, W.C.2   01-405-0741

Search Room hours: Mon.-Fri. 9.30-5;
　　　　　　　　　　Sat. 9.30-1

The national archives collections, including records of the
Lord Chamberlain's Office and the Home Office.

RAYMOND MANDER & JOE MITCHENSON THEATRE COLLECTION

The Raymond Mander and Joe Mitchenson Theatre Collections,
5, Venner Road, Sydenham, S.E.26   01-778-6730

Private collection, mainly used for commercial purposes.
Reported to be one of the largest collections of photographs, playbills, prints &c.

ROYAL INSTITUTE OF BRITISH ARCHITECTS

Sir Banister Fletcher Library,
Royal Institute of British Architects,
66, Portland Place, W.1   01-580-5533

Hours: Mon., Wed.-Fri. 10-7; Tues. 10-8.30;
　　　　 Sat. 10-5.

Accredited enquirers may receive permission to use
library.
Architectural journals, special collection of drawings.

ST. MARYLEBONE. Local Collection.

St. Marylebone District Library
(City of Westminster),
Marylebone Road, N.W.1   01-935-7766

Hours: Mon.-Sat. 9.30-9.

Considerable collection of material on Princess's and
West London Theatres; some material on other halls.

ST. PANCRAS. Local Collection.

Hampstead Central Library (London Borough of Camden)
Swiss Cottage, N.W.3.   01-586-0061-6

Hours: Mon.-Fri. 9.30-8;
　　　　 Sat. 9.30-5.

Material in the Heal Collection. Good collection of playbills, cuttings &c. on Scala Theatre throughout its history.
Some material on other theatres and music halls.

SHOREDITCH. Local Collection.

Shoreditch Central Library
(London Borough of Hackney),
Pitfield Street, N.1   01-739-6981

Hours: Mon. 9-8; Tues.-Fri. 9-7;
　　　　 Sat. 9-6

Collection on early Shoreditch theatres, and on Britannia
Theatre and other local halls.

SOCIETY FOR THEATRE RESEARCH

Society for Theatre Research,
103, Ralph Court, Queensway, W.2

The Library: 77, Kinnerton Street, S.W.1

Hours: By appointment.

Manuscripts, prints, programmes and playbills.

Book collection: *in*
University of London Library,
Senate House, Malet Street, W.C.1   01-636-4514

Hours: Mon.-Fri. 9.30-9;
　　　　 Sat. and Vacations 9.30-6.

Available to members of the society and to holders of
University of London Library tickets.
Miscellaneous collection, not comprehensive.

SOUTHWARK. Local Collection.

Newington District Library (London Borough of Southwark),
155-157, Walworth Road, S.E.17   01-703-3324

Hours: Mon.-Fri. 9.30-8;
　　　　 Sat. 9.30-5.

Considerable collection on Surrey Theatre.

STEPNEY. Local Collection.

Tower Hamlets Central Library
(London Borough of Tower Hamlets),
277, Bancroft Road, E.1   01-980-4366

Hours: Mon.-Fri. 9-8;
　　　　 Sat. 9-5.

Considerable collection, particularly on Royalty Theatre,
Wellclose Sq. and Garrick Theatre, Leman St.

STOKE NEWINGTON. Local Collection.

Stoke Newington Central Library (London Borough of
Hackney),
Church Street, N.16   01-800-1282

Hours: Mon.-Fri. 9-9;
　　　　 Sat. 9-5.

SURREY. Record Office.

Surrey Record Office,
County Hall, Penrhyn Road,
Kingston-upon-Thames, Surrey.   01-546-1050

Hours: Mon.-Fri. 9-5.20.

Sessions records.

VICTORIA AND ALBERT MUSEUM

Victoria and Albert Museum,
South Kensington, S.W.7   01-589-6371

Library: *Hours:* Mon.-Fri. 10-5.50.
Books and periodicals on the theatre arts.

Theatre Section: *see* ENTHOVEN COLLECTION

WESTMINSTER. Local Collection.

Buckingham Palace Road Branch Library,
Buckingham Palace Road, S.W.1   01-730-0446

Hours: Mon.-Fri. 10-8;
　　　　 Sat. 10-5.

Large collection of playbills, programmes and scrapbooks
on the London theatres and music halls.
(Not limited to the City of Westminster).

WESTMINSTER. Metropolitan Special Collection.

Central Reference Library,
St. Martin's Street, W.C.2   01-930-3274

Hours: Mon.-Sat. 10-8.

Comprehensive collection of books on all aspects of the theatre.

WOOLWICH. Local Collection.

Woolwich Library (London Borough of Greenwich)
Calderwood Street, S.E.18   01-854-1121

Hours: Mon.-Fri. 9-8;
         Sat. 9-5.

Name Index to Buildings

Upper case entries indicate that the building is listed under that name; lower case entries indicate that the building is listed under another name.

*indicates an illustration.

	Serial No.
QUEEN'S ARMS PUBLIC HOUSE, Haverstock Hill.	631
QUEEN'S ARMS PUBLIC HOUSE, Hackney Rd.	629
QUEEN'S ARMS PUBLIC HOUSE, Islington.	628
QUEEN'S ARMS PUBLIC HOUSE, Pimlico.	632
QUEEN'S ARMS PUBLIC HOUSE, Plumstead.	627
QUEEN'S HEAD PUBLIC HOUSE, Bethnal Green.	633
QUEEN'S PARK HALL	634
Raglan Music Hall, Borough.	90
Raglan Music Hall, Holborn.	473
RAGLAN MUSIC HALL, Southwark.	635
Railway Coffee Tavern, Whitechapel.	496
RAILWAY HOTEL, Islington.	636
RAILWAY HOTEL AND PUBLIC HOUSE, Putney.	637
RAILWAY PUBLIC HOUSE, Balls Pond.	638
RAILWAY PUBLIC HOUSE, North St., Wandsworth.	640
RAILWAY PUBLIC HOUSE, Nunhead.	639
RAILWAY PUBLIC HOUSE, Plumstead Rd.	641
Rayner's New Subscription Theatre in the Strand	766
RED BOOT COFFEE TAVERN	642
RED COW PUBLIC HOUSE, Dalston.	644
RED COW PUBLIC HOUSE, Deptford.	643
Red Cross Public House, Bethnal Green.	32
RED DEER PUBLIC HOUSE, Bethnal Green.	645
RED LION PUBLIC HOUSE, Bermondsey.	646
RED LION PUBLIC HOUSE, Clerkenwell.	650
RED LION PUBLIC HOUSE, Finsbury.	651
RED LION PUBLIC HOUSE, Greenwich.	647
RED LION PUBLIC HOUSE, Holborn.	648
RED LION PUBLIC HOUSE, Stepney.	649
RED LION AND PUNCH BOWL PUBLIC HOUSE, Finsbury.	652
RED LION AND SPREADEAGLE PUBLIC HOUSE, Stepney.	653
Regency Theatre	717
REGENT GALLERY	655
REGENT MUSIC HALL AND PUBLIC HOUSE, Westminster.	654
REGENT THEATRE, Kings Cross.	656
Regent Theatre, Kings Cross.	434
REGENT THEATRE, Soho.	657
Regent Theatre of Varieties, Hackney.	719
Regent's Park Theatre	557
RIDLEY ARMS PUBLIC HOUSE	658
RISING SUN PUBLIC HOUSE, Fulham.	661
Rising Sun Public House, Knightsbridge.	771
RISING SUN PUBLIC HOUSE, Pimlico.	659
RISING SUN PUBLIC HOUSE, Somers Town.	660
ROBIN HOOD PUBLIC HOUSE, Upper Clapton.	662
ROCK OF GIBRALTAR PUBLIC HOUSE	663
Rodney's Head Public House	611
Rooms for Concerts of Ancient Music	717
ROSE PUBLIC HOUSE, Holborn.	664
Rose and Crown Palace of Varieties	346
ROSE AND CROWN PUBLIC HOUSE, Bromley.	665
ROSE AND CROWN PUBLIC HOUSE, Drury Lane.	668
ROSE AND CROWN PUBLIC HOUSE, Finsbury.	666
ROSE AND CROWN PUBLIC HOUSE, Fort St., Tower.	669
Rose and Crown Public House, Greenwich.	346
ROSE AND CROWN PUBLIC HOUSE, Knightsbridge.	670
ROSE AND CROWN PUBLIC HOUSE, St. George St.	671
ROSE AND CROWN PUBLIC HOUSE, St Pancras.	667
ROSE AND SHAMROCK PUBLIC HOUSE, Shadwell.	672
Rose of Normandy Public House	491
Rosemary Branch Music Hall and Public House, Peckham.	564
ROSEMARY BRANCH MUSIC HALL AND PUBLIC HOUSE, Islington.	673
ROTHERHITHE HIPPODROME	674

	Serial No.
Rotunda Assembly Rooms, Southwark.	97
Royal Adelaide Theatre	5
Royal Adelphi Theatre	6
ROYAL ALBERT PUBLIC HOUSE, Wandsworth Rd.	675
Royal Albert Saloon	55
Royal Albion Subscription Theatre	819
Royal Albion Theatre, Piccadilly.	819
Royal Alexandra Theatre, Highbury Barn.	19
Royal Alexandra Theatre, Park Street.	557
Royal Alfred Theatre	853
Royal Alhambra Palace	22
Royal Amphitheatre, Astleys	38
Royal Amphitheatre and Circus, Holborn.	377
Royal Aquarium Theatre	396
ROYAL ARTILLERY THEATRE AND OPERA HOUSE	676
Royal Assembly Rooms, Woolwich.	229
Royal Avenue Theatre	588
Royal Bower Saloon	93
ROYAL CAMBRIDGE MUSIC HALL	677
Royal Camden Theatre	127
Royal Canterbury Theatre	129
Royal Circus	778
ROYAL CLARENCE MUSIC HALL	678*
Royal Clarence Theatre	434
Royal Coburg Theatre	545
Royal Comedy Theatre	170
Royal Connaught Theatre	377
Royal Court Theatre, Lower George St.	181
ROYAL COURT THEATRE, Sloane Square.	679
ROYAL CRICKETERS PUBLIC HOUSE, Old Ford Rd.	680
ROYAL CROWN PUBLIC HOUSE, St. George St.	681
Royal Denmark Theatre	266
Royal Deptford Theatre	213
Royal Duchess Theatre	46
Royal Eagle Music Hall	248
ROYAL EDWARD PUBLIC HOUSE, Hackney.	682
Royal English Opera, Covent Garden.	282
Royal English Opera House	554
Royal Foresters Music Hall	284
Royal French Circus and Britannia Saloon	104
ROYAL GEORGE PUBLIC HOUSE, Chelsea.	683
Royal Globe Theatre, Strand.	316
Royal Grove, Lambeth.	38
Royal Harmonic Hall, Knightsbridge.	289
Royal Hippodrome, Kensington.	52
Royal Holborn Empire	376
ROYAL HOTEL, Hackney.	684
ROYAL HOTEL, Stepney.	685
Royal Italian Opera, Covent Garden.	182
ROYAL KENT THEATRE	686
Royal King's Cross Theatre	434
Royal London Panorama	266
Royal Lyceum Theatre, Strand.	476
Royal Marylebone Theatre	853
Royal Music Hall	376
ROYAL OAK PUBLIC HOUSE, Barking Rd.	687
ROYAL OAK PUBLIC HOUSE, Hackney Fields.	689
ROYAL OAK PUBLIC HOUSE, Hammersmith.	688
ROYAL OAK PUBLIC HOUSE, Stepney.	690
Royal Opera, Covent Garden.	182
Royal Opera House, Covent Garden.	182
Royal Park Hall	557
Royal Park Theatre	557
ROYAL PAVILION, North Woolwich.	691
Royal Pavilion Gardens, Woolwich.	691
Royal Pavilion Hotel, Woolwich.	691
Royal Pavilion West	853
Royal Saloon, Lambeth.	38
ROYAL SOVEREIGN PUBLIC HOUSE	692
Royal Sovereign Theatre	717
Royal Standard Hotel, Victoria.	834
Royal Standard Music Hall, Battersea.	51
ROYAL STANDARD MUSIC HALL, North Woolwich.	695
Royal Standard Music Hall, Victoria.	834
ROYAL STANDARD PUBLIC HOUSE, Albion St.	693

290